The Future of the Commercial Contract in Scholarship and Law Reform

Maren Heidemann • Joseph Lee
Editors

The Future of the Commercial Contract in Scholarship and Law Reform

European and Comparative Perspectives

Springer

Editors
Maren Heidemann
Institute of Advanced Legal Studies
School of Advanced Studies
University of London
London, UK

Joseph Lee
Law School
University of Exeter
Exeter, UK

ISBN 978-3-319-95968-9 ISBN 978-3-319-95969-6 (eBook)
https://doi.org/10.1007/978-3-319-95969-6

Library of Congress Control Number: 2018955509

This Springer imprint is published by the registered company Springer Nature Switzerland AG
The registered company address is: Gewerbestrasse 11, 6330 Cham, Switzerland

Preface

This volume presents research undertaken during a research project initiated at the Institute of Advanced Legal Studies (IALS), School of Advanced Study, University of London. IALS provided an inspiring and friendly research environment where a series of successful events could be organised. We wish to thank Professor Mads Andenas for hosting this project at his Centre for Corporate and Financial Law giving scholars from all over the world the opportunity to participate. Special thanks go to the Institute's director, Jules Winterton, who very kindly supported this project over a period of over 2 years and to the staff at the IALS library and events administration, especially Ms Belinda Crothers, for their invaluable and indefatigable help and patience. We are also indebted to the University of Exeter for supporting the extension of the project.

London, UK
Exeter, UK
May 2018

Maren Heidemann
Joseph Lee

Foreword

The Autonomy of Commercial Law?

The commercial contract is not any autonomous phenomenon. It is subject to regulatory intervention and sometimes represents attempts to counteract or circumvent such intervention. It may be seen as a creature of domestic law or as an attempt to transcend it. It is subject to restatement and harmonisation, also at an international level with principles or conventions. The commercial transactions are increasingly of a cross-border and inter-jurisdictional nature. That applies to regulation of different kinds and the codification, restatement and harmonisation of commercial law itself. These parallel developments take place at varying speeds at the different levels. Party autonomy is important, but its role is only understood when account is taken of such developments.

Is a special and separate contract law for merchants in a global market necessary? Scholarship needs to develop the terminology, the doctrine and also the objectives which this law is based upon. For a long time, the choice of transnational law rules, which are often non-state law, has been marginalised and made ineffective in state court proceedings. EU reforms and proposals, including the now withdrawn Commission proposal for new Common European Sales Law, have circumvented this problem by proposing new general contract law to be used as national law. International practice in commercial dispute settlement will still remain at the forefront of promoting and modelling the use of transnational contract law.

The CCFL Research Project

This volume presents research undertaken during a research project at the Centre for Corporate and Financial Law (CCFL) at the Institute of Advanced Legal Studies (IALS), School of Advanced Study, University of London for almost 2 years. The CCFL was established in 1996, and I was its first director until 2000, and I took over again in 2007. The CCFL continues to organise and host research programmes and events, drawing together scholars from all over the world and working on a range of current research topics in corporate and commercial law. Among the outcomes of the research activities at the Centre are the monograph *The Foundations and Future of Financial Regulation: Governance for Responsibility* (Routledge 2014) by Professor Iris Chiu at University College London and myself and the edited collection by Andenas and Deipenbrock (eds), *Regulating and Supervising European Financial Markets: More Risks than Achievements* (Springer, 2016).

Dr Maren Heidemann has played a core role at the CCFL with her research and supervision of PhDs.

The research project provides European and comparative perspectives on the future of the commercial contract. Its focus is on scholarship and law reform, and it is directed by Dr Heidemann. The research project and this book brought together scholars from over ten different jurisdictions all across the globe. The volume is edited by Dr Heidemann and Dr Joseph Lee. Dr Heidemann has conceived and directed the project. I have followed their careers and scholarship for many years and supervised their PhDs at the IALS and Nottingham. They have made important contributions to international commercial law in their PhD dissertations and later. Dr Heidemann's magisterial monograph is *Methodology of Uniform Contract Law. The UNIDROIT Principles in International Legal Doctrine and Practice* (Springer, 2007) is a classic, and her book *Does International Trade Need a Doctrine of Transnational Law?: Some Thoughts at the Launch of a European Contract Law* (Springer 2012) analysed commercial contract law both national and international in view of the proposed European contract law reform. Dr Lee's publications and research council-funded larger projects have made important contributions to financial and corporate law and also in the comparative analysis they provide.

The Dichotomies of Contract Law and the Future of the Commercial Contract

The project is concerned with two fundamental dichotomies of contract law. The first is that of commercial and private (in a narrow sense) contracts. The second dichotomy is of private (in the wider sense, including commercial law) law and public law. Some time ago, some would have ventured to formulate a third dichotomy: the domestic and the European and international. In commercial law, there was always the Law Merchant *or lex mercatoria*, with its own challenges to domestic law. And contractual freedom or private autonomy would provide grounds for moving outside the domestic law paradigm. The UNIDROIT Principles and the 1980 Vienna Convention on the International Sale of Goods (CISG) of Dr Heidemann's scholarship provides a core of a such supranational contract law.

The issues of the project are complex, and different jurisdictions deal with them in different ways. Some countries have comprehensive codifications for commercial law covering in particular commercial contracts. The distinction between the private and the commercial is drawn in different ways. The relationship between commercial law and regulatory law is inherently difficult, and the doctrinal difficulties often reflect ideological and political positions. To domestic public and constitutional law the dichotomy may not have much relevance. Whether that applies to European or international law sources or not, they will not follow one of the domestic jurisdictions. German, French or common lawyers may read their systems into these sources, but that could lead one astray. At the international law level, there is some lead in harmonising aspects of commercial law, of which the UNIDROIT principles of Dr Heidemann's 2007 and 2012 monographs are but one. At the European level, consumer rights have been at the core. Both at international and EU level, much regulatory harmonisation has consequences for commercial law and may contribute to sectoral regulation which reflects the technical regular policy objectives and techniques applied in different fields. Exploring the public and public international law influence takes one to treaty interpretation, sources of law in the EU legal order and their effect in domestic law and a range of issues not traditionally seen as pressing in the commercial law context.

Financial and corporate law, Dr Lee's field, is one area where new specialised subfields of commercial contract law are emerging.

The CCFL Research Project and This Book

The first phase of the research project was on the definition and nature of the commercial contract. The commercial contract is distinct from non-commercial, private or consumer contracts. The commercial contract can also to be understood as a specialisation, a specific contract type. The second phase of the research project was on the interaction of public and public international law with substantive contract law in the commercial sphere. This interaction occurs, for instance, where contract law is codified in the form of an international treaty of which CISG is the most prominent example. Interaction also occurs where public policies influence private contract law or vice versa. The initial objective of the research project was to explore the scope of the subject and how it resonated with scholars and practitioners. The editors explain in their introduction how shared points of interest crystallised. They were in particular good faith, corporate social responsibility and contractual cooperation. They might not be the most prominent features of commercial contracts in anybody's imagination. That may be an outdated preconception.

The analysis of the future of the commercial contract falls into three main parts, as is explained in Dr Heidemann's introduction. Part I is on general theory and general aspects of commercial contract. Part II is on the commercial contract in practice with emphasis on good faith, collaboration and sustainability in commercial contracts. Part III is on the interface between public and private law in commercial contract law.

The book is timely. The chapters provide a rich source of critical analysis. The editors have managed to bring together a wide group of contributors in terms of scholarly interests and perspectives and to provide a structure for making a valuable and original book on the future of commercial law at the highest level.

Mads Andenas
Director of the Centre for Corporate and Financial Law, Institute of Advanced Legal Studies, School of Advanced Study, University of London and Professor, the University of Oslo.

University of London
London, UK
May 2018

Mads Andenas

Contents

List of Contributors

Despina Anagnostopoulou Jean Monnet Centre of Excellence "Research on Crucial Issues of European Integration", University of Macedonia, Thessaloniki, Greece

Mads Andenas Institute of Private Law, Faculty of Law, University of Oslo, Oslo, Norway

Institute of Advanced Legal Studies, School of Advanced Study, University of London, London, UK

David Christie Law School, Robert Gordon University, Aberdeen, UK

Daniele D'Alvia Birkbeck, University of London, London, UK

Jan H. Dalhuisen The Dixon Poon School of Law, King's College London, London, UK

Catholic University Lisbon, Lisbon, Portugal

UC Berkeley, Berkeley, CA, USA

National University of Singapore, Singapore, Singapore

University of Tel Aviv, Tel Aviv-Yafo, Israel

NY Bar, Albany, NY, USA

ICSID Arbitrator, Washington, DC, USA

Royal Netherlands Academy of Arts and Sciences, Amsterdam, The Netherlands

Andreas Geroldinger Faculty of Law, Department of Civil Law, Johannes Kepler University, Linz, Austria

Maren Heidemann Institute of Advanced Legal Studies, School of Advanced Studies, University of London, London, UK

Alexandra Horváthová Center for Enterprise Liability, Faculty of Law, University of Copenhagen, Copenhagen, Denmark

Sara Hourani Law School, Middlesex University, London, UK

Antonios Karaiskos Graduate School of Law, Kyoto University, Kyoto, Japan

Joseph Lee Law School, University of Exeter, Exeter, UK

Chien-Chung Lin National Chiao-Tung University, Hsinchu, Taiwan

Janwillem Oosterhuis Faculty of Law, University of Maastricht, Maastricht, The Netherlands

Catherine Pédamon Westminster Law School, University of Westminster, London, UK

Hendrik Puschmann Farrer & Co, London, UK

Clare Hall, Cambridge, UK

Johannes Kepler Universität Linz, Linz, Austria

Muriel Renaudin School of Law and Politics, Cardiff University, Cardiff, UK

Dania Thomas Adam Smith Business School, University of Glasgow, Glasgow, UK

The Future of the Commercial Contract in Scholarship and Law Reform: An Introduction

Maren Heidemann

Contents

Abstract This chapter maps out our volume on the commercial contract law in scholarship and law reform. It starts by outlining the general distinction between commercial and non-commercial contract law and by introducing and critically reflecting on recent law reform in this area of law. It then moves on to introducing and contextualising the contributions which the chapters on Parts II and III of this

M. Heidemann (✉)
Institute of Advanced Legal Studies, School of Advanced Studies, University of London, London, UK

M. Heidemann, J. Lee (eds.), *The Future of the Commercial Contract in Scholarship and Law Reform*, https://doi.org/10.1007/978-3-319-95969-6_1

volume make to scholarly debate of selected distinctive aspects of commercial contracts and of the interface of commercial contracts and contract law with public international law. The chapter concludes with an outlook and brief summary of the general findings of the research presented in this volume.

1 Introduction

Recent decades have seen new legislation in regard to contract law in countries worldwide, and also proposals put forward by the European Union (EU) in co-operation with academic scholars. Examples for the latter are the (later withdrawn) Proposal of the European Parliament and of the Council for a Regulation on a Common European Sales Law (CESL),[1] the Principles of European Contract Law (PECL)[2] and the Draft Common Frame of Reference (DCFR).[3] National jurisdictions around the world have enacted reform often responding to the need to implement or consolidate EU directives such as the UK with its Consumer Rights Act 2015, or responding to a general need to implement case law and to adapt their civil codes to the expectations of the modern civil and commercial environment such as France and Japan. All these emanations of new contract law are either based on a universal notion of contract or deal predominantly with consumer contracts. We therefore see a need to complement this activity with a focus on the commercial contract in scholarly research with a view to encouraging and informing further review and reform in the area of domestic and international commercial contract law. This chapter argues in Sect. 2 below that there has been a lack of reform in the area of traditional merchant law and commercial contract law and that the current identity based system of merchant and consumer law is an outdated concept for a modern legal system which wants to be fit for global commerce. Commercial contracts ought to be explored and defined as a separate contract type in scholarship. This volume offers a birds eye view of the potential scope of such a definition. Cross border dealings are not only a major field of application of a reformed approach to commercial contract but have also prompted the emergence of prototype rules over the past several decades which have entered general contract law and with it consumer contract law against all expectations and perhaps without sufficient premeditation in scholarship. Model contracts for domestic and international trade and more specifically rules relating to supervening events, hardship and general renegotiation duties have partly been developed by private service providers such as the International Chamber of Commerce (ICC) or national trade associations such as

[1] COM(2011) 635 final.

[2] Lando and Beale (2000). The full text can be accessed online among other sites at https://www.trans-lex.org/400200/_/pecl/.

[3] Von Bar and Clive (2010).

members of the International Federation of Consulting Engineers (FIDIC)[4] and partly by international organisations such as the Institute for the Unification of Private Law (UNIDROIT) in Rome and the United Nations Commission of International Trade Law (UNCITRAL). A universal approach to doctrine having critically evaluated these rules and assessed their value for general use should be complemented by sector specific rules. This is because the needs of international contractual business practice are not identical in all disciplines such as short term (sale of goods), long term (construction contracts) or international investment with state party involvement. This volume illustrates this by way of pinpointing selected problems taken from a range of jurisdictions across the world by looking at specialised contract types such as long term construction contracts, certain types of outsourcing, supplies, government bonds and securities as set out in Sect. 3 below. The role of public policy in commercial contract law is analysed in the context of corporate social responsibility, the notion of good faith and the protection of small and micro enterprises. A special focus is also directed at the role of domestic and international public law where it interacts directly with private substantive contract law and where states interact with private businesses directly. This is explained in Sect. 4 below. How do concepts of public international law as embodied in the 1969 Vienna Convention on the Law of Treaties (VCLT) for instance work in international commercial contract law? What is the role of international contractual dispute settlement where there are state parties involved? How is legal reasoning affected by the use of uniform law in the form of conventions?

2 The Structure of This Volume

This volume is organised in three parts. The first part contains contributions exploring the notion of merchant law and the commercial contract as distinguished from non-commercial contracts. Authors also highlight the role of commercial contracts within current settings of law reform at national and regional (European Union) level. The second part showcases selected specialised commercial contract types. The third part features contributions reflecting on the interface of public international and substantive commercial contract law from various angles. Some authors observe and explore a historic trajectory of a legal term commonly connected with commercial contracts and transactions morphing from a public into a private law concept.[5] Some focus is on the interplay of treaty law with private law and private dealings and the role of public international law reasoning in an international commercial context. This last part covers an area of legal discourse that has only been scarcely explored. The growing significance of global trade and cross border dealings conducted by private parties requires a lot more research into this type of interdisciplinary conceptual evolution. Instead, academic disciplines within the law—such as those of

[4] http://fidic.org/. See Christie in this volume.

[5] See D'Alvia and Oosterhuis in this volume.

private and public law—remain compartmentalised in this respect and stand in their own way when it comes to reconciling approaches practiced in public and private law with a view to furthering international law making, adjudication and dispute settlement. As the contributions in Part III illustrate, this may be necessary in order to reflect a historic shift from state acting to private party acting in international commerce.[6] Our research project therefore remains open to further engagement especially with this last aspect and considers itself a work in progress.

In the following, the three parts of the book are introduced with regard to their wider context and in some more detail.

3 Merchant Law in Law Reform (Part I)

Commercial contracts may be seen to form a special and separate contract type because they require specialised rules to a certain extent. This is true for both domestic and cross border (international) commercial contracts. These contracts are regularly exposed to risks that do not occur in a purely domestic and non-commercial setting. Examples are risks arising from long distance shipping, especially the carriage of goods by sea, changes in the law or factual circumstances in the course of the contractual performance (supervening events) or simply problems arising from the fact that the contracting parties are seated in different countries and have to deal with barriers arising from differences in their domestic law, international trade law or language related issues. Another difference to the domestic and non-commercial contract often arises from the content of the contract, either in relation to the actual goods traded or to be manufactured or the quality standard to be attained. This latter aspect can be explained by reference to the object and purpose of the contract.[7] Despite clear distinctive characteristics of the commercial contract no general definition of the commercial contract has been attempted in any jurisdiction. An illustration of this can be found in Articles 1 and 2 of the 1980 Vienna Convention of the International Sale of Goods (CISG), the scope provision. The CISG defines its scope using only the international aspect of the contract[8] expressly followed by an exclusion of purchases of household goods[9] and expressly excluding recourse to the 'commercial character' of the transaction.[10] This rule wants to avoid any clash

[6] See also Sect. 5 below.

[7] See Sect. 3.1 below and see Heidemann in this volume.

[8] Art. 1 (1) CISG: "This Convention applies to contracts of sale of goods between parties whose places of business are in different States:"

[9] Art. 2 CISG: "This Convention does not apply to sales: (a) of goods bought for personal, family or household use, unless the seller, at any time before or at the conclusion of the contract, neither knew nor ought to have known that the goods were bought for any such use;...."

[10] Art. 1 (3) CISG: "Neither the nationality of the parties nor the civil or commercial character of the parties or of the contract is to be taken into consideration in determining the application of this Convention."

between those jurisdictions maintaining a formally separate commercial law and those who do not which could result in a distortion or dispute of the scope provision.[11] On the basis of this, *de lege lata*, it can therefore be said that the commercial contract is a separate contract type by inverse conclusion as it merits a separate law merchant or otherwise specialised codified law in many jurisdictions.

3.1 Nature and Models of Merchant Law: Identities vs. Purpose

Continental European jurisdictions traditionally maintain separate commercial codes and even separate courts as in France[12] and partly in Germany where it is common to run special commercial 'chambers' (panels) at higher civil courts to deal with commercial cases. The United States (US) maintain the Uniform Commercial Code (UCC) at federal level as a restatement and a guide or model for the individual states to refer to in their legislation and law reform, but not as formal law. Arising from historic practice and tradition, commercial laws can be said to broadly follow a German, a French or an Anglo-American (common law) model. National laws have developed particularities of their commercial laws which today form distinct categories. They can be traced back to these three spheres of origin. The German model is traditionally 'identity based' whereas the French model is essentially 'transaction based'.[13] The common law has not developed any explicit differentiation between commercial and non-commercial private law or contracts. It can be regarded as having developed mainly on the basis of commercial cases, though, and might therefore even be regarded as using the commercial contract as a default scenario for its contract law. Historically, merchant privilege and royal protection was needed for merchant activity and success. This was granted by the king or other sovereign as delegated. Merchant law therefore developed as an expression of a class based society and embodied a degree of separation and exclusivity attributable to that class. In this context, the French system of commercial law, developed during the Napoleonic codification effort following the French Revolution of 1789 at the start of the nineteenth century, has to be seen as epitomising the 'democratic' or 'republican' alternative to the German or monarchic tradition.[14] The essence of this is the focus on the transaction rather than the person. Rather than describing a class

[11] Interestingly, Herber and Czerwenka do not refer to the merchant and non-merchant dichotomy but only to the relationship with national consumer laws which may maintain diverging categories from CISG specifying personal use as an exception to its applicability, Herber and Czerwenka (1991), pp. 23–25.

[12] See Bell et al. (2008), pp. 453–480.

[13] See in detail Heidemann (2016).

[14] English merchant law was merged into general law in the seventeenth century and special adjudication displaced. See on this McKendrick (2016), pp. 3–8. For a more detailed account and a good read on the subject see also Plucknett (1956), pp. 657 et seq.

of people this new law describes the character of a transaction as commercial or non-commercial; the so called *actes commerçants,* commercial acts. These are listed as types of contracts at the start of the *Code de Commerce*, the French commercial code.[15] They either qualify as commercial just by falling under these rules or they are further distinguished by the purpose of the transaction ('in order to resell') as in the sale of goods. This method shows two important characteristics: it uses the purpose of the transaction as a defining factor and it offers a neutral definition deflecting attention away from the person and towards the transaction. Neither characteristic is currently used to define commercial or non-commercial contracts according to the prevailing method under European Union (EU) law nor indeed national law based thereon as of course traditional merchant law as practised in other national jurisdictions. Both aspects would, however, offer different, more modern and more promising solutions to the underlying tasks at hand. More modern, because modern societies follow the republican model and a citizen state rather than the monarchic one on which the old continental European laws are based. More promising, because the person centered, identity based approach yields odd and unconvincing results at times.[16] The resulting law has consequently become the target of widespread and undermining criticism in popular opinion which erodes not only the enacted law but also the legal principles it was meant to protect such as consumer protection, health and safety laws and a generally high standard in commercial and non-commercial contractual relations.[17] A re-evaluation of the underlying factors which merit a special law governing commercial or non-commercial (consumer) transactions is therefore needed and can be based on the above described method. The law enacted to govern such transactions will be a *lex specialis* deriving its justification only from the necessities identified as typical to commercial or non-commercial transactions. Otherwise contract law is universal and applies equally to all citizens who are no longer divided by separate classes and entitlements or restrictions in a modern state design. The person centered or identity based approach does not observe this principle when it designates 'consumers' as a group of contractual partners who require privileges or protections just because they are assigned this 'label' which is based on the general assumption that they are the 'weaker party'.[18] Small and micro businesses can be powerless and victimised in the face of large business organisations as the current investigation into the Royal Bank of Scotland's restructuring unit illustrates.[19] The same applies to the description of contractual parties as 'traders' or merchants. The characteristics assigned to these 'identities' are not static or permanent in a contractual context, nor are they meant to be on the

[15] See Articles L110-1(1) and (2) of the French *Code de Commerce,* CdC.

[16] See in detail Heidemann (2016), e.g. pp. 698–699 and similar Austen-Baker (2008).

[17] See Dalhuisen in this volume who suggests the recognition and promotion of 'minimum standards' in commercial contracts.

[18] See the critique of this assumption by Austen-Baker (2008).

[19] See the Guardian newspaper of 20 Feb 2018 at https://www.theguardian.com/business/2018/feb/20/mps-publish-full-unredacted-report-into-rbs-small-business-scandal. See also Sara Hourani in this volume.

part of the EU based legislature.[20] This is precisely why continental commercial codes do not contain special rulebooks on commercial contracts but only a few individual rules. The 'German style' codifications instead open with a more or less complex description of the merchant (or 'entrepreneur' in recent terms), which can be both a natural or legal person (corporation). This is the legacy of the class system which was restructured in the French Commercial Code by starting with the definition of the commercial transaction and defining merchants as those who carry out commercial acts and make this their profession or main source of income.[21] The purpose of the transaction is a defining factor in this exercise. The purpose binds the content or object of any contract and the contracting parties together. It forms the defining relationship which is suitable to form a distinction between commercial and non-commercial. Parties can be said to have a particular attitude or relationship to the object of a contract. They may for instance purchase an item for own personal use and wanting to keep it or they may purchase an item in order to resell it. Their expectations towards the item will differ in both cases and they will place value on different aspects of the contract, for instance the quality of the item or the packaging and transportation arrangements. The purpose of the transaction defines this relationship. It is not the status of the contracting party which requires a separate law to govern the transaction but the character of this relationship, in other words the transaction, its purpose and context. In this way, commercial contract law does not seek to govern persons but transactions of a particular nature. Only in this way is it possible to explain and apply transnational uniform contract law. A person centered approach needs to describe the person—a party to an international commercial contract—to be governed by a law reaching across borders. This brings up questions of citizenship and loyalty. These are, however, not the concern of transnational commercial contract law and cannot be resolved by it. Both national and transnational commercial contract law address transactions which set themselves apart from others by aspects of context and risk, not the contracting parties. Dalhuisen calls these commercial contracts professional contracts.[22] Based on the scope provision of CISG, a reformed word pair could then be professional and private contract, rather than commercial and consumer contract or trader and consumer in the identity based system. The merchant never had a formal designated counterpart in traditional legal terminology anyway.

3.2 *The Role of Commercial Contract Law in Recent Law Reform Projects*

Jurisdictions around the world have indeed undertaken law reforms in recent years which either change their law merchant directly or impacting on it more or less inadvertently.

20 See on this Heidemann (2016). See also Austen-Baker (2008), pp. 61 and 64.

21 Art. 121-1 CdC.

22 Dalhuisen in this volume.

3.2.1 Reform of Civil and Commercial Codes in Germany and EU Consumer Law

In Germany, the latest reform of the Commercial Code (*Handelsgesetzbuch,* HGB) took place a while ago, in 1998, by way of the Trade Law Reform Act (*Handelsrechtsreformgesetz*, HRefG).[23] The aim of the reform was to simplify the existing law in particular the provisions on the definition of the merchant. Article 3 of the 1998 Reform Act removed the previous section 4 of the HGB and simplified section 2 HGB by making the merchant quality of a business the default position. This can now be disproved by a threshold provision which exempts smaller business which 'do not require a mercantile set up'. The reform was, however, by no means intended to fundamentally reform the approach taken by the HGB and shifting the starting point of the definition from the person or business (identity) to the transaction. The dichotomy merchant/non-merchant is integral to German law and affects many areas of civil and tax law. While it is not indispensable by any means, it has become an axiom of legal thinking in practice and in the minds of successive legislatures. Therefore, it must be all the more surprising that the German legislature has willingly accepted an overlapping dichotomy, that of consumer and trader brought about by EU law. This was implemented into the Civil Code[24] by way of the reform brought into effect from 2001. No explanation whatsoever is incorporated into the law as to how the relationship between the new character (identity) of trader relates to that of merchant. Clearly, a larger number of persons are caught by the notion of trader than qualify as merchants but without the safeguards and limitations that the definition of merchant is meant to maintain such as a threshold provision relating to scale and intensity of the trading activity. The qualification of a person or business as merchant entails a array of legal consequences embodied in the HGB such as reporting and accounting duties and standards spanning the life of a business from incorporation and registration to insolvency and the related criminal offences attached to a breach of some of these duties.[25] A trader, on the other hand, is in fact only a fleeting identity to be assumed mainly within one-off contractual relationships.[26] Imported from EU directives and regulations, the trader was originally always defined exclusively with regard to the respective EU legislation.[27] It was

[23] Federal Bulletin, BGBl. 1998 I Nr. 38, 1474–1484 (22 June 1998).

[24] Section 13 of the German Civil Code, *Buergerliches Gesetzbuch,* BGB.

[25] Only a merchant can commit insolvency offences.

[26] See Austen-Baker (2008), p. 61.

[27] Relevant EU Directives and Regulations open with a scope provision which stereotypically include the phrase '[f]or the purposes of this Regulation' or '[f]or the purposes of this Directive', see Heidemann (2016), pp. 679–681. Examples are Directive 1999/44/EC of the European Parliament and of the Council of 25 May 1999 on certain aspects of the sale of consumer goods and associated guarantees, [1999] OJ L 171/12; Council Directive 90/314/EEC of 13 June 1990 on package travel, package holidays and package tours, [1990] OJ L 158/59; Recital 7 and Article 3 of the Proposal for a Directive of the European Parliament and of the Council on package travel and assisted travel arrangements, amending Regulation (EC) No. 2006/2004, Directive 2011/83/EU and repealing Council Directive 90/314/EEC, COM(2013) 512 final; Regulation (EC) No.

consequently not strictly required and distinctly unnecessary on the part of the German legislature[28] to create this new word pair of consumer and trader as counterparts as a permanent fixture in German civil law. It confirms, however, the continued allegiance to this identity based concept and a missed chance to move towards a more modern law merchant.[29]

3.2.2 Reform of the Commercial Code in Austria and the Role of EU Terminology

The Austrian equivalent to the German HBG which had been largely identical since the German usurpation of the country in 1938 was reformed in 2007 and renamed *Unternehmensgesetzbuch*, UGB, (Enterprise Code).[30] Just as in Germany, the reform does not do away with the person centered approach to the dichotomy. Instead, it brings the terminology in line with EU legislation which was largely incorporated into Austrian law by way of the 1979 Consumer Protection Act (*Konsumentenschutzgesetz*). It is important to take note of the difficulty of translating the EU terminology into German. The English word pair consumer and trader is not easily implemented in the German speaking jurisdictions precisely because they already use very similar words as technical legal terms. These terms do not have direct counterparts in English because none of the Anglo-American jurisdictions operates a formally separate law merchant or has developed words like businessman, trader or entrepreneur into formal legal language with defined legal consequences attached. The EU lingo, however, clearly avoids the development of a

261/2004 of the European Parliament and of the Council of 11 February 2004 establishing common rules on compensation and assistance to passengers in the event of denied boarding and of cancellation or long delay of flights, and repealing Regulation (EEC) No 295/9, [2004] OJ L 46/1; Directive 94/47/EC of the European Parliament and the Council of 26 October 1994 on the protection of purchasers in respect of certain aspects of contracts relating to the purchase of the right to use immovable properties on a timeshare basis, [1994] OJ L 280/83; Directive 2008/122/EC of the European Parliament and the Council of 14 January 2009, [2009] OJ L 33/10; Regulation (EC) No. 593/2008 of the European Parliament and of the Council of 17 June 2008 on the law applicable to contractual obligations (Rome I), [2008] OJ L 177/12; Council Regulation (EC) No. 44/2001 of 22 December 2000 on jurisdiction and the recognition and enforcement of judgments in civil and commercial matters, [2001] OJ L 12/1; Regulation (EU) No. 1215/2012 of 12 December 2012 on jurisdiction and the recognition and enforcement of judgments in civil and commercial matters ('Brussels I Recast'), [2012] OJ L 351/1.

[28] And indeed the British in respect of the Consumer Rights Act 2015, see Sect. 3.2.3 below.

[29] Reforms of the HGB have been proposed as early as 1965 by Raiser and in 1975 by Raisch. Criticism of the existing structure is regularly voiced by scholars, to no avail, see Raisch (1965, 1975), Raiser (1969), and Schmidt (2005).

[30] The reform was effected by way of the *Bundesgesetz über besondere zivilrechtliche Vorschriften für Unternehmen (Unternehmensgesetzbuch – UGB)* as of 1 January 2007, available at www.ris.bka.gv.at/Dokument.wxe?Abfrage=BundesnormenDokumentnummer=NOR30004735; and enacted by the *Handelsrechts-Änderungsgesetz* (HaRÄG), Federal Bulletin (BGBl.) I Nr. 120/2005, available at www.ris.bka.gv.at/Dokument.wxe?Abfrage=BgblAuthDokumentnummer=BGBLA_2005_I_120.

formal and general definition of the word trader. The term is used interchangeably with the respective contractual party (seller, travel agent, airline, tour operator) in each of the directives (more rarely regulations) governing particular transactions such as time share contracts, travel or package holiday contracts or general consumer sales.[31] The legal instruments repeat the phrase 'for the purposes of this directive/regulation…' for each of their definitions thereby clearly avoiding the formation of a general meaning of the expressions used therein. The word pair consumer/trader can only be considered to have attained a customary meaning by usage but not by design.

Definitions of trader or consumer regularly incorporate an element of purpose, however, and thereby contain the promise of a new approach. EU law has the potential to serve as a pioneer for a transaction based method with the purpose of the transaction at the heart of a new definition. The insistence on fragmented and partly contradictory or at least inconsistent legislation in this area rather than proactively shaping a consistent methodology and reform is a disappointment. The recent consumer rights directive[32] could have provided an opportunity to make a fresh start in this area of law and even the Common European Sales Law (CESL) project could have been used to work on terminology and help nation states to adopt an updated version of the merchant/non-merchant dichotomy.[33] It has to be acknowledged, though, that the law as it has evolved is the result of a political process which had its origin in the early 1970s when the debate had been tinted by competing political tendencies.[34] This is regrettable and obviously means that entrenched and possibly obsolete viewpoints of a bygone era may get dragged along unchecked and unreviewed where they might not fit well any longer and not achieve the desired aims. These aims are of course to provide a legal framework for commercial dealings where needed which includes business to consumer (B2C) relations.

[31] See note 26 above.

[32] Directive 2011/83/EU.

[33] See Anagnostopoulou in this volume.

[34] The 'consumerism' debate started in the early 1970s in the US and in Europe and linked the subject to general political debate which still hinders a meaningful political and academic review of underlying concepts. See for an early contribution to the concerns raised against 'consumerism' Powers (1971). A transaction based view would arrive at different results than the identity based approach in consumer law. 'Consumer' law would cover a wider spectrum of contracting parties including professionals acting 'in the course of their business' in some cases. This contradicts a person centered view that seeks to perpetuate the character of consumer as weak and in need of privileges and protection which is often seen as a political statement defending consumers against abusive and greedy business practices (and business people), a scenario of perpetrator and victim in short. While this aim is doubtlessly justified in a modern world of mass production on a global scale the attitude reveals a possibly inadvertent adherence to the old class system with static roles for model identities which is most definitely obsolete. Consumer law must not be a vehicle to introduce new class-like divisions and classifications of equal citizens. New law can be devised in new forms. The transaction based method is clearly a more modern version of the creation of the law merchant and can be used to devise complementary law for consumers. Similar considerations have been made in the law of (international) taxation but not followed through. See Heidemann (2016) and Heidemann in this volume.

3.2.3 Reform in the United Kingdom: The Consumer Rights Act 2015

It might appear strange to head a paragraph about commercial contract law with a consumer rights legislation. However, this rather new codification in a common law jurisdiction results in a novel situation which is most likely unintended and possibly largely unnoticed. The scope of the 2015 Consumer Rights Act covers only business to consumer (B2C) contractual relationships and thereby exempts them from the general or otherwise codified law and leaves for the first time in legal history, presumably, an explicit designation of the Sale of Goods Act 1979 (SGA) as well as the Unfair Contract Terms Act 1977 (UCTA) for business to business (B2B) and consumer to consumer (C2C) dealings only,[35] a type of law merchant for the sale of goods, without an express provision to this end in the SGA. The United Kingdom (UK) does not share the conundrum of civil law jurisdictions with a separate law merchant where the arrival of the trader/consumer dichotomy competes with a pre-existing merchant/non-merchant dichotomy. Not only is there no such system in the UK[36] but the largely uncodified case law based contract law allows an easy integration of the new codification in that it does not textually collide with pre-existing provisions.

3.2.4 Reform of the French and Japanese Civil Code: Standard Contract Terms

More recent reforms of the civil and contract law have been carried out in France (2016)[37] and in Japan (2017).[38] As with the above described jurisdictions, overlap is an issue which causes contradictions and discrepancies which the legislator has not resolved. While the reform of the *Code Civil* in France was among other things prompted by the need to implement EU provisions mainly concerning consumer protection law, it is interesting to see that the Japanese legislature felt motivated in a similar way to update and reform provisions on unfair terms, standard contract forms and contracting by adhesion. As Catherine Pédamon points out in her contribution to this volume, the general contract law as codified in the French Civil Code (*Code Civil*, CC) applies to commercial contracts, too, unless there are special provisions in the law merchant, mainly found in the *Code de Commerce,* CdC. This applies to all jurisdictions which maintain a formally separate commercial law. Commercial codes typically contain only a small number of contract law provisions that differ from general contract law such as rules about silent acceptance and the role of trade usages. The purpose of the commercial codes is to establish general

[35] See Explanatory Note No. 24 to the Consumer Rights Act 2015.

[36] The law merchant is used as reference to trade usages and customs in the Sale of Goods Act (SGA) 1979 section 62(2): 'the rules of the common law, including the law merchant, except in so far as they are inconsistent with the provisions of [the SGA] … apply to contracts for the sale of goods.'

[37] See Pédamon in this volume.

[38] See Karaiskos in this volume.

rules for the incorporation of businesses, the relationship between shareholders and directors, the proper running of the business including accounting and reporting duties, commercial registers and insolvency rules. The commercial contract is not usually seen as a separate contract type. Therefore the legal consequences attached to the 'status' of merchant are not predominantly contractual[39] but largely non-contractual obligations and duties. Nevertheless, modern consumer laws distinguish between B2B and B2C contracts based on the above mentioned identity based system. In Japan, it was felt that standard contract terms needed codification outside the already existing Consumer Contract Act[40] because there was no possibility for a judicial review of such terms other than on the basis of two general provisions of the Japanese Civil Code, the good faith provision and the provision on the validity and (un)enforceability of unlawful terms. As Karaiskos describes in his contribution to this volume, an imbalance as to information and negotiating power is not exclusive to B2C situations. These can occur in B2B contracts between large business partners and their smaller and dependent counterparts, often so called small and medium sized enterprises, SMEs.[41] Particular attention was given among other points to the validity of undisclosed standard terms[42] and surprising clauses. Both reforms in Japan and in France have in common that the impact of the new rules on pre-existing systems of consumer or merchant law was not preconceived or anticipated. There is no express rule explaining the intended relationship between new and existing rules even though clashes are obvious. Interestingly, in modern reform projects, certain concepts and individual rules which used to be typical for commercial contracts have been introduced on a general basis and therefore with effect for consumer contracts, too. This is true for rules providing for contract adaptation and renegotiation as in the French reform as well as in the area of standard terms for rules allowing undisclosed terms to be validly incorporated into general contracts as in the Japanese reform.[43] These rules may be derived from business practice, custom and usage (such as the acceptance of undisclosed terms) and found to be suitable for consumer contracts, too, or they were developed in the course of projects for international commercial contracts[44] and then transferred into domestic law reform of general contract law. While it may be concluded from this that commercial law assumes a pioneering or role model function, that might be a misconception. It is more likely that the effect remained unnoticed by law makers and that the failure to distinguish commercial and non-commercial transactions is at the heart of this development.

---

[39] Discounting incorporation agreements which are regarded as (multilateral) contracts in civil law jurisdictions.

[40] See further Karaiskos in this volume.

[41] See further on this imbalance Hourani in this volume.

[42] See also Dalhuisen in this volume.

[43] See Karaiskos in this volume at Sect. 6.

[44] Such as hardship rules in the UNIDROIT Principles for International Commercial Contracts, UPICC.

4 Scholarship on Selected Aspects of Commercial Contracts (Part II)

The contributions in Part II of this volume can serve to test some of the propositions revealed in Part I as analysed above. A closer look is taken at certain contractual remedies which were thought to be suited to commercial, perhaps especially international commercial contracts but now also appear in general contract law. Rules on hardship, for instance, are not only contained in the UNIDROIT Principles for International Commercial Contracts, UPICC, but also typically included in standard contract forms issued by international trade associations in order to meet risks which are frequently incurred in international transport and shipping but less frequently in a domestic non-commercial setting. Rules on hardship and supervening events had also developed in case law on general contract law in European jurisdictions as rules of last resort in order to respond to events of an extraordinary nature affecting the public at large such as the currency devaluations following the Great Depression in the late 1920s and early 1930s or housing shortages after World War I or the like. Both the latest German as well as the French reform of the Civil Code introduced a hardship rule into the Civil Codes whereby it was intended to restate case law in this area. In the German provision[45] this aim has been exceeded and it appears to roll three remedies into one thus overlapping with rules on error and mistake as well as elevating what was a rule of last resort to a standard remedy.[46] To what extent is it common and useful to resort to contract adaptation and extensive co-operation during contractual performance of commercial contracts? Therefore, to what extent is it useful to extend express hardship rules to general contract law thereby reinforcing a previously optional instrument for hedging against certain typical commercial risks?

4.1 Cooperation, Renegotiation and Contract Adaptation

As mentioned above, this will depend on the contract type. Long term contracts in the construction industry for instance require different parameters than contracts for the sale of goods or shipping contracts. While the latter often involve a fast moving pace and a multitude of parties affected by changes and adaptations who might not be parties to the contracts to be re-negotiated[47] the former are more commonly performed in a collaborative manner which is provided for in the contract terms. This type of contract drafting and performance is discussed by David Christie in this volume who is looking at the latest version of one of the standard forms of the UK Institution of Civil Engineers' New Engineering Contract (NEC). This industry

[45] Section 313 *Buergerliches Gesetzbuch*, BGB.

[46] See Pédamon in this volume.

[47] Examples are insurers, creditors and lenders.

standard form professes to use a 'plain English' approach seeking to meet the parties' requirements. Christie sees a downside in the lack of legal clarity in this approach and analyses the legal pitfalls of re-negotiation clauses, their relationship with contractual conditions and the role of relational contract theory. His analysis highlights the interface between contractual relationships and more sophisticated arrangements that might be regarded as partnerships, joint ventures or the like. In civil law jurisdictions, the aspiration to collaborate and co-operate fulfills the criterion of pursuing a common purpose which in turn is the very definition of a partnership (*Gesellschaft*, society, *société*). The German general rule reads as follows:

> Bürgerliches Gesetzbuch (BGB)
>
> § 705 Inhalt des Gesellschaftsvertrags
>
> Durch den Gesellschaftsvertrag verpflichten sich die Gesellschafter gegenseitig, die Erreichung eines gemeinsamen Zweckes in der durch den Vertrag bestimmten Weise zu fördern, insbesondere die vereinbarten Beiträge zu leisten.

The official English translation reads:

> By a partnership agreement, the partners mutually put themselves under a duty to promote the achievement of a common purpose in the manner stipulated by the contract, in particular, without limitation, to make the agreed contributions.[48]

A duty to co-operate is at the same time a rule that has been promoted and pursued in the context of the recent CESL proposal. Art. 3 of the Annexe I of CESL (the actual Sales Law) reads:

> Co-operation
>
> The parties are obliged to co-operate with each other to the extent that this can be expected for the performance of their contractual obligations.

Likewise, Art.1:202 of the Principles of European Contract Law, PECL, reads:

> [Duty to Co-operate]. Each party owes to the other a duty to co-operate in order to give full effect to the contract.

As much as it seems to be accepted that this rule is based on the general principle of good faith in contract it has been rightly criticized as too wide and allowing undue discretion for courts to determine contractual content that they consider just in any given situation.[49] This compromises foreseeability and legal certainty for contractual parties,[50] especially in view of the unclear boundary of the codified

[48] English translation officially endorsed by the Federal Ministry of Justice and available at https://www.gesetze-im-internet.de/englisch_bgb/englisch_bgb.html#p3170.

[49] See for instance Neumann (2012), p. 517. See also Association Henri Capitant (2008), p. 77; Weller (2009), p. 517; Eidenmueller (2008), p. 539; Eidenmueller et al. (2008).

[50] As well as potentially party autonomy.

cooperation duty with the traditional civil law definition of association or partnership.

At the same time, this example illustrates that these boundaries are by no means clear cut and require reflection by the parties and the judiciary in many more contexts. Joseph Lee and Chien-Chung Lin look at two further contractual contexts in this volume which are highly relevant in commercial practice. Prof. Lin analyses the specific arrangements made in industry operating world wide, so called original equipment manufacturing (OEM) in the context of information technology. The theory of the boundary of the firm is at the heart of this conceptual discussion.[51] How can arrangements be defined as one-off contractual relationships for the purpose of the made-to-order production and supply of digital content rather than as joint ventures or part of one and the same corporate entity and therefore corporate activity? Dr Lee's analysis picks up on the nature of the firm as a contractual versus an organisational (corporate) relationship *sui generis* as is preferred in common law jurisdictions. He uses the example of intra corporate arbitrations.[52] In both analyses, the contract plays a role as one out of several options to organise commercial activity. Ronald Coase was of course an economist[53] and not as such interested in the legal nature of the firm[54] or the contract. For lawyers his theories nevertheless provide important food for thought in respect of the distinction between contract and corporation. This distinction as analysed by Lin in this volume poses questions not only of managerial diligence but also of justice and the importance of awareness of theoretical underpinning.

4.2 *Regulation and Self-Governance*

The above mentioned questions of justice in a contractual context are normally left to traditional principles of contract law and market forces. Where imbalances among contracting parties are observed on a regular basis these internalised factors may not work as desired so that intervention on the part of the legislator (regulation) may be necessary. Sara Hourani is looking at contracts between supermarkets and their suppliers. These had come under scrutiny following protracted problems with supermarkets not paying on time and effectively imposing unfavourable terms on their suppliers due to their prevailing market power. The approach taken is a gradual one with some non-binding 'soft law' guidelines being adopted by the UK Competition Commission in the form of the 'Groceries Supply Code of Practice' which is accompanied by an enforcement body hosted by the Competition Commission. This approach is reinforced by existing legislation enacted upon implementation of the

[51] This discussion was started by Ronald Coase in the early twentieth century with his publication 'The Nature of the Firm', Coase (1937).

[52] See on this for instance Solinas (2014).

[53] And a winner of the Nobel Prize for Economics in 1991.

[54] Which is shown by the use of the term firm in the legally informal but economically relevant sense.

EU 'Late Payment' Directive 2011/7/EU, the Small Business, Enterprise and Employment Act 2015. Hourani carries out a comparative exercise among common law jurisdictions in order to find out what the trajectory of this legal protection might be after the UK has left the EU prospectively in 2019 and where such protection might lie in the traditional contract laws of those countries absent EU legislation. Alexandra Horváthová examines the potential of the contract and its theory and governing law itself for the achievement of a yet wider aspect of justice in the context of free trade, corporate social responsibility, CSR. Contractual imbalances which are recognised as causing effects materialising outside the contractual relationship, perhaps even far outside the home jurisdiction, might have to be counteracted by measures based on public policy. Both authors examine to what extent this external intervention might be pre-empted or complemented by arguing on a contractual basis and exploring the contract's full potential in order to achieve certain public policy goals. Andhov looks at the contractual relations of corporations and asks what values are present in contract law which might be invoked to counteract harmful practice in international commerce. This is an important complementary analysis to the existing efforts in many jurisdictions to install legislative safeguards responding to harmful practice and 'collateral' effects in international trade such as exploitative labour provision in production countries, unsafe production facilities, corruption and many more. Most countries have provided for 'soft law' codes of practice applied by a so called 'comply or explain' method in the absence of a convincing legal basis for mandatory rules. Due to obvious problems of attribution in the causation chain of events[55] a change in business culture is intended and a reliance of respected principles of ethics and morals in commerce and general contract law. These do of course exist. Scholars in many countries are working on legal analyses that might yield a convincing answer to the problem. In the meantime, a multitude of initiatives have led to the introduction of national and international reporting standards, prizes and awards in order to raise the level of protection and prevention of harmful effects of trade in the areas of human rights, environment and markets by way of voluntary compliance and economic incentive.[56] Commercial contract law offers certain inherent answers.[57]

---

[55] One tragic example is the collapse of the 'Rana Plaza' textile factory building in Dakha, Bangla-Desh in 2013 causing over 3500 people, mostly textile workers, to be killed or injured. The flagrant breach of building regulations that led to this disaster was of course not directly attributable to the Western retailers whose suppliers were based in the building. The moral and ethical involvement is compelling though and called once again for a response on the part of retailers, by politicians, consumers and campaigners.

[56] Examples are the United Nations Global Compact, the OECD Guidelines and the standards issued by the International Labour Organisation to name a few. In the UK, stock market listed companies are required to comply with the UK Corporate Governance Code as part of listing requirements or explain why they do not comply, see Listing Rules 9.8.6. (5) and (6) of the Financial Conduct Authority (FCA), the UK supervisory body for the stock market, available at https://www.handbook.fca.org.uk/handbook/LR/9/8.html. The UK has also adapted the Proceeds of Crime Act 2002 (sections 241 and 241A) by way of the section 13 of the Criminal Finances Act 2017 expanding forfeiture rules to assets obtained in connection with human rights violations. This may not have helped the Rana Plaza building collapse case, though. See for more detail on the subject of 'transnational governance' Gless (2015), pp. 45 et seq.; Calliess and Zumbansen (2012), pp. 181–247.

[57] See Andhov in this volume. See also Austen-Baker (2008) who describes these regulatory mechanisms of contract on page 73: "In short, the contractual norm of propriety of means, coupled with

4.3 Uniform Law and Cross Border Enforcement

Commercial contracts are more often exposed to cross border situations than private or consumer contracts. A functioning international system of contractual performance and dispute settlement is therefore essential for the functioning of international trade. To what extent is classic contractual performance and related enforcement possible and desirable in this context? To what extent is it in fact practiced? Dania Thomas looks into this important aspect of classical contract theory in the context of sovereign debt recovery. Contract law itself becomes an integral part of the financial product as well as of the commercial calculus as perhaps in no other context.[58] The history and current evolvement of sovereign debt recovery also allows strong insights into the public/private relationship between private law instruments such as securities and public policy suggesting a need for continued scrutiny of commercial acting of public bodies. International disparity of laws plays a significant role in these contractual relations[59] as they traditionally do in the area of purely private cross border secured credit transactions where enforcement depends on property law. Uniform law and harmonisation have not achieved very much here at this point in time. Classic conflict of laws is used in order to stipulate the applicable national law and to try to achieve smooth and economically beneficial outcomes. Muriel Renaudin sets out past and current efforts in the area of secured credit law and the pro's and con's of each possible form of legislation and regulation at transnational level and the prospects of each of the proposals to be formally adopted and to succeed. Uniform law, especially commercial contract law which has been so successful for the past five decades, is not taking hold in the area of property, insolvency and procedural law and can therefore not deliver tailor made rules for the creation and trade of financial products, collateral and securities at transnational level.[60]

5 Commercial Contract Law and Public International Law: The Cart Before the Horse? (Part III)

The third part of this volume sheds light on a number of aspects at the interface between private and public law in the context of commercial contracts.

---

those of reciprocity and contractual solidarity, will tend to perform the role some seek to fill through regulation." Commentators generally do not consider the commercial or non-commercial nature of transactions, though. It is submitted here that the tension in consumer contracts or the failures of commercial dealings in a social context cannot be captured without making this distinction and analysing the characteristics of both commercial and private scenarios.

[58] See Thomas in this volume who throws a spotlight on recent activities of so called vulture funds and the wider practice in sovereign debt management.

[59] Practices like 'netting' do not rely on classic enforcement or performance or even offset, they are economically driven. See on this Lehmann (2017). Even within the EU classic contractual performance and traditional insolvency law seems to have been officially abandoned in the area of debt enforcement in banking relationships with the advent of the Bank Resolution Directive 2014/59/EU.

[60] See in depth Dalhuisen (2016) and Juutilainen (2018).

5.1 *Historic Trajectory*

Janwillem Oosterhuis and Daniele d'Alvia explain two components of contract and commercial transactions in a historical context which to many will be surprising and open an interesting perspective on both topics. Oosterhuis introduces the history of bills of exchange. The evolution of the bill of exchange through the history of merchant law in Europe shows that public actors have been indispensable in the creation of merchant law as we conceive of it today. Oosterhuis concludes that private actors are as capable as public actors in providing suitable law for commercial transactions that provide the required clarity and legal certainty on an international plain. The author's and co-editor's own research on this issue confirms this outcome.[61] D'Alvia reminds us of the journey of the notion of good faith through Roman legal history into our present time. The notion of good faith morphed over time from a distinctly public international law concept of the historic Roman Empire into a general clause present in most continental civil law jurisdictions and decidedly associated with private law. Both authors demonstrate that public authority and regulatory intervention is not self evidently pointed in one direction only. Private law can successfully operate as a self reliant regulatory mechanism giving little justification to public law intervention[62] contrary to the contemporary expectation that public policy can only be applied and enforced by way of regulation originating in public law. As the studies by Andhov and Hourani in this volume demonstrate, public policies are an integral part of traditional contract law when explored fully. The presence of public policies may be regarded as obvious only in public regulatory law at first sight. Regulation may then be perceived by both the regulators and the addressees as limiting, prescriptive and exclusionary. However, there are strong examples where, seemingly vice versa, public policy aims are being pursued with the means of private law.

5.2 *Contract Law in the Shape of Treaties*

Exploring contractual values and remedies are only one avenue to reveal such a mechanism concerning the content of the contractual agreement, its performance and enforcement. Another avenue has been explored, perhaps inadvertently, by the signatory states to the 1980 United Nations Convention for the International Sale of Goods (CISG). Here, states are pursuing the declared aim of world peace and economic thriving, perhaps one allowing the other, by providing for uniform law at transnational level. Similar conventions had been signed before, but not preceded by an express declaration of intentions and objectives which are clearly of a public policy nature. This seemingly paradoxical but certainly perplexing pairing of the

[61] See Heidemann in this volume.

[62] See Oosterhuis in this volume.

rather grand public policy objective typically promoted and achieved by states with the substantive contract law typically used by private parties only is explored by the author in this volume.[63] The role of object and purpose is not only an interpretation tool for treaties but is itself derived from contractual interpretation. By likening treaties to contracts[64] a powerful point is made regarding similarities in public and private acting. Some fundamental rules of interacting and indeed general principles of law can be discerned and successfully employed interchangeably in both realms. Incidentally, object and purpose are powerful tools for legislative drafting including conventions if used by design. They can at the same time shine a spotlight on the great responsibility states must observe when drafting treaties. Klabbers explores the interim obligation states assume when signing a treaty:

> Normative situations are strikingly different [from mutual or reciprocal agreements] particularly when the actors involved are not only states, but also individuals relying on the potential self-executing provisions of treaties [such as CISG] about to enter into force. In such circumstances, a test of legitimate expectations (broadly conceived) will occasionally show the same result as a test of bad faith, but without the intervening (and, in theory at least, controlling) variable of the defeat of the treaty's object and purpose.[65]

Klabbers analyses the arguments of negligence, bad faith and legitimate expectation giving rise to remedies in international treaty law. These are concepts valid in contract law, too. However, the scenario is more challenging in normative treaties because the contractarian approach cannot work when the acting parties applying the treaty are not the parties to the treaty. This is the conundrum of uniform law usually in the form of contract law conventions.

5.3 EU Financial Regulation and Investor-State Disputes

Contract law is instrumental not only in the above mentioned context of sovereign debt enforcement[66] serving private ends but also in the enforcement of regulatory law in the area of financial services adopted at EU level serving public ends. The intricate coverage of rules which has been created particularly responding to the 2008 global financial crisis serves both consumer protection and market protection. Mads Andenas analyses how contract law is not only influenced by EU financial regulation but how in reverse contract law and contracts itself as well as indeed the judiciary serve to give effect to the intended aims of the EU legislature. Due to the still prevailing fragmented nature of EU (public law) regulation private law still plays a crucial executing and gap filling role in giving effect to the policy aims pursued by the EU legislature. Finally, public and private actors meet in a more direct

---

[63] See Heidemann in this volume.

[64] As the drafters of the 1969 Vienna Convention on the Law of Treaties, VCLT, in fact did, see Klabbers (2001), pp. 305–313.

[65] Klabbers (2001), p. 293.

[66] See Sect. 4.3 above.

way in investor-state arbitrations and contractual relationships involving a private and a state party. This is often the case where states principally and exclusively act through agents in international trade for a number of reasons and more recently where states commit themselves to certain guarantees to facilitate or promote foreign investment. In both scenarios contracts are concluded seemingly on a private law basis but with public body parties which may be subject to public law only. Disputes arising out of these agreements (especially stabilisation clauses) pose questions of illegality and validity, enforceability and ethics. Where does this take the parties involved? Can the public law rule unquestionably be said to prevail or to precede the private law rule? Or are private law concepts used to explain and justify solutions found in such cases and indeed provide the procedural setting? Hendrik Puschmann and Andreas Geroldinger look at these questions in the context of arbitration clauses under the 1966 International Centre for Settlement of Investor Disputes (ICSID) Convention.

5.4 Are Treaties the Tool of Choice?

The Third Part of this volume thereby makes a strong case for a re-evaluation of well known perceptions of public and private law, their hierarchy and their respective potential for the delivery of concepts of justice and public policy aims in commercial law. Can it be that "the international community has used the wrong tool for more than a century" as Basedow asks in his 2006 essay on the role of uniform law conventions within the law of treaties?[67] The trust that the signatories of CISG and other uniform law conventions[68] place in private law may be more justified than they might have bargained for. Certain public policy aims can be achieved on the basis of inherent values of private commercial law. Public law in turn benefits from using these tools as they have arrived in public international law to perform a 'reality check' with regard to legislation and application. Incongruence between objects, purposes and content of a public or public international legal instrument can defeat a purpose just as it would in a commercial contract and it would other than in a contract also undermine the authority of the law. A qualitative issue is therefore part of any mandate to legislate including at international level. An unqualified mandate by governments or state representatives to legislate at transnational level in the form of normative treaties or to commit states by agreements in the form of treaties may not in fact exist under the doctrine of state sovereignty. This goes to the heart of concepts of statehood which certainly is beyond the scope of this volume. It is however a valid point of discussion flowing directly from the analysis of the interface of

[67] Basedow (2006), p. 731.

[68] Such as the UNIDROIT, UNCITRAL and Hague conventions on leasing and factoring, the applicable law or bills of lading.

substantive private law with public international law where commercial contract law comes closest to the law of treaties.

A historic reflection sheds more light on this point. As Basedow pointed out in 2006

> … towards the end of the 19th century the impact of the public interest in the railways was strong, at least in Europe. Most countries had nationalized the private railway companies of the pioneer phase; thus, the Contracting States of the European Railway Convention were at the same time entrepreneurs and legislators of railways law.[69]

This description shows the inherent conflict in treaties providing substantive uniform private contract and tort law. Poignantly, a protagonist and legal author of the late nineteenth century spoke of "diplomatic arrangements also called conventions"[70] thereby capturing the ambivalent relationship states have to binding international law. Other than in national contract law an element of dynamic fluctuation seems to be expected by the state signatory in the application and enforcement of conventions unlike an ordinary legal rule. The advent of the 1969 Vienna Convention on the law of Treaties (VCLT) is an expression of an evolutionary process towards a more pronounced role for the rule of law at international level. Keeping in mind the origins of our present day uniform law as expressions of the state public interest, however, puts some typical challenges in perspective that exist to this day. Some deep rooted mind sets and protective attitudes are certainly still present in legal theory such as the conception of industrial property (intellectual property rights) as a

> kind of privilege granted by each sovereign State in respect of its own territory and not reaching beyond[71]

and a ship "as a floating part of national territory".[72] The historic development has clearly moved towards a relaxation of this protective and possessive attitude to commercial assets on the part of states, a release of control and towards more trust in private actors acting out of their own rights rather than enabled by state privilege. This promises a trajectory of a greater role for uniform transnational commercial law and a modernised link between public policies and private law acting where impulses to achieve public policy aims and to promote the public interest can arise from private commercial cross border dealing as professed in the preamble of CISG and the UN declaration of a new economic order.[73] It corresponds to the expansion of the commercial sphere across the globe and the need for a level playing field.

---

[69] Basedow (2006), p. 733.

[70] Ibid. 732.

[71] Ibid.

[72] Ibid.

[73] Resolution 3201 (S-VI) adopted by the General Assembly, "Declaration on the Establishment of a New International Economic Order", 1974.

6 Conclusions and Outlook

The contributions in this volume give account of the significance of a distinction between general and commercial contract law and the proposition of a more comprehensive juxtaposition of private and professional contracts. There are a number of practical and systemic problems that arise from a lack of distinction between consumer and commercial contracts in recent law reform projects and the failure to recognise the commercial contract as a type of transaction—well defined by a different level and nature of risk undertaken—rather than assigning properties to contractual parties such as consumer or trader. The civil law reforms described in Part I of this volume show examples of this failure to distinguish causing overlap and unresolved clashes between a jurisdiction's civil and commercial codes regulating contract law. Other challenges include distorted and unforeseen effects of general legal rules imported from commercial contract law projects into general contract law such as the reformed rules on hardship and standard terms in civil codes. Important challenges in commercial contracts include ethical dimensions and desirable standards both external to the contract and internal among professional parties as demonstrated by contributions in Part II. The goal here must be to counteract preconceived limitations to commercial contracts regarding the willingness of contracting parties to adhere to standards of good faith and corporate social responsibility as inherent contractual tools rather than externally originating regulation. Like this, both potential and reach of the concept of contract itself become evident in scholarly work included in Parts I and II of this volume. Finally, academic legal doctrine has to expand beyond traditional entrenchments in public and private law and make use of the commonalities in each other's discipline. The two often neatly separated spheres come uncomfortably close to each other in investment treaty disputes and exacerbate the very question of the role of private law itself in the face of public law acting conducted by states and their commitment to public policy. This volume wants to be an invitation to continue this enquiry by pushing boundaries in the public-private discourse and encourage reliance on established concepts of contractual acting based on the idea of mutual benefit and self-determination. In this way, the roles of horse and cart may be up for reallocation.

References

Association Henri Capitant des amis de la culture juridique française and Société de législation comparée (ed) (2008) Terminologie Contractuelle Commune. Projet de cadre commun de référence. 6 Société de législation comparée, Paris

Austen-Baker R (2008) Consumer-supplier relations, regulation, and essential contract theory. J Contract Law 24(1):60–76

Basedow J (2006) Uniform private law conventions and the law of treaties. Uniform Law Rev 11:731–747

Bell J, Boyron S et al (2008) Principles of French law, 2nd edn. Oxford University Press, Oxford

Calliess G-P, Zumbansen P (2012) Rough consensus and running code. Hart Publishing, Oxford

Coase RH (1937) The nature of the firm. Economica 4(16):386–405
Dalhuisen JH (2016) Dalhuisen on transnational comparative, commercial, financial and trade law. Volume 2: Contract and movable property law, 6th edn. Hart Publishing, Oxford
Eidenmueller H (2008) Der Gemeinsame Referenzrahmen für das Europäische Privatrecht: Wertungsfragen und Kodifikationsprobleme. JZ:529–550
Eidenmueller H, Faust F et al (2008) The common frame of reference for European private law: policy choices and codification problems. Oxf J Leg Stud 28:659–708
Gless S (2015) Internationales Strafrecht – Grundriss für Studium und Praxis. 2nd Helbing Lichtenhahn Verlag, Basel
Heidemann M (2016) Identities in contract – merchant law in Europe and the future of European contract law. Maastricht J Eur Comp Law 23(4):667–701
Herber R, Czerwenka B (1991) Internationales Kaufrecht, Kommentar. C.H.Beck, Munich
Juutilainen T (2018) Secured credit in Europe. From conflicts to compatibility. Hart, Oxford
Klabbers J (2001) How to defeat a treaty's object and purpose pending entry into force: toward manifest intent. Vanderbilt J Transnational Law 34(2):283–332
Lando O, Beale H (eds) (2000) Principles of European contract law, Parts I and II. Kluwer Law International, The Hague
Lehmann M (2017) Bail-in and private international law: how to make bank resolution measures effective across borders. Int Comp Law Q 66(1):107–142
McKendrick E (2016) Goode on commercial law – 4th edition edited and fully revised by E McKendrick, 6th edn. Penguin, London
Neumann T (2012) The duty to cooperate in international sales. The scope and role of Article 80 CISG. Verlag Dr Otto Schmidt, Cologne
Plucknett TFT (1956) A concise history of the common law, 5th edn. Little Brown & Company, Boston, MA
Powers SJJ (1971) Consumerism – Caveat Vendor. Insur Couns J 38:221–225
Raisch P (1965) Geschichtliche Voraussetzungen: dogmatische Grundlagen und Sinnwandlung des Handelsrechts. CF Mueller, Munich
Raisch P (1975) Bedeutung und Wandlung des Kaufmannsbegriffs in der neueren Gesetzgebung. In: Flume W et al (ed) Beitraege zum Zivil- und Wirtschaftsrecht – Festschrift für Kurt Ballerstedt zum 70. Geburtstag am 24. Dezember 1975. Duncker Humblot, Berlin, pp 443–468
Raiser T (1969) Das Unternehmen als Organisation. Reprint 2012 de Gruyter, Berlin
Schmidt K (2005) 'Unternehmer' – 'Kaufmann' – 'Verbraucher'. Betriebsberater 60(16):837–842
Solinas M (2014) Legal evolution and hybridisation: the law of shares transfer in England. Intersentia, Cambridge
Von Bar C, Clive E (eds) (2010) Principles, definitions and model rules of European private law: draft common frame of reference (DCFR). Oxford University Press, Oxford
Weller M-P (2009) Die Vertragstreue: Vertragsbindung – Naturalerfüllungsgrundsatz – Leistungstreue. Mohr Siebeck, Tuebingen

Part I
General Theory of Commercial Contract and Aspects of Law Reform

What Does the Transnationalisation of the Commercial Contract Mean? Is There a New Model and Are There Minimum Standards? Is There a Law and Economics Perspective?

Jan H. Dalhuisen

Contents

Abstract The subject of this contribution is the model of the professional contract as it increasingly must operate in the international flows of goods, services, money, information and technology, which flows are now far larger than any domestic ones

J. H. Dalhuisen (✉)
The Dixon Poon School of Law, King's College London, London, UK

Catholic University Lisbon, Lisbon, Portugal

UC Berkeley, Berkeley, CA, USA

National University of Singapore, Singapore, Singapore

University of Tel Aviv, Tel Aviv-Yafo, Israel

NY Bar, Albany, NY, USA

ICSID Arbitrator, Washington, DC, USA

Royal Netherlands Academy of Arts and Sciences, Amsterdam, The Netherlands
e-mail: jan.dalhuisen@kcl.ac.uk

M. Heidemann, J. Lee (eds.), *The Future of the Commercial Contract in Scholarship and Law Reform*, https://doi.org/10.1007/978-3-319-95969-6_2

as manifested in particular in international supply, production and distribution chains and in international finance. Legally to continue to require the cutting up of those flows and the transactions therein into domestic pieces in the hope that they together present a proper legal framework for these economically integrated activities is no longer rational if only because these domestic laws were never made for them.

The challenge is to describe and explain the new contract (and property) model that so emerges, and the sources of law that become applicable, their balancing in the international market place by considerations of justice, social peace and efficiency if sufficiently pressing, and ultimately by public order consideration at that level. This is perceived here as the greatest challenge in the legal transnationalisation process of commerce and finance in these flows and of the professional dealings and related contracts operating therein.

1 What Is a Commercial Contract?

The commercial contract is in modern times the contract concluded between professionals in their business dealings. It assumes parties habitually entering into such contracts with others who are similarly knowledgeable in their trade or similar business with the aim of making some profit doing so.[1] Professionals in this sense are likely to be only companies or similar legal entities, not individuals and certainly not consumers. Furthermore their business is likely to be on some scale while the interests to be promoted or defended are considerable. Another feature is that these contracts increasingly operate in the international sphere and are embedded in a globalized environment which co-determines their structure and operation even if on the occasion the transaction is still purely domestic. Although in all situations where distinctions are made there are borderline cases and especially with respect to small and medium sized enterprises (SMEs), there may be justified doubts, this should not distract.

An older distinction is the one between dealings among merchants.[2] This was apt in a time when corporate activity and legal personality remained underdeveloped, which was largely the case till the latter part of the nineteenth century. In countries like Germany and France considerable authority and a set of rules developed to distinguish in this connection between merchants and non-merchants (Germany) or merchant and non-merchant activity (France). These distinctions proved problematic partly because non-merchants could engage in what was considered merchant activity, notably in signing cheques, whilst merchants would engage in much activity that was not considered typically mercantile at all. The consequence was that neither the concept of merchant nor the concept of commercial activity could comfortably be defined exclusively in terms of the other. Hence the confusion. This was borne out in countries like Germany and France, where separate commercial codes existed but most of the commercial activity remained covered by the civil codes. The commercial codes thus had

[1] See Dalhuisen (2016), pp. 60–65.

[2] See Ibid., pp. 53–59.

a limited coverage, markedly different even between Germany and France, and served in any event merely as *lex specialis* to the general system of the civil codes in the identified areas, although when corporation law and bankruptcy were included (bankruptcy only applying to merchants) or transportation and insurance were also covered, there was a fuller system, but there was never clear separation or clarity in the coverage. In countries like The Netherlands, Brazil, and earlier in Switzerland, the distinction was abandoned altogether and there were no more commercial codes. That was one way of resolving the difficulties, but as we shall see, the consequence was that all private law acquired the consumer ethos inherent in the civil codes.

The distinction remained, however, more especially important in countries like France which still had and have a special commercial jurisdiction in commercial courts and this added a procedural relevance to it. As to the nature of this law to the extent it could still be separated, a particularly aspect of commercial law both in France and Germany was and is the absence of any particular reference to the status and impact of custom and industry practices. This is entirely in line with civil law codification thinking that is suspicious of, and uncomfortable with extra-statutory sources of law. It is supported by its system thinking, but this attitude was always curious in commerce and became a considerable weakness in the codification approach. It is notably not followed in the Uniform Commercial Code in the US (Sec. 1-103) which does not seek to monopolise the law creation function in commerce and finance. It recognises many more sources of commercial law and is therefore not a codification in the civil law sense at all.[3] The law in England may now have more difficulty with custom also too, but courts at least remain pragmatic.

The discussion regarding the commercial contract should not get lost in these older distinctions, one reason why it is better simply to refer to the professional contract, which as we have seen at the beginning, has a different connotation. In common law there was never a clear commerciality notion in this regard and there was never a single overriding criterion, not in the UCC either. Traditionally, commercial law covers the sale of goods, transportation and insurance; this is historical, a matter of its origin and development. It implies another key difference: when it covers these areas it covers them in principle in full, it was never *lex specialis* to a bigger system. Arguably there is no system in common law at all. It is important to acknowledge that the common law of contract derives from commercial law in this undefined fashion, therefore from a business setting and this has clear consequences till this day as we shall see. So it is in the law of movable property. Even though in the eighteenth century the commercial law was incorporate in the common law, it always retained some independence[4] and it remains in particular more sensitive to custom as an autonomous source of law.[5] No less important was in modern times the additions that derived from the law of equity; one may think of the rescission remedies in contract law and the notion of specific performance, but also

---

[3] Cf. also Buxbaum (1994), p. 197; and Gordley (1981).

[4] See Dalhuisen (2016), pp. 16–21.

[5] Even though the notion of custom also became contentious in common law, especially in England, but less so in commercial law, see Thomas (2016), p. 11; and Book Review Dalhuisen (2017), p. 67.

of trusts, floating charges and finance sales in movable property law. Assignments and the law of set-off derive their force mainly from equity also where in business one sees the largest differences with the civil law.

In more modern times, the distinction between the commercial or professional contract and other contracts often derives from distinguishing consumer dealings which are then more specifically defined or at least described. It follows that the rest are professional dealings. That was notably the approach in the 1980 Vienna Convention on the International Sale of Goods (CISG), Article 2(a). It covers only professional sales but does do so indirectly by excluding consumer sales. Whilst in modern codifications, the distinction between commercial and non-commercial dealings is often abandoned in civil law countries—as we have seen—increasingly civil codes incorporate special rules not for business dealings but for consumers. Although a similar distinction thus results in principle like under the Vienna Convention, the danger is that in the absence of what may be called proper relationship thinking, which fundamentally distinguished between types of parties and is much more engrained in common law,[6] in civil law the consumer protection we see especially in contract law wafts over per *type* of contract (which is the civil law emphasis rather than type of relationship) to the professional sphere. That has become a great weakness of the civil law in commerce and finance and is, as we shall see, much less likely to happen under the common law of contract. In truth, civil law has become consumer law, it always was and its codes have morphed into consumer law codifications. This is connected with the fact that they have their origin in anthropomorphic nineteenth century thinking in which there was little room for corporates and business. Here a can of milk was bought for consumption, not to trade or to convert in other products. That remains in essence so till today and there is no proper distinction. It is different in the common law and this has a fundamental impact on contract law (and even on movable property law).

2 What Are the Main Features of the Common Law and Civil Law Commercial Contract Model. Extra-Contractual Rights and Obligations. Interpretation and Gap-Filling. Good Faith and Specific Performance in Civil and Common Law

Whilst considering the commercial or professional contract, later on especially in its international operation, it is helpful, even necessary to describe its main features in civil and common law. A first observation to make in this connection is that the common law of contract in its formation is not traditionally intent based,[7] and the

[6] See Bingham LJ in *Interfoto Picture Library Ltd v Stiletto Visual Programmes Ltd* [1989] 1 QB 433, 439.

[7] So still Williston explicitly as late as 1957, see Lord (1957), p. 21. The highly esteemed US Judge

civil law consensus notion in particular does not play a determining role in contract formation which depends on exchange and bargain or *consideration*, a typical commercial perception, in modern times increasingly transformed by the notion of conduct and detrimental reliance. This has important consequences in the sense that the traditional civil law failures of consensus and the defenses in this regard resulting from force, error or fraud and leading to an unenforceable contract, are not available in common law. When proper consideration is given or conduct has been detrimentally relied upon, the contract stands regardless. What is needed is a beginning of implementation;[8] there is notably no cause of action before the plaintiff has put its own money on the table, but if he has done so there is no simple way back for the other party. "I did not mean it" suggesting a void or voidable contract in civil law is no defense in common law. It is true that in equity there developed some defenses notably in the case of fraudulent and negligent misrepresentation or in the case of mutual mistake, but they are limited and depend very much on the factual situation in terms of the relief that may be granted. Although the term "rescission" is often used in this connection, it does not mean voidness per se or avoidance at the request of the party that was misled or lives under a misapprehension. Rather, in the nature of all equitable relief there is considerable judicial discretion,[9] which, may well work to a consumer's advantage but not likely for professionals.

The situation is not much different in the excuses of performance. The only true excuse in common law is the other party not performing a main condition of the contract. Under the general law, there is notably no implied force majeure or change of circumstances relief short of a force majeure or hardship clause agreed in the contract itself. Unlike in civil law, the notion of fault or blame is irrelevant. So the usual civil law excuse: "I cannot help it, it is not my fault" carries little weight in common law unless the contract so provides. The objective law dose not redistribute risk except perhaps in extreme circumstances. It always was a consumer law idea which sits easily in civil law but here again one sees a very different approach in common law which derives from its origin in commerce. The common law contract is foremost a roadmap and risk management tool, where the text, not the intent dominates, not even where parties have made some specific choices and the issue is not merely formation of the contract itself. In this approach, undiscounted risks fall where the fall. That is so for foreseeable risk where the parties could agree on a redistribution, but it also applies to unforeseeable risk. In civil law the general or

Learned Hand once remarked that even 'if both parties severally declared that their meaning had been other than the natural meaning, [but] each declaration was similar, it would be irrelevant': *Eustis Mining* Co *v Beer, Sondheimer & Co* 239 F 976 (1917). In this view, it did not make the least difference whether a promisor actually intended the meaning that the law will impose on its words.

[8] Best explained by Atiyah see Atiyah (1978): see also Atiyah (1979) reviewed by Fried (1980) and Atiyah (1981), pp. 202–215, critically reviewed by Raz (1982). The idea here is that promising itself is not a creation of the law, not truly contract formation either, but that the law will enforce a promise if the counterparty has effectively committed itself, which is ultimately expressed in the measure of damages upon breach.

[9] See Dalhuisen (2016), pp. 87–92.

objective law has here a way out unless the contract specifically provides otherwise.

In modern times in common law, entering into a contract, especially the duration commercial contract, is more like entering into a partnership and may mean assuming considerable risk. The contract will set out what the parties are going to do and the risks they take thereby are for each party to digest unless other arrangements have been made. Again, like in the case of lack of intent, the objective law does *not* help out in the case of force majeure and frustration of the contract purpose. In civil law such a situation only exists in respect of payment obligations and guaranteed performances, but it is exceptional; in common law it is normal. One can also say that in civil law terms all contractual conditions are guaranteed in common law and not excusable unless the other party does not perform or both parties have agreed otherwise. The conclusion is therefore that the cry in civil law: "I did not mean it, I cannot help it, it is not my fault" carries much less weight under common law, equity included, although it might now well be somewhat different in consumer law. This is simply the consequence of proper relationship thinking where dependency is an important issuer, also at the heart of fiduciary duties developed in equity.

We must also consider the following. In both common and civil law there may be extra contractual rights and duties. Thus, we may have pre-contractual disclosure and negotiation duties—we may also have to think of offers being binding, contractual cooperation duties and duties of care, and post-contractual renegotiation duties, but in common law, at least in professional dealings, they may mean a great deal less than in civil law. Again, the civil law of contract is anthropomorphic, nineteenth century reinforced by a twentieth century consumer law protection notions that soon expands into the professional sphere. There are no proper distinctions and there is a shortage of relationship thinking. In business, common law is much less likely to indulge. Even when it concedes extra rights and duties in this regard, often in the nature of fiduciary duties or of protection in tort, it limits the damages to direct expenses[10] and it will not readily award damages for the loss of anticipated profits or expectation damages.

This goes into interpretation and gap filling. It was already said that intent may be of importance here also in common law, thus not in formation issues but in the explanation of the road map and the risk management provisions of a contract, therefore the choices parties have made, although this intent will even then be objectivated, the perceptions of the reasonable person with a large dose of relationship thinking, quite different therefore for consumers and professionals. For the latter, the bias remains in favour of a literal interpretation of texts unless all fails, again underscoring that intent is of limited importance and not a normal correction assuming it could be established. The old parole evidence rule which is still good law, supports this too. To repeat, between professionals the common law of contract respects and furthers its nature as a road map and risk management tool and the text

[10] *Walford v Miles* 2WLR 17 (1992).

will indicate where they stand unless it does not make any longer any sense[11] or becomes manifestly unreasonable and that will not be soon between professionals. For the rest the chips fall where they fall and not much should be expected from the courts which are unlikely to help and do not encourage this kind of argument or even litigation in the matter which is made costly whilst there is appeal only with leave of the courts. Again the civil law is here more indulgent in the nature of consumer protection and relief for all.

This leads into the good faith notion which is much heralded in this connection in civil law and often seen by civil lawyers as a deficit in common law. This is a profound misunderstanding. In civil law especially of the German and Dutch variety, good faith is used as an *interpretation technique* which often suggests a reference to higher value like greater justice. In the mind of many, it then represents a mandatory norm.[12] It is particularly strong in contract where the good faith concept is meant by statute to operate in interpretation (not in property law except perhaps as to how proprietary rights are exercised as an extra statutory norm), see Sec. 242 of the German Civil Code and Arts 1134 and 1135 of the French one. In this expanded sense, good faith is often considered to confer more rights or even correct the contractual order. In civil law, it has as such been used in particular to support pre-contractual disclosure and negotiation duties, contractual cooperation duties and duties of care, and post-contractual renegotiation duties.

This may sound understandable in a consumer law context and if that is the ethos of civil law it is not surprising that good faith is strong and has become even stronger in its desire to protect weaker parties better, but the problem is that the notion then soon applies in similar ways to professional dealings—it was already mentioned and confirms at lack of relationship thinking in civil law. Common law has other, often better and more precise tools. They are fiduciary duties, the notion of reliance, or sometime implied terms of reasonableness and, if all fails, natural justice. It is true that the UCC in the US uses increasingly the notion of good faith (Sec. 1.304) but it remains more limited and is in such cases still largely subjective. In contract it does notably not mean to introduce pre-contractual or post-contractual duties. Probably more importantly it allows parties to set the standards which are only ignored if the result becomes manifestly unreasonable (Sec. 1-302(b)). Again in professional dealings that would not be soon the case. Importantly, it underscores at the same time that the concept is not absolutely mandatory, at least not in business dealings.

It is clear that common law and civil law come here from different directions, but greater relationship thinking is becoming clearer in some civil law countries also, there are green shoots, starting to distinguish business dealings and using the good

---

[11] *Chandler v Webster* [1904] 1 KB 493. See also the dictum in *Davis Contractors v Farnham* [1956] 2 All ER 145: "There is no need to consider what the parties thought, or how reasonable men in their shoes would have dealt with the situation if they had foreseen it. The question is whether the contract they did make is, on its true construction, wide enough to apply to [a] new situation; if it is not, then it is at an end."

[12] See Dalhuisen (2016), pp. 73–75.

faith concept itself to get there.[13] So is a greater concern with facts rather than systematic thinking in these matters. This good faith refinement is very necessary but it is only at the beginning of this development in civil law and has much further to go although this development may start at the same time to bridge some of the distance between the common and civil law of the professional contract.[14] But it is also true that especially in Germany there is an engrained effort ever to find more system even in good faith application with reference to *Fallgruppen* and *Funktionskreisen* which deflates these efforts towards a more practical and responsive approach leading to the necessary relationship thinking setting business dealings properly apart.[15]

Rather than seeing it always as some higher principle or norm, much better, it would seem, is to consider good faith indeed primarily as an interpretation technique through which *all* sources of law, earlier expelled in civil law by the legislative monopoly of law formation, resurface. They are fundamental and general principle (the first being of a profound nature, the latter derived from the laws of more advanced countries as a study in comparative law), custom and practices, and a more autonomous notion of party autonomy which operate besides and in appropriate cases beyond the legislative texts. Public order considerations may also surface and even the demands of justice, social peace and efficiency as autonomous extra legal considerations as we shall see.

This reminds very much of the Grotian view of law formation and operation in the pre-nineteenth century secular natural law school which approach was retained in the nineteenth century only for public international law. Art. 38(1) Statute of the International Court of Justice and Art. 53 of the Vienna Convention on the Law of Treaties are the modern expression of it. It is a view, which, it is submitted, revives in the transnationalisation of commercial and financial law, to apply to all law formation at the international level, relevant especially when we put the professional contract increasingly in its international setting, see in the next section. But even domestically in civil law countries, the monopoly of statutory law was always a myth which threatened to bar adjustment and dealing with society's contingencies and progression, although even now, such a restrictive attitude remains common and abhors innovation. It is the backbone of modern positivism, particularly strong in Europe, even in England,[16] although at least on the European continent we recognize a more accommodating attitude in interpretation and gap filling which must be

---

[13] In the Netherlands, since 2007, in contract, modern case law is moving, see HR 19 January 2007 (*PontMeyer*), NJ 575 (2007); 29 June 2007 (*Derksen/Homburg*), NJ 576 (2007); 9 April 2009 (*UPC/Land*), JOR 179 (2010): see also PS Bakker, "Uitleg van Commerciele Contracten" [Interpretation of Commercial Contracts], *WPNR* 6890/1 (2011). The idea is here indeed that the good faith notion itself may require a more literal interpretation of the commercial contract in which justified reliance plays a major role, especially if the contract is negotiated by outside law firms.

[14] See Dalhuisen (2016), pp. 63–66.

[15] See Ibid., pp. 56–61.

[16] Even in England where academia likes to line up cases and statutory texts to produce some system, see Atiyah and Summers (1987). It is very different in the US where this type of 'doctrinal' thinking is no longer favoured in academia.

liberal especially in codification countries if only for their legal texts to remain relevant, reintroducing in this manner through the back door of interpretation and gap-filling (if it can be distinguished) indeed all the non-statutory sources of law that were eliminated at the front door. That is here perceived as the essence of all interpretation in private law in civil law countries.

This leaves us in this short essay with one other important issue that distinguishes the commercial contract in common and civil law. This is the issue of performance, especially specific performance. In civil law that is a right, in common law it is exceptional (except in the transfer of real estate) and will only be granted (in equity together with injunctive relief if necessary) when damages which are the normal common law remedy for breach, cannot adequately recompense. Here it should be considered that there is much practical middle ground between the common and civil law of contract. Also in civil law it is often much better, cleaner and quicker to rely on damages. In a production process e.g. the delivery of spare parts can often not wait for quality issues to be resolved in litigation. Time pressure kills any desire for specific performance. The needed parts will be bought elsewhere and the difference in price and quality will be claimed later as damages, if necessary in litigation.

3 How Does the Professional Contract Progress in the International Flows? The Emergence of a Transnational Commercial and Financial Legal Order and Its Significance

If we accept that the size of the international flows in goods, services, money, technology, and information is now such that we may speak of a transnational legal order in which these flows operate, as is this author's view,[17] and is supported by the fact that the one in goods alone is in value now larger than the GDP of the largest countries inclusive all of the EU[18] whilst the Eurobond market is the largest capital market in the world and the international swap market the largest market of all, then transnationalisation of the law in this globalized order is immanent and is even now clearly demonstrable in the Eurobond and international repo and swap markets. This law to the extent it is private law is the modern *lex mercatoria* that is, it is posited, based indeed on the five traditional sources of law already identified being fundamental principle, custom and practices, treaty law, general principle and party autonomy, and still the basis of public international law. Even domestically, it was

[17] See also Dalhuisen (2006).

[18] Dalhuisen (2015).

argued, these sources return in any event in interpretation. It means that under the pressure of globalization and the horizontalisation of production, we place ourselves for our legal perspective increasingly in these transnational flows rather than in domestic orders. This is a paradigm shift. The reverse happened at the beginning of the nineteenth century when all law, even private law was nationalized, the law between states being the exception although even there fundamental and general principle and customary law were under pressure in favour of treaty law which required ratification and was then considered domestic law too.

There is reversal here also and the analogy of public international law formation and application in the transnational commercial and financial sphere or order to find its laws and apply them is particularly apt, although one may notice a further simplification. Above, at the beginning, the commercial contract was described as a contract between professionals. Local definitions in terms of merchant or non-merchant activity are no longer relevant. So the issue of commerciality does no longer truly arise, but neither does the issue of internationality. In this view, all professional dealings are structurally increasingly internationalised or derive their structure progressively from the international practice even if these dealings on occasion may still be predominantly domestic in contact, but they still operate and must be placed in in the international flows.

In respect of these dealings, this is the world of immanent law formation at the transnational level that, like public international law, does not depend for its formation on public authority or any other. It forms itself in an autopoietic manner[19] even if treaty law may still help or correct but this requires states to agree and strictly speaking any resulting private law remains still territorial. As such its sits uneasily in the ranking between custom and general principle and needs for its transnationality a base in the custom and practices of the trade and support through general principle which may come from many ratifications. It has so far in private law barely been successful.

It is true that the CISG has many ratifications but the commercial practice habitually excludes it because it does not sufficiently recognize itself in it. It demonstrates that there is neither a sufficient base in industry custom and practice nor even in general principle. It is too academic, was never asked for, and has a notion of fundamental breach (Art. 25) and force majeure (Art. 79) that is too subjective whilst it gives the unsatisfied buyer a possibility to unilaterally reduce the price (Art. 50). Its views on the importance of practices (Art. 9) and on its interpretation (Art. 7) are singular, demonstrating that it has little idea of its own place in the ranking of the sources of transnational law. It is barely aware of others. Its formation section is based on the conventional offer and acceptance model and consensus notion in the

[19] In Germany, sociologists (not lawyers) have more recently taken to such views, see Luhmann (1985) who noted the self-creating (autopoietic) force of all law but, although accepting the dissolution or disintegration of its system on a continuous basis, still insisted on a simplistic bilinear law/non-law matrix that was basically stabilized by states and, one must assume therefore, ultimately also caught in its system thinking. His approach did not catch on in the US but was (partly) the root of the work of G Teubner towards the modern *lex mercatoria*, see e.g. Teubner (1997).

civil law tradition. Perhaps more fundamentally, many academics do not understand the key role of custom and practices in commerce and finance and do not e.g. realise its fundamental nature in the Eurobond markets as largest capital market in the world, especially in the proprietary aspects, and in the set-off and netting facilities under the ISDA Swap Master Agreements in the interest swap markets which is the largest in the world.

Still the CISG, although merely default rule, may lay claim to more success than other projects of UNCITRAL and UNIDROIT which both mean to promote treaty law in the commercial area but have been largely a failure, the reason again being that the international practice does not sufficiently recognize itself in their texts. This has been very different in respect of the UCC in the US. Only the UNCITRAL Model Laws on international arbitration and international bankruptcy recognition may claim a following but they are only models and did not achieve treaty status nor aspired to it. The UNIDROIT Contract Principles are not a proposal for a treaty either; they mean to cover only professional dealings. As such, they come closest to the subject of this paper but their great similarity with the European Contract Principles which meant to cover both consumer and business dealings shows that it is basically a consumer inspired document still assuming an anthropomorphic legal environment like all civil law codification does towards which it is biased. So does the Draft Common Frame of Reference (DCFR), an academic effort to come to an EU codification of private law which follows in this respect (as in virtually all others) entirely the German tradition of codification and system thinking. It remains nineteenth century consumer law in its perceptions. Its sales section was in 2011 proposed to be introduced in EU law by Regulation but the project did not convince either and was quietly withdrawn in 2014.[20]

In this connection, in both commerce and finance, it must also be appreciated and can be seen that the professional contract seldom stands alone from other more purely private law concepts and exigencies. In sales, it is connected with the transfer of title, therefore property Law, which is its very purpose, in shipping with the status of the bill of lading, in payments with letters of credit and the abstract nature of the latter, in finance with the status of the eurobond as promissory note and negotiable instrument, and in repos and swaps with the set-off and netting concepts under the TBMA/ISMA Global Repo Master Agreement and ISDA Swap Master Agreements and the preferences they create in bankruptcy. The issue of transactional and payment finality should not be overlooked either in the operation of these contracts and is no less a proprietary issue. This connectedness is of the greatest importance and affects the nature of the underlying contract and the way professional contracts operate and must be considered. These contracts are likely to be part of a much bigger picture, now increasingly transnationalised in the international flows of goods, services, money, information and technology, often still ignored in academic writing. Especially in the operation of proprietary and set-off rights there is a close connect with public policy, itself increasingly transnationalised in the form of

[20] See Dalhuisen (2016), pp. 152–156.

transnational minimum standards. That should not be forgotten when these contracts start operating in the international sphere.

In fact, the more immediate question given the subject of this contribution is to what model of contract law the developing transnational law of the professional contract, derived from its various sources, will conform: is it the common law or civil law model or something in between or beyond? First it may be relevant that, besides finance, this law in these international flows is largely directed to the sales of goods, services and technology or other information. That was always much the subject of commercial law in the common law tradition as we have seen and it is not therefore strange that this law develops in a similar way at the transnational level: from situation to situation, fact to fact depending on the needs of the business community as they manifest themselves. Much will be borrowed from the common law and its method; this also comes with the English language now the lingua franca of that world. It has also an effect on the law of movable property and finality issues. This being said, even the common law of the professional contract can be better articulated and the model improved and clarified. What is different for all is that whilst operating in the transnational legal order, the contract is differently embedded, especially in fundamental principle as will be especially explored in the next section and there is also public policy to consider. It may also relate differently to the other sources of law or indeed confirm that it was always more comfortable with customary law than civil law is not as and the common law of the English variety became.

4 The Meaning and Reach of Fundamental Principle and the Challenge of International Minimum Standards

In reviving the various traditional sources of law in the transnational legal order and accepting their hierarchy in the modern *lex mercatoria*, one notices that some fundamental principles are constitutive or foundational, like the notion of *pacta sunt servanda* or the notion of property. In contract, fundamental legal principle may then also be the conduit for the introduction of newer pre-contractual, contractual, and post contractual rights and duties, helped by the other sources of law of the modern *lex mercatoria* and generally a liberal interpretation technique, whether or not under the good faith label in contract. So may be notions of justice, social peace and efficiency if sufficiently pressing and there could be overlap.

Others more closely or more directly connected with public order and policy amplify or correct, e.g. competition law principle or those principles that guard against market manipulation or fraud. They may be transnationalised in transnational minimum standards which may still compete with local policy if and when international transactions continue to come demonstrably onshore, ever less certain in an increasingly more virtual world. This may raise in particular the issue of the operation of parallel legal orders in the area of public order or public policy, which issue will not be here further explored. Rather, it is the formulation of these transnational minimum standards balancing the operation of the international market place, if only to keep it clean and its participants free from abuse, that is here perceived as one of the greatest challenges in the legal transnationalisation process and it affects directly the way of contracting and what it may achieve in the transnational professional sphere.

In this connection it may also be noted that the mercantile tradition of this law which covers shipping and attendant insurance and payments, traditionally through cheques, bills of exchange, or letters of credit, is in more modern times increasingly eclipsed by financial law that has become the more forceful force in transnational *lex mercatoria*, its formation and operation, the eurobond and swap markets were already mentioned. The importance of these markets and their potential effect on financial stability may mean that the public interest is sooner triggered and corrects, raising further the question of international standards in the international flows or financial market place, the contracts concluded therein and their operation.

Especially these facilitating or corrective aspects of fundamental principle in the transnational commercial and financial legal order may need further exploration. In this connection, increasingly reference is (additionally) made to constitutional principle or the horizontal effect of human rights or fundamental freedoms. This is a narrower but important newer perspective. The EU provides a special and prominent example in its 'mini globalisation'[21] even though globalisation and developing principle (and custom) in private law and the development of transnational minimum standards in this connection go way beyond the EU's jurisdiction. It has only limited power of private law formation which power can in its generality derive only from the exigencies of the promotion of the internal market under Article 114 TFEU, although since the Amsterdam Treaty of 1998, there is in international private law related areas original power, exercised so far in particular in the area of recognition of civil and commercial judgements (Brussels 1 Regulation) and in the area of the applicable law to contractual obligations (Rome 1 Regulation) as well as in the area of bankruptcy recognition (Insolvency Regulation). Then there are areas whether the EU uses private law tools to further its public mandate, e.g. whilst calculating damages. But even in private law, in the limited area where the EU can operate, fundamental principle may give rise to issues of supremacy and direct effect, proportionality in its application, and its effectiveness in EU law and its promotion.

The terminology is not stable, and terms like 'constitutionalisation' and 'horizontal effect' especially of human rights or fundamental freedoms may be used in this respect or even 'fundamental principle' more directly. It is then often not distinguished from general principle. In practice, EU law focusses in this connection more in particular on equality of treatment, avoidance of abuse, and probably better treatment of weaker parties, including issues of age and gender. The term 'constitutionalisation' suggests here an extension of constitutional protections into private law, relevant especially where power is exercised over others. Reference when made

[21] See in particular Temple Lang (2013) and Tridimas (2013). See earlier Koopmans (2000); see further also Adar and Sirena (2015), Bernitz and Grousol (2013). Cf. also von Bogdandy (2014).

to 'horizontal effect' is then more in particular associated with the operation of fundamental freedoms.[22] In the EU the latter now show a close connection with the Human Rights Charter.[23]

In recent times, domestically, at least the impact of human rights on private law formation had already been noted, especially in the German Constitutional Court thus advancing locally the constitutionalisation of private law.[24] In fact, in Germany it operates at several levels and may also impact (vertically) on the power of the legislature to intervene in private law through mandatory rules. In an international setting that could also affect the reach of treaty law. Respect for the freedom of contract and to own property are here especially important for business. Article 16 of the EU Charter might also be so explained. On the other hand, human rights notions of this nature facilitate state intervention in more clearly defined and limited areas, particularly in the area of consumers' and workers' protection, the respect of age and gender—it was already mentioned. They may also present a way of intro-

[22] However, horizontal effect may also arise in other contexts and instances and horizontal effect of EU legislation may also ensue when, on the basis of EU or implementing legislation directed at Member States, private rights and obligation may be newly created, varied or extinguished. It is not then an issue of correction on the basis of fundamental or general principle, although they may still surface in the interpretation of the relevant rules, *cf.* Case 36/74 *Walrave v Wielerbonden* [1974] ECR 1405, 12 December 1974; Case 13/76 *Dona v Mantero* [1976] ECR 1333, 14 July 1976; and Case 94/07 *Raccanelli v Max Planck Gesellschaft* [2008] ECR I-5939 (at N 50), 17 July 2008.

In appropriate cases, there is also horizontal effect of the four basic EU freedoms more directly, traditionally especially the free movement of persons and services when limited through the intervention of private parties or organisations, see Case C-281/98 *Angonese v Cassa di Ripsparmio di Bolzano*, 6 June 2000, now increasingly also in the case of hindrance of the free movement of goods by private parties with reference to Art 34 TFEU, see Case C-171/11 *Fra.bo v DVGW*, 12 July 2012. The truly interesting question is whether in due course EU law will intervene and promote the mutual recognition of proprietary rights rather than have them function as a bar to the free movement of (encumbered) assets.

[23] The EU Human Rights Charter is not supposed to be directly relevant unless specific and it distinguishes in this connection sharply between rules and principles (Art 52). This was politics and the distinction may prove to be hardly sustainable. In fact, many rules are never much more than principles; it depends on the level of abstraction and intellectualisation which may be found in all rules of general application. As far as the EU Charter is concerned, exception is in any event made for principles that are further developed by ECJ case law or in legislation, which are then assumed to be unconditional and sufficiently precise. This concerns in particular the implementation and interpretation of EU laws but may also affect national private law between private parties in the context of the implementation or application of EU laws.

See in this connection in particular the principle of non-discrimination and equal pay for men and women already accepted in Case 43/75 *Defrenne v Sabena I* [1976] ICR 547 below; see also Case C-426/11 *Alemo-Heron v Parkwood* ECJ 18 July 2013, in which safeguards of employees after a take-over under national law were not believed, however, to go beyond that of EU Directive 2001/23 concerning the protection of employees in view of the freedom to conduct business, precisely because of Art 16 of the Charter. In Case C-470/12 *Pohotovost v Vasuta*, ECJ 27 February 2014, the Charter (Arts 38 and 47 on consumer protection) was held not to expand the rights of consumers under Directive 1993/13. Here the specific trumped the more general.

[24] See for this concept in Germany Canaris (1998) and in England, Friedmann and Barak-Erez (2001) and Collins (2007).

ducing basic values in actions between private parties more generally and indirectly. For smaller parties in particular there may in this connection be a need for special protection against discrimination or where power is exerted against them, especially in situations of dependence. Again, this may be the horizontal effect of abuse of power. Proportionality may also figure, meaning that all public intervention must be 'fit for purpose'. Then there are procedural or due process protections, especially in state courts, potentially now arising no less in arbitrations. But proper *relationship thinking* should also enter even though in case law that seems so far hardly a priority.

However, in the perceptions of many, these are only human rights related or similar protections to the extent expressed in national instruments, and they remain therefore (in this view) state dependent (or in the EU expressed in the Human Rights Charter as laid down by the Member States). The issue is rather whether they are in a globalised or transnationalised world *autonomous* or self-executing or whether states or statist action still has the last word. Or do they denote a more open, not state-dependent framework of rights and obligations, as such becoming part of the transnational minimum standards of protection. This is so to speak the next step in this development when fundamental principle comes into its own, not merely as foundational or human rights principle, but also as a self-executing autonomous and independent source of law transnationally to supplement the modern *lex mercatoria* and correct it in sufficiently pressing cases. Again, it should allow for relationship thinking meaning that the type of private parties and the nature of their relationship need to be considered also. It should be clear that human rights protections, especially when considered in respect of weaker parties, including issues of age and gender, may be less relevant in professional dealings.

In Europe, in the EU, the Draft Common Frame of Reference (DCFR) 2008/9, already mentioned, pays some lip service in this connection to the (horizontal effect of) human rights notion in Article I-1:102(b), but again only to the extent they derive from national instruments. This is a reflection of the modern notion of constitutionalisation, but here only as a matter of interpretation of the text. The DCFR does not seem to be aware of other fundamental principles and of their status as an autonomous source of law except for the prohibition of discrimination, expressly mentioned in Articles II-2:101ff but there only in the context of contract law. The notion of good faith remains also limited,[25] still rather as the opposite of bad faith and not as an interpretation tool to reintroduce all the non-statutory traditional non-statutory sources of law, at least for professional dealings. In fact, it is clear from the Introduction, rewritten in 2009, that the DCFR does not know quite what to do with fundamental principle, except to point out that many provisions of the DCFR are expressions of them. Beyond (the horizontal effect of) human rights (contained in national instruments) and the discrimination prohibition, which are closely related, they are not given a specific mention in the text, let alone an autonomous status,

[25] see Art I-1:102 DCFR and Dalhuisen (2016), pp. 73–75.

although good faith is (wrongly in its generality) given mandatory force and thus considered fundamental in this narrow substantive sense.

In contract law, there is, however, a curious provision in the DCFR (Arts II-7:301ff), which talks about 'infringement' of fundamental principle or mandatory law and voids contracts if violating a principle recognised as fundamental in the laws of the Member States. At least in contract law, this seems to suggest the application of a higher EU public order principle derived from the laws of Member States in the nature of general principle, therefore again only to the extent recognised by them. Thus state law is here still the conduit, there are no principles beyond it and Article II-7:301 would still appear to be based on this idea: there are no common EU values per se, but apparently we can still have a common EU private law.[26] There is considerable tension here.

However this may be, the DCFR conforms in this manner to the traditional codification ethos and its formal and positivist attitudes and beliefs in black-letter rule emanating from the state or states, to be systematically applied as a matter of logic or mere technique which does not allow for extraneous considerations. Although in its Introduction it leaves the ultimate decision to others and only demonstrates that much fundamental principle is reflected in the text, the DCFR still represents the view that private law is not a carrier of values except to the extent expressly formulated by or otherwise derived from the laws of Member States. It can as such serve any regime as states remain in charge of the value system. There is no bottom-up concept of social values and a notion that they emerge in a free and vibrant society all the time and are to be respected in any civil society.

The DCFR also maintains a unitary approach to consumer and business dealings in this regard. There is no proper relationship thinking and the DCFR follows the civil law codification tradition which remains anthropomorphic and consumer law oriented. Yet its legal positivism is in vivid contrast to what EU case law itself has been doing as already mentioned. Culminating for the time being in *Mangold* in 2005[27] and in *Audiolux* in 2009,[28] the ECJ has made it clear that there are overarching fundamental principles that operate and are enforceable at the same level as the Founding Treaties and need *not* be written. In *Audiolux*, the Advocate General

[26] It contrasts with Art II-7:302, which refers to contracts infringing mandatory laws and appears to depend even more directly on the applicable national laws including those of Member States, but the article does not determine how this national law is found and even then only concerns itself with the effects (presumably in the EU).

[27] Case C-144/04 *Werner Mangold v Rüdiger Helm* [2005] ECR I-19981, upholding as fundamental principle the concept of non-discrimination on the basis of age, seen here as an elaboration of the anti-discrimination principle of Art 19 TFEU. This has become a check on private law legislation, although it may not (yet) be invoked directly between private parties, but see further also Case C-555/07 *Seda Kucukdeveci/Swedex* [2010] IRLR 346, which assumes a subjective right with reference to Art 21 (1) of the Charter on Human Rights. Non-discrimination according to nationality is no less fundamental, see Case 115/08 *Land Oberoesterreich v Cez* [2009] ECR I-10265 and also applies in private dealings under EU laws, in this case directly.

[28] Case C-101/08 *Audiolux a.o v Groupe Bruxelles Lambert SA a.o* [2009] ECR I-9823.

called them 'deeply rooted principles without which a civilised society would not exist'.[29] They are generally effective and at least in this perception also underlie private law, although again so far there is a lack of relationship thinking.[30] Regardless of the limited jurisdiction of the EU in private law formation, there is here also room for the introduction of EU private law notions, not only of damages, foremost in the determination and enforcement of public law obligations.[31] Even within the EU, this may put the whole process of the formation of private law in some different light. In this connection, it can only be repeated that in the transnational commercial and financial legal order, fundamental principle may not or no longer be EU specific. Arguably, these fundamental principles do not derive from EU law at all, at best they are recognised and further developed by it. This may apply also to foundational principle. Within the EU, this is often considered *competence creep*, potentially more so beyond it, but it is the unavoidable consequence of the EU not operating in isolation.[32] There is no 'fortress Europe' to be maintained here unless specific public order requirements or other mandatory law of an EU nature impose themselves in respect of transactions that in conduct or effect still come demonstrably on shore in the EU.

In the EU, even if the DCFR can hardly be a guide, the issue of embedding the international professional contract in fundamental transnational principle will not go away. So it is in the transnational commercial and financial legal order to sustain and develop further its *lex mercatoria*. Transnationally it is also an important way to arrive at clarification and better formulation of minimum standards.

In the US, under the due process and similar clauses in the federal Constitution, the impact of fundamental principle has long been clearer, in private law as well, at least in the elaboration and application of procedural and conflicts of laws rules. There is also the all-pervading reach of the Bill of Rights as positive law, not as mere principle. In civil society, fundamental principles of a foundational or constitutive nature or as public order amplification or corrections support the whole structure of private law, now in transnational dealings reviving particularly in the modern *lex mercatoria* where it may be seen by all who wish to see it. The drafters of the DCFR should have understood this but never considered their method. An old-fashioned codification technique was unquestioningly and uncritically adopted. But a proper consideration of methodology should have come first and would have required the authors better to understand, appreciate and evaluate other sources of

---

[29] See para 40 of the Opinion of AG Trstenjak.

[30] See also Kraus (2008), p. 54; and Metzger (2011).

[31] Notably in instances of failure of Member States to incorporate in a timely manner EU Directives at the expense of private parties, see Joined Cases C-6/90 and 9/90 *Francovich and Others v Italy* [1991] ECR I-5357; These types of cases respond to the need to make EU law fully operative or effective, sometimes believed to be another fundamental principle by itself. In Case C-47/07 *Masdar v Commission* [2008] ECR I-9761, an action for unjust enrichment against the EU was created on the basis of similar reasoning.

[32] See Prechal (2010). *Kukukdeveci v Swedex GmbH & Co KG*, Case C-550/07 ECR I-365 (2010) is often cited in this connection.

immanent law formation, above all the role and impact of fundamental principle as operating in the EU. A proper distinction between the type of parties would have followed and would have prevented the result becoming merely an expression of consumer law.

5 The Contribution of Law and Economics

It is finally also of interest to see what modern thinking in the US, especially in 'law and economics', has contributed to the discussion on modern contract law, especially the professional contract when operating in the international flows. It may be less than one might think or may have hoped for. First there is to consider the question of contract or party autonomy being an independent source of law, not a licensed notion, operating among the other sources of law in the modern *lex mercatoria*. But it also raises the question of the model that is best used to explain and simplify what is happening, especially transnationally, and to contribute to a better understanding and operation of modern contracting in the professional sphere, therefore in business transactions which are now often transnational in content, if not also in structure even when in the event the transaction still happens to be local. This poses the issue at the same time of other balancing forces, especially notions of justice, social peace, and efficiency, the last one being of special interest in business transactions. As posited above, the contract model that is used or maintained here, is itself and issue—in business together with a stronger gravitation towards efficiency—and cannot be presumed to uncritically pre-exist.[33] Neither can its operation in relation to public order and policy or minimum standards be ignored.

The view was expressed above that in such a (transnationalised) model, relationship thinking, the detrimental reliance notion, the accent on investment in the contract as precondition for the right to claim thereunder, and the distribution/management of risk in the common law mould are likely to be of special interest. In business dealings, the promotion of efficiency may even be an objective standard and risk distribution, resource allocation, and transaction costs, like the costs of lawyers and enforcement,[34] become other key elements.[35] Again, such contracts are unlikely to be intent based in the traditional way, if only because in a corporate environment only outsiders like a law firm might truly know what is in it. To enhance predictability, in commerce and finance, the notion of intent and the connected notion of blame when it comes to performance or the lack thereof may then also be limited to situations where the contract makes clear choices. Thus defences and excuses carry less weight and extra contractual rights and duties may impose themselves less forcefully and will be curtailed in a strict interpretation of texts. As

[33] Cf. Schwartz and Scott (2003), Scott (1999) and earlier Scott (1987).

[34] The notion of transactions costs is by no means fully clear, see Allen (2000).

[35] See for an early discussion, Berman (1963).

mentioned before, even good faith in the civil law sense may require this where the contract is expressed as a road map and risk management tool.

In a proper 'law and economics' analysis, it should be expected that at least amongst professionals, efficiency in terms of economic exchanges leading to a better allocation of resources and to a greater economic benefit created by enhanced co-operation and subsequent distribution of the gains between the parties trumps the notion of justice except when manifest unreasonableness results as demonstrated by the operation of the good faith concept in the UCC (Sec. 11-302(b)), again a situation unlikely to arise soon between informed parties in proper relationship thinking. In terms of promotion of social peace, the other red line may be the contract becoming socially destructive. Monopolisation and other market abuse and illicit objectives, like fraud or distinct forms of market manipulation or abuse may be an example if only to protect the integrity of the markets itself. Even the use of standard terms as an organisation tool by a contractor may have limits, obviously for consumers but even between professionals, more in particular if it manifests a dominant position. On the other hand, the extent or reach of defences and excuses may be measured again more from an efficiency point of view.[36] So may be extra-contractual disclosure, co-operation and re-negotiation duties.

It was already said that at all times, professional parties will have to be careful with whom they contract. At least in common law, entering into long time relationships may have a lot of downside that cannot be foreseen but will not lead to an excuse (of force majeure or changed circumstances) unless the contract itself so provides and otherwise only in exceptional circumstances. Such an approach may indeed align with the more modern 'law and economics' analysis of contract law and support the view that this approach (which may in terms of sources of law be supported by custom and general principle) can withstand a 'law and economics' analysis, where efficiency consideration are paramount, but the haul of new ideas was limited from the start.[37] Relationship thinking does also not appear to be a big issue. Even Posner complained about the lack of progress in contract.[38] On the other hand, empirical research has more recently even questioned some of the basic 'law and economics' tenets in contract law.[39]

At the more theoretical level, there is only one major contribution with respect to the emergence of the modern *lex mercatoria* and its operation.[40] It puts emphasis on

[36] See for the recognition of implied cooperation duties even in professional contracts, the Supreme Court of South Australia in *Alstom Ltd v Yokogawa Australia* (No 7), SASC 49 (2012).

[37] Faber (1983).

[38] Posner (2003) with a riposte by Craswell (2003).

[39] E.g. the idea that in standard contracts an 'informed minority' of term-conscious buyers is enough to discipline suppliers, see Bakos et al. (2009); Feldman and Teichman (2011), critique on empirical grounds the assumption that parties may be expected to perform their contractual duties if, and only if, the legal price of breach (damages) is higher than the cost of performance.

[40] Cooter (1994). A law-making community is here assumed to have a minimum level of control over the behaviour of its members. Group internalisation is the key but ultimately a question of maximising self-interest. The starting point is that members will not invest unless others follow. If

how the new law can be found and identified. In this view, for international commercial law to arise and to count legally, in the sense that states must accept it and back it up by coercive power (unless it has major public policy reasons not to do so): (a) the norms in a specialised business community should be empirically identifiable; (b) the incentive structure that produces or internalises the norms should be capable of being analysed (by using game theory and the notion of equilibrium) in order to determine whether those empirically found are more than social convention or moral dictates and are experienced as binding; while (c) the *efficiency* (or public good effect) of the incentive structure should be measurable using analytical tools from economics to avoid harmful laws (such as monopolistic practices, which will therefore not be enforced). Here the emphasis shifts from struggle to *rationality*, *consistency* and *predictability*.

Short of any more generic approach, there are largely unconnected newer topic specific ideas. One is that if parties have not expressed their intentions clearly, the default rule for the courts is the one that maximises the value of the transaction, even if it may be hard for judges to pin it down.[41] Another is the notion of 'efficient reliance' in such situations.[42] This notion is fact specific but it can be demonstrated that the courts have paid some attention to it although, here again, theory and practice often remain wedded to the idea of intent, which is then still preferred as the real basis of the contract. Rightly or wrongly, that often still seems the bigger issue. Again, one finds little sensitivity in 'law and economics' to relationship thinking and professional and consumer dealings are mostly not sharply distinguished.

Contract performance has also risen to the level of special interest and becomes then a question of incentives: is it more efficient or less costly not to perform? Would this be a complete defence? This connects with the question of defences and

---

upon proper signalling some co-operate and others appropriate, it means that some will make money every time, others sometimes more but other times none at all. In equilibrium, both earn the same overall, but those who co-operate have also a public good on offer, which may induce the appropriators increasingly to co-operate. Thus in this approach, the rule forms in a community when private incentives for signalling co-operation in the group align with a public good in that group. It creates momentum which shifts the equilibrium towards general acceptance. The suggestion is that when this happens the rule becomes legally enforceable.

One problem is that much private law does not operate at the level of internalisation as it is technical and must be learnt by the participants and their lawyers. Trade-offs hardly work in much of private law as it has developed and probably apply only to the bigger concepts. Once some such structures become a given, it is the innate sense, requirement of order and need to avoid contradictions that propel this law further. Businessmen learn rather than internalise and their lawyers may internalise but only after a long learning process. Conceivably, academia has here also an important role to play. External forces such as those of states may facilitate (if asked to do so), e.g. through treaty law (or similar interstate structures in organisations such as the EU), or, in regulation, impose themselves, even through the infusion of mandatory private law, which in particular also raises the problem of proper jurisdiction to prescribe in international cases, see also Dalhuisen (2016), pp. 274 et seq.

[41] Ayres and Gertner (1989).

[42] Craswell (1996) and earlier Goetz and Scott (1980).

excuses. Are we drifting towards a form of strict liability?[43] In the meantime, the measure of damages and the question whether it is different when intentions are not clearly expressed or when extra contractual duties impose themselves remains also unresolved although, again, it is recognised that a tort-like approach may sometimes be more appropriate, in particular in pre-contractual situations.[44] It was already said that at the theoretical level, the difference is that in the first case damages are based on the full performance of the contract (the monetary equivalent of specific performance resulting in expectation damages), in the latter case damages are paid to the extent necessary in order to restore the pre-contractual situation. Indeed, some inventive writing has been produced in the area of pre-contractual duties, where the accent may be on caution and on incentives to gather the right information.[45]

However, one could also put the emphasis on strategic behaviour, in particular the exploitation of delays, when there may be a game theory aspect but it has the problem that new equilibria are difficult to identify in terms of practical guidance for change and this approach soon becomes unmanageable and legally unhelpful. The possibility of expectation damages may then be a further discouragement to bargaining.[46] The research confirms here the need for a limitation of pre-contractual disclosure and negotiation duties in the professional sphere. There is also some newer literature in the area of standard terms, their binding force and its extent,[47] but the fact that they are basically an organisation technique of suppliers is mostly still overlooked. Game theory may do a little more when there is a strategic element, but again there is the practical problem with identifying equilibria.

In all of this, the engrained international dimension and character of all modern professional contract law is ignored. What is perhaps more striking is that in particular the risk management undercurrent and bias in professional dealings remains largely unexplored in these newer 'law and economics' approaches. The choices to be made are obviously efficiency driven but dependent on each party's evaluations, while the bigger issue is that much of what might happen during the contract period is barely foreseeable, as are the information and transaction costs. How the consequences are divided in terms of (objective) disclosure, (re)negotiation, and co-operation duties remains a question of default rules, which are often less than clear and in constant evolution, viz the pre-contractual and post-contractual regime, the impact of the notion of good faith and change of circumstances where again there seems to be little 'law and economics' guidance.[48] Remedies and the measure of

---

[43] See Craswell (1988a).

[44] See Craswell (2003), pp. 499ff; see also Gilmore (1974), pp. 87–89; and Atiyah (1979), pp. 1–7.

[45] See Craswell (1988b).

[46] Schwarz and Scott (2007).

[47] Plaut and Bartlett III (2012), Marotta-Wurgler and Taylor (2013), Marotta-Wurgler (2009), Murray (2012), Hillman (2002), Katz (1998) and Eisenberg (1986).

[48] Craswell (1996), p. 489 suggests that neither differences in risk preferences nor differences in belief about the market have any obvious implications for the law's choice of default rules. For this it would be necessary to identify the point at which the parties' risk aversion differed by the greatest amount, again hardly a manageable concept.

damages have caught the attention, as we have seen, but appear to be secondary, or rather only interesting in order better to force compliance with the contractual duties as they may evolve during the contract period.

In the meantime it may be noted that civil law has contributed little to this discussion. As mentioned, in contract law it follows the traditional consensus notion which is anthropomorphic, and it generally still uses the older offer and acceptance terminology, now in language largely derived from the Vienna Convention which sometimes allows conduct and reliance as an alternative to acceptance but even then does not spell out the details, in particular when this reliance is reasonable or whether it must also be detrimental. It is no surprise that under the circumstances the DCFR does not contribute either. It sticks to the Vienna Convention's approach to contract formation; in typical codification fashion it is the legislator or state that makes the choices here. How they do so and on what basis is not a matter for investigation.

6 Conclusion

The issues discussed in this paper were the model for the professional contract operating in the international flows and the balancing of the international market place in this connection to avoid abuse and keep this market and its operations clean and the applicable legal regime predictable. The sources of law and the role of fundamental principle in a foundational and correcting sense, the issue of public policy and order, and the emergence of correcting transnational minimum standards were explored. The contribution of EU law especially in the context of constitutionalisation and the horizontal effect of human rights and fundamental freedoms was considered as a guide to newer ideas operating at the transnational level and the contribution of 'law and economics' probed. It was shown that much of a challenge remains.

A better articulation of the transnational contract model operating between professionals, either in the common law or civil law tradition or in any other, was considered necessary. Its embedding in fundamental principle autonomously operating in the transnational commercial and financial legal order and the formulation of transnational minimum standards in this regard was considered the key challenge in the progression of the professional' contract in the international flows of goods, services, money, technology and information.

References

Adar Y, Sirena P (2015) Principles versus rules in the emerging European contract law. In: Rutgers J et al (eds) Rules and principles in European contract law. Intersentia, Cambridge, p 7

Allen DW (2000) Transaction costs. In: Bouckaert B et al (eds) Encyclopedia of law and economics. Edward Elgar, Cheltenham, p 893

Atiyah PS (1978) Contracts, promises and the law of obligations. LQR 94:193
Atiyah PS (1979) The rise and fall of freedom of contract. Oxford University Press, Oxford
Atiyah PS (1981) Promises, morals and law. Oxford University Press, Oxford
Atiyah PS, Summers RS (1987) Form and substance in Anglo-American law: a comparative study of legal reasoning, legal theory, and legal institutions. Oxford University Press, Oxford
Ayres I, Gertner R (1989) Filing gaps in incomplete contracts: an economic theory of default rules. Yale Law J 99:87
Bakker PS (2011) Uitleg van Commerciele Contracten [Interpretation of commercial contracts]. WPNR:6890/1
Bakos Y, Marotta-Wurgler F et al (2009) Does anyone read the fine print? Testing a law and economics approach to standard form contracts. NYU Law and Economics Research Paper 9(40)
Berman J (1963) Excuse for non-performance in the light of contract practices in international trade. Columbia Law Rev 63:1413
Bernitz U, Grousot X et al (eds) (2013) General principles of EU law and European private law. European Monographs, vol 65. Kluwer Law International
Buxbaum RM (1994) Is the uniform commercial code a code? In: Drobnig U et al (eds) Rechtsrealismus, multikulturelle Gesellschaft und Handelsrecht: Karl L. Llewellyn und seine Bedeutung heute. Duncker & Humblodt, Berlin
Canaris CW (1998) Grundrechte und Privatrecht: eine Zwischenbilanz. Stark erweiterte Fassung des Vortrags gehalten vor der Juristischen Gesellschaft zu Berlin am 10. Juni 1998. Walter de Gruyter, Berlin
Collins H (2007) Utility and rights in common law reasoning: rebalancing private law through constitutionalization. LSE Law Department, Law and Society Working Paper Series, Sept 2007(2)
Cooter R (1994) Structural adjudication and the new law merchant: a model for decentralisation. Int Rev Law Econ 14:215
Craswell R (1988a) Contract remedies, renegotiation, and the theory of efficient breach. South Calif Law Rev 61:629
Craswell R (1988b) Precontractual investigation as an optimal precaution problem. J Legal Stud 17:401
Craswell R (1996) Offer, acceptance, and efficient reliance. Stanford Law Rev 48:481
Craswell R (2003) In that case, what is the question? Economics and the demands of contract theory. Yale Law J 112:904
Dalhuisen JH (2006) Legal orders and their manifestation: the operation of the international commercial and financial legal order and its Lex Mercatoria. Berkeley J Int Law 24(1):129
Dalhuisen JH (2015) Globalisation and the transnationalisation of commercial and financial law. Rutgers Univ Law Rev 67(19)
Dalhuisen JH (2016) Dalhuisen on transnational comparative, commercial, financial and trade law, 6th edn. Hart, Oxford
Dalhuisen JH (2017) The role of arbitration in shipping law. J Int Marit Law 23(3)
Eisenberg MA (1986) Text anxiety. South Calif Law Rev 59:305
Faber D (1983) Contract law and modern economic theory. Northwestern Univ Law Rev 78:304
Feldman Y, Teichman D (2011) Are all contractual obligations created equal? Georgetown Law J 100:6
Fried C (1980) The rise and fall of freedom of contract. Harv Law Rev 93:1858
Friedmann D, Barak-Erez D (eds) (2001) Human rights in private law. Oxford University Press, Oxford
Gilmore G (1974) The death of contract. Ohio State University Press, Columbus
Goetz CJ, Scott RE (1980) Enforcing promises: an examination of the basis of contract. Yale Law J 89:1261
Gordley J (1981) European codes and American restatements: some difficulties. Columbia Law Rev 81:140
Hillman RA (2002) Rolling contracts. Fordham Law Rev 71:744

Katz AW (1998) Standard form contracts. In: Newman P (ed) The New Palgrave dictionary of economics and the law. Macmillan Reference Limited, London
Koopmans T (2000) General principles of law in European national systems of law: a comparative view. In: Bernitz U et al (eds) General principles of European community law. Kluwer Law International, Deventer
Kraus D (2008) Die Anwendung allgemeiner Grundsaetze des Gemeinschaftsrechts in Privatrechtsbeziehungen. In: Riesenhuber K (ed) Entwicklungen nicht-legislatorischer Rechtsangleichung im Europaeischen Privatrecht. Walter de Gruyter, Berlin
Lord RA (1957) Williston on contracts. Thomson Reuters, Boston
Luhmann N (1985) A sociological theory of law. Glasshouse, London
Marotta-Wurgler F (2009) Are "Pay Now, Terms Later" contracts worse for buyers? Evidence from software license agreements. J Legal Stud 38:309
Marotta-Wurgler F, Taylor R (2013) Set in stone? Change and innovation in consumer standard form contracts. N Y Univ Law Rev 88:240
Metzger A (2011) Allgemeine Rechtsgrundsaetze in Europa. RabelsZ 75:845
Murray JE (2012) The dubious status of the rolling contract formation theory. Duquesne Law Rev 50:35
Plaut VC, Bartlett RP III (2012) Blind consent, a social psychological investigation of non-readership of click-through agreements. Law Hum Behav 36:293
Posner EA (2003) Economic analysis of contract law after three decades: success or failure. Yale Law J 112:829
Prechal S (2010) Competence creep and general principles of law. Rev Eur Administrative Law 3:8
Raz J (1982) Promises, morals and law. Harv Law Rev 95:916
Schwartz A, Scott R (2003) Contract theory and the limits of contract law. Yale Law J 113:541 et seq.
Schwarz A, Scott RE (2007) Precontractual liability and preliminary agreements. Harv Law Rev 120:662
Scott RE (1987) Conflict and cooperation in long-term contracts. Calif Law Rev 75(6):2005
Scott RE (1999) The case for formalism in relational contracts. North Western Univ Law Rev 94:847
Temple Lang J (2013) Emerging European principles of private law. In: Bernitz U et al (eds) General principles of EU law and European private law, vol 65. Kluwer Law International, Alphen an de Rijn
Teubner G (1997) Breaking frames: the golden interplay of legal and social systems. Am J Comp Law 45:149
Thomas R (2016) The significance of customs, usages, and practices in the resolution of commercial disputes. In: Goldby M et al (eds) The role of arbitration in shipping law. Oxford University Press, Oxford, p 11
Tridimas T (2013) Horizontal effect of general principles: bold rulings and fine distinctions. In: Bernitz U et al (eds) General principles of EU law and European private law, vol 65. Kluwer Law International, Alphen an de Rijn, pp 213–232
von Bogdandy A (2014) Common principles for a plurality of orders: a study on public authority in the European legal area. Int J Const L 12(4):980

The Nexus of Contracts Theory and Intra-Corporate Dispute Arbitration

Joseph Lee

Contents

Abstract Arbitration has been a forum for the resolution of intra-corporate disputes (ICDs) or enforcement of corporate norms and rights in many advanced economies. The author argues that a company's constitution should be the basis for regulating intra-corporate dispute arbitration and discusses how the nexus of contracts theory can provide some foundation. The ICD arbitration clause should be drafted to define which disputes are covered and who is bound by the clause and it should provide arbitrators with specific powers, especially in the areas of evidence and interim remedies. The author examines the UK Companies Act 2006 and common law cases and suggests a legal paradigm for an ICD arbitration. ICD arbitration in China, Russia and Vietnam are also discussed in order to show different approaches to such a contract-based paradigm. ICD arbitration can become a

J. Lee (✉)
Law School, University of Exeter, Exeter, UK
e-mail: j.lee@exeter.ac.uk

M. Heidemann, J. Lee (eds.), *The Future of the Commercial Contract in Scholarship and Law Reform*, https://doi.org/10.1007/978-3-319-95969-6_3

method for international joint ventures, and the nexus of contracts theory can facilitate the advancement of this legal basis.

1 Introduction

Arbitration has been a forum for the resolution of intra-corporate disputes (ICDs) or enforcement of corporate norms and rights in many advanced economies such as the United Kingdom (UK),[1] Germany,[2] Belgium,[3] and the United States (US).[4] Nor is intra-corporate dispute arbitration new to major Asian arbitration hubs such as China[5] and Singapore.[6] Whilst courts are still considered the most suitable forum for obtaining redress and enforcing corporate norms for listed companies, many jurisdictions have already experienced intra-corporate dispute arbitration for listed companies. The theoretical underpinning and the practical model for such an arbitration have not yet provided a general consensus. In some jurisdictions, the courts have also been ambitious in providing dispute resolutions for companies and, in some way, these compete with the arbitration. The Delaware Commercial Court, the English Chancery Court, and the International Commercial Court in Singapore, are examples of an ambitious forum to attract intra-corporate dispute cases. However, even in these jurisdictions, the way in which the courts can be a better arbitration forum for resolving intra-corporate disputes between listed companies remains an under-researched topic.

In this article, the author will attempt to discuss how the nexus of contracts theory can provide a rationale for intra-corporate dispute arbitration, and how shareholder redress and the enforcement of corporate norms can be better served by intra-corporate dispute arbitration. The author will then discuss the practical difficulties for ICD arbitration for listed companies, based on the current statutory framework and case law. Some case law from outside the UK will be considered to discover whether other legal principles could offer solutions.

---

[1] *Fulham Football Club (1987) Ltd v Richards* and anther [2011] EWCA Civ 855; *Beattie v E F Beattie Ltd* 1 Ch. 708, 719–20 (CA 1938); *Hickman v Kent* [1915] 1 Ch. 881; *Exeter City Amateur Football Club Ltd v Football Conference Ltd* [2004] EWHC 831 (Ch).

[2] Borris (2012).

[3] Van Gerven (2015).

[4] *Corvex Management LP v Commonwealth REIT* Cir. Ct. Balt. May 8, 2013; Also see Coyle (2016).

[5] Gu (2013), Ali and Huang (2012) and Wang (2012).

[6] Yeo and Chew (2016).

2 The Theory of Company Law and Arbitrability of Corporate Law

The contractarian theory provides the most flexible approach to delimit an ICD, it can be regarded as the basis for company law. Academics have provided a number of theories to explain the modern form and relationships of a corporate organisation. The nexus of contract theory regards company law as a set of default rules regulating various contractual parties of a corporate organisation. According to Jensen and Meckling: '[The firm] is the legal fiction which serves as a focus for a complex process in which the conflicting objectives of individuals are brought into equilibrium within a framework of contractual relations.'[7] It is also argued that the creation of corporate personhood had four important functions: (1) continuity in the holding of contracts, (2) corporate engagement in business as an identifiable persona, (3) self-governance without the government's intervention and (4) partitioning the pools of assets.

There are also mandatory rules of company law based on this contractarian theory, and these mandatory rules are to serve the collective interest of the contracting parties, hence cannot be contracted out. For example, the compulsory directors' duties in the UK and the 'mandated regulatory conformity' of the board in EU takeovers are mandatory provisions.[8] According to the concession theory, the benefit of corporate legal personality, whereby the capital providers are not personally liable for damages caused by the company, is a privilege granted by the state; hence a company must carry out the function of serving the public interest, rather than the private interest. The communitarian theory (or the stakeholder theory) allows parties affected by corporate acts to have their interests, entitlements and rights recognised, and hence included in company law. They include employees, suppliers, consumers, and the communities affected, including government agencies. The concession theory, the stakeholder theory, and the communitarian theory would demand stronger protection to parties other than the shareholders through mandatory rules in company law. These rules, unlike other default rules, are designed to protect the public interest and interests other than those of the shareholders. They cannot be contracted out by private agreements or the company's constitution.

Yet, nexus of contracts theory can also explain the mandatory nature of some corporate law provisions. Company law serves as a standard form contract to the party, which supply the terms to the party to opt-in so that they can save the cost of bargaining over contract.[9] In other words, corporate law reduces the cost of drafting corporate contracts by providing a set of default rules that firms can adopt or reject.[10] Under Public Good Hypothesis it argues that complete contractual freedom in corporate law imposes externalities, and if the addition of customized terms by more

[7] Blair (2013).

[8] McGaughey (2015).

[9] Easterbrook and Fischel (1989).

[10] Klausner (1995).

firms will lead to disintegration of the standard form, in that way, will impose more costs. Therefore, maintenance of the public good of a standard corporate form will require a mandatory legal regime.[11] The innovation hypothesis claims that a mandatory regime may facilitate innovation of corporate charter terms. Thus a regime of mandatory law that permits the state to send such signals through revising or relaxing standard form terms may speed the process of innovation or lead to greater diffusion of innovation, and improve shareholder's welfare.[12] Under the Opportunistic Amendment Hypothesis, mandatory law as a hands-tying mechanism that provides assurance against opportunistic charter amendment by the management at the expenses of the shareholders.[13]

What is the significance of these mandatory rules to ICD arbitration? The fact that these mandatory rules cannot be contracted out by private agreements or by the company's constitution does not mean that disputes arising out of these rules cannot be submitted to arbitration. The question is why should a particular dispute arising out of company law be resolved only in the courts. Should the enforcement of these mandatory rules in company law be made publicly visible so as to advocate the 'right corporate behaviours'? Some of the rules may need to be further clarified by the courts to fill the law gap, and arbitration may deprive a legal system of this opportunity for development. This may be true, but many mandatory rules in company law are detailed, and the adjudicatory function of the courts is based on the evidence presented, rather than involving a thorough investigation in the law.

The UK has currently no clear policy for denying the arbitrability of ICDs based on the benefit of enforcement visibility. Yet, the US Securities Exchange Commission (SEC) has refused companies' registration if the companies' constitutions allow arbitration for disputes arising out corporate governance issues i.e. investors' claims for compensation against the board for wrongdoing. Contrary to this policy, many jurisdictions, such as Brazil, make ICD arbitration of a listed company compulsory. China also makes ICDs arbitration of a Chinese company listed on the Hong Kong Exchange compulsory. Thailand provides an option for listed companies to submit the dispute to the court or an arbitration.

Other than the enforcement visibility argument against ICD arbitration, company law may give exclusive jurisdiction for adjudicating a dispute to the courts. However, writing such court exclusive jurisdiction into company law may not be easy. The fact that the provisions mention a remedy to be granted by the court does not exclude the arbitrability of an IDC based on the relevant provisions. Arbitrators may have powers to grant similar remedies, if parties so agree. Even if a provision states a resolution can be declared void by the courts, so long as it does not affect the third parties' interest by avoiding the resolution, the validity of the resolution obtained by arbitration should be upheld.

---

[11] Gordon (1989).

[12] Gordon (1989).

[13] Gordon (1989).

However, if an ICD arises out of a provision that specifies both civil and criminal consequences, this ICD may not be arbitrable until the court has first ruled on it. Such an ICD is not automatically excluded from arbitration, but the arbitral award will not be binding on the court. The imposition of a criminal sanction on a party for breach of a provision, sometimes a minor one carrying a small fine or a light prison sentence, may serve the purpose of deterrent. It is arguable whether such criminal sanction is intended to be made publicly visible. There is often little scope for filling the law gap by the courts.

3 Contract-Based ICD Arbitration

In English law, party autonomy is the cornerstone of ICD arbitration[14] and is reinforced by contractual principles in company law.[15] In business associations, the company is regarded as the nexus of contractual relationships between shareholders and between the shareholders and the company.[16] The essence of such party autonomy-based corporate dispute resolution is to treat the company's constitution, which contains an arbitration clause, as a binding agreement between the shareholders and the company and among the shareholders *inter se*.[17] The parties to this corporate contract are the company and its members.[18] Other investors, such as corporate bondholders, are not considered here as privy to the company's constitution, as their relationships with the company and among the bondholders are governed by debentures—another set of contracts.[19] An arbitration clause in the constitution will bind parties privy to the company's constitution.[20] It is not certain if the constitution also makes the board collectively and its directors individually privy to the constitution.[21] In *Beattie v E F Beattie Ltd*,[22] the court ruled that the directors could not invoke an arbitration clause in the constitution when named as defendants in a shareholder

[14] Party autonomy as the basis of arbitration is also a recognised legal principle in other common law and civil law jurisdictions.

[15] Coffee (1986).

[16] Easterbrook and Fischel (1989); For a critique of this theory, see Moore (2014).

[17] This is also the approach adopted by the ECJ in Case C-214/89 *Powell Duffryn* [1992] ECR I-1745. For an American approach, see Ravanides (2008). This is similar to the New Corporate Arbitration Rules of 2003 in Italy, see Anglani and Liguori (2007).

[18] Case C-214/89 *Powell Duffryn plc v Petereit* [1992] ECR I-01745, para 10.

[19] Disputes arising out of corporate debentures have traditionally been settled through arbitration, especially for companies with a large international investor base.

[20] *Eley v Positive Government Security Life Assurance Co Ltd* (1876) 1 Ex D 88; *Hickman v Kent or Romney Marsh Sheep-Breeders' Association* [1915] 1 Ch 881.

[21] In *Beattie v E F Beattie Ltd* 1 Ch. 708, 719–20 (CA 1938), the Court of Appeal refused to stay derivative proceedings against a shareholder director on the basis of an arbitration clause stipulated in the articles, stating that the claim concerned the plaintiff in his capacity as a director, whereas he was only bound by the clause in his capacity as a shareholder.

[22] *Beattie v E F Beattie Ltd* 1 Ch. 708, 719–20 (CA 1938).

derivative suit.[23] This is because the directors were not privy to the constitution. Yet, this does not prevent the shareholder from relying on the clause, being a party to the constitution, to resolve a dispute through arbitration, i.e. bringing a derivative action in arbitration against the directors. Furthermore, because directors are bound by the rules in the constitution with regard to their appointment and removal as well as the determination of some aspects of their remuneration, it can be argued that they are bound as a party when their rights and duties are stated in the constitution. Although the UK Companies Act 2006 never affirms the corporate constitution's status as contract, the judicial attitude and academic commentators regard it as quasi-contract—an instrument that enables parties to privately order their affairs in the company and that has a binding effect, similar to a contract, on the parties.[24] It is safe to say that creditors, employees and other contractors of the company—collectively described as the company's stakeholders—are not privy to the company's constitution.[25] Therefore, without more, they are not and cannot be parties to the company's constitution and cannot invoke any provision in the agreement to enforce their interests and rights. That is to say, an arbitration clause in the company's constitution cannot be relied on by these corporate constituents to resolve a dispute. Equally, companies cannot rely on an arbitration clause in the constitution to compel an employment dispute with its employees. Creditors cannot rely on this clause to enforce a loan agreement.[26] Companies cannot use this clause to resolve a contractual or tortious dispute with the company's auditor, notwithstanding the fact that auditor is acting as the company's gatekeeper in the interest of the company. Even though the clause in the constitution cannot be relied on by non-members, the Companies Act 2006 does not preclude the inclusion of an 'outsider' party to the constitution. In addition, the duty to arbitrate could be imposed through the use of a signed employment or engagement agreement, i.e. with the directors and auditors calling for arbitration or referencing the duty to arbitrate in the company's constitution.

Careful drafting of a company's constitution is required to make ICD arbitration with non-members, i.e. company directors and company auditors, effective. First, the constitution can include the specific rights and responsibilities of the board and the specific rights and duties of the members.[27] The constitution could then specify the method for addressing any dispute arising out of these rights and obligations, such as arbitration.[28] One way of enforcing directors' duties is to bring a derivative

---

[23] See also Goldberg (1985).

[24] See Moore (2014).

[25] Investors (ex-shareholders) who sold companies' shares cannot reply on the arbitration clause in the constitution as they are no longer members of the company. They are not stakeholders nor other constituents in the same category as employees, creditors, and directors.

[26] However, it is not clear whether the arbitration clause can be relied on if a creditor's debt interest converts to an equity interest upon becoming a shareholder in the company.

[27] In this way, directors can be made privy to the constitution.

[28] This method is commonly used in the United States. The corporate bylaws are detailed and often also include the duties of board and rights of shareholders in a contested takeover bid. See case *Corvex Management LP v Commonwealth REIT* Cir. Ct. Balt. May 8, 2013.

action on behalf of the company, and the arbitration clause will cover this shareholder derivative action. Second, if the arbitration clause specifically covers shareholder derivative actions and third parties are aware of this clause in the company's constitution, it may be argued that the third parties, especially sophisticated parties such as the company's auditor, may have given implied consent to such arbitration.[29] Such an arbitration clause may be reinforced further by an arbitration clause between the company and the auditor.[30] The outcome may be that shareholder derivative action on behalf of the company against the company's auditor is covered by the arbitration clause.

However, there is a limit to such a contractual approach of using the company's constitution as the basis for ICD arbitration. It stems from the unilateral alteration of the company's constitution by a supermajority vote of the shareholders at the meeting.[31] This can arise when an arbitration clause is to be included or removed from the company's constitution by a supermajority vote of the shareholders, making the dissenting shareholders bound by the newly devised clauses in the constitution.[32] The dissenting shareholders would not be able to seek damages or an injunction against such an alteration. This may appear to be contrary to the contract approach of ICD arbitration, as the dissenting shareholders would not have redress.[33] However, the contractual notion as the basis for ICD arbitration—treating a company constitution as if it were a contract—does not necessarily treat the insertion of an arbitration clause, or removal of it, as a breach of contract by the parties.[34] Because the parties are aware of arbitration being used as an alternative forum for dispute resolution, the parties may be regarded as implicitly consenting to any change to the constitution that may result in a change of forum for dispute resolution so long as such change follows the required procedure under the Companies Act 2006, i.e. holding a general meeting.[35] Interestingly, such an alteration may give rise to an unfair prejudice suit by the dissenting shareholders against the insertion or removal of an arbitration clause.[36] The majority shareholders may also need to prove

---

[29] Hanotiau (2011); See also Junngam (2010).

[30] Sangiovanni (2006).

[31] Turkhtanov (2013).

[32] This point has never been explored in the UK.

[33] See *Suda v The Czech Republic*, No. 1643/06, October 28, 2010 49.

[34] In *Powell Duffryn v Wolfgang Petereit* Case C-214/89, European Court of Justice ruled that a jurisdiction clause in the statutes of a company is binding on all the shareholders, notwithstanding some of the shareholders against whom the clause is invoked opposed the adoption of the clause or that they became shareholders after the clause was adopted; However, such an alteration may amount to a breach of Article 6(1) of the European Convention on Human Rights. See *Suda v The Czech Republic*, No. 1643/06.

[35] In Delaware, the court held that Delaware law places shareholders on notice that boards may change corporate bylaws at any time without shareholder approval, so long as the bylaw complies with s 109 of the Delaware General Corporation Law. Also see *North v McNamara*, No. 1:13-cv-833, 2014; Boilermakers, 73 A.3d; *Corvex Management LP v Commonwealth REIT* Cir. Ct. Balt. May 8, 2013.

[36] Milman (2007).

that such amendment is 'bona fide for the benefit of the company as a whole'.[37] Paradoxically, such a dispute may need to be resolved through arbitration.

4 The Interaction Between UK Companies Act 2006 and Arbitration

In this section, the author will examine two aspects. First, how can ICD arbitration be beneficial under the current corporate governance framework, including the provisions of the Companies Act 2006. Secondly, if ICD arbitration can provide better redress, what are the practical difficulties that investors of listed companies may face?

Before deciding to use arbitration, research should be conducted to ensure that the company law statutes would not either invalidate the arbitration agreements or nullify their effectiveness—in other words, it is necessary to ascertain whether, in a given jurisdiction, the subject matter is arbitrable.[38] Hence, an arbitration clause will need to be drafted to cover the dispute. There are differences between disputes arising out of a shareholder agreement, the company constitution, and general company law. For a dispute arising out of a shareholder agreement or the company constitution, the remedies are primarily contractual. If the dispute arises out of provisions in the UK Companies Act 2006, remedies will depend on the provisions in the Act. If the remedy sought is specific performance or a temporary or permanent injunction, even though the arbitral tribunal may have such powers stipulated in the arbitration agreement,[39] the procedures to obtain such a remedy are far more complicated,[40] costly and uncertain than those for a compensatory or restitutionary remedy.[41] ICD arbitration can involve the validity of certain passed resolutions of a company.[42] If the resolution was held to be invalid due to non-compliance with the provisions in the Act, the desired remedy is to set aside the transactions executed pursuant to the invalid resolution. Injunctive relief may be sought if the transaction is executory based on a disputed resolution. Shareholders may be able to claim their loss of investment against the company, the board, or the majority shareholders if their personal rights were infringed or if the fiduciaries failed to execute their duties. To

---

[37] *Allen v Gold Reefs of West Africa Ltd* [1900] 1 Ch 656; *Greenhalgh v Arderne Cinemas Ltd* (No 2) [1946] 1 All ER 512.

[38] Chernykh (2009), Shaw (2011) and Poser (1986).

[39] In *Armstrong v Northern Eyes Inc* [2000] O. R. 48, 442, the arbitrator ruled that he had broad powers to grant both legal and equitable remedies, but not a statutory oppression remedy in the absence of the express conferral of such powers on the arbitrators by the parties. Hence, some equitable remedies can be granted by the parties so long as they agree to such conferral.

[40] Lee (2013).

[41] The party may need to apply to the court to enforce the peremptory orders given by the tribunal under s 42 of the Arbitration Act 1996.

[42] Roth (2015).

unwind the transactions, the court would need to declare the resolution invalid and to order the parties to unwind the transactions. These are powers that the arbitral tribunal would not have under the Arbitration Act 1996. This is because unwinding the transactions may affect third parties, e.g. the sale of a company asset to a third-party acquirer. Ordering a company to pass a new resolution is not within the arbitrator's power under section 48 of the Arbitration Act 1996. Furthermore, the Companies Act may not allow transactions based on an invalid resolution to be unwound.[43] This is a major difference between UK company law and German company law. In Germany, many ICDs centre on the validity of a resolution that has been passed.[44] However, in the UK, such disputes rarely arise. This is because the UK Companies Act 2006 emphasises transaction certainty. Such transaction certainty is reinforced by the Companies Act 2006 in that it specifically provides that the validity of a resolution passed should not affect the acts conducted pursuant to the resolution. For instance, if a company director is not validly appointed, his or her acts should not be invalidated because of the invalid appointment. If a company fails to comply with company procedures, such non-compliance should not invalidate the resolution. In short, what redress shareholders may be entitled to depends largely also on how the Companies Act regulates the effect of an irregular resolution.

5 The Court's Inherent Power to Grant Redress May Not Be Exclusive

There are provisions that specifically provide the courts with the power to grant particular orders or forms of redress. The English Court of Appeal has ruled that the specific provisions denoting the court's power to adjudicate do not exclude arbitration.[45] In other words, arbitration would not be in derogation of these company law provisions because the court has been mentioned only as a forum to obtain redress. The power conferred by company law to the courts would only exclude arbitration if granting such relief would have effect on a 'third party'. For instance, if an order was sought to dissolve a company, this would affect creditors' (a third party's) interests, so the arbitral tribunal would not have the power to grant such an order binding on third parties. A provision often used by minority shareholders in a closed company is s 995 regarding unfair prejudice. Under this provision, the shareholders petition the court and allege that the affairs of the company are being conducted in a way that is unfairly prejudicial to their interests.[46] If the court is satisfied with this claim, it has discretion to award a number of remedies. The fact that some of the

43 Directors' appointment and the related transactions see CA 2006, s 161(2).

44 Borris (2012).

45 *Fulham Football Club (1987) Ltd v Richards and anther* [2011] EWCA Civ 855.

46 See 'Modernising Company Law' (Command Paper CM 5553-II, 2002), para. 2.36, available at: www.dti.gov.uk/companiesbill/whitepaper.htm.

remedies may affect third parties should not preclude arbitration, as it may grant remedies other than those with third-party effects.[47] One of the remedies under s 995 is allowing the minority shareholders to bring a civil action against the board. This redress effectively bypasses the difficult issue of *locus standi*—legal standing—which has traditionally been an obstacle to minority shareholders in bringing proceedings against the board of directors, who are considered fiduciaries of the company. This procedural issue of lack of standing derives from the substantive law that sees the company as the proper person to hold the board accountable. It is questionable whether this is a remedy that an arbitral tribunal would have the power to grant. The question turns on whether arbitrators have the powers to adjudicate shareholder derivative actions. If an arbitral tribunal can adjudicate a shareholder derivative action, it should also have the power to grant such an action as a remedy.

6 Derivative Action

The shareholder derivative action is an action brought by shareholders on behalf of the company against a third party, such as the board of directors. The purpose of the action is to remedy the lack of enforcement by the company against the board of directors for failing to perform the board's duties.[48] Because the board of directors normally owes a fiduciary duty to the company and not to the shareholders,[49] a derivative action becomes an *ex post* tool used by shareholders to enforce the board's duties. Such an action is potentially an enforcement tool to prevent the board from engaging in illegal and illegitimate activities.[50] A minority shareholder can bring a derivative action and seek injunctive relief against an act of the board or an individual director.[51] Whether it is an effective action for a minority shareholder to obtain monetary compensation or an account of profits by corporate officers involved in illegal activities remains questionable. It depends on whether the corporate law provisions provide for monetary redress and whether there is sufficient financial incentive, provided by the legal regime, for the minority shareholder to institute these proceedings.[52] Under the current Companies Act 2006, which follows the principle of no reflective loss,[53] a minority shareholder who brings a derivative

[47] In *ACD Tridon Inc v Tridon Australia Pty Ltd* [2002] NSWSC 896, the court considered that a winding up order does not simply involve public policy considerations surrounding the process of winding up the company but that the operations of the order can affect third parties.

[48] Some US cases suggest that shareholder derivative action arbitration is against public policy. See *Lane v Abel-Bey* [1979] N.Y.S. 4182 25, 26.

[49] Lim (2013).

[50] Reisberg (2005).

[51] Shell (1989).

[52] Reisberg (2006).

[53] Lin (2007).

action will not receive direct monetary compensation if the board is found liable for damages to the company. As a result, there is little incentive for a minority shareholder to bring a derivative action because the legal cost required at the beginning of the proceedings, and the possibility of being responsible for the entire legal costs if the suit fails, are too high. Although the court has discretion in the ordering of costs, derivative action is uncommon in enforcing corporate governance in listed companies. In the US, the driving force for derivative suits is the claimants' lawyer, whose fees could come from the common fund of the class action settlement.[54]

In addition to the financial burden a minority shareholder must shoulder, judicial discretion in the control of the proceedings poses further legal uncertainty in a derivative action arbitration. Under the current regime, a minority shareholder must obtain court permission to continue the derivative action. Permission will be given if court action satisfies the factors specified under the provision. Based on the ruling in *Fulham Football Club (1987) Ltd v Richards and another*,[55] the mere mention of the court's power in the provisions does not preclude the arbitral tribunal from exercising a similar function, so long as such permission to continue the claim does not affect third parties. The question is whether the tribunal's decision to grant or refuse permission to continue the claim can be challenged.

A derivative action involves the shareholders (both minority and majority), the company, and the directors. Therefore, a derivative action is categorised as a set of multi-party proceedings. All the parties involved must have consented to arbitration. If a minority shareholder does not give consent to resolve the dispute through arbitration, a derivative action brought by another minority shareholder may not bind the non-consenting shareholder. In that case, the staying of non-consenting shareholders' court proceedings under s 9 of Arbitration Act 1996 may not be applied. The arbitral award will not bind the non-consenting shareholders, and hence it will not have a *res judicata* effect. To manage the risk of parallel proceedings[56] and to increase the certainty of the arbitration having a *res judicata* effect, parties should insert an arbitration clause in the company's constitution that specifically covers shareholder derivative action against the board of directors. In addition, there should also be a binding mechanism detailing how such a derivative action among minority shareholders may be brought. An arbitration institution, such as London Court of International Arbitration (LCIA), can provide specific rules, and the company can incorporate these rules into the company's constitution. These rules must also be brought to the shareholders' attention.

Based on the court's contractual approach to the parties' dispute resolution agreement, derivative action under the Companies Act 2006 does not mandate judicial approval of settlement and dismissal. The derivative suit, as many commentators have opined,[57] involves a set of procedural rules. These procedural rules are

[54] Farrar (2015).

[55] *Fulham Football Club (1987) Ltd v Richards and anther* [2011] EWCA Civ 855.

[56] Cremades and Madalena (2008).

[57] Davies and Worthington (2012).

capable of being waived or contracted out to a more flexible procedural regime based on party autonomy. The arbitration of derivative suits does not curtail substantive statutory rights conferred on the party or diminish the substantive fiduciary duty of management. If the arbitral tribunal was able be more flexible in their discretion to award costs—more friendly to shareholders—arbitration of derivative action could be used more frequently.[58]

7 Corporate Value, Shareholder Value and Social Value

Public policy, in particular investor protection, has been a basis for preventing IDC arbitration for listed companies where the public interest might thereby be reduced.[59] Hence, the public policy question much depends on behavioural assumptions regarding corporate constituents. In so doing, public policy questions could be framed as follows: would ICD arbitration enhance corporate value, shareholder value and social value? As already mentioned, ICD arbitration is rarely used in UK listed companies so the benefit of ICD arbitration for listed companies is therefore an empirical question. In increasingly shareholder-centred governance, ICD arbitration provides a forum for shareholders to enforce the board's duties instead of exercising exit strategies. To bring an ICD arbitration through a derivative action claiming a breach of the fiduciary duty owed by any director, officer or other employee of the company, the claimants need to be shareholders at the time that the proceedings are instituted. This would encourage shareholders to hold stocks for a longer term, hence fostering a longer-term investment culture.[60] For investors in a listed company, ICD arbitration provides a forum to obtain redress, such as a governance settlement, regardless of whether company law provides adequate remedies. The advantage of using arbitration is that arbitrators can mould their decision to fit the needs of the particular business problem; arbitrators can arrive at management and policy decisions that courts would not attempt to make.[61]

A UK listed company may be incorporated elsewhere and have an international shareholder base. Once its shares are traded on UK exchanges, English law becomes the applicable law for securities-related disputes. If the investor suffers damages due to the company's failure to disclose certain corporate information, such intra-corporate disputes on the misrepresentation of securities can be decided through ICD arbitration.[62] This type of arbitration can be achieved through an IPO document specifically stipulating that ICDs will be adjudicated through arbitration.

---

[58] This would also raise the question of equal treatment between both sides.

[59] Black (2012) and Ferran (2009).

[60] Shareholder engagement can facilitate long term investment. See Micheler (2013).

[61] Shell (1989).

[62] Black (2012).

ICD arbitration may be said to prevent case flows in the courts, thus reducing the precedential effect of company law cases. This has a negative effect on the development of company law by the courts. However, to what extent does the court still develop company law doctrine through case law? Most of the adjudications of company law cases take place in the lower courts, which focus on the facts rather than the law itself. As mentioned, shareholder litigation and investor securities litigation are not as prevalent in the UK as in the US, so it is difficult to argue that there is a case in the UK for such a social value enhancement. If extreme importance is attached to a legal question in English law, there is a way to apply for court review under the Arbitration Act. In this way, ICD arbitration encourages longer-term investment, attracts listing on UK exchanges, and does not compromise the existing social value of the courts developing judicial principles in company and securities law.

The growth of the private equity and hedge fund industry has significantly changed the relationship between boards and investors. Shareholder activism by private equity funds and hedge funds has attempted to remedy the deficiencies of the decoupling of ownership and control.[63] This trend of shareholder activism will continue to influence how investors engage in corporate affairs. With the ageing population of developed economies, more investment will be in private equity funds and hedge funds that focus on risk-adjusted returns rather than fixed income.[64] The increased economic pressure and fiduciary duty for private equity funds and hedge funds to monitor portfolio firms' performance and related governance means that litigation rights (claims) would be an important asset.[65] As stated, the current UK legal environment is not in favour of US style litigation-led private enforcement; thus, arbitration not only serves as an alternative catalyst for corporate governance but also reduces the negative effect of litigation-style shareholder activism. Litigation exposes listed companies to adverse publicity that could trigger irrational behaviour on the part of investors. It can also be used as excessive leverage that serves the interest of private equity and hedge funds. At the extreme, shareholder activists can abuse the litigation process, and regulation of this problem gives rise to both theoretical and practical difficulties. Unlike in the US, where pension fund and institutional shareholders undertake the primary role of litigation-led private enforcement,[66] UK institutional shareholders, holding 35% of the public market securities,[67] employ different investment strategies. Yet, a large percentage of funding for private equity and hedge funds comes from institutional shareholders. Private equity and hedge funds are in a better position to use arbitration to monitor their portfolio firms because their investments are more focused on individual firms.[68]

[63] Ryan (2000).

[64] KMPG International *Growing Up a New Environment for Hedge Funds* 2015 KPMG/AIMA/MFA Global Hedge Fund Survey 9. www.kpmg.com/growingup.

[65] Cox and Thomas (2005).

[66] Chen (2010).

[67] Office for National Statistics.

[68] Schneider and Ryan (2011).

Unlike institutional shareholders, they do not have a duty to diversify and can undertake more targeted monitoring of portfolio firms. Private equity firms often take a seat on the board, and this increases the chances that they will use arbitration to resolve disputes with the board—similar to intra-corporate disputes of private companies.

Another benefit of arbitration-led governance by hedge funds is reducing the opportunity of hedge funds to use litigation in order to profit from short selling.[69] Although arbitration is subject to disclosure at the London Stock Exchange, the confidentiality of the proceedings reduces the company's exposure to short-term trading. As a result, arbitration increases corporate monitoring, which reduces agency costs but also reduces the chances of hedge funds short-selling company shares at the expense of other investors, resulting in a principal-principal conflict.

8 ICD Arbitration and International Joint Venture

An ICD arbitration provides the benefits of confidentiality and privacy that can manage the risk of a company's operation being distracted by shareholders' claims. For an international joint venture, foreign investors may prefer arbitration to litigation fearing bias against them by local courts. However, ICDs of a joint venture in an international arbitration pose more problems than in a domestic arbitration. First, some countries many require a foreign element to be present for the initiation of an international arbitration. When a JVC consists of two companies incorporated in a single jurisdiction but with one company receiving capital directly from a company incorporate outside the jurisdiction, it is questionable whether the provision of foreign capital would be sufficient for initiating an international arbitration, according to the arbitration law in the jurisdiction of incorporation. To recognise this as an international joint venture would require the country's company law to 'lift the veil of incorporation' and see through the corporate structure of the subsidiary company that participates in the JVC as a shareholder. In some countries, the law allows parent company to enforce an arbitration agreement entered into by its subsidiary companies. In this way, a JVC's arbitration clause in the constitution can be enforced by the parent company. Following this analysis, this can be an ICD and the arbitration can come under the remit of international arbitration.

In some countries, where there is a low recognition of nexus of contract theory as the company law basis, ICDs are likely to come under the courts' exclusive jurisdictions. It might not be possible to include an ICD arbitration clause in the company's constitution. However, parties may stipulate an ICD arbitration in their shareholder agreement, hence transforming an ICD dispute into a contractual dispute.

[69] Fox et al. (2010).

There are many ways in which an ICD arbitration of a JVC can be derailed. Firstly, the resident-shareholders or the board may bring proceedings to stay the arbitral proceedings on the ground that the ICD comes under the exclusive jurisdiction of the court. Secondly, even if the parties submit the ICD to an arbitration, a party may challenge the award at the enforcement stage on the ground that an ICD arbitration is contrary to public policy. Even if these two situations do not arise, an ICD arbitration would require the company or the board to disclose information. While an international arbitral tribunal may grant an interim remedy for such disclosure, the board or the party possessing the information may refuse to comply with the order. To enforce this remedy, the enforcing party would then need to go through the domestic courts of the country of incorporation.

Unlike a contractual dispute where parties can freely decide the governing law and the jurisdiction, parties of an ICD cannot freely decide what law should govern their dispute and the jurisdiction. The governing law remains the law of the incorporation. When a company is listed in a jurisdiction other than the place of incorporation, the country of listing may apply its law. It is also possible that a court will apply the country's law based on elements other than the place of incorporation, such as the place of the headquarters, the place of main operations, or the place of residence of the majority of investors. That is to say, even if the incorporation is elsewhere and the operation is abroad, and even if the investors are residing in the country, the court may refuse to recognise an ICD arbitration in a JCV's constitution if it is incorporated abroad.

9 Other Jurisdictions

9.1 China: Differences Between Domestic-Listed Chinese Companies and Foreign/HK-Listed Chinese Companies

Chinese law permits arbitration for the resolution of intra-corporate disputes. Furthermore, it is mandatory for Chinese companies seeking listing outside China to include an arbitration clause in the company's articles of association (corporate charter) to resolve such disputes within companies listed outside China.[70] Hence, disputes between shareholders of the companies listed overseas listed, and the company, or its directors, supervisors, managers or other senior management personnel, or shareholders of domestic companies, may be resolved by methods stipulated by

[70] Article 163 of the Prerequisite Clauses of the Articles of Association of Companies Seeking a Listing Outside the Peoples' Republic of China. The law is promulgated by the Securities Office of the State Council and the State Commission for Restructuring the Economic System in 1994. It recognises the parties' autonomy in deciding the settling mechanism for confined type of disputes— disputes regarding companies listed abroad and shareholders of their overseas shares.

laws and administrative regulations, or by methods determined by mutual agreement.[71]

Furthermore, Chinese companies seeking listing in Hong Kong are also required to include arbitration clauses in the companies' articles of association. the 'Prerequisite Clauses of the Articles of Association of Companies Seeking a Listing in Hong Kong' requires companies to include an arbitration clause in their articles of association. Under this stipulation, claims or disputes between a company listed in Hong Kong and its shareholders, between the shareholders and the companies' directors, auditors or other managers, or among different shareholders, should be submitted to arbitration. The arbitral award binds all parties involved.[72] For companies listed in China, even though there is no clear rule on ICD, Chinese scholars are in favour of using arbitration to resolve disputes within domestic companies.[73]

9.2 *Russia: Legal Uncertainty*

It is increasingly common in Russia for contracts to require arbitration rather than litigation as a binding means of dispute resolution. The Russian legal system recognizes both domestic and foreign private arbitration. Russia permits domestic and international arbitration to resolve contractual disputes, however, the courts can have exclusive jurisdiction over certain types of disputes.[74] Articles 33 and 225.1 of the Russian Commercial Procedure Code (the Code) provide the commercial courts with jurisdiction over disputes related to the creation of a legal entity, its management or participation in a commercial organization. Disputes include (1) disputes relating to the establishment, reorganization and liquidation of a legal entity; (2) disputes relating to the ownership of shares or equity interests in the charter capital of business entities[,] . . . [and] creation of encumbrances [over such shares or interests] and enforcement thereof . . . ; and (3) disputes regarding claims of the founders [or] members of a legal entity . . . for damages caused by a legal person, invalidating transactions conducted by a legal entity, [and/or] the application of consequences of [such] invalidity.

The issue of arbitrability of a corporate dispute has been the subject of academic debate[75] because uncertainly arose out of several provisions of the Commercial Procedure Code which confer special subject-matter jurisdiction over "corporate

[71] Rules Regarding the Necessary Clauses in the Corporate Charter for Companies listed Overseas available at http://www.docin.com/p-70495222.html.

[72] Rules Regarding the Necessary Clauses in the Corporate Charter for Companies listed In Hong Kong, available at http://www.smartteam.hk/service/3279.html.

[73] Liu (2006).

[74] Gorbylev (2015).

[75] Pettibone (2013).

disputes" upon the commercial courts.[76] There are no provisions expressly stating that these disputes are not arbitrable. However, the Law on International Commercial Arbitration provides that any commercial dispute is arbitrable unless the law expressly provides otherwise. This language has been subject to varying interpretations and has provoked some interesting litigation.

One prominent dispute involved a large Russian metals company, OJSC NLMK, which was sued by Mr Nikolai Maximov.[77] The plaintiff claimed that NLMK owed him 9.5 billion rubles[78] as payment for certain shares sold to NLMK under a sale-purchase agreement. The agreement provided for arbitration in Russia under the rules of the International Commercial Arbitration Court (ICAC), a Russian arbitration institution. The arbitral tribunal ruled in favour of Mr Maximov, and awarded him 8.9 billion rubles[79] plus interest. NLMK appealed to the Russian courts, which is allowed under local procedural rules. The Moscow City Commercial Court overturned the ICAC award on a number of grounds. One of them is that corporate disputes may not be resolved by arbitration. Mr Maximov then appealed unsuccessfully to a higher court, the Federal Commercial Court for the Moscow Circuit, and to the Supreme Commercial Court. Both courts declined to grant relief. As a result, the lower court decision not to recognise the ICAC arbitration award stands.

However, at the same time, the same parties were engaged in separate proceedings in the same Moscow City Commercial Court in which NLMK sought a ruling to invalidate the sale-purchase agreement and to provide a remedy for the return of the purchase price to NLMK. In these proceedings, the court dismissed the complaint on the grounds that the parties had agreed to binding arbitration of their disputes. NLMK then appealed to the Ninth Commercial Court of Appeals, which reversed the lower court's decision primarily on the basis of Articles 33 and 225.1 of the Code. Mr Maximov further appealed to the Federal Commercial Court for the Moscow Circuit. This court reversed the decisions of both the Moscow City Commercial Court and the Ninth Commercial Court of Appeals and sent the case to the Moscow City Commercial Court for re-examination of the issues, based on the limitations imposed by Russian law on the submission of certain disputes to arbitration. The case is ongoing.

In view of such inconsistent judicial practice, it is difficult to see whether the Russian courts will uphold ICD arbitrations, including disputes regarding sale and purchase of shares. Some prior authority suggests that the Russian courts are only intended to have exclusive jurisdiction over disputes that have a 'public element', such as real property disputes where the decision of a state agency to register title is at issue. However, the practical consequences and limitations remain unclear.

In several other cases, the courts have refused to enforce awards rendered in disputes arising out of the sale of shares and participation interests in Russian

[76] Turkhtanov (2013).

[77] Levy (2013).

[78] Approximately US$311 million.

[79] Approximately US$292 million.

companies. In many instances, the courts found that these awards were also contrary to the public policy of the Russian Federation since they were elements of various fraudulent schemes. The practice has not been entirely consistent. In April 2013, the Federal Commercial Court for the Moscow Circuit refused to set aside an award ordering a party to pay the purchase price for the shares in a Russian joint-stock company.

9.3 *Vietnam: In Line with the Contractual Approach*

In Vietnam, a corporate dispute is deemed to involve every kind of dispute within a company: disputes between shareholders, disputes between shareholders and the management, disputes between shareholders and the company. A dispute can relate to the establishment, the operation, management activities, dissolution, merger, consolidation, division, or separation of the company.[80]

Although these disputes are usually resolved by the court,[81] the Government encourages companies to choose the methods for resolving their internal disputes.[82] Therefore, shareholders at a general meeting can decide which method is most suitable for resolving disputes.

Furthermore, Arbitration Law does not provide any restriction or prohibition against ICD arbitration. Some public companies in Vietnam put arbitration clauses in their articles of association. Despite this, in the case of insolvency, courts have exclusive jurisdiction.[83] This is because the legislators believed that public companies with more than 100 shareholders must act for the majority of shareholders and for the employees. Thus, disputes arising out of an insolvency proceeding against the shareholders cannot be an internal dispute within the company.

---

[80] Vietnam Civil Procedure Code No. 24/2004/QH11 dated June 15, 2004, which took effect from January 1, 2005 with amendment in 2011, Article 29.3. See at: http://www.noip.gov.vn/noip/resource.nsf/vwResourceList/3457A7711572E0534725767200203DDA/$FILE/CIVIL%20PROCEDURE%20CODE.pdf.

[81] The courts have jurisdiction over these disputes as set out in the Civil Procedure Code 2004, the Resolution of the Supreme Court 2005 and the Decree No. 102/2010/ND-CP.

[82] The Law on Enterprise 2005 and its guiding Circular No. 121/2012/TT-BTC.

[83] The Law on Bankruptcy No. 21/2004/QH11 dated June 15, 2004, which took effect from October 15, 2004, Article 7. See at: http://vbqppl.moj.gov.vn/vbpq/en/Lists/Vn%20bn%20php%20lut/View_Detail.aspx?ItemID=7849.

10 Conclusion

Under the nexus of contracts theory, a company's constitution provides the best basis for ICD arbitration. The constitution should be carefully drafted to define which disputes are covered and who is bound by the clause so that individual directors who are not considered privy to the constitution are able to invoke the arbitration clause. In order to provide legal certainty, company law should specify whether a company's directors will be bound by the ICD arbitration clause in the constitution. The constitution should also deal with the issue of the insertion or modification of the arbitration regime by a super-majority vote of the shareholders. Company law should also be clear on whether the principle of majority rule will apply to the arbitration clause, and whether dissenting shareholders can challenge the validity of the arbitration on the ground that they have not consented to it. As derivative actions will be one of the main potential actions, company law should clarify (1) whether the arbitral tribunal has equivalent power to the court in granting permission to continue the claim, and (2) whether an arbitration decision has the effect of *res judicata*. The parties should also stipulate in the constitution what powers, especially in the area of disclosure and interim remedies, are conferred on the arbitrators. These powers are particularly useful to the shareholders if they wish to benefit from the discovery regime that litigation would have. The constitution should also incorporate rules dealing with multiparty arbitration, especially with respect to the appointment of arbitrators and the consolidation of multiparty claims.

References

Ali S, Huang H (2012) Financial dispute resolution in China: arbitration or court litigation. Arbitr Int 28(1):77–100

Anglani A, Liguori F (2007) Italy's new arbitration laws. Eur Arbitr Rev:49–51

Black B (2012) Investor protection meets the Federal Arbitration Act. Stanford J Complex Litigation 1(1):1–50

Blair M (2013) Corporate personhood and the corporate persona. Univ Illinois Law Rev 3:785–820

Borris C (2012) Arbitrability of corporate law disputes in Germany. Int Arbitr Law Rev 15(5):161–171

Chen C (2010) Institutional monitoring through shareholder litigation. J Financ Econ 95:356–362

Chernykh Y (2009) Arbitrability of corporate disputes in Ukraine. J Int Arbitr 26(5):745–750

Coffee J (1986) Shareholder versus managers: the strain in the corporate web. Mich Law Rev 85(1):1–109

Cox J, Thomas R (2005) Letting billions slip through your fingers: empirical evidence and legal implications of the failure of financial institutions to participate in securities class action settlements. Stanford Law Rev 58:411–454

Coyle T (2016) Aggregating consumer arbitration claims after Italian colors through litigation finance and securitization of legal claims. N Y Univ J Law Bus 12(3):833–888

Cremades B, Madalena I (2008) Parallel proceedings in international arbitration. Arbitr Int 24(4):507–540

Davies P, Worthington S (2012) Chapter 17: The derivative claim and personal actions against directors. Principles of modern company law. Sweet Maxwell, London, pp 643–665

Easterbrook F, Fischel D (1989) The corporate contract. Columbia Law Rev 98:1416–1448
Farrar J (2015) The move from private enforcement to public enforcement and now the move to litigation funding of shareholder activism: are we entering a new era of access to justice in corporate law. Eur Bus Law Rev 26(1):75–94
Ferran E (2009) Are US-style investor suites coming to the UK. J Corporate Law Stud 9(2):315–348
Fox M, Glosten L, Tetlock P (2010) Short selling and the news: a preliminary report on empirical study. N Y Law Sch Law Rev 54(2):645–688
Goldberg G (1985) The controversy on the section 20 contract revisited. Mod Law Rev 48:158–166
Gorbylev S (2015) Arbitration in Russia: are there any local differences? Int Bus Law J 5:463–479
Gordon J (1989) The mandatory structure of corporate law. Columbia Law Rev 89(7):1549–1553
Gu W (2013) Securities arbitration in China: a better alternative to retail shareholder protection. Northwestern J Int Law Bus 33(2):283–324
Hanotiau B (2011) Consent to arbitration: do we share a common vision. Arbitr Int 27(4):539–554
Junngam N (2010) An MFN clause and bit dispute settlement: a host state's implied consent to arbitration by reference. UCLA J Int Law Foreign Aff 15(20):399–528
Klausner M (1995) Corporations, corporate law, and networks of contracts. Virginia Law Rev 81(3):779–797
KMPG International (2015) Growing up a new environment for Hedge Funds. KPMG/AIMA/MFA Global Hedge Fund Survey 9. www.kpmg.com/growingup
Lee J (2013) Court-subsidiarity and interim measures in commercial arbitration: a comparative study of UK, Singapore and Taiwan. Contemp Asia Arbitr J 6(2):227–247
Levy D (2013) Sentenca Arbitral, Anulacao, Russia, Efeitos, *Reconhecimento*. Revista Brasileira de Arbitragem 10(37):125–141
Lim E (2013) Directors' fiduciary duties: a new analytical framework. Law Q Rev 129(2):242–263
Lin J (2007) Barring recovery for diminution in value of shares on the reflective loss principle. Cambridge Law J 66(3):537–558
Liu J (2006) Institutional innovations of new corporate law and their impacts on the arbitration practice. Beijing Arbitr 1:47–48
McGaughey E (2015) Ideals of the corporation and the nexus of contracts. Mod Law Rev 78(6):1057–1070
Micheler E (2013) Facilitating investor engagement and stewardship. Eur Bus Organ Law Rev 14(1):29–56
Milman D (2007) Litigating domestic disputes within companies: continuity or change? Company Law Newsl 22:1–5
Moore M (2014) Private ordering and public policy: the paradoxical foundations of corporate contractarianism. Oxf J Leg Stud 34(4):693–728
Pettibone P (2013) The nonarbitrability of corporate disputes in Russia. Arbitr Int 29(2):263–274
Poser N (1986) Arbitrability of international securities disputes. Brooklyn J Int Law 12(3):675–692
Ravanides C (2008) Arbitration clauses in public company charters: an expansion of the ADR Elysian Fields or a descent into Hades. Am Rev Int Arbitr 18(4):371–454
Reisberg A (2005) Shareholders' remedies: the choice of objectives and the social meaning of derivative actions. Eur Bus Organ Law Rev 6(2):227–268
Reisberg A (2006) Derivative actions and the funding problem: the way forward. J Bus Law 3:445–467
Roth F (2015) Arbitration and company law in Germany. Eur Company Law 12(3):151–153
Ryan L (2000) Shareholders and the atom of property: fission or fusion. Bus Soc 39(1):25–48
Sangiovanni V (2006) Some critical observation on the Italian regulation of company arbitration. Am Rev Int Arbitr 7(2):281–291
Schneider M, Ryan J (2011) A review of hedge funds and their investor activism: do they help or hurt other equity investors? J Manag Gov 15:349–374
Shaw B (2011) The arbitrability of oppression claims. Advocate (Vancouver Bar Association) 69(1):21–28
Shell G (1989) Arbitration and corporate governance. N C Law Rev 67:543, 517–575

Turkhtanov A (2013) Right to fair trial as a curb on party autonomy: Russian Supreme commercial court strikes down optional arbitration clause. Arbitration 79(3):338–343
Van Gerven D (2015) Arbitration and company law in Belgium. Eur Company Law 12(3):132–137
Wang M (2012) Securities arbitration: an alternative form of dispute resolution for public investors in China. Int Lawyer 46(2):691–708
Yeo L, Chew Y (2016) The arbitration and litigation of minority shareholder disputes. Singapore Acad Law J 28(1):382–407

Civil Code Reform in Japan: Is the New Regulation of Standard Contract Terms a Desirable One?

Antonios Karaiskos

Contents

A. Karaiskos (✉)
Graduate School of Law, Kyoto University, Kyoto, Japan
e-mail: karaiskos.antonios.7c@kyoto-u.ac.jp

M. Heidemann, J. Lee (eds.), *The Future of the Commercial Contract in Scholarship and Law Reform*, https://doi.org/10.1007/978-3-319-95969-6_4

Abstract This chapter examines the issue of regulation of standard contract terms in Japan, focusing especially on the regulation newly introduced into the Japanese Civil Code after its recent reform. Starting with an introduction to the general structure of the Japanese civil law and a presentation of such regulation before the recent amendment, this chapter continues with a detailed presentation of the proposals and the outcome of the reform procedure, and analyzes the issues existing in the Act finally adopted. The author sheds lights to the problems of the new regulation, not only by taking into consideration the relevant debate in Japan, but also by conducting a comparative law analysis. The author observes that the new regulation has a dual character; on the one hand it seems not to be corresponding to the basic direction of reform as originally planned, to increase complexity, and to contain a lot of issues, but on the other hand it can also be evaluated as an important step forward. The author concludes that a positive evaluation and the future application of the new provisions in practice will be decisive in this aspect.

1 Introduction

During the recent decades, EU law has been subject to a process of harmonization, especially in the field of consumer law. This process has taken the form of a series of consumer law directives being adopted. At the same time, model rules such as the Principles of European Contract Law (PECL) and the Draft Common Frame of Reference (DCFR), as well as regulation proposals (e.g. the Proposal for a Regulation on a Common European Sales Law (CESL)) and directive proposals (e.g. the directive proposals on the supply of digital content and on contracts for online sales of goods. Regarding the withdrawal of CESL and the proposal on online sales contracts, see Anagnostopoulou in this volume) have marked a tendency towards a common civil (or at least contract) law in the EU.

The influence of such developments has not been limited to the EU. In Japan, these developments have been taken into consideration during deliberations and discussions regarding the existing legislation as well as future legislation to be drafted. The most representative example is the recent reform procedure for the Japanese Civil Code (hereinafter also referred to as the "JCC"),[1] which was recently completed with the passing of new legislation on May 26, 2017.

---

[1]Act No. 89 of April 27, 1896. An English translation of the Code can be found at the website "Japanese Law Translation" prepared by the Japanese Ministry of Justice (which however does not provide official translations), available at http://www.japaneselawtranslation.go.jp/?re=02. All websites sited in this paper have been last accessed on July 2, 2017.

During this procedure, a main issue deliberated was that of the relation between civil law and consumer law. The reform procedure provided for an opportunity to integrate into the JCC (at least a part of) the special legislation for consumer protection, currently scattered outside of the JCC. If this was realized, it would mean that such special provisions which would be moved to the JCC would apply not only to consumer contracts (contracts between consumers and businesses. Hereinafter, "B2C" contracts) as in present, but to contracts between consumers (hereinafter, "C2C" contracts) and contracts between businesses (hereinafter, "B2B" contracts), too.

The above-mentioned issue is broad, having to do with many topics, such as the introduction or not of the notion of "consumer" or "business" into the JCC, whether provisions regarding consumer contracts should be introduced into the JCC etc. The topic which has drawn most attention and has been strongly deliberated until the final stages of the reform procedure was that of the regulation of standard contract terms. The main concern was not only whether such regulation is necessary and what its content should be, but also whether it should apply only to C2C and B2C contracts, leaving B2B contracts out of its scope.

Due to the close relation of the above-mentioned concerns with the main interests of this volume, in the following, I will present and analyze the JCC reform procedure, focusing on the issue of standard contract terms. I will start by shortly describing the general structure of the Japanese civil law (Sect. 2), and continue by presenting the state of such regulation before the recent amendment (Sect. 3). I will then present an overview of the JCC reform procedure focusing on the issue of standard contract terms (Sect. 4), before analyzing the relevant content of the final Act adopted by the Japanese Diet (Sect. 5). Finally, I will consider the issues of the new provisions of the JCC (Sect. 6), and close with some remarks on the way ahead in Japan (Sect. 7).

2 General Structure of Japanese Civil Law

Before presenting how standard contract terms have been regulated in Japan until the recent reform of the JCC, in the following, I will present the relation between the JCC as a general law (Sect. 2.1) and the special laws (Sect. 2.2), especially the Consumer Contract Act (hereinafter also referred to as the "CCA"),[2] in order to provide an understanding of this basic two-staged regulation in Japan.

[2] Act No. 61 of May 12, 2000.

2.1 *The Japanese Civil Code*

2.1.1 History Overview of the Japanese Civil Code

In Japan, the JCC is the basic piece of legislation to be applied to civil transactions. After the end of *Sakoku*, namely the period of national isolation of Japan which lasted from around 1633–1853 AD, the *Tokugawa shogunate* (regime) signed treaties of commerce with Western countries.[3] According to these treaties which were signed under strong pressure on behalf of these countries, Japan was granted no tariff autonomy, and the countries enjoyed extraterritorial rights to Japan's disadvantage.

After the Meiji Restoration (*Meiji Ishin*) in 1868 which practically restored imperial rule in Japan, the new government started negotiating for a revision of the above-mentioned disadvantageous treaties. Since western countries argued that the Japanese legal system was outdated and unfair to foreigners, to do so, Japan had to be internationally recognized as a modern sovereign state. This included the necessity for western-style "modern" codes. Following this, efforts for the enactment of a Japanese Civil Code started.

The first attempts seem to have been mainly limited to preparing a Japanese translation of the French Civil Code as a basis for the works, and inviting foreign scholars to Japan to participate in the preparative procedure.[4] French legal scholar *Gustave Émile Boissonade de Fontarabie* (1825–1910) who came to Japan in 1873 and began to teach French law at the Law School of the Ministry of Justice was one of them, and was responsible for drafting much of the first Japanese Civil Code draft. The draft prepared by him in French was translated to Japanese and promulgated in 1890.

In the meanwhile, German legal science acquired prestige in Japan. A German law section was established in Tokyo Imperial University (to which the Law School of the Ministry of Justice was transferred), and finally the influence of French law was superseded by that of German law. The English and German schools of jurists, which did not share Boissonade's belief that French law was the only civilized system of law, criticized his draft. Due to such strong opposition against his draft, its putting into effect was postponed for an indefinite period, in 1892, and abolished in 1898 without being enforced.

[3] For details about the below-presented series of events that led to and the content of the procedure for the enactment of the JCC, see Uchida (2011a), pp. 706 ff.; Uchida (2011b), pp. 79 ff.; Dean (2002), pp. 109 ff.; Sato (2001); Ono (1996), pp. 27 ff.; Uchtmann et al. (1987), pp. 352 ff.; Hatoyama (1902), pp. 298 ff.; Igeta (2006), pp. 28 ff.; Chen (2011), pp. 392 ff.; Schenck (1997), pp. 52 ff. Further, for a detailed analysis of the history of the JCC and its hermeneutics, focusing on *Boissonade*, see Ikeda (2011).

[4] For a detailed presentation of the acceptance of western law in general and the influence of French law in this era, see Yamaguchi (2013), pp. 4 ff.

In 1893, three young Japanese scholars, *Nobushige Hozumi*,[5] *Masaakira Tomii* and *Kenjiro Ume* were assigned with the task of preparing a new draft. This new drafting committee followed the policy advocated by the English school and consulted many codes. In the meanwhile, the above-mentioned trade agreements have been gradually reviewed. Finally, the JCC was enacted in 1896 and came into force in 1898. From a comparative law viewpoint, the newborn JCC, which adopted the *Pandekten* system, displayed strong influence of German law, and influence from French and English law, as well as native Japanese law.[6] Especially German law has continued exerting strong influence on Japanese civil law doctrine.[7]

2.1.2 Structure and Scope

Under the above-mentioned strong influence of the German civil law, the JCC which follows the German *Pandekten* system, consists of the following five parts: Part I (General Provisions), Part II (Real Rights), Part III (Claims), Part IV (Relatives) and Part V (Inheritance). A characteristic of the JCC, both before its recent amendment which will be discussed later in this paper and after it, has been the relatively small number of its provisions.

The JCC is a general law. This means that same as the German and French civil codes (*BGB* and *Code Civil* respectively) it applies to all transactions, namely C2C, B2C and B2B transactions. As will be mentioned later in this paper, this relation between general law (the JCC in the field of civil law) and special laws has been regarded as an important factor during the reform procedure for the JCC especially in relation to the regulation of standard contracts terms. In brief, the introduction of provisions relating to the regulation of such terms in the JCC would mean that such regulation would apply to all types of contracts, in principle same as the direct regulation of standard contract terms in Germany (*Allgemeine Geschäftsbedingungen, AGB*) or in France (*conditions générales*), whereas, before the reform, only the below-mentioned specific provisions regarding some types of unfair terms existed.

[5] *Hozumi* presented the reasons for the establishment of and the contents of the Civil Code prepared by these three scholars in detail in Hozumi (1904). For a thorough analysis of Hozumi's role in this procedure, see Ishibe (2006), pp. 83 ff.

[6] More specifically, the drafters took note of the civil codes (or their drafts) of many countries including France, Germany, Prussia, Saxony, Austria, the Netherlands, Italy, Portugal, Switzerland, Graubünden, Thuringia, Montenegro, Spain, Belgium, the United Kingdom, India and the United States of America. However, they mainly transplanted the French Civil Code and the drafts of the German Civil Code. See Uchida (2011a), p. 709.

[7] A representative example of such influence can be found in the regulation of non-performance in Japan. Although the JCC only provides for delayed performance and impossibility of performance (Art. 415, 541, 543 JCC etc.), defective performance has been widely recognized by Japanese doctrine as a third type, following the relevant model of the German civil law. Regarding this issue, see Nakata (2016), pp. 107 ff.

2.2 Special Laws

Apart from the JCC as a general law in the field of civil law, there also exist special laws that have a narrower scope and apply only to certain subjects or types of transactions. For example, the Commercial Code,[8] which is a special law to the Civil Code, applies—according to its article 1—to "businesses, commercial transactions and any other commercial affairs of merchants". Moreover, the Companies Act,[9] which is further a special law to the Commercial Code, applies—according to its article 1—to the "formation, organization, operation and management of companies".

Important in this context, regarding the regulation of standard contract terms, is the existence of the CCA. The purpose of the CCA is to protect the interests of consumers, in consideration of the disparity in the quality and quantity of information and negotiating power between consumers and business operators (Art. 1). The CCA applies only to "consumer contracts", being defined as contracts concluded between a consumer and a business operator (Art. 2 para. 3), namely B2C contracts. As will be explained below, this has been the only Act—until the reform of the JCC—containing provisions for the direct regulation of unfair terms, including standard contract terms.[10]

3 Regulation of Standard Contract Terms

Following the above-presented general structure of the Japanese civil law, regulation of standard contract terms is also done at two stages: regulation by the JCC (Sect. 3.1) and regulation by the CCA (Sect. 3.2).

3.1 Regulation Under the Civil Code

Although standard contract terms have been significant and widely used in transactions in Japan for a long time, no special law (such as the German "*Gesetz zur Regelung des Rechts der Allgemeinen Geschäftsbedingungen* (*AGB-Gesetz*)" which was incorporated into the German Civil Code in 2002) regulating them has existed.

---

[8] Act No. 48 of March 9, 1899, available in English translation at the "Japanese Law Translation" website (op. cit. at note 1). All Japanese Acts mentioned in this paper are available in English translation at the same website.

[9] Act No. 86 of July 26, 2005.

[10] Regarding the history and evolvement of the regulation of such terms in Japan, see Kawakami (1988) and Karaiskos (2010). Further, for some recent developments in the same field, see Karaiskos (2015).

Therefore, issues relating to whether concrete standard contract terms have become part of a contract, as well as their validity, have been dealt with by application of general provisions or through interpretation. The two general provisions of the JCC which have been widely used for this purpose are those of Art. 1 para. 2 and Art. 90 JCC. The former stipulates that the exercise of rights and performance of duties must be done in good faith, and the latter that a juristic act with any purpose which is against public policy is void. The effectiveness of this method of dealing with an extremely wide range of related cases based on general clauses is at least disputable. Further, the regulation of the validity of the content of standard contract terms via means of interpretation by the courts has been strongly criticized, as being a "hidden regulation of standard contract terms (*verdeckte oder getarnte Inhaltskontrolle*)",[11] not based on specific provisions and lacking therefore transparency.[12]

3.2 Regulation Under the Consumer Contract Act

In view of the fact that the above-mentioned methods often could not provide for an adequate regulation of standard contract terms, specific provisions regulating unfair contract terms in general—not only standard contract terms—were established with the introduction of the CCA.[13] Contrary to the JCC, which is based on the presumption of equal parties concluding contracts under the principle of freedom of contracts, the CCA expressly recognizes, in its Art. 1, the existence of disparity in the quality and quantity of information and negotiating power between consumers and business operators.

During the preparation procedure for the CCA, the relevant developments in foreign law, especially European law, such as the adoption of the Unfair Contract Terms Directive 93/13/EEC and its transposition in the Member States were also taken into consideration.[14] The CCA includes three provisions dealing with the regulation of unfair terms: Art. 8 CCA provides for the nullity of clauses which exempt a business operator from liability for damages, Art. 9 provides for the nullity of clauses that stipulate the amount of damages to be paid by customers, and Art. 10 provides for the nullity of clauses that impair the interests of consumers unilaterally.

The establishment of these provisions was evaluated as being an important step forward.[15] However, two major issues must be pointed out in relation with the regulation under the CCA.

[11] As an opposite to "open regulation (*offene Inhaltskontrolle*)".

[12] Kawakami (1988), p. 258; Yamamoto (2007), p. 221.

[13] For an overview of the content of the CCA, see Nakata (2009), p. 806 ff. Further, regarding consumer protection in Japanese contract law before and after the enactment of the CCA, Takizawa (2009).

[14] See for example, Sumida (1999), pp. 190 ff.

[15] Ochiai (2001), pp. 114 ff.

Firstly, the scope of the CCA is narrow, and applies only to B2C contracts as mentioned above. This means that B2B contracts are not included in the scope of the CCA, and that the regulation of standard contract terms included in such contracts could be (until the recent reform) performed only through the already mentioned means of interpretation and general provisions of the JCC, mainly the above-mentioned provisions of Art. 1 para. 3 and Art. 90 JCC.

This has been regarded as especially problematic in certain situations, where the disparity in the quality and quantity of information and negotiating power which has been a basic factor leading to the enactment of the CCA, can be seen in B2B contracts as well. A representative example is that of franchise contracts between businesses, where the franchisee, although becoming a party to the contract for the purposes of a business enterprise and therefore being a business operator according to Art. 2 para. 2 of the CCA, needs special protection from the viewpoint of information and negotiating power.

Secondly, the three provisions of the CCA deal not only with standard contract terms, but with unfair terms in general. Thus, some issues which are particular to the regulation of standard terms have not been treated with specifically. Such representative issues are the requirements for the incorporation of standard terms into a contract, as well as the regulation of so-called "surprising clauses", namely clauses which the counterparty reasonably does not expect to find in the standard terms.[16] Since the scope of the CCA is not restricted to standard terms, no provision defining them exists in it.

In view of the above-presented situation before the reform of the JCC, it can be said that of the "three fortresses" of the regulation of standard contract terms that existed, namely, regulation of incorporation, regulation through interpretation and direct regulation of content,[17] only the third was expressly provided in the CCA, and the other two "fortresses" relied on general clauses or the use of interpretation methods.

4 Reform of the Japanese Civil Code

In view of the insufficiencies of the above-mentioned regulation existing before the reform of the JCC, it was inevitable that the regulation of the standard contract terms became one of the major points-at-issue during the relevant procedure. In the following, after providing an overview of the reform procedure (Sect. 4.1), I will present the deliberations regarding standard contract terms as developed in the multiple stages of the reform procedure (Sect. 4.2) and then analyze the main

[16] As I discuss later, from a comparative law viewpoint, sect. 305c para. 1 of the German Civil Code for example stipulates that clauses in standard contract terms which are so unusual that the other party does not expect to encounter, do not form part of the contract.

[17] Kawakami (1988), pp. 171 ff.

oppositions to the various drafts, mainly on behalf of businesses and legal practitioners (Sect. 4.3).

4.1 Overview of the Reform Procedure

Even though the JCC was introduced in 1896, as described above, its content dealing with the law of obligations has been surprisingly maintained basically intact. Only some partial amendments on the guarantee system were legislated along with a modernization of its language in 2004. On the other hand, in the meanwhile, social economy in Japan has dramatically changed in various aspects, and court practice has formed extensive case law through interpretation and application of the JCC.[18]

Therefore, in October 2009, the Minister of Justice consulted the Legislative Council of the Ministry of Justice for the revision of the JCC (law of obligations), and the general assembly of the Legislative Council decided to establish a "Working Group on the Civil Code (Law of Obligations)" (hereinafter, "Working Group") for this mission. The two main reasons for the reform procedure were the need to make the provisions of law of obligations in the Civil Code correspond to the changes of social economy, and the need to make especially the provisions governing contract which are deeply related to people's daily life and economic activities more understandable to the public. The need to consider global harmonization or convergence of contract law was also raised by the supporters of this reform.[19] The Working Group consisted of both academics and practitioners.[20] The relevant deliberations within the Working Group were completed in February 2015.

4.2 Deliberations Regarding Standard Contract Terms

Due to the limited space, I will not refer to the stages of this reform procedure in more detail. In the following, I will only try to present an outline of the deliberations during this process regarding the introduction of provisions relating to the regulation of standard contract terms, including the preparatory works by an unofficial academic commission. Before doing so, it is worth mentioning here that during this

[18] Indicative of the importance of such case law is the fact that in Japan, apart from the ordinary codes commercially sold, there also exist codes with short citations beside the provisions, so that the user can find important case law at a glimpse.

[19] For a detailed presentation of these reasons, as well a presentation of the Civil Code reform procedure and an assessment of the below-mentioned Draft Proposals and the Interim Draft, see. Sono (2014), pp. 107–129. For the reform procedure, see also Suizu (2011), pp. 250 ff.

[20] Information regarding the background of and the deliberations in the Working Group can be found at the website (in English) of the Japanese Ministry of Justice titled "Civil Code Reform", available at http://www.moj.go.jp/ENGLISH/ccr/CCR_00001.html.

procedure, legislations of European countries, model rules such as PECL and DCFR and international legal texts such as the United Nations Convention on Contracts for the International Sale of Goods (CISG) were also taken into consideration as comparative law models.

4.2.1 Basic Reform Policy (Draft Proposals)[21]

As already mentioned, the official procedure for the reform of the JCC started in 2009. Before this official procedure, a Japanese Civil Code (Law of Obligations) Reform Commission (hereinafter, "Reform Commission") was established in October 2006, with the purpose of devising a "Basic Reform Policy (Draft Proposals)" (*Kaisei no Kihonhoshin (Kaiseishian)*) (hereinafter, "Draft Proposals").[22] This purely private research group which was independent from the government, worked for about two and a half years, and presented the Draft Proposals in April 2009. Although the Reform Commission emphasized that these Draft Proposals are not draft provisions, it expected that due considerations would be given to them during the deliberations by the Legislative Council. In this context, it is worth mentioning that 16 of the members of the Working Group were also members of the Reform Commission. This has in fact meant a partial and unofficial continuance of the preparative procedure.

The Draft Proposals included the following three proposals regarding the regulation of standard contract terms: (1) a definition of standard contract terms (3.1.1.25), excluding individually negotiated terms from the scope of application, (2) requirements for the incorporation of standard terms to the contract (3.1.1.26), requiring that the terms are disclosed to the counterparty to be incorporated, except for cases where the counterparty is already aware of their content, and (3) a suggestion that no special provision about surprising clauses should be established (3.1.1.A), referring at the same time to a differing opinion expressed during the works, according to which a provision providing for cases where surprising clauses are not incorporated to the contract should be included.[23]

From a comparative law viewpoint, regarding the exclusion of individually negotiated terms under (1), the Draft Proposal mentions that some countries like Germany (Art. 305 German Civil Code) exclude such terms, whereas others like Netherlands (Art. 6:231 Dutch Civil Code) include them to their scope of application.[24]

Further, regarding the requirement for bringing the standard contract terms to the attention of the counterparty (hereinafter also referred to as "disclosure"), the Draft Proposals cite PECL 2:104, according to which contract terms which have not been

[21] For an analysis of the Basic Reform Policy (Draft Proposals) from the viewpoint of consumer protection, see Kihara (2012).

[22] Additional information about this unofficial Reform Commission can be found in its website titled "Japanese Civil Code (Law of Obligations) Reform Commission" (both in English and Japanese), available at http://wwr7.ucom.ne.jp/sh01/index.html.

[23] For details, see Minpo (Saikenho) Kaiseikentoiinkai (2009), pp. 80–98.

[24] Ibid, p. 85.

individually negotiated may be invoked against a party which did not know of them only if the party invoking them took reasonable steps to bring them to the other party's attention before or when the contract was concluded. The same provision stipulates that terms are not brought appropriately to a party's attention by a mere reference to them in a contract document, even if that party signs the document.[25]

As far as it concerns the necessity for a provision about surprising clauses under (3), the Draft Proposals refer to sect. 305c German Civil Code, according to which provisions in standard business terms which in the circumstances, in particular about the outward appearance of the contract, are so unusual that the other party to the contract with the user need not expect to encounter them, do not form part of the contract. Reference to Art. 2.1.20 of the UNIDROIT Principles 2004 is also made, which stipulates that no term contained in standard terms which is of such a character that the other party could not reasonably have expected it, is effective unless it has been expressly accepted by that party. Such character of a term is to be determined having regard to its content, language and presentation.

4.2.2 Interim Report of Points at Issue on the Civil Code (Law of Obligations) Reform

During its 26th meeting held in April 2011, the Working Group determined the content of an "Interim Report of Points at Issue on the Civil Code (Law of Obligations) Reform" (*Minpo (Saikenkankei) no Kaisei ni kansuru Chukanteki na Rontenseiri*) (hereinafter, "Interim Report"). Regarding the regulation of standard contract terms, the Interim Report suggested that the following issues should be further considered (No. 27, items 1 to 4): (1) the necessity of a provision stipulating the requirements for the incorporation of standard contract terms to a contract, (2) the content of a definition of the notion of standard contract terms, (3) the content of the requirements for the incorporation of standard contract terms to a contract, and (4) the modification of standard contract terms (permissibility, requirements, effects etc.).[26]

A public comment period for the Interim Report was realized from June 1, 2011 to August 1 of the same year.

4.2.3 Interim Draft for Reforming the Civil Code (Law of Obligations)

The "Interim Draft for Reforming the Civil Code (Law of Obligations)" (*Minpo (Saikenkankei) no Kaisei ni kansuru Chukanshian*) (hereinafter, "Interim Draft") was adopted in February 2013, during the 71st meeting of the Working Group.[27]

---

[25] Ibid, p. 92.

[26] The Interim Report can be downloaded from the website of the Japanese Ministry of Justice titled "'Interim Report of Points at Issue on the Civil Code (Law of Obligations) Reform' (Decided on April 12, 2011)" (in Japanese), available at http://www.moj.go.jp/shingi1/shingi04900074.html.

[27] For an overall assessment of the JCC reform and especially the Interim Draft, see Wrbka (2014).

Regarding the issue of the regulation of standard contract terms, the Interim Draft suggested the introduction into the JCC of provisions regarding the following five issues (No. 30, items 1 to 5): (1) a definition of the notion of standard contract terms, mentioning however at the same time that there also exists an opinion according to which no special regulation for standard contract terms needs to be introduced, (2) the requirements for the incorporation of standard contract terms into a contract, providing that there needs to exist an agreement for the use of standard contract terms, and their preparer needs to ensure that the counterparty is granted with the opportunity to know the content of the standard terms *by taking reasonable action* (mentioning at the same time that there also exists an opinion that disclosure of standard contract terms should be required *in principle*), (3) surprising clauses, stipulating that surprising clauses do not become part of the contract if the counterparty cannot reasonably expect them to be included in the terms, (4) modification of standard contract terms, stipulating the requirements to be met for a one-sided modification of the terms by the preparer of the terms to be allowed, and also requiring a notification of such modification to the counterparty in order for the modification to take effect (mentioning that the content of such regulation of the modification of standard contract terms needs to be further deliberated) and (5) regulation of the content of unfair contract terms, providing that standard contract terms that have become part of the contract shall be void, if they restrict the rights or expand the duties of the consumer and cause significant disadvantage to the other part (mentioning however, that there also exists an opinion that no such provision needs to be established).[28]

Despite of the quite "rich" content of the Interim Draft regarding the regulation of standard contract terms, the references made to differing opinions or to the necessity for further consideration is indicative of the controversy of this issue. A public comment procedure was realized between April 16, 2013 to June 17 of the same year.

4.2.4 Provisional Draft Bill Outline for Reforming the Civil Code (Law of Obligations)

In addition to the various opinions expressed among the members of the Working Group, the above-presented content of the Interim Draft relating to the regulation of standard contract terms was also met with criticism from outside the Working Group, as will be presented later in this paper. Reflecting such oppositions and the divergence of opinions among the members, the "Provisional Draft Bill Outline for Reforming the Civil Code (Law of Obligations)" (*Minpo (Saikenkankei) no Kaisei ni kansuru Yokokarian*) (hereinafter, "Provisional Draft Bill Outline"), adopted in

[28] The content of this proposed provision under (5) closely resembles that of Art. 10 of the CCA (with minor differences in the wording), which however applies only to B2C contracts as already mentioned, and has as effect the nullity of the clause. The Interim Draft can be downloaded from the website of the Japanese Ministry of Justice titled "'Interim Draft for Reforming the Civil Code (Law of Obligations)' (Decided on February 26, 2013)" (in Japanese), available at http://www.moj.go.jp/shingi1/shingi04900184.html. For an analysis of the relevant provisions of the Interim Draft, see Kimura (2016), p. 341 ff.

August 2014 during the 96th meeting of the Working Group, referred to the issue of standard contract terms as "pending" (No. 28).[29]

It is also noteworthy in this context that the Provisional Draft Bill Outline uses the term and notion of "formulated standard contract terms (*Teikei Yakkan*)" instead of "standard contract terms (*Yakkan*)" used in the previous documents.

4.2.5 Draft Bill Outline for Reforming the Civil Code

The "Draft Bill Outline for Reforming the Civil Code (Law of Obligations)" (*Minpo (Saikenkankei) no Kaisei ni kansuru Yokoan*) (hereinafter, "Draft Bill Outline"), adopted in February 2015 during the 99th meeting of the Working Group, proposed the introduction of four provisions relating to formulated standard contract terms (the same term and notion as in the Provisional Draft Bill Outline is used): (1) a definition of formulated standard contract terms, (2) a provision regarding the situations where an agreement regarding the incorporation of standard terms to the contract is deemed to exist, (3) a provision regarding the disclosure of the content of standard contract terms by their preparer, and (4) a provision regarding the modification of standard contract terms.[30]

Regarding (2), the requirements to be met so that an incorporation can be deemed are the following: existence of an agreement for "formulated transactions (*Teikei Torihiki*)" and an additional agreement for the incorporation of formulated standard terms, or manifestation of the incorporation of such terms by their preparer instead of such additional agreement. Further, such standard contract terms that have become part of the contract shall be void, if they restrict the rights or expand the duties of the consumer and cause significant disadvantage to the other part, in violation of the fundamental principle of good faith provided in Art. 1 para. 2 JCC.[31]

Moreover, according to (3), the preparer is obliged to disclose the content of the formulated standard contract terms only if required by the counterparty, excluding cases where the preparer has already issued a document or delivered an electronic record in which the content of the standard terms is written or recorded. If the preparer refuses to disclose accordingly, the above-mentioned provision under (2) does not in principle apply.

Finally, regarding (4), the requirements to be met for a one-sided modification of the terms by their preparer to be allowed are set, and a notification of such modification to the counterparty is required for the modification to take effect.

---

[29] The Provisional Draft Bill Outline can be downloaded from the website of the Japanese Ministry of Justice under the title "'Provisional Draft Bill Outline for Reforming the Civil Code (Law of Obligations)' (Decided on August 26, 2014)" (in Japanese), available at http://www.moj.go.jp/shingi1/shingi04900227.html.

[30] The Draft Bill Outline can be downloaded from the website of the Japanese Ministry of Justice under the title "'Draft Bill Outline for Reforming the Civil Code (Law of Obligations)' (Decided on February 10, 2015)" (in Japanese), available at http://www.moj.go.jp/shingi1/shingi04900244.html.

[31] This proposed provision also resembles that of Art. 10 CCA, even more closely than the provision proposed under the Interim Draft (see Sect. 4.2.3 above, especially (5)).

4.2.6 Draft Bill for Reforming Part of the Civil Code

The above-mentioned Draft Bill Outline was the last Draft published by the Working Group. The procedure continued with a Draft Bill for Reforming Part of the Civil Code (*Minpo no Ichibu o Kaisei suru Horitsuan*) (hereinafter, "Draft Bill") being submitted to the National Diet in March 2016.[32] Regarding the issue of regulation of standard contract terms, the Draft Bill includes the above-mentioned provisions proposed in the Draft Bill Outline, in three articles (Art. 548-2, 548-3 and 548-4).[33]

4.3 Oppositions to the Drafts

The controversy about the possibility of an introduction of provisions regulating standard contract terms into the JCC was not limited to the members of the Working Group. This perspective was met by opposition and criticism by other social actors too, especially businesses and legal practitioners. Presenting such oppositions and the relevant debate in detail would be beyond the scope of this paper. In the following, I will present the oppositions expressed by the Japanese Business Federation (*Keidanren*),[34] a major institution representing businesses in Japan, as well as consumer protection lawyers.

The Japanese Business Federation published a "Suggestion Regarding the Interim Draft for Reforming the Civil Code" (*"Minpo (Saikenkankei) no Kaisei ni kansuru Chukanshian" ni kansuru Teigen*), published in June 2013.[35] The suggestion clearly mentions that Keidanren opposes to the introduction of provisions regulating standard contract terms into the JCC.

The reasons for this are as follows:

(1) According to the Federation's understanding, the usage of standard contract terms in transactions has not been functioning as an element creating doubts about the certainty of such transactions. The point-at-issue in relevant disputes is not the legal binding force of such terms, but the fairness of individual clauses.
(2) Standard contract terms are being sufficiently regulated by respective industry laws. Further, unfair contract terms in B2C contracts are already regulated by the CCA.

---

[32] The content of the Draft Bill, as well as of the below-mentioned final Act adopted by the Diet, can be downloaded from the website of the Japanese Ministry of Justice under the title "Draft Bill for Reforming the Civil Code" (in Japanese) available at http://www.moj.go.jp/MINJI/minji07_00175.html.

[33] For an analysis of the relevant provisions of the Draft Bill, see Kimura (2016), pp. 347 ff.

[34] Information about *Keidanren* can be found in the English version of its website, available at http://www.keidanren.or.jp/en/.

[35] The content of the Suggestion can be found at the website of the Japanese Business Federation under the title "Suggestion Regarding the Interim Draft for Reforming the Civil Code" (in Japanese), available at http://www.keidanren.or.jp/policy/2013/058.html.

(3) If there are disputes about standard contract terms for issues not regulated in industrial laws, such issues should be dealt within the framework of special laws etc., and not within the JCC.
(4) Standard contract terms are intended to be used in contracts with an unspecified large number of customers, and having to take into consideration the foreseeability by each of them under a newly introduced regulation of surprising clauses, would deprive standard contract terms of their meaning.
(5) There is no need to newly introduce a special provision stipulating the invalidity of unfair contract terms. The issue is dealt with in a flexible manner by the general clause of Art. 90 JCC, and should continue being dealt by it.

Concerns have been expressed by consumer protection lawyers too, from the aspect that the introduction of provisions dealing with consumer protection into the Civil Code would result into a lowering of the consumer protection level in this field, due to the wider application of such provisions not only to B2C but to B2B and C2C contracts as well.[36]

5 The Act for Reforming the Civil Code

The Act for Reforming Part of the Civil Code (*Minpo no Ichibu o Kaisei suru Horitsu*) was adopted on May 26, 2017, promulgated on June 2 of the same year, published in the Official Gazette on the same day, and will come into force in principle within 3 years from the day of its promulgation.

The new provisions regarding the regulation of standard contract terms are the same with those included in the above-presented Draft Bill. In the following, the content of the three articles will be described more analytically in Sects. 5.1–5.3.

5.1 *Agreement Based on Formulated Standard Contract Terms*

Art. 548-2 regulates agreements based on formulated standard contract terms. This article consists of two paragraphs.

The first paragraph includes a definition of the notions of "formulated transactions" and "formulated standard contract terms". According to this, formulated transactions are transactions entered into by a specified person with an unspecified large number of counterparties, where the uniformity of the whole or a part of the content of the transaction is reasonable for both parties. Further, formulated standard contract terms are the entirety of the terms that has been prepared by the "formulated standard contract terms preparer" for using it as content of the contract for such formulated transaction.

---

[36] See for example, Takasu (2010), pp. 32 ff.; Dogauchi et al. (2010), pp. 14 ff.

According to this paragraph, there are two cases where the counterparty who has agreed to enter into a formulated transaction, is deemed to have agreed to each individual term of the formulated standard terms ("formulated transaction agreement"). Firstly, when the person agreed that the standard terms would form the content of the contract. Secondly, when the preparer of the standard terms has in advance expressed to the counterparty its intention that the standard terms form the content of the contract.

The second paragraph of this article provides for an exceptional case where certain terms are not deemed to have been agreed upon by the counterparty. According to this paragraph, notwithstanding the above-presented provision of the preceding paragraph, the counterparty will not be deemed to have agreed to a term that restricts its rights or expands its duties, and that, in light of the modes and the actual circumstances of the formulated transaction as well as socially accepted ideas with regards to formulated transactions, unilaterally impairs the interests of the counterparty, in violation of the fundamental principle of good faith provided in Art. 1 para. 2 JCC.

Insofar, this provision regulates the requirements for the incorporation of standard terms into a contract. It is the first time such an express provision is included in the JCC.

5.2 *Disclosure of the Content of Formulated Standard Contract Terms*

Art. 548-3 provides for the disclosure of the content of formulated standard contract terms. This article consists of two paragraphs as well.

According to the first paragraph, a preparer who undertakes or intends to undertake a formulated transaction, must without delay and in a suitable manner disclose the content of the formulated standard terms to the counterparty, upon a counterparty's request made either before reaching a formulated transaction agreement, or within a reasonable period after reaching such agreement. However, this obligation does not apply if the preparer has already issued a document or delivered an electronic record in which the content of the standard terms is written or recorded. According to this provision, there is no need to disclose the content of the standard terms if there has been no relevant request by the counterparty.

The second paragraph provides that, when the preparer has refused a request of the counterparty (pursuant to the preceding paragraph) for disclosure of the standard terms, made in advance of reaching a formulated transaction agreement, the provisions of the preceding Article shall not apply. This means that in such cases, the standard terms will not become a part of the contract. It must be noted here that this provision applies only to cases of refusal of a request made *in advance*, and not to cases of a refusal of requests made within a reasonable period *after* reaching an agreement. In all cases, this provision does not apply if there is a temporary electronic communication failure or other justifiable reasons for the agreement preparer's failure to disclose the content of the terms.

The main two reasons why disclosure was decided to depend on the counterparty's request are said to be the following: (a) counterparties (especially consumers) usually do not check the content of standard terms, and obliging businesses to always disclose their content despite of this would simply increase costs, but (b) at the same time, it is improper to stipulate that the counterparty is bound by the content of standard terms which it cannot even get to know.[37] These two conflicting elements were balanced with the new provision.

It is noteworthy that despite providing for the disclosure of standard terms in certain occasions, this provision does not directly stipulate the method of such disclosure, limiting itself to providing that such disclosure must be made in a "suitable manner". This of course, does not exclude the possibility of interpretation based on this provision.[38]

5.3 *Modification of Formulated Standard Contract Terms*

Art. 548-4 stipulates the cases where a one-sided modification of standard terms by their preparer is binding on the counterparty. This article consists of three paragraphs.

The first paragraph provides for the requirements to be met, so that the preparer can modify the content of standard terms, and an agreement between the preparer and the counterparty is still deemed to exist on the modified terms, even without agreeing on them with each individual counterparty (for details, see Sect. 6.1.2 below). According to the same paragraph, there are two separate requirements, and it is sufficient if one of them is met. Pursuant to the first, the modification of the terms needs to conform to the general interests of the counterparty (Para. 1 (i)). And according to the second, the modification must not be contrary to the purpose of the contract, and must be reasonable considering the necessity for modification, the properness of the content after modification, the existence or not of a clause stipulating that modifications according to this provision may occur, the content of such clause if there is one, and any other circumstance relating to the modification (Para. 1 (ii)). If either of these two requirements is fulfilled, modification is allowed and an agreement is deemed to exist.

The second paragraph provides for the necessity to notify the counterparty of such modifications. According to it, when the preparer intends to modify the terms based on the previous paragraph, the preparer needs to stipulate the effective date of such modification, and to notify the counterparty via internet or any other proper means about the fact of the intended modification, the content of the terms after modification and the effective date.

[37] Okino (2015), pp. 563 ff.

[38] Kano (2017), p. 64.

Finally, according to the third paragraph, a modification pursuant to para. 1 (ii) becomes effective, only if the above-mentioned notification is completed before the effective date.

6 Issues with the New Provisions

Although the introduction of the above-mentioned provisions into the Civil Code has been evaluated as being an important first step, there has also been skepticism and criticism.

6.1 Major Concerns

Regarding the new provisions, many issues have been pointed out. A detailed presentation of all of them cannot be covered within the confines of this chapter. Here, I would therefore like to present an overview of the major issues which are of interest in the context of this paper.

Before doing so, it is worth mentioning that one of the main reasons why such seemingly problematic provisions have been newly included, is the strong opposition of a member of the Working Group representing the business circles, which, as already mentioned, have been against the introduction of provisions regulating standard terms to the JCC. After repeated compromises of the other members to realize such introduction, the newly drafted provisions seem to have become of a content which is rather advantageous to the business circles, leading to their acceptance by the above-mentioned member.[39]

From a practical point of view, it seems that contrary to B2C contracts, where consumers are usually non-experts, in cases of B2B contracts, where both parties are usually experts (although, as already mentioned, some exceptions i.e. in cases of franchise agreements exist), the parties do not differentiate between the general agreement for the incorporation of the terms to the contract, and the individual agreements for the use of each term. Namely, businesses seem to be treating the general agreement between the parties for the use of the terms, as including such individual agreements. This means that, for businesses, B2B contracts do not fall under the notion of "standard term contracts" (or under the newly introduced notion of "formulated standard term contracts"), and are exempted from the relevant regulation.[40]

---

[39] Yamada (2016), pp. 282 ff.

[40] For example, see the relevant remarks made by the member of the Working Group representing the business circles at the 89th and 96th meeting of the Working Group, available (in Japanese) at the website of the Japanese Ministry of Justice titled "Civil Code Reform" (op. cit. at note 20).

Further, businesses also seem to have had concerns about the uniform regulation of the various types of standard terms, which involve multiple and different interests. Particularly in cases of large-scale public enterprises, the modification of standard terms has already been in fact put under regulation for its content and procedure by the existing legislation. Businesses feared of an additional regulation by the JCC which would further burden this procedure.[41]

The above-mentioned oppositions and compromises within the Working Group have led to some members of the Working Group expressing opinions that it might be better to have no provisions regarding standard terms, rather than having provisions which might have harmful effects, and that the deliberations regarding this issue will not lose their meaning as a basis for future considerations even if no provisions are included in the draft.[42]

The analysis below is restricted to the issues relating to the newly introduced provisions. Apart from these issues, there also exist other issues having to do with the lack of provisions directly regulating surprising clauses (Art. 548-2 para. 2 regulates this issue only indirectly), the relation of the regulation of unfair terms by the new Art. 548-2 para. 2 JCC and by Art. 10 CCA, the lack of a provision regarding the interpretation in favor of the consumer of terms when there is doubt about their meaning etc.[43]

6.1.1 Scope

The first major issue has to do with the scope of the problems covered by the new provisions. It is pointed out that the scope of the notion of formulated standard terms as stipulated in the new provisions is too narrow, leaving uncovered a large part of the problems which were formerly dealt with under the doctrines relating to standard terms. More specifically, it has been estimated that most B2B transactions are excluded, since they do not have to do with an "unspecified" large number of counterparties, as the number of such counterparties in B2B transactions will be "specified". Further, concerns have been shown that due to the existence of the above-mentioned requirement together with that of "formulated transactions", the new provisions will even not cover part of consumer transactions.[44]

The determination of the scope of regulation is closely connected to the legal tradition and system of each country. Therefore, a comparative law search does not

[41] See the relevant remarks made by the member of the Working Group representing the business circles at the 87th meeting of the Working Group, ibid.

[42] See for example the statements regarding this issue by Prof. *Tomonobu Yamashita* (Tokyo University then, currently Doshisha University), Prof. *Yoshio Shiomi* (Kyoto University) and Prof. *Keizo Yamamoto* (Kyoto University), as recorded in the official records (in Japanese) of the proceedings of the 93rd meeting of the Working Group (held on July 8, 2014).

[43] Regarding the last issue, Art. 5 Directive 93/13/EEC provides for example that where there is doubt about the meaning of a term, the interpretation most favorable to the consumer prevails.

[44] Kawakami (2015), p. 104.

necessarily offer results which can be used as a direct basis for consideration. However, it is worth mentioning that a quick look shows that some countries, including UK, France and Germany, provide in principle for a direct regulation of B2B contracts, too. On the contrary, as already mentioned, under the new provisions of the JCC, almost all standard terms included in such contracts are expected to be excluded from the scope of regulation.

6.1.2 Deeming the Existence of an Agreement

The second major issue has to do with an agreement of the counterparty regarding each individual term being "deemed". As already mentioned, this happens when either the counterparty has agreed to incorporate the standard terms, or when the preparer has manifested to the counterparty its intention to incorporate them. It has been indicated that this new provision is highly problematic, from the viewpoint of the underlying principle of private autonomy. This is true especially in the latter case stipulated in the provision, where the counterparty has not even expressed an intention to be bound by the standard terms. Further, the fact that an agreement of the counterparty is not "presumed" (which would mean that the presumption would be reversible) but "deemed" (which means that it is irreversible) seems to be giving to standard terms a binding force comparable to that of laws, regulations and institutions.[45]

Regarding this issue, it is asserted that despite of such wording of the new provision, since the relationship between the parties is contractual, there needs to be at least a "passive" approval on behalf of the counterparty, for example by not objecting to the incorporation of the standard terms.[46]

With the recent reform of the French Civil Code (regarding this reform, see Pédamon in this volume), provisions regarding standard contract terms were included for the first time into the Civil Code.[47] Art. 1110 para. 2 provides that adhesion contracts are contracts with general conditions which have been decided in advance by one party, without being negotiated. According to Art. 1119, general conditions invoked by one party do not have effect against the other, unless they have been brought to the other party's knowledge and that party has accepted them (para. 1). Thus, the danger of such terms being incorporated without the counterparty knowing their content is being properly dealt with.[48]

Regarding the same issue of incorporation, Art. 305 para. 2 German Civil Code provides that standard business terms only become a part of a contract if the user, when entering into the contract, (1) refers the other party to the contract to them

---

[45] Ibid, pp. 104 ff.

[46] Kano (2015), pp. 21 ff.; Okino (2015), pp. 551 ff.

[47] The problems of the new Japanese regulation when compared to such foreign legislation are analyzed in Hirose (2017), pp. 168 ff.

[48] Deshayes et al. (2016), p. 121.

explicitly or, where explicit reference, due to the way in which the contract is entered into, is possible only with disproportionate difficulty, by posting a clearly visible notice at the place where the contract is entered into, and (2) gives the other party to the contract, in an acceptable manner, which also takes into reasonable account any physical handicap of the other party to the contract that is discernible to the user, the opportunity to take notice of their contents, and if the other party to the contract agrees to their applying (this provision however does not apply to B2B contracts, according to art. 310 para. 1). Further, art. 305a provides for the incorporation of such terms in special cases.[49]

As it is clear from the above, both French and German law give importance to the other party's acceptance for the use of the standard contract terms as a general framework, and show concern for the other party as being in a weaker position compared to the preparer.

In this aspect, Directive 93/13/EEC, which regulates unfair terms in consumer contracts (B2C contracts, Art. 1) that have not been individually negotiated (Art. 3 para. 1) is also relevant. Art. 3 para. 3 of the Directive stipulates that the Annex to the Directive contains an indicative and non-exclusive list of the terms which may be regarded as unfair. Item (i) of the Annex includes in this category terms which irrevocably bind the consumer to terms with which he had no real opportunity of becoming acquainted before the conclusion of the contract.

In the UK, the Consumer Rights Act 2015 includes provisions about the regulation of unfair consumer contract (B2C contract) terms.[50] Schedule 2 Part 1 of this Act includes a list of consumer contract terms which may be regarded as unfair. Transposing Directive 93/13/EEC into UK law, item 10 of this Part refers to terms which have the object or effect of irrevocably binding the consumer to terms with which the consumer has had no real opportunity of becoming acquainted before the conclusion of the contract.

A similar provision also exists in French law. Art. R212-1 of the Consumer Code includes a list of clauses which are deemed to be abusive. According to item 1, clauses which ascertain the adherence to the contract with the consumer of clauses which are not included in the document the consumer receives, or which are included in another document to which no express reference was made by the conclusion of contract, and which the consumer was not aware of before the conclusion, are deemed to be abusive.

Also in view of the above, it is at least questionable whether the existence of such a provision in the new JCC can be justified.

---

[49] For details regarding the regulation of standard contract terms in Germany, see for example Stoffels (2015).

[50] The guidance issued by the Competition and Market Authority and available at https://www.gov.uk/government/publications/unfair-contract-terms-cma37 provides detailed information about the regulation of unfair terms in general in the UK.

6.1.3 Disclosure Requirement

The third major issue has to do with the way the disclosure requirement is stipulated. The disclosure of the content of standard terms is in principle not a requirement for the incorporation. It becomes necessary only if there is a request by the counterparty. This means that if there is no such request by the counterparty, the standard terms become part of the contract, even if no disclosure has taken place. Further, a refusal of such request for disclosure is connected to the non-application of the provision deeming the existence of an agreement, only if such request has been made prior to the contract. No such sanction against the preparer is provided in cases of refusals of requests made after the conclusion of the contract.

Professor Naoko Kano, a member of the Working Group, mentions that no sufficient explanation has been provided about why it is the counterparty which must bear the responsibility of requesting disclosure. This is especially problematic in cases of consumers, who cannot always be expected to actively engage in making such requests, although they might check the content of the terms if provided by the preparer even without request. Further, Professor Kano emphasizes that the reason indicated for this provision, namely the assertion that counterparties usually do not read the content of standard terms, is not always true, since this depends on the type of transaction (e.g. terms related to security deposits or repair fees to be paid under residential lease contracts, or cancellation terms regarding accommodation contracts tend to be carefully read by the counterparty).[51]

Regarding this issue, it is pointed out that since Art. 548-2 para. 2 stipulates that the unfairness of a term is to be judged "in light of the modes and the actual circumstances of the formulated transaction as well as socially accepted ideas with regards to formulated transactions", the non-disclosure of such term can also be taken into consideration for denying its binding effect.[52] Further, it is asserted that although no sanction against the preparer is provided in the new article for cases of refusal of disclosure requests made after the conclusion of the contract, the counterparty will be entitled to compensation. According to this opinion, in this case, pursuant to the principle of good faith, the preparer will not be allowed to claim that the counterparty's rights have been extinguished due to the lapse of a certain period, if the performance of such rights within such period was obstructed by the non-disclosure.[53]

6.1.4 Modification

The fourth major issue lies in the admission of a one-sided modification by the preparer.

[51] Kano (2017), p. 66.

[52] Kano (2015), pp. 24 ff.

[53] Okino (2015), p. 579; Kano (2015), pp. 25 ff.

According to the new provision, if the requirements are met, the preparer is not only allowed to modify one-sidedly the content of the standard terms, but also to "deem" that the counterparty has agreed to such modified content. This is problematic from a comparative viewpoint, as mentioned below. Further, also here there exists a conflict with the underlying principle of private autonomy, since the counterparty is deemed to have agreed even without making any manifestation of intention. The requirements for reasonableness and properness of the modification, as well as for notification to the counterparty do not seem to be sufficiently balancing this deficit.

From a comparative law viewpoint, item (j) of the above-mentioned Annex of Directive 93/13/EEC refers to terms enabling the seller or supplier to alter the terms of the contract unilaterally without a valid reason which is specified in the contract as being terms which may be regarded as unfair.[54]

Further, item 11 of Schedule 2 Part 1 of Consumer Rights Act 2015 in the UK provides that terms which have the object or effect of enabling the trader to alter the terms of the contract unilaterally without a valid reason which is specified in the contract may be regarded as unfair

Item 6 of Art. R212-2 of the French Consumer Code also has a similar content. According to it, clauses which reserve to the business the right to modify one-sidedly the terms of a contract relating to the rights and obligations of the parties, are presumed to be abusive.

7 Closing Remarks: The Way Ahead

As it has been presented above, the new provisions of the JCC seem to be problematic from many aspects, also when examined from a comparative law viewpoint. However, most probably this is not the only issue with the new provisions. As I have mentioned at the beginning of this paper, the main purpose of the reform procedure was twofold: making the provisions correspond to the changes of social economy, and more understandable to the public. The need to consider global trends of contract law was also unofficially indicated. It is at least questionable, to what extent the new provisions regarding regulation of standard terms have achieved these aims. It could rather be said that the new provisions mirror the dynamics and desires of the currently existing practice and of business circles. Although this is not to be automatically evaluated as being something negative or undesirable, it certainly does not match with the above-mentioned aims.

An additional question would be: have the new provisions secured a certain unification of the regulation of such terms in C2C, B2C and B2B contracts, or have they made the landscape further complex by introducing an additional system for

[54] For a detailed analysis of the provisions of the Directive, see for example Weatherill (2013), pp. 145 ff.; Nebbia (2007).

their regulation? Under the new system, there exist formulated standard contract terms which fall under the scope of the new provisions about incorporation, disclosure and modification, standard contract terms (which are not "formulated") not falling under these provisions and being therefore regulated by the general provisions of the JCC regarding these three aspects, and B2C contract terms (not limited to "standard") for which the CCA offers an additional system for regulation.

It is left to be seen, how the judicial practice (courts) will apply these new provisions. Perhaps the future application by the courts will show that the current worries and criticism about the provisions have been unnecessarily excessive. Perhaps, on the contrary, it will verify them. Maybe what is most important is to appreciate the introduction of the new provisions as being a big step to be evaluated positively, and to try to make the best use of them. Even if the provisions seem to have imperfections, an appropriate application of them might give them additional value and provide for an example worth to be taken into consideration internationally. Time will show. For the time being, the certain is that the introduction of these provisions will evoke new developments in Japan, for C2C, B2C and B2B contracts, and is worthy of further discussion.

References

Chen TF (2011) Transplant of Civil Code in Japan, Taiwan and Chine: with the focus of legal evolution. Natl Taiwan Univ Law Rev 6(1):389–432

Dean M (2002) Japanese legal system, 2nd edn. Cavendish, London

Deshayes O, Genicon T, Laithier YM (2016) Réforme du droit des contrats, du régime général et de la prevue des obligations. LexisNexis, Paris

Dogauchi H, Ikemoto S, Shiomi Y, Nakahara T, Matsuoka H, Moriwaki S, Yasunaga K, Watanabe T (2010) Saikenhokaisei o Megutte – Kigyojitsumu no Kanten kara (Regarding the law of obligations reform: from an enterprise practice viewpoint). Jurist 1392:4–45

Hatoyama K (1902) The Civil Code of Japan compared with the French Civil Code. Yale Law J 11(6):296–303

Hirose H (2017) Minpokaiseian "Teikeiyakkan" Kitei ni tsuite no Oboegaki (1) (A memo regarding the provisions on "Formulated Standard Contract Terms" in the Draft Bill for Reforming the Civil Code (1)). Aoyamahomukenkyuronshu 13:159–179

Hozumi N (1904) The New Japanese Civil Code, as material for the study of comparative jurisprudence. Tokyo Printing, Tokyo

Igeta R (2006) Reform of law in the Meiji restoration. In: Marutschke H-P (Hrsg) Beiträge zur modernen japanischen Rechtsgeschichte. Berliner Wissenschafts, Berlin

Ikeda M (2011) Bowasonado to sono Minpo (Boissonade and his Civil Code). Keiogijukudaigaku Shuppankai, Tokyo

Ishibe M (2006) Nobushige Hozumi und die Japanische Rechtswissenschaft in der Meiji-Zeit. In: Marutschke H-P (Hrsg) Beiträge zur modernen japanischen Rechtsgeschichte. Berliner Wissenschafts, Berlin

Kano N (2015) Minpokaisei to Yakkankisei (Civil Code Reform and regulation of standard contract terms). Hosojiho 67(7):1–31

Kano N (2017) Yakkan no Kaiji (Disclosure of standard contract terms). Horitsujiho 89(3):63–68

Karaiskos A (2010) Regulation of unfair contract terms in Japan. Waseda Bull Comp Law 28:13–44

Karaiskos A (2015) Recent developments in the regulation of unfair contract terms in Japan. Kansai Univ Rev Law Polit 36:85–100
Kawakami S (1988) Yakkankisei no Hori (The doctrine for regulation of standard contract terms). Yuhikaku, Tokyo
Kawakami S (2015) Saikenhokogi/Tokuron – "Teikeiyakkan" Kitei no Mondaiten – (Lectures of the law of obligations/special part: issues of the provisions on "Formulated Standard Contract Terms"). Hogaku Seminar 726:104–106
Kihara H (2012) Japan's Civil Code Reform and consumer protection. Asia Univ Law Rev 47(1):84–72
Kimura Y (2016) Yasui Hiroshi Kyoju no Yakkanron no Gendaitekiigi – Minpokaisei to Furanchaizukeiyaku ni kansuru Giron o Chushin ni (The contemporary significance of Professor Hiroshi Yasui's theory of standard contract terms: focusing on the debate about the Civil Code Reform and franchise contracts). Ho to Seiji (Law Polit) 67(1):311–380
Minpo (Saikenho) Kaiseikentoiinkai (Japanese Civil Code (Law of Obligations) Reform Commission) (2009) Shokai – Saikenhokaisei no Kihonhoshin II: Keiyaku oyobi Saikenippann (1) (Basic policy for the reform of the law of obligations – Full Commentary II: Contracts and Obligations in General (1)). Shojihomu, Tokyo
Nakata K (2009) Recent developments in Japanese consumer law. Penn State Int Law Rev 27:803–815
Nakata K (2016) Performance and monetary remedies for breach of contract in Japan. In: Wishart MC, Loke A, Ong B (eds) Studies in the contract laws of Asia I. Oxford University Press, Oxford
Nebbia P (2007) Unfair contract terms in European law, a study in comparative and EC law. Hart, Oxford
Ochiai S (2001) Shohishakeiyakuho (Consumer Contract Act). Yuhikaku, Tokyo
Okino M (2015) Yakkan no Saiyoyoken ni tsuite – "Teikeiyakkan" ni kansuru Kiritsu no Kento (Regarding the adoption requirements for standard contract terms: a study on the regulation of "Formulated Standard Contract Terms"). In: Hoshino Eiichi Sensei Tsuito "Nihonminpogaku no Aratana Jidai" (Liber Amicorum for Professor Eiichi Hoshino "A New Era of Japanese Civil Law Science"). Yuhikaku, Tokyo
Ono S (1996) Comparative law and the Civil Code of Japan (1). Hitotsubashi J Law Polit 24:27–45
Sato Y (2001) Commercial dispute processing and Japan. Kluwer Law International, The Hague
Schenck PC (1997) Der deutsche Anteil an der Gestaltung des modernen japanischen Rechts- und Verfassungswesens. Franz Steiner, Stuttgart
Sono H (2014) Integrating consumer law into the Civil Code: A Japanese attempt of re-codification. In: Keyes M, Wilson T (eds) Codifying contract law. International and consumer law perspectives. Ashgate, Surrey
Stoffels M (2015) AGB-Recht, 3. Auflage. C.H.Beck, München
Suizu T (2011) Die Schuldrechtsreform in Japan – betrachtet aus dem Blickwinkel der Kodifikationsidee. ZJapanR 32:249–260
Sumida M (1999) Shogaikoku no Rippo ni okeru Futojokorisuto (Unfair contract terms lists in foreign legislation). NBL 54 (extra issue):190–200
Takasu J (2010) Minpo (Saikenho) Kaisei o Tou – Kaisei no Hitsuyosei to Arubekisugata (Questioning the Civil Code (Law of Obligations) Reform: the necessity for and ideal content of the reform). Sakaishoten, Tokyo
Takizawa M (2009) Consumer protection in Japanese contract law. Hitotsubashi J Law Polit 37:31–39
Uchida T (2011a) Contract law reform in Japan and the UNIDROIT principles. Rev Dr Unif 16(3):705–717
Uchida T (2011b) Minpokaisei – Keiyaku no Ruru ga Hyakunenburi ni Kawaru (Civil Code Reform: contract rules will change after 100 years). Chikuma Shobo, Tokyo
Uchtmann DL, Blessen RP, Maloney V (1987) The developing Japanese Legal System: growth and change in the modern era. Gonzaga Law Rev 23:349–359

Weatherill S (2013) EU consumer law and policy, 2nd edn. Elgar, Glos
Wrbka S (2014) Japan's Civil Code Reform Plan – seen from a western perspective. Kyushu University Legal Research Bulletin. http://www.law.kyushu-u.ac.jp/programsinenglish/kulrb/stefan2.pdf. Accessed 2 Jul 2017
Yamada S (2016) Teikeiyakkan ni kansuru Saikenhokaisei no Kosatsu (A study of the reform of the law of obligations regarding formulated standard contract terms). Meijohogaku 66(3):273–294
Yamaguchi R (2013) "Mille-feuilles influences" – Reception of foreign law in the Edo-Meiji period Japan. Kyushu Univ Leg Res Bull 3:1–11
Yamamoto Y (2007) Yakkan (Standard contract terms). In: Uchida T, Omura A (eds) Minpo no Soten (Points-at-issue in civil law) (Special issue of Jurist). Yuhikaku, Tokyo

The New French Contract Law and Its Impact on Commercial Law: Good Faith, Unfair Contract Terms and Hardship

Catherine Pédamon

Contents

Abstract This chapter considers the impact on commercial law of the new French Contract Law enacted in the *Ordonnance* No 2016-131 of 10 February 2016 through the lens of three major (and relatively innovative) provisions—good faith, unfair contract terms and hardship (*imprévision*). As 'common' law of contract, the revised French Civil Code provisions apply to all contracts, whatever their classification, be they civil or commercial; inevitably they can complement or clash with those in the Commercial Code. After introducing the genesis and objectives of the French

My thanks go to Maren Heidemann for her invaluable support.

C. Pédamon (✉)
Westminster Law School, University of Westminster, London, UK
e-mail: c.pedamon@westminster.ac.uk

M. Heidemann, J. Lee (eds.), *The Future of the Commercial Contract in Scholarship and Law Reform*, https://doi.org/10.1007/978-3-319-95969-6_5

reform of contract law, the chapter analyses the commercial impact of the provisions relating to good faith, unfair contract terms and hardship successively. The author shows that commercial parties have an ever-greater incentive to draft clear terms in their contract if they want to steer away from the application of the new common law of contract and increased judicial oversight.

1 Introduction

The traditional separation of commercial law from civil (private) law is still very much alive in France, despite a noticeable trend in some countries towards merging the two,[1] and some other civil law systems where there is no such distinction.[2] French commercial law remains a distinct branch of private law; it originates from royal recognition and then formal codification in a separate code.[3] It covers

> that branch of private law which is concerned with the status of merchants (individual merchants, companies and commercial groups) as well as the regime applicable to the legal operations carried out in the exercise of their trade.[4]

The reform of Title III of Book III of the French Civil Code (*Code Civil* or CC) on contracts (*Des contrats ou des obligations conventionnelles en général*)[5] does not affect this formal division, although it does have an impact on commercial law, since the *common law of contract* governs all contracts, whatever their classification. Article 1105 CC provides that (all) contracts are subject to the general rules.[6] These general rules however are subject to specific rules, such as those in the Commercial Code that govern business contracts, in conformity with the principle *specialia generalibus derogant.*

The application of these two sets of rules—civil (private) and commercial—gives rise to different scenarios. They may complement each other as commercial law is not complete and does not govern all aspects of commercial contracts; the new con-

---

[1] See Argentinian code. See also Bell et al. (2008), p. 458.

[2] Italian and Swiss legal systems, for instance.

[3] See Bell et al. (2008), p. 453.

[4] Pédamon and Kenfack (2015), p. 1.

[5] *Ordonnance no 2016-131 du 10 février 2016 portant réforme du droit des contrats, du régime général et de la preuve des obligations*, *Journal Officiel de la République Française* (JO) of 11 February 2016. The Ordonnance was translated by Cartwright, Fauvarque-Cosson, and Whittaker: http://www.textes.justice.gouv.fr/art_pix/THE-LAW-OFCONTRACT-2-5-16.pdf. Many of the translations of the new articles used in this chapter are based on their work and the author's own translation. The *Ordonnance* was ratified by Act No2018-287 of 20 April 2018 (*Loi No 2018-287 du 20 avril 2018 ratificant l'ordonnance No 2016-131 du 10 février 2016 portant réforme du droit des contrats, du régime général et de la preuve des obligations*).

[6] Article 1105 CC—*Les contrats, qu'ils aient ou non une dénomination propre, sont soumis à des règles générales, qui sont l'objet du présent sous-titre. Les règles particulières à certains contrats sont établies dans les dispositions propres à chacun d'eux. Les règles générales s'appliquent sous réserve de ces règles particulières.*

tractual provisions apply as the default law for commercial contracts. They may also overlap, or even clash, with each other in certain contexts, requiring the courts to choose the relevant rule(s) according to their objectives and compatibility.

This chapter considers how commercial law and civil law interact with each other through the lens of three provisions of the reformed contract law. The first provision relates to the requirement that all contracts be subject to good faith—from their negotiation to their formation and performance; the second one to the new regime that governs unfair contract terms in standard form contracts; and finally, the last one to the formal recognition of hardship (*imprévision*). Each provision is discussed successively. These three provisions must be considered in the context of the reform, which is introduced first, with a focus on its genesis and objectives. A critical analysis of statutory law, positive law and legal scholarship for each selected provision has been used in this chapter.

This analysis shows that since the reform commercial parties have an ever-greater incentive to draft clear and precise terms that explain their rights and obligations in the contract if they want to steer away from the application of the new common law of contract and increased judicial oversight that is exercised for the most part as an *ultimate* recourse.

2 The Newly Reformed Contract Law: Its Genesis and Objectives

Title III of Book III on Contracts (*Des contrats ou des obligations conventionnelles en général*) had remained nearly untouched since its original iteration in 1804, forcing the courts to develop contract law outside the code through a series of judicial decisions. The *Code Civil* itself had ceased to reflect the current contractual jurisprudence. It was paradoxical that the law of contract had to be found in case law in a system of codified law and in numerous special laws; this produced a fragmented and complicated legal system. Reform was therefore urgent and the need highlighted on the bi-centenary of the Napoleonic Code.

2.1 *The Genesis of the Reform: A Need for Reform*

The abundant case law that had emerged outside the code was perceived from a civil law perspective as a source of legal insecurity—'*by essence fluctuating, even uncertain*,'—and difficult to access, by economic actors.[7] The lack of evolution of the law of contract also limited the outreach of French law in the world, be it political or economic. In economic terms, the reports '*Doing business*' published by the World

[7] *Rapport au Président de la République relatif à l'Ordonnance no 2016-131 du 10 février 2016 portant réforme du droit des contrats, du régime général et de la preuve des obligations (Rapport au Président).*

Bank portrayed French law as complex, unforeseeable and unattractive, regularly stating that common law systems were better equipped to answer the needs of international trade.[8] It highlighted the urgent need for modernising the law of contract, especially as a succession of European and international projects for the harmonisation of the law of contract was emerging,[9] and as a way of redressing the lack of understanding of the civil law tradition.

As the government was engaged in a major reform for the modernisation and simplification of law, the Chancellery pushed for the reform of the law of contract by way of *ordonnance* (decree) rather than a full legislative act.[10] It received authorisation to do so by Act No 2015-177 of 16 February 2015, within a 1-year timeframe. The sense of urgency and the extensive work already undertaken by specialists and practitioners meant that the reform was a project led by the Chancellery. The criticism that the reform would lack democratic legitimacy appears quite unfounded since political debate had already taken place before the vote of the Act authorising the Chancellery to lead the reform.[11] It nevertheless reinforces a view that the law of obligations (*droit des obligations*) is a technical matter, thus preventing it from being the flagship of a new 'political vision.'[12]

The preliminary draft that the Ministry of Justice elaborated was greatly influenced by two major academic projects—the first one written in 2005 by Professor Catala, the *Avant-projet de réforme du droit des obligations et de la prescription, dit Projet Catala,*[13] and the second one by Professor Terré between 2008 and 2013[14]—and much commentary from practitioners, businesses and academics thanks to an online public consultation in 2015. The Unidroit Principles of International Commercial Contracts and the Principles of European Contract Law also influenced the drafters. The final version of the *ordonnance* is a *compromise* between these different—and conflicting—sources. Although a compromise can be positive, it is also a perilous exercise since each source has its own logic and own set of values

[8] Djankov and McLiesh (2004). The 2004 report was critical of the 'French civil tradition' and presented the common law as the ideal model in the business world. The following reports have not been as critical.

[9] Unidroit Principles of International Commercial Law (1994 revised in 2004 and more recently in 2016); the Principles of European law of Contracts published between 1995 and 2003; and the draft European Common Frame of Reference.

[10] The Ministry of Justice received authorisation to reform the law of contract by way of *ordonnance* (decree) pursuant to the Act No 2015-177 of 16 February 2015 relating to the modernisation and simplification of law and procedures in the fields of justice and home affairs.

[11] Members of the Senate asked the *Conseil Constitutionnel* to review the constitutionality of giving the government authority to legislate on such an important topic without parliamentary debate. The *Conseil Constitutionnel* held that the authority complied with article 38 of the Constitution, which allows the government to legislate by decree in certain circumstances.

[12] For a more extensive discussion as to the choice of an *ordonnance*, see Latina (2016), pp. 615–616.

[13] *Projet Catala* (2006).

[14] *Ministère de la Justice, Projet de réforme du droit des contrats*, July 2008 and 2009. See Terré (2008).

that may clash with each other, hence some oddities in the final text.[15] Overall, the reform is an evolution, not a revolution, as it remains quite a 'conservative' revision of the Civil Code with only a few innovations.

The *Ordonnance* No 2016-131 reforming the law of contract, the general regime of obligations and the proof of obligations was finally enacted on 10 February 2016 and came into force on 1st October 2016.[16] As required, it was ratified by Act No 2018-287 of 20 April 2018, entering into force on 1st October 2018, after extensive debate in Parliament. This Ratification Act modifies certain provisions of the *Ordonnance* pursuant to two types of rules: (1) the interpretative rules that clarify the implementation of some provisions resulting from the *Ordonnance*; and (2) the substantive rules that make substantial amendments to certain provisions in the *Ordonnance*, such as the new definition of standard form contract (adhesion contract) that is considered later. The *Ordonnance* only applies to contracts concluded on or after 1st October 2016,[17] together with the interpretative rules that apply retroctively to that date. The new substantive rules however enter into force on 1st October 2018.[18]

2.2 *The Objectives of the Reform: Modernisation and Simplification*

The reform aims at modernising and simplifying the general law of contract.[19] Its primary objective as set out in the Report to the President of the French Republic (*Rapport au Président*) is to promote *legal certainty* (*sécurité juridique)* to improve the legibility, and reinforce the accessibility, of the law of contract. In a system of written law, legal certainty falls within the power of the legislature, as such this reform is in a sense the re-affirmation of the primacy of the legislature (under the

[15] Latina (2016), pp. 617–619.

[16] *Ordonnance no 2016-131 du 10 février 2016 portant réforme du droit des contrats, du régime général et de la preuve des obligations*, JO no 0035 of 11 Febr. 2016.

[17] This is in conformity with Article 2 of the CC, which states that *legislation provides only for the future; it has no retroactive effect.* (See Civ. 27 May 1861, DP 1861, 244,). It has been held that the new legislation may not govern the effects of contracts that were concluded before, except if provided expressly (Cass. Civ. 3, 3 July 1979, n° 77-15.552; Civ. 3, 11 June 1997, Bull.129, Civ. 1, 17 March 1998, Bull.115, and more recently Cass. Civ. 1re, 12 June 2013, n° 12-15.688).

[18] Only three provisions apply to current contracts from 1st October 2016; they are articles 1123 (third and fourth subparagraph), 1158 and 1183 CC—all three articles relating to the request of information about the contract (actions interrogatoires). See Francois (2016), pp. 506–509. All pre-existing contracts will continue to be subject to the law that was in force when they were concluded, including any future effects, although in practice it is likely that courts will look at the *old* provisions and their effects through the lens of the new provisions.

[19] *Rapport au Président* (2016).

auspices of the Ministry of Justice) over the judiciary, at least as proclaimed in the *Rapport au Président*.[20]

For the most part, the new law of contract is designed as a codification of consistent case law (*codification à droit constant de la jurisprudence*), a *synthesis of case law* and a *work of consolidation*. It has, however, introduced a few new provisions, such as the ability to request information about the contract (*actions interrogatoires*) or the unilateral ability of a party to terminate the contract in the case of non-performance, and only with respect of a few provisions, has it overruled existing case law (*jurisprudence brisée*). As a thread that runs throughout the new provisions from a commercial perspective, legal certainty has inhibited the creativity of the drafter in the reform.[21]

An example of greater legibility can be found in the chronological organisation of the new provisions relating to the contract from its formation to its termination that allows easier access for professionals as well as lay people. The structure and language used in Title III of the Civil Code have also been clarified, making the text more intelligible. This aim of legibility is like the 'plain legal language' developed across the Atlantic that simplifies legal language and concepts used.[22] In addition, controversial legal concepts, such as the *cause* and *obligations de faire, de ne pas faire* and *de donner* (obligations of doing, not doing and giving), have been abandoned. By contrast, commonly used practices by professionals, such as the *unilateral promise of contract* (*promesse unilatérale de contrat*), have been enshrined in the new code.

The secondary objective of the reform is reinforcing the appeal of French law in political and economic spheres.[23] Here transpires the function of contract law asserted in the reform that aims at vesting the parties with greater contractual powers and helping them pre-empt judicial proceedings either through 'consensus' (*consensualisme*) or unilateralism (*unilatéralisme*). For instance, the new provision on changed circumstances (*imprévision* or hardship)[24] pushes for a negotiated solution, such as the renegotiation of the terms of the affected contract. In addition, the new contract law officially enshrined commonly used commercial practices, such as the transfer of contract (*cession de contrat*) or the transfer of debt (*cession de dette*), and the unilateral determination of price in certain contracts (*fixation unilatérale du prix*). The objective of business efficacy runs through the new provisions and underlines, for instance, the new prerogatives granted to the contracting parties to avoid litigation or mitigate the loss without any judicial interference (*faculté de résolution unilatérale par voie de notification, exception d'inexécution, réduction du prix*), or

---

[20] *Rapport au Président* (2016). For a discussion of the new standards of interpretation that the judges have been given, see infra.

[21] Chantepie and Dissaux (2016), p. 575.

[22] See Cacciaguidi-Fady and Wagner (2006), pp. 19–32, *in* Chassagnard-Pinet (2016), p. 583.

[23] *Rapport au Président* (2016).

[24] See infra.

even to request reliable information about the contract.[25] Such 'contractual self-regulation' echoes the English libertarian approach to contract law, although with some limits in the spirit of contractual fairness transpiring from certain notions transposed from consumer law, such as a significant disequilibrium (*déséquilibre significatif*) relating to unfair contract terms. The alignment of some new contractual provisions with the commercial expectations and practices of merchants to facilitate trade blurs the distinctiveness of civil (private) law and commercial law.

The reform thus aims at finding balanced solutions that protect parties but are also economically efficient and adapted to the evolution of the market economy. An illustration of this is found in the reiteration of the twofold nature of contract as an exchange of economic value and an exchange of consent, deemed freely negotiated and performed by *informed* parties. With these two facets in mind, the first chapter on Preliminary Provisions (*Dispositions Liminaires* or the general rules governing the law of contract) asserts first the freedom of contract[26] (Article 1102 CC), its binding force (Article 1103 CC) and then good faith (Article 1104 CC). These provisions have *not* been given the value of *principes directeurs (du droit)* (general principles of law)[27] since, as the *Rapport au Président* explicitly states when commenting on this chapter,[28] making them 'general principles' would give too much discretion to the judiciary. It is however difficult to deny the 'binding force' of these preliminary provisions.

Overall, a culture of 'consensus' impregnates the new provisions of contract law as conciliatory—or negotiated—solutions outside a judicial setting are promoted. Parties have an incentive to exercise their freedom of contract through clear and precise terms as nearly all the new provisions are optional, except those relating to matters of public policy, such as good faith and the elements of a valid contract, which are mandatory. This extended contractual freedom is however under the control of the judge who emerges as the *ultimate recourse*.[29] The introduction of (new) flexible, open-ended, standards, such as *reasonable, significant imbalance, excessive advantage* and *disproportion,* in certain provisions allows the judge to *assess* the fairness of the contractual relationship. These standards inspired from common law and international instruments on commercial contract law show the considerations that the courts must keep in mind—the respect of contractual freedom as facilitating economic efficiency within the limits of contractual fairness. In this respect, the *Ordonnance* sets the scene for a new contractual narrative that contracting parties and judges are expected to co-write.

---

[25] Article 1183 CC with respect to a possible termination of the contract. With respect to third party, Articles 1123 and1158 CC define the right of third parties to request information ('interrogate') the concerned parties about the contract.

[26] Whose value is constitutional.

[27] See definition of *Directeur, directrice* in Cornu (2016).

[28] *Rapport au Président* (2016) states that the Preliminary Provisions do not have a superior value that would give judges increased power of interpretation.

[29] Mekki (2016a) No 1–3, p. 1.

Whilst pushing for a socio-economic understanding of contract to facilitate trade, the reform also enshrines the principle of good faith that governs all contracts for the sake of a more level playing field.

3 Good Faith: An Overall Principle That Applies to All Contracts, Civil or Commercial

Good faith is not new in French contract law. It now has an article on its own. Article 1104 CC, in a minimalist formulation, provides that

> [c]ontracts must be negotiated, formed and performed in good faith. This provision is a matter of public policy.

What is new is the place where this *principle* is now stated. As already mentioned, it is in the first chapter on Preliminary Provisions, together with the freedom of contract (Article 1102 CC), and its binding force (Article 1103 CC). A contract, be it civil or commercial, is subject to good faith.

This principle now applies to the whole life of the contract—from its negotiation, which is a (formal) addition, to its formation, which is also new, and its performance. Article 1112 CC, for instance, expands the requirements of good faith to the commencement, continuation and breaking off of pre-contractual negotiations.[30] Although it consists mainly of a consolidation of case law, it still raises a number of questions as to the meaning of good faith as it has not been defined.

Good faith remains a polymorph concept, leaving its potentiality to judicial interpretation. Despite fears of excessive judicial intervention and against some preconceived ideas about the outreach of this principle, French judges have actually used good faith with moderation. It is neither an abstract and open-ended principle nor a one size fits all concept.[31] It aims (1) first at guaranteeing that the consent given by the parties is *free* and *informed*, thus targeting bad faith and other defects in consent, hence for example the new duty of disclosure in the formation of contract in Article 1112-1 CC; and (2) second at preserving the exercise of the rights of the parties in the contract whilst respecting its 'economic balance,'[32] hence the new ability for one party to request the renegotiation of the contract in changed circumstances in Article 1195 CC, for example. Two remarks must be made—the first one is that the focus here is on the contract *stricto sensu* and the behaviour of the parties in the negotiation, formation and performance of the contract to act in good faith. Good faith is therefore a *general standard of conduct;* it is not an abstract value

[30] See infra for a discussion of Article 1112 CC.

[31] By contrast, see for a comparative analysis of good faith in English and German law, Teubner (1998).

[32] *Dans la loyauté contractuelle, 'le critère pertinent n'est pas la morale de la sociabilité, mais plus prosaïquement le respect du but économique recherché*', Stoffel-Munck (2000). Contra, Chazal (2003), p. 114.

imposed upon in the interest of a broader public policy.[33] The second remark deals with the new rules, such as Articles 1112-1, 1165, and 1195 CC,[34] which embody variations of good faith without any explicit reference to good faith and which the judge has to apply as such. In light of these remarks, what is the scope of application of good faith and its effects? What are the duties that derive from good faith?

3.1 The Scope of Application and the Effects of Good Faith

Even in pre-contractual negotiations, as already mentioned, the expectation is that parties behave in accordance to good faith. Article 1112 CC, as modified by the Ratification Act, provides that

> the commencement, continuation and breaking-off of pre-contractual negotiations are free. They must mandatorily satisfy the requirements of good faith. In case of fault carried out during the negotiations, the reparation of the resulting prejudice shall cover neither the loss of benefits expected from the contract that was not entered into nor the loss of the chance of obtaining these benefits.

The amendment brought by the Ratification Act (i.e. '*nor the loss of the chance of obtaining these benefits*') is considered as an interpretative rule that comes into effect retroactively as of 1st October 2016. Pursuant to Article 1102 CC, the parties are free to contract or not, but this has to be done in good faith, refraining from improper bargaining tactics that would mislead the other party. Any negotiations that are engaged or continued while the decision not to contract is already made gives rise to damages.[35] In case of a wrongful termination of pre-contractual negotiations, the aggrieved party is however only entitled to damages covering, for example, the expenses incurred during the negotiations, but may not obtain compensation for either the lost benefits deriving from the non-conclusion of the contract or the lost opportunity of obtaining these benefits.[36] Good faith extends to the formation and performance of the contract too. How has it been enforced and how will it be implemented?

---

[33] Leggatt (2016) available at: https://www.judiciary.gov.uk/announcements/speech-by-mr-justice-leggatt-contractual-duties-of-good-faith/. The author disagrees with Justice Leggatt's claim that good faith is imposed upon the parties in the interest of a broader public policy in French law (at paras 7 and 9).

[34] See infra for a discussion of these articles.

[35] Cass. Com. 18 June 2002, no 99-16.488.

[36] *Affaire Manoukian*, Cass. Com 26 Nov. 2003, Nos 00-10.243 and 00-10.949; D. 2004.869, note Dupre Dallemagne; JCP 2004, I, 163, obs. Viney; JCP E 2004, 738, obs. Stoffel-Munck; RDC 2004. 257, obs. Mazeaud; RTD civ 2004.80, obs. J. Mestre and Fages.

Overall, judges have used good faith to limit certain contractual excesses, especially disloyal or fraudulent conduct of parties.[37] In a decision of 1999, the *Cour de Cassation* prevented a creditor from terminating a contract pursuant to a termination clause after he had ignored the non-performance for a certain period of time.[38] This is what Article 1165 CC aims at when it requires that the party that fixes the price unilaterally be able to justify it. Good faith is an instrument, which ensures that a level playing field exists between the parties—it is not paternalistic as the '*cause*' used to be, but it is an incentive for the parties to implement the rules of the game fairly. For example, in a (fairly exceptional) decision reached by the Commercial Chamber of the *Cour de Cassation* on 3 November 1992 in *Huard,*[39] the *Cour de Cassation* upheld the obligation to renegotiate the contract in a case of changed circumstances that had caused an economic imbalance in the performance of the contract (i.e. price deregulation followed by the intensification of competition). The Court grounded its decision on good faith as stated in the old Article 1134 al 3 of the Civil Code. However, since the new Article 1195 CC provides for hardship, it is likely that the courts will now use that provision (rather than the principle of good faith).[40]

In addition, the *Cour de cassation* has consistently limited the scope of application of good faith. It has rejected the claim that good faith can overturn the terms of the contract, or even the rules of the Civil Code or any other special rules. In a decision of 2009, it held that

> if the rule according to which the agreements must be performed in good faith allows the judge to punish the disloyal usage of a contractual prerogative, it does not authorise it to affect the substance itself of the rights and obligations legally agreed upon by the parties nor to move away from the mandatory provisions of the status of commercial leases.[41]

This is a position that the *Cour de Cassation* has followed overtime, thus restricting the effects of good faith on commercial contracts.[42]

---

[37] Cass. Civ. 3, 21 March 2012, No 11-14. 174; Bull. civ. No 49; RDC 2012. 753, obs. Laithier; ibid. 807, obs. Deshayes.

[38] Cass. Civ. 1, 16 Febr. 1999, No 96-21.997; Bull. civ. I, No 52.

[39] Cass. Com. 3 Nov 1992, No 90-18.547, Bull. civ. IV, No 338; JCP ed. G 1993.II; 22614, note Virassamy; Defrenois 1993 1377, obs. Aubert; RTD civ. 1993.124, obs. Mestre; Contr. Conc. Consom. 1993, No 45, obs. Malaurie-Vignal.

[40] See infra for a discussion on hardship.

[41] Cass. Civ 3, 9 Dec 2009, No 04-19.923; Bull. civ. III, No 275; RDC 2010.561, obs. Laithier; ibid.564, obs. Mazeaud.

[42] Com., 10 July 2007, JCP 2007.II.10154, note Houtcieff, D.; D. 2007, p. 2844, note Gautier, p. 2839, note Stoffel-Munck. The Commercial chamber quashed the decision of the lower court on the basis of the now old Article 1134 al 1 and 3 of the CC and held that "in deciding this way, whereas if the rule according to which the contracts must be performed in good faith enables the judge to punish the disloyal use of contractual provision, it does not authorise him to affect the substance itself of the rights and obligations legally agreed upon between the parties, the Court of appeal has violated, by wrong application, Article 1134 al 3 and by refusing to implement it, Article 1134 al 1." The judges of the lower court had rejected the request of the beneficiary of a guarantee (*garantie de passif*) on the ground that as manager and main shareholder, he had exposed

It is likely that it will continue to do so since the newly codified provisions on good faith enshrine existing case law. Parties may set limits (or extensions) to good faith in their contract although they may not exclude it as it is a mandatory rule of public policy (Article 1104 sub-para 2 CC). So, what are the duties that good faith entails?

3.2 Duties Deriving from Good Faith: The Usual Ones

Good faith can be used in a positive manner to impose a number of *implied* duties[43] upon the contracting parties, such as the duty of disclosure (*devoir d'information*), the duty of loyalty (*devoir de loyauté*), the duty of co-operation (*devoir de coopération*) and even, for a few authors, duties of fraternity or altruism.[44] It is important to note that none of these duties, with the exception of the duty of disclosure in pre-contractual negotiations, have been formally enshrined in the *Ordonnance*. They however transpire through certain articles and in certain types of contracts that are for the most part commercial, such as long-term contracts, and can be found in case law.

For example, Article 1112-1 CC provides that

> the party who knows of a piece of information which is of decisivel importance for the consent of the other party must inform her so long as this party legitimately does not know this information or relies on the other party.' Nevertheless, this duty to inform does not apply to an assessment of the value of the act of performance. Information is of decisive importance if it has a direct and necessary relationship with the content of the contract or the status of the parties. (...)

This article codifies current case law and asserts a (formal) pre-contractual duty of disclosure. It reflects the trend supporting more transparency in commercial relationships[45] and the increasing economic value given to information.

In terms of nature of this duty, it can be held that it is non-contractual since the article is enshrined in Chapter II (Formation of contract). Certain authors however overcome the temporal criteria and instead link the duty to the performance of the contract by focusing on the underlying economic exchange—rather than the exchange of consent—so central to the contract.[46] Finally this duty may be a variation of good faith as a standard of conduct. As such, it would explain why this obligation is mandatory.

---

the company to the risk of tax penalty referred to in the guarantee and thus he could not, without violating his good faith, benefit from the guarantee.

[43] For a discussion on the distinction between duty and obligation, see Mekki (2016b), p. 1207; Chazal (2003), p. 104. Although there is no reference to an actual duty of good faith, it has been understood that good faith creates a duty that precedes, and perhaps outlives, a valid contract.

[44] Mazeaud (1999), p. 603, No 6; also from the same author (2003), p. 295.

[45] See Article L. 330-3 and R. 330-1 and 2 of the Commercial Code.

[46] Chazal (2003), p. 99, spec. p. 111.

More precisely, the definition in Article 1112-1 CC aims at reassuring professionals that only certain pieces of information must be disclosed i.e. those that have *a necessary and direct link to the content of the contract or the status of the parties*—and that the seller *knows of. A contrario*, the non-disclosure must be intentional, thus highlighting the role of *intentionality* in the performance of this obligation.[47] In addition, the article clarifies that the obligation does not relate to the estimated value of the act of performance (goods or services).[48] Reciprocally, the buyer also has a duty to inquire (*devoir de se renseigner*) as ignorance of the information or reliance on the other party must be *legitimate*. How legitimacy will be assessed is still unclear but it refers to an assessment of the *conduct* of the party in accordance with good faith. The judge will have the last word on the interpretation of this Article and the implementation of the new legal standards referred to, such as legitimately or decisive importance, in Article 1112-1 CC.

In terms of remedies, the breach of this obligation may cause the termination of the contract pursuant to Article 1130 CC and the following articles relating to the defects in consent. This is in addition to the damages for the loss of an opportunity to contract (or not) on different terms.[49]

In practice, it is common for commercial parties to do some due diligence and exchange a disclosure letter, which is part of the contractual process. Now they must now also comply with the statutory duty of disclosure in the Civil Code. How compatible Article 1112-1 CC is with special rules of disclosure in the Commercial Code (Com.C), such as the mutual duty of information between the commercial agent and the principal, is an issue that courts will settle on a case by case basis.

In addition to this duty, good faith includes the more traditional duty of loyalty[50] and duty of co-operation.[51] Loyalty[52] is commonly found in insurance contracts,[53] commercial agencies and employment contracts where trust is intrinsic to the commercial relationship between the parties. In the *Chevassus* case of 24 November 1998, for example, the *Cour de Cassation* asserted the obligation to give the means to charge competitive prices to the agent in a commercial agency agreement.[54] The

---

[47] Cass. Civ. 1, 28 May 2008, No 07-13.487; Bull. civ. I, No 154.

[48] This is conformity with the current *Baldus* case law: Cass. Civ 1, 3 May 2000, No 98-11.381; Bull. civ. I, No 131; Cass. Civ. 3, 17 Jan 2007, No 06-10.442; Bull. civ. III.; D. 2007.1051, note Mazeaud; ibid.1054, note Stoffel-Munck; JCP 2007, II, 1042, Note Jamin; RTD civ. 2007.335, obs. Mestre and Fages.

[49] Cass. Com., 31 Jan 2012, No 11-10.834 (non- published); Cass. Com. 10 July 2012, No 11-21.954, Bull civ. IV, No 149, Bull. Joly 2012, 767, note Stoffel-Munck.

[50] Cass. Com. 27 Febr. 1996, Bull. n° 65. See also Cass. Com. 30 Oct 2007 (non- published), pourvoi n° 06-20.944; Cass. Com. 20 Jan 2015, non publié, pourvoi n° 13-24.231. Mestre (1986), p. 101; Picod (1988).

[51] Cass. Civ. 24 Sept. 2002 (non- published) pourvoi No 99-13.537.

[52] See definition of *loyauté* in Cornu (2016).

[53] In an insurance contract, duty of loyalty and sincerity of the insured to the insurer, see Cass. Civ 1., 28 March 2000, Bull. civ. I, No 101.

[54] Cass. Com., 24 Nov 1998, No 96-18.357, Bull. civ. IV, No 277; *Defrénois* 1999.371, obs. Mazeaud; JCP ed G.I. 143, note Jamin.; RTD civ 1999.98, obs. Mestre, J. and 646, obs. Gautier.

refusal by a party to comply with this obligation could amount to a violation of good faith making him contractually liable, or a breach of an obligation defined in the Commercial Code. In a recent case of 2017, the *Cour de Cassation* held that the conduct of the commercial agent constituted a breach of a non-compete obligation pursuant to Article L. 134-3 Com.C as the commercial agent had to perform his obligations with loyalty.[55] It is important to note that Article L. 134-4 Com.C states in its second paragraph that the relationship between the commercial agent and the principal is governed by a *duty of loyalty* and *a mutual duty of information*. By contrast with loyalty, co-operation is a restricted duty that arises in certain types of contract only, such as long-term supply contracts, franchise agreements and employment contracts. This duty is not formally recognised and has a limited scope of application; its focus is on the (negative) effects of the absence of such co-operation and, as a result, the expectation of an active behaviour from the contracting party to permit the performance of the contract.

Despite the fears—and erroneous claims -[56] about good faith as being a hindrance to freedom of contract, good faith is rather inherent to this freedom as parties, even commercial parties, may pursue their commercial interests on a more level playing field according to certain rules of conduct.[57] As acknowledged by Leggatt J,

> the essence of trade and commerce is reciprocity which benefits both parties and makes each party better off. To achieve such mutual gain, the parties agree to cooperate with each other in various ways. Contract law facilitates such cooperation by giving it legal backing.[58]

Overall French courts have used, and are likely to continue to use, good faith as a mechanism to control the *conduct* of the contracting parties in all types of contracts; it reflects a concern that parties give a consent that is free and *informed* and perform their obligations in the spirit of the contract. Certain kinds of contracts, such as standard form contracts, however are subject to further judicial scrutiny due to their inherently asymmetrical nature so that any imbalance in the rights and obligations of the parties may be redressed. A new provision in the Civil Code now deals with unfair contract terms and comes as an addition to existing commercial provisions. This article has caused much controversy.

Three companies had entered into a commercial agency contract with an agent for the exclusive sale of their products to importers, wholesalers and retailers in the Indian Ocean. A little while after, it emerged that the (potential) clients of the appointed agent could purchase their products directly from purchasing pools in mainland France. The agent then terminated all commercial relationships with the principals and asked for damages.

[55] Cass. Com. 29 March 2017, No 15/26476, LD May 2017, obs. S.B.

[56] Leggatt (2016) available at: https://www.judiciary.gov.uk/announcements/speech-by-mr-justice-leggatt-contractual-duties-of-good-faith/. The author disagrees with Justice Leggatt's claim that '*good faith limits (the Parties') freedom in making contracts in the first place*' (at 7).

[57] Campbell (2014), p. 485.

[58] Leggatt (2016) available at: https://www.judiciary.gov.uk/announcements/speech-by-mr-justice-leggatt-contractual-duties-of-good-faith/.

4 Overlapping, or Even Contradictory, Provisions on Unfair Contract Terms in Civil and Commercial Law

Traditionally, pursuant to the social contract theory, a contract was an exchange of consent *necessarily fair*[59] entered into freely by the parties.[60] As stated by one author, "who says contractual says just" ("*Qui dit contractuel dit juste*").[61] The contract was considered as a bargain detached from its circumstances, above and beyond economic and financial circumstances. This view of contract has now been subject to numerous qualifications. In practice, most contracts are negotiated in an economically constrained environment between parties of unequal bargaining power: for example, between consumers and professionals, small suppliers and large retailers, powerful principals and small agents, just to name a few... These contracts are often imbalanced to the detriment of the weaker party in economic or social terms. This raises

> the central question in general contract law of the proper balance to be struck between respecting the freedom of parties to choose the terms of their transaction and controlling unfair terms inserted into contracts by stronger parties.[62]

In the contract law reform, the control of unfair terms in the hands of the judge has gained in legal legitimacy as it is now enshrined in a new provision, which seems to guarantee an *economic balance* in *imbalanced* contracts with the *proviso* however that it only applies to certain terms in standard form contracts. Article 1171 CC, as amended by the Ratification Act, strikes down as invalid (not written)

> any non-negotiable term determined in advance by one of the parties that creates a significant imbalance (*déséquilibre significatif*) in the rights and obligations of the contracting parties to a standard form contract.[63]

The new reference to '*non-negotiable term determined in advance by one of the parties*' is considered as a subtantive rule that enters into force on 1st October 2018. The previous version of Article 1171 CC therefore continues to apply to contracts concluded between 1st October 2016 and 30 September 2018, but it is likely that courts interpret the 'old' provision in light of the new one. The novelty of Article 1171 CC lies in its more restrictive scope of application since it now applies to *any* non-negotiable pre-determined contract term in a standard form contract, whatever the nature of the contract, civil (private) or commercial. Following strong protest from business, this article was confined first to standard form contracts, and then

---

[59] Pédamon and Chuah (2013), p. 36.

[60] Rousseau (1762).

[61] Fouillée (1880), p. 410; see also Spitz (2007), p. 281.

[62] Collins (2008), p. 2 with respect to the 1993 Directive on unfair terms in consumer contracts.

[63] Article 1171 CC, as amended by the Ratification Act, provides that "(i)n a standard form contract, any non-negotiable, determined in advance by one of the parties, term which creates a significant imbalance in the rights and obligations of the parties to the contract may be deemed invalid [*réputée non écrite*]. The assessment of significant imbalance does not concern either the main subject-matter of the contract nor the adequacy of the price to the obligation."

following the debate in Parliament, to non-negotiable pre-determined contract terms.[64] Pursuant to Article 1110 CC also modified by the Ratification Act, a standard form contract (or adhesion contract) is a contract which contains a set of non-negotiable terms, determined in advance by one of the party. This new definition also enters into force on 1st October 2018, leaving the standard form contracts concluded between 1st October 2016 and 30 September 2018 governed by the original version resulting from the *Ordonnance* that only refers to general terms that are not subject to negotiation. This temporal application may give rise to quite a few issues as non-negotiable pre-determined terms are commonly used between professionals in certain sectors, such as the retail industry and ecommerce. A contract term must therefore meet three conditions to be deemed non written (invalid); it must (1) be non negotiable; (2) determined in advance by the other party; and (3) creating a significant imbalance. The non-negotiability is therefore decisive to characterise a standard form contract and check if Article 1171 CC may apply.

The sanction of unfair contract terms (*clauses abusives*) is not new in French law, but it is a novelty in the Civil Code. It was originally introduced in the Consumer Code in 1978 and has been re-asserted over several articles (Articles L. 212-1. L. 212-2, L. 212-3 and L. 241-1 and L. 241-2) in the newly codified Consumer Code that entered into force on 1st July 2016.[65] These provisions are similar to the ones in the newly reformed Civil Code; they aim at controlling the fairness of the terms in a contract between professionals and consumers or *non-professionals*, meaning professionals that enter into a contract *that has no direct relationship* with their professional activity.[66] The notion of significant imbalance is also found in Article L. 442-6 Com.C, but in a different manner, so how compatible is Article 1171 CC with Article L. 442-6, I, 2° Com.C?

4.1 *Article L. 442-6, I, 2° of the Commercial Code as a Competitive Tool*

The Commercial Code refers to the notion of *significant imbalance* as a tool to prevent commercial practices that distort competition between commercial parties and as an instrument to control the *economic balance* of certain types of commercial

[64] For a critical discussion of unfair terms in standard form contracts, see Bicheron (2015), Boffa (2015) and Revet (2015).

[65] Articles L. 212-1 to 212-3; L. 232-1, L. 241-1 to L. 241-2, L. 822-4 to L. 822-6, L. 822-9 and L. 822-10 in the Consumer Code.

[66] For a rejection of the application of these statutory provisions to a merchant with respect to a contract for the supply of electricity—see Cass. Civ. 1, 24 Jan 1995, D. 1995, J, 327, note Paisant; D. 1995. Somm. 229, obs. Delebecque; D. 1995. Somm. 310, obs. Pizzio; to a glass maker with respect to a contract for the supply of water, see Civ. 1, 3 Jan. 1996, D. 1996. 228, note Paisant; D. 1996. Somm. 325, obs. Mazeaud; RTD Civ. 1996.609, obs. Mestre.

relationships.[67] Before the reform of the Civil Code, Article L. 442-6, I, 2° Com.C was the only protection for the weaker party in asymmetrical commercial relationships. This article provides that a producer, merchant, manufacturer, or any person registered on the Commercial registry may be liable for, and obliged to remedy the loss caused by, subjecting, or attempting to subject, a commercial partner to obligations causing a *significant imbalance* in the rights and obligations of the parties.[68] It mainly targets the retail industry, including all activities of supply or distribution of goods or services, as this industry commonly uses standard form contracts that comprise terms, which might be detrimental to the 'commercial partner'.[69] This provision applies to other sectors too, but quite rarely.[70]

Different notions in this article need to be clarified. First, the notion of 'submission'—it is established by reference to the bargaining power of the parties.[71] Courts look at the facts to establish if unjustified and non-mutual obligations have been imposed upon one party.[72] *A contrario*, the evidence of actual negotiation of the terms in the standard form contract may avoid the application of the article.[73] Second, the notion of 'commercial partner'—this notion must be considered in its context. In a decision of 2017, the Paris Court of Appeal defines the notion of '*commercial partner*' quite strictly by stating that a partner is a professional with whom a business enterprise/venture maintains commercial relationships to undertake any activity that involves

> a common and mutual will to carry out together actions in activities of production, distribution or services, as opposed to the wider notion of economic agent or the more restrictive notion of contracting party.[74]

This decision sets two criteria for a commercial partner – the first one is the duration of the commercial relationship that must be stable and well-established, and the second one the common will of the parties to carry out a commercial activity of

[67] Act No 2008-776 of 4 August 2008 for the modernisation of the economy. For a general discussion of Article L. 442-6, I, 2° of the Commercial Code, see Pédamon and Kenfack (2015) at No 642.

[68] Article L 442-6 Com. C, as amended by Act n ° 2010-874 of 27 July 2010—"I. Make the party liable, and force him to remedy the damage caused, the act by any producer, trader, industrial or person registered in the Commercial Registry: 1° (…); 2° To impose, or attempt to impose, upon a trading partner obligations creating a significant imbalance in the rights and obligations of the parties; (…)." The Constitutional Council has declared that this article was 'conformed' to the Constitution in a decision of 13 Jan 2011; see Cons. Const., 13 Jan 2011, No 2010-85 QPC, Dalloz actualité, 19 Jan. 2011, obs. Chevrier; D. 2011.415, note Picod; ibid. 392, Chron. Chagny; ibid. 2823, obs. Roujou de Boubee, Gare, Mirabail and Potaszkin; RTD Civ. 2011. 121, obs Fages RTD Com. 2011. 655, obs. Bouloc.

[69] See article L. 410-1 of the Commercial Code.

[70] CA Paris, 29 Oct 2014, No 13/11059, RJDA 2015, No 146.

[71] CA Paris, 29 Oct 2014, No 13/11059, RJDA 2015, No 146.

[72] Ibid.

[73] CA Paris 19 April 2017, No 15/24221, LD May 2017, P.1, obs. N.E.

[74] CA Paris 27 Sept. 2017, No 16/00671; also CA Paris 21 Sept. 2016, No 14/06802, LD Oct. 2016, p.1, obs. N.E.

production, distribution or services over a length of time. In terms of relationships, the article mainly targets the relationship between suppliers and retailers. A *contrario*, occasional actions, such as the lease agreements of the case that related to occasional transactions with a limited object and timeframe, do not fall within the definition of *commercial partnership*. In addition, any banking and financial services activities are excluded from the scope of application of the article, pursuant to that decision of 2017, as these activities already pertain to the Monetary and Financial Code (*code monétaire et financier*). The Cour de Cassation has confirmed this exclusion with respect to Article L. 442-6 I 5 Com.C.[75] Similarly, company relationships are not covered pursuant to a series of decisions by the *Cour de Cassation*.[76]

Third, the notion of imbalance—this notion is central. Recently, the *Cour de cassation* confirmed the interpretation of the Court of Appeal that considered the contracts *in concreto* and as a whole—rather than term by term—in light of the *economy* (*l'économie*) of the contract so that the imbalance caused by one term can be offset by another.[77] The notion of *significant imbalance* qualifies as a *lack of reciprocity* (*absence de réciprocité*) or a lack of common will that can be aggravated by a lack of consideration/compensation (*absence de contrepartie*); it can apply with respect to a term for the revision of price or a term on the rate for the supply of service.[78] In another recent decision, the *Cour de cassation* held

> that Article L. 442-6, I, 2° of the Commercial Code authorises a judicial control of the price on the basis that this price does not result from a free negotiation and characterises a significant imbalance in the rights and obligations of the parties.[79]

This is a striking difference with Article 1171 CC. Wary of the potential for an explosion of commercial disputes around imbalance where pricing is challenged, commercial judges have interpreted the scope of application of Article 442 6, 1, 2° Com.C in a restrictive manner.[80] In addition, a series of terms is illegal *per se*, such as the return of unsold products,[81] the asymmetrical revision of prices,[82] the unilateral and automatic termination of the contract, without notice and indemnity,[83] for example.

In sum, Article L. 442-6, I, 2° Com.C is an instrument of control in asymmetrical commercial relationships for combating market failures.[84] Issues surrounding the scope of application of Article L. 442-6, I, 2° have given rise to an increasing

[75] Cass. Com. 25 Oct. 2017, No 16-16839.

[76] Cass. Com. 8 Febr. 2017, No 15-23050; Cass. Com. 11 May 2017, No 14-29717

[77] Cass. Com. 25 Jan. 2017, No 15-23547, LD Febr. 2017, obs. N.E.

[78] Cass. Com. 27 May 2015, No 14-11.387.

[79] Cass. Com. 25 Jan. 2017, No 15-23547 – *qu'il suit de là que l'article L. 442-6, I, 2° du code de commerce autorise un contrôle judiciaire du prix, dès lors que celui-ci ne résulte pas d'une libre négociation et caractérise un déséquilibre significatif dans les droits et obligations des parties.*

[80] Cass. Com. 25 Jan. 2017, No 15-23547, LD Febr. 2017, p. 1, obs. N.E.

[81] CA Paris 4 July 2013, No 12/07651.

[82] CA Paris 11 Sept 2013, No 11/17941.

[83] CA Paris 20 Nov. 2013, No 12/04791.

[84] Behar-Touchais (2015). See for a discussion of unfair contract terms in B2B transactions involving Micro and Small Businesses in English law, Australian law and US law, Hourani in this volume.

number of disputes, often without much success. As a consequence, courts have recently given a strict and restrictive interpretation of this article and limited its application to complex commercial relationships, such as those in the retail sector (*secteur de la grande distribution*).[85]

Given the number of special texts already dealing with unfair terms in contracts between consumers and professionals and between professionals, how and when will Article 1171 CC apply? In a decision of 2017,[86] the *Cour de cassation* applied the adage *specialia generabilus derogant* strictly, so any special text prevailed over the general provisions in the Commercial Code, and furthermore over the common law of contract in the Civil Code. It however appears that this adage is often used in an opportunistic manner by the courts and that its application still raises questions.[87]

4.2 How Compatible Is Article L. 442-6, I, 2° of the Commercial Code with Article 1171 of the Civil Code?

By generalising the provision relating to unfair contract terms in *standard form contracts*, the Ministry of Justice has clearly made a political decision that reflects one of the objectives of the reform to fight contractual unfairness. Article 1171 CC gives the judge a tool to control contractual imbalances caused by non-negotiable pre-determined term, especially as the article does not define either the notion of *significant imbalance*. Guidance may however be found in the way civil and commercial courts have applied Article L. 212-1 of the Consumer Code and Article L. 442-6, I, 2° Com.C respectively. Inevitably some gaps remain, since, for instance, the commercial courts have focused on the relationship between suppliers and retailers in the retail industry, leaving aside the relationship between agents and principals, and franchisees and franchisor?[88] Will the civil courts refer to the commercial case law by analogy? How contradictory or complementary are these two sets of provisions then?

First, the two sets of provisions pursue different objectives. The commercial provision seeks to protect the *weaker* party in an asymmetrical sustained commercial relationship with the ultimate aim at regulating the overall competition of the relevant industry and other markets affected by these (unfair) commercial practices.[89] The Civil law provision has a more modest objective—i.e. to protect the weaker party forced to agree upon non-negotiable pre-determined terms in a standard form contract—but its outreach is broad as it can apply to commercial contracts between

[85] CA Paris 25 Nov 2016, No 16/08557, LD Jan 2017, P. 1, obs. S.C. In this case, the Court of Appeal held that the provisions relating to commercial leases are exclusive from a joint (or alternative) application of Article L. 442-6 of the Commercial Code.

[86] Cass. Com. 11 May 2017, No 14-29717, LD June 2017, obs. N.E.

[87] Ibid.

[88] CA Paris, 7 June 2013, RTD com. 2013. 500, obs. Chagny.

[89] Cass. Com. 25 Jan. 2017, No 15-23547, LD Febr. 2017, p. 2, obs. N.E.

professionals. In addition, Article 1171 CC is less constraining from a procedural perspective than the equivalent commercial provisions given that Article L. 442-6 I 2 Com.C requires that any claims be lodged with only one of the 8 commercial courts (*tribunaux de commerce*), the Court of Appeal of Paris being the exclusive court of appeal.[90] The court backlog is a concern, which can explain the current narrow judicial interpretation of Article L. 442-6 I 2. By contrast, the conditions of application of Article 1171 CC are less constraining than its equivalent commercial provisions. As Article L. 442-6 I 2 Com.C retreats, the scope of application for Article 1171 CC expands as the default provision, thus applying to commercial relationships between professionals that are not subject to Article L. 442-6 I 2.

Article L. 442-6, I, 2° Com.C raises questions as to the enforcement of Article 1171 CC—should the term that causes the imbalance be a non-negotiated albeit negotiable term or should it be a non-negotiated non-negotiable one? Could one term be offset by another? Whereas the Consumer Code explicitly refers to an objective interpretation of the term against the other terms of the contract, the Commercial Code refers to a subjective one. Quite confusing really!

In addition, Article 1171 CC excludes explicitly

> either the main subject-matter of the contract or the adequacy of the price to the performance

from the assessment of *significant imbalance*. This exclusion contrasts with Article L. 442-6, I, 2° Com.C, which authorises such control[91] as the price is an essential term in the commercial relationship. It is however the same as the one that is found in the Directive on Unfair Contract Terms in consumer contracts.[92]

In terms of remedies, the contrast is also striking. Pursuant to Article 1171 CC, the court is only able to *declare the term as invalid*, striking it out and leaving the rest of the contract unaffected, thus relying on the general law of contract to fill in the gaps left by the invalidity of the term. It is confined to a mechanical or procedural application of the article. This remedy is the same in the Consumer Code. In contrast, the commercial provisions offer a range of remedies—from the tort liability of the party responsible for the damages and the payment of a civil fine (*amende civile*) to an administrative fine (*amende administrative*) and the nullity of the illegal terms.[93] This range of remedies reveals the gravity of these terms (and practices) in the eyes of the legislator in the commercial sphere.[94]

Overall, the Civil Code provision—i.e. Article 1171 CC—applies as a fall-back position if the special provisions—i.e. Article L. 442-6, I, 2° Com.C—do not bite.

---

[90] Art L. 442-6 I 2 requires that any claims be lodged only with specific jurisdictions that are one of the eight commercial courts (*tribunaux de commerce*) and on appeal, the Court of Appeal of Paris, which has an exclusive competence to hear these claims.

[91] See supra.

[92] Art 4(2) of the European Directive 93/13/EEC.

[93] Cass. Com. 6 Febr. 2007, no 04-13.178, Bull. civ. IV, No 21; Cass. Com. 13 Jan.2009, No 08-20.411.

[94] See also for Japanese law, Karaiskos in this volume.

How and when exactly it applies is likely to be decided on an *ad hoc* basis. This new civil law provision holds however a symbolic significance since the judge is now able to ensure that the rights and obligations of the contract be *balanced* in standard form contracts. The *threat* of judicial intrusion into the contract should be an incentive for the commercial parties to anticipate and clearly (and fairly) allocate the risks in the contract in clear and precise terms. If the stronger party fails to do so, the judge is *the ultimate recourse* for the weaker party. Such a threat also exists in the new provisions dealing with hardship.

5 The *Imprévision* or How the Civil Code Now Reflects a More Realist View of Commercial Contracts

A novelty of the reform is that the new text in its Article 1195 CC embraces the theory of *imprévision* or theory of hardship that had been rejected since the *Canal de Craponne*[95] in 1876 despite many attempts to introduce it.[96] Although this is a novelty, it follows in the footsteps of the legislator who had already inserted such a concept in the Commercial Code with respect to the sale of raw agricultural and food products.[97] Article L 441-8 Com.C, as modified by the Act No 2015-990 of 6 August 2015, adopts a new and original approach to changed circumstances by focusing on the *obligation of renegotiation* by the parties.

Pursuant to this article, the parties must undertake to renegotiate the price if there is a change of circumstances in the prices of raw agricultural and food products that affects significantly the cost of production.[98] The contract must include a term relating to the methods of renegotiation of the price. Although it is common that the parties insert a renegotiation clause in their commercial contract, this clause is now required by statute. Any violation of the conditions set out in Article L. 441-8 Com.C regarding this renegotiation clause is punished by a fine.[99] The renegotiation

[95] Cass. Civ., 6 March 1876, DP 1876.1.193. In contrast, see the case-law of administrative courts, such as *Gaz de Bordeaux*, CE 30 March 1916, Recueil Dalloz 1916.3.25.

[96] For a comparative and general development on hardship in transnational commercial contracts, see Pédamon and Chuah (2013). See also Cass. Com. 3 Nov 1992, *Huard* RTDC 1993.124; Cass. Com. 24 Nov 1998, *Chevassus-Marche* RTDC 1999.98; CA Nancy 26 Sept 2007 *Novacarb,* D. 2008.1120; Cass.Com 29 June 2010, *Soffimat* JCP 2010, ED g. 1056.

[97] Act Hamon of 17 March 2014 (Act n° 2014-344 of 17 March 2014).

[98] This Article covers the contracts whose performance exceeds 3 months for the sale of products listed in the 2nd subparagraph of Article L. 442-9, and supplemented, if need be, by decree. This Article refers to these products whose "prices of production can be significantly affected by the fluctuation of prices of agricultural raw and food products."

[99] The fact of not foreseeing a renegotiation clause in conformity with the first two subparagraphs of this article, of not respecting the time allowed in the 3rd subparagraph, of not preparing the minutes envisaged in the same 3rd subparagraph or violating trade secrets or business confidentiality during the renegotiation, shall be liable of a fine of no more than 75,000 Euros for a natural person and 375,000 Euros for a legal person. The fine is imposed in the conditions set in article L.

of these contracts must be performed in good faith within 2 months at the latest (or by a time specified in the contract) from the changed circumstance. It must respect confidentiality in industrial and commercial matters, and aims at a fair distribution between the parties, and all the members in the supply chain, of the increase or reduction of the production costs resulting from these changes.

This provision raises some questions—i.e. what if the conditions for the obligation of renegotiation are met, but the renegotiation fails or leads to an unsatisfactory outcome? As the article remains silent about the consequences of failed negotiations, the new Article 1195 CC applies as the default rule. The conditions and effects of this article need to be considered carefully.

5.1 The Conditions of Application of the New Article 1195 of the Civil Code on Hardship: All About Re-Negotiation

In a long and fairly complex paragraph, Article 1195 CC provides that

> (i)f a change of circumstances that was unforeseeable at the time of the conclusion of the contract renders the performance excessively onerous for a party who has not agreed to bear the risk, that party may ask the other contracting party to renegotiate the contract. This party continues to perform her obligations during the renegotiation. In the case of rejection or failure of renegotiation, the parties may agree to either terminate the contract as from the date and on the terms they determine, or ask the judge by common agreement to set about its adaptation. In the absence of agreement within a reasonable period, the judge may, upon the request of one party, revise the contract or terminate it, as from a date and on the terms that (the judge) determines.

Although French law is now aligned with most European laws, especially German and Italian law, and European and international principles, such as the Principles of European Contract Law (PECL) and the UNIDROIT Principles of International Commercial Contracts (PICC),[100] which provide specifically for hardship, Article 1195 CC nonetheless shows the legislator's reluctance to limit the binding force of contract and give powers to the judge over the contract. The objective of the provision is instead to instill a dialogue between the parties so that they reach an agreement to either revise the contract terms or terminate the contract terms in light of the changed circumstances. How realistic is this consensual quest? The recourse to the judge is the ultimate option, the last resort, in this context. In that sense, it is quite different from §313 of the German Civil Code or *Bürgerliches Gesetzbuch* (BGB) under the heading *Störung der Geschäftsgrundlage* (Interference

465-2. The maximum fine is doubled in the event of a repeated breach within a period of 2 years from the date from which the first decision became final.

[100] UNIDROIT Principles 2016 available at http://www.unidroit.org/instruments/commercial-contracts/unidroit-principles-2016.

with the basis of the transaction—change of circumstances),[101] where the remedy available is direct judicial adaptation of the contract.

In terms of conditions, the sets of provisions in German and French law are however quite similar, although not as specific; they relate to (1) an unforeseeable change of circumstances at the time of conclusion of the contract; (2) rendering the performance excessively onerous; (3) for a party that had not agreed to bear that risk.

First of all, the changed circumstances must be unforeseeable at the time of conclusion of the contract. It is unclear from the text if the unforeseeability must be assessed objectively or subjectively. Some authors compare this element with the requirement in the definition of *force majeure*—i.e. the reasonable unforeseeability of the circumstance that renders the performance of the contract impossible—and conclude that the objective interpretation is the only way to give (business) efficacy to the article.[102] Nevertheless, coming from a subjective tradition of interpretation, and given that Article 1195 CC is drafted in a laconic manner, courts may consider the extent to which the parties actually foresaw the occurrence of the changed circumstance. This opens the door to a fact-intensive investigation as French courts would have to assess the foreseeability in light of the specific commercial contract between professionals. In American law, for instance, hardship in the sale of goods is not a legal or judicial concept; it is a term to describe a fact. American courts use a fairly subjective and fact-intensive test to assess if the events were foreseeable risks.[103] An *objective unforeseeability* would however avoid disputes of facts as to whether the changed circumstances were foreseeable at the time of conclusion of the contract. In a sophisticated commercial world, what is unforeseeable anyway?

Second, the effects of the changed circumstances must render the performance of the contract 'excessively onerous.' There is no reference to a fundamental alteration of equilibrium of the contract as in Article 6.2.2 (Definition of hardship) PICC, but instead to one of its manifestations—i.e. an excessively onerous increase in the cost

---

[101] § 313 BGB refers to 'the contractual basis' (*Grundlage des Vertrags*). This article has been translated in English by Geoffrey Thomas and Gerhard Dannemann and is available at www.iuscomp.org/gla/statutes/BGB.htm.

§ 313 BGB—Interference with the basis of the transaction

(1) If circumstances upon which a contract was based have materially changed after conclusion of the contract and if the parties would not have concluded the contract or would have done so upon different terms if they had foreseen that change, adaptation of the contract may be claimed in so far as, having regard to all the circumstances of the specific case, in particular the contractual or statutory allocation of risk, it cannot reasonably be expected that a party should continue to be bound by the contract in its unaltered form.
(2) If material assumptions that have become the basis of the contract subsequently turn out to be incorrect, they are treated in the same way as a change in circumstances.
(3) If adaptation of the contract is not possible or cannot reasonably be imposed on one party, the disadvantaged party may terminate the contract. In the case of a contract for the performance of a recurring obligation, the right to terminate is replaced by the right to terminate on notice.

[102] Chantepie and Latina (2016), p. 445.

[103] Pédamon and Chuah (2013), Chapter 3.

of performance. Typically, it is the case where the dramatic rise in the price of raw materials causes a substantial increase in the cost of production.[104] The Civil Code remains silent about the second manifestation of hardship characterised by a substantial decrease in the value of performance received by one party, as considered in Article 6.2.2 (Definition of hardship) PICC. Is this covered then?

Finally, only the party who has not agreed to bear the risk may trigger the application of this article. This condition appears in Article 6.2.2 (Definition of hardship) PICC that provides that, in addition to other requirements, "*(d) the risk to the events was not assumed by the disadvantaged party*." French courts already consider the contractual or statutory allocation of the relevant risks having regard to all the circumstances of the specific case. This is an important qualifier as French law[105] like German law and even English law hold the party enduring the hardship to its word if the contract was one which was highly speculative in the first place.[106] In a fairly recent decision,[107] the *Cour de Cassation* held that the appellate court had failed to ascertain whether the increase in the cost of raw materials that the seller complained of amounted to abnormal fluctuations in the relevant market. The Court of Appeal had held that the seller

> assumed the risk that the performance of its obligation would become more onerous.

It did not consider if the increase in the cost of raw materials exceeded "the normal risks of increase" that the seller bore.[108] It concluded that the seller could not prove that the price increases it suffered amounted to hardship and, even if it had been able to do so, it was not allowed to suspend performance pursuant to the PICC. The risk that needs to be considered is the risk to the changed circumstances—i.e. the risk of abnormal price fluctuations. If this case was to be decided under the new Article 1195 CC, it is likely that the courts would reach the same conclusion as

---

[104] See *Société Dupiré Invicta Industrie v Société Gabo*, Cass. Com. 17 Febr 2015 (non published). For a discussion of the use of the PICC to interpret hardship claims under the CISG, see Ferrari et al. (2017). See also *Scafom International BV v Lorraine Tubes S.A.S*, Belgiam Cass. Com 19 June 2009, available in English at http://cisgw3.law.pace.edu/cases/090619b1.html. This case has been subject to extensive comments in Pédamon and Chuah (2013).

[105] *Société Romay AG v. SARL Behr France*, Cass. Civ. 30 June 2004, RTDC 2004.845, obs. Delebecque; Pan. 2004.2281, obs. Witz. See translation available at http://cisgw3.law.pace.edu/cases/040630f1.html:

> As a professional who is familiar with the practices of international trade, it was for [Buyer] to provide contractual mechanisms of guarantee or revision of contract. (...) (I)n the absence of such provisions, it was for [Buyer] to bear the risk of non-performance without being able to benefit from the provisions of Article 79 CISG (...).

[106] The *Oberlandesgericht* Hamburg (28 Feb 1997, No 167, CISG-online 261 cited by Schwenzer (2008), p. 715, did not exempt a seller from liability under Article 79 of the CISG although the market price for the goods, iron molybdenum, from China, had risen by 300%. The Court reasoned that the sector was notorious for price fluctuations and that that fact was known to the parties. As such, a higher threshold must be applied as to what constitutes hardship. See Pédamon and Chuah (2013), p. 30.

[107] Cass. Com. 17 Febr 2015, No 1501, available at http://www.cisg.fr/decision.html?lang=fr.

[108] Ibid, p. 2.

the conditions of application are similar. Would the effects of hardship be the same then?

5.2 *The Effects of the New Article 1195 of the Civil Code: Contractual Solutions First, Judicial Recourse Last*

In terms of consequences, Article 1195 CC reaffirms a preference already established by the courts that contractual solutions are preferable to judicial ones.[109] By contract, in German law, §313(1) BGB gives an explicit right to the aggrieved party to ask for the contract to be adapted (*Anspruch auf Anpassung des Vertrags*) since

> adaptation may be claimed in so far as (…) it cannot be reasonably expected that a party should continue to be bound by the contract in its unaltered form.[110]

It is however quite unclear whether § 313 BGB gives rise to a right of renegotiation. The majority view is that § 313(1) BGB merely gives the aggrieved party the right to ask the court to adapt the contract; it does not require renegotiation of the contract.[111] Once judicial proceedings have commenced, it is open to the court to discuss with the parties how to adapt the contract, and in the last resort, revise the terms of the contract. It is important to note that this judicial ability has not been used in commercial contracts recently. This contrast with Article 1195 CC, which insists on the right to request a renegotiation from the other party with a view of finding, within a reasonable time, a common solution. There is no obligation to renegotiate but only a right to request a renegotiation. This departs from previous case law that had emerged in favour of an obligation to renegotiate.[112] The other party can refuse to take part in any renegotiation, but that would be to its detriment as the affected party could request that the contract be terminated or revised by the judge, as provided for in the article. The incentive to renegotiate, or at least to engage with each other, is strong but that does not mean that the parties have to reach an agreement either.[113] In any case, this has to be done in good faith,[114] so that the request to renegotiate is not a purely tactical manoeuvre and, once the request

[109] Aynès (2005), No 30.

[110] For a discussion of the right to adapt the contract in German law, see Pédamon and Chuah (2013), p. 30.

[111] For a discussion of the minority view, following a decision dated 30 Sept 2011 that held that "the right (of the aggrieved party) to the adaptation of the contract obliges the other party to cooperate to this adaptation," see Pédamon and Chuah (2013), p. 30.

[112] For a discussion on the emergence of an obligation to renegotiate in French law, Pédamon and Chuah (2013) pp. 37–48.

[113] This duty to renegotiate is also being discussed in Italy and the Netherlands as for the time being, the statutory provisions in these countries do not provide for one. In Germany, in a decision of 30 September 2011, the *Bundesgerichtshof* held that "the right (of the affected party) to the adaptation of the contract obliges the other party to cooperate to this adaptation."

[114] See supra for a discussion of good faith.

has been made, both parties must act in a constructive manner, as explained in the Comments under Article 6.2.3 (Effects of hardship) PICC. However, in a recent French decision, the seller was unable to prove that the buyer had violated the principle of good faith when it failed to renegotiate the price as it postponed meetings to discuss the situation.[115]

Despite the excessive cost, but in order to discourage fraudulent claims and opportunistic behaviour, the affected party must continue to perform the terms of the contract during the renegotiation. The same requirement appears in Article 6.2.3 (Effects of hardship) PICC that '*(t)he request for renegotiation does not in itself entitle the disadvantaged party to withhold performance.*' How can this be achieved as performance of the contract as originally concluded has become financially '*excessively onerous*'? The obligation to perform in these conditions could however lead to a *significant imbalance* of the rights and obligations of the parties to the contract (if it relates to a non-negotiable pre-determined term in a standard form contract).[116] It could also be a breach of good faith and equity pursuant to Article 1194 CC if the conduct of one party is excessive,[117] but this might be difficult to prove.

Upon rejection or failure to reach an agreement, the parties may agree to either terminate the contract, or jointly ask the judge to set about its adaptation. This illustrates the legislator's objectives that the parties find a common solution—either to renegotiate or terminate the contract—for their own sake as the exercise of party autonomy. Either option is available to the parties, and terminating the contract instead of renegotiating might be the best commercial solution for them.

As the ultimate solution, however, in the absence of agreement within a *reasonable* period, the judge may, upon the request of one party only, revise the contract or terminate it, as from a date and on the terms that the judge determines. It is only then that the court is entitled to step in when the parties have failed to reach an agreement. It is not clear which agreement the legislator is referring to, but it is likely that it is only once the parties have not been able to agree to either terminate or request the judge to adapt the contract after a 'reasonable period of time', that the judge may be able to revise or terminate it. French courts, as German courts, might be reluctant to adapt the terms of the contract unless there is a hardship clause in the contract.[118] In that case, courts give effect to the contractual term.

It is important to note that Article 1195 CC is not a mandatory provision, so parties may define their own terms relating to hardship. In practice, commercial parties commonly insert price variation clauses aimed at adjusting prices when there are sudden and unexpected market fluctuations, material adverse change (MAC) clauses

[115] Cass. Com. 17 Febr 2015, No 1501, available at http://www.cisg.fr/decision.html?lang=fr.

[116] See supra for a discussion of unfair contract terms.

[117] Article 1194 CC—'*Contracts create obligations not only in relation to what they expressly provide, but also to all the consequences which deride from equity, practice or legislation.*'

[118] In *Scafom International BV v Lorraine Tubes S.A.S.*, the court of first instance noted the absence of such clause. In an Italian case, *Ravennavi S.P.A. v Handitankers*, 19 May 2011, the Ravenna court also noticed the failure of the parties to insert a hardship clause.

or even general hardship clauses. These clauses can be quite extensive and spell out the procedure that needs to be followed to reach a satisfactory outcome. They seek to adapt the terms of the contract automatically if certain events occur. More generally, since Article 1195 CC expressly states that it does not apply to a party who has assumed the relevant risk, parties to most commercial contracts may include language specifically defining the 'risk of hardship' and allocating this risk between the parties contractually. If the parties stay silent however, the new provisions may apply as the fall-back position. In the *Scafom* and the *Société Dupire Invicta Industri* cases, some courts held the absence of such clause against the aggrieved party. Pursuant to the spirit of Article 1195 CC, the incentive is that the parties find a contractual solution, or at least reach an amicable outcome to changed circumstances, so as to avoid judicial intervention. The judge is the ultimate recourse where the dissension between the parties is such that any form of collaboration is not possible. Until now French judges have been extremely reluctant to step into the contract and even more so to revise the contract. They would rather see themselves as assisting parties in their contractual ventures. In that sense, Article 1195 CC reflects a more realistic and pragmatic vision of contract law.

6 Conclusion

The new French contract applies as the common law of contract law, or the default law relating to contract, whatever the classification—civil or commercial—of the contract. Intrinsically it has an impact on commercial law. As this Chapter has demonstrated through the provisions relating to good faith, unfair contract terms and hardship, the commercial and civil law provisions either complement each other or overlap, or even clash. Although the principle *specialia generalibus derogant* enshrined in Article 1105 of the Civil Code might help to discern which conflicting rule should apply, it is unlikely to be enough, so the judge with whom the claim has been lodged will have to decide first on this matter.

In keeping with the new culture of consensus that the *Ordonnance* has instilled in the law of contract, and the importance given to contractual clauses, there is now a greater incentive for commercial parties to insert clear and precise terms into their contracts in which they explain and contextualise their rights and obligations. With the parties taking more responsibility for their contractual relationship, the French judge is then left to play the ultimate, residual, role as overseer of the fair performance of the contract.

References

Aynès L (2005) L'imprévision en droit privé. Rev Jur Com 397
Behar-Touchais M (2015) Un déséquilibre à deux vitesses ? La Semaine Juridique (21):603

Bell J, Boyron S, Whittaker S (2008) Principles of French law, 2nd edn. Oxford University Press, Oxford
Bicheron F (2015) N'abusons pas de la clause abusive. Gaz Pal 119–120:24
Boffa R (2015) Juste cause (et injuste clause). Brèves remarques sur le projet de réforme du droit des contrats. D. 335
Cacciaguidi-Fady and Wagner (2006) Searching for clarity, vol 37. Peter Lang Publishing, Berne, pp 19–32
Campbell D (2014) Good faith and the ubiquity of the 'Relational' contract. Modern Law Rev 77(3):475–492
Catala P (2006) Avant-Projet de Réforme du Droit des Obligations (Art 1101 à 1386 du Code Civil) et du Droit de la Prescription (Art 2234 à 2281 du Code Civil). Paris, Documentation française, 2006. Translation available at http://www.justice.gouv.fr/art_pix/rapportcatatla0905-anglais.pdf
Chantepie G, Dissaux N (2016) Rapport introductif. RDC, 3 Sept 2016, p 575
Chantepie G, Latina M (2016) La réforme du droit des obligations. D. 2016
Chassagnard-Pinet S (2016) Le vocabulaire. RDC, 3 Sept 2016, p 583
Chazal J-P (2003) Les nouveaux devoirs des contractants. Est-on allé trop loin? in La nouvelle crise du contrat. Dalloz, Thèmes et commentaires, 99–133, spéc 114 et seq
Collins H (2008) Standard contract terms in Europe: a basis and a challenge to European contract law. Wolters Kluwer
Cornu G (2016) Vocabulaire juridique. Association Henri Capitant. PUF, Quadrige
Djankov S, McLiesh C (2004) Doing business in 2004: understanding regulation. The World Bank, Oxford University Press 217, Report No 27147
Ferrari F, Gillette CL, Torsello M, Walt SD (2017) The inappropriate use of the PICC to interpret hardship claims under the CISG. IHR 3:97–102
Fouillée A (1880) La science sociale contemporaine. Paris
Francois CL (2016) Application dans le temps et incidence sur la jurisprudence antérieure de l'ordonnance de réforme du droit des contrats. D. 2016, chron. pp 506–509
Latina M (2016) Apprécier la Réforme. RDC, 3 Sept 2016
Leggatt J (2016) Contractual duties of good faith. Lecture to the Commercial Bar Association on 18 October 2016. https://www.judiciary.gov.uk/wp-content/uploads/2016/10/mr-justice-leggatt-lecture-contractual-duties-of-faith.pdf. Accessed 1 Oct 2017
Mazeaud D (1999) Loyauté, solidarité, fraternité: la nouvelle devise contractuelle ? in Mélanges Fr. Terré. Dalloz, PUF, Litec, p 603, No 6
Mazeaud D (2003) Le nouvel ordre contractuel. RDC 2003, p 295
Mekki M (2016a) Incidences de la réforme du droit des obligations sur le droit des sociétés, II. Les Clauses. Rev Soc, 563
Mekki M (2016b) The general principles of contract law in the "Ordonnance" on the reform of contract law. La Law Rev 76:4
Mestre J (1986) D'une exigence de bonne foi à un esprit de collaboration. RTD civ. 1986, p 101
Pédamon C, Chuah J (2013) Hardship in transnational commercial contracts, A critique of legal, judicial and contractual remedies. Paris, Netherlands
Pédamon M, Kenfack H (2015) Droit Commercial, 4th edn. Dalloz, France
Picod Y (1988) Le devoir de loyauté dans l'exécution du contrat. JCP 1988, I, 3318
Rapport au Président de la République relatif à l'Ordonnance no 2016-131 du 10 février 2016 portant réforme du droit des contrats, du régime général et de la preuve des obligations (2016) JO of 11 February 2016
Revet T (2015) Le projet de réforme et les contrats structurellement déséquilibrés. D. 2015. 1217
Rousseau (1762) Of the Social Contract
Schwenzer I (2008) Force majeure and hardship in international sale contracts. Vic Univ Wellingt Law Rev 39:709
Spitz J-F (2007) Qui dit contractuel dit juste: quelques remarques sur une formule d'Alfred Fouillée. RTD civ. 2007, 281

Stoffel-Munck Ph (2000) L'abus dans le contrat. Essai d'une théorie. Bibliothèque de droit privé, Tome 337. LGDJ, France

Terré F (2008) Pour une réforme du droit des contrats. Dalloz, France

Teubner G (1998) Legal irritants: good faith in British law or how unifying law ends up in new divergences. Modern Law Rev 61(1):11–32

The Withdrawal of the Common European Sales Law Proposal and the European Commission Proposal on Certain Aspects Concerning Contracts for the Online and Other Distance Sales of Goods

Despina Anagnostopoulou

Contents

D. Anagnostopoulou (✉)
Jean Monnet Centre of Excellence "Research on Crucial Issues of European Integration",
University of Macedonia, Thessaloniki, Greece
e-mail: danag@uom.gr

M. Heidemann, J. Lee (eds.), *The Future of the Commercial Contract in Scholarship and Law Reform*, https://doi.org/10.1007/978-3-319-95969-6_6

Abstract The chapter examines the reasons why the 2011 European Commission Proposal on Common European Sales Law (CESL) was so important for the formation of the contract at European level, and the reasons why it was withdrawn by the European Commission. It then focuses on the 2015 Online Sales of Goods (OSG) Proposal and demonstrates its drawbacks and its innovations in comparison with the CESL proposal and the existing European Union (EU) consumer legislation. In both cases, the reactions of the Member States and EU Institutions are discussed in order to show that the time has not come for a comprehensive body of an EU contract law, covering the full cycle of a contract. The chapter explains the importance of the Digital Single Market and the holistic approach taken by the European Commission in order to attain it. It presents the legal mosaic that may be created in comparison e.g. with the Consumer Sales Directive 1999/44/EC (CSD) and the Consumer Rights Directive 2011/83/EU (CRD), the legal fragmentation of the markets and the role of the EU principle of subsidiarity. It analyses the innovative provisions of the draft OSG proposal and demonstrates their advantages and disadvantages. The author believes that flexibility is necessary during the final negotiation of the OSG text, so that the "play of 20 questions" stop and that this Directive of total harmonisation in most aspects of the formation of the consumer contract finally be adopted. Minimum harmonisation in one or two fundamental issues that otherwise would lower the level of consumer protection in many Member States, may be used in combination with a data basis in the e-justice portal of the European Commission as a less harmful measure. The author concludes that certain "compensating to the consumer" provisions of the proposal must be amended to strike a fair balance between the interests of the seller and the consumer, since the US experience has shown that the motivation of the seller is also very important for the growth in e-commerce. Last but not least, the author criticizes the attempted fragmentation of the contract types in several categories according to the method of sale. The reactions of the stakeholders and the EU institutions were so strong that the European Commission amended its OSG proposal on 31st October 2017, and extended the provisions of the initial OSG proposal to all types of consumer contracts, face-to-face and online ones, repealing Directive 1999/44/EC and establishing a true "CSD+" (word used by Professor H. Beale) which covers the majority of B2C transactions for the sale of goods.

1 The Problem That the CESL Proposal Aimed to Solve

The formation of a European Union (EU) Contract Law occurs in bits and pieces. It is usually national laws that determine the form that a contract takes and the rights and obligations of the contracting parties. However, since 1979 the European Union has gradually adopted Directives that aimed to harmonise certain aspects of contract law in order to protect consumers in the Common Market and, since 1987, in the

Internal Market. These Directives aimed however, at minimum harmonisation, allowing Member States to adopt stricter measures in favour of consumer protection.[1] This was a piecemeal and gradual approach over many years,[2] leading to the prominent example of the Consumer Sales Directive 1999/44/EC (CSD).[3] The effort to adopt a full harmonisation Directive on consumer rights met the resistance of the Member States and the consumer organisations and led to the adoption of the Directive 2011/83/EC (CRD),[4] which applies mainly to distance and off-premises contracts but governs only pre-contractual information,[5] time of delivery and withdrawal rights of the consumers.[6]

Legal instruments of the emerging EU private international law aimed at favouring the consumer's interests in the EU in cross-border disputes regarding the jurisdiction of national courts and the determination of applicable law. The Brussels Convention on Jurisdiction and the Enforcement of Judgments in Civil and Commercial Matters (1968) and its replacing and repealing EU Regulations[7] aimed at protecting the weaker party and provided that a consumer may bring proceedings against the seller either in the courts of the Member State in which the seller is domiciled or in the courts for the place where the consumer is domiciled.[8] The 1980 Rome Convention Convention on the Law Applicable to Contractual Obligations provided that the applicable law in consumer contracts is that of the Member State of habitual residence of the consumer. This provision was strengthened by Regulation (EC) 593/2008 (Rome I), which clearly states that when a trader deals with a consumer in the consumer's Member State of habitual residence or directs its activities towards that State, the consumer is protected by the

[1] See for example Directive 85/577/EEC of 20 December 1985 to protect the consumer in respect of contracts negotiated away from business premises; Directive 97/7/EC of the European Parliament and of the Council of 20 May 1997 on the protection of consumers in respect of distance contracts; and Directive 93/13/EEC of 5 April 1993 on unfair terms in consumer contracts, O.J. L95/29 (21 April 1993).

[2] Twigg-Flesner (2016), p. 4.

[3] Directive 1999/44/EC of the European Parliament and the Council of 25 May 1999 on certain aspects of the sale of consumer goods and associated guarantees, O.J. L171/12 (7 July 1999).

[4] European Commission (2014).

[5] Art 6 h-k, 7 (3), 8(4) and 8(8) of the Consumer Rights Directive 2011/83/EC. See Watson (2016), p. 252.

[6] Beale (2016), p. 5.

[7] Council Regulation (EC) No 44/2001 of 22 December 2000 on jurisdiction and the recognition and enforcement of judgments in civil and commercial matters, O.J. L12/1 (16 Jan 2001), Preamble para 13 and Art 16 para 1. Repealed by Regulation (EU) No 1215/2012 of the European Parliament and of the Council of 12 December 2012 on jurisdiction and the recognition and enforcement of judgments in civil and commercial matters, O.J. L351/1 (20 Dec 2012), Preamble para 14, 18–19, Art 18 para 1.

[8] Magnus and Mankowski (2007), p. 312; Anagnostopoulou (2012), pp. 627 ff.

mandatory rules of that State's law.[9] These consumer protective provisions, however, may have a deterring effect on traders who do not want to confront the differences between the laws of the Member States, obstructing them from engaging in e-commerce.[10]

In the framework of its 2010 Digital Agenda and in order to promote e-commerce,[11] in 2011 the European Commission submitted a proposal for a Regulation in order to establish a uniform but optional Common European Sales Law (CESL).[12] The proposal aimed to create a second[13] (not 28th) uniform optional contract law regime,[14] co-existing with the national contract laws, which the consumer would choose by e.g. clicking a "blue button".[15] The proposal aimed to approximate the national contract laws of the Member States not by requiring amendments to the first national contract-law regime, but by creating a second optional contract-law regime for cross-border contracts within its scope. It was like an optional EU Civil Code that would assist Small and Medium Enterprises (SMEs)[16] to use only one set of rules for all countries for cross-border sales.

The scope of the CESL proposal included Business to Business (B2B) (only for SMEs) and Business to Consumers (B2C) transactions as well as digital content supply. Its Annex contained 183 articles on general principles of contract law, pre-contractual duties for the seller to provide information; the conclusion of a contract including formal requirements; the right of withdrawal and its consequences; avoidance of the contract as a result of mistake, fraud, threat or unfair exploitation and the consequences of such avoidance; rules of interpretation of the contract content and effects; the assessment and the effects of unfairness of contract terms; the rights and obligations of the parties; remedies for non-performance; restitution after avoidance or termination or in the case of a non-binding contract; prescription and preclusion of rights; supplementary common rules on damages for loss; interest for late payment; sanctions available in the event of breach of the obligations and duties arising under its application etc.

---

[9] Regulation (EC) No 593/2008 of the European Parliament and of the Council of 17 June 2008 on the law applicable to contractual obligations, O.J. L177/6 (4 July 2008), Preamble paras 23–25 and Art 6 para 2. Anagnostopoulou (2012), pp. 167 ff. For the meaning of the concept "direct its activities" see Court of Justice of the EU, Case C-190/11, *Mühlleitner,* ECLI:EU:C:2012:542. See Beale (2016), p. 5.

[10] Beale (2016), p. 1.

[11] Anagnostopoulou (2013a), pp. 121 ff.

[12] European Commission (2011).

[13] COM (2011) 635 at p. 8.

[14] Basedow (2011), pp. 25–37.

[15] Schulte-Nölke (2007, 2011).

[16] Recommendation 2003/361 of the Commission concerning the definition of micro, small and medium-sized enterprises, O.J. L124/36 (20 May 2003).

The CESL was intended to become an optional European Civil Code, based on the multiannual work of the Ole Lando Commission and the Principles of European Contract Law (PECL),[17] inspired by the UNIDROIT Principles[18] and the 1980 UN Convention of International Sales of Goods (CISG).[19] CESL was in line with the European Commission proposals since 2001[20] and was based on the work for the Draft Common Frame of Reference.[21] What was most important in CESL was that it provided for an optional uniform EU contract law, discussed by academics for years, covering the full cycle of a contract.[22]

The proposed CESL optional instrument was also envisaged in the Digital Agenda of the European Commission Strategy "Europe 2020" and was included under the Digital Single Market pillar thereof.[23] However the CESL proposal was not welcomed:

The National Parliaments of the EU Member States were the first to resist the CESL proposal. According to the Protocol no 2 attached to the Lisbon Treaty (2009), all EU legislative proposals have first to be reviewed by the National Parliaments, but only for their conformity with the principles of subsidiarity and proportionality, before being debated in the Council and the European Parliament that both have to agree on the proposal's content.[24] Therefore, the National Parliaments had to debate and decide in 8 weeks' time whether the Commission proposal infringed the principle of subsidiarity and proportionality.[25] Indeed, the National Parliaments from Austria, Belgium, Bulgaria, Germany and United Kingdom objected to the legislative proposal and adopted reasoned opinions that the CESL proposal infringed the principles of subsidiarity and proportionality. The

---

[17] Lando and Beale (2000, 2003).

[18] See http://www.unidroit.org/english/principles/contracts/main.htm.

[19] Adopted in 11 April 1980 and entered into force on 1 January 1988 with 89 Contracting Parties in 2018. In the EU, only the United Kingdom, Ireland, Portugal and Malta have not signed CISG.

[20] European Commission (2001) and European Commission (2003). The latter concluded in the aim of identifying areas in which the diversity of national legislation in the field of contract law may undermine the proper functioning of the internal market and the uniform application of Community law (p. 45).

[21] Study Group on a European Civil Code/Research Group on EC Private Law (2009).

[22] European Commission (2011) Preamble of the CESL Proposal COM(2011) 635, para. 6.

[23] European Commission (2010). Action 13: Complementing the Consumer Rights Directive, Digital Agenda for Europe, at <http://ec.europa.eu/information_society/newsroom/cf/fiche-dae.cfm?action_id=171&pillar_id=43&action=Action%2013%3A%20Complementing%20the%20Consumer%20Rights%20Directive>.

[24] Protocol no 2 on the Application of the Principles of Subsidiarity and Proportionality attached to the Treaty establishing the European Union (Treaty of Lisbon) put into effect in December 2009.

[25] According to Art 5 para 3 of the Treaty establishing the EU, "Under the principle of subsidiarity, in areas which do not fall within its exclusive competence, the Union shall act only if and insofar as the objectives of the proposed action cannot be sufficiently achieved by the Member States, either at central level or at regional and local level, but can rather, by reason of the scale or effects of the proposed action, be better achieved at Union level." Thus the principle of subsidiarity seeks to safeguard the ability of the Member States to take decisions and action.

House of Commons of the United Kingdom highlighted that through the introduction of the optional CESL, national consumer protection also becomes optional; the Austrian Federal Council regarded it as incompatible e.g. because it reopened issues on which there was no consensus; the Bulgarian National Assembly regarded it as disproportionate; and the German *Bundestag* thought it infringed the principle of subsidiarity and increased legal uncertainty.[26]

The European Economic and Social Committee (EESC) welcomed the CESL proposal but questioned subsidiarity and proportionality. The EESC has also raised issues such as the inter-relation between the optional instrument and European private international law, including overriding national mandatory provisions and public policy rules; the protection of SMEs in relation to multinationals; and the need for accompanying measures such as European model contracts.[27]

The discussions in the Council of the European Union, the EU co-legislator, reflected also the national reaction to CESL. Indeed, the Council never finished the first reading, due to the reactions of the same Member States.[28] The first discussion in the Council took place in December 2011 and confirmed that:

> among the aspects of the proposal that require thorough discussion were the personal, material and territorial scope of the proposal, the complexity of linking the proposal with the different national legal systems, the details and consequences of choice of the instrument, the consequences of an invalid choice, the consumer protection rules relating to the choice and the reporting obligations of Member States.[29]

In June 7–8, 2012, the Ministers held an orientation debate in which a divergence of national views emerged, relating to the legal basis of and the actual need for the proposed CESL, as well as its scope. Anyway, there was overall agreement that work had to start on the examination of the substance of the Annex to the proposal and the extent to which the individual parts of the proposal would work towards removing the actual practical obstacles to the internal market.[30] The Council never approved the CESL proposal since "several member states have voiced criticism that the Commission proposal would create an unnecessarily complicated system that would deter stakeholders" from using it, that a less intrusive approach might be more appropriate and that there was considerable scepticism from business and consumer organisations.[31]

---

[26] Facts provided by Grigorova Ilieva (2013).

[27] European Economic and Social Committee (2012). See also Cordero-Moss (2016), p. 487 ff.

[28] See legislative procedure 2011/0284 (COD).

[29] Council of the European Union, Press Release, 3135th Council meeting, Justice and Home Affairs, Brussels, 13–14 December 2011, available at http://europa.eu/rapid/press-release_PRES-11-491_en.htm?locale=en.

[30] European Commission, Press Release, http://europa.eu/rapid/press-release_PRES-12-241_en.htm?locale=en.

[31] Council of the European Union, Note from Presidency to Council, Brussels, June 1, 2012. Doc. 10611/12 JUSTCIV 210 CONSOM 85 CODEC 1496, DG D 2A, CG/BM/dd, p. 4. See also Cygan (2016), pp. 13–16.

In contrast to national reactions, the European Parliament discussed the text in its Committees and approved the CESL proposal it in its first reading in 26 February 2014. Indeed, 416 votes out of 751 were in favour. However, the European Parliament requested several amendments in order to restrict its scope only to B2C distance contracts including, however, online contracts and services provided using the so-called "cloud".[32]

Several academics have approached the CESL proposal with a critical eye: Professor E. Posner emphasized that if the CESL proposal was adopted, transaction costs would rise; while "its consumer protection provisions would make it unattractive for businesses".[33] Professor J. Basedow found that there emerged too many transactions excluded from CESL's scope, not justified by a general market perspective, because of considerations confined to the Internal Market and to consumer protection aims, that rendered the technical implementation of these exclusions defective.[34] Others have claimed incompatibility with the Rome I Regulation 593/2008.[35] Professor E. Arroyo Amayuelas (2016)[36] considered that the CESL proposal added "a further layer of complexity to the system".

In addition, consumer organisations feared that in the end of the legislative process, there would be such a substantial reduction in the consumer *acquis* in order to get the CESL proposal voted in the Council, and that ultimately CESL would lose its optional character and would become a binding European civil code.[37]

After all these reactions, in December 2014 the newly elected European Commission withdrew the proposal and promised a new initiative.[38] In its Political Guidelines for the Next Commission, the Commission president Jean Claude Juncker promised "ambitious legislative steps towards a connected digital single market ... by modernizing and simplifying consumer rules for online and digital purposes".[39] In the words of Professor J. Smits,[40] "the demise of CESL left the European private law community uncertain about the future of European contract law".

---

[32] See legislative procedure 2011/0284 (COD)—26.2.2014 Text adopted by Parliament, 1st reading/single reading.

[33] Posner (2012).

[34] Basedow (2012) An EU law for cross-border sales only – its meaning and implications in open markets, Max Planck Private Law Research Paper No. 12/20, pp. 43–44.

[35] Regulation (EC) No 593/2008 of the European Parliament and of the Council of 17 June 2008 on the law applicable to contractual obligations, O.J. L177/6 (4 July 2008). Fleischer (2012), pp. 235–252. See further arguments in Anagnostopoulou (2013b), pp. 293 ff.

[36] Arroyo Amayuelas (2016), p. 485.

[37] Beale (2016), p. 5.

[38] Király (2015). pp. 31–32.

[39] Mańko (2016), p. 2.

[40] Smits (2016b), p. 2.

2 The New 2015 Proposals and the Changed Context

On May 6, 2015, the European Commission announced the Digital Single Market Strategy.[41] It included a legislative initiative for better access for consumers and businesses to online goods and services across Europe".[42] Indeed, on December 9, 2015 the European Commission submitted a package of proposals with common objectives, composed of:

(a) a Communication on "Digital contracts for Europe - Unleashing the potential of e-commerce"[43];
(b) a proposal of a Directive "on certain aspects concerning contracts for the supply of digital content", included in its Communication COM(2015) 634 (hereafter called also DCD)[44]; and
(c) a proposal of a Directive "on certain aspects concerning contracts for the online and other distance sales of goods" included in its Communication COM(2015) 635 (hereafter called also OSG).[45]

The new proposals substitute the optional and comprehensive CESL proposal with total harmonisation Directives. They have the same aim with CESL, namely to eliminate the most important obstacles in relation with the divergence in national contract laws in cross-border online sales and reduce the resulting legal uncertainty and additional costs paid by businesses.[46]

The European Commission had examined five policy alternatives and opted for a directive of full harmonisation in order to reduce contract-law related costs for traders and untap the potential of e-commerce.[47] The OSG and DCD proposals were presented as building on a number of amendments made by the European Parliament in its first reading concerning the CESL proposal, e.g. the restriction of its scope to online and other distance sales of goods.[48]

In order to justify its proposals, the European Commission established that in 2015, the EU traders were hindered from selling online in other Member States because of differences in national contract law rules (39% of EU retailers selling online) and the cost of cross-border dispute resolution (49% of EU retailers selling

[41] European Commission (2015a), pp. 4–5.

[42] Mańko (2016), p. 2.

[43] European Commission (2015c).

[44] European Commission (2015d).

[45] European Commission (2015e).

[46] Council of the European Union, Presidency Progress Report no 6150/16 JUSTCIV 17 CONSOM 30 DIGIT 10 AUDIO 12 CODEC 165, available at: http://data.consilium.europa.eu/doc/document/st-6150-2016-init/en/pdf.

[47] See European Commission (2015c, f).

[48] Beale (2016).

online).[49] On the other hand, it has been found that, in 2015, 65% of EU citizens were already shopping online, but most of them opting for local traders.[50] These figures demonstrated to all involved in the legislative procedure the dynamic of e-commerce.

Both proposed legal instruments were part of the EU strategy for a Digital Single Market (DSM) in Europe and aimed at the faster development of the DSM in the interest of both consumers and businesses. The Digital Single Market Strategy (6 May 2015) aims to abolish all main obstacles to the functioning of the Digital Single Market.[51] The European Commission has already presented proposals for its attainment:

- the draft Directive on the role of platforms[52];
- the European Cloud Initiative that would help unlock the power of big data[53];
- the draft Directives aiming to reduce the cost related to the Value Added Tax (VAT) procedures on cross-border e-sales in several Member States[54];
- the draft Regulation aiming to reduce the high cost of cross-border parcel delivery[55];
- the possibility of solving consumer disputes online through the Online Dispute Resolution Platform (ODR) which was put into effect in 2016[56];
- the review of the Consumer Protection Co-operation Regulation (EC) 2003/2004 on cooperation between national authorities responsible for the enforcement of consumer protection laws[57]; and
- the revised online-friendly Small Claims Regulation.[58]

[49] See Flash Eurobarometer 396 "Retailers' attitudes towards cross-border trade and consumer protection" (2015) and Flash Eurobarometer 413 "Companies engaged in online activities" (2015) Breakdown by sector (B2C only), both cited by European Commission (2015e), p. 2.

[50] Europe's Digital Progress Report 2016—Use of internet, p. 4.

[51] European Commission, Commission Staff Working Document Impact Assessment, Accompanying the document proposals for directives of the European Parliament and of the Council (1) on certain aspects concerning contracts for the supply of digital content and (2) on certain aspects concerning contracts for the online and other distance sales of goods, SWD(2015) 274 final/2, 18 Dec 2015, p. 18. http://data.consilium.europa.eu/doc/document/ST-15251-2015-ADD-1-REV-1/en/pdf.

[52] European Commission (2016c).

[53] European Commission (2016a)

[54] European Commission (2016d).

[55] European Commission (2016b).

[56] Directive 2013/11/EU of the European Parliament and of the Council of 21 May 2013 on alternative dispute resolution for consumer disputes and amending Regulation (EC) No 2006/2004 and Directive 2009/22/EC, O.J. L165/63 (18 June 2013).

[57] European Commission, Proposal for a Regulation of the European Parliament and of the Council on cooperation between national authorities responsible for the enforcement of consumer protection laws, COM(2016) 283 final, 25 May 2016.

[58] Regulation (EU) 2015/2421 of the European Parliament and of the Council of 16 December 2015 amending Regulation (EC) No 861/2007 establishing a European Small Claims Procedure and Regulation (EC) No 1896/2006 creating a European order for payment procedure, entered into force on July 14, 2017.

The above initiatives constitute a holistic approach for the attainment of the Digital Single Market and will "optimise the effects of the fully harmonised substantive rules put forward in the draft Directives" on digital content and online and distance sales.[59]

However, the proposed Directives on online sales of tangible goods and digital content were met with criticism. First, the proposals were quite unexpected since the European Commission had promised (just) a modification of the existing CESL proposal.[60] Second, by contrast to the CESL proposal, the proposed legal acts were neither optional nor a comprehensive set of rules[61] i.e. covering the full cycle of a contract. Instead, they contain a targeted, fully harmonised set of specific rules.[62] Third, using total harmonisation Directives was like resurrecting an approach which was disliked by the Member States and hampered the adoption of the Consumer Rights Directive 2011/83/EU (CRD) in 2011.[63] Fourth, a full harmonisation Directive would oblige Member States in which there are already rules of higher level of consumer protection allowed e.g. by the Consumer Sales Directive 1999/44/EC (CSD) to lower their standards. The fact that the OSG proposal provides for full harmonisation of rules already foreseen as minimum harmonisation provisions in CSD and CRD is upsetting Member States which have already adopted a higher level of protection and will have to lower it to the common uniform standard only for cross-border online sales of tangible goods to consumers.[64] An example of higher consumer protection is the free choice of the remedy granted by six Member States to their consumers in case of non-conformity of the sold product to the e-contract, instead of the proposed obligatory two-step system obliging the consumers to allow first the seller to repair or replace the product and if not, to ask for the termination of the contract.[65] Another example is the obligatory reduction of the seller's liability period (the period in which a fault has to appear before a consumer can make a claim) to 2 years, when in the UK the seller is liable for 6 years.[66] Fifth, the 2015 proposals fragmented the 2011 proposal of a Regulation on CESL into two Directives, setting divergent rules sometimes. Sixth, the OSG proposal restricted harmonisation to only consumer contracts (B2C) and regulated only selective aspects.[67]

---

[59] European Commission, Commission Staff Working Document, Impact Assessment Accompanying the document Proposals for Directives of the European Parliament and of the Council (1) on certain aspects concerning contracts for the supply of digital content and (2) on certain aspects concerning contracts for the online and other distance sales of goods, SWD/2015/0274 final/2, p. 18.

[60] Arroyo Amayelas (2016), p. 486.

[61] European Commission (2015d), p. 2.

[62] European Commission (2015c), p. 6.

[63] Twigg-Flesner (2016), p. 9.

[64] Smits (2016b), pp. 2–3.

[65] See Sect. 4.2 below.

[66] UK Parliament, point 5.39.

[67] Beale (2016), p. 7.

2.1 The Digital Content Directive (DCD): A Short Presentation

The definition of digital content is very important and is left deliberately broad in order to encompass all types of digital content.[68] Digital content supply occurs when consumers e.g. buy music, films, e-books or applications, computer programs, digital games, cloud services and social media.[69] The draft DCD extended the definition of "digital content" to cover digital services and for the first time included contracts for cloud computing and social media. The digital content is supplied in exchange for a price or other counter-performance than money (Art 6). The proposed full harmonisation Directive on Digital Content will apply to both domestic and cross-border contracts. The draft DCD provides for:

- the time in which digital content must be supplied (Art 4);
- the definition of the conformity of the digital content to the contract (Art 5);
- the remedies for delay and non-conformity in a hierarchical order, from repair to termination of the contract in serious cases (Art 12);
- the right of the consumer to retain back his data which he has supplied or the trader has kept after the contract has been terminated (Art 13);
- the trader's right to modify digital content that is to be supplied over a period of time and the consumer's rights to terminate the contract if the consumer is not satisfied with the modification (Art 15).[70]

In addition, the draft DCD aims to strengthen the enforcement of the provisions of the Directive by obliging the Member States to grant rights to certain bodies to take action before the national courts, such as national bodies, consumer organisations, or professional organisations (Art 18).

The DCD proposal is quite likely to be adopted,[71] since only the Netherlands and the UK have recently adopted relevant legislation which is not as much articulated as the proposed rules.[72] However, its provisions for the supply of digital content "in exchange for data as counter-performance"[73] other than money (in the form of personal data or any other data) has triggered the response of the European Data Protection Supervisor (EDPS) after the request of the Council of

[68] European Commission (2015d), p. 11.

[69] Smits (2016b), p. 2.

[70] Beale (2016), p. 9.

[71] Beale, p. 8. Smits (2016b), p. 3.

[72] European Commission (2015d), p. 3.

[73] See Article 3 of the draft DCD "This Directive shall apply to any contract ....and in exchange, a price is to be paid or the consumer actively provides counter-performance other than money in the form of personal data or any other data".

the European Union. In his Opinion, dated 27 June 2017,[74] the EDPS warned against:

> "any new provision introducing the idea that people can pay with their data the same way as they do with money. Fundamental rights such as the right to the protection of personal data cannot be reduced to simple consumer interests, and personal data cannot be considered as a mere commodity" ... "such rules will overlap with the recently adopted data protection framework (the 'GDPR') and the new e-Privacy legislation under discussion" as well cause "confusion as to the precise function of the data in a given transaction".

According to the EDPS, the DCD will upset the careful balance negotiated by the EU legislator on data protection rules and will put at risk the coherence of the Digital Single Market.

Following this Opinion, and taking into account that many National Parliaments objected to the same provision,[75] no one can be certain of the successful adoption of the draft DCD, at least in the form proposed, despite the non-existence of relevant specific legislation in 26 Member States.

2.2 *What Does the Online Sales of Goods (OSG) Proposal Provide for?*

The scope of application of the 2015 OSG proposal is less broad than the scope of the 2011 CESL proposal since the draft OSG will not apply:

- to Business to Business (B2B) transactions or Business to SMEs;
- to the sale of physical carriers such as DVDs and CDs incorporating digital content in such a way that the goods function only as a carrier of the digital content and
- to distance contracts for provision of services.[76]

---

[74] Regulation (EU) 2016/679 of the European Parliament and of the Council of 27 April 2016 on the protection of natural persons with regard to the processing of personal data and on the free movement of such data, and repealing Directive 95/46/EC (General Data Protection Regulation), O.J. L119/1 (4 May 2016). In addition, the current Directive 2002/58/EC of the European Parliament and of the Council of 12 July 2002 concerning the processing of personal data and the protection of privacy in the electronic communications sector (Directive on privacy and electronic communications), O.J. L201/37 (31 July 2002) will be repealed by the Proposal for a Regulation of the European Parliament and of the Council concerning the respect for private life and the protection of personal data in electronic communications and repealing Directive 2002/58/EC, COM (2017) 10 final (Regulation on Privacy and Electronic Communications), 10 Jan 2017.

[75] E.g. the Dutch Eersten Kamer der Staten-Generaal, Opinion on the application of the Principles of Subsidiarity and Proportionality, ST 13742 2016 INT—2015/0287 (OLP).

[76] However, it applies to goods like household appliances and toys where the digital content operates as an integral part of the goods (smart television sets). In addition, where a sale contract provides both for the sale of goods and the provision of services this Directive will apply only to the part relating to the sale of goods (mixed contracts). See European Parliament, summary of the proposal, p. 2.

Its scope covers only cross-border Business to Consumers (B2C) sales (Art 1 para 1) and thus coincides partly with the Consumer Sales Directive 1999/44/EC (CSD) and the Consumer Rights Directive 2011/83/EU (CRD) which both cover online sales as well.[77] The only differentiation of the OSG proposal is that it will apply exclusively to online sales and distance contracts. Therefore, what is an online or distance sales contract is an essential criterion for the application of the draft OSG. According to Art 2 para 7 of the draft OSG,[78] this concept requires an organised distance scheme with no simultaneous physical presence of seller and consumer and an exclusive use of one or more means of distance communication, including via internet, up to and including the time at which the contract is concluded until the contract is concluded. However, the consumer is unable to ascertain whether the offer he/she received is part of a broader scheme.[79] In addition, interpretation problems have already arisen with the implementation of the CRD which had included the same concept.[80]

The OSG proposal provides for a full harmonisation:

- of the conformity criteria for the goods;
- of the hierarchy of the remedies, available to consumers;
- of the periods for the reversal of burden of proof, extended from 6 months to 2 years; and
- of the "legal guarantee", i.e. consumer rights vis-à-vis the seller in the case of non-conformity of the goods which exists at the time of delivery.[81]

The OSG proposal deals also with the "commercial guarantee" which is, however, subject to minimum harmonisation only, as in the CSD.[82] The commercial guarantee is offered by the seller or the producer on a voluntary basis, above the standard set out by the legal guarantee, which must be legally binding and provide consumers with certain information.[83]

---

[77] Smits (2016a), p. 7.

[78] The provision duplicates the definition in Art 2 para 7 of CRD 2011/83.

[79] Smits (2016a), p. 7.

[80] European Commission (2017d) p. 6 where the European Commission found difficulties in interpreting some provisions such as "the notion of outside the 'business premises' in off-premises contracts (Art 2 para 8), the distinction between a digital content contract and a contract for paid online services...".

[81] For the distinction between the legal guarantee and the commercial guarantee see European Commission (2007) Communication, on the implementation of Directive 1999/44/EC of the European Parliament and of the Council of 25 May 1999 on certain aspects of the sale of consumer goods and associated guarantees including analysis of the case for introducing direct producers' liability, COM(2007) 210 final, 24 April 2007, pp. 6 and 9.

[82] Mańko (2016), p. 6 and Preamble of the Draft OSG, para. 14.

[83] European Commission (2007), p. 9.

3 A First Evaluation of the Proposal

3.1 *Another Piece of the Mosaic?*

The EU legislation already includes Directives which harmonise substantive consumer contract law, which are not in principle amended by the draft OSG. The relevant consumer *acquis* is consisted of:

- The Directive 1999/44/EC on certain aspects of consumer sales (CSD)[84];
- The Directive 2000/31/EC on certain aspects of e-commerce (E-CD)[85];
- The Directive 2011/83/EU on consumer rights (CRD)[86]; and
- The Directive 93/13/EEC on unfair contract terms.[87]

The draft OSG mostly affects the Directive 1999/44/EC and supplements the other three. In fact, many of the draft OSG provisions have their origin in CSD 1999/44/EC, some come from the CRD 2011/83/EU[88] or the proposal for a Regulation on a Common European Sales Law. So the question is how the draft OSG fits in this mosaic and what new rules it brings to the EU e-consumers.

3.2 *Relationship with CSD 1999/44/EC*

The Directive 1999/44/EC (CSD) "on certain aspects of the sale of consumer goods and associated guarantees" is a minimum harmonisation Directive which applies to all consumer sales transactions: online or offline, at a distance or face-to-face, cross-border or domestic. Its policy choices and rules have strong resemblances to the UN Convention on the International Sales of Goods (CISG), especially Art 35 and 45 CISG.[89] The CSD established the general liability of the seller in case of breach of

[84] See above footnote 4.

[85] Directive 2000/31/EC of the European Parliament and of the Council of 8 June 2000 on certain legal aspects of information society services, in particular electronic commerce, in the Internal Market ('Directive on electronic commerce'), O.J. L178/1 (17 July 2000).

[86] Directive 2011/83/EU of the European Parliament and of the Council of 25 October 2011 on consumer rights, amending Council Directive 93/13/EEC and Directive 1999/44/EC of the European Parliament and of the Council and repealing Council Directive 85/577/EEC and Directive 97/7/EC of the European Parliament and of the Council, O.J. L304/64 (22 Nov 2011).

[87] Council Directive 93/13/EEC of 5 April 1993 on unfair terms in consumer contracts, O.J. L95/29 (21 April 1993). The Directive 93/13/EEC applies to all consumer contracts indistinctly without any exception. It is a minimum harmonisation directive and does not apply to the price and description of goods. It may also be affected by the OSG proposal. Mańko (2016), p. 4.

[88] See Art 2 para 7 and para 14 and Art 18 CRD.

[89] Anagnostopoulou (2012), p. 222. Troiano (2008).

contract according to the CISG model of the breach of contract and non-conformity of the goods to the contractual terms.[90]

The CSD is affected by the OSG proposal since the latter focuses on key rights and remedies that are already set out in CSD, some in an extended way (e.g. the right to cure) and some in a brief manner (e.g. the right of termination).

The European Commission itself declares that the basis for the new OSG rules is the minimum harmonisation rules of Directive 1999/44/EC.[91] In fact, the OSG proposal is a new version of the CSD with certain amendments, added rights[92] and clarifications,[93] which will apply uniformly to all Member States. In the words of Professor H. Beale,[94] the OSG proposal is a "CSD+".

As a version of the CSD, the OSG proposal does not change the criteria for establishing conformity with the contract and requirements for conformity of the goods, i.e. establishing whether the goods are "fit for purpose" and free of fault, as Art 2 para 2 of the CSD 1999/44/EC provides. The OSG proposal follows also the innovative hierarchy introduced by the CSD on the remedies to be chosen by the consumer according to the principle of the primacy of *in natura* performance before the right of price reduction or termination (Art 3 para 3 CSD). This hierarchy of remedies is not foreseen in the CISG[95] and is similar to German rules on specific performance.[96] Such hierarchy has been accepted in many Member States following the adoption of the CSD.[97]

Clarifications on the consumer rights provided by CSD are given by the OSG proposal e.g. on the obligation of the seller to take back the replaced goods at the seller's own expense (Art 10 para 1), and the non-obligation of the consumer to pay for any use made of the replaced goods prior to replacement (Art 10 para 3),[98] except if it exceeds regular use and only up to the price originally paid.[99] This draft provision reflects also the case law of the Court of Justice of the European Union.[100] However, there are many doubts expressed for this consumer obligation by the

---

[90] Christopoulou (2008), p. 405.

[91] European Commission (2015e), p. 3 and European Parliament, Summary Content, 2015/0288(COD) – 09/12/2015 Legislative proposal, p. 1.

[92] See Sect. 4 on the innovations of the draft OSG.

[93] European Parliament, Summary Content, 2015/0288(COD) – 09/12/2015 Legislative proposal, p. 1.

[94] Beale (2016), p. 12.

[95] See below Sect. 4.2. See Christopoulou (2008), p. 411.

[96] Schmidt-Kessel and Silkens (2016), pp. 132–133.

[97] ECC-NET, Summary of facts on the legal guaranty of conformity and commercial warranties. https://www.europe-consommateurs.eu/fileadmin/user_upload/eu-consommateurs/PDFs/PDF_EN/REPORT-_GUARANTEE/tableau_EN_Legal_commercial.pdf.

[98] Smits (2016a), p. 6.

[99] Mańko (2016), p. 6.

[100] CJEU Case C-404/06, *Quelle AG v Bundesverband der Verbraucherzentralen und Verbraucherverbände*, ECR 2008, p. I-2685, ECLI:EU:C:2008:231.

EESC Opinion[101] and by the European Commission in its 2017 evaluation of the CRD 2011/83/EC.[102]

The impact of the OSG proposal on CSD seems to be only for cross-border online and distance sales. Therefore, the CSD 1999/44/EC will in principle be amended by the OSG proposal mainly to exclude from its scope distance sales contracts.[103]

3.3 Relationship with Directive 2000/31/EC

The Directive 2000/31/EC or the e-Commerce Directive obliges Member States to ensure that the electronic form does not hamper the legal effect of e-contracts in any way. It also sets out detailed information rights of the buyer before concluding an electronic contract, which are mandatory in the case of consumer contracts, but may be waived if both parties are professionals.[104] The Directive 2000/31/EC established the principle that the seller will apply the law of the Member State of his/her establishment (principle of the country of origin) except if there are mandatory requirements of general interest (e.g. public health) invoked by the Member State of destination (Art 3 para 4).[105] There are many proponents of this principle that support its implementation in online sales of goods as well.[106] However, this option (listed as option no 2) was not chosen by the European Commission.[107]

3.4 Relationship with the Consumers Rights Directive (CRD) 2011/83/EU

The Directive 2011/83/EU on consumer rights introduced fully harmonised rules for distance (online) and off-premises contracts for goods and services, as well as for digital content contracts. The CRD also amended certain provisions of Directive 93/13/EEC on unfair terms in consumer contracts and Directive 1999/44/EC on certain aspects of the sale of consumer goods and associated guarantees.[108]

---

[101] European Economic and Social Committee (EESC) Opinion (2016), para 4.2.5.10.

[102] European Commission (2017a, b, c, d) Evaluation, p. 6: In CRD the Commission found that there were difficulties in interpreting some provisions such as "the calculation of the diminished value of goods in cases consumers exercise their right of withdrawal after having used the goods more than necessary to establish their nature, characteristics and functioning (Art 14 para 2)".

[103] Art 19 para 1 of the OSG Proposal.

[104] Mańko (2016), p. 4.

[105] Anagnostopoulou (2013a), p. 116.

[106] See for example UEAPME, Position Paper on contract rules for online purchases of digital content and tangible goods.

[107] European Commission (2015e), p. 10.

[108] European Commission (2017d) p. 2.

The CRD 2011/83/EU has fully harmonised key rules of distance contracts such as:

- pre-contractual information, as an obligation incumbent on sellers (Art 6);
- formal requirements regarding the contract (Art 7 CRD);
- right of withdrawal, without invoking any reason, within 14 days (Art 9 ff);
- default rules: on the passing of risk once the goods are actually delivered to the consumer; and on time of delivery, which has to be 30 days since the contract, without covering modalities of delivery (Art 18 CRD)[109]; and
- ancillary rights such as the right of the consumer not to be charged additional fees for using a specific payment method (Art 19 CRD).[110]

The CRD 2011/83/EU has been criticised for leaving many aspects unharmonised, e.g. legal guarantees.[111] In addition, it allows some regulatory choices to Member States. According to its 2017 Evaluation by the European Commission, 20 Member States exempt off-premises contracts from CRD if the price is below 50€ (Art 3 para 4 CRD), while seven Member States apply a simplified information regime for repair or maintenance works not exceeding 200€ if explicitly requested by the consumer (Art 7 para 4 CRD).[112] This evaluation shows the disparity of national legislative choices once a Directive gives such discretion. The CRD is not formally amended by the OSG proposal.

4 The Innovations by the 2015 OSG Proposal

4.1 Conformity of the Goods

As was originally provided for in the Directive 1999/44/EC, the goods must primarily conform to what was promised in the contract. The initial concept of conformity in CSD extended the traditional concept of liability for defective products to include liability for any public statements, e.g. advertising. According to the CSD, the seller may prove that he/she was not aware of such statements, or that the statements did not influence the decision of the consumer to buy or that the statement was corrected before the sale took place.[113]

[109] Smits (2016a), p. 5.

[110] Mańko (2016), p. 4.

[111] Anagnostopoulou (2013a), p. 122.

[112] European Commission (2017a, b, c, d) Evaluation, p. 3. For more detailed information, see tables at: http://ec.europa.eu/justice/consumer-marketing/files/overview_regulatory_choices.pdf.

[113] Mańko (2016), p. 2.

However, the draft OSG presupposes a direct reference of public statements to the content of the contract, thus controlling only pre-contractual statements which are an integral part of the contract (Art 4 para 1 c).[114]

The draft OSG also clarifies that, as a default rule, the conformity of the goods would be assessed not only with regard to the contract terms but also after taking into account a combination of subjective (Art 4 OSG) and objective criteria (Art 5-7 OSG).[115] In the absence of explicit contractual terms specifying the conformity criteria, the goods must conform to these objective criteria which include incorrect installation and third party rights.

Indeed, due to previous case law,[116] the draft Directive also states that a lack of conformity resulting from an incorrect installation of the goods (by the seller or under his/her responsibility) is to be regarded as a lack of conformity of the goods themselves if the reason for the incorrect installation is in the sphere of the seller.[117]

The draft Directive contains an additional conformity requirement that the goods must be clear of any third-party rights, including those based on intellectual property. This requirement was not included in the CSD.[118]

In addition, the proposed OSG specifies at which time the conditions for the lack of conformity must be fulfilled in order to incur the seller's liability for non-performance.[119] Generally, that is the time of passing of risk, where the consumer or a third party designated by the consumer, obtains control over the goods; or when the installation is completed; or after a reasonable time has passed for installation which cannot exceed 30 days from the time of passing of risk (Art 8 para 2).[120]

All the above OSG provisions are very useful clarifications, which could be used also in case the CSD was amended since they are not useful only in a digital environment, but also to face-to-face transactions.

4.2 *Hierarchy of Remedies Versus Free Choice of Remedies and Time Limit of the Liability (Article 9 of the Draft OSG): Deterioration of Consumer Protection?*

The draft OSG, following the example of CSD 1999/44/EC, limits the right to reduce the price or terminate the contract by providing a hierarchy of remedies and giving the seller a clear right to cure (e.g. to repair or to replace the good). By

---

[114] Ibid., p. 5.

[115] European Parliament, Summary Content, p. 2.

[116] See Court of Justice of the EU, Joined Cases C-65/09 and C-87/09, *Gebr. Weber GmbH v. Jürgen Wittmer and Ingrid Putz v Medianess Electronic GmbH*, 16 June 2011 (on tiles and dishwasher installed), ECR 2011, p. I-05257, ECLI:EU:C:2011:396.

[117] European Parliament, Summary Content, 2015/0288(COD) - 09/12/2015 Legislative proposal.

[118] Mańko (2016), p. 5.

[119] European Parliament, Summary Content, 2015/0288(COD) - 09/12/2015 Legislative proposal.

[120] Ibid., p. 2.

contrast, the draft CESL, following the example of CISG, had provided for a free choice of remedies, based on its optional character. In this way, CESL had put the seller in the most inconvenient position and strengthened the consumer's rights by according the possibility of easy termination and price reduction.[121] This turned out to be one of the most controversial points of this proposal. Learning from this experience, the model of the CSD was retained in the OSG.[122]

The draft OSG lists the remedies for lack of conformity the consumers have available by fully harmonising the order in which remedies could be exercised in an obligatory two-step remedy system of primary remedies and secondary remedies[123]:

1. the first step is for the consumer to ask the seller for the goods to be repaired or replaced, within a reasonable time[124] and without any significant inconvenience; the seller however may refuse the remedy proposed by the consumer if he/she deems it disproportionate.[125]
2. if the repair or replacement remedies are not successful, and the lack of conformity is not or cannot be remedied through repair or replacement by the seller, only then in a second step, the consumer should be entitled to a price reduction or to terminate the contract.[126]

The aim of this two-step system is to keep the contract intact for as long as possible and thus reduce costs while giving a second chance to the seller to properly perform the contract.[127] This is why the two-step system of hierarchy of remedies has found support by business associations but was rejected by the vast majority of consumer associations which favour a free choice of remedies.[128] However, the European Commission insists on this hierarchy and has presented a recent consumer survey demonstrating that 77% of EU28 consumers agree that it is reasonable for a seller to offer a repair or replacement—and not a refund—when a problem with a product occurs for the first time.[129]

---

[121] Schulte-Nölke et al. (2012) Remedies for buyers in B2C contracts: general aspects, European Parliament, PE 462.460, p. 16.

[122] COM(2015) 635, pp. 2–3.

[123] Mańko (2016), p. 3.

[124] European Economic and Social Committee (EESC) Opinion (2016), p. 10: "The notion of 'reasonable time' is a subjective one, and provides leeway for differing transpositions on this key subject, which is incompatible with maximum harmonisation. For example, in countries such as Bulgaria, France, Portugal and Luxembourg, the time period is 30 days; in Hungary, Romania, Greece and Estonia it is 15 days. The provision should establish a period corresponding to the maximum applying in some EU countries - 15 days".

[125] Mańko (2016), p. 3.

[126] European Parliament, Summary Content, 2015/0288(COD) - 09/12/2015 Legislative proposal.

[127] Smits (2016b), p. 3.

[128] Mańko (2016), pp. 5–6.

[129] Consumer market study on the functioning of Legal and Commercial Guarantees for consumers in the EU (2015) as mentioned by the Impact Assessment.

As already mentioned, the same two-step system is also established by the Consumer Sales Directive but Member States had the possibility to opt for higher protection. Indeed, six Member States (Greece, Cyprus, Croatia, Portugal, Lithuania, Slovenia) were allowed by the CSD to provide for a free choice of the consumer to demand price reduction or rescission of the contract without having first to ask the seller to repair or replace the product.[130] According to the European Economic and Social Committee, the proposed hierarchy of remedies excludes as an initial option the possibility of the product being returned immediately to the seller and would deteriorate consumer rights in six Member States, which have not followed the hierarchy of remedies.[131] In addition, the UK and Ireland have granted the consumers an immediate right to termination (the short term "right to reject" of 30 days).[132] This right would have to be abolished if a hierarchy of remedies was established across the EU in case of adoption of the OSG proposal.

The European Commission in its OSG proposal was aware of this deterioration of consumer protection. It stated in its Impact Assessment, this deterioration:

> … would be partially counterbalanced by the right of withdrawal from the contract for any reason foreseen in the Consumer Rights Directive 2011/83/EC, for a period of 14 days after delivery. In Ireland the situation and consequences will be the same as in UK as regards the current long-term right to reject.[133]

A further deterioration of consumer protection in all Member States is evident, since the proposed OSG maintains the time limit of 2 years for the availability of the remedies in a total harmonisation provision, thus reducing liability periods and the consumer protection level in some Member States. For example, the liability and limitation periods for remedies are aligned at 6 years in England, Wales and Northern Ireland and 5 years in Scotland.[134]

Finally, the OSG proposal does not include any rule on damages caused by the termination or from the non-performance itself, e.g. compensation in case that the consumer is obliged to purchase a more expensive product from another seller. In this way the consumer must have recourse to the divergent national laws on compensation. However, this is a serious omission since the draft DCD includes such rule (Art 16).[135] If the product is defective, the consumer may certainly ask for damages on the basis of the Product Liability Directive 85/374/EEC[136] which however

---

[130] Mańko (2016), p. 3 and European Economic and Social Committee (EESC) Opinion (2016).

[131] EESC Opinion (2016), para. 4.2.5.7.

[132] Smits (2016b), pp. 3–4.

[133] Impact Assessment, Annex 8.

[134] UK Parliament, Documents considered by the Committee on 10 February 2016 - European Scrutiny Contents, 5 Digital Single Market: Consumer contract rights for the online sale of goods. The Minister's Explanatory Memorandum of 5 January 2016, Policy Implications, point 5.39. https://publications.parliament.uk/pa/cm201516/cmselect/cmeuleg/342-xxii/34208.htm.

[135] See Smits (2016b), p. 5.

[136] Directive 85/374/EEC of the Council of 25 July 1985, on the approximation of the laws, regulations and administrative provisions of the Member States concerning liability for defective products O.J. L210/29, 7 August 1985.

includes certain restrictions in Art 9, e.g. property damage, other than the product, less than 500 Euros.[137]

4.3 *The Counterbalances to the Obligatory Hierarchy of Remedies to the Consumer's Advantage*

The draft OSG introduces new rules, not included in CSD 1999/44/EC, in favour of the consumer:

(a) The consumer does not need to notify the seller of the lack of conformity as soon as he/she discovers the lack of conformity in 2 months after delivery of the product as Member States were permitted to impose to consumers by Art 5 para 2 CSD.
(b) The consumer has the right to withhold performance (payment) until the goods are brought in conformity (Art 9 para 4 OSG).[138]
(c) The consumer may terminate the contract even if the defect is minor.[139]
(d) The consumer will be entitled to termination and refund or continuation with the contract and price reduction (second step remedies) if the seller does not repair or replace the goods within a reasonable time, or without any significant inconvenience to the consumer; or if the seller declares that he/she will not complete repair or replacement in reasonable time or if it is clear that the seller will not complete such remedy in time (Art 9 para 2-3 OSG).[140]
(e) The seller pays all expenses in case of termination: He/she must reimburse the price within 14 days from notification, bear the costs of reimbursement (banking fees) and pay the expenses for taking the goods back, which the consumer has to send in 14 days after termination of the contract (Art 10).[141]

These rights clearly protect the consumer at the expense of the seller. Some are reasonable, e.g. withholding the payment until the seller has brought the goods into conformity, but some are excessive. The most striking example is the right to terminate the contract even if for a minor defect e.g. a scratch, which should be condemned. Such a right was excluded by Directive 1999/44/EC in its Art 6 para 3. In addition, CISG allows termination only in fundamental breach of contract. Professor M. Stürner (2016) suggests that the right of withdrawal for a minor lack of conformity is unjustified and infringes the principle of good faith, according to which the conduct of contracting parties is governed by a positive obligation of good faith.

---

137 See Beale (2016), p. 14. For the restrictions of the Directive see Alexandridou (2008), pp. 382–383; Anagnostopoulou (2012), p. 430.

138 European Parliament, Summary Content, 2015/0288(COD) - 09/12/2015 Legislative proposal.

139 See Art 13 OSG. European Commission (2015e), pp. 3, 13 and 15.

140 Mańko (2016), p. 5.

141 Ibid., p. 6.

This principle would be undermined in case the contract was terminated due to a minor non-conformity.[142] Professor J. Smits considers unacceptable the argument invoked by the Commission that the mere possibility for the consumer to terminate the contract gives a strong incentive for the seller to remedy a lack of conformity at an early stage since it will turn unjustifiably at the expense of the seller's interest.[143]

In addition, the draft OSG eliminates the so-called 2-month notification duty of the consumer in case of non-conformity which was optional for the Member States to impose according to Art 5 para 2 of the CSD 1999/44/EC. Though the elimination will bring change to 17 Member States that have imposed such duty in consumer sales, it will simplify cross-border sales in favour of the consumer who will not lose his/her rights for remedies in case he/she does not notify the lack of conformity within 2 months of discovery.[144] On the contrary, the European Association for Craft, Small and Medium-sized Enterprises (UEAPME), representing SMEs, considers the longer this period is, "the harder it will be to identify the link between non-conformity and the defect. In other words, if the period to notify the trader is too long, the defect could also have been caused by misuse or general wear and tear".[145]

4.4 On the Reversal of the Burden of Proof (Art 8 Para 3 OSG)

The Consumer Sales Directive 1999/44/EC provides that if the consumer complains about a lack of conformity of goods sold within 6 months, the seller has the obligation to prove that the goods were in conformity to the contract (reversal of burden of proof). The draft OSG (Art 8 para 3) proposes an extension to the reversal of the burden of proof from 6 months to 2 years. This would mean that the consumer will have the benefit of a presumption that the goods were defective when delivered for a period of 2 years after delivery (increased from 6 months) and it would be for the supplier, not the consumer, to prove that the goods were in conformity at the time of sale. This provision is new since the Annex of the CESL proposal did not include it (Art 105 second sentence).

The argument used in favour of this extension is to ensure both a higher awareness of consumers and an easier enforcement of EU consumer rules (draft OSG, preamble, para 33). Professor J. Smits warns that such rule will incite a consumer not to exercise reasonable care in handling the product (e.g. a computer), since he/

[142] Stürner (2016), p. 8.

[143] Smits (2016a) p. 13.

[144] Smits (2016b), pp. 4–5.

[145] See UEAPME, Position Paper. http://www.ueapme.com/IMG/pdf/UEAPME_position_on_Contract_Rules_for_online_purchases_of_digital_content_and_tangible_goods.pdf.

she would have the right to ask for repair or replacement for 2 years and its pervasive effect will clash with national legislation which holds the seller liable for non-conformity for e.g. 5 years for durable consumption goods to the detriment of the consumer.[146] Professor M. Stürner considers that this is a de facto guarantee of the product's being in a good situation (*Haltbarkeitsgarantie*) which does not exist in face-to-face sales and thus brings an unjustified divergence.[147] In addition, these time limits neglect the existing guarantee periods in some Member States (Finland, Netherlands, Sweden and the UK) which take into account the durability and built-in obsolescence of products.[148] The European Economic and Social Committee (EESC) points out that the Commission has not provided for the suspension of the legal guarantee during the repair or replacement period, which most Member States provide in their national legislation e.g. for periods of repair as well as mediation, arbitration and legal recourse. In addition, where there is a replacement, the replaced product should benefit from a new and identical guarantee period as of the moment it is delivered.[149]

The provision therefore is under serious discussion and could also be considered as excessive at the expense of the seller.

5 Reactions During the EU Legislative Procedure

5.1 The Reaction of the National Parliaments

National Parliaments have strongly reacted to the proposal. They have issued 12 reasoned opinions,[150] making the OSG proposal rank fourth at the general reaction of National Parliaments to EU legislative proposals.[151] Most of the opinions from National Parliaments agreed on the need for an EU-wide appropriate level of consumer protection. However, several National Parliaments emphasised the fragmentation that will result from the proposals between online and other distance sales of

146 Smits (2016b), pp. 3–4.

147 Stürner (2016), p. 10, who makes reference to the judgment of the Court of Justice of the European Union: Case C-497/13, *Froukje Faber versus Autobedrijf Hazet Ochten BV*, judgment of 4 June 2015, ECLI:EU:C:2015:357, para 69–75.

148 ECC-NET, Summary of facts on the legal guaranty of conformity and commercial warranties.

149 European Economic and Social Committee (EESC) Opinion (2016), para 4.2.5.8.

150 In addition, the Commission received 11 reasoned opinions on the proposal for a Directive on certain aspects concerning contracts for the supply of digital content (COM(2015) 634). Eight of the opinions covered both proposals. See Annual Report, p. 6.

151 See Annex 2 to the European Commission, Report on Relations of the Commission with the National Parliaments, pp. 4–5: "Six opinions, from the CZ Senát, the FR Sénat, the LU Chambre des Députés, the AT Bundesrat, the PT Assembleia da República and the RO Senat jointly concerned COM(2015) 634 and COM(2015) 635. The NL Eerste Kamer sent two opinions which both jointly concerned COM(2015) 633, COM(2015) 634 and COM(2015) 635".

goods, and face-to-face sales and commented upon the proposed new rules concerning the reversal of the burden of proof, liability for damages as well as on the proposed two-year legal guarantee period.[152] In particular:

- The French *Sénat* had initial reservations and continued the political dialogue, despite the Commission's response, by sending on 7 March 2016 a "European Resolution" to the Council against Art 3 OSG requesting that the Member States would continue ensuring a higher level of protection for their citizens, otherwise the proposal would infringe the principle of subsidiarity.[153]
- The Italian Chamber of Deputies welcomed the proposal pointing out many issues that should be changed, like the excessive burden of proof on the seller, the need to avoid uncertainty with e.g. setting a period for the consumer to notify the defect etc.[154]
- The Austrian *Bundesrat* (Federal Council) rejected the OSG proposal. It considered it as "a complicated parallel guarantee regime that is not materially justified … leading to an unnecessary fragmentation of the law".[155]
- The *Oireachtas* Joint Committee on Jobs of Ireland condemned the fact that the OSG proposal creates a dual regime which prioritises the Digital Single Market over domestic markets and the consumer certainty. Consumers should continue to avail of existing remedies of higher consumer protection. The Irish Joint Committee has also offered various solutions, e.g. obligation of the online retailers to notify the Member State on which they are based at the moment of e-purchase.[156]
- The Romanian Senate has welcomed the proposal and asked for more harmonisation to cover the legal vacuum for certain contractual matters.[157]
- The UK criticised the creation of two sets of rules existing for online and other distance sales of goods and for offline purchases. This could create differences in the rights enjoyed by consumers depending on whether they bought their goods online or offline. Though the proposal retains many of the same rights that are set out in the CSD 1999/44/EC and implemented in the UK in the Consumer Rights Act (2015), there are some differences between the statutory remedies available to consumers in the proposal and those in the 2015 UK Consumer Rights Act.[158]

[152] See European Commission, Annual Report 2016, pp. 6–7.

[153] Council of the European Union, Opinion on the application of the Principles of Subsidiarity and Proportionality, ST 6893 2016 INIT—2015/0287 (OLP).

[154] Council of the European Union, Opinion of the Italian Chamber of Deputies (*Camera dei Deputati*), 9566/16, 18 May 2016.

[155] Council of the European Union, Opinion of the Austrian Federal Council of 31 March 2016 (7758/16).

[156] Council of the European Union, Opinion of the Joint Committee on Jobs, Enterprise and Innovation of the Houses of Oireachtas in Ireland, 5755/16, January 2016, p. 4.

[157] Romanian Parliament Senate (2016).

[158] UK Government (2016) and UK Parliament (2016).

In its replies, the European Commission stressed the need to eliminate differences between national consumer contract law rules in key areas and argued that full harmonisation at European level, combined with a high level of consumer protection, is the only one capable of meeting the two objectives of legal certainty and consumer confidence. The Commission stated in its 2016 Annual Report[159] that:

> the overall level of consumer protection would remain very high in all Member States, since a possible decrease of the national level of consumer protection on a few specific points in certain Member States would be compensated to a certain extent by other rules in the proposal providing for a higher level of consumer protection, for example through the extension of the reversal of the burden of proof from six months to two years.

These facts show the increased interest of the National Parliaments in the OSG proposal and their reactions, as well as the attitude of the European Commission to propose in the draft OSG, provisions with a consumer compensating character.

5.2 *The Response of the EU Institutions*

The European Economic and Social Committee (EESC) issued its Opinion on 20 July 2016. The EESC did not support full harmonisation but rather favoured minimum harmonisation. It pointed out the problem of the Treaty legal basis, opting for Art 169 TFEU. It pointed out the difference between online and offline sales. In its consultative Opinion, the EESC made many comments, e.g. on subjective concepts, such as 'reasonable', 'significant inconvenience' etc.[160]

The European Parliament Committees started to discuss the draft OSG in early 2016. The European Parliament Internal Market and Consumer Protection Committee (IMCO) issued a draft report on the OSG proposal on 18 November 2016. The European Parliament's response is not yet finalised. The Draft Report, on which many amendments were submitted, emphasizes that the OSG proposal would create a fragmented legal framework, and that there is a need to introduce uniform rules for both online and face-to-face consumer sales. The rapporteur agrees with the approach of maximum harmonisation and suggests moving to maximum harmonisation for both online and offline consumer sales.[161] The Draft Report amends the OSG proposal in many points in a critical manner, by e.g. deleting the possibility of termination of the contract in minor defects.

159 See European Commission (2017c), Annual Report 2016, p. 7.

160 European Economic and Social Committee (2016) on the DCD and OSG Proposals.

161 European Parliament, Committee on the Internal Market and Consumer Protection (Rapporteur Pascal Arimont) Draft Report on the proposal for a Directive of the European Parliament and of the Council on certain aspects concerning contracts for the online and other distance sales of goods, PE 593.817v03-00, 18 Nov 2016.

In the Council, numerous Member States indicated that the EU should: (a) avoid to create different rules between the online sales and the offline sales of goods, and (b) wait for the quality evaluation of the existing consumer directives, especially CSD 1999/44/EC in the framework of (REFIT),[162] a process launched by the European Commission in order to make EU law simpler, more effective and coherent and to reduce regulatory costs. Other Member States have underlined the importance of coherence both in the field of EU contract law in general and between the two proposals.[163] The Council is currently discussing the OSG proposal within the Working party on Civil Law Matters (Contract law).[164]

The above reactions of the Council and, in particular of the European Parliament, which are both co-legislators, demonstrate that the OSG proposal should be amended in order to reflect the real needs for e-commerce.

6 Overall Evaluation

6.1 Introducing CESL Through the Back Door and Extending the Proposal to Face-to-Face Sales?

Some consumer organisations accuse the European Commission of "introducing parts of the CESL through the backdoor after all, pursuing an alternative strategy of small steps, apparently betting on the self-created need and hence sufficient political leverage".[165] They accuse the European Commission that it would subsequently eliminate the then existing inconsistencies and fragmentation between online and offline purchases by simply expanding the scope of the OSG proposal to cover all sales channels.[166] The amendment of the CSD is feared by some Member States as well.[167]

These arguments are not really out of place since the Consumer Sales Directive 1999/44/EC, as one of the six important legal instruments of EU Consumer law,[168]

---

[162] European Commission, Communication "EU regulatory fitness", COM(2012) 746 final Strasbourg, 12.12.2012. See more at http://ec.europa.eu/info/law-making-process/evaluating-and-improving-existing-laws/refit-making-eu-law-simpler-and-less_en.

[163] Council of the European Union, Presidency Progress report no 6150/16 JUSTCIV 17 CONSOM 30 DIGIT 10 AUDIO 12 CODEC 165, available at: http://data.consilium.europa.eu/doc/document/st-6150-2016-init/en/pdf.

[164] See Opinion of the European Data Protection Supervisor (2017), point 8.

[165] Leupold (2016).

[166] Ibid.

[167] See Council of the European Union, Opinion of the Austrian Federal Council of 30 March 2016 (7758/16), p. 5.

[168] The Unfair Contract Terms Directive 93/13/EEC, the Sales and Guarantees Directive 1999/44/EC, the Unfair Commercial Practices Directive 2005/29/EC and the Injunctions Directive 2009/22/EC.

are now under review by the Regulatory Fitness and Performance Check (REFIT)[169] and the final report on the results was published in May 2017.[170] Then, the European Commission should amend the CSD and align it with the OSG, something which is approved by commentators[171] but not welcome by the National Parliaments.[172]

In addition, the proposal already contains draft new rules that usefully clarify the rights provided by the CSD 1999/44/EC. The academics urge the Commission to apply these clarifications also to face-to-face sales.[173] Of course a "one size fits all" approach might not be appropriate in all circumstances.[174] However, creating an unjustifiked differentiation in the treatment of online and offline sales of goods is considered unacceptable by many.[175] The importance of ensuring a coherent legal framework throughout the EU for both online/distance and face-to-face sales of goods has been emphasised by the European Commission.[176] Therefore coherence seems to be a common aim for all stakeholders.

6.2 *Market Fragmentation*

Both the DCD and the OSG proposals are leading to further fragmentation of the European contract law. The issue of fragmentation between the markets has been raised almost from every EU institution, National Parliaments, and stakeholders.

Modern contract law is divided between e.g. sale of goods, supply of services and leasing. These categories are further subdivided in sales B2B, B2C, C2C.[177] The above subcategories are each further divided in cross-border sales and domestic sales. Each of the above divisions are divided in on online and offline markets.[178] Online markets, domestic and/or cross-border, may now be subdivided to contracts for the supply of digital content and distance contracts on sales of movable goods, each with its own rules, domestic or European, with minimum or maximum EU

---

[169] European Commission, COM(2012) 746 final Strasbourg, 12.12.2012.

[170] Leupold (2016), Refit "fit for purpose"? https://vkiakademie.wordpress.com/2016/09/28/refit-fit-for-purpose/. See the results of REFIT in http://ec.europa.eu/newsroom/just/item-detail.cfm?item_id=59332.

[171] Smits (2016a), p. 4.

[172] Council of the European Union, Opinion of the Austrian Federal Council of 30 March 2016 (7758/16), p. 5.

[173] Smits (2016a), p. 3.

[174] Watson (2016), p. 252.

[175] European Economic and Social Committee (EESC) Opinion (2016), para 1.8.

[176] See European Commission (2017c), pp. 6–7.

[177] Hesselink (2016), p. 519; Mańko (2016), p. 4.

[178] Smits (2016a), p. 5. Compare European Law Institute (ELI) approach as cited by Mańko (2016), p. 9.

harmonisation.[179] Sometimes in the same Directive, there may be provisions with either minimum or maximum harmonisation, e.g. CRD 2011/83/EU. The OSG proposal also causes confusion because some rules contained in previous Directives are of minimum harmonisation e.g. for limitation periods for exercising consumers' rights, commercial guarantees and the right of redress for the seller.[180]

This labyrinth may confuse sellers with multiple channels of distribution.[181] This is even more true, since the OSG and the DCD proposals contain sometimes different rules and use different terms (e.g. seller or supplier, consumer, commercial guarantee).[182] There could also be problems with the scope of each contract, which performs the role of the traffic policeman between conflicting rules, and may not easily be distinguished from other kind of contracts.[183]

Professor J. Smits suggests that the Commission could rethink its policy to separate the two proposals.[184] In my opinion, the form is not the problem, whether there are two proposals or one. The problem is the substance. The rules should be carefully reviewed, so that they are not different between the OSG and DCD proposals, without a substantial reason. And they should not be different from other Directives on consumer protection without a fundamental reason.

6.3 *Contract Fragmentation*

The proposal and the existing Directives deal only with specific problems in specific sectors and do not cover the full cycle of the contract in cross-border transactions which is usually the formation of the contract, invalidity, interpretation, performance, non-performance and remedies.[185] Each Directive has its own substantive scope, mostly off-premises sales, while the Consumer Sales Directive 1999/44/EC deals with both face-to-face sales and distance sales.

Fragmentation would be less likely to occur if the legislative act of maximum harmonisation covered with contractual default rules more contractual remedies as well as the formation and contents of the contract; and if the scopes of application and substantive rules of various Directives were more uniform.[186]

Indeed, the OSG proposal does not cover a wide variety of topics included in the CESL proposal, e.g. damages for non-performance (Art 159 ff CESL); change of

---

[179] Twigg-Flesner (2016), p. 13.

[180] Draft Directive, Preamble Recital 14. See also Smits (2016a), p. 7.

[181] Smits (2016a), p. 8.

[182] Ibid.

[183] Stürner (2016), pp. 2–3.

[184] Smits (2016a), p. 16.

[185] Hesselink (2016), p. 519.

[186] Smits (2016a), p. 6.

circumstances (Art 89 CESL); anticipatory breach (Art 116 CESL); or damages for non-performance (Art 159 ff CESL).[187]

The draft OSG proposal includes an express exception of the "rules on formation, validity or effect of contracts, including the consequences of the termination of a contract" and certain aspects of its enforcement (Art 1 para 4).[188] This exception has its model in CRD 2011/83/EC.[189] However, it is feared that national contract law divergences on this matter may cause confusion and distortion of competition. Thus the proposal does not really produce a "level playing field", as promised by the European Commission, and is not a true total harmonisation.[190]

Contract fragmentation however is a necessary technique in order to apply the EU principles of subsidiarity and proportionality and overcome the national resistance to producing a European Civil Code. The United States, which is a federation of states, use the comprehensive Uniform Commercial Code (UCC), created in 1952 by the American Law Institute and the National Conference of Commissioners on Uniform State Laws.[191] The UCC is not federal legislation, but is adopted by the states. The UCC covers all aspects of a contract and was amended several times, the last one being in 2012. To adopt a legal instrument like UCC has proven not to be easy for the European Union, after the recent fruitless efforts on the non-binding Draft Common Frame of Reference and the optional CESL.

Dealing only with certain aspects of contract law, however, does not lead to failure of the EU contract law. The most prominent example is the 1980 CISG which deals only with certain aspects of the contract cycle, but has been extremely successful for B2B transactions all over the world.

6.4 What Is the Best Way to Proceed? A de facto CSD Recast?

Should the Commission proceed by way of a CSD recast, a Regulation, the country of origin principle, or model contract rules? The OSG proposal could be characterized as a *de facto* recast of Consumer Sales Directive limited only to online and distance contracts.[192] In this way the 1999 CSD will apply only in face-to-face contracts where Member States will be entitled to continue applying higher standards thus introducing a dual regime.[193] However, many ask for an update of the CSD to

[187] Smits (2016a), pp. 6–7.

[188] See EESC (2016) Opinion, para 2.4.

[189] See Art 3 para 5 of CRD Directive 2011/83/EC: "This Directive shall not affect national general contract law such as the rules on the validity, formation or effect of a contract, in so far as general contract law aspects are not regulated in this Directive".

[190] Stürner (2016), p. 2.

[191] Anagnostopoulou (2012), pp. 230–232.

[192] Mańko (2016), p. 1.

[193] Mańko (2016), p. 4.

reflect the needs of online purchase such as the English Barristers' Association.[194] The European Association of Craft, Small and Medium-Sized Enterprises (UEAPME)[195] has also asked only for CSD ameliorations and not for new legislation.

Is the form of a Directive of total harmonisation suitable? The European Economic and Social Committee (EESC) supports the idea of two separate Directives of minimum harmonisation or the optional model contracts certified with the trust mark of the EU, which was considered as "option number five" of the European Commission.[196] The European Law Institute (ELI), which has contributed greatly with its Statements during the CESL negotiations, argued that there should be a Regulation jointly covering the cross-border sale of tangible goods and digital content applicable to all types of sales (including B2B) in an electronic environment.[197] Others, especially professional organisations, supported the country of origin principle of the trader that would allow the e-traders to sell abroad under their home legislation.[198]

However, this discussion has already been conducted during the CESL proposal procedure. No matter the legal instrument, the EU has to proceed in order to attain the Digital Single Market. Since the CESL proposal was rejected because it was in the form of Regulation, the Commission has now opted for its proposals the form of a Directive. The "play of 20 questions" must be stopped.

The aim should be to proceed with flexibility and caution. Whatever the form or fragmentation, what counts is the substance of the rules, with direct effect or with Member State discretion, whether with total or minimum harmonisation, according to the results of the negotiations during the legislative procedure.

7 Conclusion: The Aims of the Single Market and the High Protection of the Consumer and Comprehensiveness vs Fragmentation

One of the core aims of the European Union is the establishment and the better functioning of the Internal Market and since 2010 of the Digital Single Market. According to Professor Schulte-Nölke (2007) the very term "market" insinuates

---

[194] Mańko (2016), p. 9.

[195] See UEAPME, Position Paper. http://www.ueapme.com/IMG/pdf/UEAPME_position_on_Contract_Rules_for_online_purchases_of_digital_content_and_tangible_goods.pdf.

[196] See points 1.4–1.6 and 3.1.4. of the Opinion. For the five options, see European Commission (2015d), p. 9.

[197] European Law Institute (ELI) approach as cited by Mańko (2016), p. 9.

[198] Mańko (2016), pp. 8–9, referring to UAPME, the EU SME Federation, Eurocommerce, the Austria Economic Chamber, the Polish Business Federation, the European and International Federation of Booksellers etc. For the theoretical justification of this approach see Grundmann (2013), p. 225.

the negotiation, formation and performance of contracts, especially cross-border.[199] Though the contract is a central tool in the Internal Market, there is no autonomous self-standing EU contract law system, instead the formation of the contract and remedies is based mainly on EU consumer law.[200] The reasons for this situation is the old 1958 Treaty principle for the attribution of EU powers and more recently (1993) the principles of subsidiarity and proportionality guaranteed since 2009 by the National Parliaments. Therefore, the EU contract law and national contract law are deeply intertwined resulting in a multi-layered system.[201] The EU Digital Agenda aims to change this structure and overcome the patchwork of different rules, from a multi-level origin, either international and EU, or national laws, in strengthening consumer rights.[202] Therefore, it seems that the current challenge for the DSM would be to develop a sufficiently autonomous conception of contract law justice in the EU.[203] To adopt a legal instrument like the Uniform Commercial Code in the US has proven not to be easy in Europe, after the recent efforts on the non-binding Draft Common Frame of Reference and the optional CESL. Especially if one takes into account the strong and persistent reactions of the National Parliaments which have emerged as the guarantors of the national contract law.

However, the fact that for the moment the biggest bulk of e-commerce (54%) is carried out by multinational firms established in the United States while only 4% represents EU based cross-border e-commerce[204] demonstrates that the EU has to hurry to adopt the proposed Directives if it wants to unleash the potential of the Digital Single Market.[205] In fact, it is already too late. The United States are the leaders in the e-commerce and digital technology thanks to their fundamental approach that the private sector should lead in e commerce, allowing industry self-regulation while the government should avoid undue restrictions on e-commerce. This "hands-off" approach was already established in 1997 in the US with the Presidential Directive on E-Commerce".[206]

Is the EU approach in the right direction? It is evident that all stakeholders disagree with the OSG proposal. Despite the "counterbalances" proposed for the benefit of the consumer, consumer organisations react. They warn about the blocking

---

[199] Schulte-Nölke (2007).

[200] Hesselink (2016), p. 523.

[201] Smits (2016a), p. 5; Hesselink (2016), p. 523.

[202] Anagnostopoulou (2013b), p. 210.

[203] Hesselink (2016), p. 534.

[204] European Commission factsheet, "Why we need a Digital Single Market", https://ec.europa.eu/commission/sites/beta-political/files/dsm-factsheet_en.pdf.

[205] European Commission (2015c) Digital contracts for Europe - Unleashing the potential of e-commerce, COM(2015) 633, Brussels, 9 Dec 2015.

[206] Anagnostopoulou (2017) referring to Wunch-Vincent (2016), pp. 103–105.

effect of a fully harmonised regime lowering the current level of consumer protection.[207]

The game is not over yet and the EU institutions continue with the negotiation of the Proposals. The aim should be to strike a fair balance between the interests of the sellers and the consumers.

On the one hand, the OSG proposal deteriorates consumer protection in many Member States which have enacted stricter measures due to the previous authorisation by CSD. It would be unfair to lower the standards and thus minimum harmonisation must be allowed in one or two very important issues, at least for some transition period. Instead of lowering the high protection of the consumer in those Member States, there could be less burdensome measures, according to the principle of proportionality (Art 5 para 3 TEU). For example, a data basis in the e-justice portal of the European Commission could inform sellers of such national measures.

On the other hand, some of the draft provisions of the OSG proposal "raise consumer protection standards to an unjustified level", e.g. the extension of the period of reversal of the burden of proof in case of non-conformity from 6 months to 2 years or the right to terminate the contract even for minor defects[208] or the abolition of the Member States' discretion to oblige the consumer to notify the seller of the defect within 2 months after detecting it. These "counterbalance" provisions are not supported by consumer organisations and deteriorate the interests of the seller in an unjustified way. Therefore they should not be included in the final Directive.

The US experience has shown that the motivation of the seller is also very important for the growth in e-commerce. And e-commerce is very important for the internal market, an aim of the Treaty on the Functioning of the EU (Art 3). In addition, deterioration of consumer protection cannot be allowed, since a high level of consumer protection is another aim of the Treaty on the Functioning of the EU. The above aims must be both safeguarded and balanced with each other, in order not to provoke market fragmentation and an irrational labyrinth. The strong reaction of stakeholders and EU co-legislators to market fragmentation, have led the European Commission to submit an amended proposal of a Directive that would encompass online and offline sales and will repeal CSD 1999/44/EC.[209] The proposal COM (2017) 637 final is a major step towards simple, uniform and efficient rules on consumer sales. Adopted on October 31, 2017 the new Commission proposal extends the scope of application of the OSG proposal to all sales of goods, face-to face or electronic ones, between business and consumers (B2C), making the above fears expressed by certain stakeholders come true. Being more than a recast of CSD 1999/44/EC, the new Sale of Goods proposal (SGP) is a

[207] Council of the European Union, Opinion of the Austrian Federal Council of 30 March 2016 (7758/16), p. 5.

[208] Council of the European Union, Opinion of the Austrian Federal Council of 30 March 2016 (7758/16), p. 5.

[209] European Commission (2017e).

"CSD+" (in the words of Professor H. Beale in 2016).[210] The 2017 proposal becomes thus an embryon B2C European "CISG−" instrument which puts an end to the legal categorization of the contract in accordance with the channel of consumer sale.

References

Alexandridou E (2008) Consumer protection law. Sakkoulas Publishers, Thessaloniki

Anagnostopoulou D (2012) Law of international transactions: the European dimension (in Greek). A. Sakkoulas, Athens

Anagnostopoulou D (2013a) E-commerce in international and European Union law: the policy of the European Union on digital agenda and strategy 2020. Hell Rev Eur Law Foreign Ed 2013:109

Anagnostopoulou D (2013b) EU policies and Common European Sales Law. In: Bitzenis A, Vlachos V (eds) Proceedings of the international conference on international business, May 16–18, 2013, pp 283–301

Anagnostopoulou D (2017) The digital agenda of the European Union and the digital policies of the US. In: Zacher L (ed) Technology, society and sustainability – selected concepts, issues and cases. Springer International, Basel

Arroyo Amayuelas E (2016) The idea of an optional contract code. In: Twigg-Flesner C (ed) Research handbook on EU consumer and contract law. Edward Elgar, Cheltenham, pp 463–486

Basedow J (2011) Fakultatives Unionsprivatrecht oder: Grundlagen des 28. Modells. In: Festschrift für Franz Jürgen Säcker. CH Beck, München, pp 25–37

Basedow J (2012) An EU law for cross-border sales only – its meaning and implications in open markets, Max Planck Private International and Comparative Law, Research Paper No. 12/20, pp 43–44

Beale H (2016) The future of European contract law in the light of the European Commission's proposals for directives on digital content and online sales. IDP Revista de Internet, Derecho y Política 23:3–20. https://doi.org/10.7238/idp.v0i21.3085

Christopoulou C (2008) Consumer sale. In: Douvlis V, Bolos A (eds) Consumer protection law (in Greek). Sakkoulas Publishers, Athens, p 401

Cordero-Moss G (2016) Standard contract terms as an alternative to legislation. In: Twigg-Flesner C (ed) Research handbook on EU consumer and contract law. Edward Elgar, Cheltenham, pp 487–507

Council of the European Union (Justice and Home Affairs), 3455th meeting of the 10 11 March 2016

Court of Justice of the EU, Case C-190/11, *Daniela Mühlleitner v. Ahmad Yusufi και Wadat Yusufi*, 6 Sept 2012, ECLI:EU:C:2012:542

Court of Justice of the EU, Case C-404/06, *Quelle AG v. Bundesverband der Verbraucherzentralen und Verbraucherverbände,* 17 April 2008, ECR 2008, p. I-2685, ECLI:EU:C:2008:231

Court of Justice of the EU, Joined cases C-65/09 and C-87/09, *Gebr. Weber GmbH v. Jürgen Wittmer and Ingrid Putz v Medianess Electronic GmbH*, 16 June 2011, ECR 2011, p. I-05257, ECLI:EU:C:2011:396

Court of Justice of the European Union, Case C-497/13, *Froukje Faber v. Autobedrijf Hazet Ochten BV,* 4 June 2015, ECLI:EU:C:2015:357

[210] Beale (2016), p. 9.

Cygan A (2016) A step too far? Constitutional objections to harmonisation of EU consumer and contract law. In: Twigg-Flesner C (ed) Research handbook on EU consumer and contract law. Edward Elgar, Cheltenham, pp 13–54
European Commission, Communication, European Contract Law, COM(2001) 398, Brussels, 11 July 2001
European Commission (2003) Communication, a more coherent European Contract Law, An Action Plan, COM(2003) 68, Brussels, 12 Feb 2003
European Commission (2007) Communication to the Council and the European Parliament on the implementation of Directive 1999/44/EC of the European Parliament and of the Council of 25 May 1999 on certain aspects of the sale of consumer goods and associated guarantees including analysis of the case for introducing direct producers' liability, COM(2007) 210, Brussels, 24 April 2007
European Commission (2010) Communication, Europe 2020: a strategy for smart, sustainable and inclusive growth. COM(2010) 2020 final, Brussels, 3 March 2010
European Commission (2011) Communication, proposal for a regulation of the European Parliament and of the Council on a Common European Sales Law, COM(2011) 635 final, Brussels, 11 Oct 2011
European Commission (2012) Communication, EU regulatory fitness, COM(2012) 746 final, Strasbourg, 12 Dec 2012
European Commission (2014) DG justice guidance document concerning Directive 2011/83/EU of the European Parliament and of the Council of 25 October 2011 on consumer rights, amending Council Directive 93/13/EEC and Directive 1999/44/EC of the European Parliament and of the Council and repealing Council Directive 85/577/EEC and Directive 97/7/EC of the European Parliament and of the Council, DG Justice, Brussels, June 2014
European Commission (2015a) Communication, a digital single market strategy for Europe, COM(2015) 192 final, Brussels, 6 May 2015
European Commission (2015b) Commission staff working document. A digital single market strategy for Europe - analysis and evidence communication from the commission, COM(2015) 192 final
European Commission (2015c) Communication, digital contracts for Europe - unleashing the potential of e-commerce, COM(2015) 633, Brussels, 9 Dec 2015
European Commission (2015d) Communication, proposal for a directive "on certain aspects concerning contracts for the supply of digital content", COM(2015) 634, Brussels, 9 Dec 2015
European Commission (2015e) Communication, proposal for a directive of the European Parliament and of the Council "on certain aspects concerning contracts for the online and other distance sales of goods", COM(2015) 635, 2015/0288 (COD), Brussels, 9 Dec 2015
European Commission (2015f) Commission staff working document, impact assessment, Brussels, 18 Dec 2015
European Commission (2016a) Communication, European Cloud Initiative - Building a competitive data and knowledge economy in Europe, COM(2016) 178 final, Brussels, 19 April 2016
European Commission (2016b) Proposal for a Regulation of the European Parliament and the Council on cross-border parcel delivery services, COM(2016) 285 final, Brussels, 25 May 2016
European Commission (2016c) Communication, Online Platforms and the Digital Single Market Opportunities and Challenges for Europe, COM(2016) 288 final, Brussels, 25 May 2016
European Commission (2016d) Proposal for a Council Directive amending Directive 2006/112/EC and Directive 2009/132/EC as regards certain value added tax obligations for supplies of services and distance sales of goods, COM(2016) 757, Brussels, 1 Dec 2016
European Commission (2017a) Commission staff working document accompanying the document communication from the commission to the European Parliament, the Council, the European Economic and Social Committee and the Committee of the Regions on the Mid-Term Review on the implementation of the Digital Single Market Strategy "A Connected Digital Single Market for All", SWD/2017/0155 final

European Commission (2017b) Staff Working Document SWD(2017) 154 final, accompanying the document report from the Commission to the Council and the European Parliament, Final Report on the E-Commerce Sector Inquiry, COM(2017) 229, Brussels, 10 May 2017

European Commission (2017c) Report from the Commission, Annual Report 2016, on relations between the European Commission and National Parliaments, COM(2017) 601 final, Brussels, 30 June 2017

European Commission (2017d) Report on the application of Directive 2011/83/EU of the European Parliament and of the Council of 25 October 2011 on consumer rights, amending Council Directive 93/13/EEC and Directive 1999/44/EC of the European Parliament and of the Council and repealing Council Directive 85/577/EEC and Directive 97/7/EC of the European Parliament and of the Council, COM(2017) 259, Brussels, 23 May 2017

European Commission (2017e) Amended proposal for a Directive of the European Parliament and of the Council, on certain aspects concerning contracts for the online and other distance sales of goods, amending Regulation (EC) No 2006/2004 of the European Parliament and of the Council and Directive 2009/22/EC of the European Parliament and of the Council and repealing Directive 1999/44/EC of the European Parliament and of the Council, Brussels, COM(2017) 637 final, Brussels, 31 Oct 2017

European Commission factsheet, "Why we need a Digital Single Market". https://ec.europa.eu/commission/sites/beta-political/files/dsm-factsheet_en.pdf

European Data Protection Supervisor, Opinion on the Proposal for a Directive on certain aspects concerning contracts for the supply of digital content, (2017/C 200/07), O.J. C200/10 (23 June 2017). https://edps.europa.eu/sites/edp/files/publication/17-03-14_opinion_digital_content_en.pdf

European Economic and Social Committee (2012) Opinion on the Proposal for a Regulation of the European Parliament and of the Council on a Common European Sales Law and the Communication from the Commission to the European Parliament, the Council, the European Economic and Social Committee and the Committee of the Regions: A Common European Sales Law to facilitate cross-border transactions in the single market, INT/600 – CESE 800/2012, Brussels 29 March 2012

European Economic and Social Committee (2016) Opinion on the 'Proposal for a directive of the European Parliament and of the Council on certain aspects concerning contracts for the supply of digital content' (COM(2015) 634 final — 2015/0287 (COD)) and the 'Proposal for a directive of the European Parliament and of the Council on certain aspects concerning contracts for the online and other distance sales of goods' (COM(2015) 635 final — 2015/0288 (COD)), O.J. C264/57, 20 July 2016

European Parliament, Committee on the Internal Market and Consumer Protection (Rapporteur Pascal Arimont) Draft Report on the proposal for a directive of the European Parliament and of the Council on certain aspects concerning contracts for the online and other distance sales of goods, PE 593.817v03-00, 18 November 2016

European Parliament, Summary Content, 2015/0288(COD) – 09/12/2015 Legislative proposal

Fleischer H (2012) Optionales europäisches Privatrecht ("28. Modell"). Rabels Zeitschrift für ausländisches und internationales Privatrecht 76:235–252

Grigorova Ilieva E (2013) The proposal for a Common European Sales Law: does the European Union need this optional common code? https://www.cisg.law.pace.edu/cisg/biblio/ilieva.html

Grundmann S (2013) Costs and benefits for an optional European Sales Law. Common Mark Law Rev 50:225

Hesselink MW (2016) Contract theory and EU contract law. In: Twigg-Flesner C (ed) Research handbook on EU consumer and contract law. Edward Elgar, Cheltenham, pp 508–534

Király M (2015) The rise and fall of common European sales law. ELTE Law J 2:31–42

Lando O, Beale H (2000) Principles of European contract law, Parts I and II, Part III. Kluwer Law International, The Hague

Lando O, Beale H (2003) Principles of European contract law, Parts I and II, Part III. Kluwer Law International, The Hague

Leupold P (2016) Refit "fit for purpose"? 28. Sept 2016. https://vkiakademie.wordpress.com/2016/09/28/refit-fit-for-purpose
Magnus U, Mankowski P (eds) (2007) The Brussels I regulation. Sellier European Law Publishers, München
Mańko R (2016) Contracts for online and other distance sales of goods (February 16, 2016). European Parliamentary Research Service, PE 577.962, EU legislation in progress, Briefing. http://www.europarl.europa.eu/RegData/etudes/BRIE/2016/577962/EPRS_BRI(2016)577962_EN.pdf
Posner EA (2012) The questionable basis of the Common European Sales Law: the role of an optional instrument in jurisdictional competition (May 1, 2012). University of Chicago Institute for Law & Economics Olin Research Paper No. 597. Available at SSRN: https://ssrn.com/abstract=2049594 or https://doi.org/10.2139/ssrn.2049594
Research Group on the Law of Digital Services, Discussion Draft of a Directive on Online Intermediary Platforms, EuCML, Issue 4/2016, 164-169
Romanian Parliament Senate (2016) Opinion regarding the Proposal for a Directive of the European Parliament and of the Council concerning contracts for the supply of digital content and the Proposal for a Directive of the European Parliament and of the Council on certain aspects concerning contracts for the online and other distance sales of goods, 5937/2016, 1 March 2016
Schmidt-Kessel M, Silkens E (2016) Breach of contract. In: Plaza Penades J, Martines Velencoso L (eds) European perspectives on Common European Sales Law. Springer International, Basel, p 111
Schulte-Nölke H (2007) EC law on the formation of contract – from the common frame of reference to the 'blue button'. Eur Rev Contract Law 3(3):332–349
Schulte-Nölke H (2011) Der Blue Button kommt: Konturen einer rechtlichen Infrastruktur für den Binnenmarkt. Zeitschrift für Europäisches Privatrecht 19:749
Schulte-Nölke H, Zoll F, Charlton S (2012) Remedies for buyers in B2C contracts: general aspects, European Parliament, Directorate General for Internal Policies-Policy Department C: Citizens' Rights and Constitutional Affairs, PE 462.460, p 16. http://www.europarl.europa.eu/RegData/etudes/note/join/2012/462460/IPOL-JURI_NT(2012)462460_EN.pdf
Smits J (2016a) The New EU proposal for harmonised rules for the online sales of tangible goods (COM (2015) 635): conformity, lack of conformity and remedies (February 12, 2016). European Parliament Committee on Legal and Parliamentary Affairs, briefing note PE 536.492, European Union Publications Office, February 2016; Maastricht European Private Law Institute Working Paper No. 2016/01. Available at SSRN: https://ssrn.com/abstract=2731811
Smits J (2016b) New European Union proposals for distance sales and digital contents contracts: fit for purpose? (February 17, 2016). Zeitschrift für europäisches Privatrecht 2016, pp 319–324 and in a doc file, pp 1–6. Available at SSRN: https://ssrn.com/abstract=2733815
Study Group on a European Civil Code/Research Group on EC Private Law (2009) Principles, definitions and model rules of European private law: Draft Common Frame of Reference (DCFR). Sellier, Munich
Stürner M (2016) Stellungnahme zu den Kommissionsvorschlägen COM(2015) 634 und COM(2015) 635 im Rahmen der öffentlichen Anhörung des Ausschusses für Recht und Verbraucherschutz des Deutschen Bundestages, 4 May 2016. https://www.bundestag.de/blob/422106/efd7cdf67eb00e2c82d577d7c480bcfb/stuerner-data.pdf
Troiano S (2008) The CISG's impact on EU legislation. Internationale Handelsrecht 6:222
Twigg-Flesner C (2016) Introduction: EU consumer and contract law at a crossroads. In: Twigg-Flesner C (ed) Research handbook on EU consumer and contract law. Edward Elgar, Cheltenham, pp 3–11
UEAPME Position Paper on Contract Rules for online purchases of digital content and tangible goods. http://www.ueapme.com/IMG/pdf/UEAPME_position_on_Contract_Rules_for_online_purchases_of_digital_content_and_tangible_goods.pdf
UK Government call for views, Draft directives on the online sale of digital content and tangible goods, January 2016

UK Parliament, Documents considered by the Committee on 10 February 2016 - European Scrutiny Contents, 5 Digital Single Market: Consumer contract rights for the online sale of goods. The Minister's Explanatory Memorandum of 5 January 2016, Policy Implications, point 5.39. https://publications.parliament.uk/pa/cm201516/cmselect/cmeuleg/342-xxii/34208.htm

Watson J (2016) Withdrawal rights. In: Twigg-Flesner C (ed) Research handbook on EU consumer and contract law. Edward Elgar, Cheltenham, pp 241–265

Wunch-Vincent S (2006) The WTO, the internet and trade in digital products: EC-US perspectives. Hart, Oxford, pp 103–105

Part II
Selected Aspects of Commercial Contract Law in Practice: Good Faith, Collaboration and Sustainability in Commercial Contracts

Original Equipment Manufacturing Contract and Three-Way Bargaining: Cooperation, Control, and the Opportunism Within

Chien-Chung Lin

Contents

Abstract This chapter discusses the original equipment manufacturer (OEM), a model of large-scale industrial production that is popular today in many sectors of industry, especially in the information technology industry. An OEM's contractual setting usually involves a three-party negotiation, which includes a product design company/brand owner, an OEM, and a component supplier. The underlying logic of the OEM model is the delegation of manufacturing tasks to different players with

C.-C. Lin (✉)
National Chiao-Tung University, Hsinchu, Taiwan

M. Heidemann, J. Lee (eds.), *The Future of the Commercial Contract in Scholarship and Law Reform*, https://doi.org/10.1007/978-3-319-95969-6_7

different skill sets or specialties for a better allocation of resources. However, this contractual design also entails much complexity in its coordination, as modern manufacturing often has dozens or hundreds of units or steps before a final product is complete.

The author further discusses the phenomenon of the "technical service charge" contract, which is a side agreement between an OEM and a component supplier that allows the OEM to receive a payment or rebate from the component supplier even though there is no real exchange of goods or services involved. The technical service charge contract exemplifies the commercial opportunism and dynamics of adjustment at work in the multi-party supply chains of modern-day manufacturing. Examining this contractual design sheds light on how contracting parties extract benefit from the arrangement.

1 Introduction

An original equipment manufacturer, or OEM (sometimes referred to as original equipment manufacturing; both shortened to OEM hereinafter),[1] is a model of large-scale industrial production that is popular in many sectors of industry, including textiles, automobiles, and consumer electronics, to name a few. The OEM contract is omnipresent in the modern information technology (IT) industry.

From a legal standpoint, an OEM's contractual setting represents an interesting dynamic. Three parties or roles are often involved: a product designing company/brand owner (BO), an OEM, and a component supplier (CS). The product designer/BO (who often appears as the final seller and who promotes the products under its own brand) controls the sale and/or marketing of the final product, along with key patents in its product in many cases, and the power that comes from being a buying party. The whole process of delegating manufacturing (sometimes referred to as outsourcing) begins as the OEM takes an order from the BO and executes it as required. In the early days of such an arrangement, the OEM may only produce

[1] OEM is a term that is used in several ways that are slightly different from each other and sometimes even conflicting. For example, in Wikipedia, OEM is a company that "makes a part or subsystem that is used in another company's end product." See https://en.wikipedia.org/wiki/Original_equipment_manufacturer. Accessed 23 June 2017. In Merriam-Webster's dictionary, OEM means a company "that produces complex equipment (as a computer system) from components usually bought from other manufacturers." See https://www.merriam-webster.com/dictionary/OEM. Accessed 23 June 2017. According to Investopedia, in its traditional meaning, OEM means "a company whose goods are used as components in the products of another company, which then sells the finished item to users." However, in a newer definition from Investopedia, OEM refers to "the company that buys products and then incorporates or rebrands them into a new product under its own name." See Original Equipment Manufacturer—OEM Definition, Investopedia at http://www.investopedia.com/terms/o/oem.asp. Accessed 23 June 2017. The company in the second definition of OEM in Investopedia is termed brand owner in this article, to avoid confusion.

parts for the BO, and after receiving parts from the OEM, the BO assembles them on its own. Later, as the OEM evolves and shows superior ability to produce and integrate parts more cheaply, the OEM may assume a larger portion of production, including manufacturing parts and assembling them into the final product. An OEM that is sophisticated enough in its operations may even take on the design work or propose product ideas to a BO when the BO is not sure which product strategy to develop or the OEM is expanding its production business to serve multiple BOs in the same line of business. The outsourcing structure, at this stage, often extends to involve more CSs who specialize in producing certain key parts. OEMs who reach this level of sophistication also cultivate their capability to manage and assemble parts in a more efficient and timely fashion, with good quality control, and provide a so-called "total solution" to BOs. For BOs, this arrangement involves delegating a large portion of production and its processes to other producers and so allows BOs to focus more on research and development, scientific innovation, or brand managing and marketing, while leaving manufacturing to partners who are more capable in managing production costs.

From both a managerial and a legal perspective, the efficient coordination of complex production, when thousands of parts or components from different suppliers are involved, presents an inevitable challenge. What complicates things even more is when the traditional two-layer OEM model (BO to OEM, OEM to CS) transforms, as it does in some areas such as IT. Conceptually, in a two-layer outsourcing situation, two basic approaches exist alternatively; call them Model I and Model II. In the first approach, a BO allows an OEM to sub-delegate by conducting negotiation directly with a CS, and the BO needs only to decide whether the OEM's price quote is attractive enough to be accepted. This approach allows the OEM to enter into its own contractual relationship with the CS, facilitating an OEM's control over the CS and allowing the OEM more maneuverability in determining the profit that it can earn (Model I). In the second approach it is the BO that negotiates with a CS directly (typically a key CS that supplies critical parts), which eliminates any contractual relationship between the OEM and the CS. The purpose of the second approach is so that a BO can exercise tighter control over every portion of production, including the supply of satisfactory components (Model II).

In practice, it is not rare to see a BO bypass an OEM and deal with separate CSs directly (Model II). The BO's logic in circumventing an OEM is either to save cost or to gain more control over the needed parts, in terms of quantity, quality, price, timeliness, and possibly part interchangeability. This move on the part of a BO, in theory, changes vertical organization into a horizontal one between BO and OEM. In this situation, a BO signs separate contracts with the OEM and the CS, using contracts to require both OEM and CS to cooperate and coordinate.

Presumably, OEMs lose their buying power and work merely as an assembly factory (AF) when BOs choose the latter arrangement, i.e., cutting a deal directly with key CSs. But at the daily operational level, as the BO might be thousands of miles away, some challenges to oversight crop up. In a less known but highly prevalent practice (especially in the information technology (IT) OEM production ecology as it exists currently in Asian countries), many OEMs routinely demand and receive a payment or rebate, in the name of a "technical service charge," or TSC, from key CSs, even though there is no formal or contractual relationship between the OEM and the CS. This result, when it happens, suggests that an OEM coerces these payments and uses them to compensate its low profit margin when the BO chooses to negotiate directly with key CSs. A more interesting part of this practice is that sometimes it is carried out with the BO's knowledge and maybe even approval.

This TSC, a practice routinely observed in the IT industry, warrants further investigation into its contractual design from a theoretical perspective. In Model II an OEM/AF can still use its inspection power when components are delivered to the OEM's warehouse and waiting to be assembled as a leverage to "extract" additional payment from the CS. This is so because the BO may be far away from the production bases in Asia, so it is often difficult to exercise on-site scrutiny to determine which side, OEM or CS, is correct in a dispute. In this situation, the TSC works, in fact, as an institutionalized payment or a facilitating tool, or even a "bribe," for the OEM/AF within the business structure that results from Model II.

Thus, the question becomes whether or how this practice can be justified structurally or economically. Alternatively, this practice can be viewed, in a more friendly way, as a form of compensation, as an OEM shoulders the responsibility of inspecting and making sure all components received are qualified on the BO's behalf and also has the overall responsibility of completion and delivery before a product is sold to a retail customer. In an outsourcing structure, the OEM/AF insists or reasonably expects more flexibility as well as power when it shoulders much of the responsibility of completing the final products, especially when the BO is a faraway principal and delegates most of the task to it.

As I propose in this article, the TSC is a practice or a tool that facilitates three-party negotiation and allows more dynamic adjustment in modern-day IT production, in which the price for both the component and the final product, the specifications, and the production schedule can all be very volatile and uncertain. This rebate, in effect, and its structure illustrate the complexity of a three-party contract and its negotiation, as well as the commercial power structure that undergirds it. By examining the desirability and efficiency of this "self-adjustment" structure, this article uses the TSC as an example to explore the multilayer contract structure and its boundaries in today's mass industrial production. As part of the conclusion, I argue that a contractual disruption like a TSC is designed to overcome the difficulties inherent to Model II, be they contractual or organizational, and to create a possible strategic balance among relevant actors, corresponding to the prevailing power structure, as a result.

This article proceeds as follows. Section 2 examines the OEM contract and offers a closer look at how modern multinational corporations create global supply chains to enhance their production capability and efficiency, and the organizational and contractual arrangements at work in this setting. A case study of Apple's supply chain is used to illustrate how OEM contracts feed the omnipresent global manufacturing model we see today. Section 3 offers a brief account of the concept of "contract versus organization" in traditional organizational economics, with a review of leading academic literature in this area. This review provides the theoretical groundwork for reconsidering how the traditional understanding of a firm's "boundary" changes in light of mass production coordination bound by contracts with serial adjustment. In Sect. 4 I discuss a sample of a TSC contract collected from an electronics manufacturing company and the context of its usage. In addition, some newspaper articles revealing that Apple initiated contact with its CS for price renegotiation in 2016 provide a lens to observe how a large BO such as Apple Inc. stepped in and utilized an under-the-table arrangement like the TSC for the BO's benefit. The goal of this article is to reveal a dynamic process in contract negotiation in the rapidly changing industrial setting and the interaction between the legal forms adopted and this setting. The OEM structure stands in the middle of the traditional dichotomy of "contract versus organization" while working amorphously to serve a special need of the relevant parties. In this sense, it shows that the contract/organization choice is actually more of a continuous spectrum than a dichotomy.

2 Global Supply Chain and the OEM Model

Global production has been one key feature of the post–World War II industrial order. Comparative advantages in different countries, international political alliances, and lower transportation costs have all contributed to its prevalence. As companies adventured into foreign lands to seek cost reduction and later teamed up with local entrepreneurs to form joint ventures to avoid local hassles, many multinational conglomerates started to shed their production function along the way by delegating it to foreign manufacturers or partners. By doing so, these multinational conglomerates slowly shifted their focus to the high margin parts of their business, mostly product creation (research and development), brand management, marketing and sales, etc. Meanwhile, multinational conglomerates increasingly relied on their able partners for production and used well-designed contracts to maintain and secure smooth production for a myriad of products in a fashion that suited their corporate strategy at relatively low cost.

This strategy has proven successful for decades following World War II. Upon gaining more experience in production, manufacturing entrepreneurs also evolve and grow vertically or horizontally. For example, a manufacturer may consolidate different competitors or component provision functions and provide a complete product, instead of only some parts of it. Or it may acquire research or design capabilities to become an ODM (original design manufacturer). At this point, these manufacturing entrepreneurs, as authorized manufacturers, can even propose a new product or work as an OEM for multiple BOs, even though these BOs may be in fierce competition with one another at the consumer product level.

2.1 Models of OEM

To construct a supply chain, a BO generally adopts one of two strategies. The first model (Model I) allows an OEM more latitude in offering product ideas and in its actual manufacturing. In this model, an OEM controls much of the whole process of production, and that often includes the most important functions: component procurement and decision making. The second model (Model II), by contrast, gives less latitude to an OEM. One key feature in the second model is that the BO often controls the purchases of major components directly, deciding which producers to purchase from and the price to pay, as well as the quantity and quality and other key terms such as delivery. By doing that, the BO can effectively reduce the role of its OEM and the cost for components by direct negotiation if the BO is equipped with the necessary negotiation skill and the right operational knowledge. In this scenario, the OEM works more like an AF and has less decision power in terms of the specifications of components and from whom the components should be purchased. A variation of Model II is sometimes described in OEM jargon as "assigned vendor assigned price," or AVAP. Basically, in AVAP, a BO will first negotiate price and quantity with a CS. When a deal is agreed on, the BO may notify the AF (sometimes referred as a vertical integrator) that the AF can purchase a certain quantity of components at a specific price directly from the CS on the BO's behalf.[2]

The reason why a BO chooses the second route—buying components by direct negotiation—is not always clear. Logically, the BO may do so from a belief that it, not the OEM, has better knowledge of which CS has a superior cost-performance structure, on the one hand; or, on the other hand, the BO may believe that it has the needed negotiation skill to cut the price more effectively compared to an OEM. Both assumptions make little sense, especially when considering the facts that the OEM is generally in a position closer to the actual manufacturing process and has more direct access to CSs to evaluate them and their products. However, the second model survives in situations when a BO believes that it is in a dominant position in terms of negotiation or has substantial power over the final product market, and that power can extend to the component market.

Due to the confidential nature of commercial contracts, many of the contractual arrangements remain undisclosed, and it is not easy to ascertain how many major BOs or what percentage of OEM arrangements follow the second model. One widely reported example opting for the second model is Apple. To better understand the real-world dynamics of this model, it is worth looking at the example of Apple—the largest capitalized company in the world—to understand how this model is used and its underlying rationale.

[2] Xu (2012), pp. 13–14.

2.2 *Case Study: Apple's Value Chain*

2.2.1 The Making of a "Supply Chain King"

Apple Inc. is one the largest companies in the world that focuses on consumer electronics, software, and online services.[3] It sells a range of related software, services, accessories, networking solutions, and third-party digital content and applications.[4] It was valued at 773.68 billion U.S. dollars as of March 2017; it was valued at roughly 350 billion near the end of 2011; and it was valued at around 50 billion back at the end of 2005, another 6 years prior. Apple's value had been consistently less than 10 billion U.S. dollars since its founding in the early 1980s, all the way through 2003. The year 2004 marked the start of its astonishing rise in stock price that continues today.

Behind Apple's success and its popular products such as the iPod, iPhone, and iPad, its manufacturing arm had not received much notice until recently. Termed "the largest, fastest and most sophisticated manufacturing system on earth," Apple has been mastering its value chain,[5] with a successful global production model that matches the speed of its innovation.[6] The fast, cost-effective, and flexible manufacturing system, mostly based in China and taking advantages of low wages and a versatile supporting system there, plays a crucial role in the success of this global corporate giant.

Any success, especially one of this magnitude, has its reasons. Basically, a smart phone like Apple's star product iPhone has many key components in it, such as the processor, case, camera, display, and memory. However, the difficulty in maintaining an efficient supply chain for putting together a complex IT product like the iPhone is often understated. One research report about iPhone 6's supply chain, published in September 2014, reveals some hard facts about iPhone 6's supply chain. The supply chain spreads out to 31 countries, with the top five locations being China (349 suppliers), Japan (139 suppliers), USA (60 suppliers), Taiwan (42 suppliers) and South Korea (32 suppliers), and the manufacturing occurs mostly in China or the neighbouring Asian area.[7] In the same vein, Apple for the first time

[3] Apple has been the largest company in the world by market capitalization since late 2011, taking this position from ExxonMobil. See https://en.wikipedia.org/wiki/List_of_public_corporations_by_market_capitalization. Accessed 23 June 2017.

[4] Company Profile: Apple Inc. Available at http://www.reuters.com/finance/stocks/companyProfile?rpc=66&symbol=AAPL.O. Accessed 23 June 2017.

[5] Value chain is a concept that includes a set of interrelated activities a company uses to create a competitive advantage. The idea was pioneered by Michael Porter in his influential book Competitive Advantage in 1985.

[6] Duhigg and Barboza (2012).

[7] A useful and widely circulated overview of Apple iPhone 6's supply chain is "How & Where iPhone Is Made: Comparison of Apple's Manufacturing Process," available at http://comparecamp.com/how-where-iphone-is-made-comparison-of-apples-manufacturing-process/. Accessed 23 June 2017.

published a key suppliers list in 2012 (a list consisting of 156 companies, accounting for 97% of all of Apple's suppliers[8]) and currently publishes its top 200 suppliers.[9] But Apple's list only contains suppliers with which Apple does business directly.[10]

Details of Apple's supply chain first came under heavy public scrutiny when a series of suicides happened inconveniently at Honhai/Foxconn, Apple's key manufacturing partner in China, in 2010.[11] Since the 2010 Foxconn suicide event, the secretive manner that Apple used to manage its supply chain has transformed dramatically. Since then, Apple has paid close attention both to efficiency in its supply chain and to its public image and responsibility. It started to issue detailed supply chain responsibility reports—"progress reports"—annually to guarantee that its supply chain partners meet the heightened standard of public safety, working conditions, and provide other measures such as environment protection and worker's education.[12]

It is not hard to imagine the difficulty in coordinating and dealing with hundreds of suppliers in the pipeline, having to watch their performance and progress closely. Similarly important, a company like Apple needs to closely monitor potential firms for emerging technologies, as they are crucial in the fast-changing and densely competitive landscape of the IT industry.[13] Apple has succeeded in managing its vast network of suppliers so far and thus has been dubbed the "King of Outsourcing."[14]

---

[8] Wingfield and Duhigg (2012).

[9] Apple Inc., Supplier List, February 2017, at http://images.apple.com/supplier-responsibility/pdf/Apple-Supplier-List.pdf. Accessed 23 June 2017. Obviously these lists that Apple publishes do not include many of the secondary suppliers, i.e., suppliers without a direct contract with Apple.

[10] To fill out one's view of Apple's supply chain, a breakdown of the bill of materials shows the estimated price of all main components of the iPhone and their relationship to the whole. See http://www.supplychain247.com/article/apples_supply_chain_cost_of_making_the_iphone_7 (citing leading research institute IHS Markit's report and estimate of a base model iPhone 7's bill of materials at $219.80 U.S. dollars). Accessed 23 June 2017.

[11] The Economist (2010). Much attention was drawn to Apple's powerful OEM Foxconn Electronics by an article published by The New York Times in 2012. This article was written response to a series of worker suicides in Apple's OEM Foxconn in China in 2010 and raised questions about safety and labor conditions there. By looking into the reasons for the serial suicides, this article provides a peek into Apple's complex outsourcing structure. See Duhigg and Barboza (2012).

[12] Apple Inc., Supplier Responsibility, at http://www.apple.com/supplier-responsibility/. Accessed 23 June 2017.

[13] For some overview of Apple's procurement policy and its endeavor to develop an ecosystem of suppliers, see Apple Inc., Apple and Procurement, at http://www.apple.com/procurement/. Accessed 23 June 2017. Surprisingly, if one looks back to 2011, 6 years prior to the time of this writing, Nokia was still the leading smart phone vendor in the world. (It ranked number one through the first quarter of 2011, shipping 23.8% of all smart phones to customers that season, while Apple owned 18.3% of the smart phone market.) However, Nokia disappeared completely from the market in the third quarter of 2012, merely 18 months later. Nokia's precipitous fall exemplifies the stiff competition and volatility of the consumer electronics industry. Statista (2017).

[14] See http://www.supplychainopz.com/2013/01/is-apple-supply-chain-really-no-1-case.html and https://supplychainminded.com/apple-supply-chain-strong-iphone-6-closes/. Accessed 23 June 2017. Similarly, IT research firm Gartner ranked Apple's supply chain as the best supply chain in the world from 2009 to 2014. In 2015 and 2016, Apple was listed in the "Master" category for its

2.2.2 Supply Chain Management and Resource Allocation: Outsourcing with Lots of Hands-on Attention

As the backbone behind the iPhone's success, the role of Foxconn, the mighty manufacturing partner of Apple's iPhone, is to provide so-called FATP, which means final assembly, testing, and packaging.[15] Reportedly, it takes about 400 steps to assemble the iPhone, including polishing, soldering, drilling, and fitting screws. Foxconn's Zhengzhou manufacturing site can reportedly produce 500,000 iPhones a day, or roughly 350 per minute.[16]

Behind the apparent success of Apple's supply chain management, several legal maneuvers are in place to ensure its continuation. First, the tremendous market success that Apple and its popular products, like the iPhone and iPad, enjoy gives Apple great leverage over its OEMs and further along to its CSs. In this regard, notably, Apple makes contracts directly with key CSs and has a clear policy to use Model II. In particular, it is widely suspected that Apple opts for an "assigned vendor assigned price" model for most of the key components it uses and puts it into its master contract with its OEMs. By doing this, presumably, it can extend its leverage and market dominant position to cut a better deal with CSs, believing it can do this job better compared to its OEMs. In this way, Apple optimizes its supply chain and exerts direct control, via contracts, over its CSs.[17]

Second, reports repeatedly claim there is a strong tie between Apple and its OEM/assembly partner Honhai/Foxconn (famous for its strong disciplinary approach in production and its capability to manage dozens of factory, each equipped with tens or even hundreds of thousand of workers), but Apple is clearly aware of both the benefits and the perils in relying on a single OEM. It strategically seeks a competitor, as an alternative, to allow competition in the assembly section. Similar logic followed its adding an additional A-series chip supplier other than Samsung for its iPhone 6 and later models.[18] These efforts, in addition to its already strong grip over CSs and direct negotiation, are of particular importance when viewing Apple's heavy reliance on its supply chain and its gigantic investment in an industry in which speed and quality are almost everything. All combined, as a winner in outsourcing, Apple is extremely careful in its supply chain management, finding a delicate balance in all its needs and concerns. That probably helps explain how it has built one of the strongest (as well as one of the most complicated) supply chains in the world to support its business empire.

"sustained supply chain leadership over the last 10 years." See http://www.gartner.com/newsroom/id/3323617, http://www.gartner.com/technology/supply-chain/top25.jsp and http://www.supplychainopz.com/2013/01/is-apple-supply-chain-really-no-1-case.html. Accessed 23 June 2017.

[15] Barboza (2016b). Investigative reporter Barboza provides an interesting inside look into Honhai/Foxconn's deep-rooted management skill in China and its efficiency.

[16] Barboza (2016a).

[17] Australian Institute of Company Directors (2015). The tactics that Apple uses to control its suppliers include a long-term exclusive contract and prepayment to negotiate better price terms.

[18] See http://comparecamp.com/how-where-iphone-is-made-comparison-of-apples-manufacturing-process/. Accessed 23 June 2017.

3 OEM Structure and the Theory of the Firm

3.1 Coasean Theory

Since Ronald Coase's seminal thesis in 1937, "The Theory of the Firm,"[19] the boundary of the firm has been a central issue of study in corporate law and economics literature. Many distinguished economists and legal scholars have devoted much effort to delineating what constitutes the raison d'être, as well as the resilient prevalence, of capitalist firms and, more broadly, what economic rationales lie underneath a myriad of organizational schemes.

As widely noted, Ronald Coase first approached the issue from the angle of transaction costs and laid the foundation for the modern discussion of organizational economics. Basically, in Coase's view, a firm exists to avoid various transactional costs, especially the cost of learning about the terms, as well as the counterparty, of the exchange.[20] In addition, the cost of haggling over the terms of exchange is another important type of transaction cost. Both costs tend to be large if the transaction is a long-term one.[21]

Coase's line of argument continues as follows: to overcome these costs, a firm expands its reach to include certain production functions within its organization, in the hope that it can avoid the need for frequent transactions and hence reduce the associated costs. Put in other words, by bringing an exchange conducted outside the firm on the market to within the firm internal to its organization, a firm reduces its overall transaction costs.

But in Coase's thesis, the extent to which a firm will continue to expand itself to further this goal of lowering costs is a key question. Despite the incentive for a firm to grow in size by internalizing more transactions that it originally conducted on the open market, and thus relieve itself of constant haggling, the key question that concerned Coase was how far a firm would or should go in this direction. The answer, or the boundary of a firm's expansion according to Coase, is determined by the balance of "the costs of marketing in the open market" and "the costs of organising in another firm."[22] Put differently, in Coase's words, a firm will tend to become larger relative to certain conditions:

(a) the less the costs of organising and the slower these costs rise with an increase in the transactions organised;
(b) the less likely the entrepreneur is to make mistakes and the smaller the increase in mistakes with an increase in the transactions organised;
(c) the greater the lowering (or the less the rise) in the supply price of factors of production to firms of larger size.[23]

[19] Coase (1937).

[20] Ibid.; Hart (1989).

[21] Hart (1989), p. 1760.

[22] Coase (1937). p. 395.

[23] Ibid., pp. 396–397.

That is to say, the ability to organize and to keep the price of production of relevant factors lower are keys factors that determine the size of a firm. This postulation was later refashioned by Alchian and Demsetz, in their work "Production, Information Costs, and Economic Organization," into a formulation that focuses on how to control the monitoring costs.[24] In other words, a firm only exists because it can reasonably lower its monitoring cost when producing internally; otherwise it would be wiser to buy than to internalize.

In Alchian and Demsetz's view, a joint production takes a careful assessment or monitoring of each member's contribution, and this monitoring or assessment forms a different kind of transaction cost within the company or organization when transactions are replaced by long-term employment or ownership. In particular, bringing market transactions into a firm, or to use organizational authority to replace market negotiations, creates an enhanced need for monitoring and monitoring cost—another kind of transaction cost. In this sense, the boundary of a firm is determined by its monitoring capability.[25]

In another line of discussion, scholars' attention centers on what constitutes transaction costs. In theory, transaction costs include those arising in "making" an agreement and "leaving" an existing transaction (and finding another one to replace it). This is the area of thought to which Professor Oliver Williamson contributes in his work "The Economic Institutions of Capitalism,"[26] which focuses on "relationship-specific investments," a contractual arrangement in which one party may find it particularly difficult to leave once the original arrangement is agreed on and much of the investment cannot be easily transformed or moved to a different use. In that sense, transaction costs include not only learning and haggling but also leaving an agreement without much loss. These costs, in some sense, all imply different degrees or forms of opportunism that one party may exploit. Bringing transactions within a firm, as Williamson argues, may help reduce these costs and thus avoid opportunism that may occur.[27]

3.1.1 Comment

This brief introduction to the theory of the firm provides insights into OEM models. OEM structure, when fitted into theories of the firm, poses interesting questions. First, coming along at a later time than when theory of the firm was developed, OEM structure has proliferated with the wave of "lean production" popularized in the 1990s, but it was the "integration wave" that served as the backdrop for developing firm theory.[28] Firm theory and its refinements were developed in a context where

[24] Alchian and Demsetz (1972), pp. 777, 783.

[25] Ibid.

[26] See, generally, Williamson (1975, 1985).

[27] Hart (1989), p. 1763.

[28] See Wikipedia, Lean Manufacturing, https://en.wikipedia.org/wiki/Lean_manufacturing. Accessed 23 June 2017.

multinational conglomerates constantly expanded after World War II and gained an unprecedented political/economic influence. How far can or should these conglomerates continue with the expansion/integration strategy is the main concern in the various formulations of firm theory. But, against a different background, the OEM structure started to prosper in the 1980s at a time of rational "reshaping" of production lines and business organizational downsizing. So, how or to what extent theory of the firm can explain the outsourcing phenomenon and the OEM structure is an issue warranting further scrutiny.

Second, the outsourcing phenomenon and the OEM structure emphasize one unique feature: the other party in the bargaining. In IT-industry OEM, many of the suppliers provide only one or a small set of components with highly specialized features and functions. In this setting, the investigation cost is relatively low and the monitoring is rather straightforward—simply checking whether the delivered products fulfill the specifications and the described function. Further, companies in the IT industry tend to be related, and the degree of information and knowledge sharing is high. This is true probably because potential cooperation opportunities exist and the founders of those companies have a common technological background. If this observation holds true, learning the products or the counterparty in the exchanges would be relatively easy, thus reducing the need or cost of monitoring, as well as reducing asset specificity. Naturally, these features of the IT industry all fit the firm theories mentioned earlier and thus reduce the need to integrate other's production into one's firm. These features (product standardization, shared knowledge base, and the ecology and its close environment of companies involved) also adequately explain the current organizational arrangements in the IT industry today.[29]

3.2 *Asset Complementarity and Opportunism Revisited*

Led by Grossman and Hart, a property rights approach to the firm provides a different angle on the OEM discussion. This view concentrates on the power/surplus allocation after the original contracts are signed, i.e., the ex post distribution, or more precisely, the opportunism problem when contracts are incomplete. In this view, because contracts—ex ante negotiation—are inherently incomplete, ex post residual rights of control will play a determining role and in turn dictate the ex post bargaining power and the division of ex post surplus in a relationship. The logic goes on and posits that the division will, in turn, affect the incentives of actors to

[29] However, even when contracts are used as the means of obtaining needed parts, the purchase often tends to be, in the IT industry, a mid- or long-term, but not a one-time, relationship. Using contracts to manage a mid- or long-term relationship adds some twists to the original calculation and makes it more complex. In the view taken here, seeing this recurring possibility in fact changes the original contractual features and leads to arrangements closer to organization-like territory. I take up this point at more length later in the article.

invest in that relationship ex ante.[30] Put differently, a firm would and should set its boundary along the line of ownership of the residual assets that it wishes to hold on to. This strategy will help produce the desired amount of ex post bargaining power, or, in plainer words, a better position when renegotiation or negotiation beyond the original contract is needed.

Why is the ownership of residual assets so important? In Grossman and Hart's observations, assets start to become complementary to each other when a contract starts to bind different assets together and form a relationship. In some situations, after a relationship is formed and takes root, some assets become highly complementary to each other and hard to replace. In this situation, those highly complementary assets should be owned by the same entity to avoid the renegotiation problem and possible opportunism.[31] In this line of thought, asset complementarity is the key concept that defines the boundary of assets that should be included in the firm for the purpose of avoiding opportunism or the hold-up problem. In Professor Hart's own words, when viewing this issue from the other end, "in the absence of significant lock-in effects, non-integration is always better than integration."[32]

3.2.1 Comment

A property rights approach to the firm correctly points to the concern of incomplete contract and the hold-up problem that arises therefrom. As the emphasis on opportunism clearly becomes the focus, however, whether pointing to the ownership of the residual asset is the best, or the only, solution is still unclear. Notably, asset specificity can be a two-way phenomenon. If it is true, the mutual lock-up (then giving rise to mutual adjustments) or the long-term relationship that allows the possibility for retaliation both show potential in solving this problem, at least at different levels or to various extents. In the following analysis, the example of the IT industry outsourcing to OEMs, exemplified by the Apple-Honhai relationship, provides an interesting case study of highly interdependent value chain production in the real world. This discussion, in turn, will test how strong these theories hold for OEMs.[33]

[30] Hart (1989), p. 1766.

[31] Ibid., p. 1770.

[32] Ibid.

[33] Grossman and Hart (1986), Holmstrom and Tirole (1989) and Hart and Moore (1990).

4 Technical Service Charge, Opportunism, and a Dynamic Game

4.1 *Side Bargaining*

The TSC goes by many names, but, in essence, it is a contract between the main sub-contractor, often an OEM,[34] and other CSs in which the main sub-contractor demands a payment (roughly 3% of the goods/components delivered, charged annually) from the CSs. In most cases, it can take place no matter whether there is any formal or direct procurement contract between the main sub-contractor and the CSs or not. The purpose of this contract is to guarantee a smooth reception of goods/components from the CS to the main sub-contractor, as the former needs clearance to enter the latter's warehouse to make a delivery. CSs may face a serious problem if the delivery of goods is delayed or rejected for any reason, generally an unnecessary or stretching inspection exercised by the main sub-contractor that creates unwanted delay. In truth, TSC is a payment made by a CS for the right to be left alone.

As a prevalent practice in the IT industry, a typical TSC contract looks straightforwardly simple. According to the sample contract acquired by the author, it is a two-page document of rudimentary form and titled "Contract" without further specification. The key terms in a TSC contract basically contain only the following stipulations:

- The OEM, as an international electronics manufacturing company, is willing to help promote the CS's products. It will provide needed technical support and other assistance to further the goal of a smooth adoption of the CS's product in the manufacturing process. (Preamble)
- In the case when the CS's products are used, be it directly purchased by OEM or BO, the CS will pay OEM ___ percentage [left blank] of the value of the overall products shipped to the OEM as the "technical service charge." The TSC is calculated annually and paid at the end of each year. (Article 1)
- The contract's duration is from 01/01/2016 to 31/12/2017. The contract is on a rolling basis and will automatically extend another year at the end of each year. Each party can express its intention of not extending the contract one month before the last day of the effective date of the contract. (Article 2)
- Other typical provisions, such as a non-assignment clause (Article 3), method/address of notice (Article 4), and confidentiality (Article 5).
- Termination and amendment of the contract, if needed, will be conducted based on the written consent from both sides of the contract. (Articles 6 & 7)

---

[34] The main sub-contractor can be a large AF and is in most cases. When all manufacturing work is outsourced to one main sub-contractor, that sub-contractor is customarily called, in the IT industry, an OEM.

- Applicable law and forum. It includes Taiwanese law and court as the default in the sample contract. (Articles 8 & 9)
- Signatures and dates.

Basically, a TSC contract is loose and ill defined, even by the local standard (mostly in China, Taiwan, and other Asian countries where electronics OEMs reside). In particular, it does not provide much detail about the actual content of service that will be provided by the party who receives the delivered merchandise, i.e., the OEM. Several experienced legal counsel professionals in the OEM/EMS (electronics manufacturing service) sector that the author interviewed expressed their views on the TSC based on their own experience. Their observations can be summarized as followed:

- As a procedural matter, they opined that the sample contract the author acquired and examined is boilerplate and quite similar to those they have encountered in their careers. They agreed that the TSC is a common practice and has been in place for more than a decade. Key CSs (who supply components that account for 10% or more of the overall material cost, such as display, hard drive, CPU, and RAM in notebook manufacturing; or processor, display, memory, metal case, and camera in smart phones) will tend to be asked to agree on a TSC contract, with a few exceptions.
- In its function, a TSC works as a rebate for the OEM firm, as one interviewee described it. However, all the interviewees similarly pointed out that, in order to avoid the impression of paying a commercial bribe, the vague term of TSC is used instead.
- A TSC is generally demanded by an OEM when a BO opts for Model II and conducts direct procurement. That means, if opting for Model I, an OEM will integrate a TSC into the purchase negotiation without a making separate demand.
- One legal specialist with more than 15 years' experience as OEM in-house counsel used an adage, "cost—and its change—may be small, but the overall impact is not," to describe the mentality shared in the industry around this practice. Namely, even when each component may cost only a few cents less without a TSC, in aggregate the arrangement leads to multimillion-dollar profits. This is true considering that a top notebook OEM may manufacture around 30–40 million units per year under different brands.[35]
- Whether the existence of a TSC is known to the BO is unclear. But as the case of price-cutting renegotiation by Apple in 2016 shows (discussed below), it may be naïvely one-sided to assume a BO's unawareness of this practice. The ecology of the IT industry and the OEM supply chain's intimate interdependence suggest that the TSC may be carried out with a business-savvy BO's awareness or even approval.

[35] See Wikipedia, List of Laptop Brands and Manufacturers, https://en.wikipedia.org/wiki/List_of_laptop_brands_and_manufacturers. Accessed 23 June 2017.

Interestingly, CSs in this ecology (especially small- or medium-sized suppliers) seem resigned to this practice. Their acquiescence may be attributable to several reasons. First, for participants in the ecosystem, the long-followed practice has become an "industry rule" that participants have gotten used to despite its semi-coercive nature. Second, any unnecessary delay in the whole production process, even a small one, can incur huge liability and economic loss. In this sense, the threat posed by the OEM, remote or not, still has its bite. Conversely, a good relationship with the OEM can provide additional benefits to the CS. Those include a better communication channel with the OEM to learn about business opportunities and stay apprised of industrial trends. In a competitive world, a small advantage, accumulated over time, may lead to long-term success. At a minimum, in a situation where an OEM has direct purchasing power and the particular component market is competitive or the product's performance-cost structure is similar, an OEM is likely to purchase from a CS with which it has a good relationship.[36] In all, as both the CS and the OEM have invested a huge amount of capital in this area, the nature of the repeated game prevents the negotiation from breaking up, and often the CS side may yield. Third, as commonly observed, a CS generally enjoys a higher profit margin, possibly 15%, as an OEM has 5% only (in contrast to 40% or more profit for the BO). In this setting, comparatively, a CS still has more room to compromise vis-à-vis an OEM. As a result, the demand for a TSC generally prevails, with or without the direct purchase relationship between the OEM and CS.

4.2 Collaboration and the "Contract Versus Organization" Distinction

4.2.1 Close Collaboration Between BO and OEM

In an area such as sophisticated IT manufacturing, it is common to see a BO send a group of engineers to station inside an OEM facility for close monitoring and for making design modifications as needed.[37] This practice is particularly common when a complex product project faces imminent launch. In this case, the BO needs to make sure that all designs, no matter whether originated with the BO or an ODM,

[36] In the IT industry, securing a timely acquisition of key components may also be crucial to a BO, especially when new technology is embodied in those components. Because new components will affect the overall experience of a product, the goal is to acquire those key components as quickly as possible. For an OEM, similarly, getting familiar with new components' performance and characteristics will give it advantages in quickly completing the manufacture of a product. This is critical in an industry where change is rapid and competition is fierce. In this situation, a "good relationship" between BO and OEM comes closer to being two-way reciprocity than one-sided reliance.

[37] See Oliver (2012). Some of the literature on supply-chain management places much emphasis on monitoring suppliers. In fact, Apple is a frequent case cited as taking an intensive approach to such monitoring.

can reasonably work at an efficient rate of production. Similarly, the performance of a product, the modifications needed, and the resolution of any other problems arising in manufacturing all require close cooperation from both sides. Sometimes key issues such as abandoning a design idea, modifying a major design, or changing some production process have to be put forward and determined by the BO and OEM jointly. The intensive back-and-forth discussion by the engineers from the BO and the OEM requires teamwork to guarantee feasibility and timely problem solving. In reality, to meet the competitive market conditions, this intensive collaboration is qualitatively little different from any intra-firm collaboration.

4.2.2 The Dynamics in Collaboration and Its Fluidity

This intensive cooperation further complicates the idea of "outsourcing." What good is it to a BO if it has to pay so much attention to the OEM that it loses the cost saving of outsourcing? Or put differently, to what extent is an OEM still an independent company if the monitoring is very high? The answer to this question may be multifold. If looking from a more neutral angle, the level of monitoring simply reflects the fact that each product (or each company) has its own strategy, which in turns defines the relationship between OEM and BO, which finds its own balance. Surely from the angle of the OEM/ODM, a higher degree of autonomy (including more design work or latitude) often means a larger room for profit, and thus it becomes the goal of its business strategy. This combination is clearly observed in the notebook industry, as the main OEM/ODMs control large parts of the overall work. However, a different story can be seen in Apple's iPhone. In that case, the design of the iPhone is held tightly at Apple's headquarters in California, and its OEM work is substantially delegated to Honhai/Foxconn in China. This guarded form of cooperation, largely exclusionary of others, is built on long-term cooperation as well as the iPhone's past success.[38] From this perspective, different modes of cooperation or bargaining can coexist that strike their own balance between the anticipated result and the monitoring cost. The verdict in deciding among different modes of cooperation really depends on the nature of the product, namely, the structure of the market and market power of the product.

Similar indeterminacy can be seen in the choice of Model I or Model II. The decision of opting for Model I or Model II is not a static but rather a dynamic one. The task of purchasing rests on who ultimately has greater bargaining power over the key CSs, which in turns decides what model to follow. For example, if the OEM can successfully convince the BO that it can acquire key parts at a lower price because it also acts as an OEM for other BOs and can use quantity to bargain down

[38] See Bibey (2014). In fact, to speak of true exclusiveness is an overstatement. In terms of OEM or AF, Apple does use two OEMs, Honhai and Pegatron, at least since 2014. Pegatron, interestingly, enjoys roughly half the order by estimation. The reason Foxconn is mentioned more often owes to a series of New York Times stories and, possibly, to the fact that Pegatron is responsible for smaller iPhones and Honhai, the bigger and more expensive ones.

the price, the BO may agree to Model I and let the OEM make the purchase of that component directly. But, if the BO for any reason (such as better bargaining skill or the desire to maintain more control over the whole process) considers itself a better deal maker, it may bypass the OEM and negotiate directly with key CSs in preference for Model II. To sum up, the decision between these two models depends on the actual combination of characteristics of all players, products, and market features; thus it is a dynamic one.

4.3 A Structure Based on Power

4.3.1 Acquiescence Analyzed

The TSC still leaves puzzles unsolved. Whether, or to what extent, do BOs really know or tolerate the extraction of value from CSs by an OEM, by way of a TSC, is an issue to be determined. As discussed earlier, as this practice is widely used and has been in place for many years, it is hard to imagine a powerful BO being unaware of it. However, it is possible for a BO to maintain the status quo because the payment is made by a CS to an OEM without harming the price quote it receives from the CS. In addition, it also helps reduce the OEM's resistance when BO and OEM negotiate their price and the OEM knows it can find some other source of revenue to compensate its low margin in the OEM contract.

With that said, the TSC from CS to OEM still means a possible concession a CS may be willing to make to maintain its commercial production. In light of this, a rational BO, if powerful enough, may want to use this knowledge and extract more profit from a CS's quote, i.e., take away some of the pie originally divided between the CS and OEM. To the surprise of many, this is the action Apple took with its iPhone 6.

4.3.2 Ad Hoc/Ex Post Adjustment by a BO

Around the third quarter of 2016, stories about Apple "renegotiating" with its CSs to accept a price cut started to surface.[39] This action was taken by Apple around July 2016 following two consecutive quarters of shrinking profit for Apple.[40] Clearly, the purpose of these renegotiations was to protect Apples falling profit, and these renegotiations and price cuts were agreed to without much resistance, or so it appeared from the outside.

If this renegotiation happened as reported, two reasons may explain Apple's result. One is time sensitivity in the IT industry that makes both sides amenable to compromise to avoid the cost of uncertainty and delay when time pressure is strong.

[39] See Dou (2016) and Lovejoy (2016).

[40] See Webb (2016) and Leswing (2016).

The other, and probably the more important reason, may be that most suppliers are eager to get an order from Apple, for both its leading position in the market and for the vast quantity of components involved. These reasons make it seem that Apple, as a BO, was able to demand a less profitable price for its suppliers to increase its own profit margin when needed. Moreover, other stories have reported similar tactics used by Apple to gain the upper hand in negotiation.[41]

4.3.3 Renegotiation and TSC: Power Structure Matters

The renegotiation process displays a pattern similar to the TSC. The existence of a TSC may suggest to a BO that it can exert a similar squeeze to boost its own profit. From a legal perspective, a renegotiation between BO and CS is carried out despite the fact that a formal contract is already in place and binding. The result of renegotiation, as well as that of a TSC, explicitly indicates that neither ex ante contractual arrangement (as seen in Apple's renegotiation with CSs) nor a non-contractual relationship (as seem in the TSC, a "created" contract without any meaningful exchange from OEM in an economic sense, to be more precise) can protect a weaker party from coercion by the stronger party, with the inevitability of a looming opportunism in a long-term relationship. The opportunism originally exploited by the OEM (i.e., Honhai in this case) was transferred to the BO, the larger and more powerful role in the whole chain of contracts, when it sees fit to exercise it. In different terms, it is the residual right of a key asset (in the case of Apple's iPhone the asset inheres in its design, marketability, brand image, and probably some patents) that determines bargaining power.

It is thus obvious what really matters. No matter the organizational structure of a corporation or a group of corporations, owning the "key assets"—the ability to design and market a superior product and the size of economic resources owned and under control—is the real determining factor. In other words, if one owns more power in this distribution, it really does not matter so much where the formal organizational or corporate line is drawn. A powerful player can still direct, to different degrees, how other parties allocate their resources and set prices through contractual arrangements, ex ante or ex post alike. That is, a similar result can be achieved even without direct ownership being in effect.

Thus, the possible, as well as the real, limits or boundaries of a firm are measured by its bargaining power. Its power penetrates organizational or contractual arrangements when necessary and sets its outer boundary and the extent of its reach. In this way, what defines the boundaries of the firm is its economic power, whether BO, OEM, or CS. And a company only stops where its power ends, be that boundary a formal organizational one or not.

---

[41] See Randewich (2014) and Hein (2014).

5 Conclusion

No matter how a firm should be viewed from the transactional cost theory of Coase or its later modifications, a modern-day firm, if powerful enough, can exert control beyond the boundaries of its business organization as defined by corporate law. As a tool, contracting with an OEM or other outsourcing arrangement extends a firm's reach beyond its organizational lines and reshapes the view of a firm today.

As discussed herein, the TSC is an unusual but prevalent practice in the OEM structure. TSCs highlight the power structure of each relevant player in a supply chain. The fact that a TSC uses a contract's guise even when no real economic exchanges exist tells a vivid story about how firms pierce the original legal arrangement and create one of their own. TSCs and similar renegotiation also evidence how power dynamics in the real world reshape not only the corporate/organizational borderline of a firm but also a contractual obligation that used to delimit the reach of legal influence. Put differently, the TSC defies the traditional distinction of "contract versus organization" as an explanatory theory of the firm and argues for an alternative narrative: power structure remains the key element in all production relationships, though they may rely more on organization, contract, or neither.

It is true and frequently noted that a contract is often a power structure. But this article has taken the argument a step further and in another direction. As the power structure does not stop where no formal contractual relationship exists, it creates one of its own. The TSC shows that it is not a contract that enables power but rather vice versa. If this view holds, to say a firm is a series of contracts or a nexus of contracts does not actually point to the heart of the matter. In fact, it is not the place or the person or the cost of contracts that defines a firm per se; it is the power behind all contracting and negotiating that does.

References

Alchian AA, Demsetz H (1972) Production, information costs, and economic organization. Am Econ Rev 62(5):777–795

Australian Institute of Company Directors (2015) A case study of Apple's supply chain. 11 Sept 2015. http://aicd.companydirectors.com.au/advocacy/governance-leadership-centre/governance-driving-performance/a-case-study-of-apples-supply-chain. Accessed 23 June 2017

Barboza D (2016a) An iPhone's journey, from the factory floor to the retail store. The New York Times, 29 Dec 2016. https://www.nytimes.com/2016/12/29/technology/iphone-china-apple-stores.html. Accessed 23 June 2017

Barboza D (2016b) How China built 'iPhone City' with billions in perks for Apple's partner. The New York Times, 29 Dec 2016. https://www.nytimes.com/2016/12/29/technology/apple-iphone-china-foxconn.html. Accessed 23 June 2017

Bibey C (2014) Apple supply chain strong as iPhone 6 closes in. SupplyChain247. 21 Aug 2014. http://www.supplychain247.com/article/apple_supply_chain_strong_as_iphone_6_closes_in/supply_chain_optimization. Accessed 23 June 2017

Coase R (1937) The nature of the firm. Economica 4(16):386–405

Dou E (2016) Apple squeezes parts suppliers to protect margins. The Wall Street Journal, 1 Sept 2016. https://www.wsj.com/articles/apple-squeezes-parts-suppliers-to-protect-margins-1472713073. Accessed 23 June 2017
Duhigg C, Barboza, D (2012) In China, human costs are built into an iPad. The New York Times, 25 Jan 2012. http://www.nytimes.com/2012/01/26/business/ieconomy-apples-ipad-and-the-human-costs-for-workers-in-china.html. Accessed 23 June 2017
Grossman SJ, Hart OD (1986) The costs and benefits of ownership: a theory of vertical and lateral integration. J Polit Econ 94(4):691–719
Hart O (1989) An economist's perspective on the theory of the firm. Columbia Law Rev 89(7):1757–1774
Hart O, Moore J (1990) Property rights and the nature of the firm. J Polit Econ 98(6):1119–1158
Hein B (2014) Court docs reveal how Apple treats its suppliers (badly). Cult of Mac. 7 Nov 2014. http://www.cultofmac.com/302445/unsealed-court-docs-reveal-apples-strained-relationship-gtat/. Accessed 23 June 2017
Holmstrom BR, Tirole J (1989) The theory of the firm. In Schmalensee R, Willig R (eds) Handbook of industrial organization, vol 1. Handbooks in Economics 10. North-Holland, Amsterdam, pp 66–133
Leswing K (2016) Apple is squeezing suppliers to keep its profits high, says analyst. Business Insider, 9 Aug 2016. http://www.businessinsider.com/apple-is-squeezing-suppliers-says-rbc-2016-8. Accessed 23 June 2017
Lovejoy B (2016) Foxconn, Pegatron & other Apple suppliers reportedly under pressure as Apple squeezes margins. 9to5Mac. 5 July 2016. https://9to5mac.com/2016/07/05/foxconn-pegatron-apple-margins/. Accessed 23 June 2017
Oliver S (2012) Under Tim Cook, Apple cracking down on supply chain management. Appleinsider, 18 June 2012. http://appleinsider.com/articles/12/06/18/under_tim_cook_apple_cracking_down_on_supply_chain_management. Accessed 23 June 2017
Randewich N (2014) GT Advanced says fell victim to "bait-and-switch" by Apple. Reuters, 7 Nov 2014. http://www.reuters.com/article/us-gt-advanced-tech-bankruptcy-apple-idUSKBN0IR2G220141107. Accessed 23 June 2017.
Statista (2017) Global market share held by leading smartphone vendors from 4th quarter 2009 to 4th quarter 2016. Statista, the Statistics Portal. https://www.statista.com/statistics/271496/global-market-share-held-by-smartphone-vendors-since-4th-quarter-2009/. Accessed 23 June 2017
The Economist (2010) Light and death: suicides at Foxconn. The Economist, 27 May 2010. http://www.economist.com/node/16231588. Accessed 23 June 2017
Webb A (2016) Apple forecasts second sales drop as iPhone woes deepen. Bloomberg, 27 Apr 2016. https://www.bloomberg.com/news/articles/2016-04-26/apple-forecasts-another-sales-decline-as-iphone-demand-cools
Williamson O (1975) Markets and hierarchies: analysis and antitrust implications. Free Press, New York
Williamson O (1985) The economic institutions of capitalism: firms, markets, relational contracting. Free Press, New York
Wingfield N, Duhigg C (2012) Apple lists its suppliers for 1st time. The New York Times, 13 Jan 2012. http://www.nytimes.com/2012/01/14/technology/apple-releases-list-of-its-suppliers-for-the-first-time.html. Accessed 23 June 2017
Xu EY (2012) Defining new business models for the mobile device supply chain. Master's thesis, Massachusetts Institute of Technology

Uncertainty, Speculation, Subjectivity: The Expanding Judicial Role in Sovereign Debt Workouts

Dania Thomas

Contents

D. Thomas (✉)
Adam Smith Business School, University of Glasgow, Glasgow, UK
e-mail: Dania.Thomas@glasgow.ac.uk

M. Heidemann, J. Lee (eds.), *The Future of the Commercial Contract in Scholarship and Law Reform*, https://doi.org/10.1007/978-3-319-95969-6_8

Abstract This chapter situates a discussion of the NML decision against Argentina within a wider political economy context to better understand the expanding judicial role in sovereign debt workouts. The observed surge in debt demand, growing debt to Gross Domestic Product ratios in debt states increasingly reliant on refinancing their budgetary deficits and a fragmenting consensus that sustained the informal debt workout process so far indicate that sovereign debt speculators that drive demand are making investment decisions in conditions of uncertainty. This paper delineates the political economy contexts in which these speculators evolved as legal subjects. In modern debt markets, the common law courts have become instrumental in entrenching the subjectivity of the debt speculator. This role is an overlooked factor that explains their expansive influence on sovereign debt workouts.

1 Introduction

The jury is still out on the actual impact of recent decisions[1] against Argentina in distressed asset fund enforcement litigation, on sovereign debt workouts. On the face of it these were straightforward contract interpretation disputes. The US courts relied on common sense and simple logic to interpret a standard, boilerplate term in sovereign bond contracts—the *pari passu* clause[2]—to eventually enforce the contracts. This approach belies the significance of the decisions reflected in the ongoing and sustained critical reaction to them.[3] It was argued that this "non-expert"[4]

[1] NML Capital, Ltd v Argentina, No 08 Civ 6978 (TPG) (SDNY 23 Feb 2012); NML Capital, Ltd v Argentina, 699 F3d 246, 264 (2d Cir 2012); NML Capital, Ltd v Argentina, No 08 Civ 6978 (TPG), 2012 US Dist LEXIS; 167272 (SDNY 21 Nov 2012); NML Capital, Ltd v Argentina, 727 F3d 230 (2d Cir 2013), cert denied 134 SCt 2819 (16 June 2014).

[2] The clause was contained in the prospectus of Argentina's defaulted bonds as follows: "[t]he Securities will constitute…direct, unconditional, unsecured and unsubordinated obligations of the Republic and shall at all times rank *pari passu* without any preference among themselves. The payment obligations of the Republic under the Securities shall at all times rank at least equally with all its other present and future unsecured and unsubordinated External indebtedness." Gulati and Scott (2013).

[3] Thomas (2017), Miller and Thomas (2007), Bai (2013), Gelpern and Gulati (2006) and Weidenmaier and McCarl (2014). Outside the courtroom, the litigation strategies of the so called 'vulture funds' were also widely condemned. In his speech to the United Nations in 2002, Gordon Brown the then Chancellor of the Exchequer said "We particularly condemn the perversity where Vulture funds purchase debt at a reduced price and make a profit from suing the debtor country to recover the full amount…". (Quoted after Jones (2009)). This was followed in a G8 meeting in 2007, where ministers expressed similar concerns and agreed to work with the Paris Club. In that year the Paris Club committed to exclude creditors who refused to participate in debt restructuring from purchases of debt on the secondary market. This was followed by a similar EU-wide agreement in 2008. This sentiment resurfaced in the Doha Declaration on development calling for similar action. In the UK, this led to legislative enactments in 2008 and 2010. Debt Relief (Developing Countries) Act 2010; Debt Relief (Developing Countries) Bill, (2010), followed by a Euro zone legislation aimed at restricting holdout intervention in debt workouts.

[4] Buchheit and Gulati (2017) "As a matter of contract interpretation of the *pari passu* clause, the decision was certainly wrong. The largest trade association representing bondholders, underwriters,

interpretation was 'plain wrong'[5] and contrary to past market practice. On this, there was clear water between the experts including academics such as Joseph Stiglitz,[6] seasoned practitioners like Lee Buchheit,[7] the US government,[8] and the 'non-expert judges'.

The dust has since settled but for all intents and purposes, the court did play an instrumental role in resolving the enforcement problem: a problem that is a feature of the systemic architecture and which the official sector (International Monetary Fund (IMF)), informal market associations, creditors and debtor states had failed to resolve for over three decades. The judicial resolution however came with consequences. Once the interpretation established a route to enforce the contracts, the court followed through and proceeded to customise a remedy that would not only affect third party claims but would even injunct the US clearing system to bring Argentina—a sovereign state—to the negotiating table. The longterm implications of this judicial method are still unravelling.

As far as the courts were concerned no one knew what the exact meaning of the clause was or indeed why these clauses migrated from corporate into sovereign bonds?[9] The courts were resolute in their refusal to reference past market practice to interpret the clause. The exercise of their discretion—an integral part of the common law method—did not require them to follow the experts nor assume that any outcome should reproduce meanings established in the past. They were standing in the shoes of the litigating creditors. They were interpreting the clause through the eyes of investors choosing to lend in conditions where repayment prospects were non-existent. The petitioners were speculative investors. Their decisions to buy distressed debt were based on risks that could neither be precisely defined nor measured against historical data. It is revealing that the judges take their approach over the historically informed and carefully reasoned explanations drawn from market practice that informed expert opinions on alternative meanings of the clause.[10]

The speculators that spearhead enforcement litigation have been doing so since the securitization of sovereign debt in the 1980s.[11] They form a subset of debt investors[12] that have historically driven debt demand. They specialize in 'buying cheap

issuers and financial intermediaries felt compelled after the NML decision to promulgate model *pari passu* clauses for use in sovereign bonds that expressly disavow the court's ratable payment interpretation of the provision."

[5] Buchheit and Gulati (2017).

[6] See Joseph Stiglitz' Amicus Brief in support of petitioner dated 24 March 2014 in petition to the United States Court of Appeals for the Second Circuit.

[7] Bucheit and Pam (2004).

[8] Amicus brief filed by the US Government Arg 4112842 Argentina v NML Amicus 120913.

[9] Buchheit and Gulati (2011).

[10] The decision has been referred to as "a perversion of international law in a New York City court" http://foreignpolicy.com/2014/08/03/a-short-history-of-vultures/.

[11] Fisch and Gentile (2004).

[12] "A speculator is a person who trades derivatives, commodities, bonds, equities or currencies with a higher than average risk in return for a higher-than-average profit potential. Speculators take

and selling dear' and rely on the courts to realise their gains.[13] By changing US law, this case was a high point in legitimizing their speculative investment strategies. By standing in their shoes, facing down a 'uniquely recalcitrant debtor', the NML courts eventually ensured that their "high-risk-high-return" gamble paid off.[14] For the lead litigant NML, its pay-out amounted to '$2.426 billion—a total return of approximately 1270%.'[15] (NML initially paid 23–28 cents on the dollar for distressed bond purchases between 2001 and 2008, lending Argentina $177 million in total.) The bond purchases in question were made in the period when Argentina had just defaulted on its debt payments. There was no foreseeable prospect of investors getting paid, let alone getting returns of over 1000%.[16] What was also clear here was that there was no risk-based metric to quantify the probability of repayment. This was clearly a high-risk gamble but much more it requires us to question the assumptions that inform our understanding of the role of the 'non-expert' judges in sustaining sovereign debt demand.

Do 'non-expert' judges have a distinct expertise in 'coping with the unknown'?[17] If they do, this raises further and unique questions. Is the absence of expertise a distinct form of governance of decisions made in conditions of uncertainty? Can this explain their expansive influence on sovereign debt workouts in external debt crisis? In this context, are common sense and logical consistency, technologies of 'non-expert' governance?

This paper offers a new perspective to the ongoing debate on the salience of the expanding judicial role in sovereign debt workouts. It has been argued for instance that this unprecedented expansion can be ignored as the ramblings of a 'grumpy judge' or confined to the actions of a 'uniquely recalcitrant debtor'. Others have argued that the implications are wide ranging

> with systemic effects in its dis-incentivising impact on the majorities that coalesce to sustain the current ad hoc debt restructuring process.[18]

large risks, especially with respect to anticipating future price movements, in the hope of making quick, large gains." https://www.investopedia.com/terms/s/speculator.asp. A sovereign debt speculator is a high risk investor in sovereign debt instruments. Investopedia https://www.investopedia.com/terms/s/speculator.asp.

[13] In October 1995, Elliott Associates L.P. purchased approximately $28.7 million of Panamanian sovereign debt for the discounted price of $17.5 million. The case made its way from a district court in Manhattan to the New York State Supreme Court, which sided with Elliott. Panama's government had to pay the firm over $57 million, with an additional $14 million going to other creditors. …' Guzman (2016).

[14] King (2016).

[15] Guzman (2016).

[16] The decision to default was taken in the context of social and economic meltdown. At the time of the default, Argentinian GDP declined rapidly, unemployment rose to 21.5% and the poverty rate reached a historical peak of above 45% Guzman (2016).

[17] King (2016) and Crook (2016).

[18] Gelpern (2016).

Debt restructurings or workouts are a crucial and necessary step for a debtor to regain access to financial markets[19] both before and after default.[20] There have also been concerns that this non-expert intervention upsets the balance between creditor rights and debtor protections that sustain the 'chemistry' that has so far bought both parties to the negotiating table. The courts have skewed this balance in favour of creditors leading to possibly innovative countervailing responses by sovereign debtors[21] to restore the chemistry.[22] In these views however, non-expert judges are viewed as being relevant only to the extent that they interfere in the 'chemistry' that sustains debt workouts or solely as a mechanism relied on by creditors to counter opportunistic debtor behaviour.[23] Their "non-expert intervention" is viewed as the proverbial 'straw that can break the camel's back'—disruptive but marginal in the larger scheme of complex events that trigger a crisis and stymie eventual resolution. This chapter is the beginning of a sustained attempt to understand the 'non-expert' judicial role within the context of the wider political economy shifts[24] noted in the context of other changes[25] in the systemic infrastructure that threaten voluntary and informal debt workouts.

This paper takes a different view. It argues that the decisions reveal an emerging modality of governing economic activity—speculative investment decisions—undertaken in conditions of radical uncertainty.[26] Does the significance of the courts lie in the constitution of the speculative investor as a legal subject?

---

[19] Over the past 20 years or so there have been widespread debt workouts. However, sovereign debt workouts differ fundamentally from corporate restructurings for several reasons. First there is no international bankruptcy law for sovereigns and countries are assumed to have unlimited liability as they are not subject to liquidation or reorganisation as provided in bankruptcy statutes. If and when they start debt negotiations involves series of negotiations between a debtor and its creditors who eventually devise a voluntary debt workout. This is further complicated by political factors in the debtor states and the terms on which International Lender of Last Resort support is provided by international organisations such as the International Monetary Fund (IMF). The challenge here is to arrive at an outcome that restores market confidence and allows a debtor to regain market access. The process is marked by pathologies that impedes these outcomes such as delays in the debtor state recognising a problem with debt sustainability; delays in debt negotiations and entering a restructuring programme pre-emptively without effectively restoring debt sustainability, Buchheit et al. (2013) and Das et al. (2012).

[20] As far as the debtor sovereign was concerned, the decision was their only route back into capital markets. Once the court found them no longer "recalcitrant", they regained access to external capital markets after 16 years. The concerns raised about the impact of judicial intervention on debt workouts is not discussed here. Buchheit and Gulati (2017).

[21] For instance Argentina proposed innovative ways in which to avoid the injunctions that prevented the government from fulfilling its debt obligations, such as payments re-directed away from the US payment system to domestic clearing systems.

[22] Bucheit and Daley (2014).

[23] Fisch and Gentile (2004).

[24] There are exceptions. Streeck (2014) offers a sociologists' account of the Eurozone debt crisis set within a wider political economy context.

[25] Recent research, for instance shows that the institutions that coalesced to sustain voluntary debt workouts are losing their influence. Gelpern (2016).

[26] According to Mervyn King "radical uncertainty," means the kind of uncertainty that statistical analysis cannot deal with. King (2016).

The focus of this paper is on external debt issued in the US by sovereign debtors. This subset of debt issuances is partial but significant.[27] The resolution of crises and the conditions in which debtors can re-access capital markets are forbiddingly complex events and there is no attempt here to simplify this social, political, and economic complexity. The judicial role in the face of this complexity is limited and arguably its expansive scope significant. This role is not confined to the point at which courts actually get involved in post-default litigation. In the absence of statutory constraints or standstills, the further questions raised here are about how far 'non-expert' judges will go to protect creditor rights, dismantle debtor protections, at what costs to third party rights and the systemic infrastructure that has so far sustained debt workouts.

The following section sets the context to justify this discussion of the expanding judicial role. This is followed by a section that discusses how the strong assumption of rationality in theorisations of crises lends itself to a limited view of the courts thereby overlooking the salience of judicial intervention as a modality of governing decision-making in conditions of uncertainty. This discussion is followed by a historical overview of the central role of the sovereign debt speculator operating in conditions of uncertainty and the changing modalities of governance of decision making in conditions of uncertainty. This is followed by a discussion of market resistance to proposals for reform that attempted to restrict the judicial role and conclusions.

2 Setting the Context: Changes in Debt Demand

In 2014, the McKinsey report "Debt and not much deleveraging" warned that

> Global debt has grown by $57 trillion and no major economy has decreased its debt-to-GDP ratio since 2007.[28]

High government debt in advanced economies was one of three areas of concern highlighted in the report. The same report noted that in the wake of the massive official interventions to reverse the post-2008 downturn in developed economies, in contrast to highly indebted countries, in financial markets had regained their health. This return to health signals an increase in investment activity and this explains the recent upswing in debt demand 3 years after the report was released.[29] Recent

---

[27] Empirical evidence on global issuances indicates that there are four main legal jurisdictions that govern debt issuances—the US, the United Kingdom (UK), Germany and Japan. Domestic debt issuances are generally much larger than foreign bond issuances. In the case of Mexico for instance, '[a]s of June 2015, close to 80% of the total debt was issued in local markets and domestic currency, while in 1995 80% of the debt portfolio was external debt', Díaz De León (2016), p. 13.

[28] Dobbs et al. (2015).

[29] See Allen (2018). There is emerging scholarship explaining these long term trends.

nuanced and contextualised political economy scholarship for instance situates high debt to GDP figures as evidence of the increasing reliance of states on debt to meet budgetary deficits or Wolfgang Streeck's 'debt states.'[30] This combined with evidence of long term trend that show the rate of return on capital has historically exceeded the rate of economic growth and output[31] indicates that 'debt states' are here to stay. In the absence of a statutory sovereign debt restructuring framework and the fracturing of the 'norms and alliances'[32] that sustained debt workouts (Gelpern's modular framework) for over half a century, debt crises can potentially destabilize the world economy. As far as the sovereign debt demand is concerned, for both sovereign debtors and creditors, decision-making in conditions of uncertainty and sovereign debt speculators have become the new normal.

2.1 *Trends in Capital Flows and Speculation*

If history is any guide, the early signs of 'a desperate hunt for yield'[33] by speculative investors do not bode well for the world economy. However, in the face of clear signs that debt demand is being driven by intense speculative activity, history is of limited use in predicting the extent and nature of the correction when it inevitably comes. So far, this new 'Gold rush'—has seen record net inflows of $68.9 Billion into emerging markets in 2017 (doubling the previous spike in 2012). In this rush, investors are overlooking 'deteriorating credit quality with downgrades in 2017 of debt issued by China, Brazil, Turkey, South Africa, Nigeria, Chile, Ecuador and Lebanon. A similar trend was seen in earlier forays into high risk frontier economies in Asia, Africa and Latin America for higher yields.[34] In Latin America it is unclear whether Venezuela already in selective default on its debt payments is an early warning sign of an imminent correction mediated by the courts. When viewed through the lens of uncertainty and speculation it appears that the best we can hope for is that debtor governments, markets and international Lenders of Last resort such as the IMF and central banks' (official sector's) predictions about the future can only be 'roughly right' rather than 'precisely wrong'.[35]

[30] Streeck (2014).

[31] Picketty (2014).

[32] Gelpern (2016).

[33] See Whittall (2017).

[34] Countries such as Mongolia, Paraguay and Rwanda never had access to capital markets. In response to enhanced demand issued foreign currency denominated debt with maturities ranging from 6 to 10 years, B-rated low risk debt. See The Brookings Institution (2013).

[35] King (2016).

2.2 Debt States

The movements of capital mentioned above take place against the backdrop of economies transforming from tax states into "debt states"—"a state which covers a large possibly rising part of its expenditure though borrowing rather than taxation".[36] In debt states, sovereign debt is never repaid but refinanced. Refinancing in the aftermath of a debt crisis relies on sustained debt demand in all foreseeable future states of an economy. It is not surprising then that responses to manage high debt to GDP ratios (by the official sector) are defined by uncertain demand. The corresponding debtor government anxiety about uncertain demand arises from the real fear that access to capital markets will be lost if there is any sign of 'recalcitrance' on their part. This fear leaves budgets reliant on refinancing facing uncertain futures—futures in which harm to their economies are neither avoidable nor statistically calculable and as recent trends indicate a future reliant on the governance of decision-making in conditions of uncertainty. The intervention by the European Central Bank is an example of debt-demand-anxiety- driven interventions aimed at incentivising sovereign debt speculators.[37]

2.3 Official Sector Anxiety

The governments of debt states are overtly reliant on central banks who in turn rely on monetary policy tools to loosen credit market constraints for example by reducing interest rates to artificially stimulate demand.[38] The problem here is that once these massive interventions are underway there are limited avenues for central banks to extricate themselves from markets and states that have now become reliant on cheap money. A recent example of an intervention in conditions of uncertain demand that was first marked by official sector anxiety and then evidence of speculative excess is the European Central Bank (ECB) response to the Eurozone debt crisis.[39] The gist of which involves diverting taxpayer funds from the eurozone economies to buy back bonds of distressed peripheral country debt (Greece) held by creditors in core economies (Germany) in open market operations unprecedented in scope and scale.

The monthly influx of open market operations amounting to 60 billion Euros[40] was formulated to artificially stimulate demand for peripheral debt. This artificial stimulus depresses the interest rates at which debtor governments can borrow. This

[36] Streeck (2014), p. 72.

[37] Ibid.

[38] So called open market transactions, OMTs.

[39] See for a discussion of the effect of these in the context of judicial review Heidemann and Thomas (2016).

[40] van Lamoen et al. (2017).

intervention papered over the weakness of a monetary union that brought together fundamentally unequal states.[41] The problem of peripheral indebtedness is not resolved but pushed out into an uncertain future. The artificially stimulated demand is at the cost of increasing the debt to GDP ratios of economies that qualified for this scheme—which of course will have to be re-financed on maturity. The ECB intervention is in effect creating a risk-free lending environment leading to creditor moral hazard which was arguably one of the factors that led to the Eurozone debt crisis in the first place.[42] In any event, the management of debt states cannot countenance creditor losses. Open market operations currently sustain debt demand. This keeps debtors happy as they avoid default and creditors happy by ensuring their high-risk-high-returns gamble pays off albeit at the cost of increasingly unsustainable debt burdens.

The following section explores how the problem of sovereign debt is theorised and how the assumptions made in the economics literature about the law limit an appreciation of the currently observed expansive influence through the courts on sovereign debt workouts.

3 Theorising the Problem of Sovereign Debt: The Law in Economic Reasoning

The relatively modern phenomenon of debt states define debt flows driven by speculative investors. Sovereign debt speculators engage in high-risk-high-return activity in conditions of uncertainty. Though this reliance tides sovereign states over, the sting in the tail is that the speculation on which they rely on is destabilising and will eventually tip them into crises—and so the cycle continues. It is at the point at which debt default is imminent that is either a 'rush to the courthouse' by creditors choosing to enforce their contractual claims or to central bank intervention that obviates this judicial role (or papers over the threat) as discussed above. It is here that the courts play a pivotal role in confining the central problem of sovereign debt to protecting creditor rights. This section discusses the possibility that by doing so, the litigants also make decisions in conditions of uncertainty. This section examines the role of the law in economic reasoning and draws out the limiting assumptions that restrict a full understanding of the expansive influence of 'non-expert' judges on sovereign debt workouts.

This section questions the strong assumption of rationality in the economics literature that has so far defined the central problem of sovereign debt—why do sovereigns repay? It will be argued here that this assumption relies on a thin filleted description of the law. The law and legal institutions—contracts and the courts—are under-theorised in this literature. The starting assumption in this literature is that the

[41] Blyth (2013), Ch. 3.

[42] Ibid.

law is functional and the courts are impartial umpires that apply the law to resolve a contractual dispute—complete the contracts. In the aftermath of default, the law forms the backdrop to the negotiations and the contract terms as expressed in the boilerplates should be enforced. This reappraisal of economic reasoning is justified by parallel trends[43]—a significant increase in litigation[44] and the gradual dismantling of sovereign defences to creditor suits in enforcement litigation. It will be argued here that the positivist and functional view of the law overlooks the historical links between private law, debt demand and sovereign debt speculators. In doing so, this literature overlooks the possibility that the courts are actually giving both the willful, defaulting debtors and speculative investors rhetorical form with reference to a fixed, immutable debt obligation?

3.1 Crises Triggers

Economic historians of crises rely on an evidence based approach to critique the rationalist assumption in mainstream economic reasoning. In his classic and influential work *Manias, Panics and Crashes*, the economic historian Charles Kindleberger reveals evidence of the inherent irrationality of crises. He relies on historical evidence to counter the alternative but dominant discourse defined by Milton Friedman amongst others that explains crises as a failure of 'rational expectations'. For Kindleberger the historical evidence shows that '[r]ationality is an …a priori assumption rather than a description of the world.'[45] In his description of the anatomy of a typical crisis he reconciles the particular interests of historians with the general interests of economists through the work of Hyman Minsky, a monetary theorist who emphasised the fragility of the monetary system and its "propensity to disaster".[46] His justification for adopting this model is that it "lends itself effectively to the interpretation of economic and financial history."[47] Minksy's model is presumed on the inherent 'instability of the credit system'. In addition, Minsky's focus is on "the role of debt structures in causing financial difficulties."[48] This focus on speculation is the main motivation to draw on Kindleberger to re-assess the assumptions in the economics literature about the role of contracts, private law and the courts in a debt crisis.

The key elements of a crisis Aliber and Kindleberger identify are: instability of credit and expectations that leads to speculation followed by monetary expansion

[43] Schumacher et al. (2018).

[44] Most of the litigation was in response to the Argentine default and this increase has been attributed to the removal of the champerty defence by US Courts in 2004. Guzman (2016).

[45] Aliber and Kindleberger (2015), p. 24.

[46] The Minsky model makes it a "lineal descendant …of a host of classical economists including John Stuart Mill, Alfred Marshall, Knut Wicksell and Irving Fisher", Syll (2014).

[47] Aliber and Kindleberger (2015).

[48] Syll (2014); Aliber and Kindleberger (2015), p. 24.

corresponding to a precipitous rise in asset prices (bubbles) with the eventually drastic fall in asset value and ends with market revulsion evidenced by a rush into money. According to them, the historical evidence 'allows for no other interpretation than occasional irrational markets [rather than irrational individuals] and destabilising speculation'[49] as the two main triggers of crises. The identification of irrationality and speculation as triggers of crises in Aliber and Kindleberger's work acknowledges the centrality of decision-making by sovereign debt speculators in conditions of uncertainty.

3.2 *Risk and Radical Uncertainty*

In his discussion of crisis Meryvn King, the Governor of the Bank of England at the time of the 2008 financial crisis, highlights the centrality of radical uncertainty in markets. Unlike for radical uncertainty, risk assessments rely on probabilities which can be calculated for risks that can be precisely defined and measured against historical data. By definition there is no similar method to predict whether investment decisions made in conditions of uncertainty will pay out.

It follows then that in the face of radical uncertainty, "it is better to be roughly right than precisely wrong." Being roughly right, he argues, requires simple rules of thumb and an open mind, rather than misleadingly precise mathematical solutions—the approach which financial regulation (like economics as a whole) tends to rely on. ... If we do not know how the world works, there is no unique right answer, only a problem of coping with the unknown." Decision making in conditions of uncertainty relies on what Mervyn King describes as "simple rules of thumb and an open mind..." rather than mathematical precision. The business strategy of sovereign debt speculators requires them to make investment decisions in (and profit from) conditions of radical uncertainty.[50] In the context of debt states, it is assumed here that risk-based probability analysis is marginal to the investment strategies of sovereign debt speculators. As King states in his discussion of radical uncertainty,

> we do not know how the world works, there is no unique right answer, only a problem of coping with the unknown.

This section draws on risk and uncertainty as two forms of indeterminacy that inform investment decisions in this market to highlight the significance of the expansive influence of 'non-experts' in sovereign debt workouts. In Frank Knights framework "risk is viewed as the statistically calculative and predictive model that is descended from positivism...Uncertainty is the non-statistically calculable

[49] Aliber and Kindleberger (2015).

[50] Probabilities can be calculated for risks that can be precisely defined and measured against historical data. Radical uncertainty here refers to the kind of uncertainty that statistical analysis cannot deal with.

model."[51] Recent work by Pat O'Malley[52] for instance links uncertainty to "the creative activity of the entrepreneur."[53] When viewed through the lens at the intersection of uncertainty and irrationality, Aliber and Kindleberger's historical evidence of crises is centred on the sovereign debt speculator. They clarify this with the observation that

> the enormous external debt of developing countries ... can be traced to the speculative activities of multinational banks swollen with dollars created through a serious mistake in monetary policy…[tumbling] over one another in trying to uncover new foreign borrowers and practically forced money in the less developed countries.[54]

It is the activity of the speculator that drives demand and eventual default or correction. At the time Aliber and Kindleberger note that, this speculative activity led to defaults by Zaire and Peru with Argentina, Brazil and Mexico set to follow. Despite historical evidence, the significance of sovereign debt speculator and the governance of decision-making in conditions of uncertainty do not inform the key questions that dominate the sovereign debt literature in economics—the problem of weak enforcement or why do sovereigns repay in the face of weak enforcement.

3.3 Weak Enforcement

In the economics literature on sovereign debt crises, the main problem—weak enforcement—is a function of the law. This refers to the absence of legal powers invested in the US courts to attach sovereign's assets situated within its boundaries to satisfy judgements made in favour of external creditors. The systemic problem here is the absence of an international sovereign bankruptcy framework, so creditors cannot force a debtor into involuntary insolvency. Further in the face of sovereign law protections in international law, there are limits on the extent to which creditors can liquidate a sovereign's asset to enforce their claims. Against this backdrop of weak enforcement, the assumption in the literature is that sovereigns have unlimited liability and default is a rational act evidencing an unwillingness to repay. Debtors are also modelled as unified market actors assuming away the complex relationship between a government and its citizens—a key factor influencing the debtor's decision to default on its debt.[55] This literature assumes away historical evidence of irrationality, and the centrality of the sovereign debt speculator as drivers of crises. The focus of this literature is to predict the debtor's behaviour as rational market actors.

---

[51] O'Malley (2000), p. 462, quoted after Turner and Holton (2015).

[52] Ibid.

[53] Ibid., p. 462.

[54] Aliber and Kindleberger (2015), p. 21.

[55] Reinhart and Rogoff (2009).

3.4 Reputational Models

This early generation of influential literature focused on the question of why sovereigns repay in conditions of weak enforcement. This work assumed away any institutional context. Eaton and Gersowitz for instance showed that the availability of capital market access would induce debt repayments.[56] They concluded that sovereigns repay to preserve their reputations. This explains why they regain access to capital markets in the aftermath of a crisis. Reputation per se however overlooks the institutional hardwiring that underpins international lending. This literature presents the problem of sovereign debt outside a framework that actually accounts for the immutable relationship between the debtor and each of its creditor. So for instance, they assume that creditors and debtors are homogeneous rational actors. They assume away the marked distinction between debtor (borrowing) and creditor (lending) states and overlook historically established capital flows set in place by colonisation and imperialism. This model overlooks the significance of the jurisdiction in which debt disputes are litigated and the currency in which debt is denominated.[57] This influential early model also assumes away the centrality of the speculator in driving debt demand.

3.5 Institutional Models

The gaps in the reputational models were partially closed by new models that focused on legal institutions. These drew out the significance of creditor rights in international lending to explain the rational decision of a sovereign debtor to repay against the backdrop of weak enforcement. They assumed that the debtor references the past and this could be the basis on which investors should predict their future behaviour—repay or willfully default. More importantly the assumption of rationality in these models was as strong as the earlier literature.

Bulow and Rogoff for instance, specifically discuss the rights of creditors to seize the assets of a debtor situated outside its legal jurisdiction (otherwise protected by international law) as a key factor that ensures repayment.[58] Though this extension factors in the salience of legal rights, the starting presumption remains—the sovereign debtor makes a rational decision not to pay its creditors in acknowledgment of their rights. Reputation is not a constraint here. This conclusion is premised on the assumption that the courts will perform their role and enforce creditor rights. Further, the assumption of enforceable creditor rights in all states of the world obviates a discussion of the speculator and the active intervention by sovereign governments to stoke speculation to sustain debt demand.

[56] Eaton and Gersovitz (1981).

[57] Reinhart and Rogoff (2009).

[58] Bulow and Rogoff (1989).

Unlike companies, sovereigns are assumed to have unlimited liability for the debts they incur, the issue is not therefore whether or not each sovereign has a capacity to pay (it is assumed they do) but whether or not each sovereign is willing to pay.[59] Here actual enforcement relies on some institution to make sovereigns repay, otherwise the assumption is that they will not.

Debt obligations must therefore be enforced either by military conquest by creditor (or lending) states such as the US[60] or through the courts. In either case the debtor must be made to repay though the modality by which this is achieved shifts over time. The following section discusses the political economy drivers to draw out distinct modalities of governance. When viewed from the perspective of speculative investors the presumption here is that the courts should further the investment strategies sophisticated investors have developed over the past 20 years as a hedge against default.[61]

It is consistent with this literature to assume that bond contracts have evolved to limit opportunistic behaviour by sovereign debtors. The contracts for instance specify the creditors' right to file suit and can enforce claims against the debtor under specified conditions as typically bond contracts will contain a waiver of sovereign immunity clauses and choice of law terms that specify the jurisdiction in which claims can be made. The 'institutional' models conflate the role of private law, contracts and the courts and do not allow for the possibility that sovereign debt speculators evolved as legal subjects in specific political economy contexts. In this literature, in response to the question—why do sovereigns repay contracts—the courts are acknowledged as being essential to the 'functioning of capital markets.'[62] However, what is missing here is an exploration of whether over time and driven by changes in the political economy the courts constitute the subjectivity of the sovereign debt speculator with reference to a willingly defaulting debtor to sustain this 'functioning.'

The strong assumption of rationality is implicit in both notions of 'opportunistic default' and 'willingness to pay'. This literature assumes away the historical evidence that irrationality and speculation trigger crises. This literature also obscures a discussion of differing modalities of governing enterprising activity in conditions of uncertainty. More importantly, the economic literature assumes that the debtor and creditors are rational actors and are recognised as such in the law.

It is argued here that there are two levels at which the law operates. The first is the familiar enforcement role. When viewed against the business cycle or 'a full revolution of the economic wheel'.[63] The courts come into play at specific point at a particular part of the cycle—the initial upswing of demand after the downturn[64]—the

[59] The assumption that sovereigns default because they are unwilling to pay is based on a prior simplification in which a government and its populace is defined as a coherent market actor (Reinhart and Rogoff 2009), p. 53.

[60] See Sect. 4.1 below.

[61] Reinhart and Rogoff (2009), p. 56.

[62] Fisch and Gentile (2004).

[63] Aliber and Kindleberger (2015), p. 13.

[64] This is a narrower part of the cycle discussed by Kindleberger, ibid.

point at which the 'revulsion' or the rush into money in the aftermath of a crisis is reversed either through voluntary debt workouts or repayment. Here the courts intervene to threaten attachment of payments flowing to third parties and disrupt debt negotiations. There is however a second level at which the courts play a critical part in reinforcing the wider paradigm of governance by constituting sovereign debt speculators as legal subjects. At this level, the law ensures that their returns arising from investment decisions in conditions of uncertainty are realised. This constitutive role has ex ante effects on sovereign debt markets as these are pivotal in sustaining debt demand. In the absence of a full account of the judicial role, interventions to counter the disruptive effects of litigation are confined to proposals that seek to marginalise the courts through statutory or market-driven initiatives. These proposals overlook a fuller appreciation of the conditions in which the sovereign debt speculators are constituted as legal subjects. The following section revisits the early days of the formation of capital markets to highlight the centrality of these speculators as drivers of debt demand to understand better the centrality of the courts in the constitution of them as legal subjects.

4 Debt Demand and the Rise of the Sovereign Debt Speculator: A Historical Overview (1870–2017)

The modalities of enforcing debt obligations undertaken in conditions of uncertainty have varied since the formation of capital markets in the US (and earlier where colonial governments during the nineteenth century routinely enforced debt obligations to further colonial imperatives).[65] An historical examination of sovereign lending reveals that the modalities of enforcement have changed from direct military intervention, official sector intervention culminating in the expansive judicial role. This section delineates how the speculator who profits from investment decisions made in conditions of uncertainty begins to evolve as a legal subject during this period. In the historical record, this subjectivity is evident at the intersection of private law, debt obligations, the rise of speculators with private capital and the wider geopolitical interests of the US state. It is argued here that the current ad hoc debt market driven debt resolution process is the historical culmination of the gradual accretion of rights to protect the speculator. In modern debt markets the courts have entrenched the subjectivity of the speculator. The courts replaced the role played by the US government in the early days of the formation of capital markets.

The discussion here covers the period that begins with the formation of US capital markets. Given space constraints, the discussion of each period is confined to one or two key changes. The time periods are not self-contained and overlap significantly with continuities and differences as discussed. In the early periods, the US government actively encourages the enterprising spirit and the speculative instinct

[65] Perez and Weissman (2006).

to sustain debt demand. This role is then taken on by the official sector including the IMF and as argued here eventually by the courts.

In the early days of "dollar diplomacy", the push to initiate and sustain debt demand was informed by the anxiety of the US Government in establishing and then maintaining its geopolitical influence in Latin America. This was followed by the middle period that saw the establishment of the IMF and securitization of sovereign debt markets in the 1980s both moves sustained demand triggered by the threats to the US banking system as widespread defaults became inevitable.

4.1 US Imperialism and the Orbit of Debt Obligations

Historically, sovereign debt markets have been marked by interconnected relationships between the government and private interests. This period saw the establishment of "dollar diplomacy" formulated as a market driven initiative to maintain the geo-political influence in of the US government Latin America. This initiative operated outside a treaty framework. To sustain demand in the face of geopolitical uncertainty, the US government played a critical role in ensuring that private debt obligations were enforced and debts were paid either fully or in part through negotiated debt workouts.

In the early part of this period, the expansion of American influence 'throughout the Caribbean and Pacific' was 'armed intervention and military occupation.'[66] Debt obligations were relied on to counter the European threat that competed with US foreign policy interests in the region and to do so in ways that reduced the costs of full scale military intervention. Mitchener and Weidenmier highlight the enhanced reliance by the US government on debt obligations to extend its "sphere of influence in the Caribbean, Central America, and smaller countries of South America" and "to cement U.S. commercial and political objectives."[67] In their empirical examination of the Roosevelt period at the turn of the twentieth century, the authors found

> historical evidence [to] suggest that direct intervention as well as the threat of gunboat diplomacy increased the probability of debt workouts by Central American and Caribbean countries.[68]

The military option was costly and denied the US government the legitimacy they needed to maintain an administrative presence in Latin America.[69] Gradually overt military action was supplemented by other forms of control that included the

[66] "The U.S military seized territories and sponsored regime changes in the 1890s (...Brazil, Nicaragua, Santo Domingo, and Panama) making way for the Morgan family banking interests to profit through purchase and control of the Panama Canal Company", Mitchener and Weidenmier (2005), p. 12.

[67] Mitchener and Weidenmier (2005), p. 659.

[68] Ibid., p. 686.

[69] See above Sect. 3.4.

creation of debt obligations. This form of control was at the cost of the political sovereignty of debtor states. The governments of debtor states

> were often obliged to modify elements of public administration and political institutions. They had to agree to transform their economies and accept the advice and direction of financial experts whose judgements would take precedence over their own. Further, the power and influence of the financial experts restrained groups who opposed U.S. foreign control.[70]

In the early days of "dollar diplomacy" historian Emily Rosenberg, describes how

> [the] sovereignty of borrowing states was further impaired by the importation of economic experts who advised debtor governments about how to transform their economies in ways that benefited the United States.[71]

These were the early days of sovereign lending that relied in large part on speculative investors actively encouraged to invest, that is engage in decision-making in conditions of uncertainty.

Perez and Weissman also highlight the influence of financial experts during the presidency of Theodore Roosevelt (1901–1909). This influence they argue was "illustrative of the convergence of finance, commerce and public policy."[72] In this period,

> financial loan transactions were the primary means for securing U.S. financial and political leverage throughout Latin America.[73]

Though the external debts were secured through private banks

> the terms of these "controlled" loans were negotiated with the participation of government officials who obtained concessions in the form of control over the borrowing state's economy.[74]

In this period, the US government continues to play a direct role through the threat of military action and geopolitical influence in the region as the modalities of governing decision-making in conditions of uncertainty. This role reflected its foreign policy imperative: to establish its influence in the region and limit the costs of this expansion to placate domestic resistance. Debt obligations become the new geopolitical front of US imperial expansion. Facilitating the conditions for the emergence of the sovereign debt speculator.

This is a period where there is clear historical evidence of the inter-linkages between private capital and US foreign policy interests. Loans and debt contracts would become the softer informal mechanisms that would define 'non-military' interventions by the US government. By bringing countries into the orbit of debt obligations, there had to be a steady demand for debt. Given the historical uncertainty

---

[70] Perez and Weissman (2006), p. 12.

[71] As quoted in Perez and Weissman (2006).

[72] Ibid., p. 10

[73] Ibid., p. 11.

[74] Ibid.

of lending to sovereigns in the region this incipient demand could not be taken for granted. The achievement of US foreign policy imperatives relied on sustained debt demand. Any disruption in demand would impede the expansion of its geo-political influence. Disruptions were minimised with the U.S government's 'chief long-run strategy in the region—to promote 'peace and regional security' as a public good.[75] This strategy reduced 'the incidence of conflict in Central America and the Caribbean, encouraged export growth and revenue collection in the region.'[76] This public good was essential to sustain debt demand in the face of the uncertainty of lending to sovereigns and sustain demand. A foretaste of the role that would be eventually played by the IMF in member states as discussed later in this section.

4.2 *The Dominance of Contracts*

The shifting modality of US intervention—direct military action to expanding the orbit of debt obligations—led to a key change. In the absence of an overarching treaty framework, this shift establishes the centrality of private law in protecting the interests of the sovereign debt speculator. The political economy conditions at the time led to the gradual accretion of legal rights. This would eventually coalesce into legal subjectivity of the speculator. Debt obligations that specified the rights to protect speculative investors were a strategic intervention as part of US imperialism, debtor states were vassals with no comparable private law protections. Later their rights as sovereign states in international law would be whittled down by US courts in sovereign debt litigation. The central issue in the law would eventually become about protecting their rights. Contract law and the courts would become key modalities of governing decision-making in conditions of uncertainty.

In her discussion of this period Rosenberg finds clear evidence that contract law has always served political interests. In her discussion on the early days of "dollar diplomacy" Rosenberg shows that

> loans negotiated as private contracts between sovereign debtors and private creditors functioned in aid of U.S. capital interests.[77]

Further, she also notes that

> the rhetoric of contract law, particularly in relationship to sovereign debtors and private creditors, … conceal relationships of power under the guise of contract provisions such as mutuality.[78]

---

[75] As the authors argue this was because of the decline of European influence in the region. Mitchener and Weidenmier (2005), p. 690.

[76] Though "the threat of gunboat diplomacy or lost sovereignty made credible by prompt U.S. intervention in Santo Domingo, led many Central American and Caribbean countries to settle long outstanding defaulted debts", ibid. The generation of peace and stability as a public good was against the backdrop of a real and ever present threat of military intervention.

[77] Perez and Weissman (2006), p. 48.

[78] Ibid.

When in fact contracts were an essential part of establishing US imperial interests in the region, when private law rights debt obligations were skewed in favour of creditor protections.

In addition to Rosenberg, other examinations of sovereign debt reveal that private law is often valorised as offering benefits such as "[p]redictability, stability, order, harmonization" making contracts "important factors in banking transactions and contract enforcement."[79] There is an assumption of equality between contracting parties when in reality contracts in this political economy context are arrangements to protect creditor rights with reference to debt obligations of sovereign states. Perez and Weissman highlight the one characteristic that is relied on to distinguish private law—its "perceived indifference to the political".[80] Thus

> private law provides the basis for 'utterly non-political arguments'

and

> change[s] the nature of any dispute from hotly ideological to seemingly neutral and objective.[81]

Private law concepts are characterised as being impartial and having no regard to redistributive concerns similar to those raised by government regulation.

The analysis provided here exposes the implicit assumption of political neutrality and equality between contracting parties by revealing the constitutive role of the law in the context of the overarching modalities of governance that sustains lending in conditions of uncertainty. The early days of sovereign lending in Latin America reveal the foundations of what would eventually drive the formation of the sovereign debt speculator as a distinct legal subject—the bearer of legal rights that arose and were defined with reference to the debt obligations of sovereign debtors. The sovereigns now dependent on debt and sensitive to debt demand would become an integral part of Gelpern's module framework. Eventually, the US government expands its sphere of influence beyond Latin America the sovereign debt speculators and the recalcitrant debtor come into their own as legal subjects in contract law.

4.3 Debt Imperialism Beyond Latin America

The overarching foreign policy imperatives that relied on uncertain debt demand set the conditions for the entrenchment of the sovereign debt speculator. Private law and state policy would form the contours of their legal subjectivity. Speculative excess and crises would become the abiding legacies of this imperial period. Defaults became a constant feature of sovereign debt markets. In the Cold War, the main thrust of US foreign policy was to ensure the development and expansion of

[79] Perez and Weissman (2006), p. 46.

[80] Ibid.

[81] Ibid.

market economies rather than to assess the abilities of countries to repay their debts. The focus was on incorporating states into the orbit of debt capital. The unsustainable debt and the enhanced threat of sovereign defaults became a side show in the larger context in which US interests required "sustained loans to Third World countries."[82] The sovereign debt speculator becomes a central part of this initiative as evidenced in their increased power *vis à vis* the US state.

The situation in the early days where the US government could rely on private capital to further its strategic geo-political interests as discussed above was changing and additional attempts had to be made to incentivize debt demand. The government aggressively pushed commercial banks otherwise wary of exposing themselves to the uncertainty of lending to sovereigns. The inherent conservationism of the banks resisted attempts by the US government to actively foster speculation. This included regulators exhorting banks and other private companies to keep aside relatively petty concerns about lending risks and to further the national interest instead. Perez and Weissman note that

> the banks that experienced the pressure of regulatory agencies were those that were reluctant to extend financing to countries of strategic importance to the United States.[83]

Once the extent of sovereign over-indebtedness, the threat to the commercial banks that had overextended themselves and through them the threat to the American banking system was becoming evident, there was a further push to extend more loans leading to the formulation of the Baker plan in the 1980s.[84] This period also saw the development of a secondary debt market[85] when overexposed banks swapped their loans for other assets thereby removing high risk debt instruments from their books. Secondary market transactions fostered the business model of distressed asset investors (a subset of sovereign debt speculators) who would subsequently drive enforcement litigation.

4.4 The Baker Plan

The Baker plan involved loans by US banks conditional on debtor countries undertaking "market oriented" reform policies such as deregulation, privatization and liberalization of trade.[86] The Baker plan was widely perceived as a failure as it increased the

> debts of sovereigns who were already burdened with debt payments they could not make.[87]

---

[82] Perez and Weissman (2006), p. 32.

[83] Ibid., 33.

[84] See Sect. 4.4 below.

[85] Power (1996).

[86] Perez and Weissman (2006), p. 34.

[87] Ibid., 35.

Default risk still remained high and non-performing debt could not be shifted from the banks' books. This however did not stop the Federal Reserve from encouraging banks to issue Baker loans in return for favourable treatment. Banks were for instance, incentivized through tax breaks if they undertook Baker Loan transactions. In a continuation from the past, the government was actively encouraging speculation in conditions of uncertainty about repayment.[88] However, to counter the emerging backlash that would imperil US foreign interests in Latin America and reduce the demand for US manufactured goods in these cash-strapped countries. The US soon realised that much more was required to be done than the Baker Plan.

The Plan reached a limit on debt demand as the main actors here were US commercial banks. As Anna Gelpern notes commercial banks who were for the past 60 years repeat players in the market would be replaced by bond holders rather than commercial banks. The bond holders "as a rule sought to profit from bonds, not the relationships." To meet the need for increased debt demand the floodgates were opened with the adoption of the Brady Plan.[89] With the advent of the distressed asset investors, the homogeneity that characterised the earlier period when commercial banks were the main speculative investors and would soon become a thing of the past.

4.5 *The Brady Initiative*

The failure of the Baker Plan necessitated the formulation of the Brady initiative. This initiative was market-based and sought to address the incipient debt crisis that would inevitably follow the lending boom in the Baker plan period. With the active encouragement of the U.S government the Brady plan expanded the set of lenders from a relatively few US commercial banks to several thousand bondholders located across the world. They were drawn to risky but highly profitable investments. This was like a coral bloom awakening to the opportunities of untold returns from lending to sovereigns. This bloom would soon turn into a speculative feeding frenzy that would eventually tip East Asian economies into crises.

The Brady plan

> encouraged private creditors to provide debt relief through the conversion of loans into ..., bonds and the promotion of debt-equity schemes in addition to some debt reduction and forgiveness.[90]

For the commercial banks loaded with debt, this would ensure that their 'slate was wiped clean' and opened up more lending and borrowing opportunities. In this

---

[88] Banks were also being encouraged to invest in the real economy in the countries to which they were extending loans. This led "to the expansion of banking interests in other sectors such as manufacturing and service." Ibid. 36.

[89] See Sect. 4.5 below.

[90] Perez and Weissman (2006), p. 36.

environment '[n]ew loans confirmed a country's creditworthiness and this perception attracted even more loans'.[91] The implementation of this initiative was encouraged by the US Congress with the

> International Debt Management Act which directed federal banking regulatory agencies to provide "the widest possible latitude with respect to debt restructuring by commercial banks with high exposure to third-world debt."[92]

The post-default revulsion was managed with interventions to facilitate debt workouts and refinancing. This significant change in sovereign lending set in place the conditions for the emergence of 'debt states' as mentioned earlier.

The Brady plan was aimed to override prudent behaviour (encourage sovereign debt speculators) as

> regulators facilitated the implementation of the Brady Initiative through pressure on banks reluctant to engage in new loan restructuring.[93]

This initiative was also

> the first …to address the debt crisis in a coherent and systematic manner…though it was difficult to assess the benefits for [less developed countries][94]

This period was followed by a series of statutory interventions aimed at maintaining the strategic dominance of the US in the Cold War. Perez and Weissman note that these interventions were not always facilitative as far as market interests went and "appear to overshadow and limit, if not conflict, with market transactions."[95] The baton had shifted from the US government to sovereign debt investors.

4.6 *The Role of the IMF*

In the period that followed the securitization of sovereign lending and the development of sovereign debt markets, international institutions such as the IMF gradually replaced direct US intervention to sustain debt demand. This was a period when the possibility of strategic default by debtors in distress was reined in and creditor participation actively encouraged in a context that saw widespread debt workouts. This led to a proliferation of 'non-contractual' mechanisms with the IMF playing a critical role in maintaining the balance between debtor protections[96] and creditor

---

[91] Ibid.

[92] Ibid., 37.

[93] Ibid., 38.

[94] Perez and Weissman find that "these countries had to sell off state ownership in their industries and firms." Ibid., 38.

[95] Ibid., 42.

[96] As Gelpern notes "A country that could not pay its debts first turned to the IMF, which typically offered financial support for up to 3 years, conditioned in economic reform. The IMF indicated what budget savings the country could achieve, which implied a 'financing gap' to be filled by new lending and debt relief from other creditors." Gelpern (2016).

rights—the 'chemistry' that ensured debt workouts becomes part of the systemic infrastructure now underpinned by the IMF.[97] The debtors were assured of access to lender of last resort funding and it became instrumental in bringing creditors to the negotiating table.[98] This crucial IMF role led to the development of a new kind of expertise and by the 2000s

> this role was well-understood by a small core of repeat players: finance officials in debtor and creditor countries, staff and management at multilateral institutions, experts at credit rating agencies, big law and financial firms and smaller, specialized investors.[99]

For sovereigns in need of debt refinancing the IMF became the gatekeeper to capital markets access. The IMF relied on a combination of threats and the provision of lender of last resort support to bring parties to the negotiating table.[100] During this period, given the informal institutional arrangements in place debtors and creditors had "few good alternatives to negotiation."[101] Another key mechanism in play at the time was the use of what Gelpern refers to as 'cross-conditionality' by the Paris Club and the IMF.[102] In this period, there were a few creditor driven initiatives such as the International Institute of Finance (IIF) and other market bodies which provided a market -based support for investment decisions in conditions of uncertainty.

Against this backdrop, the courts were playing an increasingly important role. In post Brady Plan bond markets, vulture funds have achieved spectacular victories both through the courts and legislative intervention. First, absolute sovereign immunity protections in international law were replaced by a restrictive theory of sovereign immunity that allowed funds to attach sovereign commercial property governed by US law.[103] Second, all sovereign defences to creditor suits have been gradually dismantled.[104] Finally, the courts have consistently held that international political considerations and the refusal of holdouts to participate in a debt restructuring would not bar recovery.[105] The courts were establishing a position that was moving away from the more nuanced way in which market actors were viewing the relationship between lenders and sovereign debtors. For instance, Elena Duggar, a Moody's Senior Vice President, was of the view that 'the vast majority of sovereign defaults are driven by 'capacity to pay' rather than 'willingness to pay' issues. The courts were taking a view that was closer to mainstream economic reasoning as discussed

---

[97] Gelpern (2016), p. 50 and Sachs (1995).

[98] Ibid.

[99] Ibid.

[100] Ibid.

[101] Ibid.

[102] As Gelpern notes this informal regime that "came together in the mid-1990s was under threat and by 2016, its survival cannot be taken for granted." Hence the opening up to other modalities of governance. See also Sachs (2003).

[103] Fisch and Gentile (2004), p. 1079.

[104] Gathii (2006) and Fisch and Gentile (2004).

[105] Gathii (2006).

above where the starting premise was that as rational individuals, debtor sovereigns were willingly choosing not to pay.

The following section revisits market resistance to proposals that sought informal modalities of governance that defined sovereign debt demand for over a century. A key component of this resistance was to ensure a continuing role for the common law courts.

5 Market Resistance to Proposals for Reform: Reinforcing the Sovereign Debt Speculator as Legal Subject

This section maps two key debates over a 5-year period to reform the ad hoc sovereign debt restructuring process. These debates occurred in the period leading up to the *NML* decisions and were informed in the main by distressed asset fund enforcement litigation. They highlight the resistance of relevant market actors to an international sovereign bankruptcy procedure and the eventual adoption of what would be an ineffective contract change—the adoption of Collective Action Clauses in all future debt issuances. In response to the contract change, some market actors voiced concerns about the effectiveness of this change Duggar from Moody's for instance noted at the time that

> the decision to default is governed by economic and financial developments at the time of sovereign distress rather than by the specifics of the bond covenants.

It is argued here that the courts play a small but crucial role in the modular framework. The sovereign debt speculator the bearer of legal rights now had to be protected by contracts and the courts from 'recalcitrant' and wilfully defaulting debtors.

5.1 *The Rey's Report*

Much before the Argentine debt default of 2001, an earlier sovereign bankruptcy proposal was set aside in favour of contract change by G10 governments in the "Rey's Report" of 1996.[106] This rejection was justified on the ground that sovereign debtors would be left unprotected if an international bankruptcy court was established. Such a court would not work for four reasons.

> First, it would 'neither [be] appropriate nor possible to replace the authorities responsible for the economic policies of a sovereign state with a "new management", or to take possession of a state's non-commercial property.[107]

---

[106] Group of Ten (1996).

[107] Ibid., pp. 14–15.

Second, '[t]he need for additional protection from creditors has not in the past been a serious problem for sovereign debtors. Such debtors have few assets to seize and some of them benefit from sovereign immunities.'[108] The third reason was concerns about the impact on negotiation required to resolve a crisis and the potential impact on sovereign rights. Finally, the report was confident that

> [m]any of the same results (sought by debtor states) could in principle be achieved in more informal ways that would not require such fundamental institutional reform.[109]

One of the objectives[110] of the Report was to ensure

> disruptive legal action by individual creditors does not hamper a workout that is underway, while protecting the interests of the creditor group.[111]

Instead of replacing the courts by a bankruptcy mechanism, the mandate of the G10 working group was restricted

> to consider how sovereign debt contracts could be modified in order to make the resolution of debt crises more orderly.[112]

The market solution endorsed here and the resistance to a formal bankruptcy court would both be subsequently picked up in subsequent reform debates.

5.2 *The Sovereign Debt Restructuring Mechanism (SDRM)*

This debate followed the Argentine debt default a year earlier. This was the largest debt default in the history of sovereign lending[113]and sovereign debt speculators were threatening to delay the first of three voluntary debt restructurings to claim full repayment through the courts.

The ongoing enforcement litigation against Argentina would define the two countervailing—official sector and market-based—responses discussed here. Early in 2002, the then First Deputy Managing Director of the IMF, Anne Krueger proposed 'A new Approach to Sovereign Debt Restructuring (SDRM).[114] The proposal was expressly motivated to counter the successful use of the courts by a holdout

---

[108] Ibid.

[109] Ibid.

[110] The other objectives were "… (i) to foster early dialogue, coordination, and communication among creditors and a sovereign caught up in a sovereign debt problem; (ii)to ensure that there are effective means for creditors and debtors to re-contract, without a minority of debt-holders obstructing the process; …", ibid.

[111] Ibid.

[112] Ibid.

[113] Guzman (2016).

[114] Krueger (2001).

fund (Elliot) to get paid in full.[115] Elliot had convinced a court to issue an *ex parte* order that threatened ongoing payments made by Peru to its creditors.[116] Unlike the earlier contract change validated in the Rey's report, the SDRM, was not a market-driven initiative. This proposal was developed on the template of domestic statutory municipal and corporate insolvency frameworks.[117] The SDRM would in effect restrict the influence of the US courts on debt workouts. With hindsight it appears that Krueger was attempting to delink speculative behaviour from unrestricted access to the courts.[118] An insolvency court of this kind would fundamentally change the legal rights and entitlements of sovereign debt speculators—their centrality as legal subjects that kept the ad hoc framework in place was under challenge. The SDRM was exposing the unequal relationship between debtors and sovereign debt speculators that had been erased by the assumed neutrality of contract law. This change threatened to dismantle the framework that had coalesced to entrench the subjectivity of the debt speculator who had driven debt demand for over a century of private lending.

The market rejection of this proposal was swift. Their solution mirrored the earlier Rey report recommendation—a market-driven alternative premised on contract change. This response left creditors with full access to the courts and marginalised any possibility of statutory change.[119]

[115] Elliot is the parent company of NML capital who had successfully relied on the courts to win spectacular victories. In October 1995, Elliott Associates L.P. purchased approximately $28.7 million of Panamanian sovereign debt for the discounted price of $17.5 million. When Panama's government asked for a restructuring of its foreign debt in 1995, the vast majority of its bondholders agreed. Not Elliott. In July 1996, Elliott Associates, represented by one of the world's most high-profile securities law firms, filed a lawsuit against Panama in a New York district court seeking full repayment of the original $28.7 million—plus interest and fees. The case made its way from a district court in Manhattan to the New York State Supreme Court, which found in favour of Elliott. Panama's government had to pay the firm over $57 million, with an additional $14 million going to other creditors. It was a ground breaking moment in the modern history of finance. By taking the case to a New York district court, Elliott broke with long-standing international law and custom, according to which sovereign governments are not sued in regular courts which are thought to be meant to deal with questions internal to a nation state. Further, the presiding judge accepted the case—another break with custom. It set the stage for two decades of such cases, including Argentina's default. Elliott's case against Panama upended established international norms about how to negotiate sovereign default…, see Guzman (2016).

[116] In her talk, Krueger stated "But the more recent success of an aggressive legal strategy employed against Peru by a vulture company called Elliott Associates underlines the power that holdout creditors retain. The threat of disruption remains likely to deter countries from seeking a necessary restructuring for longer than is desirable either for the country itself or for the international community." See also Guzman (2016).

[117] Through a modification of the IMF statute as suggested in the Buchheit et al (2013).

[118] Referred to as "defanging the vultures," see Wigglesworth (2013).

[119] Miller (2002).

5.3 The Taylor Intervention

In his keynote speech to the Emerging Markets Trade Association's (EMTA) Annual conference on 5 December 2002,[120] John Taylor, the then Under Secretary for International Affairs at the US Treasury, provided a brief overview of the US Treasury's proposal for new Collective Action Clauses (CACs)[121] in sovereign bond documentation. This approach he argued was market-based and worked without the need for a centralised bankruptcy authority. He cited supply side (debtor) issues and lay the blame for the problems sought to be addressed on flawed official sector intervention. He argued that the current arrangement impedes the ability of the market to adequately price in the possibility of a debt workout and increases the susceptibility of debtor countries to crises, because of more complicated official and private sector decision-making.

Taylor did not expressly attribute this market-driven approach to resolving the litigation problem as Krueger had done earlier. In fact, he stressed that "[r]ogue creditors were not even mentioned in one of his previous speeches." He also dismissed the criticism that the CAC solution was focused on a "not so bad" rogue creditor issue. In situations in which CACs are not triggered, the role of the US courts would remain unchanged. This market-driven initiative entrenched the sovereign debt speculator as legal subject and the ad hoc framework establishing the courts as a central governing of decision-making in conditions of uncertainty.

In the same event, the Emerging Markets Traders Association's (EMTA) Executive Director Michael Chamberlin explicitly dismissed the SDRM proposal. He appeared to be playing to the gallery of sovereign debt speculators who could be relied on to sustain debt demand. According to him,

> [u]nfortunately, the focus on restructuring bonds has distracted attention from the larger picture of how best to meet the financing needs of developing economies.

The SDRM, Taylor argued was

> a bad idea that will drive investors away from developing economies and drive up their borrowing costs.[122]

[120] http://emta.org/template.aspx?id=5498.

[121] Collective Action Clauses are clauses that replace the unanimous consent clauses that were preferred by creditors in US law issuances. These clauses allow a majority of bondholders of a specific bond series to bind the rest to changes in the payment terms of bonds. IMF Staff (2014) and Gelpern and Gulati (2013).

[122] For a discussion on this debate as basically being about the perceived trade-off between ex-post and ex-ante efficiency see the Brookings Report (2013).

5.4 The Market Adopts CACs

CACs received the endorsement of the US Government. Creditor bodies such as the International Capital Markets Association (ICMA) and EMTA made moves to embed this new consensus by proposing the wording for new clauses. In 2004, the International Primary Market Association (IPMA) published a standard form of collective action clauses[123] for use in sovereign bond issues governed by English law and use a fiscal agent structure.[124] This proposal would be endorsed by six market associations[125] and by G20 governments later that year.[126] The ICMA reissued the standard CACs in August 2014.[127]

Sovereign debt demand would continue to be driven by sovereign debt speculators that operated in conditions of uncertainty. In the event of a dispute, the courts would remain pivotal in ensuring their high risk-high-return gambles pay off. Debtor states that impede the achievement of these pay offs with their "recalcitrance" will be disciplined by no access to capital markets. This meant that sovereign states began lining up to officially eschew the idea of a formal debt restructuring framework. This period saw a surge in the inclusion of CACs in bond documentation.[128] Mexico started the ball rolling[129] less than 3 months after Taylor's keynote. This move was viewed favourably by the US government.[130] Brazil, Israel, Lebanon,

[123] In August of that year ICMA issued standard second generation CACs and a *pari passu* clause to avoid the NML outcome in future debt issuances. In October, the IMF releases a report endorsing the second generation ICMA, CAC In October, the Republic of Kazakhstan adopted the second generation CAC and the *pari passu* clause. Mexico was the next big emerging market issuance that followed the lead of Khazakstan. On November 18, 2014 they "issued the first New York-law, SEC-registered sovereign bond with the new second generation CACs...ranking clauses...and incorporate the change from a fiscal agency agreement that was in place since 1992 to a trust indenture, most recently amended in 2015." In November 2014, G 20 leaders endorsed ICMA's second generation CACs at the Brisbane Summit.

[124] ICMA 'Standard Aggregated Collective Action Clauses ("CACs") For The Terms And Conditions Of Sovereign Notes' available at http://www.icmagroup.org/Regulatory-Policy-and-Market-Practice/Primary-Markets/primary-market-topics/collective-action-clauses/; ICMA 'Standard Pari Passu Provision For The Terms And Conditions Of Sovereign Notes' available at http://www.icmagroup.org/Regulatory-Policy-and-Market-Practice/Primary-Markets/primary-market-topics/collective-action-clauses/.

[125] The Bond Market Association; Emerging Markets Creditors Association; Emerging Markets Traders Association (EMTA); Institute of International Finance; International Securities Market Association; Securities Industry Association.

[126] See note 120 above.

[127] See notes 120 and 121 above.

[128] "Since March 2004, sovereign issues containing CACs grew to represent more than 90% of total value of new issues, and 40% of the value of the outstanding stock of bonds from emerging market countries, largely reflecting the increase in sovereign bonds issued under New York law that included CACs." International Monetary Fund (2004), p. 44.

[129] Mexico adopted a 75% threshold for voting on amendments to payments and other significant 'reserved matters' (Díaz de León 2016), p. 14.

[130] http://emta.org/template.aspx?id=5498.

Mexico, Peru, the Philippines, and Turkey followed.[131] CACs in US law bond issuances gradually becoming standard market practice with "no observable impact on pricing."[132]

5.5 *The Limits of CACs*

Despite the consensus that settled so quickly, CACs were not the panacea they were made out to be.[133] It is hard to overestimate Taylor's intervention as it removed any serious discussion or debate about the possibility of SDRM like institutional solutions being discussed in the foreseeable future.[134] As far as the official sector is concerned, the Taylor intervention minimised concerns that CACs "were not the fast fix for the fundamental dysfunctions of sovereign debt."[135] For instance, CACs were triggered and had failed to work in Argentina in 2001 and Uruguay in 2003. Further market investors such as PIMCO were cautioning that CACs would not in a default situation live up to the hype.[136] In any event, CACs did not cover legacy debt and was ineffective in containing the surge in speculative activity as evidenced in the desperate hunt for yield highlighted earlier.[137]

The limitations of CACs was reinforced by Moody's, one of the three main bond ratings agencies,[138] in their investor advice on the new clauses. In their view

> the introduction of ... aggregate CAC clauses ...does not systematically alter the probability of default or prospective recoveries by enough to justify applying a rating differentiation to bonds containing the new modified clauses.[139]

The benefits, if any, of the contract changes were unclear. This raises the question, why did US markets capitulate[140] and accept a solution that would according to

---

[131] Brazil initially adopted a CAC with an 85% voting threshold for reserved matter amendments and then adopted Mexico's CAC.

[132] International Monetary Fund (2004), p. 44.

[133] https://www.pimco.com/insights/viewpoints/viewpoints/collective-action-clauses-no-panacea-for-sovereign-debt-restructurings.

[134] Though there have been several proposals that have been made since then with marginal engagement by the mainstream policymakers such as Brookings, the United Nations Conference on Trade and Development (UNCTAD) and other agencies of the United Nations.

[135] Gelpern (2016).

[136] Gelpern (2016), p. 131.

[137] See Sect. 2.1 above.

[138] The other two bond rating agencies are Standard and Poor (S&P) and the Fitch group.

[139] Moody (2015).

[140] This was without doubt a significant shift for another reason. The changes were accepted in a legal tradition that had resisted collective rights to establish individual rights fiercely defended in the pre-Chapter 11 period. As Buchheit and Gulati note in their classic paper, the individual rights tradition was unique to US law and this was now making way for a different tradition of collective rights. US law seemed to be moving closer to the collective rights tradition established in UK law; Buchheit and Gulati (2011).

key market actors not work? One reason is that there was no appetite for constraints on the speculative impulse and the enterprising spirit inherent in an SDRM-type formal institutional framework.[141] An impulse that was actively encouraged by an almost unbroken line of first US Government, then official sector interventions. The market bodies resisting the SDRM also stoked the deep-rooted anxiety of debt states about demand. Investor associations such as EMTA and ICMA and significant speculative distressed asset funds such as Elliot (and later NML) start playing pivotal roles in entrenching the subjectivity of the sovereign debt speculator. The extent this would become evident in official sector responses to the Eurozone debt crises.

After the Greek debt workout,[142] Eurozone sovereigns adopted model CACs[143] in all issuances after 1 January 2013. Immediately thereafter, as mentioned above, the ECB enters into an unprecedented and potentially unlimited quantitative easing programme to contain the multiple sovereign debt crises. In line with the consensus established after the Taylor intervention, European institutions categorically excluded the possibility of debt workouts and have instead offered an implicit guarantee to "do what it takes"[144] to avoid default. When viewed from this perspective, it is interesting that the debates discussed in this section were bookended by two legal challenges—first, Elliot and later Argentina, both instances of the expanding judicial role in a changing political context.

6 Conclusions

This chapter is motivated by the resolution by the US courts of a contract interpretation dispute—a dispute where admittedly no one knew the meaning of a widely used boilerplate clause. It is argued here that this resolution opens up a lens into understanding better the interface between contracts, the common law and the courts and the conditions in which sovereign debt investors make investment

141 Miller (2002).

142 In March/April 2012, Greece underwent the first "major debt restructuring in Europe since the defaults preceding World War II", Zettelmeyer et al. (2013), p. 2. In the absence of cross-series aggregation CACs only 17 of the 36 series eligible for restructuring were successfully restructured. Holdout creditors obstructed the operation of CACs in the remaining series. This left unstructured claims worth 6.5 billion Euros (30% of the foreign debt). The ongoing cases and the decision in the New York courts were instrumental in determining the future course of official sector intervention in the Eurozone. The Greek government eventually repaid the holdouts in full and retrospectively modified its majority domestic debt to introduce CACs that would eventually settle the repayment crisis. In addition, the Greek government had to accept programme conditionality imposed by the so called 'Troika' consisting of IMF, ECB and the Commission of European Union. It was clear at the time that in the absence of mechanisms to rein in the holdouts the successful Greek debt work out did not offer any guarantee of similar successes in the future. The maintenance of enforcement choices would require sustained official sector intervention; see ibid.

143 Model CACs were significantly different from the ICMA CACs.

144 https://www.ecb.europa.eu/press/key/date/2012/html/sp120726.en.html.

decisions. These decisions are not the outcome of risk-based probability assessments but decisions made in conditions of radical uncertainty. The first question raised here is whether 'non-expert' judges are better equipped to govern decision-making in these conditions? Though there is no analysis of the common law here, this possibility sets the ground for further questions to be examined—for instance are common sense and logical consistency modalities of 'non-expert' governance central to sustain debt demand in conditions of radical uncertainty.

This chapter then proceeds to understand better the political economy factors that have led to the US courts playing this expansive role in sovereign debt workouts. It questions the functional assumptions about the law that dominate mainstream sovereign debt scholarship and relies on historical evidence to highlight the critical constitutive role of contracts and contract law in sustaining debt demand. It explores the possibility that in the context of debt states, contracts and contract law have entrenched the subjectivity of the sovereign debt speculator—a role now played by the courts. This paper concludes by highlighting that the constitutive role of the courts is critical to sustain debt demand. However, this role also threatens debt workouts with wider implications on the world economy given current concerns around the long term sustainability of debt states.

References

Aliber RZ, Kindleberger CP (2015) Manias, panics and crashes: a history of financial crises, 7th edn. Palgrave Macmillam, London

Allen K (2018) African debt markets thrive as investors hunt for yield. Financial Times, 23 Feb 2018. https://www.ft.com/content/6e71b16a-17df-11e8-9e9c-25c814761640

Bai J (2013) Stop them circling: addressing vulture funds in Australian law. Sydney Law Rev 35(4):703–730

Blyth M (2013) Austerity: the history of a dangerous idea. Oxford University Press, Oxford

Bucheit LC, Daley E (2014) Minimizing holdout creditors: carrots. In: Lastra R et al (eds) Sovereign debt management. Oxford University Press, Oxford

Bucheit LC, Pam JS (2004) The pari passu clause in sovereign debt agreements. Emory J 53:869–913

Buchhcit LC, Gulati M (2011) Drafting a model collective action clause for eurozone sovereign bonds. Cap Mark Law J 6(3):317–325

Buchheit LC, Gulati GM (2017) Restructuring sovereign debt after NML v Argentina. Cap Mark Law J 12(2):224–238

Buchheit LC, Gelpern A et al (2013) Revisiting sovereign bankruptcy. https://www.brookings.edu/research/revisiting-sovereign-bankruptcy/

Bulow J, Rogoff K (1989) Sovereign debt: is to forgive to forget? Am Econ Rev 79(1):43–50

CrookC(2016)Theeconomicsofradicaluncertainty.TheformerBankofEnglandheadurgesthefinance industry to rethink risk. Bloomberg Opinion, 31 March 2016 Economics. https://www.bloomberg.com/view/articles/2016-03-31/mervyn-king-writes-the-book-on-radical-uncertainty

Das US, Papaioannou MG et al (2012) Sovereign debt restructurings 1950–2010: literature survey, data, and stylized facts. IMF Working Paper 12 203. https://www.imf.org/external/pubs/ft/wp/2012/wp12203.pdf

Díaz de León A (2016) Mexico's adoption of new standard in international sovereign debt contracts: CACs, pari passu and a trust indenture. Cap Mark Law J 11(1):12–24

Dobbs R, Lund S et al (2015) Debt and (not much) deleveraging, Series McKinsey Global Institute, February 2015. http://www.mckinsey.com/global-themes/employment-and-growth/debt-and-not-much-deleveraging

Eaton J, Gersovitz M (1981) Debt with potential repudiation: theoretical and empirical analysis. Rev Econ Stud 48(2):289–309

Fisch JE, Gentile CM (2004) Vultures or vanguards: the role of litigation in sovereign debt restructuring conference on sovereign debt restructuring: the view from the legal academy. Emory Law J 53:1043–1113

Gathii JT (2006) The sanctity of sovereign loan contracts and its origins in enforcement litigation. George Wash Int Law Rev 38:251–325

Gelpern A, Gulati M (2006) Public symbol in private contract: a case study. Wash Univ Law Rev 84(7):1627–1715

Gelpern A, Gulati M (2013) The wonder clause. J Comp Econ 41(2):367–385

Gelpern A (2016) Sovereign debt: now what? Yale J Int Law 41:45

Group of Ten (1996) The resolution of sovereign liquidity crises. A report to the ministers and governors prepared under the auspices of the deputies, Series Bank for International Settlement, May 1996

Gulati M, Scott RE (2013) The three and a half minute transaction: boilerplate and the limits of contract design. University of Chicago Press, Chicago

Guzman M (2016) An analysis of Argentina's 2001 default resolution CIGI paper No. 110 – October available at https://www.cigionline.org/sites/default/files/documents/CIGI%20Paper%20No.110WEB_0.pdf

Heidemann M, Thomas D (2016) Judicial review in the Eurozone – the court system as regulator? The case of the sovereign debt crisis. In: Andenas M et al (eds) Regulating and supervising European financial markets. More risks than achievements. Springer, Heidelberg, pp 337–364

IMF Staff (2014) Strengthening the contractual framework to address collective action problems in sovereign debt restructuring, Series International Monetary Fund. https://www.imf.org/external/np/pp/eng/2014/090214.pdf

International Monetary Fund (2004) Global financial stability report. Market developments and issues series IMF, 13 Sept 2004. https://www.imf.org/External/Pubs/FT/GFSR/2004/02/index.htm

Jones M (2009) MPs move to outlaw vulture funds. BBC Newsnight, 6 May 2009. http://news.bbc.co.uk/1/hi/programmes/newsnight/8034749.stm

King M (2016) The end of alchemy: money banking and the future of the global economy. W.W. Norton, London

Krueger A (2001) International financial architecture for 2002: a new approach to sovereign debt restructuring national economists' club annual members' dinner, November 26, 2001

Miller M (2002) New clauses, new courts, or no action? IIE Policy Brief

Miller MH, Thomas D (2007) The judge, the vultures and creditor rights. World Econ 30(10):1491–1509

Mitchener KJ, Weidenmier M (2005) Empire, public goods and the Roosevelt corollary. J Econ Hist 65(3):658–692

Moody (2015) Announcement: Moody's answers frequently asked questions on new ICMA sovereign bond clauses. Global Credit Research, 17 March 2015. https://www.moodys.com/research/Moodys-answers-frequently-asked-questions-on-new-ICMA-sovereign-bond--PR_320871

O'Malley P (2000) Uncertain subjects: risks, liberalism and contract. Econ Soc 29(4):460–484

Perez LA, Weissman DM (2006) Public power and private purpose: odious debt and the political economy of hegemony. N C J Int Law Commer Regul 32(4):699–747

Picketty T (2014) Capital in the twenty first century. The Belknap Press of Harvard University Press, Cambridge

Power PJ (1996) Sovereign debt: the rise of the secondary market and its implications for future restructurings. Fordham Law Rev 64(6):2701–2772

Reinhart CM, Rogoff KS (2009) This time is different: eight centuries of financial folly. Princeton University Press, Princeton
Sachs JD (1995) Do we need an international lender of last resort? Frank D. Graham Lecture, Princeton University, April 20, 1995. Columbia University Academic Commons
Sachs JD (2003) The roadblock to a sovereign bankruptcy law. Cato J 23:1
Schumacher J, Trebesch C et al (2018) Sovereign defaults in court. European Central Bank (ECB) Research paper series - working papers 2135
Streeck W (2014) Buying time: the delayed crisis of democratic capitalism. Verso, London
Syll LP (2014) The Keynes-Minsky-Kindleberger theory of financial crises. Wordpress Economics, 11 Sept 2014. https://larspsyll.wordpress.com/2014/09/11/the-keynes-minsky-kindleberger-theory-of-financial-crises/
The Brookings Institution (2013) Annual Report 2013. Brookings
Thomas D (2017) Sovereign debt as a commodity: a contract law perspective. Osgood Hall Law J 54(2):419–464
Turner BS, Holton RJ (eds) (2015) The Routledge international handbook of globalization studies: second edition. Routledge, London
van Lamoen R, Mattheussens S et al (2017) Quantitative easing and exuberance in government bond markets: evidence from the ECB's expanded asset purchase program. DNB Working Paper 548, March 2017. https://www.dnb.nl/en/binaries/Working%20Paper%20No.%20548_tcm47-353673.pdf
Weidenmaier M, McCarl RM (2014) Creditors' remedies. In: Lastra R et al (eds) Sovereign debt management. Oxford University Press, Oxford
Whittall C (2017) Hunt for yield fuels boom in another complex, risky security. The Wall Street Journal, 22 October 2017. https://www.wsj.com/articles/hunt-for-yield-fuels-boom-in-clos-1508673601
Wigglesworth R (2013) Lee Buchheit: crusader for financially stricken countries. Financial Times, 28 May 2013. https://www.ft.com/content/f0c2519c-c79e-11e2-9c52-00144feab7de
Zettelmeyer J, Trebesch C et al (2013) The Greek debt restructuring: an autopsy. Econ Policy 28:513–563

Approximation of Secured Credit Laws in Global Economies: Methodological Challenges

Muriel Renaudin

Contents

Abstract The principal aim of this volume is to explore commercial contract law in scholarship and legal practice, to discuss new research agendas and provide a forum for debate of topical issues that might benefit from further attention by scholarship and legislatures. This chapter on methodological challenges within the approximation of personal property security law regimes raises what is a key contemporary problem as commercial legislations continue to grow out of national boundaries. It raises some of the most challenging issues in this area of commercial law due to its dependence on baseline concepts of insolvency and property laws and

M. Renaudin (✉)
School of Law and Politics, Cardiff University, Cardiff, UK
e-mail: RenaudinM1@cardiff.ac.uk

M. Heidemann, J. Lee (eds.), *The Future of the Commercial Contract in Scholarship and Law Reform*, https://doi.org/10.1007/978-3-319-95969-6_9

because of the vast differences within the laws of national legal systems in these areas. This chapter thus contributes to a topic of central importance to any project of law reform on an international level in commercial law. In particular, in the context of multiple projects for the approximation and modernisation of personal property security law, this chapter proposes to analyse some of the methodological challenges that have arisen as a result of these initiatives. It is argued that there are still outstanding challenges and obstacles to the comprehensive approximation and modernisation of personal property security law. The analysis sketches out and critically considers four methodological challenges connected to the justification of approximation of law projects, the appropriation of international endeavours and the issues of legitimacy and enforcement within the emergence of a transnational personal property security law framework.

1 Introduction

In this era of transnationalisation of legal relations, law is being subject to significant mutations and challenges. This is especially true of the regulation of commercial transactions, and in particular personal property security law, which has been the focus of several attempts at modernisation and approximation in the recent years.[1] Having a similar and modern legal regime across national jurisdictions is in principle a desirable goal for commercial actors and likely to promote economic prosperity. Harmonised and unified modern laws would increase confidence for traders and investors which should in turn constitute a positive factor for the growth of the economy.[2] It is argued that the adoption of a uniform legal regime should also encompass the principles of a modern and predictable law for secured transactions. Promoting access to credit has indeed been a priority for national and international law reformers seeking to promote economic activity and economic growth. Several international organisations such as the European Bank for Reconstruction and Development (EBRD), the United Nations Commission on International Trade Law (UNCITRAL) or the International Institute for the Unification of Private Law (UNIDROIT) have thus encouraged the approximation and modernisation of personal property security law regimes through the enactment of model laws and

[1] The European Bank for Reconstruction and Development (EBRD) Model Law on Secured Transaction (1994), the International Institute for the Unification of Private Law (UNIDROIT) Convention on International Interests in Mobile Equipment and the Protocol to the Convention on International Interests in Mobile Equipment on Matters specific to Aircraft Equipment (2001), the United Nations Commissions on International Trade Law (UNCITRAL) legislative Guide on Secured Transactions (2007) and more recently the UNCITRAL Model law on Secured Transactions 2016 reflect some of the major attempts at the international level.

[2] See for example the UNCITRAL Report of the Secretary General on the draft legislative Guide on Secured Transactions in February 2002 available at http://www.uncitral.org/uncitral/en/commission/working_groups/6Security_Interests.html.

legislative guides. But as many projects for the approximation and modernisation of law continue to flourish and as the law continues to grow out of national boundaries, this chapter proposes to analyse some of the methodological challenges that have arisen from these initiatives. It is argued that there are still outstanding challenges and obstacles to the comprehensive approximation and modernisation of personal property security law. Firstly, this chapter reasserts that the case for the approximation of personal property security laws is not absolute[3] and that, despite a converging trend,[4] there are still unresolved obstacles to the recognition of a sound theoretical justification for the approximation of personal property security law regimes. The case within which the modernisation and approximation of law was built has also dramatically changed. The beginning of the millennium was marked by historic economic events such as the 2008 economic crisis, the transformation of planned economies to more liberal models in Eastern Europe, and more recently, the perceptible slowdown in global trade and noticeable emerging protectionism.[5] Further, the argument based on legal culture remains strong, especially in the field of personal property security law, baseline concepts of which are rooted *par excellence* in national property and insolvency laws. This argument is also reinforced by the fact that many international approximation of law projects in the field of secured credit law are modelled on the principles of Article 9 of the American Uniform Commercial Code (UCC) the rationale of which has yet to be proven from a legal perspective. The legal transplant of a foreign legal model thus appears to be the chosen methodology for the approximation and modernisation of the law rather than legal harmonisation.[6] There is no doubt that Article 9 UCC encompasses features of a modern and predictable legal regime for secured transactions but that should not in itself justify and prescribe the need to modernise and approximate the law along the same lines.[7] What works in one particular jurisdiction may not work in another. The American regime encompasses specific views on key policy issues that may not be reasonable to import within the cultural legal context of other jurisdictions. The literature demonstrates that the importation of foreign legal models within national laws and/or international law may raise significant difficulties due to the differences

---

[3] See for instance Boodman (1991), p. 43; Legrand (1996), p. 52; Stephan (1999), p. 743; Walt (1999), p. 671.

[4] On the convergence of commercial legislations, see for instance Mistelis (2001).

[5] See the note from the Secretary-General of the Organisation for Economic Co-operation and Development (OECD) entitled "Contribution of Trade and Investment to Increased Productivity, Growth, Jobs and Inclusiveness" available at http://www.oecd.org/officialdocuments/publicdisplaydocumentpdf/?cote=TAD/TC(2016)6/REV1doclanguage=en. The United States have recently pulled out of a major trade agreement namely the North American Free Trade Agreement (NAFTA) and the British government has indicated its willingness to leave the European Single Market.

[6] Legal harmonisation involves the action of coordinating different legal rules from different legal systems to eliminate and accommodate differences whereas legal transplant "[...] consists in the introduction, in national legal systems, of statutes and principles belonging to other systems, be they legal rules of other countries or customs whose acceptance is widespread". See Carbonara et al. (2007), p. 2.

[7] See for example Mattei (2003), p. 385.

in socio-legal context and in legal culture, such as the differences underlying Common law and Civil law systems.[8] Secondly, this chapter discusses the ongoing issue of appropriation[9] and proposes to investigate the suitability of current forms of international instruments, namely international conventions and soft law instruments such as model laws or legislative guides, that might enable a successful approximation of law in the field of personal property security. Furthermore, the body of international law that is emerging from the international law making process raises further challenges for the approximation and modernisation of personal property security law. The analysis thus questions whether the nature of a transnational commercial law operating within a distinct legal order beyond the state would be better suited to regulate international personal property security law. It is argued that the recognition of such an autonomous transnational personal property security law together with the recognition of a commercial legal framework within which to operate remains uncertain because of further methodological challenges, primarily embodied in the lack of state sovereignty and lack of coercive powers to enforce property rights.

2 Prolegomena: The Approximation and Modernisation of Personal Property Security Law Regimes

A security can be defined as a right over property to guarantee the repayment of a debt or to guarantee the performance of some other monetary obligation. As a general rule, secured claims get priority over unsecured claims. If the debtor defaults, the secured creditor is thus entitled to the asset representing the security in priority over other unsecured creditors. Without a regulated framework for secured credit and its priority system, the *pari passu* principle would apply, that is a principle of equal repayment amongst all creditors. Hence, a security creates an incentive for lenders as it gives secured creditors a priority for the repayment of money lent over other unsecured creditors. Finch explains:

> The normal rule in a corporate insolvency is that all creditors are treated on an equal footing - pari passu - and share in insolvency assets pro rata according to their pre-insolvency entitlements or the sums they are owed. Security avoids the effects of pari passu distribution by creating rights that have priority over the claims of unsecured creditors.[10]

The priority system enshrined in secured credit law regimes creates an exception to the principle of equality of repayment. This derogatory treatment may be

[8] See example Montesquieu (1748), Book One, Chapter Three; Kahn-Freund (1998), p. 7; Teubner (1998), p. 11; Legrand (1997), p. 111.

[9] See for example Chinkin (1989), p. 850; Boyle (1999), p. 901; Shaffer et al. (2008); Gopalan (2008), p. 327.

[10] Finch (1999), p. 634.

considered unfair for unsecured creditors[11] and contrary to the principles of social justice but some argue that the rationale for the priority system can be grounded on the notions of property rights and freedom of contract.[12] It is further argued that the availability of security and its priority system may reduce risks for creditors, support economic activities and contribute to the growth of the economy.[13] If the institution of secured lending is desirable, it is contended that promoting access to credit through the modernisation of personal property security law regimes would constitute a significant factor in economic growth.[14] Economists and financial institutions further argue that an efficient and modern personal property security law regime should take a liberal approach by removing restrictions on the taking of a security.[15] In the international context, the yearly published Doing Business Reports of the World Bank also confirm this postulate.[16] As a result, it is contended that an efficient and modern personal property security law regime should give access to credit to a wide range of individuals and commercial actors at lower costs and should be framed within a secured and predictable set of rules.[17] Hence, it is not surprising that in this quest to become more competitive, many jurisdictions, including England and Wales, introduced law reform proposals aiming at the modernisation of personal property security law.[18]

An illustration of potential uncertainties within the law of secured credit and insolvency can be drawn from the English legal framework, particularly, within the distinction between the fixed and floating charge. A floating charge can be defined as a global security over a companies' fund of assets, including present and future

[11] On the debate over the rationale for secured lending, see for instance Jackson et al. (1979), p. 1143; Schwartz (1981), p. 1; Schwartz (1984), p. 1051; Buckley (1986), p. 1393; Shupack (1989), p. 1067; Schwartz (1994), p. 2073; LoPucki (1994), p. 1887; Hudson (1995) p. 47; Carlson (1998), p. 1635.

[12] McCormack et al. (2017), p. 112.

[13] See for example Gullifer and Raczynska (2016), p. 271; Levine (2005), p. 865.

[14] Levine (2005), p. 865.

[15] See for example the studies on the legal origin thesis of the LLSV group (Rafael La Porta, Florencio Lopez de Silanes, Andrei Shleifer and Robert Vishny) (1997, 1998), p. 1113.

[16] See for example World Bank Doing Business Report 2017 (2017).

[17] Gullifer (2016).

[18] Some provinces of Canada reformed their personal property security laws modelled on the American Article 9 UCC. Ontario was the first Canadian province to adopt a PPSA modelled on Article 9 UCC. It was adopted in 1967 but the Act did not come into effect until 1973. New Zealand reformed its law in 1999 (Personal Property Security Act 1999). In England and Wales, the Law Commission considered the need for reform with respect to company charges, and issued a Consultation Paper in June 2002 (Registration of Company Security Interests: Company Charges and Property other than Land—Law Commission Consultation Paper No 164) which was followed by a Consultative Report published in August 2004 (Company Security Interests: A Consultative Report, Law Commission Consultative Report No176). A final Report was published in 2005 (Company Security Interests, Law Commission Report No 296, Cm 6654). France also reformed its secured credit Law in 2006 with the Ordinance No 2006-346 dated 23rd March 2006.

assets. The security will thus float over a changing pool of assets until a triggering event does occur (crystallisation). The great advantage of the floating charge is that it allows a debtor to provide the secured creditor with a wide security and to continue to deal with the charged assets in the course of business without the lender's consent and until crystallisation which predominantly happens when a receiver or liquidator is appointed.[19] The floating charge is thus a great device for the borrower. It provides him with a great degree of freedom but may leave the creditor at greater risks of not getting repaid. Indeed, the holder of a floating charge will usually be paid out once other categories of creditors (fixed-charge holders, preferential creditors, expenses of the insolvent estates and unsecured creditors ring-fenced funds) have been paid. In contrast, the holder of a fixed charge is paid out of the proceeds of sale of the charged assets which may place him in a more advantageous position upon the debtor's insolvency. The uncertainty in the law stems from the characterisation of a charge as being floating or fixed. The characterisation of the floating charge has indeed been problematic and has been a recurring topic of debate in courts over the years. Particularly, the question emerged whether a security created over present and future book debts paid into a company's current account with a bank was a fixed or a floating charge. In *Westminster plc v. Spectrum Plus Limited & Ors*,[20] the House of Lords decided that such a security had to be floating because the bank did not have enough control over the account to completely block it which, if it did, would have enabled the creation of a fixed charge. The case of *Gray and others v. G-T-P Group Limited*[21] is another illustration of the difficulties underlying the uncertain distinction between floating and fixed charge. In this case, the High Court had to determine whether the creation of a trust had to be characterised as a fixed or floating charge. Most significantly, the High Court had to determine whether such a security could fall within the ambits of the Financial Collateral Arrangements Regulations 2003 which exempts the financial collateral arrangement from the registration requirements under the Companies Act 2006. In the *Gray* Case, assets were placed in an account following a declaration of trust for the purpose of securing certain liabilities. The High Court clearly confirmed that such an arrangement was a charge and should be registered pursuing Section 860 of the Companies Act 2006. The Court then considered whether this security was floating or fixed. It was reaffirmed that:

> … the essential element in determining the difference between a fixed and a floating charge is the chargor's ability without the chargee's consent to control and manage the charged assets. That ability is present in this case.[22]

Thus, it was concluded that the trust created for the purpose of security had to be characterised as being a floating charge, which was, under the circumstances of the case, void for lack of registration.

---

[19] Crystallisation can also occur upon 'ceasing to do business', 'enforcing the security' or upon the occurrence of a particular event agreed in a clause (automatic crystallisation).

[20] [2005] UKHL 41.

[21] [2010] EWHC 1772.

[22] See Para 31[2010] EWHC 1772.

Looking at the wide range of modernisation endeavours in the field of personal security law, Article 9 of the UCC is often presented as a model of success in encompassing the characteristics of a modern secured credit law regime. Article 9 of the UCC adopts a functional approach to the regulation of a unitary security device, the security interest. It encompasses a wide range of coverage, including all categories of personal property, tangible and intangible, and all types of parties. One of the most interesting features of the Article 9 security interest lies in the fact that its scope is delimited according to the function served, so that the parties can freely apply the most suitable structure for their transactions. Article 9 of the UCC provides for a single functional system together with the recognition of a single set of rules, a notice filing system and a first to file priority rules, applicable to the security interest.

Many international organisations such as the EBRD, UNIDROIT or UNCITRAL adopted international instruments modelled on the unitary and functional approach of the American secured credit law regime.[23] The need to become ever more competitive has also led national law reformers to opt for reforms encompassing some of the features of Article 9 UCC. Jurisdictions such as some provinces of Canada,[24] Australia,[25] and New Zealand[26] adopted an Article 9 UCC type regime but European jurisdictions such as France,[27] Belgium,[28] Italy[29] and England and Wales[30] adopted a more nuanced approach. There is thus a noticeable convergence of the law towards the American model but a true assimilation of an Article 9 type regime through the approximation of law remains uncertain.

3 Justifications

The case for the approximation of law is not uncontested. On the one hand, advocates see it as likely to achieve substantial reductions in the cost of cross-border transactions and provide more certainty and clarity in the applicable law for the

[23] See for example the recent adoption of the UNCITRAL Model Law on Secured Transactions (2016).

[24] See for example the Personal Property act of Ontario 1990.

[25] Personal Property Security act 2009.

[26] Personal Property securities Act 1999.

[27] The Ordinance of 23rd March 2006 reforming French Secured Credit law added a new chapter to the French Civil code. On the French Law reform, see Simler (2006), p. 124.

[28] Law of 24th June and 11th July 2013 reforming personal property security law regime.

[29] Law 3rd May 2016, 'Decreto- Legge 3 maggio 2016, n. 59, Disposizioni urgenti in materia di procedure esecutive e concorsuali, nonche' a favore degli investitori in banche in liquidazione'.

[30] Companies Act 2006 (Strategic Report and Directors' Report) Regulations 2013 clarifies which charges are registrable and improve registration procedures. On the development of the English secured credit law framework, see De Lacy (2012), pp. 3–82.

international business community. But on the other hand,[31] sceptical theorists see in the approximation of law process a form of disguised protectionism and national hegemony.[32] Further challenges to the argument for the approximation of secured credit laws are based on cultural and economic grounds.

3.1 *The Case for the Harmonisation of Secured Credit Law*

Many arguments have been advanced in favour of an approximation of commercial laws, and emphasis will particularly be given on the reasons that have forged the consensus for the approximation of secured credit law regimes.[33] Arguments based on a cost-benefit rationale would seem to provide strong incentives in support of an approximation of secured credit law regimes. It is argued that the approximation of commercial laws is desirable because of negative externalities and jurisdictional interface.[34] Negative externalities would impose extra costs on contracting parties that could be avoided with an approximation of laws.[35] These costs within commercial activities include the costs of negotiations, drafting and enforcing commercial contracts, translation costs, search and information costs.[36] One crucial contractual aspect for traders is to find the best legal system that will provide them with security and certainty at cheaper cost. From that perspective, it is arguable that the implementation of modern and more uniform secured credit law regimes would reduce the costs of credit at domestic and international level.

It is further argued that within the jurisdictional interface, interaction and communication between commercial participants will be problematic in the absence of an approximation of laws.[37] An approximation of laws would enable the international commercial community to communicate and interact using the same legal language. Of course, conflict of law rules already help in providing more certainties for traders at the international level in the way they can now ascertain the applicable law but this is not always possible. The rule of the *lex situs,* for example, in the context of a security created in mobile equipment, is arguably not adequate. Further, the conflict of law rules does not eliminate all the costs. Creditors are not guaranteed that their security will be valid and enforceable within the national applicable law. Thus, contractual parties will generally spend substantial time and money in translation

---

[31] See for example Boodman (1991), p. 43; Legrand (1996), p. 52; Stephan (1999), p. 743; Walt (1999), p. 671.

[32] Leebron (1996), p. 64.

[33] On this point see Schmitthoff (1968), p. 551; Goode (1991), p. 54; Fox (1991–1992), p. 593; Leebron (1996), p. 64; Kronke (2000), p. 13; Goode (2001), p. 751; Smits (2002–2003), p. 79; Kronke (2003), p. 11; Lando (2003), p. 123.

[34] Leebron (1996), p. 75.

[35] Ibid. p. 78.

[36] Schmidtchen et al. (2004).

[37] Leebron (1996), p. 75.

work and in searching and analysing the commercial law of a particular foreign jurisdiction if it appears to be the applicable law to the case. Thus, an approximation of secured credit law regimes would seem to reduce these costs and would also provide more certainty with respect to the applicable law.

Approximation of laws is not only justifiable through a costs-benefits rationale; it has also been justified because of the values it would promote such as fairness and transparency within international transactions.[38] It is often contended that different legal rules can lead to unfair results for some participants.[39] In the field of secured credit law, this argument can be exemplified with the different registration requirements of a security created over movable property. For instance, a French or English lender does not need to register a property based security such as simple retention of title clause to be valid. Across the Atlantic, an American lender would need to file his purchase money security interest to perfect the security.[40] Registration may be presented as a burdensome requirement but some will argue that it provides more certainty and predictability for creditors by avoiding the issue of the debtor's false wealth. An approximation of laws would mitigate the production of unfair results by subjecting creditors and debtors to similar sets of rules. The question of the approximation of property-based security such as the English or French retention of title clauses in line with the American purchase money security interest has widely been discussed in a context of law reforms.[41] However, it is to be reasserted that reconciliation between the different national secured credit law regimes, particularly of retention of title, remains a true *casus belli* within the approximation of law endeavours.[42]

Although one could see substantial advantages in the approximation of secured credit law regimes, it has also been argued that uniformity of law is a mixed blessing.[43] There is always the risk, linked to the recognition of a single legal rule to be applied at the international level that uniformity might lead to the adoption of inefficient rules, which might ultimately increase the costs imposed on contracting parties.[44] In particular, the efficiency of the law as an international standard has been questioned. The risk being that an approximation of secured credit law regimes, modelled on a particular foreign legislation, may not produce similar efficient results in other recipient national legal systems. For example, the recognition of uniform rules could still lead to substantial divergences following their implementation and interpretation within national legal systems, thus leaving the establishment of uniform rules unproductive and fruitless. Finally, even if a nation was to implement the new uniform law, commercial participants, lacking information and

---

[38] Ibid. pp. 84–89.

[39] Ibid. p. 84.

[40] Art. 9-324 UCC.

[41] See on this point Gullifer (2007).

[42] For example, the UNCITRAL Legislative Guide for Secured Transactions provides the option to include or exclude property based securities from the unitary regime.

[43] Walt (1999).

[44] Walt (1999), p. 672.

familiarity with the new law, could be deterred from applying it which could, again lead to inefficiencies in the adoption of the uniform legal rule.[45]

3.2 *Regulatory Competition*

In the absence of a sound and absolute theory on the approximation of secured credit law regimes, some authors have argued that the diversity in legal methods for structuring secured financing may enhance economic activities through regulatory competition. In this sense secured credit could be envisaged as a marketable product that would enable national jurisdictions to compete with one another.

For example, in the context of the EU, and in light of the achievement of the Common Market, the question emerged whether the harmonisation of secured credit laws was desirable or whether the diversity of legal regimes which allows for more innovation in secured credit and which allows for a wider choice for structuring finance, should be preserved.[46] In other words, would competition between secured credit law regimes better support the development and growth of economic activities within the Common Market than legal harmonisation? Given the limited success at the harmonisation of EU secured credit laws,[47] and given the recent draft of the Common Frame of Reference[48] 'optional toolbox' for traders, competition of national legal systems would appear to be the current *statu quo*.[49] On the one hand, it is arguable that a competition of legal regimes could end up in distorted and unfair competition towards legal regimes with lower legal standards. The reason is that some jurisdictions might be deterred from investing in some Member States because their secured credit law regimes might offer lower standards. Jurisdictions with less efficient secured credit legislations may appear less attractive to investors than other jurisdictions offering more modern legal regimes.[50] On the other hand, it is arguable that diversity in national legal regimes would enable Member States to experiment and innovate in their quest to find an efficient and predictable secured credit law. It is arguable that the preservation of diversity in legal systems would also allow legal reformers to provide for more innovation within secured credit law regimes and would also avoid the risk of enacting an inefficient legal regime with the approxima-

---

[45] Walt (1999), p. 673.

[46] Sykes (2000), p. 257.

[47] See I.A.2. with respect to the Directive 2000/35/EC of the European Parliament and of the Council of 29th June 2000 on Combating Late Payment in Commercial Transactions, OJ L 200, 8.8.2000. See Article 4 on retention of title clauses.

[48] The Draft Common Frame of Reference (DCFR) prepared by the Study Group on a European Civil Code and the Research Group on EC Private Law has been published in February 2009. The CFR will also include a Book IX on Proprietary Security Rights in movable assets. See Eidenmüller et al. (2008), p. 665.

[49] On the CFR, see for instance Beale (2008). See also Reich (1992), p. 861.

[50] See Lando (2000), p. 61.

tion of law. Ultimately, it is argued that a competition of legal systems will enable the best law to survive and may serve as basis for the law of the community.[51] Legal diversity would also be consistent with the preservation of legal culture.

3.3 Legal Culture

The argument based on legal culture is significant in explaining the obstacles to successful comprehensive approximation of secured credit law regimes. In the field of secured credit, there are substantial differences among national legal cultures and policy choices regarding the extent to which a security should be recognised (if at all). In jurisdictions where the institution of security is recognised, the validity requirements for a security can also vary. These requirements will usually reflect different policy choices in different legal cultures. For example, common law jurisdictions are generally described as sympathetic to the concept of party autonomy and self-help. These jurisdictions have thus developed a more liberal attitude towards security. As a result, a security can generally be taken subject to a minimum of formality over both present and future assets to secure existing and future obligations. A functional approach is also generally followed where the concept of a universal security usually prevails. By contrast, civil law jurisdictions have been more cautious towards the recognition of a universal security and in their approach towards non-possessory security, such as the non-possessory pledge. These jurisdictions have been particularly concerned about the false wealth phenomenon where the debtor can remain in possession of an asset subject to a security. So in these jurisdictions, there are, in varying degrees, requirements of specificity and individualisation of assets, the requirement for a new post-acquisition act of transfer to give in proprietary effects to security taken on future assets, requirements of notice to the debtor as a condition of the validity (not merely priority) of an assignment of debts, and restrictions on self-help remedies such as possession and sale of the asset.[52]

The difficulty is that, despite diversity in national legal approaches and in underlying policies towards the regulation of secured credit, many approximation and modernisation of law endeavours opted for a model based on the principles of American Article 9 UCC. The reason is that Article 9 UCC is often described as a model of success in encompassing the features of a modern regime for secured credit and in promoting economic efficiency. Article 9 UCC enables wide access to credit within a certain and predictable legal framework for creditors and debtors. Such legal regime would in turn promote the growth of the economy. But given the legal and cultural divergences, the legal transplantation of a particular foreign legal model should be envisaged with caution within the context of the approximation and modernisation of law. The international legal reformer should avoid systematic

[51] See Schmitthoff (1968).

[52] Goode (1998a), p. 48.

standardisation through the process of legal transplantation of the law of the strongest or the richest. As explained above, regulatory competition would also enhance legal competitiveness and would also promote legal reforms. Legal diversity and legal culture are to be protected against hasty law reforms solely motivated by economic imperatives. Legrand argues that law is cultural, and that in a world of plurality of cultures, there cannot be a universal law.[53] In attempts at the approximation and modernisation of law, the international legislator cannot ignore the legal language or the historical and political context.

4 Appropriation and the Choice of Legal Instruments

Goode identifies at least nine instruments by which unification of the law may be achieved:

> … (1) a multilateral Convention without a Uniform Law as such; (2) a multilateral Convention embodying a Uniform Law; (3) a set of bilateral Treaties; (4) Community legislation – Typically, a Directive; (5) a Model Law; (6) a codification of custom and usage promulgated by an international non-governmental organization; (7) international trade terms promulgated by such an organization; (8) model contracts and general contractual conditions; (9) restatements by scholars and other experts.[54]

Although all these instruments aim at the harmonisation and unification of the law through the enactment of a supra national legal rule, they generally offer different degrees of flexibility to the interested states. International conventions have generally been the preferred method used to achieve unification of the law at the international level notwithstanding their restrictive nature, but model laws, restatements and other soft law instruments have recently become the panacea for successful international unification and harmonisation owing to their greater flexibility.

Considering the wide range of legal instruments for unification, one of the many challenges for international organisations is to determine whether a specific type of legal unification instrument can be identified which might constitute an adequate legal method to achieve a successful approximation and modernisation of secured credit law regimes.

4.1 International Conventions

International conventions have long been the preferred method to achieve unification of the law at the international level mainly because of their binding nature.[55] Abbott recognises that:

---

[53] Legrand (1997).

[54] Goode (1998b), p. 54.

[55] Shaffer et al. (2008).

> [b]y using hard law to order their relations, international actors reduce transactions costs, strengthen the credibility of their commitments, expand their available political strategies, and resolve problems of incomplete contracting.[56]

International conventions generally consist in the enactment of provisions aiming at the unification of conflict of law rules or in the enactment of provisions embodying a substantive law regime. For example, in the field of secured credit, the Cape Town Convention on International Interests in Mobile Equipment and associated protocols[57] opted for a uniform regime regulating the creation and recognition of an international interest in high value mobile equipment and did not opt for a regime aiming at unifying conflict of law rules.[58]

International conventions provide for a strong level of uniformity of the law with a unique supra national legal instrument that once ratified by states, is legally binding. Arguably, international conventions could provide a successful method for the modernisation and approximation of secured credit law regimes pursuing the achievement of a high ratio of ratifications. Evidently, such efforts would require a strong consensus among all participating states on the question of secured credit. The attempt to reach such consensus is however uncertain given the different legal and cultural approaches towards secured credit and given the various existing national secured credit law regimes. Even if a consensus was possible on the shape of a single legal regime for secured credit, it is arguable that uniformity would not be guaranteed if a consistent interpretation across participating states' courts was not followed.[59]

International conventions are not the product of national draftsmen but their adoption still requires a certain consensus among participating states. Given the diversity of national secured credit law regimes and the diversity among national baseline property and insolvency law principles, the success of an international convention to approximate and modernise the law would ineluctably require its drafters to accommodate the existing differences of national legal regimes to maximise state ratifications. International legislative efforts should thus attempt to establish the best available solution that would be acceptable for all, that would be consistent with the various national legal cultures and the diverse national legislations. In reality, powerful lobbies are commonly used by states' representatives within the international law making process, in an attempt to promote the exportation of their own

[56] Abbott et al. (2000), p. 422.

[57] Convention on International Interests in Mobile Equipment (Cape Town, 2001); Protocol to the Convention on International Interests in Mobile Equipment on Matters Specific to Aircraft Equipment (Cape Town, 2001) and the Luxembourg Protocol to the Convention on International Interests in Mobile Equipment on Matters Specific to Railway Rolling Stock (Luxembourg, 2007).

[58] On this point see Espinola (1997), p. 9; Fleisig (1999), p. 253; Cuming (1998), p. 365; De La Peña (1999), p. 347; Foëx (1999), p. 409; Cuming (1998); Davies (2002); Goode (2002), p. 4; Deschamps (2002), p. 17; Davies (2003), p. 151; Goode (2004), p. 757; Honnbier et al. (2004), p. 3; Saunders et al. (2006).

[59] On the assessment of international conventions as successful instruments of unification at the international level, see Kronke (2000), at p. 13.

laws to other jurisdictions which raises the obvious issue of legitimacy.[60] Such an approach towards the international law making process would also run the risk of a low level of ratification or the risk for international conventions to remain dead letters.

Simply concluding an international convention just constitutes an indication of the potential adhesion of states and will only become legally binding if officially ratified by states. As Goode has already highlighted:

> [t]he treaty collections are littered with conventions that have never come into force, for want of the number of required ratifications, or have been eschewed by the major trading States. There are several reasons for this: failure to establish from potential interest groups at the outset that there is a serious problem which the proposed convention will help to resolve; hostility from powerful pressure groups; lack of sufficient interest of, or pressure on, governments to induce them to burden still further an already over-crowded legislative timetable; mutual hold-backs, each State waiting to see what others will do, so that in the end none of them does anything.[61]

The UNIDROIT Convention on International Finance Leasing 1988 has only been ratified by ten countries[62] and the UNIDROIT Convention on International Factoring 1988 has only been ratified by seven countries.[63] The Cape Town Convention on International Interests in Mobile Equipment was much more successful and has been ratified by thirty-two countries. But, the Convention is restricted in its application to the regulation of an international security interest created in a particular class of assets, that is high value mobile equipment.

The possibility for states to derogate from the main text of the convention may also clearly undermine the goal of uniformity within unification of law efforts.[64] Considering the vast amount of divergences in national secured credit law regimes, the substantive unification of secured credit law regimes using an international convention would bear the risk of states introducing some opt-outs provisions or simply not proceeding to its ratification at all.[65] For example, Article 39 of the Cape Town Convention provides that each participating states can decide that certain rights and interests will have priority over international interests by introducing specific declarations. The loss of uniformity related to amendments explains the reason why international conventions usually have a limited scope and only cover a specific area of law. As a result, international conventions generally remain rather fragmentary in their nature and most of them only concern one specific area of commercial law such as one special type of contract or one specific legal regime. Even the very well-known United Nations Convention on Contracts for the International Sale of Goods

---

[60] See Sect. 5 below.

[61] Goode (1997a), p. 232.

[62] The list of contracting states is available at http://www.unidroit.org/english/implement/i-88-l.pdf.

[63] The list of contracting states is available at http://www.unidroit.org/english/implement/i-88-f.pdf.

[64] Wool (1997), p. 49.

[65] See on this point Vogenauer (2009), p. 3.

contains legal gaps as for example on the validity of the international contract in question or about the repercussions of State control over the import and export of certain goods.[66]

The regime embodied in the Cape Town Convention is no exception as it enables creditors to create an international global security interest in high value mobile equipment together with the recognition of the notice filing[67] and a first to file priority rule. The international interest so created does not replace a security introduced under the law of a Member State as they can validly coexist. Nonetheless, if the international interest is validly registered, it will have priority over the national security.[68] Previous developments have identified some of the difficulties in attempting to reach a consensus on the question of secured credit, especially considering the existing differences between legal systems.[69] Thus, on this occasion the choice to solely unify an aspect of secured financing[70] without requiring states to modify their national legislations proved to be a success. In this respect, the Cape Town Convention on International Interests in Mobile Equipment and Associated Protocols[71] constitutes a significant achievement for the unification of the law of secured credit in respect of these specific types of assets. Conversely, it is also arguable that the decision to opt for a series of separate conventions to regulate the creation of an international security interest relative to specific types of assets could reduce the economic benefits of the proposed new scheme to no more than a limited variety of assets.[72] Indeed, it is to be recognised that a successful modernisation based on the use of international convention would not be entirely satisfactory unless it could be extended to other categories of assets for secured credit.

Finally, international conventions could also fail in their endeavours to approximate the law if not interpreted uniformly. It is explained that:

> [t]he principal objective of an international convention is to achieve uniformity of legal rules within the various States party to it. However, even when outward uniformity is achieved following the adoption of a single authoritative text, uniform application of the agreed rules is by no means guaranteed, as in practice different countries almost inevitably come to put different interpretations upon the same enacted words.[73]

---

[66] Bonell (1997), p. 11.

[67] The Cape Town Convention has introduced an international register (CTIR) in respect of security created in aircraft equipment. Information is available at https://www.internationalregistry.aero/irWeb/pageflows/work/UserDocumentation/DownloadUserDocumentationController.jpf?language=English.

[68] Goode (2004), p. 758.

[69] Goode (1998a), p. 48.

[70] This aspect of secured credit law was for many jurisdictions left unregulated (for example in France) which facilitated the adoption and ratification of the Convention.

[71] The Protocol to the Convention on International Interests in Mobile Equipment on Matters Specific to Aircraft Equipment (Cape town 2001) and the Luxembourg Protocol to the Convention on International Interests in Mobile Equipment on Matters Specific to Railway Rolling Stock (Luxembourg 2007) but not yet in force.

[72] Stanford (1999), p. 248.

[73] Munday (1978), p. 450.

For example, it might be unnatural for a civil lawyer to understand and interpret a convention using the concept of 'security interest' when civil law jurisdictions do not recognise interests in property but only rights in property. In that respect, it is interesting to note that the UNCITRAL Model Law on Secured Transactions did not use the American Article 9 UCC terminology of 'security interest' but adopted the term of 'security right'.[74]

4.2 Model Laws and Restatements

Soft law international legal instruments[75] have recently become the panacea for the harmonisation and modernisation of private law. Soft law instruments can cover a wide range of legal instruments and include model laws, restatements, legislative guides, international trade terms such as those produced by the International Chamber of Commerce (ICC), or International Contracts Terms (ICT). As opposed to international conventions, states are not the sole actors in the making of soft law legal instruments. Private law scholars, academics, and organisations representing businesses and industries now also take part in the adoption of international legal standards which can raise questions as to the legitimacy of the rule making process.[76]

The use of soft law legal instruments has been the object of significant debates among academics. It has been argued that the increase in the use of soft law "… might destabilize the whole international normative system and turn into an instrument that can no longer serve its purpose."[77] Others have argued that soft law is desirable as it would constitute a step towards the recognition of hard law.[78] Partisans of the use of soft legal instruments generally recognise that it would lower contracting costs by avoiding the lengthy negotiation process required with international conventions. The non-binding nature of soft law instruments would allow more flexibility in dealing with legal and cultural diversity. Further, these instruments would provide more flexibility in the amendment process which would ease and speed the adaptation to modern commercial and financial environment. By avoiding the ratification and cumbersome amendment process, soft law instruments might be quicker and simpler to draft. Finally, it is arguable that soft law instruments might be used as a step forward to the recognition of legally binding instruments.[79]

[74] For instance, terminologies issues have been extensively analysed in the *travaux préparatoires* of the UNCITRAL Legislative Guide on Secured Transactions. See for instance, Riffard (2006), p. 107.

[75] For a description of the features of soft law instruments see for example Shaffer et al. (2008).

[76] See McCormack (2011).

[77] Weil (1983), p. 423.

[78] Reinicke et al. (2000), p. 75.

[79] Trubek (2005).

These instruments of unification have particularly been used in the United States of America. The American Law Institute has used restatements and model laws extensively as legal methods to clarify, modernise, and improve the law.[80] The success of restatements and model laws as a legal method to reform and approximate the law aroused significant interest from other international entities. The success of the American Uniform Commercial Code, and particularly of Article 9 in relation to secured transactions, in spreading uniformity and modern legislation across the American States[81] clearly inspired many international entities to create similar legal instruments to be used in other jurisdictions.[82] Indeed, recent international approximation and modernisation projects have essentially taken the form of soft law legal instruments such as restatements and model laws. For instance, UNCITRAL recently enacted a Model Law on Secured Transactions[83] which constitutes one of the major initiatives in the field of secured transactions. Previous initiatives conducted by UNCITRAL have already been successful in approximating and modernising the law by using soft law legal instruments. The successful UNCITRAL Model Law on International Commercial Arbitration (1985 as amended in 2006) has served as a model for legislative reforms in many jurisdictions such as Canada, Germany or Australia.[84] The UNCITRAL Model Law on Procurement of Goods, Construction and Services (1994) has also served as a model for legislation particularly in many new emerging economies such as jurisdictions from Africa and jurisdictions from the former Soviet Union.[85] Finally, the Model Law on Electronic Commerce has also successfully served as a model for legislative reforms in many jurisdictions such as China, India and the United States.[86] These examples clearly illustrate the success of soft law legal instruments such as model laws and restatements as legal methods for modernising and approximating the law in specific areas of commercial law.

Soft law legal instruments are not binding and, thus, do not require any ratification, but states are offered the choice to adopt and modify some of their provisions

[80] See *e.g.*, the American Law Institute.

[81] Vogenauer (2009), p. 5.

[82] See fn. 2.

[83] The text of the UNCITRAL Model Law on Secured Transactions is available at http://www.uncitral.org/uncitral/en/uncitral_texts/payments/Guide_securedtrans.html.

[84] Legislation based on the UNCITRAL Model Law on International Commercial Arbitration as adopted in 1985 has been adopted in 74 jurisdictions.

[85] The UNCITRAL Model Law on Procurement of Goods, Construction and Services is available at http://www.uncitral.org/uncitral/uncitral_texts/procurement_infrastructure/2011Model.html.

[86] The Model Law on Electronic Commerce is available at http://www.uncitral.org/uncitral/en/uncitral_texts/electronic_commerce/1996Model.html. The Model Law has also been adopted in the Bailiwick of Guernsey (2000), the Bailiwick of Jersey (2000) and the Isle of Man (2000), all Crown Dependencies of the United Kingdom of Great Britain and Northern Ireland; in Bermuda (1999), Cayman Islands (2000), and the Turks and Caicos Islands (2000), overseas territories of the United Kingdom of Great Britain and Northern Ireland; and in the Hong Kong Special Administrative Region of China (2000).

or to disregard them completely.[87] Another purpose of restatements and models laws is that they can encourage party autonomy by offering the opportunity to parties to adopt the legal regime as the governing law for their contractual relationships. This is a substantial advantage in using these legal instruments as legal methods to modernise the law at the international level. Naturally, soft law instruments can also serve as model legislations for national legal reforms as it has just been demonstrated. Owing to more flexibility, the use of soft law instruments may offer the potential to successfully reform and modernise the law. On the other hand, it is arguable that the high degree of flexibility offered by model laws and restatements is obtained at the expense of the successful achievement of complete unification of the law. In effect, the nature of model laws and restatements does not impose any ratification amongst potential participating States of the dispositions to be adopted. States remain free to adopt, modify and reject altogether the dispositions of a model law.

By avoiding the difficulties underlying the adoption of international conventions and by providing more flexibility for states to adhere to their provisions and, more flexibility to adapt to modern commercial transactions,[88] model laws and restatements would seem to offer a better vehicle for the successful modernisation and approximation of secured credit law regimes.

5 The Recognition of a Transnational Secured Credit Law: Legitimacy and Enforcement Challenges

5.1 Definitions

Originally, trade customs, embodied in the expressions of *lex mercatoria* or law merchant, were considered to constitute an autonomous source of law used to regulate commercial activities. During the nineteenth century the notion of sovereignty emerged and the idea that law could only emerge from the state. It was also during this time that codification spread as an expression of this national sovereignty. Illustrations of this movement of codification can be found with the enactment of civil codes in Europe such as the Napoleonic French civil code in 1804, The Spanish civil code (1888) or the German BGB (1900). With the transnationalisation of international commercial dealings, a new body of commercial law emerged at the

[87] Vogenauer (2009), p. 4.

[88] See Gopalan (2004), p. 310 where the author states that: "[t]his is a vehicle for harmonization that has assumed tremendous importance following the successful reception of the UNIDROIT Principles of International Commercial Contracts. Without a doubt, the tremendous flexibility offered by restatements has contributed to their recent allure. Parties can adopt them on a voluntary basis, and they serve many important functions. For example, the UNIDROIT Principles of International Commercial Contracts as viewed as "neutral" contract law principles in that they reflect a balance of interests and have not been formulated by any government."

international level which suggested a resurgence of the concept of *lex mercatoria* which is still the object of fervent debates.[89] The question of the emergence of a new *lex mercatoria* is part of a debate that is central for a number of scholars and academics.[90] In particular, underlying ambiguities remain over the definition, content, source and scope of the *lex mercatoria* which suggest the need for caution in the use of this terminology. The expression *lex mercatoria* is sometimes used interchangeably with the terminology of transnational commercial law which is defined as the "... law which is not particular to or the product of any one legal system but represents a convergence of rules drawn from several legal systems".[91] Yet the *lex mercatoria* and transnational commercial law must be distinguished. It is explained that:

> The phrase "transnational commercial law" is used to describe the totality of principles and rules, whether customary, conventional, contractual or derived from any other sources, which are common to a number of legal systems, while the phrase "*lex mercatoria*" is used to indicate that part of transnational commercial law which is unwritten and consists of customary commercial law, customary rules of evidence and procedures and general principles of commercial law, including international public policy.[92]

Thus the *lex mercatoria* is here taken to represent the corpus of unwritten law that is emerging at the international level through international usages and customs. Accordingly, the *lex mercatoria* only represents a small part of transnational commercial law which extends to international conventions, model laws and other international uniform principles.

5.2 *The Suitability of Transnational Commercial Law to Govern Modern Secured Transactions*

Would an autonomous transnational commercial law be more suited to enable the recognition of modern secured credit laws than domestic legislations? This question must be assessed in the light of the requirements of modern commerce and certainly does not aim to suggest that national legislations are inefficient. Naturally, domestic laws would still apply in purely domestic commercial transactions. Also, if transnational commercial law was not yet available in relation to specific aspects of international secured credit, domestic law would still be relevant following the application of traditional conflict of law rules.

As with legal unification, the recognition of international standards would clearly avoid conflict of law issues and thus avoid the complexities generated by the

[89] See for example Flanagan (2004), p. 297.

[90] On the debate on the *Lex Mercatoria* see for instance Berman (1988), p. 221; Highet (1989), p. 613; Kahn (1992), p. 413; Drobnig (1995), p. 223; Berger (1997), p. 943; Bonell (1998); Dalhuisen (2006), p. 129.

[91] Goode (1997b), p. 2.

[92] Ibid. p. 3.

existence of different legal regimes. Further, by avoiding conflict of law issues, transaction costs and legal risks would also arguably be reduced. Traditional conflicts of law rules do not always provide the certainty that the creation of a security in one jurisdiction will be enforceable in a foreign jurisdiction. This is particularly true for securities created in movable assets which are likely to easily cross boundaries. In that respect, the Cape Town Convention now enables creditors to create and enforce their security in high value mobile equipment at the international level. Although the success of international conventions largely depends upon the degree of adherence and ratifications of states to be successful, this example demonstrates that the emergence and recognition of an autonomous transnational secured credit law regime would similarly avoid conflict of law issues.

In addition to avoiding conflict of law issues, the flexibility of transnational commercial law would ease the formulation of international legal standards to regulate areas of secured transactions where domestic legislations have left significant legal gaps. For instance, the Cape Town Convention filled in the legal gap in relation to the creation and enforcement of an international security in movable equipment such as aircraft or railway rolling stocks which did not exist under some domestic legislations.

The recognition of an autonomous *corpus* of law to regulate international secured transactions would arguably be better attuned to the requirements of modern international commercial transactions. This is because transnational commercial law generally adopts a functional approach to the formulation of international legal standards. The functionalist approach designs law according to the desired objective, overlooking, to a certain extent, cultural, social and political elements inherent to state values. At the outset, it is arguable that transnational commercial law would be better suited to provide modern secured credit law regimes for international commercial participants than domestic legislations where legal culture is often said to constitute a significant obstacle to approximation and modernisation of law. Conversely, it is arguable that whatever the legal pattern in which secured credit law regimes emerge, a legal culture, representing specific policy choices and other specific interests will colour the legal norm. The draft of a secured credit law cannot be neutral and will always reflect fundamental policy choices. The question is thus to determine who is to make these choices. Should they solely remain with the state or could they also be considered within a distinct international legal framework by non-state entities and private actors? After all, there is always the risk that private actors decide to promote, through the recognition of transnational commercial law, specific policy decisions reflecting the position of powerful economic jurisdictions at the international level. In the field of secured credit, it is quite clear that most of the existing transnational legal instruments, such as the EBRD Model law on Secured Transactions or the UNCITRAL Model Law on Secured Transactions and other international principles already reflect the principles enshrined in Article 9 of the American UCC. There is the risk that the international law making process becomes the tool of legal political strategy.[93]

---

93 Cohen (2008), p. 770.

5.3 *The Challenges Facing the Recognition of a Transnational Secured Credit Law Beyond the State*

If transnational secured credit law could in theory be successful in providing a modern secured credit law, the next challenge is to determine how this autonomous body of law would operate in the international context. This section argues that the recognition of an autonomous transnational commercial law to regulate international secured transactions would create some difficulties related to the legitimacy and enforcement of these new sources of law.

The privatisation of the law-making process leads to significant concern as to the legitimacy of this new autonomous body of law, or transnational commercial law.[94] The recognition of the autonomy and legitimacy of transnational commercial law is still the topic of fervent debates amongst scholars and academics. It is questioned:

> Is there an anational lex mercatoria, a "global law without a state"? The debate seems infinite. Some argue that the rules, institutions, and procedures of international arbitration have now achieved a sufficient degree both of autonomy from the state and of legal character that they represent such an anational law. Others respond that whatever law merchant may exist is really state law – dependent on national norms and the freedom of contract they provide, and on the enforceability or arbitral awards by national courts.[95]

In the field of secured credit law, it is arguable that the case for the recognition of legitimate and autonomous sources of law is uncertain. In effect, the regulation of secured credit, which also involves the regulation of property law, remains a fundamental function of the state. The extent to which owners can exercise their property rights is restricted by state law. For example, the fundamental principle of the *numerus clausus* recognised in many Civil law jurisdictions restricts the creation of certain property rights. The regulation of property law remains a prerogative of the state, which arguably renders the recognition of an autonomous transnational secured credit law quite uncertain.

If a distinct autonomous transnational commercial law could provide a transnational regime for secured transactions, a distinct international commercial legal framework would also need to be identified for this autonomous secured credit law to operate. The recognition of such a distinct legal order is admitted by many legal academics in relation to transnational commercial law.[96] Some authors recognise the existence of such a distinct legal order and talk about an 'international commercial and financial order'[97] that may have emerged following the phenomenon of internationalisation and globalisation of commercial transactions.

---

[94] On this point see *e.g.*, Franck (1988), p. 705; Zumbansen (2002), p. 400; Rodl (2008), p. 743; Basedow (2008), p. 703; Riles (2008), p. 605.

[95] Michaels (2007), p. 447. See also Mazzacano (2008).

[96] On this point see Berger (1997), p. 91; Cranston (2007), p. 600. See also Dalhuisen (2007), p. 211.

[97] Dalhuisen (2007), p. 134.

Legal orders have been defined as "… participatory social structures or communities that spontaneously produce their own laws".[98] The state can be cited as the most important legal order. Domestic legislations operate in their own national legal framework with their own enforcement mechanisms. If a relevant legal pattern can be identified, one would still need to determine whether the international secured transaction in question should be subjected to the law of this 'international commercial and financial order'. In other words, one would have to establish in which situations this autonomous secured credit law should supersede domestic legislations and how this autonomous secured credit law regime could be enforceable.

The recognition of this autonomous body of law to successfully operate in a distinct legal pattern, 'the international commercial and financial order' as proposed by Dalhuisen, would also need to be recognised as legally binding.[99] In this respect, the New York Convention of the Recognition and Enforcement of Foreign Arbitral Awards[100] is fundamental in providing guidance on enforcement mechanisms for transnational commercial law. Yet, it is arguable that the enforcement of an autonomous transnational secured credit law is to be doubted.

It is to be observed that in the field of international trade and international contract, party autonomy plays a major role in the legitimisation and enforcement of transnational commercial law. Commercial participants often choose transnational law as the governing law for their transactions. In England and France for example, the use of certain international usages to govern private dealings is open to traders as implied contractual terms.[101] General principles such as *pacta sunt servanda* and party autonomy are also recognised worldwide. The international commercial community often chooses transnational commercial law standards to govern international transactions through arbitration and reference to international usages. Could party autonomy also play a major role in the recognition of an autonomous secured credit law which would enable the creation and recognition of an international security in personal property?[102] Again, it is arguable that the recognition and enforcement of this international security in personal property would generate some difficulties in relation to the creation of proprietary rights and third parties. For instance, Civil law jurisdictions generally retain a restrictive approach to the recognition of proprietary rights through the *numerus clausus* principle. Secured transactions create proprietary rights which are enforceable *erga omnes*. Private parties cannot modify rules affecting transfer of property and freely create new proprietary

---

[98] Ibid. p. 132.

[99] Ibid. p. 161.

[100] The Convention is widely recognised as a foundation instrument of international arbitration and requires courts of contracting States to give effect to an agreement to arbitrate when seized of an action in a matter covered by an arbitration agreement and also to recognise and enforce awards made in other States, subject to specific limited exceptions. The text of the Convention is available at http://www.uncitral.org/uncitral/en/uncitral_texts/arbitration/NYConvention.html.

[101] Chuah (2005).

[102] Dalhuisen (2008), p. 354.

rights. It is thus arguable that contractual choice of law may thus be ineffective in legitimising and enforcing transnational secured credit law.

It is further proposed that an international court should be created to support the recognition of this autonomous transnational law and enable it to operate. The idea of an international commercial court to support transnational commercial law has already been suggested by some academics.[103] Could this international court be competent in enforcing international security interests? In the field of secured credit and property laws, it would seem difficult to see how the decisions of such a court would be recognised and enforceable in other legal orders, particularly national legal orders, unless this international court was internationally recognised by states under an international treaty.

The recognition of an autonomous transnational secured credit law operating within a distinct legal framework appears to be quite illusory. In particular, such recognition would create significant difficulties related to the legitimacy and enforcement mechanisms. Beyond the theoretical difficulties of recognising an autonomous secured credit law regime, it is fundamental to highlight the political impact on the recognition of autonomous sources of international commercial law. In effect, the formulation of secured credit law regime reflects fundamental political social and economic interests that are often overlooked by functional imperatives at the international level. Accordingly, the prospects for modernisation of secured credit law regimes through the recognition of an autonomous secured credit law regime appear to be limited. Secured credit law remains cultural, attached to the economic, social and political values of the state.

6 Conclusion

Following the multiplication of international initiatives in drafting international legal standards in the field of secured credit, the analysis has attempted to identify recurrent methodological challenges to the successful modernisation and approximation of personal property security laws. This chapter identified four methodological challenges that were recognised in the context of the approximation and modernisation of secured credit law regimes. In the absence of a sound theoretical justification for the approximation of law and given the strong legal cultural argument, it was concluded that the success of current and future approximation of law endeavours remains uncertain. Further, an analysis of current methods of appropriation such as the use of international conventions or soft law instruments demonstrated that a successful approximation and modernisation of the law is not always successful in the field. The analysis thus questions whether the nature of a transnational commercial law operating within a distinct legal order beyond the state would be better suited to regulate international secured credit law transactions. It is argued

[103] Ibid.

that the recognition of such an autonomous transnational secured credit law together with the recognition of a commercial legal framework within which to operate remains uncertain because of further methodological challenges, primarily embodied in the lack of state sovereignty and lack of coercive powers. The nature of transnational commercial law may be better suited to regulate international secured credit transactions in light of the requirements of modern commerce than under domestic legislations and private international law rules. Even where a particular national secured credit law regime can clearly be identified following the application of traditional conflict of law rules, substantial uncertainties may still arise for the commercial actors who may not be able to enforce their security in a foreign jurisdiction. The legal formalism and territorial nature of domestic legislations showed that it is often inadequate to fit with the requirements of modern legislations on secured transactions. The dynamic nature of transnational law would enable the recognition of more modern legislations that would adapt faster and more effectively to modern commercial practices. Assuming that a modern secured transactions law could arise from transnational commercial law, it was further questioned whether the recognition and enforcement of an autonomous corpus of law that would regulate international secured transactions could be possible. In this respect, the recognition of an autonomous body of law to regulate secured transactions outside the framework of a state may be limited. In particular, this situation evidently raises doubts about implied the question of the legitimacy of these new non-territorial sources of law to become legally binding without the intervention of the state.

The analysis explained that the regulation of secured credit largely affects baseline concepts of insolvency and property law. The regulation of property law remains a fundamental function of the state and it is difficult to see how an autonomous transnational secured credit law regime could be recognised and enforceable outside the national framework. The recognition of an autonomous transnational secured credit law regime would require the identification of a distinct legal order operating with appropriate enforcement mechanisms. In the field of proprietary rights, the emergence of enforcement mechanisms outside the framework of the state appears to be unlikely. Accordingly, the recognition of a distinct international commercial legal pattern that might enable the creation and enforcement of a security at the international level remains uncertain. Particularly, the enforcement of an international autonomous regime would create difficulties, especially in light of the creation of proprietary rights and third parties.

Beyond the theoretical difficulties underlying the recognition of an autonomous transnational secured credit law regime, mainly related to the lack of state sovereignty and coercive powers, it is fundamental to also highlight further obstacles to the recognition of legal reforms beyond the state, such as the reinforcement of legal pluralism and significant conflict of interests in the field of secured credit. Secured credit law is cultural, attached to certain economic, social and political values, even in the international context. The nature of secured credit makes it a complex area for law reform. Secured credit law is based on grounding concepts of insolvency and property and it also encompasses a certain legal culture, particular policy choices and fundamental interests which make it difficult to reform, particularly in the light of an approximation of law.

This is the grand challenge of law; to strike a balance between the requirements of modern commerce and the respect of legal culture, fundamental interests, and particular policy choices. In the field of secured credit, transnational commercial law instruments are essentially the products of private actors which often represent the political and economic values of powerful economic nations. Many secured credit law reform initiatives at the international level are based on the American Article 9 model. The modernisation of secured credit law regimes through legal reforms should not be the result of political economic strategy. There is always the risk that private actors, engaged in the making of the law, will produce projects more influenced by political economic power than legal expertise.

References

Abbott KW et al (2000) Hard law and soft law in international governance. Int Organ 54(3):421–456

Basedow J (2008) The state's private law and the economy - commercial law as an amalgam of public and private rule-making. Am J Comp Law 56(3):703–722

Beale H (2008) The nature and purposes of the common frame of reference. Juridica Int 14:10–17

Berger KP (1997) The *Lex Mercatoria* doctrine and the UNIDROIT principles of international commercial contracts. Law Policy Int Bus 28:943–990

Berman HJ (1988) The law of international commercial transactions (*Lex Mercatoria*). Emory J Int Disp Resol 2(2):235–310

Bonell J (1997) An international restatement of contract law, 2nd edn. Transnational Law Publishers, New York

Bonell MJ (1998) UNIDROIT principles and the *Lex Mercatoria*. In: Carbonneau TE (ed) Lex Mercatoria and arbitration. Juris Publ., Kluwer Law International, pp 249–255

Boodman M (1991) The myth of harmonisation of laws. Am J Comp Law 39(4):699–724

Boyle A (1999) Some reflections on the relationship of treaties and soft law. Int Comp Law Q 48(4):901–913

Buckley FH (1986) The bankruptcy priority puzzle. Va Law Rev 72(8):1393–1470

Carbonara E et al (2007) The paradox of legal harmonization. George Mason Law Economics Research Paper No 05-40; Minnesota Legal Studies Research Paper No. 07-14. Available at https://ssrn.com/abstract=870519

Carlson DG (1998) Secured lending as a zero-sum game. Cardozo Law Rev 19:1635–1741

Chinkin CM (1989) The challenge of soft law: development and change in international law. Int Comp Law Q 38:850–866

Chuah J (2005) Law of international trade, 3rd edn. Sweet Maxwel, London

Cohen ES (2008) Constructing power through law: private law pluralism and harmonization in the global political economy. Rev Int Polit Econ 15(5):770–799

Cranston R (2007) Theorizing transnational commercial law. Texas Int Law J 42:597–617

Cuming RCC (1998) The draft UNIDROIT Convention on international interests in mobile equipment. Uniform Commer Code Law J 30(4):365–398

Dalhuisen JH (2006) Legal orders and their manifestation: the operation of the international commercial and financial legal order and its *Lex Mercatoria*. Berkeley J Int Law 24(1):129–191

Dalhuisen JH (2007) Dalhuisen on transnational and comparative commercial, financial and trade law, 3e rev edn. Hart Publishing, Oxford

Dalhuisen JH (2008) Customs and its revival in transnational private law. Duke J Comp Int Law 18(2):339–370
Davies IR (2002) Security interests in mobile equipment. Dartmouth, Ashgate, London. Reprinted (2018) Routledge, Abingdon
Davies IR (2003) The new Lex Mercatoria: international interests in mobile equipment. Int Comp Law Q 52:151–176
De La Peňa N (1999) Reforming the legal framework for security interests in mobile property. Unif Law Rev 4(2):347–360
De Lacy J (2012) The evolution and regulation of security interests in personal property in England. In: De Lacy J (ed) Personal property security law reform in the UK: comparative perspectives. Routledge-Cavendish, London, pp 3–82
Deschamps M (2002) Les Règles de Priorité de la Convention et du Protocol du Cap. Unif Law Rev 7:17–48
Doing Business Report 2017 (2017) Getting credit: legal rights "Two approaches to developing an integrated secured transactions regime". http://www.doingbusiness.org/reports/case-studies/2016/gc-legal-rights
Drobnig U (1995) The use of the UNIDROIT principles by national and supra-national courts in UNIDROIT principles for international commercial contracts: a new Lex Mercatoria? ICC Publication n. 490/1. ICC, Paris, pp 223–232
Eidenmüller H et al (2008) The common frame of reference for European private law – policy choices and codification problems. Oxford J Leg Stud 28:659–708
Espinola SA (1997) Le Financement de Biens d'Equipement Serait Facilité Par Une Nouvelle Convention Internationale. J OACI 52(8):9–22
Finch V (1999) Security, insolvency and risk. Mod Law Rev 62(5):633–670
Flanagan PM (2004) Demythologising the law merchant: the impropriety of the Lex Mercatoria as a choice of law. Int Comp Com Law Rev 15:297–312
Fleisig HW (1999) The proposed UNIDROIT Convention on mobile equipment: economic consequences and issues. Unif Law Rev 4(2):253–264
Foëx B (1999) La Réserve de Propriété Dans l'Avant-projet de Convention d'UNIDROIT: un Point de Vue Suisse. Unif Law Rev 4(2):409–424
Fox EM (1991–1992) Harmonization of law and procedures in a globalized world: why, what, and how? Antitrust Law J 60:593–600
Franck TM (1988) Legitimacy in the international system. Am J Int Law 82:705–759
Goode RM (1991) Reflections on the harmonisation of commercial law. Unif Law Rev 1:54–75
Goode RM (1997a) International restatement of contract and English contract law. Unif Law Rev 2(1):231–248
Goode RM (1997b) Usage and its reception in transnational commercial law. Int Comp Law Q 46:1–36
Goode RM (1998a) Security in cross-border transactions. Texas Int Law J 33:47–52
Goode RM (1998b) Transcending the boundaries of earth and space: the preliminary draft UNIDROIT Convention on international interests in mobile equipment. Unif Law Rev 3(1):52–76
Goode RM (2001) Insularity or leadership? The role of the United Kingdom in the harmonisation of commercial law. Int Comp Law Q 50:751–766
Goode RM (2002) The Cape Town Convention on international interests in mobile equipment: a driving force for international asset-based financing. Unif Law Rev 7:3–16
Goode RM (2004) The Cape Town Convention on international interests in mobile equipment. In: Hartkamp AS et al (eds) Towards a European Civil Code. Chapter 41, pp 757–767
Gopalan S (2004) Transnational commercial law. Fred B Rothman Co, Colorado
Gopalan S (2008) A Demandeur-Centric approach to regime design in transnational commercial law. Georgetown J Int Law 39(2):327–382
Gullifer L (2007) Retention of title clauses: a question of balance. In: Burrows A (ed) Contract terms. Oxford University Press, Oxford, Ch 14

Gullifer L (2016) Secured transactions law reform, principles, policies and practice. Hart Publishing, Oxford, pp 1–3
Gullifer L, Raczynska M (2016) The English Law of personal property security: under reformed? In: Gullifer L, Akseli O (eds) Secured transactions law reform principles policies and practice. Hart Publishing, Oxford, pp 271–296
Highet K (1989) The Enigma of *Lex Mercatoria*. Tulane Law Rev 63(3):613–628
Honnbier B et al (2004) The Convention of Cape Town: the creation of international interests in mobile equipments. Eur Rev Priv Law 12(1):3–8
Hudson J (1995) The case against secured lending. Int Rev Law Econ 15:47–53
Jackson TH et al (1979) Secured financing and priorities among creditors. Yale Law J 88(6):1143–1182
Kahn P (1992) La *Lex Mercatoria*: point de vue francais après quarante ans de controversies. McGill Law J 37:413–427
Kahn-Freund O (1998) On uses and misuses of comparative law. Mod Law Rev 37:1–27
Kronke H (2000) International uniform commercial law conventions: advantages, disadvantages, criteria for choice. Unif Law Rev 5:13–21
Kronke H (2003) Congrès du 75ème Anniversaire d'UNIDROIT – Harmonisation Mondiale du Droit Privé et Intégration Economique Régionale : Hypothèses, Certitudes et Questions Pendantes. Unif Law Rev 8:11–27
Lando O (2000) Optional or mandatory Europeanisation of contract law. Eur Rev Priv Law 8:59–70
Lando O (2003) Principles of European contract law and UNIDROIT principles: moving from harmonisation to unification? Unif Law Rev 8:123–133
Leebron DW (1996) Claims for harmonization: a theoretical framework. Can Bus Law J 27:63–107
Legrand P (1996) European legal systems are not converging. Int Comp Law Q 45:52–81
Legrand P (1997) The impossibility of legal transplants. Maastricht J Eur Comp Law 4:111–124
Levine R (2005) Finance and growth: theory and evidence. In: Aghion P, Durlauf S (eds) Handbook of economic growth, 1st edn. Elsevier, Amsterdam, pp 865–934
LLSV group (Rafael La Porta, Florencio Lopez de Silanes, Andrei Shleifer and Robert Vishny) (1997) Legal determinants of external finance. J Financ 52(3):1131–1150
LLSV group (Rafael La Porta, Florencio Lopez de Silanes, Andrei Shleifer and Robert Vishny) (1998) Law and finance. J Polit Econ:1113–1155
LoPucki LM (1994) The unsecured creditor's bargain. Va Law Rev 80(8):1887–1966
Mattei U (2003) A theory of imperial law: a study on U.S. hegemony and the Latin resistance. Indiana J Global Leg Stud 10(1):383–448
Mazzacano P (2008) The Lex Mercatoria as autonomous law. CLEA 2008 Meetings Paper, CLPE Research Paper No. 29/2008. Available at http://ssrn.com/abstract=1137629
McCormack G (2011) Secured credit and the harmonisation of law: the UNCITRAL experience, 1st edn. Edward Elgar Publishing, Cheltenham
McCormack G, Keay A, Brown S (2017) European insolvency law reform and harmonization, 1st edn. Edward Elgar Publishing, Cheltenham
Michaels R (2007) The true Lex Mercatoria: law beyond the state. Indiana J Global Leg Stud 14(2):447–468
Mistelis L (2001) Is harmonisation a necessary evil? The future of harmonisation and new sources of international trade law. In: Fletcher I, Mistelis L, Cremona M (eds) Foundations and perspectives of international trade law. Sweet Maxwell, London, pp 3–27
Montesquieu C (1748) De L'Esprit des Lois. Reprint (2016) Wentworth Press, US
Munday RJC (1978) The uniform interpretation of international conventions. Int Comp Law Q 27(2):450–459
Reich N (1992) Competition between legal orders: a new paradigm of EC law? Common Mark Law Rev 29(5):861–896
Reinicke WH et al (2000) Interdependence, globalization, and sovereignty: the role of non-binding international legal accords. In: Shelton D (ed) Commitment and compliance. The role of non-binding norms in the international legal system. Oxford University Press, Oxford, pp 75–114

Riffard JF (2006) Le Guide Législatif de la CNUDCI sur les Opérations Garanties. Un Pas Décisif vers un Droit des Sûretés Mobilières Harmonisé. In: Picod Y, Crocq P (eds) Le Droit des Sûretés à l'Epreuve des Réformes, Collection Droit et Procédure. Edition juridiques et techniques, Paris, pp 107–125

Riles A (2008) Anti-network private global governance, legal knowledge, and the legitimacy of the state. Am J Comp Law 56(3):605–630

Rodl F (2008) Private law beyond the democratic order - on the legitimatory problem of private law beyond the state values. Am J Comp Law 56(3):743–768

Saunders A et al (2006) Innovation in international law and global finance: estimating the financial impact of the Cape Town Convention. NYU Working Paper No FIN.06.001. Available at http://papers.ssrn.com/sol3/papers.cfm?abstract_id=1293636

Schmidtchen D et al (2004) Conflict of law rules and international trade, a transaction costs approach. Discussion Paper published by the Centre for the Study of Law and Economics. Available at http://papers.ssrn.com/sol3/papers.cfm?abstract_id=545763

Schmitthoff CM (1968) The unification or harmonisation of law by means of standards and general conditions. Int Comp Law Q 17(3):551–570

Schwartz A (1981) Security interests and bankruptcy priorities: a review of current theories. Oxf J Leg Stud 10(1):1–38

Schwartz A (1984) The continuing puzzle of secured debt. Vand Law Rev 37(5):1051–1070

Schwartz A (1994) Taking the analysis of security seriously. Va Law Rev 80(8):2073–2088

Shaffer G et al (2008) How hard and soft law interact in international regulatory governance: alternatives, complements and antagonists. Society of International Economic Law (SIEL) Inaugural Conference 2008 Paper. Available at http://ssrn.com/abstract=1156867

Shupack PM (1989) Solving the puzzle of secured transactions. Rutgers Law Rev 41(4):1067–1130

Simler P (2006) La réforme du droit des sûretés - Un Livre IV nouveau du Code civil. JCP éd. G, n° 13, I: 124

Smits JM (2002) The harmonisation of private law in Europe: some insights from evolutionary theory. Ga J Int Comp Law 31(1):79–100

Stanford MJ (1999) Broader or a narrower band of beneficiaries for the proposed new international regimen: some reflections on the merits of the convention/protocol structures in facilitating the former. Unif Law Rev 4:242–252

Stephan PB (1999) The futility of unification and harmonization in international commercial law. Va J Int Law 39(3):743–798

Sykes AO (2000) Regulatory competition or regulatory harmonization? A silly question. J Int Econ Law 3:257–264

Teubner G (1998) Legal irritants: good faith in British law or how unifying law ends up in new divergences. Mod Law Rev 61(1):11–32

Trubek DM (2005) 'Soft law', 'Hard law', and European integration: towards a theory of hybridity. Jean Monnet Working Paper. Available at http://www.law.wisc.edu/facstaff/trubek/HybridityPaperApril2005.pdf

Vogenauer S (2009) Commentary on the UNIDROIT Principles of International Commercial Contracts (PICC). Oxford University Press, Oxford

Walt S (1999) Novelty and the risks of uniform sales law. Va J Int Law 39:671–705

Weil P (1983) Towards relative normativity in international law? Am Univ Int Law Rev 77(3):413–442

Wool J (1997) Rethinking the notion of uniformity in the drafting of international commercial law: a preliminary proposal for the development of a policy-based unification model. Unif Law Rev 2(1):46–56

Zumbansen P (2002) Piercing the legal veil: commercial arbitration and transnational law. Eur Law J 8:400–432

Capturing Collaboration in Construction Contracts in Their Commercial Context

David Christie

Contents

Abstract This chapter examines the way in which the idea of "collaboration" or cooperation can be facilitated by a standard form contract which has "collaboration" as its explicit goal. This is done by contrasting the approach of that contract with another standard form contract which does not have an explicitly "collaborative" approach. This examination is put in its wider context within construction law and the surrounding commercial context in order to identify lessons for the way in which legal frameworks can promote and capture ideas of collaborative working.

D. Christie (✉)
Law School, Robert Gordon University, Aberdeen, UK
e-mail: david.christie@rgu.ac.uk

M. Heidemann, J. Lee (eds.), *The Future of the Commercial Contract in Scholarship and Law Reform*, https://doi.org/10.1007/978-3-319-95969-6_10

1 Introduction

Construction law is a useful prism for the consideration of the future of commercial law. This is for a number of reasons.

Firstly, the industry itself is in UK terms significant and successful. It makes up around 6.5% of the UK economy.[1] There is, therefore, an economic interest for all in ensuring that the industry operates smoothly. This operation can be made more difficult by the technically demanding nature of the work which the industry carries out and the project management of the range of different specialisms which are active within it. 'Disagreements' of some form or another are inevitable in construction projects.

If issues arise then dealing with them—whether they become full blown "disputes" or not—requires a detailed understanding of the management of parties' relationships and the legal framework in which they operate. There are some features which are found within construction industry practice which can help manage that. For example, the use of standard form contracts, produced and drafted by ostensibly neutral parties (and attempting to balance the various interests involved) is common. The shared and recognised language which comes from this and other features has no doubt contributed to the rise of "construction law" as a distinctive discipline.[2]

The second reason why construction law is a useful prism for examining commercial contracts is that there has been less academic assessment and critique of construction law and linking it into the underpinning ideas within the broader spectrum of the law than some other areas of law.

That does not mean that there has been no discussion; and there are some particularly interesting recent developments on this front[3] but there is scope to build on this and test out ideas within an area of law where there are detailed legal rules but where the underpinning of conceptual ideas is still being explored. There may be a link between this development and other areas of commercial law, where the legal position has arisen by the institutionalisation of rules and, more broadly, the more inchoate 'understandings' which help to manage the business which the contracting parties have entered into.[4]

This paper will look at a particular concept which is important within the sphere of construction law and of growing importance elsewhere: collaboration. The way in which this is given effect to in the legal sphere is unclear.

In particular, this chapter will look at the operation of a standard form of contract which is recognised as being "collaborative" within the industry. The way in which

---

[1] House of Commons Briefing Paper Construction Industry: Statistics and Policy Number 01432, 6 October 2015 See p. 3.

[2] This is discussed in more detail below.

[3] See for example, Bell (2016).

[4] See Oosterhuis in this volume.

its terms help facilitate "collaboration" will be explored in context with legal doctrine.

There are, clearly, a number of ways in which "collaboration" could be examined as a sociological or behavioural issue. The present analysis will seek to identify (i) what actions a party has to perform under a contract (which is the sort of thing a client might ask their lawyer) and following that (ii) how that might promote collaboration.

Part (ii) will be done by comparing the actions required by two different standard form contracts: one which is considered to be collaborative and one which is not.

The final part of the chapter will be to put these discussions in the wider context and draw conclusions. One important factor which is relevant to these issues but which is dealt with elsewhere is the use of "good faith" type obligations in promoting collaboration.[5] The recent case of *Costain Limited v Tarmac Holdings Limited*[6] suggests that the boundary of good faith might be anything which does not go beyond the parties' self interest.[7] That still leaves matters open to some interpretation. Moreover, the discussion here will focus on how collaboration is fostered by the operation of the contract itself; rather than the precise interpretation of the good faith type obligations.[8]

Before engaging in the present exercise, it is necessary to provide some background to establish construction law in its wider context and to develop the idea of collaboration.

1.1 Defining Construction Law

As noted above, construction law is an interesting discipline for the academic since, many leading commentators are practitioners.[9] While this is not necessarily unusual it does show the focus is on the literal "business end" of the law rather than engaging in philosophical, jurisprudential or conceptual reflection.

A construction project is usually complex both from a technical point of view and in terms of the intertwining relationships involved.

---

[5] See D'Alvia in this volume and Christie (2017) for a discussion in the specific issues arising in standard form construction contracts.

[6] [2017] EWHC 319 (TCC).

[7] Ibid at para. 124.

[8] Although these inform the overall approach.

[9] The two leading textbooks on Construction Law, namely *Hudson on Building and Engineering Contracts* (13th Ed. Sweet and Maxwell) and *Keating on Construction Contracts* (10th Ed. Sweet and Maxwell) are both the work of leading construction chambers, Keating Chambers and Atkin Chambers: rather than academics. The leading textbook on construction adjudication is written by Sir Peter Coulson, a judge of the Technology and Construction Court. Professor John Uff is a practicing barrister and leading expert in this field as well as the author of a leading student textbook, *Construction Law*. There are others.

By way of example, even the installation of a kitchen can involve three or four different specialisms (usually held by four of five different individuals): the designer, the electrical specialist; the plumber and the fitter. That ignores the technical work that goes into designing the basic kitchen and appliances. The person who wants the new kitchen has to find an arrangement that encompasses all of these people, who will be dealing with matters of which the others involved have varying degrees of interest or knowledge. That involves a set of overlapping contractual arrangements.[10]

The contractual arrangements usually have to envisage some degree of flexibility or change control.[11] Change is an important feature of construction law and practice as a result. This can result from changes to the work scope which can be driven by changing preferences of the party seeking the work; issues with the work when more information is found out; to correct errors in design or planning and so on. For clarity, "change" in this context relates to change of the scope of the work, rather than to the change of the underlying terms of the contract or the obligations of the parties.[12] To this end, most standard form construction contracts—and bespoke building contracts—will have specific provisions setting out a mechanism by which the scope of the work can be changed, and how to take account of the consequences of that in terms of additional cost for the work and the time taken to complete as a result of those changes.

There are, of course, all sorts of issues that arise from the complex, multi-party arrangements in construction projects and these arise from common law, primary legislation or the various heavily regulated aspects of construction activity, such as "health and safety".[13]

As a result of all this, and perhaps unsurprisingly, there is a significant amount of litigation and other dispute resolution arising from construction contracts. In England and Wales, there is a specific, specialist, division of the high court—the Technology and Construction Court—where disputes between construction companies form a very significant part of its business. In addition, construction contracts[14] provide for a statutorily mandated form of (non-court) dispute resolution: construction adjudication.[15]

Construction law therefore covers a number of issues. It draws on the general law of contract and the wider law of obligations, often in the context of its own ecosystem of the interpretation of its standard form contracts,[16] as well as particular legislation and dispute resolution processes.

---

[10] The precise allocation of risk (especially for the design) is something which can be dealt with through a number of different routes of procurement.

[11] Work has been done in the USA and Canada on work to measure the impact of change on construction contracts. For a survey on the position in English law see Miller and Cohen (2002).

[12] The distinction is explained briefly in the introduction to Fischer (2013), pp. 211–212.

[13] See for example, the Construction (Design and Management) Regulations 2015.

[14] As defined in s. 104 of the Housing Grants, Construction and Regeneration Act 1996 (as amended)—it encompasses most things which would be conventionally understood as construction work.

[15] S. 108 Housing Grants, Construction and Regeneration Act 1996 (as amended).

[16] Uff (1993).

In this respect, construction law represents:

> primordial soup in the "melting pot" of the law — a thick broth consisting of centuries-old legal theories fortified by statutory law and seasoned by contextual legal innovations reflecting the broad factual 'realities' of the modern construction process[17]

This chapter, to strain the metaphor, is focussed on identifying the recipe for collaboration. Indeed, on reflection, perhaps a soup is also a good way to identify "collaboration": as a coming together of different ingredients to deliver a satisfying end result.

1.2 Collaboration: Background

Although opinions can vary as to what it precisely means, the core idea of "collaboration" seems to be the creation of a mechanism which facilitates the smooth working together of different parties for mutual gain of some sort. The difficulty is that parties to traditional construction contractual arrangements frequently operate on the basis of having opposing commercial incentives: the contractor, builder, or, for example, electrical engineer is looking to maximise profit while the employer is looking to do the same, that is have the work completed as cheaply as possible.

Frequently, these ideas are brought out by ensuring that the parties have incentives to work together: often through some arrangement of sharing risk and reward. There are a variety of mechanisms which can be deployed to work on this, for example, through the use of joint venture arrangements where parties form a group to deliver work. This tends to bring together parties on one "side" of the transaction—and in particular those involved in the construction side.[18] This can be done to allow specialists to be brought in, who can deal with particular items of work or to share the financial risk in large projects. In this case, of course, the Joint Venture's commercial incentives are generally still opposed to the person procuring the work (which might also be a joint venture—or partnership of various commercial and financial interests).

Another common example of collaborative working is known as Alliancing and Partnering.[19] In these instances, the employer and the construction parties work

[17] Bruner (2007), pp. 13–145 quoted by Gerber (2010).

[18] For example, on Crossrail, various joint venture companies have been awarded contracts for different sections of the tunnelling works. An example close to home for the present writer is the Aberdeen Western Peripheral Route (or Bypass)—one of the longest road's currently under construction in the UK is being constructed by a joint venture of the large construction companies of Balfour Beatty, Carillion and Morrison Construction: https://www.transport.gov.scot/projects/aberdeen-western-peripheral-route-balmedie-to-tipperty/aberdeen-western-peripheral-route-balmedie-to-tipperty/#.

[19] It is interesting that in the fourth edition of the NEC contracts—its "partnering" option is going to be explicitly called "collaboration".

across the ‘divide’ to identify areas and ways in which their commercial areas are aligned—and take steps to effect these in their relationship. One of the most common ways to do this is through “pain/gain share” provisions where by the costs of risks arising are shared as are any extra benefits which might be realised where efficiencies are achieved.[20]

In these cases, the incentive to collaborate is a commercial and financial one. What is interesting is to consider how collaboration can be encouraged or facilitated while parties retain their traditional incentives.

One option is to engage the parties early on in the process and involve them in the preparation of the project.[21] That changes the structure of the process of developing the project without really changing the fundamental dynamic between the parties (aside from the benefits of sharing the design process and encouraging communication which flow out of the process).[22]

More broadly, in construction projects, this misalignment of viewpoints had led, over time, to an unhealthy and inefficient atmosphere: projects were carried out in an atmosphere of conflict.[23] The need to resolve this was a key finding of the Latham Report which was carried out by Sir Michael Latham in the early 1990s—as part of a joint effort by the construction industry and the government to identify ways to improve the construction industry.[24]

Latham called for an end to this atmosphere—and for parties to work together better.

In terms of how this was done, a key idea was to promote cooperation[25] and “collaborative working” has come to embody this ideal. While collaborative working has subsequently been adopted as a goal, across sectors (from the oil and gas industry to education), it has been an issue and aim in the construction industry for some time. Whether that has been successful or not might still be open for debate but a recent survey recorded that 52% of contractors, 44% of clients and 42% of consultants felt that they had worked in at least some collaborative projects in the previous 12 months. (Although there was divergence over what that actually meant).[26]

This drive for collaboration or cooperation is not unique to the construction sector but fits with wider ideas to promote cooperation in contract law. For example, Article 3 of the Draft Common Frame of Reference contains an obligation “to cooperate with each other to the extent that this can be expected for the performance of

[20] There is an interesting discussion of the legal content of partnering arrangements in PD Begg (2003).

[21] The effectiveness of this is discussed by Mosey (2010).

[22] Both of which are relevant to collaboration as will be seen below.

[23] This theme runs through the Latham report. (Sir Michael Latham *Constructing the Team: Joint Review of Procurement and Contractual Arrangements in the UK Construction Industry* HMSO 1994).

[24] Appendix 1 of Latham Report at p. 113.

[25] The Foreword to Latham Report calls for Team-Work and “Win Win Solutions” or, as Sir Michael prefers the attitude of Lewis Carroll’s Dodo: “All will win prizes” (see p. v of the Report).

[26] See NBS *National Construction Contracts and Law Survey* 2015 at p. 14.

their contractual obligations."[27] Details as to the expectations of parties to cooperate in a construction contract are set out in more detail in the relevant section of the DCFR.[28]

Similar obligations are found in the draft Common European Sales Law[29]—and are linked to the hardship provisions in Unidroit.[30] The equivalent duties in the Principles of European Contract Law[31] are explicitly linked to good faith obligations. The difficulty is how to transfer these broadly framed duties into specific actions by the parties.

This difficulty arises because the actual content and extent of obligations to cooperate are unclear. So, for example, the Draft Common Frame of Reference provides for duties of cooperation in construction contracts[32] but these are limited to the implication of specific tasks (such as providing access to the site of the works) which are necessary for the execution of the works in the project.[33] These are already recognised and have been for some time in the UK.[34] Further duties are suggested[35] but the idea of collaboration is less tangible than this and scope of the obligations is unclear. There is a suggestion in recent case law that the obligations of "mutual trust and cooperation" found in the NEC 3[36] might only reflect this pre-existing underlying position but that there is also the possibility that this might go further.[37]

2 Facilitating Collaboration in Construction Contracts

The question then is how to encourage collaboration where parties do not have the incentive to collaborate? This will depend on the parties' commercial relationship but the structure and language of the contract is also relevant.[38]

The present discussion of this will examine the change mechanism in the suite of standard form contracts which is growing in popularity: the third edition of the New

---

[27] von Bar and Clive (2009) (Outline edition) at p. 230 (Book III 1:-104).

[28] von Bar and Clive (2009) at. Book IV Part C Chapter 3, pp. 1707–1711.

[29] Proposal for a Regulation on a Common European Sales Law, COM(2011) 635 final, available at: http://eur-lex.europa.eu/LexUriServ/Lex UriServ.do?uri=COM:2011:0635:FIN:en:PD at p/29 (preamble para. 31 and article 2.

[30] Article 6 of the Unidroit Principles of International Commercial Contracts.

[31] Lando and Beale (2000) Available at: https://www.trans-lex.org/936000/_/duty-to-notify-to-cooperate/.

[32] von Bar and Clive (2009) at. Book IV Part C Chapter 3, pp. 1707–1711.

[33] Ibid.

[34] Ramsey and Furst (2016) at para. 3-063.

[35] von Bar and Clive (2009), pp. 1707–1711.

[36] Clause 10.1 of the NEC 3—see below.

[37] Costain Limited v Tarmac Holdings Ltd [2017] EWHC 319 (TCC) at paras. 123 and 124 (and see Sanderson (2017) for a comment on this case).

[38] The present author has examined another aspect of this—namely the use of a clause requiring the parties to cooperate in a spirit of mutual trust and cooperation in Christie (2017).

Engineering Contract (now known as "NEC 3") and in particular the Engineering and Construction Contract. For ease, since the provisions are similar across the suite, in this chapter "NEC 3" will be used as short hand for the provisions in the Engineering and Construction Contract. At the time of writing, a new edition of this suite of contracts had been announced and was published in June 2017. Thus far, it does not appear that the provisions under discussion here will be radically changed[39] and since the precise terms of the new edition are yet to be published at the time of writing, the discussion will focus on the third edition—which has the further benefit of having been used for around 10 years and so been the subject of detailed consideration and commentary.

The NEC 3 can fairly be said to promote collaboration for three reasons.

1. It is a specific and central goal of those who draft the contract itself.[40]
2. The approach of its predecessor—the second, broadly similar edition (NEC 2) was endorsed by Latham as being helpful towards the goal of collaborative working[41]
3. In a survey of contractors – 67% of those who said they had worked collaboratively gave the reason that they had worked in a contract which had a clause requiring parties to cooperate in a spirit of "mutual trust and cooperation".[42] Such a clause is an important feature of the NEC 3.[43] Even if it is not possible to extrapolate that the respondents on the survey were talking about the NEC 3 specifically—the JCT (as will be seen below) has a similar clause—the fact that that clause is central to the NEC 3[44] provides further support for the idea that it is a "collaborative" form of contract.

In terms of the impact of this revision of the suite, the NEC 3 has been increasingly widely used. In 2011, it was the contract which was used "most often" by respondents in 16% of projects. By 2015 that had increased to use "most often" in 30% of all reported projects. It was the suite of contract used for the delivery of the London 2012 Olympics and for Crossrail,[45]—as well as gaining international usage: particularly in Hong Kong.[46] This reflects the growing success of the form and its approach.

---

[39] NEC Users Group Newsletter No. 84 April 2017.

[40] Dr Martin Barnes, Preface Engineering and Construction Contract, NEC 3 April 2013.

[41] Latham Report, para. 5.19 at p. 39.

[42] NBS Survey n. 26 at p. 14.

[43] Indeed, it was introduced at least partly as a result of the recommendations of Latham (see point 4 of para. 5.20 of the Latham Report).

[44] Clause 10.1 of the NEC Engineering and Construction Contract 3rd Edition, 2013 edition.

[45] See case studies on the NEC website https://www.neccontract.com/Case-Studies for details.

[46] See, for example, the "Special Hong Kong Issue" of the NEC Users Group Newsletter, Issue 68 September 2014. There is an interesting discussion to have in the future about the way in which the cultural ideas which a particular form of contract takes with it can influence or be influenced in a different legal culture from its "home" jurisdiction (i.e. the one in which the contract was drafted).

There is enough general acceptance of the collaborative nature of the NEC 3 and it has been successful enough in its approach, that it can be treated as an example of collaborative practice, for the purposes of providing a benchmark for comparison.

The question is how that "collaboration" is shown in the terms of the contract itself and then how that is analysed to translate the idea of collaboration into a legal doctrine.

In order to establish and demonstrate how the approach of the NEC 3 is different, another standard form of contract will be looked at, the Joint Contracts Tribunal's ("JCT") standard form of building contract ("SBC").

This suite of contracts is of longer standing than the NEC 3[47] and takes a more traditional approach to contracting. The 2011 SBC does include an obligation towards working "cooperatively", but this is found in a Schedule. So although an enforceable term of the contract (if not contracted out of) it has less of the rhetorical impact than the broadly equivalent position in the NEC 3.[48]

More pertinently, perhaps, the JCT state their aims to be to "Minimise the transaction cost of entering into a contract" and "Provide benchmark provisions in standard form contracts"[49] rather than collaboration.

One of the key ways in which these aims are met is said to be through the "clarity" of the JCT's provisions: a point which is emphasised on its web page.[50] Whether or not this is intended to be a direct contrast with the more novel approach taken by the NEC 3 suite, it is certainly the case that the JCT is long established and widely used. However, its dominant position as the most commonly used standard form in UK construction is weakening.[51] A new JCT suite was released in late 2016 which was said to contain collaborative elements. That said, in terms of the basic contractual terms, this new addition appears to use largely the same structure, albeit with some changes. Since the 2011 suite had been established and used, the discussion will focus on it as the main comparator to the NEC 3.

In particular, the SBC is used since in that standard form the contractor is not intended to be responsible to the client for a significant amount of the design of the works; it reflects the most traditional approach. References in what follows to the JCT will be to the 2011 SBC.

The comparison between the two forms will look at three aspects. Firstly, the major differences in approach between the two forms; secondly, some of the novel clauses and mechanisms within the NEC 3 will be contrasted with the JCT to explore the impact these differences might have and thirdly, the two contracts'

---

[47] The first edition of the JCT Suite of contracts was issued in 1931 (although it was not known as the "JCT" until 1997 – http://corporate.jctltd.co.uk/about-us/our-history/. The first edition of the New Engineering Contract was 1993.

[48] See discussion on the interpretation of this clause in Christie (2017).

[49] See http://corporate.jctltd.co.uk/products/about-our-contracts.

[50] Ibid.

[51] The NBS Survey at n. 26 suggests that the JCT contract was used "most often" in 2015 by 39% of organisations surveyed; down from 60% in 2011.

different approaches to change management will be examined in detail. These differences will then be discussed in their wider commercial context.

The focus is on change management since this is one of the key sources of conflict in construction projects.[52] For example, some 11,000 claimed changes were at the heart of one of the claims in the disputes arising from the delays and cost overruns in the rebuilding of Wembley Stadium, in London.[53] These changes were said to arise from the poor design of the steelwork in the new stadium which then had to be altered later—leading to changes in the costs, and delay while issues were resolved. The claim later settled but not until after parties had spent tens of millions of pounds on legal and associated fees.[54]

More recently, there was a significant dispute arising from the need to re-design a tunnel which was to carry the main road south from Spain into Gibraltar underneath the runway of Gibraltar airport.[55] This re-design only happened after construction had been underway for two and a half years (of an initially two year project).[56] The changes here related to complications with the project, in particular issues around the foreseeable level of contamination under the runway.

In addition, change management is one area where the two contracts have a clear difference of approach and so is worthy of examination in that respect, too.[57]

2.1 *"Project Management Tool" Instead of a "Set of Obligations"*

There has been much commentary on the operation of the NEC in general.[58] A particularly pithy description is that it is

> a project management tool rather than a set of obligations.[59]

---

[52] Without wishing to labour the NBS Survey, 50% of respondents said that extensions of time were a main issue in dispute in the previous 12 months—and it is suggested that this is a form of change caught by what is discussed here. A further 42% said that "Valuation of Variations" was the main issues in dispute. These are not mutually exclusive categories See p. 24 of the NBS Survey.

[53] See "£253m legal battle over Wembley delays", The Guardian newspaper 16 March 2008.

[54] Final whistle for £253m Wembley row, Building Magazine 25 June 2010. Jeffrey Brown (2012) draws a contrast between this project and the London 2012 which although not without some disputes, is generally thought to have been delivered successfully. The London 2012 Olympics did, of course, use the NEC 3 suite of contracts.

[55] Previously the main road had had to close when a plane landed on the Rock.

[56] *Obrascon Huarte Lain SA v Her Majesty's Attorney General for Gibraltar* [2014] EWHC 1028 (TCC) appealed at [2015] EWCA Civ 712.

[57] For example, the payment provisions in each contract follow a similar pattern as a result of the requirements of s. 109–113 of the Housing Grants, Construction and Regeneration 1996 (as amended).

[58] See e.g. Gould (2008), p. 291.

[59] A pithy tweet from the NBS/Bond Dickinson "Which contract" conference, 7 October 2014.

In terms of the present discussion, the description "project management tool" can neatly be applied to the NEC 3 suite while, at the same time contrasting it with the "set of obligations" paradigm which could describe the JCT provisions—especially with their core focus on "risk allocation."[60]

Both parties can, of course, make whatever changes to the terms of the contract they wish but the basic structure of the two suites is that each contains main standard terms, covering the work to be done, as well as particular sections which allow the parties to insert their commercial preferences over particular parts of those standard terms (the contract price, the level of damages and so on).

The NEC 3 suite sets itself apart from the JCT by attempting to force parties more closely to engage in choices as to the contents and the provisions these documents—rather than accepting them out of habit or by default. This is because a number of 'boiler plate' or standard commercial devices need to be opted into, rather than simply being the default provision.[61]

In addition, the NEC3 strives to be in "plain English" making it easily understood by all who use it; rather than a jargon-filled-specialist document.[62] While the JCT's language is not particularly unclear there is, for example, a significant amount of cross referencing and relatively intricate language which can make it difficult to read and follow.

This use of "plain" language in the NEC 3 was the source of initial criticism of the document but more recently the judiciary have indicated that they are happy to work with it.[63] The use of "plain language" ties in with the idea that the intention of these contracts is that they are intended to be documents which are read and used— "not put in a drawer" and left.[64] By encouraging use of the contract in this way, it can make the NEC 3's framework more focussed on the active operation of its terms (a manual): rather than remaining a passive allocating rights that can be called upon if necessary.

2.2 *Innovations of Traditional Contractual Mechanisms?*

The JCT contract largely sets out mechanisms to cover traditional issues such as quality, cost, time and termination. The NEC 3 has these and also two further features, which are particularly worth noting.

---

[60] See the JCT "About our contracts page" at n. 24. This is not to say that the NEC does not deal with risk allocation; it does—but in terms of the founding approach, there is a distinction.

[61] A point emphasised by Robert Gerrard, NEC 3 Users Group Secretary, in a talk given at Robert Gordon University, Aberdeen on 6 April 2016.

[62] See Gould (2008), p. 288 and discussion of the language by Rosher (2015), pp. 316–317.

[63] See e.g. Akenhead J in *Atkins Ltd v Secretary of State for Transport* [2013] EWHC 139 at para. [9].

[64] A point reaffirmed and explained by Buckley (2016), p. 17.

Firstly, as indicated above, Clause 10.1 of the NEC 3 gives particular prominence to the requirement that the parties need to work together in a spirit of mutual trust and cooperation. While a similar provision is made in the JCT 2011 Standard Building Contract it is somewhat buried in the Schedule to the main contract.[65] It is central to the NEC 3. It still seems particularly important to the promotion of collaboration.[66] However, the NEC 3 provision is within the standard terms (and indeed in the first substantive clause) while the JCT equivalent is expressly optional.[67] The "rhetorical impact" of the difference in emphasis is important in the way it frames the working culture under the contract.[68]

Secondly, clause 16 of the NEC 3 contains what is called the "early warning mechanism." Under that clause, if parties identify a risk[69] then there is a process for the parties to meet and discuss the risk (in a "risk reduction meeting") and what steps can be taken to mitigate it.[70] This is aimed at bringing the parties together—and increasing the flow of information.[71] One criticism of this provision is that it does not have mandatory effect: it is permissive in that it provides that there "may" be a meeting, and no outcome from this meeting is prescribed beyond "cooperation" to work out what to do. It requires the parties to engage with the process in order to make it a success.

The JCT 2011 does not contain such a provision. Changes and risks are dealt with under the change mechanism, which is set out below at Sect. 3.

Along with the emphasis on being a 'project management tool' these two differences indicate a requirement for a degree of proactivity and engagement by the parties under the NEC 3 when compared with the traditional JCT approach.

Of course, parties are not bound by the particular terms of either suite and are free to amend as much as they can agree. However, the basic choice of contract will to some extent influence the approach which will be taken to the work. It is therefore important to look at how unamended versions of these contracts operate. Choosing a form will, to a significant extent, require a choice as to the overall approach. At the very least, a full understanding of the picture offered will be helpful in understanding what changes might be made, and their impact. Commentators tend to suggest that the use of wholesale amendments to the NEC 3 ought to be discouraged.[72]

---

[65] Para. 1 of Schedule 8 of the JCT 2011 Standard Form of Building Contract.

[66] See discussion in my article Christie (2017).

[67] Eighth recital of the contract particulars of the JCT SBC 2011 with quantities, page 7. It should be said that it is an "opt out" system and that the NEC 3 contract can, of course, be amended to remove clause 10.1 but the difference in emphasis is important here as it speaks to the overall style.

[68] See Christie (2017), pp. 101–102.

[69] Described in Clause 16.1 as "a matter which could increase the total of the prices, delay completion, delay meeting a Key Date or impair the performance of the works in use".

[70] Clause 16.3 NEC 3.

[71] Information flow is a recognised requirement in collaboration by contractors in the NBS Survey at p. 15 (81% of respondents agree that collaboration enables information sharing). The linked idea of "good faith" is often paired with "honesty" in the literature.

[72] see Gould (2008), p. 311 ("*Put simply, wholesale amendments to the standard form through the use of Z clauses should normally be resisted.*").

3 Change Mechanisms

In terms of specific parts of the contracts, there is a clear contrast between the NEC and the JCT in the way in which they facilitate the exchange and provision of information. This is particularly clear in the way in which the contracts discuss changes: especially those relating to changes in the timing for delivery of the project and delay.

3.1 Change Under the JCT

The JCT deals with "change" in two principal ways. The first of these could be termed as changes which arise from the external environment, causing delay or changes to work scope in order to cope with new or previously unknown conditions. The second source of change—which is linked—is where the change comes from within the project team as a result either of a change in the needs or desires of those involved in the project or where it is driven in response to outside factors, indirectly by some of the external environmental factors.[73] There is therefore clearly overlap in how these are dealt with.

In terms of "external" changes, clause 2 of the 2011 JCT SBC provides for the general obligations which relate to the carrying out of the work and that includes dealing with events which cause potential delays (Clause 2.26) and the discovery of errors or discrepancy in the design (2.13).

Taking this further, in terms of delays, in the JCT standard form of building contract, clause 2.27 provides for the provision of notices "forthwith" by the contractor when it appears that there might be a delay to the work and identifying the cause of the delay; this notice must highlight if appropriate if the cause of delay falls within the specific risk events (known as "Relevant Events" (clause 2.29)) for which the "Employer" (the person named in the contract as having responsibility for the works) has responsibility. This notice provision provides for an initial notification, to be followed up with further information "as soon as practicable" after the initial notice, and for the notification "forthwith" of any material changes or any other material which might be required by the Architect/Contract Administrator ("A/CA").

Traditionally, although the Architect has been an agent of the Employer under the contract, they also had an independent role in managing the project and, importantly, in confirming ("certifying") the valuation of works[74] and therefore the amount which the contractor would be paid for doing the work. As time has gone on, the

[73] The issue who bears the risk of cost and delay which arise from theses changes can be dramatically different, hence (although under a different form of contract) the debate about the foreseeability of ground conditions in the Obrascon case (see n. 56 above).

[74] This independent role is discussed in the case of *Sutcliffe v Thakrah* [1974] AC 727.

project management role of the Architect has separated from the more traditional design based function and so a "contract administrator" will fulfil those project management functions.[75]

Clause 2.28 then provides that the architect will reach a fair and reasonable assessment of any extension of time (assuming it is within the Employer's risk allocation (that is, it's a Relevant Event)) which decision on that assessment is to be notified "as soon as practicable" (in the words of the clause) or within 12 weeks. The only requirement as to the information to be found in that notification is identification of the delay attributable to each Relevant Event.

That deals with the impact in terms of the time taken to do the work. The cost consequences of this are dealt with in a separate clause, clause 4.23. That provides a similarly binary exchange between the Contractor and the Architect/Contract Administrator over the assessment (or "ascertainment" as it is termed in the contract[76]) of the "loss and expense" (the direct costs) which have been incurred as a result of delays to the work.

There is provision for the A/CA to revisit the awards of extensions of time after completion of the work (as long as within 12 weeks of completion).[77]

The process in clause 2 of the contract can then be broken down as follows:

1. Notice to be given when there might be a delay to the work
2. Followed up with further information "as soon as practicable"
3. Notification of any "material changes" or information as "reasonably required"
4. Architect reaches "fair and reasonable" assessment of extension of time "as soon as practicable or" within 12 weeks

As noted, the information passes one way (contractor to A/CA) and the instruction comes back along the same route.

In the event that there is a change to the works which is driven internally, either by a change in focus or need by the Employer or in response to external factors, this is dealt with by a third clause: clause 5 which deals with changes to the contract in the form of variations.

This clause provides a lengthy definition of variations, which covers changes to the works, the materials to be used, the working arrangements or the removal of work from scope.[78] There is a footnote[79] that the Contractor's right to object to a variation is contained within a different clause of the contract: meaning that there is a need to read across a number of pages to gain the full picture.

---

[75] The extent to which this role has to be impartial was discussed in *Costain Ltd v Bechtel Ltd* [2005] EWHC 10108 (TCC).

[76] See clause 4.23 JCT SBC 2011.

[77] Clause 2.28.5 JCT SBC 2011.

[78] The potential for an omission to lead to lower profit margins can mean that the ability to instruct a variation which omits work has to be expressly provided for see discussion in Ramsey and Furst (2016) at paras. 4-055 and 4.056.

[79] Footnote 53 on p. 63 of the JCT SBC 2011.

The provisions for variations to be dealt with in this manner are complex and cross reference to other provisions and schedules. Having set out the definition, the clause then provides three methods of valuation of the variations. Each has a different process depending on the source of the variation:

- Valuation by agreement of Employer and Contractor where this has been instructed by the Architect, or the variation has come from the Employer in the specified ways (and no process is set out for how agreement is to be reached)[80]
- Valuation by the Quantity Surveyor on a fair and reasonable basis where the Contractor has not submitted a quote[81]
- Valuation by the Quantity Surveyor where the Contractor has not submitted a quote after an instruction to do so[82]

The process for valuation is detailed Clause 5.6.1 and Schedule 2. This prescribes detail about the contents of valuations in terms of what needs to be included and the extent to which allowances are to be made.[83]

As an initial conclusion, it can be said that the position is complex but there is limited scope for discussion between the relevant parties, at least to the extent that this is provided for in the contract.

3.2 NEC 3—Compensation Events: Clause 6

By contrast, in the NEC 3 contract, the broadly equivalent provisions dealing with change are found in one place, Clause 61, and this clause encompasses delays and changes to work scope as well as the valuation of the impact of those changes. Clause 61 provides for either the project manager or the contractor to raise the issue (the project manager under the NEC 3 fulfilling the equivalent function to the A/CA under the JCT SBC[84]). It then provides for the project manager to seek an estimate of the cost and time impacts of the potentially delaying events. There is provision for the submission of more than one quotation if the project manager does not like the original submission (see clause 62). Furthermore, there is scope for the project manager's assessment to be made on the basis of stated assumptions if the project manager does not feel that any available forecasts are sufficiently certain to provide the basis of their assessment. In that situation, there is scope to change the assessment if the assumptions are "later found to have been wrong".[85] However, if a

[80] Clause 5.2.1 JCT SBC.

[81] Clause 5.3 JCT SBC.

[82] Under clause 5.3 JCT SBC 2011 at p. 64.

[83] The position is complex but well summarised in Ndekugri and Rycroft (2002). Although this deals with the 1998 Edition of the contract, the position is broadly the same under subsequent editions of the JCT contract.

[84] See *Costain v Bechtel* [2005] EWHC 1018.

[85] Clause 61.6.

forecast made as a basis for the process is shown to be wrong, then there is no revision.[86] This creates some finality but also some scope for flexibility—with, crucially, transparency as to what has changed or has not.

The process in clause 6 is as follows:

1. Notification by PM or Contractor[87]
2. Discussion of how to deal with the event[88]
3. Quotations for time and cost changes are to be provided within 3 weeks of instruction to do so
4. Two weeks for a reply to the quotation which can include submission of a revised quotation[89] and which period can be extended[90]
5. Notification of the acceptance of the quotation or—if the timescales are not met—this is deemed to have occurred if not done timeously[91]

Importantly, the contract sets out timings in which these notices are to be provided (and the impact of this is discussed below).

3.3 *Discussing the Differences: Decision Making*

It is clear that there is more interaction provided for in the NEC 3 provisions than in the JCT equivalent. Express provision is made in the NEC 3 for discussion and dialogue, the JCT focusses on notices being provided by one party to the other. It can also be said that more detail is required in the NEC on what the basis for the information provided is. While the JCT has the opportunity for a review of extensions of time 12 weeks after completion, providing some flexibility in the decision making: the basis for the reasoning to be applied is far less clear as it is left to the A/CA's discretion.

The communication provided for in the JCT is rather binary in the sense that the contractor raises the issue and the architect responds with their view. The scope for dialogue in this instance is limited (clause 2.27.3) to a situation where there is a "material change" on the side of the contractor; although the "reasonably required" provisions on the part of the Architect do give scope for information to be sought by them. In addition, there is little incentive to highlight delays which are not within the scope of Relevant Events or Relevant Matters and the decision on whether or not something is a Relevant Event lies with the A/CA.

---

[86] Clause 65.2.

[87] Clause 61.1.

[88] Clause 62.1.

[89] Clause 62.3.

[90] Clause 62.5.

[91] Clause 65.1.

By contrast, under NEC 3, the assessment which the project manager is to make is governed by clauses 63 and 64. This generally specifies and limits the particular outcomes which the PM is to apply to different sources of claim. It also makes the programme of the works (which sets out what is to be done and when) an important part of the process. Project Management under the NEC 3 relies on the programme strongly and provides for different approaches to assessment depending on the status of the contract programme, at any point in the project process.

The way in which the NEC 3 approaches information sharing is a key difference and how this impacts collaboration is set out below.

3.4 Discussing the Differences: Conditions Precedent and Timing?

One of the key distinctions, in terms of the legal rules which apply, is the requirement—under the NEC 3—for a time bar to operate if certain notifications in the change provisions are not made. This means that if some of the notices are not served within a particular time period, then the right to make the notification (and the remedies which then arise from that) may fly away. The process the NEC 3 sets out also specifies consequences if parties do not follow it. As a result, aside from the 'soft' impact of encouraging communication, there is a further and 'harder' legal requirement to effect communication.

The force of these, and the extent to which they mean that rights are lost for non-compliance with the contract comes from on the extent to which the provisions on these processes constitute "conditions precedent" that is, whether compliance with these procedures is needed in order to gain the remedies sought or, if the procedures are not complied with, the entitlement to any remedy is lost.

The traditional position was that under construction contracts claims—and valuation of variations—were dealt with after the event with the benefit of hindsight. This was said to lead to disputes, and the approach in the 1998 version of the JCT—as is reflected in the 2011 suite too—was to try and agree the valuation up front. This was described as "innovatory" in a commentary on those provisions at the time they were in use.[92]

It is not thought that failure to comply with the mechanisms in the JCT would lead to the loss of the relevant rights.

This 'innovation' continues into the present versions of the JCT contract and the thrust of it is also found in the NEC 3 with—as mentioned—the added use of timescales to force parties to make notification in particular periods.

The specific timescales and other measures mean that the NEC 3 provisions may well be considered conditions precedent—requiring the operation of the process before any entitlement arises.[93] By contrast, the provision in clause 2.28.5 of the

---

[92] Ndekugri and Rycroft (2002), p. 333.

[93] See discussion in Gould (2008), pp. 301–304 and Champion (2008).

JCT that decisions of extensions of time can be revisited at the end of the project weakens the argument that the process in Clause 2.26 is made up of conditions precedent—and so there is less obligatory force behind the need to comply with the timescales provided for in that contract (which are, in addition, indicated but not specified in general terms). The condition precedent promotes compliance with the mechanism and sharing of information.

This has caused some controversy. For example, Champion has suggested that the strict notification provisions within the NEC 3—supported by what he calls the "drop dead" time bar provisions may, in fact, operate against the collaborative atmosphere which the NEC 3 otherwise tries to promote.[94] Champion puts forward a "view held by many engineers and project managers" that the requirement to serve a notice can—essentially—distract parties from cooperating to complete a project. Where they would usually "agree to put aside differences temporarily to get the job finished. Requirements to serve notice can break that approach."[95] Presumably by bringing issues into the foreground that which might otherwise have been suppressed can annoy or at least distract parties from getting on with the job. In this context, the natural question—as Champion poses it—is

> with the draconian effect of the failure to serve a timely notice, where does this leave the requirement in clause 10.1 that employer, contractor and project manager are to work in a spirit of mutual trust and cooperation?[96]

On this view, the collaborative arrangement is threatened by the formality of the notification regime.

An answer to that in the context of the NEC 3 is that if parties comply with the need to cooperate and have mutual trust *alongside* the notice provisions then parties, operating in that spirit, will take full account of both obligations and that helps to prevent the service of notices becoming deemed to be or seen as adversarial. In this case, if the notifications are served as a factual statement—in a spirit of cooperation, adequately explored and supported—and, supported (for example) by the early warning notification system so they do not come as a surprise, there does not seem to be any reason why this in itself necessarily drives adversariality. Nor does it require parties to act against their self-interest: simply to continue to operate the contract. This highlights the benefits of the overall process, discussed above, which places weight on the exchange of information.

Another possible issue for collaboration which arises in terms of the time bar clause is that, while the use of prospective valuation of variations is generally considered positive and helps to avoid disputes at a later date; the time bar provisions within the NEC 3 run the risk that the valuations agreed before the work is done are locked in and cannot be changed.[97] That could lead to an erosion of the parties' relationship and disputes. As Ennis points out, though, the project manager can state

[94] Champion (2008).

[95] Champion (2008), p. 216.

[96] Champion (2008), p. 219.

[97] See discussion by Ennis (2016), p. 312.

assumptions which form the basis of the valuation (clause 61.6) leaving scope for the valuation to be changed if the assumptions change. It is suggested that this is a more transparent way of facilitating change when compared with the JCT's sweep up provisions in clause 2.28.5 in respect of extensions of time. In that latter case, the basis for any change (or failure to change) is difficult to interrogate—it is left in the discretion of the A/CA.[98] Furthermore, while Ennis himself suggests that this approach (of making valuations somewhat provisional and based on assumptions) might not be something that "Purist NEC aficionados" will like because it "strikes at the root of NEC 3's prospective valuation philosophy"[99] and that the use of the assumptions "can be criticised for simply kicking the can down the road"[100] it does, in fact, demonstrate the differences between the NEC 3 and the JCT approach clearly and without necessarily undermining collaboration. This is because under the NEC 3 there is compulsion to serve notices within prescribed timescales and the decision making process is more open. It is suggested that any "NEC purists" who might object to the use of clause 61.6 are not purists to its overall aims to be an effective tool for the parties working together. If operated as intended, the NEC balances the use of time bars/conditions precedent with the "assumptions" clause and the overall obligations to mutual trust and cooperation to promote communication, clarity and flexibility.

This does highlight the value placed on transparency by the NEC 3: if you want to make a claim, you need to be forthcoming about it and need to lay the notices on the table, as it were. Trust and transparency go hand in hand.

4 Evaluation: Changing NEC and JCT

There are clear differences of approach, therefore, between the way in which the JCT and the NEC 3 contracts facilitate discussion around changes and the difference between them might reveal how the NEC 3 operates collaboratively.

As has been set out above, there is evidence to support the claim that the NEC 3 is collaborative in its intent and approach. Assessing how that approach differs from a less collaboratively focussed contract, such as the JCT, is worthwhile to see what lessons there might be for wider practice.

The key differences are as follows.

Firstly, there is more focus on the process and format for the exchange of information in the NEC when compared with the JCT. That is not, of course, to say that there is no framework within the JCT but it does not provide for how and when the information is to be exchanged in any particular detail; nor does it provide for the character of the information to be exchanged. That may require a looser framework

[98] One reason which might be suggested for the need to increase 'formal' collaboration could be a perceived breakdown in the confidence of the in the independence of the A/CA.

[99] Ibid at p. 313.

[100] Ibid.

for operation and project management or, alternatively, an additional informal framework (arising from, for example, the parties' conduct) being interposed to fill the gaps.

Secondly, following on from this, in terms of ensuring collaboration amongst parties with competing commercial interests, the mandatory framework of the NEC may serve to create a stronger incentive for parties to work more closely together and information exchange. Failure to comply with the condition precedent clauses can entail loss of rights and the framework is in place to ensure that parties face consequences for failing to operate the system.

Thirdly, there is more flexibility in terms of the resolution of change events in the NEC 3 rather than the JCT since it forces parties to discuss the outcomes of the compensation events rather than forcing them into a more constrained process of valuation. In practice, much of the underlying substance of these discussions may be the same; relying on the same sort of underlying documentation but the NEC 3 approach seems to be more geared towards forcing the parties to engage, compared with the JCT's approach of forcing the parties to follow a pre-agreed path.

That is not to say that the NEC framework is flawless; far from it—and the flaws are well known.[101] For example, (i) while there is a mechanism to amend the contract, it can be difficult to make substantial amendments without causing problems throughout the rest of the contractual scheme[102] and (iii) there are significant gaps in the contract's operation and wording where its compulsory force weakens.[103]

Crucially, there are likely to be cost implications involved in the detailed management and information exchange provided for in the NEC, compared with the "lighter touch" of the JCT. Champion also points out that:

> the potential impact of time-bar clauses for contractors is potentially far reaching, impacting how projects are organised, how their commercial matters are managed, how their staff are trained and how their in-house legal teams supports the project teams. One wonders how many contractors embarking upon NEC 3 have realised this.[104]

The far reaching impact of the NEC 3 is well captured in the quote. The time bar clauses are not the only part of the NEC 3 which have required that change in attitudes. Of course, the NEC 3 has grown in use and popularity since Champion wrote the above but the underlying idea that NEC 3 takes commitment from all parties to make it work, remains the same. As a reflection of the broader context, the drive for cooperation is also recognised as a being the source of additional work in the DCFR as

[101] Rosher (2015) sets out a number of loopholes at pp. 319–322.

[102] Gould (2008) cautions against this at p. 311.

[103] By way of example of the Early Warning Notice mechanism in clause 16, the parties are obliged to cooperate to work out what should be done. This cooperation is to occur at a meeting—but there is no specification as to when the meeting will be or what consequences arise if the meeting does not happen. In clause 62, discussed above, if the Project Manager does not seek further quotations—there is no particular consequence. (There are consequences where a quotation is instructed but no more—but that require the threshold to be crossed first).

[104] Champion (2008), p. 215.

> keeping written records of all the essential communications that take place is costly, but may lead to important savings in dealing with quality problems and other potential disputes later on[105]

As the DCFR points out, this requires on the scope of the project to justify the extra expense.

In terms of making contracts more collaborative, the NEC model would suggest that the framework has a focus on facilitating communication and information sharing with consequences for failure and mechanisms which encourage flexibility, as much as setting out the parties' rights and responsibilities. As has been noted, this seems to assist a collaborative result if parties are willing to put the effort and resources into making it work.

5 Three Points in the Context of Contract Doctrine

The idea of collaboration seems to have echoes in three propositions which are found in current thinking on the developments of contract law and practice and which appear to be highly relevant in construction law.

These three propositions are (i) the extent to which commercial contracts, especially construction contracts, seek flexibility (ii) the 'relational contract' and (iii) the way in which the parties understand of their mutual positions to form a "psychological contract" which lies outside the mere words of their legal arrangement.[106] It would be possible to map all three in a Venn diagram showing overlaps between the ideas which are inherent in each of them. Flexibility and understanding of the context in which the formal contract operates are both strong ideas in the relational contract.[107]

5.1 Flexibility

Bell has noted that parties to construction contracts place a great deal of value on flexibility. As he explains

> It may be challenging for lawyers to accept the observations of empirical studies that commercial people do not naturally do business in 'in the shadow of the law' – that is under the assumption that their transactions may be litigated. However this perspective also opens up prospects including a more explicit recognition of the desirability of upholding contractual structures which place at the heart of the parties' agreement a flexible working relationship seeking mutually advantageous outcomes.[108]

---

[105] Book IV. Part C Services – D p1708. – It is noted that the "may" in this sentence is doing a lot of work in justifying the up front expense for greater efficiency in the future. It might perhaps be the source of further quantitative assessment.

[106] This psychological contract is recognised as a tool for performance management—rather than creating obligations (although there is scope for a cross over). The way in which the legal contract interacts with the psychological contract is, however, interesting.

[107] There is relevant discussion on some of these issues in Collins (2016).

[108] Bell (2016), p. 6.

This is echoed in the broader commercial sphere by Legatt J (as he was) speaking extra- judicially when he said:

> I think there is sometimes a tendency of English commercial lawyers to view commerce as if it were a kind of Darwinian struggle in which everyone is trying to gain at the expense of those with whom they do business and where, even when parties have made a contract, that does no more than set limits on the pursuit of profit at the other party's expense.[109]

Instead, Leggatt J says, echoing Bells' thoughts, parties are looking to cooperate for mutual benefit and the contract provides the "legal backing" for that cooperation.[110]

A key point which both Bell and Leggatt J make is that there is still a need for the parties' relationship to be placed within the framework provided by the contract: neither Bell nor Leggatt J suggest that there ought not to be a contract in place. Moreover, while it seems like common sense to understand that commercial organisations like flexibility; "uncertainty" is often considered to be something the business world dislikes. It is striking in this context to note the stress which the JCT- places on "clarity" in introducing the aims of that suite of contracts.[111] Clarity is synonymous with certainty, in many ways. This emphasis on the clarity of its framework is reflected in its change mechanism (as discussed above) and presumably reflects the desire of the cross industry representation from which its drafting committee is drawn.

These discussions are also captured in the DCFR—and the need to balance freedom, security, justice and efficiency.[112] In particular, the need to balance "certainty or flexibility" is explicitly recognised.[113] Certainty is said to generally "mean security."[114] It is, however, striking that the DCFR recognises contracts for the provision of construction services are an example of the long term contract where need for flexibility means that "the reverse is true"[115] and that

> true security comes from the knowledge that there are fair mechanisms in place to deal with changes in circumstances.[116]

Taking these together, to the extent that the construction industry would prefer flexibility, the NEC 3 approach might strike that balance in favour of flexibility. However, there may be that there is a trade off in terms of efficiency—at least up front—arising from the document management requirements which this striking of a balance imposes.

---

[109] Leggatt (2016) at para 26.

[110] Ibid.

[111] See http://corporate.jctltd.co.uk/products/about-our-contracts.

[112] von Bar and Clive (2009).

[113] von Bar and Clive (2009) Principle 22 at p. 47.

[114] Ibid.

[115] Ibid.

[116] Ibid.

5.1.1 Balancing Act

The NEC 3's collaborative—rather than adversarial—approach in balancing between flexibility and certainty is clearly illuminated when the balance between four further contrasting ideas is examined—by reference to the particular contract clauses.

5.1.1.1 Process Focus as Opposed to Focus on Substance

As seen above, the NEC 3 contract mechanism spells out a process; while the JCT provisions are less specific on the process. To some extent this runs against the idea of commercial flexibility and collaboration highlighted above: the NEC 3 provisions require action from the parties; compared with the JCT SBC.

The NEC 3 framework of obligations also creates certain requirements as to the substance of the communications—such as the requirement to state assumptions. This might assist communication through the depersonalisation of the information: it is the assumptions which are wrong; not the person.[117]

The framework of active engagement required by the NEC 3 could be termed "active flexibility": the parties are operating within constraints but these are constraints to deal with the present; rather than constraints imposed by the terms of an agreement in the past.

While it might be said that the process of the NEC3 impinges on the parties' flexibility: it is focussed less on their particular legal rights and more on the process of maintaining their relationship. To the extent that parties' rights are impacted, this is as a result of the conditions precedent ensuring compliance with the process: the benefit of that is that the framework is clear. In addition, it would be wrong to suppose that a process—even if detailed—is undesirable simply for its detail. The key is "buy in" which requires recognition of the need to put in the right resources and, more broadly, commitment to the collaborative process. That does not mean that only the NEC 3 approach can foster collaboration—the key is the parties relationship, but there is a difference in the level of detail which the contract contains and which helps to maintain the relationship.

5.1.1.2 Attention to Detail Rather Than a Minimal Framework

By contrast the JCT tends to leave more to the parties to sort things out without the intervention of a contractual process: it sets a basic framework and a basis for dealing with change. The parties, to a significant extent, must decide what detail is required or provided and—within the contractual terms—when that should be. The timescales are not provided.

As such, there is no reason—on the face of the contract—why that cannot be operated collaboratively but the impetus to act proactively is not there.

[117] "Separating the people from the problem" which is described as one of the five key things to do when attempting a negotiation, see Fisher and Ury (1991), p. 37.

What is interesting is the contrast with the commercial drivers for those parties to the contracts. The recent work of Bell discussed above attempts to identify the way in which legal theory can be applied in the context of construction law. His suggestion is that construction practice prefers a minimalist approach, which is (by reference to Jonathan Morgan):

> contract law is as simply, clear and strict – formalist – as it can be made, commercial preferences are best satisfied.[118]

In this sense, the JCT fits the bill. The JCT suite aims for 'clarity'. The JCT suite has a set of contracts of long standing usage which mean that its concepts and language are generally well understood and been discussed case law. The NEC, by contrast, is in its very name "new".

The answer to that would be that the use of conditions precedent adds an element of compulsion which helps create certainty by forcing action and that, by contrast, the lack of detail in the JCT leaves it open to the parties to drift away from the contract. That gives flexibility; but a lack of clarity about the framework does not necessarily meet the requirements of the parties.

In achieving flexibility, crucially, the bilateral nature of the relationship needs to be recognised. Unilateral flexibility—where a party can do what it wants, unfettered—might be a goal or desire for commercial parties (although neither Bell or Leggatt LJ suggest this) but it is likely to cause problems if it does not take place within the parameters of their bilateral relationship. The parameters and framework for that relationship will be found within the contract. The aim of 'flexibility' requires flexibility of the contract in the way it facilitates *bilateral* flexibility: that is, within some sort of contractual (or similar) framework.

This then feeds into the second issue of principle and theory, namely the way in which contracts can be understood to allow some sort of flexibility and that is the idea of the "relational" contract.

5.2 Relationality

The idea of the "relational" contract was developed by MacNeill[119] but has grown in recent years. Leggatt J refers to it as the means of providing some of the flexibility sought by commercial parties, and in particular to argue for the increased use of good faith in English law.[120]

---

[118] Bell (2016), p. 5.

[119] The brief summary of his work in Stone and Devenney (2015) at Chapter 1.6 pp. 13–15 is a useful summary and the critique by Eisenberg (2000) is a useful way of capturing some of the academic debate on this topic.

[120] Leggatt (2016) especially at paras. 27 to 43. Leggatt J also referred to relational contracting in his judgement on implying terms of good faith into certain contracts in the case of *Yam Seng Pte Ltd v International Trade Corp Ltd.* [2013] EWHC 111 (QB) at para. 142.

Briefly, the theory of the relational contract draws on the idea that all contracts must be understood in their context as part of a wider network of communications and relationships between people. Flowing from this, is the idea that single transactions (for instance of buying and selling things) are the foundation of commerce and the traditional approach of contract law is to the understandings and approaches of the contracting parties as to relatively singular "one off" events (or "as-if discrete" transactions as MacNeill terms them).[121] By contrast, many commercial relationships—such as under construction contracts—are longer term and encompass the need for flexibility to meet changing circumstances. The interest of the parties is focussed on the output from their relationship than the gain from a one-off transaction. MacNeill's idea recognises that all contractual relationships need to take account of the context in which they operate and in particular that there are two paradigms which exist at opposing ends of a spectrum. The paradigms are what McNeill terms "as-if discrete" transactions and relational contracts which involved repeated interactions. The

> "primary" distinctions are that "relational contracts…give rise to an intensification in exchange relations…Primary among these are (1) role integrity (2) contractual solidarity and (3) harmonization with the social matrix, especially the internal social matrix".[122]

There is a recognition that this model is better able to deal with what he had earlier termed the "constant clash in modern economic structures between the need for stability and the need to respond to change".[123]

The communication facilitated by the NEC 3 suite can help in ensuring that the 'internal social matrix' is managed effectively: by encouraging parties to engage with each other. In terms of the relational aspect of the NEC 3 suite, this has been discussed at length and in detail by McInnis[124] but the focus is on the "good faith" aspect of the contract, rather than the mechanism for managing changed circumstances around the work.

McInnis does however identify four concepts at the heart of relational theory namely: "society, exchange, choice and futurity".[125] He defines these concepts as follows:

> *Society* is the context in which contracts operate and thus establishes the boundaries for contractual relationships. *Exchange* is the broadest means of promoting the distribution of goods and services…exchange here is not market-orientated but socially orientated the parties' obligations toward each other are determined less by their respective promises than by their relationship. *Choice*…is a central concept but only one of several bases for explaining and understanding the binding force of contract. Lastly *futurity* is how the projection of exchange into the future is encapsulated here.[126]

---

[121] MacNeill (2000).

[122] Ibid at 897.

[123] MacNeill (1978). In this article, MacNeill suggests a variety of responses which American contract law had to resolving this difficulty (see pp. 865–873) some of which have feature in the NEC 3—especially the discussion around agreements to agree at pp. 870–873—but the promotion of communication suggested in the change mechanism seems to go beyond this.

[124] McInnis (2003).

[125] McInnis [2003] ICLR 128 at 130.

[126] Ibid.

These ideas would seem to fit the concept of a collaborative contract: promoting the working together of parties in the structure, language and approach of the contract, as much as any relational paradigm.

So, while boundaries of these ideas, as defined, do not focus on the transfer of information—ideas of a 'social' framework, of the exchange as the basis of relationships and futurity in terms of moving the exchange through time all seem to fit with the process set out in the NEC 3 as discussed in particular.[127] The JCT with its focus more on the allocation of risk and of certainty is a less natural fit into these ideas.

The need to manage a parties' relationship over a longer period is important to the relational contracting paradigm. For this reason, the idea of good faith in contracts has become intertwined with that idea—as it creates a possibly less formal space to allow the parties to maintain their relationship.[128] Collaborative working patterns, more generally, recognises this.

In particular, the need to manage change is, perhaps, more pronounced in construction projects than it is in other commercial transactions. Construction projects are complex: both in terms of the underlying subject matter and in terms of the management of the personnel involved. While 'good faith' can have some role in managing the ups and downs of a commercial relationship, there is scope to recognise other techniques. It is suggested that the mere recognition of variation mechanisms, such as those discussed in this chapter, have some role to play in creating relational contracts: the parties contractual relationship does not change in terms of their underlying obligations, but there is an agreed mechanism in which changes to the scope of the work can occur. That allows some flexibility.

More broadly, case law has increasingly begun to recognise that there might be a need to approach interpretation of "relational contracts" differently. In case law in England and Wales, "relational" contracts are—essentially—considered to be those which are long term.[129] The Court of Appeal have recently discussed rules of interpretation for "long term contracts"[130] and in giving the leading judgement on a case around the interpretation of such a contract, Moore-Bick LJ identified that it could be appropriate to adopt a more flexible approach to the interpretation of this sort of contract. He said

> I accept that, particularly because of its long term nature, the court should seek to construe [the contract] to enable flexibility to meet changing circumstances. ...a flexible approach may best match the reasonable expectations of the parties. [131]

At the same time, Moore-Bick LJ stressed the need to take the language of the contract itself as the "starting point".[132] The Court of Appeal also distinguished this

---

[127] Admittedly in an article which has putting the NEC 3 into a relational contract at its focus.

[128] See Campbell (2014), pp. 488–490 and the discussion by Leggatt (2016) at [53] above.

[129] See e.g. *Yam Seng Pte Limited v International Trade Corporation* [2013] EWHC 111 (QB) at para.124.

[130] *Globe Motors, Inc &Ors v TRW Lucas Varity Electric Steering Ltd* [2016] EWCA Civ 396.

[131] Para. 75.

[132] Para. 76.

"flexible" approach to interpretation from the implication of a term which might bring in some scope of "flexibility" such as a good faith obligation.[133] The clear desire for flexibility and collaborative behaviour in the NEC 3 ought to help the courts to engage with a more flexible approach to interpretation—it can clearly be seen as being part of the parties' 'reasonable expectations' given the context and approach of the NEC 3.

This would fit with the UK Supreme Court decision in *Wood v Capita Insurance Services Limited* [134] which held that

> Textualism and contextualism are not conflicting paradigms in a battle for exclusive occupations of the field of contractual interpretation.[135] Rather, the lawyer and the judge when interpreting any contract can use them as tools to ascertain the objective meaning of the language which the parties have chosen to express their agreement.[136]

Reading these together, there is clear scope to use the long term nature of the contract as a tool for interpretation, especially where the desire for flexibility in contracting is recognised in construction law in general and the NEC 3 suite in particular.

Importantly, however, the clear provisions of the NEC 3 avoid one of the difficulties which MacNeill foresaw in applying these traditional approaches to contractual interpretation. On MacNeill's analysis the classical contract law which focusses on the "discrete" transactions paradigm breaks down in longer term relational contracts because the original understandings of the parties do not deal with changing circumstance. Instead here can be a drift to

> stretching consent far beyond its actual bounds and by fictions to squeeze later changes within an initial consent framework[137]

The 'stretching' of consent comes around because parties have not actually agreed to the new circumstances—but are being put in the position of the law treating them as if they had. As a result, MacNeill considers the "objective agreement" in American contract law to be the "greatest" of these fictions.[138] For MacNeill consent must be based on the subjective knowledge of the parties. This has been criticised as too narrow an understanding of "consent" and inconsistent with other arguments made.[139]

However, whatever the interpretation of "consent", from a contract management point of view, the more that parties can be made aware of changes and be forced to some extent to engage with that process can only help to engage the parties with the

---

[133] Para. 67.

[134] [2017] UKSC 24.

[135] To some extent that this runs counter to the dichotomy expressed by MacNeill between a context led interpretation of relational contracts and the more classical interpretation of "as-if discrete" contracts.

[136] [2017] UKSC 24 at para. 13.

[137] MacNeill (1978), p. 901.

[138] Ibid at p. 884.

[139] Barnett (1992).

way change affects their contract. The NEC 3 approach which facilitates that communication, discussion and agreement of changes is therefore particularly useful—however the parties' state of mind is characterised.

The collaborative approach of the NEC 3 as a whole can be seen as an example of the relational paradigm.

5.3 The "Psychological Contract"

Flowing from wider ideas in employment law, there is a recognition of the importance of the "psychological contract" between the employer and the employee. Understanding psychological contracts is considered important in managing performance and maximising outputs from employees:

> The psychological contract has emerged as an important framework for understanding employees' wellbeing, attitudes and performance.[140]

It is suggested that this is a further, useful, tool for understanding the collaborative contract. That term is not defined with precision but has been described as

> the full set of beliefs that employees have concerning the continuing exchange relationship with their employer. In other words, everything he or she can expected from the employer and everything that the employer can expect of him or her.[141]

The link between employment contracts and the "relational" contracting paradigm is also recognised since both relate to building an understanding of the full context of the parties' relationship, beyond the formal terms of it. In this way, it demonstrates a practical dimension to the understanding of the relational contract as a mechanism for promoting good performance by parties to a contract and building trust.

At the same time, this idea has links with the understanding both Leggatt J and Bell capture above: that commercial parties (especially those in 'relational' contracts) develop understandings about their, and the other parties, conduct through the operation of their relationship. Effective use of the psychological contract is thought to have a benefit to business performance.[142]

There are, of course, differences between employment law and construction law. For example, the contract of employment owing to its origins in the law of master and servant, draws on implied terms of trust and confidence to a higher degree[143] than is recognised in construction contracts.

It is a useful idea, however, in understanding how a party's formal legal/contractual relationship must be seen its broader context. Maintaining the parties' relation-

[140] Ibid p. 33.

[141] Middlemiss (2011), p. 32.

[142] CIPD Factsheet (2016).

[143] Middlemiss (2011), pp. 38–44.

ship requires a broader understanding of the parties' respective expectations than merely what is contained within the terms of the parties' agreement.[144] Much of the force of the "psychological contract" in employment law relates to the idea that "reward" in employment has both financial and non-financial meanings as well as the integral role of employment to the individual's understanding of themselves.

In construction law—and other commercial arrangements—"reward" is more closely linked to payment and the circumstances of payment are provided for in statute (at least in the UK).

Further, the "work" done on one construction project is less likely to be as integral to the construction company's understanding of itself than it is for an individual's employment (although a construction company will also have some sense of its brand values and mission, no doubt—which would have relevance here).

The facilitation of exchange of information, even if it is limited to some extent, and the requirement to engage parties in the issues arising has value in terms of building the understanding of each parties' position. This can be of value in maintaining whatever "psychological contract" exists between them: improving performance and managing disputes.

6 Conclusion: The Wider Commercial Collaborative Environment

The NEC 3 is widely considered to promote 'collaboration'. The discussion above brings out a number of key ways in which it does so. Understanding this in terms of legal theory and practice, it can be seen how the NEC 3 approach facilitates bilateral flexibility and within the parameters of the so called relational contract.

The exchange of information helps in building up the idea of the psychological contract. Understanding how this operates can be a useful step in their successful understanding and management of their commercial relationship.

In terms of the impact of these steps in the wider area of construction law as it sits both within and separate to the overall branch of the law which deals with commerce (especially the law of commercial contracts), the lessons are reasonably clear.

Firstly, there is a clear message that engagement is encouraged. In the NEC 3, this is done through a framework of exchanging information focussed on dealing with changes and enforcing those through the 'drop dead' payment provisions. The context of this engagement needs to be managed and the NEC 3 does this by also reminding parties of their obligations to trust and cooperate with each other (and thereby to try and defuse the tensions which arise from following the mandated process) and also by allowing some flexibility to deal with changing circumstances such as a valuation change.

---

[144] The link between this issue and the wider issues around the legal interpretation of contracts within the context of the "factual matrix" is worth further reflection.

In the NEC 3 this engagement is also found in the language and the approach of the contract as a whole: it wants to be accessible and forces the parties to think about what they are doing. That said parties need to be aware of, and comfortable with, the commitment required to engage with each other in this way.

Secondly, if these ideas are understood, it is hard to see a reason why they would require a relatively rigid framework for enforcement but could take place in the less rigid atmosphere of the JCT: as long as they are controlled. Parties consider that a contractual term to work together in a spirit of mutual trust and cooperation facilitates collaboration—but it does not necessarily take a contractual provision to facilitate it. The discussion shows how the NEC 3 requires different behaviour compared to other contracts. In taking inspiration from that, it can be seen that the NEC 3 sets out ground rules in the contract but these are not necessarily appropriate to every contract. Working with the NEC 3 needs a significant commitment. That commitment does not necessarily need the NEC 3 as the basis for the parties' contract. The way the NEC 3 encourages engagement can inspire further consideration and discussion. The balance between clarity and flexibility is at the heart of this discussion reflecting on that balance is recommended to parties to construction contracts and beyond.

References

Atkin Chambers (2015) Hudson on building and engineering contracts, 13th edn. Sweet and Maxwell, London

Barnett RE (1992) Conflicting visions: a critique of Ian MacNeill's relational theory of contract. Va Law Rev 78:1175

Begg PD (2003) The legal content of partnering arrangements in the construction industry available. https://core.ac.uk/download/pdf/1576017.pdf

Bell M (2016) Contract theorists: what did they ever do for us in construction law? May 2016, D189 available on www.scl.org.uk/papers

Brown J (2012) Legal disputes: the Olympics and Wembley. Building Magazine, 10 February 2012

Bruner PL (2007) The historical emergence of construction law. William Mitchell Law Rev 34:1

Buckley W (2016) NEC 3 – not to be left in the drawer. Construction Law August/Sept 2016

Campbell D (2014) Good faith and the ubiquity of the relational contract. Modern Law Rev 77(3):475

Champion R (2008) Variations, time limits and unanticipated consequences. Const Law J 24(3):208

Chartered Institute of Personnel and Development (CIPD) Factsheet (2016) The psychological contract

Christie D (2017) How can the use of mutual trust and cooperation in the NEC 3 suite of contracts help collaboration? Int Constr Law Rev 34(2):93

Collins H (2016) Is a relational contract a legal concept? In: Degeling S, Edelman J, Goudkamp J (eds) Contract in Commercial Law. Lawbook Co, Thomson Reuters, Sydney

Eisenberg MA (2000) Why there is no law of relational contracts. Northwest Univ Law Rev 94(3):805

Ennis C (2016) Prospective claims for variations under FIDIC: evidential and procedural issues and comparison with the NEC3 regime. Constr Law J 32(3):303

Fischer C (2013) Unilateral variations in construction contracts. Constr Law J 29(3):211

Fisher R, Ury W (1991) Getting to yes: negotiating agreement without giving in, 2nd edn. Penguin, New York

Gerber P (2010) The teaching of construction law and the practice of construction law: never the twain shall meet? Leg Educ Rev 20(1&2):59

Gould N (2008) NEC3: construction contract of the future? Constr Law J 24(4):286

House of Commons Briefing Paper Construction Industry: Statistics and Policy Number 01432

Lando O, Beale H (2000) Principles of European contract law. Kluwer Law International, The Hague

Leggatt J (2016) Contractual duties of good faith. Lecture to the Commercial Bar Association, 18 October 2016. Available at https://www.judiciary.gov.uk/wp-content/uploads/2016/10/mr-justice-leggatt-lecture-contractual-duties-of-faith.pdf

MacNeill IR (1978) Contracts: adjustment of long term economic relations under classical, neo-classical and relational contract law. Northwest Univ Law Rev 72:854

MacNeill IR (2000) Relational contract theory: challenges and queries. Northwest Univ Law Rev 94:877–907

McInnis A (2003) The new engineering contract: relational contracting, good faith and cooperation. Int Constr Law Rev 20(1):128. (Part 1) and 20(2):ICLR 289 (Part 2)

Middlemiss S (2011) The psychological contract and implied contractual terms: synchronous or asynchronous models? Int J Law Manage 53(1):32

Miller J, Cohen L (2002) One change too many! Is there any position for the American concepts of "cardinal changes" and the "cumulative impact doctrine" in English law? Constr Law J 18:378

Mosey D (2010) Early involvement trumps partnering. Constr Law 21(1):14

Ndekugri I, Rycroft M (2002) Variations under the JCT standard form of building contract. Constr Law J 18(4):310

Ramsey V, Furst S (2016) Keating on construction contracts, 10th edn. Sweet and Maxwell, London

Rosher P (2015) NEC3 contracts: partnering benefits, drawbacks and adaptation under French law. IBLJ 4:311

Sanderson K (2017) Mutual trust and cooperation. NEC 3 CMS Law- Now eAlert: 20 March 2017. Available http://www.cms-lawnow.com/ealerts/2017/03/mutual-trust-and-cooperation-under-the-nec?cc_lang=en&ec_as=5A246833783F4575B8A1E0075AB2C4FE

Stone R, Devenney J (2015) The modern law of contract, 11th edn. Routledge, London

Uff J (1993) Standard contract terms and the common law. Constr Law J 9(3):108

Uff J (2013) Construction law, 10th edn. Sweet and Maxwell, London

von Bar C, Clive E (eds) (2009) Draft common frame of reference principles, definitions and model rules of European private law. Sellier, Munich

Commercial Contracts and Corporate Social Responsibility Values: A European Perspective and an Attempt of a Normative Approach

Alexandra Horváthová

Contents

Abstract The topic of corporate social responsibility (CSR) has been captioned under many names and forms while emphasizing the role of business in society. According to CSR proponents, corporations should create value for their shareholders in a way that it also creates value for society. The CSR notion has become present in commercial as well as contractual relationships. Yet, its legal normative rationale continues to be challenged. This chapter analyses the position of contract from a modern contract law theory reflecting on the evolution of contract law theory and the understanding of contract as a social concept. CSR in this chapter is represented by a set of values and thus it is analysed to what extent values have been an element of contracts. Ultimately, this chapter analyses the position of European legal frameworks, the CESL, the PECL and the DCFR. The chapter carries out an

A. Horváthová (✉)
Center for Enterprise Liability, Faculty of Law, University of Copenhagen, Copenhagen, Denmark
e-mail: alexandra.andhov@jur.ku.dk

M. Heidemann, J. Lee (eds.), *The Future of the Commercial Contract in Scholarship and Law Reform*, https://doi.org/10.1007/978-3-319-95969-6_11

inquiry into the state of the European common contract law frameworks and their embracement and inclusion of values. The chapter through normative determination aims to show that the modern contract law theory supports inclusion of CSR values into the contracts. The same trend is visible in the European contract law frameworks.

1 Introduction

This chapter carries out an inquiry into the state of the European common contract law frameworks and their embracement of values, in particular Corporate Social Responsibility (CSR). The concept of CSR is understood as a form in which the values of the parties manifest. CSR represents pillars of our consideration for human rights and environment and other values, as the concept itself continues to develop as well. The aim of this chapter is to offer a normative support for the further development of existing contract law theories towards inclusion of CSR values. It seeks to provide a synopsis of a persuasive normative theory of contract law, evolved from accepted contract law theory that allows, facilitates and enforces values, and thus could later serve as a backbone for inclusion of CSR provisions into contracts.

It is often argued that not only is CSR a soft law construct, but it is also a voluntary undertaking of companies beyond law and thus unenforceable. This chapter does not engage in the position of CSR within the national or global legal systems or its legal character. This chapter approaches CSR from a slightly different angle, it perceives CSR as a certain set of values that has developed over the time together with the society and whether embraced by the national contract law norms or not, these CSR values are already present in the general contract law theory. Given that the contracts represent primarily social constructs, due to the evolution of our values in the society, including those of CSR, it is natural that also these values affect the contract and form a part of it.

This chapter builds on the notion that our ideas of what a corporation is and how it governs its relationships through contract law has been largely constructed by a liberal theory. According to this theory, the corporations and their relationships are not absolute and greatly depend on the societal perceptions. Corporations are constructs, which we, the communities and nations are free to reject and develop as we choose. It is the overall appeal of this chapter that as we, the people, deepen and broaden our knowledge and considerations for values, so should the law of contracts do.

The starting point of this chapter is in the understanding of CSR as a set of values. Values for human rights, for environmental protection, for certain standard of living and wage or for childhood and education. This chapter uses the term "value" to reflect on the content of CSR, without going into particularities. It inquires into the meaning of value, both in a contractual scholarship as well as philosophy. Given that the chapter perceives contracts as active social constructs, the inclusion of values into contracts is instinctive. Thus, the understanding of "value" is essential. Ultimately, within the normative part, the concept of value is further used to substantiate for inclusion of corporate social responsibility values in modern contracts.

The section three subsequently provides an analysis of the classical contract theory and its development towards modern contract law theory and thus to show from a normative perspective where CSR values come in. It is the aim of contract law theories to illuminate the concept of contract, to help us understand what a contract is and why we understand the contract law in a particular way. There are additional fields that complement our understanding, such as sociology, cultural studies, philosophy or economics that provide an angle to the development of law and its concepts. A contract, shall thus be understood as not only a legal concept dependent only on the contractual parties, but also as a social construct that continuously undergoes evolution.

Once the normative understanding has been set up, the chapter moves to identify the position and the reference to the values, including CSR values, in the modern common European contract law frameworks, such as the Principles of European Contract Law (PECL), the Draft Common Frame of Reference (DCFR) and the Common European Sales Law (CESL). It is well understood that this legal frameworks are of a soft law character. Nevertheless, they all together with CESL show a gradual reflection and inclusion of CSR values in the European contract law.

The focus of this chapter is to first show the theory support for inclusion of the CSR values within the contract law and subsequently present through the analysis of existing common European contract law frameworks this development. This chapter concludes with a reflection on the relevance of inclusion of CSR values in the contract and the role of European contract law frameworks for application and enforceability of CSR across Europe.

2 CSR as a Set of Values

Since Milton Friedman in 1962 in his Capitalism and Freedom declared that 'the responsibility of business is to increase its profits,[1] the literature on corporate social responsibility (CSR) has grown exponentially. Academics coming from diverse research fields have put forward several of arguments why CSR should or should not be of a concern for the corporate world, and if so to what extent.[2] Confining itself to a selective review and limited length, the purpose of this section is to present CSR as a certain set of values that is to be embraced by contracts under the modern contract theory.

CSR is present in life of a company in various forms, be it internal guidelines, CSR reporting, public statements, but also in a form of a contract, where one contractual party requires the other to adhere to respect certain set of values and act

[1] Friedman (1963).

[2] Henderson (2001).

accordingly. This section does not elaborate on the practicalities of how these sets of values should be incorporated in a contract. It rather explains what values should be understood under the notion of CSR, as for many it might only represent a buzzword. Yet, a certain level of abstraction is necessary, given that this chapter does not purely speak of one national law.

First, it has to be emphasized that CSR is a subject that has connection with many areas of law and therefore it often remains undefinable. From a perspective of law, international law and European Union law, corporate law and corporate governance, tort law and contract law, procedural law, labour law, environmental law and human rights as well as criminal law contain the components of CSR.[3] Nowadays, many international guidelines and conventions address obligations of multinational corporations towards CSR, continuing with their dispersion.[4] It has been argued that the multinational corporations play an important role in the investment process that has been shaping the world economy and thus contributed to the development across the world. Therefore, the multinational corporations should also play a pivotal role in positively shaping the business environment and their adherence to certain set of standards and values. Moreover, more states through extraterritorial effect of their national laws also encompass a part of CSR and apply a strict liability of corporations for a respective breach.[5] CSR truly represents a legal discipline of its own.

Focusing now on CSR as a set of values, it is a concept that entails a set of values present in diverse human rights, environmental as well as anti-corruption treaties, and conventions or as well in individual constitutions of majority of states. Given the broad scope of these legal instruments, it is challenging to specify the particular values. However, the UN has clearly incorporated the values within the UN Global Compact,[6] covering four areas that represent the four pillars of CSR: (1) human rights, (2) labour rights, (3) environment and (4) anticorruption. Irrespective of the fact that the UN defines them as principles, these principles represent values for protecting human rights, protecting environment, labor law or integrity in business. These ten UN values (principles) entail the correlation with ideals, prosperity of society as well as a determined activity towards the protection of them. They are derived from the most respected international declarations and thus serve as the highest ideals that have been proclaimed to support the affluence of the entire society.[7]

---

[3] Lambooy (2014).

[4] E.g. Universal Declaration of Human Rights, UN Global Compact, UN Guiding Principles on Business and Human Rights, OECD Guidelines for Multinational Enterprises, European Convention on Human Rights, EU Charter of Fundamental Rights, United Nations Convention against Corruption, ILO Conventions combines with the ILO MNE Declaration or Aarhus Convention.

[5] E.g. Foreign Corrupt Practices Act of 1977, 15 U.S.C. ch. 2b §78a et seq.; Sarbanes-Oxley Act 2002, Modern Slavery Act of 26 March 2015 or UK Bribery Act of 8 April 2010.

[6] Available online at: <https://www.unglobalcompact.org/>.

[7] The ten principles are derived from the Universal Declaration of Human Rights, the International Labour Organization's Declaration on Fundamental Principles and Rights at Work, the Rio Declaration on Environment and Development, and the United Nations Convention against Corruption.

Some may challenge the binding character of these principles/values for contractual parties. Yet, this is not the scope of this chapter. The primary purpose of this chapter is to show that due to the development of the society, its acceptance of certain values on the highest level, the contract law theories further develop towards inclusion of CSR values. The CSR values should be understood as not purely mercantile, but those emphasizing and supporting human rights, solidarity and social responsibility to others, not only to the shareholders or investors in the corporation.

3 Values in Contracts

Under the modern contract law theory, contract law is formed on diverse sets of principles and values.[8] Contract is perceived as not only an economic institution between two or more parties, but also a social one. Hence, a contract continues to continually develop together with a society, as its values do, reflecting on the necessity of environmental and human protections and the indisputable evolution of values. Karl Klare, Friedrich Kessler and Jay M. Feinmann in the modern contract theory emphasize the "social control".[9] Having such control on our mind, we should expand the basic principle of the liberal theory of contract as Charles Fried stated—"we secure in what is ours"[10] towards the further step "we protect what is ours". This step might not only reflect the development of our values, but also progress of our awareness of our rights, acknowledgments of the environmental reality and essentially our need for survival.

In commercial relations it is hard to define what a value is. Value is often perceived purely economically or from a mercantile perspective; what value/profit does a contract bring to a party. For many, contracts are legally enforceable promises and only few actually search for 'value' within these promises other than monetary. To that end, one of the most influential works in contract law theory of Charles Fried also stipulates that contracts serve moral ends, not only monetary.[11] Undoubtedly, it is easier to value things in monetary terms and to calculate costs and benefits, while perceiving the economic gain as the sole motivation for a transaction.[12] Yet, some theorist have included within their theories the search for values. Besides Fried, scholars such as James Penner, Liam Murphy and Charlie Webb acknowledge the moral function of a contract. However, they question what that function is. Penner argues that a moral basis for the law of contract is not in the morality of promises, but in the morality of agreements more generally, as he argues that contracts are best

---

[8] See Sect. 4.

[9] Gilmore (1974), pp. 1–14; Feinman (1983), p. 834.

[10] Charles Fried advocated a theory, where the binding force of contract is based on the moral obligation to keep promises, which in turn is based on the Kantian concept of autonomy.

[11] See generally Fried (2015).

[12] On the perspective of the economists see also Katz (2014), p. 176.

understood as involving agreements rather than promises.[13] Murphy distinguishes three functions contract law might have with respect to the moral sphere. The relevant for the purpose of this section is Murphy's third function, where contract is deployed instrumentally to promote social welfare. Murphy focuses not on the primary promises of the parties, but on possible remedies. He asks what remedy is better for society as a whole, with a focus on contract law's role in supporting the social practice of making and keeping agreements.[14] Charlie Webb also introduces an interesting argument, which however seems circular. Webb states that contracts entail promises because legal obligations claim to be moral obligations and so to voluntarily undertake a legal duty to perform a contract is also to voluntarily undertake a moral duty to do so. Thus, as long as contracts involve the voluntary assumption of obligations, whatever their content, these obligations are moral obligations.[15] This argument also shows the merits of legal obligations and the fact that they have throughout the time evolved, often from moral obligations assumed and accepted by the society. In addition, Charlie Webb observed that aside of the moral legal obligations, also the law's technical rules that do not require or invite appeal to value, they earn a place in our reasoning and decision-making only on the back of norms which get there on their merits—values.[16]

None of these scholars actually clearly elaborates on what they understand by "value". Rather, they seem to presume that values refer to moral principles. In summary, based on the contemporary contract scholarship, it is argued that contracts also implicate values or moral principles and that a complete account of contract law must attend to those values or principles as well. Yet, who is to determine what the values are? I would argue that only society might. Moreover, as the contracts dwell on the evolution of society, these values will never stop to evolve as long as the society itself progresses.

3.1 *Defining Values: A Philosophical Perspective*

To understand the values are, there are several research challenges that have to be considered. Should this quest be based on empiricism, philology or ontology? What kind of data should be taken into account? The word value has been used in various contexts, from natural sciences as mathematics, logic and economics to social sciences, such as philosophy, religion and art. Proclaiming additional value than just a monetary, a direct recourse to an in-depth analysis of the definition of value is required. This purpose will be fulfilled by the article on Definition of Value written

---

[13] Penner (1996).

[14] Murphy (2014).

[15] Webb (2014).

[16] Webb (2014), p. 135.

by Osbourne.[17] According to Osbourne, who considers naturalistic as well as non-naturalistic theories, he finds that in naturalistic theory "value" is synonymous with "good and evil" due to its independency from the theological and transcendental implications of those words in the ancient philosophy. Values represent ideals, whereas the absolute values are the absolute ideals of truth, beauty and goodness. From ideals the value moves to represent "satisfaction", "enjoyment," an "attitude" taken up towards an object which is valued. Furthermore, it is possible to distinguish from individualistic conceptions also the "social" definitions. The social definitions fall into two sub-categories. First, a value is the object for socially approved ideals or purposes or second, it is conduciveness to the prosperity of society.[18] This understanding of values would be intrinsically compatible not only with the notion that values in context of contract theory refer to generally approved values, but also that the value reflects not only an individual's monetary gain, but rather the prosperity of a society en banc.

Osborne when analysing the non-naturalistic theory discovers two branches, an idealistic and a realistic. In the light of idealistic theories value is defined by only one ultimate concept—"oughtness". Oughtness is an absolute and underived factor in the structure of reality, referring to things that "ought to exist".

> And where their existence or non-existence depends upon the voluntary action of a moral being, he is morally obliged to further the existence of that which is most "fitting" or "ought most" to exist.[19]

The values represent certain standards that a members of a society should reach.

Even though each individual bears his and her own values and perceives their application in different form within their contractual relationship, the above-stated philosophical analysis is significant. It entails the correlation of values with ideals, prosperity of society as well as a determined activity towards the two. In connection with this understanding, contract law theory should embrace the position of values within the understanding and interpretation of contract.

4 Towards Modern Contract Law Theory

Setting aside values for a second, if we aim to understand, what contract law represents today and how contract law has been developed, it is necessary to go back in both history and philosophy to comprehend what has been the role of the contract, whether this role has changed through the time and how is the contract and contact law perceived today. Legal theory recognizes multiple theories of contract law, general theories of contract law and theories about specific features of contract law. These stem from different philosophical approaches and diverse legal systems. The

---

[17] Osborne (1931).

[18] Ibid. p. 436.

[19] Ibid pp. 443–444.

theories are naturally interlinked. Each of them aims to explain various doctrines that have been used to draft, apply and interpret contract law.[20]

There is a major difference between "classical" and "modern" contract law and between the common and civil contract law. Starting with the first group, classical contract law is usually understood to be the law of contract as developed during the nineteenth century and the first half of the twentieth century.[21] The classical contract law is believed to have been shaped by the conditions created in the wake of the industrial revolution and the existing social and economic outlook at the time. The theory was centred around the individual as the source of the creative power of his will and state.[22] Yet, the nature and the enforcement of the will was often defined by the courts of equity. Even though the contract law's corner stone principle of contractual freedom was effective and vigorous, it was not omnipresent. The courts, particularly the courts of equity, have interfered[23] to the extent that they were perceived arbitrary and uncertain.[24] Therefore, more pronounced and clear rules were needed and on that basis, the modern contract law was initiated in the Anglo-Saxon legal system.

Undisputed was the aspiration of the classical contract law in the Anglo-Saxon system to develop a general body of contract law applicable to all types of contracts in order to provide the highest degree of stability and predictability to ensure the parties' ability to rely on the binding effect of a contract.[25] In England and the United States, it was only at the end of nineteenth century when Pollock started to systematize contract theory. Blackstone devoted only a few pages to contract. Even though Pollock initiated the systematization, he did not assert large philosophical, political or economic principles to support his theory. He stated that such theories were not the concern of jurists, as "their business is to learn and know, so far as needful for their affairs, what rules the State does undertake to enforce and administer, whatever the real or professed reasons for those rules may be."[26] Yet, the movement continued. These pieces were later advanced by the more sophisticated theories of modern contract law developed by Lon L. Fuller's and William Perdue Jr. in 'The Reliance Interests in Contract Damages' in 1936,[27] followed by 'Contract as Promise: A Theory of Contractual Obligations', written by Charles Fried. Fried systematically explored the normative foundation of contract law and attempted to

---

[20] According to Smith, we could divide the contract theories into several, including *promissory* theories, *reliance* or *transfer* theories. Smith further, based on the normative question, stipulates *utilitarian* theories, *rights-based* theories. For more on general contract law theories *see* Smith (2004).

[21] See e.g. Gilmore (1974), p. 6; Friedman (1965), pp. 20–24; Beatson and Friedman (1997), p. 7.

[22] Cohen (1933), p. 558 or Williston (1921).

[23] For more details on equitable contractual principles, see Sherwin (1991).

[24] Powell (1790), p. 229.

[25] Beatson and Friedman (1997), p. 10.

[26] Pollock (1896), pp. 26–27.

[27] Fuller based his theory on three interests, expectation, reliance and restitution. See Fuller and Perdue (1936).

explain the main contract doctrines on a unified moral basis, through the Kantian moral autonomy.[28]

Like classical contract law theory, modern contract law aims to achieve a fundamental objective—to ensure that voluntary agreements between private parties are legally binding. Modern contract law as a concept is characterized by an increased control over the contractual regime. Not from a perspective of limiting the contractual freedom, but from the perspective of insuring the procedural supervision over the contract formation and substantial supervision over the content of the contract.[29] Regulators and courts became part of the contract with confining the *caveat emptor* idea and with ensuring that the contract during its formation is free from elements that would vitiate parties' consent.[30] Some stated that it was a necessity to adapt contract law to the realities of a market economy.[31] Even if some may object to this historical interpretation,[32] it is not the aim of this chapter to resolve this perpetual argument. Nevertheless, the nineteenth century wake of individual freedoms and the development of market economy together with the necessity of easily accessible contractual principles continue to provide a narrative for the development of the modern theory of contract law in the Anglo-Saxon world. Moreover, English law has influenced the attempts for further harmonization of European contract law (*e.g.* the DCFR), not only by common EU projects, but also through decision-making of the Court of Justice of the European Union, thus the relevance of the common law contract law theory introduction.

In continental Europe, the Romans attempted to systematize contract law as a set of promises and transactions. Since then diverse legal theories have started to emanate across Europe.[33] Yet, due to the breakup of the Roman political system and the ensuing Middle Ages, the advancement of legal theories was postponed until the Modern Period.[34] The states of modern Europe in late eighteenth century initiated the codification processes of their national private laws.[35] The leading principle present in all national laws across Europe has been freedom of contract.[36] In German and French scholarship, the freedom of contract is understood as the most significant manifestation of private autonomy and thus as assurance of individual liberties.[37] In France, the traces to the importance of this concept go back to the

[28] Fried (2015).

[29] As examples, serve the Restatement (Second) of Contracts in the United States or Implied or Unfair terms in the United Kingdom.

[30] Beatson and Friedman (1997), p. 13; Horwitz (1974), p. 945.

[31] Verplanck (1825); in his essay Verplanck asserts diverse difficulties and contradictions to be found in existing legal contractual doctrines of "the question of the nature and degrees of equality required in contracts of mutual interest".

[32] Gordley (1993), ch. 8.

[33] See generally Zimmermann (1996), pp. 508–558.

[34] Farnsworth (2006), p. 907.

[35] Zimmermann (2005), p. 5.

[36] Grundmann (2005), p. 194; In general see Schulte-Nölke (2009).

[37] Basedow (2008), p. 903.

French Revolution's declaration of human rights.[38] However, in neither of the European jurisdictions is the freedom of contract absolute as it is restricted by certain substantial values prevalent in these jurisdictions.[39]

The relevance of modern contract law theory for this chapter lies in understanding two of its main components. First is the evolution of contract law towards its conceptualization. The need for a general body of contract law applicable to all parties involved that would secure parties' trust, contractual stability and predictability. Contractual parties should be able to rely on a clear set of rules ensuring the binding effect of a contract. Otherwise the main purpose of a contract wanes. This argument continues to be relevant even today for building the common market representing the support for the systemization of law in the European Union.[40] The second important factor of the contract law theory development is the understanding of contract in the light of the above conceptualization, i.e. in the light of principles, policies and values. Understanding that a contract is not only an economic transaction between two parties, but also a political and social institution.[41]

In order to show the application of this normative analysis on practical development of a legal framework, I now move to the assessment of the existing European contract law legal frameworks. In this way, it will be possible to assess to what extent the values represent a part of the further conceptualization of EU private and contract law.

5 European Legal Frameworks and CSR

In the European Union, a clear reference to the three-letter abbreviation—CSR—took place in March 2000, when the EU in the Lisbon Agenda decided to concentrate on CSR as a way of linking economic, employment and social goals that lie at the core of its agenda.[42] The Lisbon Agenda was designed to make the European Union "the most competitive and dynamic knowledge-based economy in the world, capable of sustainable economic growth with more and better jobs and greater social cohesion."[43] This agenda was later developed into a White Paper on promoting a European framework for Corporate Social Responsibility.[44] This period has been

[38] Jacques Ghestin (1994), para 134 et seq.

[39] Waddams (2013).

[40] Section 5 and below.

[41] In eighteenth century, beliefs about contract law emphasized the relations between the individual and the community. People were determined by social hierarchy and the reciprocal ties of social obligation among members of community-defined standards of behavior. Feinman (1983).

[42] Schutter (2008).

[43] European Commission, Promoting a European Framework for Corporate Social Responsibility: Green Paper (COM) 2001 366 final.

[44] Commission of the European Communities, "Communication from the Commission Concerning Corporate Social Responsibility: A Business Contribution to Sustainable Development" COM (2002) 347 final.

concluded in 2004, which was declared the European Year for Corporate Social Responsibility. This clear endorsement of CSR and the values that the notion stands for are naturally not surprising given that in numerous previous documents throughout the 1990s has the European Union stipulated its interest in addressing broader societal well-being, the welfare of employees, stakeholder model of corporate governance and its devotion to human rights protection.[45]

With the worldwide move on the integration of CSR values, including among many the ILO Declaration on Fundamental Principles and Rights at Work in 1998, the Rio Declaration on Environment and Development in 1992 or the UN Global Compact in 2000, the EU also progressed that direction. EU aimed to create a forum for intra-sectorial communication, stakeholder dialogue, exchange and dissemination of information about CSR as well as education on CSR. Yet, in 2006, the European Commission clearly stipulated that Europe remains company-led and that CSR remains voluntary.[46] The EU was not ready for any greater dossier than just political.[47] There was no sign of additional regulation and CSR continued to be perceived as purely voluntary.[48] The Commission failed to understand what CSR really meant.

The change in the policy came only 5 years later. In 2011, the European Commission embraced a new strategy on CSR.[49] Within this new strategy, the Commission adopted a new, extremely broad definition of CSR—"the responsibility of enterprises for their impacts on society"—and politically endorsed the position of CSR within the Social Business Initiative as well as the EU social dialogue. A clear acknowledgment of the UN Guiding Principles was established. The Commission stipulated that it "expects all European enterprises to meet the corporate responsibility to respect human rights, as defined in the UN Guiding principles." The Commission further promised new guidance for implementation of the UN Guiding Principles.[50] In regard to the latest development, the Commission issued in 2015 the Staff Working Document on Implementing the UN Guiding Principles.

---

[45] See e.g. Maastricht Treaty of 1992, Treaty of Amsterdam of 1997, Fannon (2003) and Búrca (2015) chapter 11.

[46] Communication of the Commission "Implementing the Partnership for Growth and Jobs: Making Europe a Pole of Excellence on CSR", 136 Final of 22 March 2006.

[47] Commission's vice president and commissioner for enterprise and industry, Gunter Verheugen states that "A controversial discussion has been finished at its heart: does CSR require a legal framework or should it be purely voluntary? We're not going to create any new bureaucracy but we will rather pursue a partnership approach." He further stated "There will be no monitoring, no benchmarking, no naming and shaming, no reporting requirements. It is completely voluntary. We will never have a regulatory framework for CSR because it is a philosophy, a concept". Cited in Amao (2011), p. 65.

[48] Ibid.

[49] Communication from the Commission on a Renewed EU Strategy 2011–14 for Corporate Social Responsibility COM (2011) 681 final.

[50] Ibid.

Besides policy documents, the EU adopted in 2014 Directive 201/98/EU on non-financial reporting.[51] This directive is applicable from January 1, 2017 and covers simply large corporations with over 500 employees.[52] One of the main rationales behind this directive was to provide shareholders and other stakeholders with a comprehensive view on the activities of large corporations, including listed companies, banks, insurance undertakings and other companies with more than 500 employees. These companies have the obligation, in their management reports, to disclose their policies, development, risks and impact of their activity, relating to, as a minimum, environmental, social and employees matters, respect for human rights, anticorruption and bribery maters.[53] Given that the directive is applicable only from January 1, 2017, it is only this year to see and observe the depth and the quality of respective reports. Nevertheless, this report represents a substantial move towards greater compliance and possibly responsibility and even though in 2006 reporting was not attainable, 11 years later the situation has changed.

Based on the above, one can see the gradual development of the EU policies towards CSR and the present embracement of CSR. With the economic development, also the development of social and human rights values took place. Moving from the general EU policies to existing legislative framework and drafts of Common European Sales Law in Europe, the following sections will provide the reader with an analysis of each of the three developed and how do they reflect on CSR values and whether certain included principles promote pro-CSR contractual interpretation.

5.1 Towards Harmonisation of Private Law in Europe

Harmonisation of private law in general and contract law in particular in the European Union has been a large and difficult mission. This mission has initiated several projects that are to a great extent interconnected. The principal aim of these projects was the smooth functioning of the EU internal market.[54] Contract law in each of the Member States is based on national legislative traditions, customs, unwritten principles of law, and many decades or in some case centuries of case law of the national courts or at least the highest courts. Thus, the EU contract law has been described as a 'patchwork' or 'pointillist'[55] lacking coherence,[56] transparency and normative clarity.

[51] Directive 2014/95/EU of the European Parliament and of the Council of 22 October 2014 amending Directive 2013/34/EU as regards disclosure of non- financial and diversity information by certain large undertakings and groups.

[52] Article 29a of the Directive 2014/95/EU.

[53] Article 19a of the Directive 2014/95/EU.

[54] Staudenmayer (2002).

[55] Riesenhuber (2005), p. 308.

[56] Röttinger (2006), p. 816.

To pin point what exactly had initiated the EU harmonisation process is difficult. The academic inclination towards comparison and harmonisation of the European contract law started already in 1980, when a group of lawyers formed the Commission on European Contract Law (CECL). CECL was formed by independent academics from 15 European Union countries who hoped to distil the general principles from the national laws and thus bring about a systemic harmonization of the contract law in the European Union.[57] The first official statement from an EU authority came in 1989 and then again in1994, when the European Parliament passed resolutions requesting the preparatory work for drafting a European Code of Private Law.[58] According to Professor Lando, the European Commission at the beginning supported the work of CECL, but it later withdrew its support. At that time, the European Council also did not show any interest in CECL's work.[59]

Only in 1999 during a European Council meeting in Tampere, the European Council mentioned its intention to work towards a European harmonisation of civil law. The European Council requested an overall study "[on] the need to approximate Member States' legislation in civil matters in order to eliminate obstacles to the good functioning of civil proceedings."[60] In regard to the wording of the request, one may observe uncertainty as it is rare that the approximation of substantive laws aims to eliminate obstacles to the proper functioning of civil proceeding. The European Council expected a report back by 2001. This report released by the Commission was believed to be inconclusive as to defining the specific obstacles that had to be removed, while calling for further examination.[61]

In 2003, the European Commission in the Action Plan 'A More Coherent European Contract Law', proposed two strategies for the future direction of the European Contract law.[62] The first one was a systematization and consolidation of the acquis directives by a consolidation of common principles and definitions in a so-called 'Common Frame of Reference—CFR'. The second one was a 'non-sector—specific optional instrument' of contract law, a contract code, including also other areas of law closely related to contracts.[63] For some academics, this proposal seemed too farfetched and the issue of the EU's competence was raised. However, that issue is not of a concern for this chapter.

[57] Lando (1998), p. 810.

[58] Resolution on Action to Bring into Line the Private Law of the Member States, Eur. Parl. Res., 1989 O.J. (C158) 400; Resolution on the Harmonization of Certain Sectors of Private Law of the Member States, Eur. Parl. Res., 1994 O.K. (C205) 518. The preamble of the 1989 Resolution stated that "unification can be carried out in branches of private law which are highly important for the development of a Single Market, such as contract law..."

[59] Lando (1998), p. 811.

[60] Section 39, available online at: <http://www.europarl.europa.eu/summits/tam_en.htm>.

[61] Commentary of the UK Parliament on the Draft Common Frame of Reference, available online at: <https://www.publications.parliament.uk/pa/ld200809/ldselect/ldeucom/95/9505.htm>.

[62] Communication from the Commission to the European Parliament and the Council—A more coherent European contract law—An action plan, 12 February 2003, COM (2003) 68 final.

[63] Communication on European Contract Law, 11 October 2004, COM (2004) 651 final.

Given the extensive literature on the genesis, aims, procedures applied of the European harmonization projects this section will not devote itself further to detailed analysis of the above.[64] The following sections will only briefly describe each of the projects, while focusing on the assessment of the extent to which the values represent a part of these legal frameworks.

5.1.1 Values in the Principles of European Contract Law

The Principles of European Contract Law was a product of CECL. In the Introduction of PECL, CECL stipulated five "benefits" of PECL and five "purposes" for which they were designed.[65] The primary purpose of the PECL was to facilitate the cross-border trade within Europe and strengthen the Single European Market.[66] At the time of PECL preparation, the European Union's contract law was fragmented and uncoordinated. Most of these laws were adopted as directives that governed very specific areas, e.g. unfair contract terms, home sale or consumer protection. The purpose of PECL was to serve as a combined information on the contract law of European countries and the common core of the European systems. They were intended to be applied as general rules of contract law in the European Union.[67] The aspiration was that the PECL would provide a basis for a future European Civil Code: "One objective of the Principles of European Contract Law is to serve as a basis for any future European Code of Contracts."[68]

Understanding that the individual national laws differ, CECL approached PECL project through principles instead of a classical civilian code. The Principles were reflected in the articles. The CECL group presumed the presence of common core of European contract law and the PECL represented a form in which CECL tried to restate it.

Looking at PECL and its reference for values in broad understanding, one can find the traditional contract law values, including freedom of contract, good faith, fair dealing and the duty to cooperate.[69] PECL introduces the excessive benefit and unfair advantage of a contractual party. PECL provides that a party may avoid a contract if at the time of the conclusion of the contract (1) it was dependent, (2) it had a relationship of trust with the other party, (3) was in economic distress or (4)

---

[64] See e.g. Alpa (2004); Weatherill (2004); Riesenhuber (2005); Lurger (2005) or Stefan Vogenauer (2006).

[65] PECL, Introduction, p. xxi.

[66] Ibid.

[67] PECL, Article 1:101 (1). CESL was influenced by existing harmonization approaches, namely the Uniform Commercial Code (UCC) and the UNIDROIT Principles, where the UCC represents the unitary law for different US states and the UNIDROIT Principles were an attempt to provide for a worldwide uniformity in contract law. *See* Hesselink (2001).

[68] PECL, p. xxiii. Also an explicit reference is stated to the European Parliament Resolutions calling for the preparation of a European Code of Private Law, see above fn. 55.

[69] PECL, Articles 1:102, 1:201 and 1:202.

had urgent needs (5) was improvident, (6) ignorant, (7) inexperienced or (8) lacking in bargaining skills, while the other party knew or ought to have known of this.[70] In addition, PECL provides for a court discretion to adapt the contract under the light of good faith and fair dealing.[71] Thus, introducing indirectly a possibility to employ an objective party (a court) to assess the fairness of the contractual terms. PECL pushes a step forward the good faith and cooperation, a step towards more of a Scandinavian concept of fairness of all contract terms.[72]

When looking for PECL referring to values within a contract, which is a separate group than the contract law values per se, PECL is silent. However, there is an interesting development between the conflicts of contractual parties' autonomy versus solidarity. PECL stipulates the "freedom of contract" at its core. Parties are free to agree on their contractual terms within the limits of laws and good faith and fair dealing. Yet, the question is how broadly we understand "fair dealing" and how we approach it. Does the law leave it for the free market to take care of the inequality or is an intervention advisable? In different countries, different approaches have been undertaken and the fairness has been interpreted differently.[73] PECL stipulates that also the contract itself shall be interpreted with an emphasis on promotion of good faith, fair dealing, certainty and uniformity.[74] However, the most interesting provision of PECL, showing the inclination of PECL and thus also of the EU towards solidarity and fairness is present in the Article 4:109.[75] Having on mind that PECL's aim was to introduce principles of the future EU Contract Code, the fact that PECL indirectly positions fairness and solidarity above the contractual freedom is significant.

5.1.2 Values in Draft Common Frame of Reference

In 2003, the European Commission published an Action Plan on a More Coherent European Contract Law.[76] This action plan aimed to advance the harmonisation of the European private law by developing a 'Common Frame of Reference' (CFR), which had the aspiration to facilitate the cross-border trade in the Union. Instead of

---

[70] PECL, Article 4:109 (1).

[71] PECL, Article 4:109 (2) and (3).

[72] Hesselink (2001), p. 10.

[73] Kennedy (1997).

[74] PECL, Article 1:106 (1).

[75] Also Article 4:110 on Unfair Terms not Individually Negotiated provides legal remedies for contractual imbalance in the parties' rights and obligations. The value of this provision is nowadays found in the consumer law.

[76] European Commission, Communication from the Commission to the European Parliament and the Council: A More Coherent European Contract Law: An Action Plan (2003) OJ C63/1. Before the action plan, the EU Commission published a Communication on European Contract Law that is perceived as the first stone for CFR, available online at: <http://eur-lex.europa.eu/legal-content/EN/TXT/PDF/?uri=CELEX:52001DC0398&from=EN>/. In 2002 an academic Acquis Group was established.

the CFR, the Draft Common Frame of Reference (DCFR) was published in 2009. It is important to emphasize that there is a difference between the CFR and the DCFR, as the DCFR is only an academic proposal.[77] Numerous legal scholars of international private law, EU law and comparative law prepared the DCFR, while using PECL as its foundation.[78] In its structure, the DCFR represents a typical Continental civil code. However, its content differs from all known national civil codes as it includes Books on secured transaction law, franchise and trust; legal tools that are often dispersed within national legal systems and often even unregulated. Thus, one could assume that the Uniform Commercial Code also served as an inspiration for the DCFR drafters.

The DCFR discusses contract law principles and elements across multiple jurisdictions, indicating the different traditions among civilian jurisdictions and comparing the civilian systems on each point both with each other and with English law. In the Action Plan on European contract law, the European Commission has announced that it envisages adopting a legal framework such as the DCFR, which will be instrumental in revising the Union acquis and could provide the basis for an optional European Code of Contracts.[79] The European Commission stated in its presentation of the proposal for a Common Frame of Reference that "contractual freedom should be the guiding principle; restrictions should only be foreseen where this could be justified with good reasons."[80]

The DCFR is a non-binding instrument that sets out fundamental principles of contract law, definitions of contract terms, and coherent model rules for diverse contracts. The DCFR is based on the Union *aquis* and on the best practices in the Member States' jurisprudence. The key idea behind the DCFR was to identify the common problems in contract law and to seek appropriate solutions based on a common understanding across the European jurisdictions. The DCFR represented a draft "European Civil Code" that revised and reconceptualised the contract law laid down in the PECL from the perspective of the law of obligations.[81]

From the beginning, the DCFR refers to values as part of the "fundamental principles and values", based on which the model rules are built.[82] The DCFR stipulates a distinction between principles, fundamental principles and underlying principles where the first is part of 'principles, definitions and model rules' and the second reflects the values.[83] The third group of underlying principles reflects the four principles of freedom, security, justice and efficiency that represent the four

[77] DCFR, Introduction, sec. 1.

[78] Study Group on a European Civil Code and Research Group on the Existing EC Private LAW (*Acquis Group*), Draft Common Frame of Reference: Principles, Definitions and Model Rules of European Private Law (Munich, Sellier European Law Publishers, 2009).

[79] European Commission (2003, 2004).

[80] European Commission (2003), p. 16.

[81] DCFR, Introduction, sec. 8, see also Hesselink (2009), pp. 919, 923.

[82] DCFR, Introduction, sec. 11.

[83] Compare DCFR, Introduction, sec. 9, 10 and 11.

corner stones of the DCFR.[84] Considering the fundamental principles, it is emphasized that private law is one of those fields of law that is guided by deep-rooted principles that not only serve for DCFR's structure, but also for its interpretation. The fundamental principles are also referred to as overriding principles that include protection of human rights, the promotion of solidarity and social responsibility.[85] The word 'overriding' clearly emphasizes the standing of these principles/values in the entire DCFR. Moreover, the DCFR stipulates the relevance of 'social justice' as a correction for market failures.[86]

The DCFR distinctly places a high value on the protection of human rights, while recognizing its ultimate nature as being referred to as "overriding principles". The rules of the DCFR are to be read in the light of any applicable instruments guaranteeing human rights and fundamental freedoms.[87] This provision is placed as the second in regard to the 'interpretation and development' section. In the commentary, it is stated that this provision presents a reminder that human rights serve overriding laws and may provide defences to liability not specifically mentioned in the DCFR. The Commentary stipulates that those parts of a contract contrary to the human rights laws are of no effect.[88] This principle is also reflected in the Books II and III in the rules on non-discrimination. Moreover, in the Introduction to the DCFR the promotion of solidarity and social responsibility are stated to be 'of a great importance to the DCFR'.[89] Nevertheless, they are not directly reflected upon in the Books covering contractual relationships.[90]

Human rights and fundamental principles are in the EU Member States protected predominantly by constitutional law. Thus, in national legal systems, the power attributed to fundamental rights in the interpretation of contract law rules will depend on the relationship between constitutional law and private law.[91] To what extent have the private parties comply with the objectives of these values? The German Federal Constitutional Code, the Italian Constitutional Court together with the Italian Supreme Court as well as the Dutch Supreme Court have recognised a reciprocal effect of fundamental constitutional rights and private law regulation since 1950 by reading the provision of private law in the light of constitutionally protected rights.[92] It has been the role of judiciary in these three EU Member States to safeguard the human rights in private disputes. Professor Mak states that the wording of Article I.-1:102(2) of the DCFR seems to allow for a variety of mostly

[84] DCFR, Introduction, sec. 15.

[85] Ibid, sec. 16.

[86] Ibid, sec. 11.

[87] DCFR, Article I-1:102(2).

[88] DCFR, pp. 134–135.

[89] DCFR, Introduction, sec. 18.

[90] The word solidarity in this context has to be distinguished from the solidary liability.

[91] See Mak (2009), p. 517.

[92] Ibid, pp. 517–520.

indirect effects of fundamental rights in contract cases.[93] However, reading this article together with the introductory remarks of the drafters and the commentary, I believe that the DCFR supports a direct effect of values stemming from fundamental rights in the contracts, providing judiciary with the power of oversight. Even though the DCFR represents only a model and an academic creation, it has found its use in different areas, including teaching European private law as well as adjudicating or arbitrating international cases.[94]

5.1.3 Values in Common European Sales Law

Moving from PECL and the DCFR to the latest attempt of harmonisation of contract law in Europe—the Common European Sales Law (CESL)—it is necessary to start with an understanding, why the European Commission initiated this project and what were its aims, given also other endeavours that have been present in the EU. One may challenge CESL's inclusion into this chapter given its failure of being adopted. However, that failure was predominantly political and given that this chapter aims to show and support the presence of CSR values within the EU contract law frameworks, it is important to reflect also on CESL as one of the most coherent and most recent attempts.

In July 2010, Viviane Reding, on behalf of the European Commission proclaimed the intent of adopting a pan-European contract law.[95] The European Commission stated that the primary aim of CESL was to further contribute to the developing of the EU's internal market for goods and related services.[96] A year later, the Commission published a draft regulation on a Common European Sales Law, proposed to operate as an optional supplement to national law.[97] Thus, the idea was that CESL would operate in parallel to the existing national contract law. However, this work rendered unsuccessful. Despite the full preparation of the proposal regulation, on 16 December 2014 the EU Commission withdrew the proposal. The stated reason by the First Vice-President Frans Timmermans for the withdrawal of CESL was the need for its modification in regard to use of e-com-

---

[93] See Mak (2008), p. 562.

[94] See Tajti (2014).

[95] Green Paper form the Commission on policy options for progress towards a European Contract Law for consumers and business, COM (2010) 348 final.

[96] Proposal for a Regulation of the European Parliament and of the Council on a Common European Sales Law ("Proposal"), COM (2011) 635 final, 4, which states the following: "*The overall objective of the proposal is to improve the establishment and the functioning of the internal market by facilitating the expansion of cross-border trade for business and cross-border purchases for consumers. This objective can be achieved by making available a self-standing uniform set of contract law rules including provisions to protect consumers, the Common European Sales Law, which is to be considered as a second contract law regime within the national law of each Member State.*"

[97] Proposal for a Regulation of the European Parliament and of the Council on a Common European Sales Law, COM (2011) 635 final.

merce.[98] Since then, CESL has been mentioned in the Commission's digital single market strategy. However, a number of EU Member States as well as scholars opposed the adoption of CESL. The UK submitted to the European Parliament a Reasoned Opinion stipulating the principles of subsidiarity and proportionality being breached by possible adoption of CESL.[99] Numerous scholars have put forward concerns in regard to a necessity and relevance of CESL.[100]

Yet, it is not the purpose of this section to analyse the reasons that rendered CESL paralyzed. It is important to assess whether and to what extent has CESL evolved from PECL and to what extent there are any similarities with the DCFR with respect to the inclusion of non-mercantile values in contracts.

In the Proposal for the CESL Regulation, first the grounds and objectives of the Proposal are stipulated. As mentioned above, the main objective was to improve establishment and the functioning of the internal market by facilitating the expansion of cross-border trade for business and cross-border purchases for consumers. Thus, CESL would have been applicable to both business-to-business and business-to consumer transactions as long as the parties would agree on CESL to govern their cross-border contracts.[101] Thus, throughout CESL, the additional protection for consumers is present.[102]

Similarly, CESL refers to three pillars, (1) freedom of contract, (2) good faith and fair dealing and (3) co-operation, as do the DCFR and PECL.[103] On the other hand, in comparison to the DCFR, CESL refers to its respect for human rights only in the recital 37. Further, in the text of the regulation, there is no direct reference to the protection of human rights or solidarity as overriding principles or as tools for interpretation. Thus, except for additional protection for consumers which represents a

---

[98] See Eric Clive, 'Proposal for a Common European Sales Law withdrawn', European Private Law News, posted on January 7, 2015, available online at: <http://www.epln.law.ed.ac.uk/2015/01/07/proposal-for-a-common-european-sales-law-withdrawn/>.

[99] See Carla Salazar, 'Opinion to the reaction of UK government and legal groups to the withdrawal of the Common European Sales Law (CESL), available online at: <http://blogs.escript.law.ed.ac.uk/contractlaweurope16/2016/10/12/opinion-to-the-reaction-of-uk-government-and-legal-groups-to-the-withdrawal-of-the-common-european-sales-law-cesl/>; See also the Impact Assessment of the UK Ministry of Justice, available online at: <https://consult.justice.gov.uk/digital-communications/common-european-sales-law/results/cesl-impact-assessment.pdf>. For arguments in favor of the CESL, see Hans-Wolfgang Micklitz (2013), pp. 23–27. For arguments in favor of the CESL, see Hans-Wolfgang Micklitz (2013), pp. 23–27.

[100] E.g. Horst Eidenmüller (2012).

[101] CESL, Article 3.

[102] E.g. The consumer has to be provided with specific information on the application of the CESL before the agreement, see CESL, Annex II. Article 10 also stipulates penalties for breach of the information obligation; Consumers have to be aware of the complex set of charges and costs, see CESL, Article 14; CESL also included specific provision governing the off-premises contracts and distance contracts, which obliges the seller to provide additional information as well as acquire a confirmation of the consumer's consent and other requirements. Moreover, also the burden of proof in regard to the information provided is shifted and is bore by the seller, see CESL, Article 26.

[103] CESL, Articles 1–3.

great part of CESL, there is a complete lack of direct reference to CSR values within the text. Nevertheless, there are two relevant articles, which show a normative support for further development of contract law in the light of CSR values.

First interesting articles that could bring CSR values indirectly into the contractual relationship are Article 68 and 69 CESL that introduce implied terms and pre-contractual statement. According to Article 68, additional contract term may be implied by (1) the nature and purpose of the contract, (2) the circumstances in which the contract was concluded and (3) good faith and fair dealings. Naturally, question remains how we understand and interpret good faith and fair dealings between two private parties. This is often dependent on the practice, industry and region in question. However, the most interesting is the Article 69, according to which contract terms can be derived from certain pre-contractual statements, "about the characteristics of what is to be supplied". Article 69 provides that a statement made to the other party or made publicly is incorporated as a term of the contract, unless the other party "was aware… that the statement was incorrect or could not otherwise be relied on." Hence, both public and private statements, through advertisement, online CSR statements become relevant as they become part of a contract. Statements on labor law considerations and no child labor, no forced labor, no discrimination in production of a product might become perceived as a certain pre-contractual statement and thus be incorporated as a term of the contract. This rule was first introduced in consumer contract law on the ground that consumers were often subject to unfair marketing techniques that would induce them to enter into a contract based on misleading and untrue pre-contractual information. This information would be later omitted in the final contract.[104] Yet, even though the origin of this provision finds its place in consumer law, CESL aimed to apply it broadly and apply the same standard of fairness between two business parties. How broadly this article would be interpreted by courts is debatable and remains unanswered.

The other interesting Article, introduced in CESL that can affect the above stated understanding and use of Articles 68 and 69 is Article 4(1) stipulates that the new regime of contract law has to be interpreted autonomously without reference to national legal orders. Article 4(2), modeled on Art I.-1:102(4) DCFR, requires those issues within the scope of the regime but not expressly regulated to be settled in accordance with the principles underlying it. Article 4(2) is a gap filling provision, indicating who has the power to fill the possible gaps in CESL and its application and interpretation. This provisions limited the scope of interpretation for both national courts as well as the CJEU to interpret the European contract law only in accordance with the principles of CESL and the EU law. Creating thus a 'closed system'.[105] The CESL drafters aimed to clearly restrict the national courts from applying national law principles when interpreting CESL. The rationale for such restriction is hard to find due to the scarcity of publicly available *travaux prépara-*

---

[104] Cafaggi (2013), pp. 318–319. Similar provision is present in the Consumer Sales Directive, 1999/44/EC, O.J. 1999, L 158/60 in Art. 6(1) and in the Time-Sharing Directive 2008/122/EC, O.J. 2009, L33/10 in Article 5(2).

[105] Busch (2016), p. 35.

toires. Hence, one could only assume that the creation of a closed system for interpretation of the legal tool—CESL—that aimed at improving the establishment and the functioning of the internal market, was to limit the principles to those of the EU law itself. Among these are primarily the fundamental rights, proportionality, legal certainty and solidarity. Statements, proclamations of contractual parties of their law and human rights abiding nature and behavior thus would not be only part of marketing, advertising or yearly reports, but could be perceived as part of a contract. Moreover, not only that they would form part of the contract, but where the content would remain uncertain, it would have to be interpreted in the light of the general principles of the EU law and CESL. This would be also supported by the recital 37 of the CESL and the Regulation's proclamation of respect for EU fundamental rights.[106]

6 Relevance of the European Legal Frameworks and Challenges for Application of CSR in Europe: Value and Enforceability

One may claim that the above stated discourse is inconsequential as none of the projects for contract law harmonization in the European Union has been markedly successful. Either the regulation was not adopted or only the academic version has been supported. At the same time, some may claim that if parties wish to include anything into their contracts, they are free to do so under the principle of contractual freedom. The inclusion of any contractual provision that is not contrary to the obligatory provisions of law or morals is obviously complimentary. Nevertheless, the enforcement of such provision would be questionable due to its possible ambiguity or a court's difficulty in interpreting the provision due to the lack of any doctrinal support. Only those contractual provisions are relevant which are enforceable. In most cases the enforcer is a court or an arbitral tribunal. Thus, only with the support of courts and arbitral tribunals provisions including CSR values may become "real". In order for a court or a tribunal to (1) comprehend a meaning of such contractual provision, which is usually broad and ambiguous and (2) interpret it correctly, without a specific statutory support, the court or tribunal would need a certain theoretical framework, a contract law doctrine within which it can interpret such contractual clause. This chapter aimed to provide such theoretical framework and development of contractual doctrine. It shows a change of the contract law theory, supported by the modern law theory as well as natural evolvement of European contract law frameworks. By identifying the position of CSR values within the existing European contract law, the article also showed the future of commercial contracts in the European Union.

---

[106] See Wielsch (2014), p. 384, 'principles underlying 'the CESL therefore requires a broader understanding that reaches beyond principles expressly stated in the Articles 1–3 CESL. For restrictive interpretation, see Yehuda Adar (2013), p. 32.

Even though the European Union at this moment faces existential challenges, the analysis of the three common European projects shows that the European Union and the legal scholars as well as professional contributors to the above stated frameworks accept and understand the position of other than just mercantile values in contracts. The legal scholars and contributors coming from individual Member States perceive values for respect of human rights, solidarity and social responsibility as a part of further conceptualization of the EU contract law. Even though the frameworks have not been adopted, they clearly indicate the respect for CSR values. Thus, I believe once the EU will decide to strengthen the common market and the trade of goods and services and adopt a binding legal tool, these values will form a part of it, as they do in the DCFR or CESL.

The rationales for devotion to European contract law harmonization are multiple and diverse. Direct reference to respect of fundamental rights in CESL and the DCFR, and interpretation of the implied terms and pre-contractual statements in light of European Union law is of a great importance and extremely important step for the contract law in the European Union. It is essential to remember that one part of the identity of the European Union, beside purely an economic union, is a space for protection of fundamental (including human) rights. The European Union law, with all its directives and regulations, is a legal order shaped by fundamental rights.[107] Through direct reference and inclusion of CSR values as part of common contractual frameworks and later on cross-border contracts, these values will further contribute to adoption and better understanding of CSR values within European contract law. As such they will transcend into national private laws and thus common practice within the European Union would be created. The values would converge gradually as a result of Europeanisation and common practice within the European Union.[108]

7 Conclusion

In the eighteenth century, contractual obligations arose not solely from an agreement, but from implied community standards of behaviour.[109] In the nineteenth and twentieth century, it was the furtherance of individual freedoms and the development of market economy that contributed to the more simple access to the contractual principles, reflecting community standards. These pertain even until today, as the nature of doing business and ways of contracting differ from nation to nation or

[107] For many decades the EU law has been supplemented by fundamental rights developed judicially by the CJEU in a case law that draws on the constitutional tradition common to the Member States as well as international legal tools for the protection of human rights, namely the European Convention on Human Rights. The regard for the human rights in the EU has been also codified in all of the Treaties since the Treaties of Maastricht. Currently, the Treaty on European Union, in Article 2 reaffirms the central role of fundamental rights among the values the EU is founded on.

[108] Lando (2000), p. 361.

[109] Ibid. p. 831.

even region to region. Stefano Rodotà also observed the great importance of the civil codes in Europe, as having 'played an essential role in the development of the national State, representing the real Constitution of civil society'.[110] Irrespective of whether it is the civil codes in civilian jurisdictions or the jurisprudence in common law jurisdictions, they both embody norms of behaviour with a moral as well as an empirical character that can be restated as a legal principle to direct the courts in the resolution of disputes.[111]

Law as a legitimate ideology and as an expression of legal consciousness recognizes that contract law in society has different functions. A powerful function of contract law is to present a system of belief, which affirms the legitimacy of the existing social order. We observe more and more an endeavour from different groups towards harmonisation, unification or some other form of codification. The broad application of codes with directly stipulated legal principles has substituted the various original theories with the objective of easing the practice as well as understanding of contract law. The common legal frameworks by implementing and introducing the relevance of additional values and fundamental principles that mirror the recognized pillars of the CSR principles shape the economic affairs. As shown by the development of the frameworks' reflection on values and fundamental principles, it is evident that there is growing consideration for CSR values.

Unfortunately, none of the discussed three frameworks has been substantially successful. They have lacked political support in order to effectively shape the contractual relationships in the European Union. Nevertheless, the development for CSR considerations and placement of human rights protection is undisputable and it reflects also the position of human rights protection in the Union *acquis*, realizing that also contractual parties within the relationship are bound to not only respect, but also protect these values. Values entail the correlation with ideals, prosperity of society as well as a determined activity towards the protection of them. They are derived from the most respected international declarations and thus serve as the highest ideals that have been proclaimed to support the affluence of the entire society. It seems natural that they should be protected also by private parties, be it an international corporation or an individual entrepreneur.

In conclusion, the inclusion of CSR values to the contract law in the European Union Member States could contribute to building a closer social and political Union complementing the economic cooperation of the Member States by increasing the relevance and reference to the values that should be common for all contracting parties across the Union. The future of commercial contracts goes hand in hand with the development of the contract law that should reflect on the development of the society. Development of the society is a far more complex process than simple economic growth. It involves economic, social, environmental, political and legal considerations. These have to be taken into consideration as we speak about the development of contract law and its future.

---

[110] Rodotà (2006), p. 118.

[111] Feinman (1983), p. 837.

References

Alpa G (2004) Harmonisation of contract law and the plan for a European civil code. Eur Bus Law Rev 15:33–40
Amao O (2011) Corporate social responsibility, human rights and the law. Routledge, Abingdon
Basedow J (2008) Freedom of contract in the European Union. Eur Rev Priv Law 6:901–923
Beatson J, Friedman D (1997) Introduction: from 'classical' to modern contract law. In: Good faith and fault in contract law. Oxford University Press, Oxford. https://doi.org/10.1093/acprof:oso/9780198265788.003.0001
Busch C (2016) Identification of gaps and gap-filling under the Common European Sales Law - a model for uniform law instruments? In: Ciacchi AC (ed) Contents and effects of contracts - lessons to learn from the Common European Sales Law. Springer, Dordrecht
Cafaggi F (2013) From a status to a transaction-based approach? Institutional design in European contract law. Common Mark Law Rev 50:311–330
Cohen RM (1933) The basis of contract. Harv Law Rev 46:553–592
Craig P, De Búrca G (2015) EU law: text, cases and materials, 6th edn. Oxford University Press, Oxford
European Commission (2003) Communication from the Commission to the European Parliament and the Council: a more coherent European contract law - an action plan, COM (2003) 68 final
European Commission (2004) European Contract Law and the revision often acquis: the way forward, COM (2004) 651 final
Fannon IL (2003) Working within two kinds of capitalism: corporate governance and employee stakeholding: US and EU perspectives. Hart Publishing, Oxford
Farnsworth AE (2006) Comparative contract law. In: Mathias R, Reinhard Z, Farnsworth EA (eds) The Oxford handbook of comparative law. Oxford University Press, Oxford. https://doi.org/10.1093/oxfordhb/9780199296064.013.0029
Feinman MJ (1983) Critical approaches to contract law. UCLA Law Rev 30:829–860
Fried C (2015) Contract as promise: a theory of contractual obligation, 2nd edn. Oxford University Press, Oxford
Friedman M (1963) The social responsibility of business is to increase its profits. The New York Times Magazine
Friedman ML (1965) Contract law in America: a social and economic case study. University of Wisconsin Press, Madison
Fuller LL, Perdue WR (1936) The reliance interest in contract damages: 1. Yale Law J 46:52–96. https://doi.org/10.2307/791632
Gilmore G (1974) The death of contract. Ohio State University Press, Columbus
Gordley J (1993) The philosophical origins of modern contract doctrine. Oxford University Press, Oxford
Grundmann S (2005) European contract law(s) of what colour? Eur Rev Contract Law 2:184–210
Hans-Wolfgang Micklitz NR (2013) The commission proposal for a "Regulation on a Common European Sales Law (CESL)" - too broad or not broad enough? In: Moccia L (ed) The making of European private law: why, how, what, who. Verlag Dr. Otto Schmidt, Cologne
Henderson D (2001) Misguided virtue: false notions of corporate social responsibility. The Institute of Economic Affairs, Great Britain
Hesselink MW (2001) The principles of European contract law: some choices made by the Lando commission. Glob Jurist Front 1:1–68
Hesselink M (2009) The Common Frame of Reference as a source of European private law. Tulane Law Rev 83:919
Horst Eidenmüller NJ, Kieninger E-M, Wagner G, Zimmermann R (2012) The proposal for a regulation on a Common European Sales Law: deficits of the most recent textual layer of European contract law. Edinb Law Rev 16:301–357

Horwitz MJ (1974) The historical foundations of modern contract law. Harv Law Rev 87:917–956. https://doi.org/10.2307/1340045
Jacques Ghestin GG (1994) Traité de droit civile - Introduction générale, 4th edn. Libr. Gen de Droit et de Jurisprudence, Paris
Katz AW (2014) Economic foundations of contract law. In: Klass G, Letsas G, Saprai P (eds) Philosophical foundations of contract law. Oxford University Press, Oxford
Kennedy D (1997) A critique of adjudication: Fin de Siecle. Harvard University Press, Cambridge
Lambooy T (2014) Legal aspects of corporate social responsibility. Utrecht J Int Eur Law 30:1–6. https://doi.org/10.5334/ujiel.bz
Lando O (1998) The common core of European private law and the principles of European contract law. Hastings Int Comp Law Rev 21:809
Lando O (2000) Some features of the law of contract in the third Millenium. Scand Stud Law 40:343–402
Lurger B (2005) The future of European contract law between freedom of contract, social justice, and market rationality. Eur Rev Contract Law 1:442–468
Mak C (2008) The constitution of a Common Frame of Reference for European contract law. Eur Rev Contract Law 4:553–565
Mak C (2009) The constitutional momentum of European contract law. Eur Rev Priv Law 4:513–529
Murphy L (2014) The practice of promise and contract. In: Klass G, Letsas G, Saprai P (eds) Philosophical foundation of contract law. Oxford University Press, Oxford
Osborne H (1931) Definition of value. Philosophy 6:433–445
Penner JE (1996) Voluntary obligations and the scope of the law of contract. Legal Theory 2:325–357
Pollock F (1896) A first book of jurisprudence for students of the common law. Macmillan and Co., London
Powell JJ (1790) Essay upon the law of contracts and agreements X. P. Byrne, J. Moore, J. Rice and W. Jones, Dublin, Ireland
Riesenhuber K (2005) System and principles of EC contract law. Eur Rev Contract Law 3:297–322
Rodotà S (2006) The civil code within the European "constitutional process". In: Hesselink MW (ed) The politics of a European civil code. Luwer Law International, The Hague, p 115
Röttinger M (2006) Towards a European code Napoleón/ABGB/BGB? Recent EC activities for a European contract law. Eur Law J 12:807–827
Schulte-Nölke CBECH (2009) Principles, definitions and model rules of European private law. Sellier European Law Publishers GmbH, Munich
Schutter OD (2008) Corporate social responsibility European style. Eur Law J 14:203–236
Sherwin EL (1991) Law and equity in contract enforcement. Md Law Rev 50:253–315
Smith AS (2004) Contract theory. Oxford University Press, Oxford
Staudenmayer D (2002) The commission communication on European contract law: what future for European contract law? Eur Rev Priv Law 10:249–260
Stefan Vogenauer SW (2006) The harmonisation of European contract law: implications for European private laws, business and legal practice. Hart Publishing, Oxford
Tajti T (2014) Systemic and topical mapping of the relationship of the Draft Common Frame of Reference and arbitration
Verplanck GC (1825) An essay on the doctrine of contracts. The Lawbook Exchange, Ltd, Clark
Waddams S (2013) The Draft Common Frame of Reference in relation to English contract law. In: Devenney J, Kenny M (eds) The transformation of European private law: harmonisation, consolidation, codification or chaos? Cambridge University Press, Cambridge
Weatherill S (2004) European contract law: taking the heat out of questions of competence. Eur Bus Law Rev 15:23–32
Webb C (2014) Contract as fact and as reason. In: Klass G, Letsas G, Saprai P (eds) Philosophical foundations of contract law. Oxford University Press, Oxford

Wielsch D (2014) The function of fundamental rights in EU private law - perspectives for the Common European Sales Law. Eur Rev Contract Law 10:365–389
Williston S (1921) Freedom of contract. Cornell Law Q 6:365
Yehuda Adar PS (2013) Principles and rules in the emerging European contract law: from the PECL to the CESL, and beyond. Eur Rev Contract Law 9:1–37
Zimmermann R (1996) The law of obligations: Roman foundations of the civilian tradition. Oxford University Press, Oxford
Zimmermann R (2005) The new German law of obligations: historical and comparative perspectives. Oxford University Press, Oxford

Towards a Fairer Trading System for Micro and Small Businesses Post-Brexit? Comparative Aspects with Other Common Law Systems

Sara Hourani

Contents

S. Hourani (✉)
Law School, Middlesex University, London, UK
e-mail: S.Hourani@mdx.ac.uk

M. Heidemann, J. Lee (eds.), *The Future of the Commercial Contract in Scholarship and Law Reform*, https://doi.org/10.1007/978-3-319-95969-6_12

Abstract This chapter explores the position that the English legislature and courts would have on the issue of imposing unfair contract terms on Micro and Small Businesses (MSBs) in the post-Brexit era. The chapter looks into the extent that current applicable law and developments in English contract law offer protections for contractual trading with MSBs. In the presence of current legal gaps with regards to such protections that often lead to abuse by larger corporations there might be some solutions available in the current law to deal with the invalidation of unfair contract terms in Business to Business (B2B) transactions involving MSBs, however these still do not deal with the issue in its entirety and are also met with limitations. Given the uncertain developments on this matter after Brexit the chapter considers a brief comparative analysis with other common law jurisdictions on the issue as they might influence possible future reforms. The comparative analysis consists of examining the protections available on imposing unfair contract terms on small businesses in the Australian and the US legal systems. This chapter thereby analyses what possible solutions can be raised in dealing with this pressing issue after Brexit by considering these comparative results.

1 Introduction

According to a statement made by the Department for Business Innovation and Skills (now part of the Department for Business, Energy and Industrial Strategy) in 2015, micro and small businesses made up to 99% of businesses in the UK and had a combined turnover of £655 billion.[1] It has been reported since that the number of these enterprises has risen in 2016 to constitute over 99% of the UK private sector businesses.[2] Micro and small businesses (MSBs) therefore form part of the UK's economic backbone as they are one of the key contributors to the current economy. A micro entity is defined in Section 384A of the Companies Act 2006 as consisting of not more than ten employees and having not more than £632,000 in turnover. Whereas a small business is defined in Section 382 of the same Act as consisting of not more than 50 employees and having a turnover of not more than £10.2 million. For the purpose of this chapter, MSBs will also encompass Medium enterprises that are defined in Section 466 of the same Act as not consisting of more than 250 employees and having a turnover not exceeding £36 million net or £43.2 million gross. The importance of MSBs has been gaining momentum as in the age of the digitisation of commerce the number of such businesses is on the rise.[3]

[1] Call for Evidence on Protection of Small Businesses When Purchasing Goods and Services by the Department for Business Innovation and Skills.

[2] According to the Federation of Small Businesses (FSB) small businesses accounted for 99.3% of all private sector businesses at the start of 2016 and 99.9% were small or medium-sized (SMEs). More information available at https://www.fsb.org.uk/media-centre/small-business-statistics.

[3] See The Chartered Trading Standards Institute E-Commerce Crib Sheet for Local Authority Regulators of January 2017 https://www.tradingstandards.uk/media/documents/news--policy/lead-officer/e-commerce-crib-sheet-for-regulators-v-10.pdf.

Despite their important contribution to the economy, MSBs remain as weaker parties in commercial agreements with larger companies due to their weaker bargaining position that has an impact over the negotiations and performance of their business contracts. MSBs have been undergoing a number of commercial pressures that include the imposition of unfair contract terms into their agreements with larger corporations. Thus, unfair commercial practices such as late payments are being imposed as part of the contract or during the performance of the contract. Other abusive terms and practices that are being imposed on MSBs consist of terms that make it hard for a business to cancel a long-term contract, terms that commit the business to paying price increases and terms that require full payment in advance for goods or services among others.[4]

The main reasons behind the vulnerability of MSBs with regards to their larger business counterparts are the lack of time, expertise, information, sufficient capital for access to legal advice, experience and economic independence.[5] Moreover, the majority if not all unfair contract terms are imposed in standard form contracts with the MSBs which means that the MSB is not given a chance to negotiate the terms of the business agreement.[6] However, even if given a chance to negotiate contract terms MSBs would not have much room for negotiation due to the greater market power that the larger corporation has in comparison. This means that the position that MSBs have on the market then is similar to that of a consumer as a party who is worthy of more contractual protection.[7] The imposition of unfair contract terms on MSBs normally have detrimental effects as this can lead to capital constraints and even the closure of the business itself due to the emergence of cash flow problems.[8]

1.1 The Legal Issues with Unfair Contract Terms in B2B Contracts Involving MSBs

The legal dilemma currently faced by MSBs in the UK is that there is a legal gap for protections against the imposition of unfair contract terms upon them. The only available legal instrument that applies to such terms in Business to Business (B2B) contracts is the Unfair Contracts Terms Act (UCTA) 1977. However, the UCTA is limited in its scope of application as it only applies to exclusion and limitation of liability clauses that are deemed as unfair. There were suggestions for implementing

[4] See Schleper et al. (2017), p. 98 for case examples of the use of these contract terms.

[5] See Hesselink (2008), p. 32.

[6] See Van Loock (2014), p. 89.

[7] Dias Simões (2014), p. 19.

[8] According to a study carried out by the FSB half (52%) of small firms have been affected by unfair contract terms with suppliers, costing them nearly £4 billion in the last 3 years. Results available at http://www.fsb.org.uk/media-centre/press-releases/unfair-contract-terms-costing-small-firms-billions.

unfair contract terms protections for micro businesses by a UK Law Commission report of 2005,[9] but no further action was taken on the matter.

The concern for the protection of micro and smaller businesses as weaker parties in business transactions with larger corporations was voiced by the European Parliament and the European Commission in 2006.[10] Although no further action was taken by the European institutions on the issue, recital 13 of the Directive 2011/83/EU of the European Parliament and of the Council on consumer rights states that Member States are competent to apply the Directive to scopes beyond consumer rights. The Directive suggests that Member States have the liberty of choosing to apply the rules of the Directive to legal persons or natural persons such as start-ups or SMEs.[11] However, the UK did not adopt this suggestion and there remains a legal gap with regards to the protection of MSBs against unfair contract terms. It will be seen nevertheless in Sect. 2.2.3 of this chapter that other European measures have been adopted to tackle certain aspects of this issue.

Given this legal gap, the Federation of Small Businesses (FSB) has called for improved protections for MSBs when buying goods and services.[12] The FSB has called for the Government and regulators of energy, financial services and telecoms to focus on small business vulnerabilities and suggested that Trading Standards[13] should also be given the power to take action against suppliers imposing unfair terms.[14] A call for evidence for purchasing goods and services by MSBs was made by the Government in 2015, but no further action was taken upon the issue so far with regards to unfair contract terms.[15]

Therefore, it remains clear that one of the issues in need of legal regulation concerns unfair contract terms imposed in B2B contracts where MSBs are involved. The rising importance of MSBs in the UK economy demonstrates the need for current legislation to keep up with the regulation of trade involving these smaller entities. The introduction of such reforms has been met with concern from the Government as it stated that MSBs do not only act within their quality as customers, but mainly as business suppliers which shows the difficulties in shaping legal protections for these smaller businesses.[16] Whilst it is true that MSBs are not

---

[9] See The Law Commission and the Scottish Law Commission (law com no 292) (scot law com no 199) (2005).

[10] See European Parliament (2005), pp. 109–112.

[11] Official Journal of the European Union L 304, 22 November 2011, 65.

[12] See Fletcher et al. (2014).

[13] Trading Standards offices are governmental authorities that have the duty to ensure consumer protection and support legitimate business activity.

[14] FSB press release on unfair contract terms costing small firms billions, available at https://www.fsb.org.uk/media-centre/press-releases/unfair-contract-terms-costing-small-firms-billions.

[15] See Call for Evidence on Protection of Small Businesses When Purchasing Goods and Services by the Department for Business Innovation and Skills.

[16] Ibid.

necessarily weaker parties in all business contexts, these entities still require further protection on the contractual front.[17]

1.2 Aims and Objectives of the Chapter

Given the trend of 'Europeanisation' that has introduced the application of notions of fairness in contracts as a result of the influence of EU law especially in the context of consumer contracts and the protection of weaker parties to the contract more generally, the question that ensues is what position the UK Government will have on the imposition of unfair contract terms on MSBs post-Brexit. This question is important as legal developments on this issue could have an important impact on the viability of small businesses and consequently on the economy as a whole. The arguments advanced in this chapter argue that an improved regulation of trade involving MSBs would encourage an increase in their creation which would lead to boosting trade and economic development.[18]

This chapter thereby aims to explore the position that the English legislator and courts would have on the issue of effectively imposing unfair contract terms on MSBs in the post-Brexit era. The discussion aims to analyse whether there are solutions to this issue as a result of the current legal developments in English contract law with regards to the protection of weaker parties to the contract. In this light, the chapter seeks to observe what position other common law systems such as Australia and the US have adopted on this particular matter given that they are also potential future trading partners with the UK that could eventually influence the development of English rules on contracts. This chapter consequently seeks to analyse what the future of unfair contract terms with MSBs in English law could be and what legal reform in the post-Brexit era could bring to the issue.

In order to answer these questions, the chapter will first examine in Sect. 2 the legal developments, the current applicable law and potential solutions to the use of unfair contract terms in B2B contracts with MSBs in English contract law. In Sect. 3, the chapter will carry out a comparative observation of the approach of the issue in the Australian and US legal systems. Finally, Sect. 4 will effect an analysis of the comparative results of this chapter's discussion in order to show a potential outcome that English law could have on the issue of unfair contract terms after Brexit.

[17] See Dias Simões (2014).

[18] A poll by the Forum of Private Business (FPB) has said the growth of UK SMEs is being undermined by spiralling costs of doing business, suffocating red tape and bullying tactics from big companies, available at http://www.howardworth.co.uk/red-tape-and-bullying-from-big-firms-continue-to-affect-smes-4453/.

2 The English Legal Framework on Unfair Contract Terms in B2B Contracts: Recent Developments, Current Law and Potential Solutions

2.1 *The Legal Developments on Unfair Contract Terms in B2B Contracts in English Law*

The most recent legislative initiatives that have been introduced for a more extensive policing of unfair contract terms in B2B contracts with MSBs include the Groceries Supply Code of Practice (GSCOP). Nonetheless, more transparency on payment methods used by larger companies has been imposed by the Small Business, Enterprise and Employment Act 2015. Also, the EU adopted Directive 2011/7/EU on combating late payment in commercial transactions in February 2011 that succeeded the 2000 late Payment Directive.[19] This legal instrument was transposed into English law through the Late Payment of Commercial Debts Regulations 2013. Although these last texts do not directly govern unfair contract terms, they do have as their objective to tackle the late payments problem which is normally an abusive term used in contracts with MSBs as mentioned at the beginning of this chapter.[20]

2.1.1 The Groceries Supply Code of Practice (GSCOP)

The Groceries Supply Code of Practice (GSCOP) came into force in February 2010 to replace the Supermarkets Code of Practice. The GSCOP was created as a result of a recommendation by the UK Competition Commission due to the inefficiency of its predecessor. It is a commercial code of practice and does not have a legislative value, however, it is true that the role of the Grocery Adjudicator increases its enforcement value.

The Supermarkets Code of Practice was first suggested by the Competition Commission as the outcome of an inquiry conducted by the Commission.[21] The inquiry found that supermarkets were acting contrary to public interest by reducing the choice and quality of goods. The inquiry was started as a request by the Office of Fair Trading (OFT) after a number of complaints for abusive behaviour by supermarkets was filed by suppliers. The OFT thereafter introduced the Supermarkets Code of Practice to deal with the abusive behaviour of supermarkets with regards to the suppliers in 2002.

The Supermarkets Code of Practice applied to supermarkets that benefited from at least 8% of grocery purchases which in fact consisted of the UK supermarket chains

---

[19] Directive 2000/35/EC of the European Parliament and of the Council of 29 June 2000 on combatting late payment in commercial transactions.

[20] See Sect. 1 of this chapter.

[21] Shears (2013), p. 60.

of Asda, Safeway, Sainsbury and Tesco. The Code of Practice applied to contracts that these major supermarkets concluded with suppliers. In trying to control unfair contract terms and practices the Supermarkets Code of Practice imposed a number of principles that needed to be respected by the supermarkets in question. The Code stated that there would not be undue delay in payments, that there would be no retrospective reduction in price without reasonable notice, and that a supermarket should not directly or indirectly require a supplier to reduce the agreed price of or increase the agreed discount without reasonable notice among other provisions. If a claim of breach of any of the provisions of the Code ensued, the parties necessitated to first attempt to resolve the matter themselves. If this was to fail then the parties had to go through mediation, and if that failed again then the case could have been advanced to the OFT's Director General either by the supplier itself or by their trade body.

However, as part of an independent audit in 2005, it was shown that supermarkets did not change their abusive practices therefore demonstrating the inefficiency of the Supermarkets Code of Practice. It appeared that the Code was being breached without any reports or claims being raised regarding the breach.[22] In its 2004 review of the efficiency of the Code, the OFT reported that the inequality of bargaining power between the MSB supplier and the supermarket meant that the supplier felt pressured not to make any claims unless there was hard evidence against the supermarket, which was very difficult to achieve given the context. Therefore, the Supermarkets Code of Practice had failed to control the imposition of unfair contract terms on the MSB grocery suppliers mainly due to the fear of the economic consequences of making a complaint.[23]

In 2008, the Competition Commission recommended to replace the above text with the GSCOP and to also establish a special adjudicating body to tackle complaints arising from the application of the GSCOP. The GSCOP applies to ten UK retailers who have a turnover in the groceries market that goes over one billion GBP. These retailers are Tesco, Asda, Sainsbury's, Morrisons, Waitrose, M&S, Aldi, Lidl, Iceland and the Co-op.[24] The Code applies to these retailers and their direct suppliers.[25]

The GSCOP introduced a somewhat revolutionary provision that governs the Code as a whole. This provision is the principle of fair dealing that is imposed under Section 2 of the Code and stipulates that:

> a Retailer must at all times deal with its Suppliers fairly and lawfully. Fair and lawful dealing will be understood as requiring the Retailer to conduct its trading relationships with Suppliers in good faith, without distinction between formal or informal arrangements, without duress and in recognition of the Suppliers' need for certainty as regards the risks and costs of trading, particularly in relation to production, delivery and payment issues.

---

[22] Ibid, p. 62.

[23] Ibid, pp. 62–63.

[24] The Groceries (Supply Chain Practices) Market Investigation Order, 2009, Schedule 2 available at http://webarchive.nationalarchives.gov.uk/20111108202701/http://competition-commission.org.uk/inquiries/ref2006/grocery/pdf/revised_gscop_order.pdf.

[25] Ibid, p. 63.

It can be argued that this provision imposes the obligation on the retailer not to impose terms that are contrary to ideals of good faith or fairness, which means that the retailer would not be able to impose terms that are deemed unfair.

This is considered to be a big step in protecting MSBs as there is generally a rejection to apply a general duty of good faith and fair dealing in English contract law,[26] especially in the context of B2B contracts. This general provision on the duty to act in accordance with standards of fairness specifically states that the retailers are not allowed to use undue commercial pressure on the suppliers who are normally MSBs to make them accept terms that are detrimental to them. This includes terms that affect the costing of goods and payment times.

To this effect, the following sections of the GSCOP provide a clear obligation for the retailer not to vary supply agreements retrospectively, to pay suppliers within a reasonable time, not to oblige suppliers to contribute to marketing costs, not to make them pay for shrinkage, not to put additional payments on the suppliers for better positioning of goods unless this is related to promotions, to provide compensation for forecasting errors, to take due care when ordering for promotions and there are limited circumstances for payments as a condition of being a supplier among other provisions.[27] The retailers that come under the application of the GSCOP are not allowed to enter into or perform a supply agreement unless the Code's standards are incorporated and that such agreements would not include any stipulations contrary to the Code's standards.[28]

The GSCOP is considered to be more successful than its predecessor due to the amelioration of the dispute resolution procedure that the parties, and more particularly the suppliers, can be benefit from. The GSCOP is accompanied by the Groceries Code Adjudicator Act 2013 which established the powers of the Code Adjudicator to be able to police the dispute arising from the application of the Code.[29] According to the Groceries Code Adjudicator Act 2013 the adjudicator has the power to arbitrate the dispute,[30] the Adjudicator can open investigations for suspected breaches of the GSCOP by a large retailer if there has been a complaint by a supplier,[31] and in cases where he finds that there has been breach by the retailer of the Code he has the power to make recommendations, publish information in the aim of naming and shaming the retailer in question and to impose fines.[32] In addition, in order to deal with the intimidation issue that suppliers felt under the Supermarkets Code of Practice, the Grocery Adjudicator can use evidence forwarded by third parties including whistleblowers and trade associations to carry out investigations against

[26] See Sect. 2.2.2 of this chapter.

[27] For a more extensive understanding of the provisions of the GSCOP see the GSCOP available at https://www.gov.uk/government/publications/groceries-supply-code-of-practice/groceries-supply-code-of-practice#no-delay-in-payments.

[28] Shears (2013), p. 63.

[29] Ibid.

[30] Section 2 of the Act.

[31] Section 4 of the Act.

[32] Section 6 of the Act.

retailers who have been accused of using unfair trading practices with their suppliers.[33] Also, the Adjudicator has the duty of confidentiality with regards to the identity of the complainant supplier in order to encourage suppliers to feel confident enough to file claims against breaches by the retailers.[34]

In sum, it can be argued that the GSCOP has further developed the controls over unfair contract terms in contracts with MSB suppliers in comparison to the Supermarkets Code of Practice. This is mainly through the fairness principle that is imposed throughout the GSCOP, but most importantly through the innovative dispute resolution procedure of the Groceries Adjudicator that allows for more MSB suppliers to be encouraged to file claims against retailers and the powers that the Adjudicator has in order to enforce the application of the GSCOP by the retailers. This new dispute resolution procedure has also allowed for a stronger enforcement of the Code and its application by the larger retailers in question.

Nevertheless, the GSCOP has limitations with regards to the advancement of the law on unfair contract terms in B2B contracts involving MSBs in English law as it only applies to grocery retailers and these retailers with a turnover in the groceries market of over one billion GBP.[35] Thus, for the retailers that do not cover the groceries sector, for grocery retailers who do not meet this threshold, or for larger businesses that are not retailers they would still be legally able to impose unfair contract terms on MSBs. Also, questions of the efficiency of the GSCOP ensue with regards to its efficacy as only a small number of claims have been raised for its breach by suppliers.[36]

2.1.2 The Small Business, Enterprise and Employment Act 2015: More Transparency on Payment Methods by Large Companies

In order to further tackle unfair practices suffered by MSBs as a result of their imposition by large businesses the Small Business, Enterprise and Employment Act 2015 was created. One of the areas covered by this Act includes the issue of late payments by these larger corporations. The Small Business, Enterprise and Employment Act 2015 was enacted in order to render the UK a more attractive place to start a business, particularly a small business, by aiming to reduce a number of market barriers that these small businesses face when trying to compete and grow on the market.

---

[33] See Schedule 2 of the Act.

[34] Section 18 of the Act; this has given some successful results as for example Tesco was named and shamed for its breach of the GSCOP for delays in payment as can be seen at https://www.gov.uk/government/news/tesco-breached-code.

[35] The GSCOP has been praised to be one of the most successful texts within the EU Member States for policing unfair contract terms in B2B contract as can be seen from the final report of 26 February 2014, prepared for the European Commission, DG internal market, DG MARKT/2012/049/E, on the study on the legal framework covering business-to-business unfair trading practices in the retail supply chain.

[36] See the retailers' GSCOP reports for 2014–2015 available at http://www.britishbrandsgroup.org.uk/upload/file/GSCOP%20retailer%20compliance%20report%202015-16.pdf.

The Act touches on a number of issues such as business payment practices and other issues dealing with transparency regarding corporate activities.

Concerning the business payment practices issue, Section 3 of the Act imposes on large companies the obligation to publish their payment practices and performance. This provision aims to put pressure on large businesses to make timely payments and avoid to impose late payment terms in their contracts, especially when dealing with MSBs. This obligation also has the objective to make large companies avoid any payment deductions that are seen as unfair. Although this provision adds more pressure on large businesses to be more transparent with their payment practices and performance, this does not add any sanctions for such unfair practices through which unfair contract terms are imposed on MSBs.

2.1.3 The Late Payment of Commercial Debts Regulations 2013

The Late Payment of Commercial Debts Regulations 2013 is the transposition of the EU Directive 2011/7/EU on combating late payment in commercial transactions. The Directive was developed with the idea of protecting SMEs from the abusive payment practices that larger companies impose on them as Article 1 of the Directive clearly explains. Article 7 of the Directive provides that contract terms or practices relating to late payment are considered to be unfair. Article 7 states that "Member States shall provide that a contractual term or a practice relating to the date or period for payment, the rate of interest for late payment or the compensation for recovery costs is either unenforceable or gives rise to a claim for damages if it is grossly unfair to the creditor."

The Directive also made a distinction between payments due by public authorities and those by private entities. It provides that public entities need to ensure payment is made within 30 days or in exceptional circumstances within 60 days.[37] Whereas private entities need to pay their invoices within 60 days unless otherwise agreed and provided that this would not be grossly unfair within the meaning of Article 7.[38]

In this light, the English transposition of the above Directive also imposes the same rules for payment terms with SMEs.[39] Section 2 subsection 5 of the Act adopted the fairness test and partly disposes that a contract term or practice on late payment is grossly unfair if the circumstances of the case show anything that is a gross deviation from good commercial practice and contrary to good faith and fair dealing. Therefore, it can be argued that the 2013 Regulations have managed to demonstrate that abusive contract terms and practices that impose late payment in the contract or its performance are considered to be unfair and would consequently not be applicable in English law. What is interesting in this amendment of the Late Payment of Commercial Debts (Interest) Act 1998 is that good faith and fair dealing

[37] Article 4 of the Directive.

[38] Article 3 of the Directive.

[39] See Section of the late payment of commercial debts regulations 2013.

are taken into account when determining whether a term or practice relating to late payment is legally valid or not. Moreover, although a company is allowed to pay within a delay that exceeds 60 days of the invoice if there is an agreement on this basis, this agreement is still subject to the fairness test of the Regulations.[40] The Regulations state that such terms would be invalid whether they are part of standard terms contracts or individually negotiated agreements.[41]

As it has been observed, English law has introduced a number of very much needed legal developments to further control unfair contract terms in B2B contracts especially those that affect MSBs. The GSCOP introduced more rigour in the application of its principles and code of conduct with MSBs in order to avoid the imposition of certain unfair contract terms on MSBs, the Small Business, Enterprise and Employment Act 2015 allows for more transparency with regards to the payment methods and practices that larger companies have with MSBs and the Late Payment of Commercial Debts Regulations 2013 impose a strict regime on rendering inapplicable unfair contract terms that touch on late payment.

2.2 *The Statutory and Common Law Mechanisms Applicable to Unfair Contract Terms in B2B Contracts in England*

2.2.1 The Unfair Contract Terms Act 1977

The Unfair Contract Terms Act 1977 (UCTA) was enacted by Parliament to deal with unfair contract terms, and more specifically to regulate unfair exemption and restriction of liability clauses for B2C and B2B contracts. It is the only legislative text that currently controls unfair contract terms for B2B contracts in English law. A term imposing an exclusion or limitation of liability is subject to the UCTA as well as the scrutiny of the incorporation and construction tests. The UCTA exercises direct control over the substance of the terms that it governs as opposed to applying a particular method in regulating unfair terms, as the incorporation test does.

The Act established some prohibitions in sections 2(1), 3, 6 and 7 under which the terms caught by them would be void. For example, section 6 prohibits the exclusion or restriction of liability with regard to implied terms relating to the transfer of a good title to the goods, compliance of the goods with their description, delivering goods of satisfactory quality and goods which are fit for the specific purpose communicated to the seller, and in cases of sale by sample, that the delivered goods correspond to the sample in consumer contracts.[42] Nevertheless, the same provision allows for the exclusion or limitation of liability in commercial contracts as long as it satisfies the requirement of reasonableness found in the Act. Moreover, other

[40] See Section 2(3C) of the Regulations.

[41] See Section 3(4) of the Regulations.

[42] These are the implied terms under Sections 12–15 of the UK Sale of Goods Act 1979.

provisions of the UCTA are also subject to a test of reasonableness in respect of which they refer to, thereby making this test key to the functioning of the Act.[43]

Section 11(1) of the UCTA disposes that:

> in relation to a contract term, the requirement of reasonableness…is that the term shall have been a fair and reasonable one to be included having regard to the circumstances which were, or ought reasonably to have been, known to or in the contemplation of the parties when the contract was made.

This test has a broad scope of interpretation as it refers to what the courts would assess as being fair and reasonable in relation to the terms concerned. Moreover, the test specifies that the term should also have been fair in being incorporated into the contract, which also implies that there should be some compliance with standards of fair dealing.

Notwithstanding the wide meaning of what could be perceived as being fair and reasonable, the UCTA and the courts have developed guidelines to help in indicating what would constitute a reasonable term in the sense of section 11. Schedule 2 of the UCTA provides that guidelines which should be taken into account are the bargaining positions of the parties, whether there were alternative means by which the customer's requirements could have been met, whether the customer received an inducement, whether the customer had an alternative choice of contracting with another business offering better terms, whether there was transparency of the term, whether compliance with an exclusion or restriction of liability at the time of the conclusion of the contract was practicable and whether the goods were manufactured, processed, or adapted to the special order of the customer.

The courts have also identified further indications used for assessing whether a contract term under the UCTA is reasonable. Thus, it has been concluded that it would be taken into account by the courts whether the task in respect of which liability is being exempted or limited is a particularly difficult one.[44] Moreover, the 'practical consequences' of the decision regarding the reasonableness of the term are considered broadly by the courts.[45] This means that the courts take into account the financial impacts upon the parties by deciding whether or not the term is reasonable, such as looking into whether there was any insurance available to cover the liability.[46] The courts also generally qualify terms as being unreasonable if they cover a wide scope of liabilities.[47] Finally, the term is usually concluded to be unreasonable if it excludes or restricts liability for fundamental breach.[48] These guidelines contribute to curtailing the wide scope of the reasonableness test. However, they are not exhaustive and still give discretion to the courts in assessing what is reasonable. Also, the guidelines in Schedule 2 of the Act are only applicable to the

---

[43] See McKendrick (2011), p. 205.

[44] *Smith v Eric S Bush* [1989] 2 All ER 514 at 531.

[45] Ibid.

[46] Willett (2007), paragraph 2.127.

[47] *Balmoral Group Ltd v Borealis (UK) Ltd* [2006] 2 Lloyds Rep. 629.

[48] Willett (2007), paragraph 2.127.

meaning of reasonableness in sections 6(3), 7(3) and (4), 20 and 21. Nevertheless, they still help in pinning down the meaning of reasonableness within the context of the UCTA, which could be seen as an English common law characteristic in dealing with general tests and standards of fairness and reasonableness.[49]

Other provisions of the UCTA which help in considering the reasonableness of an exemption or restriction of liability clause are sections 11(4), 13 and 17. Section 11(4) deals with limitation of liability clauses and specifies that regard should be given to the resources available to the person imposing the clause for meeting the potential liability, and whether it was possible for this party to cover himself by insurance in deciding the validity of the term. Section 13 applies to duty defining clauses and extends the scope of section 2 of the Act concerning the exemption or limitation of liability for negligence.[50] Section 17 provides more detail regarding which terms would be considered to be unreasonable. For example, in section 17(1)(b), it is stated that:

> any term of a contract which is a consumer contract or a standard form contract shall have no effect for the purpose of enabling a party to the contract in respect of a contractual obligation, to render no performance, or to render a performance substantially different from that which the consumer or customer reasonably expected from the contract, if it was not fair and reasonable to incorporate the term in the contract.

In consequence, it can be observed from the above analysis that the general test of reasonableness under the UCTA covers a wider number of exclusions and/or restrictions of liability clauses. Considering the limitations of the incorporation and construction tests, a general test of reasonableness would be applicable to a larger variety of unfair clauses. Therefore, it can be stated that this general test under the UCTA responds to the need for more flexibility, as the context and facts of exemption or limitation of liability clauses differ from one another. Nonetheless, the application of this general test is only confined to terms imposing an exclusion and/or limitation of liability subject to the UCTA. Thus, the UCTA alone does not provide further legal protections to MSBs against unfair contract terms that do not exclude or limit liability.[51]

2.2.2 The Incorporation and Construction Tests

There is no general principle of good faith that acts as an overriding duty in English contract law, which means that there is no obligation on the parties to the contract to take each other's interest into account when entering into or performing a contract. Albeit this is not necessarily true for consumer contracts anymore, it still applies as an underlying ethic to B2B contracts including those where MSBs are involved. This specific ethic is the adversarial position of the parties that English contract law is based upon whereby commercial parties to a contract are encouraged

[49] See McKendrick (2011), p. 198.

[50] Ibid.

[51] See Van Loock (2014), pp. 104–105 and pp. 128–131.

to have a 'cut-throat' approach to negotiating and performing contractual agreements. This means that parties do not have to take into account the legitimate interests or expectations of the other party.[52] Thus, the imposition of a duty of good faith on the parties would be incompatible with this position, where the parties would have to consider each other's contractual interests or expectations.

Historically there was no legal protection against the inclusion of unfair contract terms in English Law. However, the law started to develop a number of mechanisms to invalidate certain abusive contractual terms, specifically if they excluded or limited liability of one of the parties in an unfair manner. Two main mechanisms were developed by the courts to deal with these unfair clauses for both B2C and B2B contracts; the incorporation and the construction mechanisms.

Under the incorporation test the concerned terms would not be given any legal effect for they would have not been duly incorporated into the contract. However, the incorporation test only applies to unsigned documents.[53] In cases of signed documents or contracts, the purchaser is bound by his signature and the terms would not be assessed against the incorporation mechanism.[54] The notion 'unfair terms' for the purposes of the incorporation test is confined to the understanding of terms that impose unfair obligations or exclude or limit liability for important breaches that are not transparent to the buyer. Thus, according to the test, for a term to be valid it must have been validly incorporated into the contract. This means that the term or terms had to be reasonably brought to the attention of the buyer at or prior to the time of the conclusion of the contract.[55] Namely, the party imposing the terms must have done what was reasonably sufficient to draw the terms to the attention of the other party.[56] What is considered to be reasonable notice depends upon the facts and circumstances of each individual case.[57]

Notwithstanding, terms that are regarded as particularly onerous or unusual must be fairly and reasonably brought to the attention of the buyer as individual terms.[58] This was held in *Interfoto Picture Library Ltd v Stiletto Visual Programmes Ltd.*[59] On the facts of the case, the plaintiffs concluded a contract with the defendants for lending transparencies which were delivered with a note containing the conditions. Condition 2 stipulated that all the transparencies had to be delivered within 14 days of delivery, otherwise there would be a charge of a GBP 5 holding fee plus value added tax for each transparency retained by the defendants each day thereafter. The defendants had not read the conditions, as the plaintiffs had not drawn them to their

---

[52] Brownsword (1999), p. 15.

[53] See Wang (2015), p. 14.

[54] There are a number of limited exceptions to this rule, such as *non est factum* [this is not my deed]; See *l'Estrange v Graucob Ltd* [1934] 2 KB 394.

[55] McKendrick (2011), p. 158.

[56] See *Parker v South Eastern Railway* (1877) 2 CPD 416; Ibid, p. 159.

[57] McKendrick (2011), p. 159.

[58] Willett (2007), paragraph 2.111.

[59] [1989] QB 433.

attention. It was concluded by the court that where a penalty clause was out of step with market norms and was not brought to the special attention of the other party, it would not be incorporated into the contract.[60]

As it can be observed, the incorporation test has limitations regarding the scope of its application to unfair contract terms. Such limitations relate, for example, to the coverage of the test, as it does not apply to documents that have been already signed, and where unfair terms would apply to the contract in such situations. Also, this mechanism does not require that contracts are transparent in their entirety, meaning that they should be available, clearly formulated, in clear sized print, in plain intelligible language, and so on.[61] Furthermore, the incorporation test does not cover all types of unfair terms, as unfairness in the sense of the test is limited to what is not drawn to the reasonable attention of the buyer. In other words, if there is sufficient transparency of the term, the term would qualify as having been incorporated into the contract, and thereby as being fair in this context. Thus, in the face of these limitations, the law further developed other tests to deal with unfair contract terms.

The second test that was developed to be applied to a term in assessing its fairness is the construction of the term test. The construction test also implements requirements of a more general objective of fairness and of establishing fair terms in contracts. In doing so, it has a strict approach towards the construction of exemption clauses. In cases of ambiguity, exclusion or limitation of liability clauses are usually construed *contra proferentem* by the courts. This means that they would be interpreted against the party seeking to rely on them. Namely, the exemption clause has to cover the damage or relevant liability that is being invoked in question.[62] For example, in *Wallis, Son and Wells v Pratt and Haynes*,[63] the exemption clause stipulated that the sellers gave "no warranty express or implied" with regard to the description of the goods.[64] It was held by the court that the clause did not cover the breach as the clause only covered breaches of warranties, but not breaches of conditions as was the case in the circumstances of the dispute, since the description of the goods is a condition.

Therefore, the courts assess whether intent from the wording of the clause is:

> clear, unambiguous and incapable of misleading.[65]

Nevertheless, the strict construction of exclusion of liability terms has been criticised in *Photo Production Ltd v Securicor Transport Ltd*.[66] In this case, Lord Diplock stated that such an approach should not be applied to exemption clauses which are clear and unambiguous in terms of covering the breach in question. Thus,

---

[60] Also see *Thornton v Shoe Lane Parking Ltd* [1971] 2 QB 163; and *AEG (UK) Ltd v Logic Resources Ltd* [1996] CLC 265.

[61] Willett (2007), paragraph 2.111.

[62] Ibid, paragraph 2.112; McKendrick (2011), p. 189.

[63] [1911] AC 394.

[64] McKendrick (2011), p. 190.

[65] *Mannai Investment Co Ltd v Eagle Star Life Assurance Co Ltd* [1997] 3 All ER 352 at 377.

[66] [1980] AC 827.

it is not an absolute that exemption clauses would necessarily be strictly construed in such a manner as to not give legal effect to the exclusion of liability concerned.

Also, there are limitations to this test in terms of rendering inapplicable terms that are deemed to be unfair. An illustration of this is where the term in question covers fundamental breach or an exemption of an important liability in a clear and unequivocal manner.[67] According to the construction method, such a term could still be qualified as applicable, and thereafter as fair due to the lack of ambiguity in reading it. However, the law on controlling unfair contract terms for both B2C and B2B contracts further developed and the standards set by statutes circumvent the limitations posed by the incorporation and construction of terms tests.

2.2.3 Other Common Law Solutions

In the absence of a more extensive legal framework to protect MSBs from unfair contract terms that do not fall under the scope of the UCTA and the other common law mechanisms for controlling such terms under English law, economic duress is a mechanism that already exists in the current law and that can be applied to controlling such terms. Economic duress is one of the tools used by the English courts in order to set aside a contract in cases of extreme imbalance or unfairness affecting the contract.

Economic duress is a type of duress which ensues when one party to the contract uses their superior economic power in an illegitimate manner in order to pressure the other party to accept certain terms that are to their financial detriment.[68] Economic duress was first recognised by Kerr J in *Occidental Worldwide Investment Corporation v Skibs A/S Avanti (The Siboen and the Sibotre)*.[69] Case law has been in constant development on the question of assessing the elements that compose economic duress.[70] More recently, it was established in *R v A-G for England and Wales*[71] that the wrong of duress consists of two elements; pressure amounting to compulsion of the will of the victim and the illegitimacy of the pressure.

Therefore, according to this statement, duress controls and regulates problems of fairness with regard to lack of free consent and illegitimate pressure to contract. In addition, the pressure must have been sufficient to have induced the party to enter into the contract, and there must have been a lack of an alternative choice or course of action for the victim.[72] Henceforth, it is important to establish a causal link between pressure used by the defendant and the consent given by the claimant to conclude or renegotiate the contract in order to establish duress.[73]

[67] Willett (2007), paragraph 2.112.

[68] McKendrick (2015), p. 294.

[69] [1976] 1 Lloyd's Rep 293.

[70] See McKendrick (2010), p. 636.

[71] [2003] UKPC 22.

[72] See Treitel (2011), p. 445, paragraph 10-009.

[73] McKendrick (2010), p. 636.

The illegitimacy of the pressure concerned in cases of economic duress is assessed according to the nature of the pressure and the nature of the demand which the pressure applied is to support.[74] In line with this assessment, on one hand, if the threat from the pressure is unlawful, this would give rise to duress.[75] On the other hand, in circumstances where the threat is lawful but is used to support an unlawful demand, it may amount to duress.[76] Notwithstanding, cases of threatened breach of contract are particularly problematic, as it is not always clear whether such threats are lawful or not, thereby leading to duress. In this context, the issue arises of how the courts should decide in which situations the party is entitled to make such threats, as these could be part of the normal cut and thrust of commercial practice. It was held in *North Ocean Shipping Co Ltd v Hyundai Construction Co Ltd (The Atlantic Baron)*[77] that pressure exerted under the form of a threatened breach of contract would amount to economic duress.

Moreover, it has been suggested by some scholars that there has to be an element of bad faith in order to determine whether the pressure is unlawful.[78] Thereafter, a threat to breach a contract encompassing bad faith is likely to affect the consent of the other party and to constitute economic duress.[79] This would mean that economic duress can be used as a tool to prevent the larger corporations from pressuring the MSB into accepting contract terms that are deemed as unfair or that would be very detrimental to them. However, there needs to be a threat to breach the contract by the larger corporation or an illegitimate form of pressure for the MSB to accept the problematic terms for economic duress to apply. This can limit the possibility of invalidating the unfair terms in question on the basis of duress if the pressure is not considered to be illegitimate, or that the demand to impose the terms upon the claimant is seen to be lawful by the courts. Namely, there is no established understanding of what illegitimate pressure means in a commercial context. This adds more uncertainty regarding whether economic duress can be considered as an adequate tool to control unfair contract terms imposed on MSBs.

Despite the advancements in the law to deal with the issue of unfair contract terms imposed on MSBs, there are still gaps as these legal developments do not cover all MSBs or unfair contract terms. For example, the Late Payment of Commercial Debts Regulations 2013 has a robust system for dealing with terms relating to late payments but are only limited in their application to these terms. In light of this legal lacuna in English law, the question arises as to whether there is a solution that currently lies in the mechanisms and developments of English contract law to deal with this issue. In answering this question, the next sub-section will discuss the whether there are any such solutions, even if partial, to further protect MSBs from these terms.

---

[74] This was stated by Lord Hoffmann *in R v A-G for England and Wales* [2003] UKPC 22 at 16.

[75] McKendrick (2011), p. 298.

[76] Ibid.

[77] [1979] QB 705.

[78] See Burrows (2010) in McKendrick (2011), p. 299.

[79] See McKendrick (2011), p. 299.

2.3 *Potential Solutions to the Unfair Contract Terms in B2B Contracts with MSBs Issue in the Current Law in England?*

The question that this discussion is raising is whether it would be possible to use contract interpretation for invalidating unfair contract terms or at least for limiting their effect by protecting the parties' expectations to the contract and taking into consideration their respective bargaining positions with each other. It has been observed in Sect. 2.2.2 of this chapter that English law has already developed the contract construction test by using the *contra proferentem* approach for the courts to determine whether an exclusion or limitation of liability clause is unfair or not. However, the limitation of this test is that it only applies to exclusion and limitation of liability contract terms. So the question would be whether it would be possible to extend this test beyond these specific terms to other terms that do not exclude or limit liability but that are deemed as unfair by applying the more general tool of contract construction to these.

Contract interpretation is used as a tool in English law in cases of conflict over the performance of the contract as a whole or a specific clause in the contract.[80] In such cases, the clause would normally be ambiguous or unclear thus requiring an objective interpretation given by the courts made from the stand point of a reasonable person. Consequently, it can be argued that in cases of ambiguity or lack of clarity surrounding certain clauses that are deemed as unfair by one of the parties there is the possibility for that party to approach the courts in order to interpret the clause in question.

There has been more flexibility introduced into this mechanism in recent years as the courts started accepting to take into account other aspects surrounding the contract such as the context of the conclusion and performance of the agreement by the parties.[81] The traditional approach consisted of the traditional four corners rule where the courts would only be able to abide by the four corners of the contract to interpret it without having the possibility to have recourse to other information in order to interpret the clause or contract in question.[82] The move towards a more contextual approach in contract interpretation was seen in the case of *Investors Compensation Scheme v West Bromwich Building Society*[83] where Lord Hoffmann held that:

> interpretation is the ascertainment of the meaning which the document would convey to a reasonable person having all the background knowledge which would reasonably have been available to the parties in the situation in which they were at the time of the contract.[84]

---

[80] See Beale (2009), Chapter 13, Section 3.

[81] See Hooley (2013), pp. 65–90.

[82] See *Lovell and Christmas Ltd v Wall* (1911) 104 LT 85.

[83] [1997] C.L.C. 1243.

[84] Ibid.

Lord Hoffmann placed an emphasis on the importance of the background information to the contract when interpreting it. This case is considered to have played a key role in the shift of the doctrinal development from a traditional towards a contextual approach in contract interpretation.[85]

This development continued through other major cases such as *Rainy Sky S.A. v Kookmin Bank*[86] where the court held that it is important to take context into account when interpreting a contract, especially in cases of commercial contracts. In this case special significance was placed on interpreting the contract according to its commercial context and business common sense.[87] It was stated by the Supreme Court in *Rainy Sky* that it is important to give the contract an interpretation that is in line with its business common sense in order to better reflect the parties' expectations from the agreement. Furthermore, the developments in contract interpretation saw their peak in the High Court case of *Yam Seng Pte Ltd v International Trade Corporation Ltd.*[88] In this case, Justice Leggatt stated that good faith was an implied duty which governs the performance of the contract by the parties.[89] The judge discussed that the context of the contract would consist of taking into account the honesty and expectations of the parties when executing the contract.[90] Further, Justice Leggatt stated that a key aspect of good faith is the observance of generally accepted standards of commercial dealing.[91] Therefore, according to Justice Leggatt's reasoning the parties to a commercial contract would need to take into account each other's expectations in order to have a satisfactory performance of the contract.

These developments that have affected the mechanism of contract interpretation in English law can be used in situations where one of the parties, perhaps the MSB, is suffering from an imposition of an unfair contract term by its larger counterpart. The context of the parties' bargaining positions can be taken into account by the courts when assessing how to interpret the disputed term in question. Also, with regards to interpreting the context of commercial agreements in accordance with business common sense, unfair commercial practices which are found in contract terms can be interpreted in such a way as to not affect the MSB party to its detriment. It has been observed in Sect. 2.1 of this chapter that certain practices and contract terms that impose a change in the payment terms or late payment are considered to be unfair even in a commercial context. Since these have already been recognised as unfair commercial practices and terms by the legal instruments discussed in Sect. 2.1, then the courts already have legal sources indicating what contract terms are considered to be as contrary to business common sense which

[85] Brownsword (2015), p. 533; McKendrick (2016), p. 377.

[86] [2011] UKSC 50.

[87] Ibid at paragraph 40.

[88] [2013] EWHC 111 (QB).

[89] See ibid at paragraph 153.

[90] Ibid at paragraphs 141 and 142.

[91] Ibid at paragraph 138.

requires a stricter interpretation of these terms. Moreover, when interpreting the disputed contractual term according to this developed logic of contract interpretation in English law, the courts need to ensure that the expectations of both parties are reflected. This means that contract terms that have been imposed on the MSB party in a way that does not reflect their expectations should be interpreted in a way that it should, which might lead to minimising the effects of the unfair contract term in question.

For example, this logic can be applied in a situation where a contract term is ambiguous with regards to payment to the MSB which can potentially lead to payment changes or late payment. If the above logic of contract interpretation is applied, then this contract term can be interpreted in favour of the MSB by taking into account all of the above factors and thereby reducing the effect of the unfair contract term in that specific circumstance.

Although contract interpretation could be a potential solution for tackling unfair contract terms in B2B contracts with MSBs, this method does carry a number of limitations that affects its effectiveness to generally control such terms. First, this method would only apply to cases where the contractual clause is unclear or ambiguous to necessitate its interpretation by a third party adjudicator. Second, contract interpretation might lessen the effect of the clause in question or interpret it in a way that might not be too detrimental to the parties, however, the courts might not have the power to invalidate it.

Third, the English courts are normally reticent to interfere with the freedom of contract that parties dispose of especially in the context of commercial contracts.[92] In the need to promote certainty in commercial dealings, the courts are normally quite discouraged to interpret the contract in a way that would lead to rectification rather than interpretation. The recent Supreme Court case of *Arnold v Britton*[93] held that the contract needs to be construed in a manner that gives importance to the language used by the parties.[94] This means that the Supreme Court might set back the trend of applying a more traditional approach in contract interpretation rather than allocate a meaning to the contract term that takes other factors into account.[95] Protecting the parties' reasonable expectations through contract interpretation has also been criticised for being elusive and vague which endangers the certainty of the agreement.[96]

Further, the case of *Yam Seng Pte Ltd v International Trade Corporation Ltd* was not very well received as there has been a lot of criticism against it mainly for the reason that there is no general duty of good faith that applies in English law, especially in a commercial context.[97] This criticism has however been confirmed in the recent Court of Appeal case of *MSC Mediterranean Shipping Company SA v*

---

[92] See Van Loock (2014), p. 130; Lawson (2005).

[93] [2015] UKSC 36.

[94] Ibid at paragraph 19.

[95] Also see *Marks and Spencer plc v BNP Paribas Securities Services Trust Company (Jersey) Ltd* [2015] UKSC 72 and *Wood v Capita Insurance Services Ltd* [2017] UKSC 24 on this point.

[96] See Barnes (2011), p. 197.

[97] See for example Carter and Courtney (2016), pp. 608–619.

Cottonex Anstalt[98] where it was stated that there is a preference for the law to develop along established lines rather than apply a general organising principle.[99] The court added that establishing and applying a general principle of good faith would undermine the certainty that parties have to the contract.[100] Fourth, there is no protection against inequality of bargaining power in English law as there is no legal principle of unconscionability in its law of contracts. There have been a number of objections against the inclusion of such a doctrine in English law that is mainly based on the importance of certainty of contract and the adversarial position of the parties to a commercial agreement.[101]

As it has been observed so far in the English legal system, there are gaps in the law in dealing with the issue of protecting MSBs against unfair contract terms. The question that ensues is to what extent Brexit will have an impact over developments on this matter as the influence of EU law will cease. In this context, it would be important to understand how other common law jurisdictions deal with this issue and whether there are any legal developments in those systems to control unfair contract terms with MSBs. It can be argued that it would be important to observe the position that other common law systems have on the issue outside a European influence, as 51% of cases on contracts in England refer to other legal systems, and more particularly, they refer to common law systems.[102] Thus, the next section will discuss this issue in the Australian and US legal systems.

3 A Comparative Observation of Unfair Contract Terms in B2B Contracts with MSBs in Other Common Law Systems: The Australian and US Examples

3.1 Legal Developments on the Issue of Unfair Contract Terms with MSBs in Australian Law

Australian law has very recently introduced a legislative text for protecting small businesses against unfair contract terms in B2B contracts with larger corporations. The Treasury Legislation Amendment (Small Businesses and Unfair Contract Terms) Act 2015 came into force on 12 November 2016. This Act is an extension to the current protections against unfair contract terms in consumer contracts. The Australian Productivity Commission first recommended the inclusion of legislative protections against unfair contract terms for both consumer contracts and contracts

98 [2016] EWCA Civ 789.

99 Ibid at paragraph 45.

100 Ibid.

101 McKendrick (2015), pp. 306–307.

102 Burrows (2014).

with small businesses in a report in 2008.[103] This report was mainly inspired by the laws on unfair contracts with consumers in the State of Victoria, but also as a result of the implementation of similar laws in the UK through the Unfair Terms in Consumer Contracts Regulations 1999.[104] However, even though the draft legislation on unfair contract terms was to apply to both consumers and small businesses, the final draft only imposed such protections for consumer contracts.[105] Due to the recognition of need to protect small businesses in a contractual context though, the Australian Competition and Consumer Commission (ACCC) suggested to extend the protections for unfair contract terms to small businesses.[106]

The main reasons for this extension consisted in the fact that small businesses were recognised to have a weaker bargaining position in comparison to their larger counterparts which created a power imbalance from a contractual perspective.[107] This is due to the use of standard form contracts in most cases with small businesses which means that they do not have a chance to negotiate the contract in actuality and that their consent to the contract is not secured or protected by the law.[108] Also, the Australian Treasury consultation paper on the proposed new legislation for small businesses cited US research that stated that only around 4% of survey participants who were small businesses reported reading standard form contracts.[109] This was stated to be due to having less access to information and advice as well as having less experience which puts small businesses in a vulnerable position when entering into agreements with larger businesses.[110] The new Treasury Legislation Amendment (Small Businesses and Unfair Contract Terms) Act 2015 thereby reformed the Australian Consumer Law as the new rights of the small businesses have been added and both work in tandem.

The new 2015 Act applies to standard form contracts that are entered into with a small business. A small business is referred to as one consisting of less than 20 employees according to Section 12BF of the Act. Although there is no specific definition in the legislation of what standard form contracts are, they are known to be 'take it or leave it' contracts whereby the party accepting it would only adhere to accept it without having the possibility to negotiate any of the terms involved.[111] The Australian Consumer Law adds some explanations of what standard form contracts are such as whether one of the parties has all the bargaining power or whether the contract was negotiated by both parties in Section 27 without adding a specific defi-

---

[103] Phillips (2016), p. 343.

[104] Australian Treasury (2009) The Australian consumer law: consultation on draft provisions on unfair contract terms. Canberra: commonwealth of Australia.

[105] See Van Esch (2015), p. 93.

[106] Phillips (2016), p. 343.

[107] See Consumer Affairs Australia, and New Zealand (CAANZ), Treasury, Implementation of the Australian consumer law, Report on Progress IV.

[108] Phillips (2016), p. 345. Also see Simons and Geer (2014), p. 433; Casson (2016), p. 76.

[109] Australian Treasury (2014) Extending unfair contract term protections to small businesses: consultation paper. Canberra: commonwealth of Australia, p. 9.

[110] See Phillips (2016), p. 345.

[111] See Casson (2016), p. 76.

nition of what these are. The contract concluded with the small business needs to also cover a certain threshold with regards to the amount of money it covers. Section 12BF of the Treasury Legislation Amendment (Small Businesses and Unfair Contract Terms) Act 2015 provides that contracts with small businesses that have an upfront contract price of AUD 300,000 or less, or AUD 1,000,000 or less where the term of the contract is for more than 12 months are covered under the new Act.

A contract term is considered as unfair in the sense of the new Act and the Australian Consumer Law if it causes a significant imbalance in the parties' rights and obligations in the contract, if it is not reasonably necessary to protect the legitimate interests of the party who would be advantaged by the term and if it would cause detriment to a party if it were to be applied or relied on.[112] In determining whether a term is unfair the courts could also take into account the extent to which the term is transparent and the sense of the contract as a whole.[113] A non-exhaustive list is also provided by the Australian Consumer Law, which also extends in its application to contracts concluded with small businesses now, gives examples of what terms are considered to be unfair. For example, according to these legal texts, a term that avoids or limits performance of the contract by the party imposing the terms is unfair, or a term that varies the terms of the contract is also considered to be unfair, a term that varies the price payable under the contract without the right of the other party to terminate the contract is unfair too. It must be noted that the new Act covers unfair contract terms with small businesses when they acquire and supply goods and/or services.[114] This means that the new Act offers protections to small businesses when they enter into commercial agreements with other businesses. If a contract term is found to be unfair by the court then the remedy against this would to render it as void. Section 23 of the Australian Consumer Law and Section 12BF(2) of the new Act provide that the unfair term may be severed from the contract to the extent that the contract can be performed without it.[115]

The Australian legal system has been the first system globally to introduce such a specific protection for small businesses against unfair contract terms. The Treasury Legislation Amendment (Small Businesses and Unfair Contract Terms) Act 2015 blended with the Australian Consumer Law provide a fairness test for the courts to apply which is seen as a welcome step to the protection of vulnerable businesses. Now small businesses that fit within the definition of this legislation can benefit from such protections and perhaps reduce the issues that they were facing before the enactment of this text. However, the Act does come with its limitations for the protection of small businesses more generally. The protections afforded by the new legislation does not extend to MSBs that have more than 20 employees but are still vulnerable entities on the market. The legislation does not apply to individually negotiated contracts or terms which can be a gap that can be used by the larger

[112] See Section 24 of the Australian Consumer Law.

[113] Ibid.

[114] See Section 31 of ibid.

[115] See Casson (2016), p. 77.

companies to impose unfair contract terms on MSBs. The limitation of the application of the new protections with regards to the amount covered in the contract also acts as an obstacle towards a more general protection of all contracts that MSBs conclude with larger companies.

Definite progress has been made in Australian law with regards to the protection of MSBs against unfair contract terms nevertheless there are still numerous gaps as discussed in this section. In the absence of a legal framework to protect MSBs coming under these gaps, they have the possibility of pursue a case for unconscionable conduct.[116] However, this still remains as an uncertain solution to the issue of unfair contract terms imposed on more vulnerable commercial parties. This is the method that US law has developed in order to tackle such terms as will be discussed in the next subsection of this chapter.

3.2 *Tackling Unfair Contract Terms in B2B Contracts with MSBs in US Law Through the Doctrine of Unconscionability*

There is no explicit law on unfair contract terms in US law, however, unconscionability is a fundamental doctrine that is applied to protect parties to an agreement against unconscionable or unfair contract terms. The doctrine of unconscionability finds its roots in equity, however it only started being more widely used from the 1960s in the US.[117] The popularity of the doctrine led to its codification within the UCC and the US Restatement Second of Contracts. Prior to this codification, the courts had developed different legal devices to protect contracts from being affected by abusive behaviour, especially during the bargaining process.[118] The courts were using public policy and principles drawn from equity and tort to save the weaker party to the contract from unfair contractual bargains.[119] Namely, legal tools such as fraud, misrepresentation, duress and undue influence were developed by the courts in order to control these abuses but were still not sufficient to protect all abuses.[120] A contract was only policed by the courts if it was affected by these recognised abuses or if it was contrary to public policy. The courts were more reticent to apply notions of fairness to police the contract and widen their scope due to their application of the fundamental principles of certainty and freedom of contract.

However, with the increased use of standardised contracts in practice there was a rise in issues relating to the inequality of bargaining power between the parties to

---

[116] See Van Esch (2015), p. 93.

[117] See Mallor (1986–1987), p. 1065.

[118] Ibid, p. 1068.

[119] Swanson (2001), p. 361.

[120] Mallor (1986–1987), p. 1068.

the contract.[121] The consent of the weaker party to the contract was affected due to many obstacles such as not having sufficient power to negotiate the terms of the contract or not having sufficient time to revise and read the contract in its entirety.[122] These issues resulted in an initial legal response from the courts as they started controlling the imposition of unconscionable terms in these standardised contracts either through interpreting contracts against the party imposing the terms or rendering the contract as void due to lack of mutual consent and/or consideration.[123] In recognition of this legal gap, given the inadequacies in applying the classical doctrines and critical of the way that the courts handled unfair contract terms arising from the inequality of bargaining power between the parties to the contract, the drafters of the UCC included the doctrine of unconscionability in the code.[124] The main objective of the doctrine of unconscionability as incorporated into the UCC is to rectify abuses in standard form contracts and other contracts for the sale of goods too, and it applies to both consumer and commercial contracts.

This doctrine is incorporated within § 2-302 of the UCC and provides that:

> (1) If the court as a matter of law finds the contract or any clause of the contract to have been unconscionable at the time it was made the court may refuse to enforce the contract, or it may enforce the remainder of the contract without the unconscionable clause, or it may so limit the application of any unconscionable clause as to avoid any unconscionable result.

According to this provision, contracts or terms that are considered to be unconscionable by the courts are not applicable. Namely, the courts have the power to modify or withhold the enforcement of contracts that contain unfair contract terms.[125] Therefore, the UCC tackles unfair contract terms through their interpretation by the courts then rendering them as void. The courts tend to adopt a stricter approach when applying this provision to commercial contracts due to difficulties in assessing whether there is an unequal bargaining power between the parties.[126] However, there is a number of successful cases where a merchant invoked the presence of unconscionability in a contract.[127]

Despite the developments on protecting contracting parties against unfair contract terms in US law, there are a number of limitations that touch on the doctrine of unconscionability as it is currently codified within the UCC. One of the major weaknesses that affect the application of this doctrine relate to the lack of a definition of what unconscionability is.[128] Cases that preceded the codification of the UCC confirmed the equitable historical roots of the doctrine, but these do not help in

---

[121] Ibid, p. 1069.

[122] See ibid.

[123] Ibid, pp. 1069–1070.

[124] Nottage (1996), p. 258; Mallor (1986–1987), p. 1070.

[125] Mallor (1986–1987), p. 1070.

[126] DiMatteo and Rich (2005–2006), p. 1082 and see Nottage (1996), p. 258.

[127] Mallor (1986–1987), p. 1066.

[128] Ibid, p. 1070 and see Murray (2014), p. 264.

providing a modern meaning to the doctrine.[129] There is currently no direction given to the courts for how to apply this provision.[130] This why the manner in which this doctrine needs to be implemented by the courts has been the subject of major scholarly discussion.[131] This lack of guidance has resulted in difficulties with how to implement the doctrine in practice which eventually led to the adoption of different approaches in its application by the courts.

The courts started applying the doctrine by basing their reasoning on the procedural and substantive elements of unconscionability.[132] The case authority that established this is *Williams v Walker-Thomas Furniture Co*[133] and was later reinstated in a 2002 case which held that the courts must look for two factors when considering whether there is unconscionability; first, there must be unfairness in the formation of the contract and second, there must be a case of excessively disproportionate terms.[134] The first factor being the procedural element, and the second being the substantive element.[135] Nevertheless, one of the questions that the courts were faced with consisted of how they should apply the doctrine in cases where one factor is more overtly present and evident but the other is not.[136] This was questioned for example by the Arizona Supreme court where it held that a balancing approach between both factors needs to be applied in order to establish whether there is unconscionability present in a contract.[137] This court also stated that some courts held that establishing either of these factors would be sufficient to hold a term as unconscionable.[138] Other courts have also emphasised the importance of the substantive ground in establishing whether there is unconscionability such as in the case of *Brower v Gateway 2000, Inc.*[139] However, there is still no clear position in theory and in practice on how to establish whether there is unconscionability.

Certain scholars have debated whether emphasis should be placed on the procedural aspect rather than on both factors to establish the presence of the abusive contract or clauses.[140] Certain scholars such as Professor Hillman also raised the question of whether unconscionability should apply to B2B contracts since merchants normally have the same bargaining power and can protect themselves against the imposition of abusive terms in the contract.[141] However, Hillman did admit that

---

[129] Swanson (2001), p. 361.

[130] See Nottage (1996), p. 258; DiMatteo and Rich (2005–2006), p. 1068.

[131] DiMatteo and Rich (2005–2006), p. 1068.

[132] Ibid, p. 1072.

[133] 350 F.2d 445 (D.C. Cir. 1965).

[134] *Sitogum Holdings, Inc*, 800 A.2d at 921.

[135] See Murray (2014), pp. 265–266.

[136] DiMatteo and Rich (2005–2006), p. 1073.

[137] *Maxwell v Fid. Fin. Sers., Inc*, 907 P2.d 51, 58 (Ariz. 1995).

[138] DiMatteo and Rich (2005–2006), p. 1074.

[139] 676 N.Y.S.2d 569 (N.Y. App. Div. 1998).

[140] See Hillman (1981) and Leff (1967).

[141] See Mallor (1986–1987).

there are exceptions to these cases where merchants share the same characteristics as those of consumers and the doctrine would have to then apply to these.[142]

Based on this observation, there is currently no clarity on the manner in which the application of the doctrine of unconscionability should be effected which also means that there is no clarity regarding the extent to which the doctrine can be applied to protect MSBs against unfair or unconscionable terms. This vagueness has meant that the doctrine is rarely invoked by the courts due to being seen as grossly interfering with the freedom of contract.[143] There was an attempt for the revision of the unconscionability provision in the UCC that had started in the 1980s and 1990s but it did not culminate in much change.[144]

What can be said though is that the courts did show their willingness to protect some of these in certain cases as already mentioned earlier in this section. Also, the discussions behind the attempted revision of Article 2 of the UCC on unconscionability showed an opposition towards the enforcement of a more protective application of the doctrine in favour of consumers alone.[145] Actually, the importance of the protection of business parties against such terms was emphasised.[146] In the meanwhile, courts are in the process of expanding this doctrine and including when it comes to its application to contracts with MSBs.[147] However, it still remains that not many cases are normally decided on the basis of unconscionability as courts cautiously apply it[148] due to the ambiguities surrounding it and due to not wanting to impede over established fundamental principles of contract law, especially in a commercial context, which puts MSBs at a certain risk of suffering from unfair contract terms.

After having carried out an analytical study of the issue of unfair contract terms imposed on MSBs in English law, Australian law and US law, the next section of this chapter will consider the comparative conclusions relevant to this analysis and to what extent MSBs will be granted protections against this problem in a post-Brexit era.

4 Comparative Conclusions on the Issue of Unfair Contract Terms with MSBs: What Next After Brexit?

As it has been mentioned throughout this chapter, the issue of having a legal gap with regards to protecting MSBs against unfair contract terms in English law is a pressing matter. The research conducted in this chapter has sought to analyse what

142 Ibid.

143 DiMatteo and Rich (2005–2006), p. 1072.

144 Swanson (2001), p. 372.

145 Ibid, p. 399.

146 Ibid.

147 See Posner (1995), p. 306.

148 Swanson (2001), p. 361.

the situation with regards to this matter is in other major common law jurisdictions, notably the Australian and US jurisdictions, in order to gain an understanding of whether there are any common trends that English law might share with them. This is particularly significant so as to get an understanding of potential directions that English legislation and courts could take on the issue after the UK leaves the European Union and EU law diminishes in its influence. As the issue of unfair contract terms imposed on MSBs in England is a pressing matter, it is important to further develop the law on this and not have this compromised after Brexit. This crucial need for protection stems from the concern that MSBs to have a sustainable economic growth.

From the analysis conducted in this chapter, it is clear that all three legal systems tend to protect MSBs against certain types of unfair contract terms. There is a trend to protect certain interests of smaller businesses at a contractual level albeit there are limitations to that. The common approach that the three legal systems use in dealing with unfair contract terms consists of having court control. The Australian and US legal systems have shown that they embraced legal developments on unfair contract terms to eventually protect smaller businesses through a favourable court attitude towards these protections. The English system has developed controls on unfair contract terms through the courts such as the common law mechanisms for dealing with these and other piecemeal solutions such as duress. Moreover, it has been raised in this chapter that contract interpretation by the courts can be used as a method for further controlling unfair contract terms affecting MSBs in English law. The second degree of similarity also lies between the English approach and Australian approach as both systems have adopted piecemeal solutions that specifically deal with controlling certain unfair contract terms affecting MSBs.

If a hard Brexit occurs in the sense that EU law would cease to have any influence and effect over English law, then all of the protections that have been advanced through EU law will diminish. This includes rules on late payment that have been seen as a development of the protection of MSBs against unfair contract terms through the EU Directive 2011/7/EU on combating late payment in commercial transactions as discussed in Sect. 2.2.3 of this chapter. This would also mean that the European *aquis* or the Europeanisation of English contract law which has introduced more extensive norms of fairness will cease to have any effect.[149] The Europeanisation of English law can be particularly seen in the development of consumer law and the standards of fairness that apply to consumers to protect them against unfair contract terms.[150] This influence had also started to extend beyond the consumer context as was seen in the case of Yam Seng v ITC mentioned above in Sect. 2.3.

Therefore, the results of this comparative analysis show that although contract interpretation by the courts can be used as a tool for further extending the protection of unfair contract terms for contracts with MSBs, English courts have demonstrated

149 See Twigg-Flesner (2013).

150 See Macmillan (2016), pp. 420–430 and for more extensive reading see Giliker (2015), pp. 237–265.

that they are more reticent in assessing these issues especially when it comes to B2B contracts as opposed to the Australian and US courts. Also, this reticence will only increase after Brexit as courts will probably go back to adhering to a more adversarial approach when applying principles of contract law and will be less keen on introducing more flexibility through notions of fairness to protect the weaker commercial party to an agreement. The most probable option for dealing with this issue in English law would be through specific rules or regulation. The Australian developments on unfair contract terms applying to small businesses seem like a good example that might eventually influence English law to adopt a similar text. Nevertheless, if the courts are reticent to support such protections, especially in the absence of European protections, this might create further difficulties to adopt such a legal instrument. Thereby, in the absence of a robust legal framework to protect MSBs against unfair contract terms, it might very well be the case that the UK courts and legislation would not adopt any protections for MSBs against such terms after Brexit.

What is yet to come will depend on the economic policies that the UK will be adopting post-Brexit, however, it is clear that there is great uncertainty looming over the fate of contractual protections afforded to MSBs in English law. What is certain though is that immediate legal reform is needed in order to deal with these legal discrepancies which only have a negative effect over the overall economy.

References

Australian Treasury (2009) The Australian consumer law: consultation on draft provisions on unfair contract terms. Canberra: Commonwealth of Australia. Available at: http://archive.treasury.gov.au/documents/1537/PDF/The_Australian_Consumer_Law_Consultation_Paper.pdf

Australian Treasury (2014) Extending unfair contract term protections to small businesses: consultation paper. Canberra: Commonwealth of Australia. Available at: https://www.treasury.gov.au/ConsultationsandReviews/Consultations/2014/~/media/E53165D4D8B24B4799395680E68FE0B0.ashx

Barnes R (2011) Commerciality and the construction of commercial contracts: some observations on the use of legal reasoning. In: Twigg-Flesner C, Puig GV (eds) Boundaries of commercial and trade law. Sellier, Munich

Beale H (ed) (2009) Chitty on contracts. Sweet & Maxwell, London

Brownsword R (1999) Positive, negative, neutral: the reception of good faith in english contract law. In: Brownsword R, Hird NJ, Howells G (eds) Good faith in contract: concept and context. Ashgate Publishing Limited, Aldershot

Brownsword R (2015) Smith & Thomas: a casebook on contract, 13th edn. Sweet & Maxwell/Thomson Reuters, London

Brownsword R, Hird NJ, Howells G (eds) (1999) Good faith in contract: concept and context. Ashgate Publishing Limited, Aldershot

Burrows A (2014) The influence of comparative law on the english law of obligations. Oxford Legal Studies Research Paper No. 31/2015. Available at: https://papers.ssrn.com/sol3/papers.cfm?abstract_id=2605921

Call for Evidence on Protection of Small Businesses When Purchasing Goods and Services by the Department for Business Innovation and Skills, March 2015. Available at: https://www.gov.uk/

government/uploads/system/uploads/attachment_data/file/433139/bis-15-209-protection-of-small-businesses-when-purchasing-goods-and-services-call-for-evidence.pdf
Carter JW, Courtney W (2016) Good faith in contracts: is there an implied promise to act honestly? Camb Law J 75(3):608–619
Casson J (2016) Small business and unfair contract terms: changes on the horizon. Law Soc NSW J (20):76
Commissions Act 1965 (Cm 6464 SE/2005/13)
Consumer Affairs Australia, and New Zealand (CAANZ), Treasury, Implementation of the Australian consumer law, Report on Progress IV (2013–2014), December 2014
Dias Simões F (2014) SMEs in the common European sales law. In: Loos M, Samoy I (eds) The position of small and medium-sized enterprises in European contract law. Intersentia, Cambridge
DiMatteo L, Rich B (2005–2006) A consent theory of unconscionability: an empirical study of law in action. Fla State Univ Law Rev 33:1067
Directive 2000/35/EC OF THE European Parliament and of the Council of 29 June 2000 on combatting late payment in commercial transactions. OJ L 2000, 200/35
European Parliament (2005) Resolution on European contract law and the revision of the acquis: the way forward (2005/2022 (INI)), Official Journal of the European Union, 1 December 2006
Fletcher A, Karatzas A, Kreutzmann-Gallasch A (2014) Small businesses as consumers: are they sufficiently well protected? A report for the Federation of Small Businesses. ESRC Centre for Competition Policy, Norwich
Giliker P (2015) The influence of EU and European human rights law on English private law. Int Comp Law Q 64:237–265
Hesselink M (2008) The values underlying the draft common frame of reference: what role for fairness and 'social justice'? (Study; No. PE 408.312). European Parliament, Directorate General Internal Policies of the Union, Brussels
Hillman R (1981) Debunking some myths about unconscionability: a new framework for UCC section 2-302. Cornell Law Rev 67:1
Hooley R (2013) Controlling contractual discretion. Camb Law J 72(1):65–90
Lawson R (2005) Exclusion clauses and unfair contract terms. Sweet & Maxwell, London
Leff A (1967) Unconscionability and the code-the emperor's new clause. Univ Pa Law Rev 115:485
Loos M, Samoy I (eds) (2014) The position of small and medium-sized enterprises in European contract law. Intersentia, Cambridge
Macmillan C (2016) The impact of brexit upon English contract law. King's Law J 27(3):420–430
Mallor J (1986–1987) Unconscionability in contracts between merchants. Southwest Law J 40:1065
McKendrick E (2010) Contract law: text, cases and materials, 4th edn. Oxford University Press, Oxford
McKendrick E (2011) Contract law, 9th edn. Palgrave Macmillan Law Masters, London
McKendrick E (2015) Contract law, 11th edn. Palgrave Law Masters, London
McKendrick E (2016) Contract law: text, cases and materials, 7th edn. Oxford University Press, Oxford
Murray J (2014) The judicial vision of contract: the constructed circle of assent and unconscionability. Duquesne Law Rev 52(2):263
Nottage L (1996) Form and substance in US, English, New Zealand and Japanese law: a framework for better comparisons of developments in the law of unfair contract terms. Vic Univ Wellington Law Rev 26:247
Phillips K (2016) Does Australia's unfair contracts act limit or enhance contractual freedom? Econ Aff 36(3):258–272
Posner E (1995) Contract law in the welfare state: a defense of the unconscionability doctrine, usury laws, and related limitations on the freedom to contract. J Leg Stud 24(2):283
Schleper M, Blome C, Wuttke D (2017) The dark side of buyer power: supplier exploitation and the role of ethical climates. J Bus Ethics 140:97–114. https://doi.org/10.1007/s10551-015-2681-6

Shears P (2013) The groceries supply code of practice: fairness for farmers? Int J Agric Manage 3:1. https://doi.org/10.5836/ijam/2014-01-08

Simons J, Geer T (August 2014) The end of 'unfairness' in commercial contracts: proposed extension of 'unfair contract terms' laws to business to business transactions. Governance Directions

Swanson C (2001) Unconscionable quandary: ucc article 2 and the unconscionability doctrine. NM Law Rev 31:359

The final report of 26 February 2014 prepared for the European Commission, DG internal market DG MARKT/2012/049/E on the study on the legal framework covering business-to-business unfair trading practices in the retail supply chain. Available at: http://ec.europa.eu/internal_market/retail/docs/140711-study-utp-legal-framework_en.pdf

The law commission and the Scottish law commission (law com no 292) (scot law com no 199) (2005) Unfair terms in contracts: Report on a reference under section 3(1)(e) of the Law Commissions Act 1965 (Cm 6464 SE/2005/13)

Treitel (2011) In: Peel E (ed) The law of contract, 13th edn. Sweet & Maxwell/Thomson Reuters, London

Twigg-Flesner C (ed) (2013) The Europeanisation of contract law: current controversies in law, 2nd edn. Routledge, Abingdon

Twigg-Flesner C, Puig GV (eds) (2011) Boundaries of commercial and trade law. Sellier, Munich

Van Esch P (2015) Extending unfair contract term provisions for standard form contracts to small businesses. Altern Law J 40(2):93–96

Van Loock S (2014) Unfair terms in contracts between businesses: a comparative overview in light of the common European sales law. In: Loos M, Samoy I (eds) The position of small and medium-sized enterprises in European contract law. Intersentia, Cambridge

Wang FF (2015) The incorporation of terms into commercial contracts: a reassessment in the digital age. J Bus Law:87

Willett C (2007) The role of contract law in product liability. In: Grubb A, Howells G (eds) The law of product liability, 2nd edn. LexisNexis, New York

Part III
Commercial Contract Law at the Interface Between Private and Public Law: Interactions, Influences and Impacts

From Public Law to Private Law: The Remarkable Story of *bona fides*

Daniele D'Alvia

Contents

Abstract This Chapter examines the evolving principle of good faith. The informing legal principle has shaped the law of contracts for centuries and it has been introduced for the first time under Roman law. Therefore, this Chapter illustrates the origins and evolution of the Roman concept of *bona fides* until the modern evolution of the same principle under the CISG and UPICC at International level as well as the PECL, CFR and CESL at European level. In this light, a new dimension of *bona fides* is discovered in its private dimension. The aim of this Chapter is to highlight the different perspective of the study of *bona fides* from public law to private law.

The author is thankful to the invaluable support of the Max Planck Institute in Hamburg

D. D'Alvia (✉)
Birkbeck, University of London, London, UK

M. Heidemann, J. Lee (eds.), *The Future of the Commercial Contract in Scholarship and Law Reform*, https://doi.org/10.1007/978-3-319-95969-6_13

Indeed, a privatisation of good faith can be seen as a natural development, but at the same time its construction as a general clause has privatised its meaning contributing to a possible denaturalisation of the entire concept.

1 Introduction

The principle of good faith is controversial and there is a lack of comparative studies on this topic.[1] Undoubtedly, the concept is very broad and it is not recognised by every legal system in Europe, although the majority take this into account due to common Roman law origins (Sect. 2). For this reason, I intend to explore the meaning(s) of good faith under contract law and in commercial dealings in order to establish whether the original meaning of good faith has changed or has been unaltered.

Certainly the principle of good faith has become important in European Union law especially in relation to its evolution as a new principle of protection of the weak contractual party, often the consumer. To this end, a specific directive is examined, namely the Directive on distance marketing of consumer financial services[2] in order to assess how the information duties that are now imposed on the supplier of financial services can be constructed as the reception of general clauses of good faith. This illustration is only an instance that represents a specification of the general evolution of good faith that is outlined in Sects. 3 and 4 where such evolution is studied through European and International developments such as the United Nations Convention on Contracts for the International Sale of Goods (CISG), the *Unidroit* Principles of International Commercial Contracts (UPICC), the Principles of European Contract Law (PECL), the Common Frame of Reference (CFR) for an European Code of contract law, and finally the withdrawn EU Proposal for a Common European Sales Law (CESL)[3] in order to highlight the double construction of good faith as a general principle and as a general clause. The latter would bring the arguments on good faith towards a new light that can be understood as a private dimension of good faith where judges are deputed to play a central role, namely, what I term a 'private approach' to good faith (Sect. 4).

---

[1] Zimmermann and Whittaker (2000). The authors highlight that one of the most important comparative law textbooks, that by Zweigert and Koetz "An Introduction to Comparative Law" lacks a chapter on the principle of good faith. This is because it is extremely difficult to carry out a comparative study of a legal principle that does not have any mandatory definition and can be even vague in some cases.

[2] Directive 2002/65/EC concerning the distance marketing of consumer financial services and amending Council Directive 90/619/EEC and Directive 97/7/EC and 98/27/EC (2002) OJ L. 271/16.

[3] Proposal for a Regulation of the European Parliament and of the Council on a Common European Sales Law [2011] COM (2011) 635 final 2011/0284.

Finally, consolidating arguments are provided under Sect. 5. The conclusion is the discovery of the illusion of one single meaning of good faith in order to break down the disillusion of different meanings. This reason is explained as the different qualifications of good faith have contributed to denaturalise its inherent meaning and has brought to a privatisation of that universal principle of law by which *bona fides* is represented in its highest expression.

2 An Overview of Roman Legal History

This section will give a brief overview of the Roman legal history[4] to introduce the reader who is not familiar with Roman law to the historical background on which the legal principle of *bona fides* has developed during the centuries. Certainly Roman law has always been regarded as the outcome of a remarkable legal history that is closely linked to the stages of the political history of the Roman Empire. The origins of Rome are seen in the Monarchy period in the eighth century B.C. to 509 B.C. This period was followed by that of the Republic from 509 B.C. to 27 B.C. which is further divided into the early Republic and later Republic until its last development during the phase of the Empire from 27 B.C. to 565 A.D. This last period is further divided into so called Principate and the Dominate. This macro-division can be regarded as a common understanding of Roman legal history according to Jolowicz (1972), Mousourakis (2007) and Grosso (1965).

The conventional division of the three major phases of the Roman legal history should not be read as a static segmentation, but as an evolutionary process that is dynamic in nature and evolves continuously. This has led some authors to propose a more coherent framework of Roman legal history capable of reflecting the different functions of the law-making process.[5] This alternative historical framework classifies the broad stages of Roman legal history as follows: the Archaic period

[4] The expression Roman legal history can directly give rise to the concern to firstly define the concept of Roman law. Notwithstanding, the term 'Roman law' can be misleading because as it has been noted by Orestano (1961, p. 511) there are at least six different connotations of Roman law such as Roman law as Roman legal history; Roman law as Roman tradition; Roman law as European *ius commune*; Roman law as the study of pandects; Roman law as '*romanistica*' that means the study of the history of Rome; and finally Roman law as '*romanesimo*' that means the identification of ideals and political tendencies that were born in Rome and that have further inspired the ideology of other generations. However, within these several meanings, Orestano constructs the *Corpus Iuris Civile* as the highest summary and explanation of Roman law intended as Roman legal history, and on the other hand it can be conceptualised as the starting point of all the other different meanings. In this section I would like to introduce the reader to the first meaning of Roman law, namely Roman law in the sense of Roman legal history.

[5] Biondi (1972) and Johnston (1999). In particular, the classification of Roman legal history, although conventional can vary in accordance to the different perspectives that are taken into account such as the evolving conception of ownership, the contractual obligations, the development of public law etc. For this reason, a more coherent structure based on the development of law functioning has been proposed.

from the Monarchy to the early Republic; the pre-classical period from the later Republic and the earlier years of the Principate; the classical period that represents the central years of the Principate from the first century A.D. to the middle of the third century A.D.; and finally the post-classical period from the later part of the Principate to the Dominate.

Within this historical context, the principle of *bona fides* is shaping in its dimension as a legal, social and ethical principle that is incorporating essentially Roman society in its interactions with other populations and furthermore it is the expression of the same '*romanesimo*'[6] as a pure ideology on the meaning of being Romans. Consequently, an early evolution of the concept of *bona fides* derives from this social dimension that Rome starts to experience from the first relationships with *Latini* in Italy until the years of its expansion and influence on the Mediterranean Sea with the first Punic Wars. It is during the overwhelming expansion of the *imperium* of Rome that the *bona fides* became a binding legal principle that is capable of taking into account for the first time in law the economic interests of the foreigners, the so-called *peregrini*. In the following I will outline this legal history and highlight the importance of *bona fides* as an influential principle for both the *peregrini* as well as the *cives*, the citizens of Rome during the years of the late Republic and Principate. This is also an original approach to the study of Roman legal history that tries for the first time to understand Roman society as the product and expression of an informing principle that has possibly shaped the same appreciation of Roman law in terms of Roman legal history through the principle of *bona fides*.

I will finish the section by discussing the evolving nature of the principle of *bona fides* in contrast to the similar, but different concept of equity.

2.1 The Evolving Principle of Fides in Roman Legal History

During the pre-classic period (third century B.C.) when Rome is extending its influence across the Mediterranean Sea, the commercial transactions between *cives romani* (the Roman citizens) and *peregrini* (foreigners or strangers) are growing in importance. Indeed, even before the pre-classical period the interactions between the *cives romani* and other populations, namely the *Latini* in Italy gave rise to the fundamental question of how to guarantee a peaceful coexistence between Romans and foreigners.

Essentially, the successful expansion of the Roman Empire through the *imperium romanum* was sustained by allowing foreign populations to retain the application of their own domestic law. This meant that every population had the right to apply the law of its own *civitas*: the Romans were expected to follow their *ius civile* namely "the entire body of Roman law, irrespective of its sources",[7] while the *peregrini* (non-Romans or foreigners) should have lived in accordance with the laws of

[6] Orestano (1961), p. 511.

[7] Mousourakis (2003), p. 22.

their own city. In particular, the *ius civile* identified the original community of *cives*, namely Roman citizens so that the *ius civile* represented the *ius* that was applied and followed by *cives*. To this end, the strict bond between *ius civile* and *cives* was reflected in its ancient name *ius quiritium* in order to identify the *quirites*, namely the early Romans that were differentiated into two groups: the *gentes* and the *familiae*. The main features of this *ius civile* are its spontaneous development and its strong link with the religion. Indeed, in the Ancient period, there was an overlap between *fas* and *ius*, namely between religion and law that was not so clearly defined and distinguished (Watson 1992). Subsequently, the jurisprudence was laicised and the *ius* becomes an external element of recognition of powers and entitlements in respect of the formation of the original groups (for instance, the *pater familiae* was in charge of a *dominium* that was exercised on goods and people under his authority, this *dominium* was formally recognised by the *ius*, although the source of law of that *dominium* was inside the same constitution and creation of the roman family: for this reason the *ius civile* was always imbued with religious aspects).

The comprehensive ideal by which the *peregrini* could retain their own applicable law to govern disputes as well as commercial transactions between non-romans was intended to preserve the freedom of populations who were not properly organised in cities as well as that of the defeated who were considered as subject to the authority of Rome, the so called *dediticii*.

Furthermore, these relationships and contacts posed another legal issue, specifically how to regulate the interactions and contacts between Romans and *peregrini*. This issue has been considered also as one of the main reasons for the development of Roman law from an international point of view, and for the establishment of the well-known *ius gentium* (*i.e.* the modern law of nations). Aside from the relationships between the Romans and *Latini* that were regulated inside the *Foedus Cassianum*,[8] the contacts between the Romans and *peregrini* were firstly mentioned in the Twelve Tables.[9] For instance, the reference to the *status dies cum hoste* was

[8]The Romans had with the *Latini* a special relationship because they had with Romans the so called *ius commercii*, and with the *Latini prisci* also the *ius connubii*, namely the possibility of having a marriage with Roman citizens; essentially it could be said that the *Latini* were a federation of Italian populations that tried to merge in order to oppose the new hegemonic power of Rome. Nonetheless, after the battle of lake Regillus (499 B.C.) the consul Spurius Cassius entered into a new *foedus*, namely a new federation that had to be composed of the *Latini* and the Romans that will be referred to as *Foedus Cassianum* capable of assimilating Romans and *Latini* in their rights. In other words, their rights were equated and the legal institutions that were available for Roman citizens were extended also to *Latini* in accordance with the new *Foedus*. Therefore, the *Latini* were not properly *peregrini*.

[9]The Twelve Tables were enacted in 450 B.C. and it can be said that they represented the main source of knowledge in Roman private law (Johnston 1999, p. 2), although the Twelve Tables did not survive and, therefore, we possess only a fragmented knowledge of them through the evidence provided by Cicero and Livy. Historically, in 462 B.C. there was an important power struggle between the plebeians and the patricians, who formed the two major social classes of the Roman population. In particular, the Tribune C. Terentilio Arsa, who was an official representative of the plebeians proposed to set up a special committee of five lawmakers (*quinque viri legibus de imperio consular scribendis*). Years later, in 457 B.C. the number of lawmakers grew to ten (*decemviri*)

related to the solution of disputes between Romans and *peregrini*. Certainly, the qualification of *hostis* that subsequently would be interpreted as an enemy if the populations were at war with Rome (Mousourakis 2003) was originally identified in the Twelve Tables as the *peregrinus, qui suis legibus utitur* (Kent 1938), and especially referring to all the populations with whom there was friendly relationships. Specifically, Cicero in his first Book the *De Officiis* mentions and confirms this original definition of *peregrini*.[10]

2.2 *The Ethical Dimension of* bona fides

Within international relationships an important role was played by the *fides* that had a broad meaning, ancient origins and was known even before the period of the early Republic.[11] *Fides* was considered to denote a comprehensive content. It related to *deditio in fidem* (to be subject to the influential power of the other) as well as to the free discretion of the winner to which the defeated was subjected, and also to the protection of a particular expectation of a third party, and finally to the conception of an idea of equal and balanced relationships between private parties. Particularly, the term *fides* can reveal in the English language different meanings as well such as "faith, belief, confidence, reliance, belief without evidence or proof, and belief

---

and the Tribunes enacted the *Lex de Aventino publicando*. In 451 B.C. the *decemviri* enacted the Twelve Tables. This was one of the most important achievements of the plebeians that they had for the first time a 'codified law' (indeed, the Twelve Tables were not a codification in the modern sense as for instance the *Code Napoleon*; it was more a sort of delimitation and specification of the *ius* as it was recognised as a completely formed entity before the enactment of the Twelve Tables). For the first time, this brought a form of legal certainty in the form of rights and delimitation of obligations that were written down into a law. This enactment has always been regarded as a *quid unicum* in Roman legal history (Grosso 1965).

[10] For enemy (*hostis*) meant to our ancestors what we now call 'stranger' (*peregrinus*). This is proved by the usage in the Twelve Tables: 'or a day fixed for trial with a stranger' (*hostis*). And again: 'Right of ownership is inalienable for ever in dealings with a stranger' (*hostis*). What can exceed such charity, when he with whom one is at war is called by so gentle name? And yet long lapse of time has given that word a harsher meaning: for it has lost its signification of 'stranger' and has taken on the technical connotation of 'an enemy under arms' (Miller 2016, paragraph 37).

[11] In particular, in the Ancient period the *ius civile* had a religious connotation that was specifically illustrated by the *dominium* that was expressed by the *paterfamilias*. The *familia* was an important minor social group of the initial Roman society and a bigger aggregation of people was centred on the *gens*. The *gens* as well as the *familia* were the initial aggregation of people who pre-existed the Roman society that was later called *civitas* and identified by its citizens, namely the *cives*. Indeed, it is inside the *gens* and specifically among the people who formed the *gens*, namely the *gentiles* that other social figures were identified in the so called *clientes* (essentially, vassals) who were under the protection of the patron and they were entrusted to his *fides*, namely they were in charge of looking after his lands and subject to particular duties such as the *obsequium*, the *officium* and the *pietas* (Grosso 1965). Furthermore, the *ius civile* was originally overlapping with *fas*. Therefore, the breach of *fides* was intended not only as a legal violation, but specifically as a reprehensible behaviour that was against the *voluntas dei* (Mousourakis 2007).

based on testimony or authority".[12] As a result, the open-ended meaning of *fides* can show a main understanding of the word in terms of trust, faith and belief, namely all terms that are intimately connected to a religious character or dimension. Indeed, the *fides* is primarily an ethic concept to which the law attributes a juridical and legal meaning that can also be reflected into the production of legal effects such as in the case of *usucapio* or adverse possession in Roman law (Biondi 1972, p. 267). Indeed, here the *fides* is a central concept for the *usucapio* that aims to guarantee the transfer of ownership or the achievement of profit only to a faithful possessor, who has to act in good faith at the moment he or she acquires the possess of a specific item,[13] albeit the *mala fides* can supervene at a later stage. This latter circumstance does not have any legal effect and cannot prejudice the final transfer of ownership, because the main concern is to guarantee that at the start of possession, the possessor does not prejudice the interests of any third party. In this sense, it is possible to appreciate what can be defined as an ethical dimension of *fides* in the form of moral respect to others' private interests.

2.3 The Origin of Good Faith in the Pre-Classical Period

The main legal instrument to regulate the relationships between the Romans and *peregrini* was the treaty.[14] In this light, in the first international treaty of the Roman legal history between Rome and Cartago there was a specific mention to *publica fide* (the public good faith). It is stated there that the commercial transactions entered into by Roman merchants and the Carthaginians should be concluded by virtue of a public transaction, involving a *grammateus*, essentially a public notary, in order for

[12] Lesley Brown (1993), p. 908.

[13] Specifically, in Roman law and still today in modern Italian law (see article 1147 of the Italian Civil Code according to which: '*è possessore di buona fede chi possiede ignorando di ledere l'altrui diritto*' that means the possessor in good faith is the one who has no intention to cause a prejudice to the right of a third party) there is a strict separation between possession and ownership, so that to get the possession of a specific item it is sufficient that the possessor acts in good faith from the moment he or she starts to possess otherwise the profits deriving from such item as well as the *usucapio* shall be prevented. This is to guarantee an ethical behaviour that is expressed into the subjective idea of good faith, namely the consciousness to possess without the intention to cause prejudice to any other third party in the following terms: '*(…) el poseedor está protegido en su posesión con los interdictos. Si la posesión es de buena fe, el poseedor hace suyos los frutos. La possessio ad usucapionem hace que el poseedor mediante la prescripción adquiera la propiedad. El poseedor, por el hecho de serlo, conserva el objeto mientras se aclara la cuestión de su propiedad.*' Bravo González and Bravo Valdés (2004), p. 233.

[14] The principal difference between the *Foedus Cassianum* and an international treaty such as the one with Cartago was mainly focused on a different perspective of the commercial transactions. Indeed, in the *Foedus Cassianum* the validity of commercial agreements was recognised due to the shared values between *Latini* and Romans, while the treaties with Cartago immediately recognised the different *ius* of each city, therefore, different applicable laws to different citizens. Hence, the treaty became the legal instrument by which the rights of foreign populations were recognised by Romans.

the transaction to be protected by the *publica fide*. It is clear that under this first understanding, *fides* had a public dimension, namely the commercial transaction was rendered trustworthy by means of *publica fide*. This public dimension of *fides* was also apparent in the Ancient period when *ius* and *fas* were overlapping and the components of the *familia* were under the supervision and *fides* (protection) of the *pater familia*.

As we have seen the commercial transaction was considered valid because it was rendered and carried out in front of a public notary who was able to give public trust to such agreement. Specifically, the trust is the fundamental feature to grant a protection to those relationships. Undoubtedly, from the point of view of Rome, the *peregrini* were not able to defend their rights through *legis actiones*,[15] therefore, jurisdiction in relation to the *peregrini* was exercised outside the restrictions and forms provided by means of the *ius* of the *civitas*. Briefly, Romans gave trust to foreign judges to solve disputes among *peregrini*.

These international relations were dominated by the *fides* that informed either the free discretion of the judges of the foreign cities and also the physical persons with whom the Romans were used to carry out commercial transactions. It is from this moment that a new objective dimension of *fides* is established, namely the idea of *fides bona* or *bona fides* (Grosso 1965), synonym of morality and commercial fairness that was the core ideal of any commercial transaction: this *bona fides* was binding and informed the new *iudicium bonae fidei*. Legal institutions of Romans were applied to the *peregrini* (at least the *traditio* and the *stipulatio*, but this latter only in forms that were different from *sponsio*); on the other hand foreign legal institutions were recognised by Roman law, but prevalently a new set of legal institutions and commercial agreements started to develop under the *bona fides* dimension, namely under a commercial fairness that was intended as the main principle on which any international commercial transaction was based, and in particular the consensual contract of sale (*emptio venditio*) played a key role in this regard.[16]

---

[15] The Roman law of procedure is mainly divided into three stages in the light of Roman legal history: the period of the *legis actio* procedure, the period of the formulary system and the period of the *cognitio extraordinaria*. The *legis actio* procedure was literally an action based on the law. It means that if there was not a specific action in order to protect a particular interest of the plaintiff, the latter could not start a trial and borne the damage. The most important feature is that only Roman citizens were entitled to a *legis actio* (du Plessis 2010; Mousourakis 2007; Marrone 1994).

[16] In particular, the good faith or *bona fides* in this light was the outcome of the emergence of the consensual contract of sale (*emptio venditio*) that characterised this phase of the Roman legal history in terms of underpinning the Roman commerce with foreign populations. The new feature of this agreement was focused on superseding the formalities that were imposed and required in the *stipulatio*, namely the formal orally contract that was concluded by question and answer. Indeed, according to Johnston (1999, p. 80) there were at least three main advantages that the *emptio venditio* could achieve only through the good faith or *bona fides* that contributed to the production of automatic effects of the contract of sale. To this end, '(1) the seller impliedly warranted his title to the goods, so that the buyer who was dispossessed by a person who turned out to be the true owner was automatically able to sue the seller for breach of contract (…) this development illustrates the significance of the fact that sale was a 'good faith' contract. What this meant was that the parties'

2.3.1 The Evolution of Good Faith in the Pre-Classical Period

In 242 B.C., at the end of the first Punic war, Rome imposed the creation of a new *praetor*, the so-called *praetor peregrinus*.[17] His jurisdiction was extended either to the disputes arising between foreigners as well as between Romans and foreigners (respectively *ius dicere inter peregrinos* and *ius dicere inter cives Romanos et peregrinos*). This can provide an evidence of the growing importance of disputes between Romans and foreigners.

The *bona fides* between Romans and foreigners was a binding principle and the Roman magistrate, namely the *praetor peregrinus* recognised this binding nature in order to give legal effect to the commercial transactions. It is not by chance that under this new jurisdiction, a new trial *per formulas* has been created as opposed to the *legis actiones*. Indeed, the *bona fides* is always a binding legal principle that is recognised by the Romans and that is capable of adapting Roman legal institutions for the relationships between *cives* and *peregrini*. Therefore, it is coherent that a binding principle that was observed between Romans and foreigners should have commenced to be applied also amongst the Romans.[18] This was the start of a new

dealings with one another were assessed in any eventual litigation on the basis of what good faith demanded; and so, without any need for adding further express promises or undertakings (...) (2) the seller impliedly warranted the quality of the goods. Initially the buyer took the risk of defects in the goods. If he wanted a guarantee against particular defects, he would have take it expressly by *stipulatio*. Only if the seller had fraudulently concealed the presence of defects in the goods would the buyer have a remedy, as this was of course a breach of good faith. (...) (3) Once agreement had been reached on the essentials of the contract, the object sold and its price, the risk of accidental loss or destruction passed to the buyer. (...) It has been regarded as strange that the buyer became liable at such an early point in the transaction, since he would not become owner until the goods were actually conveyed to him, for example by delivery. The result is that, at a time at which he did not own the goods, he was at risk if they were lost or destroyed in certain circumstances. (...) So the sorts of risk which the buyer assumed on conclusion of the contract were for destruction by earthquake, flooding or fire (so long as the seller was not responsible for it). (...) The terms just discussed were (ultimately) implied in every contract of sale. But it was possible to introduce further terms ('pacts') into the contract. This could be done without need for additional stipulation, because sale was a 'good faith' contract. One aspect of this was that, where the parties had entered into pacts in conjunction with the sale, the tenor of those pacts should be observed'.

[17] The *praetor* should be likened in contemporary terms to an international arbitrator in an international arbitration (Costa 1990).

[18] Indeed, *fides* was an ancient roman concept that existed even before the enactment of the Twelve Tables as it has been mentioned before especially in relation to the transfer of ownership by *fiduciae causa* in the solemn forms of *mancipatio* and the *in iure cessio* where the failure to give back the subject matter of the sale was considered a fraudulent act (*i.e.* a *fraudatio*) against the *fides*. So that the duty to give back the subject matter of the sale was originally based on the trust of the other party and later it was penalised as *ut inter bonos bene agier oportere et sine frudatione*. In particular, the *mancipatio*, the *in iure cessio* and the *stipulatio* were all formal agreements that were part of the *ius civile* as that law that was applied only between roman citizens (Marrone 1994). The most important of them because also the oldest that was later recognised by the Twelve Tables was the *mancipatio* that was used to transfer the ownership of goods as well as to acquire status rights (for instance, the will was made by virtue of the *testamentum per aes et libra*) and rights on people (a famous case was the *coemptio* of the woman, who became part of the family of the husband by virtue of the *conventio in manum* that was a form of *mancipatio* in relation to people).

trial *per formulas* that had its genesis in the jurisdiction of the *praetor peregrinus* and was later extended to the *praetor urbanus*.[19] When the *praetor* had to deal with disputes between Romans and foreigners, the *legis actiones* could not be used because they were reserved only for Roman citizens, therefore those disputes were regulated initially by an arbitration panel (the *reciperatores*) and subsequently by the *imperium* of the *praetor* by virtue of a special procedure that was divided in two phases: *in iure* and *apud iudicem*. Essentially, the ruling of the *praetor* was mainly based on the *bona fides*, therefore it was perceived as an established rule *in iure*, namely before the *praetor* who fixed the litigation programme into the formula[20] and then it would have been applied and assessed by the judge (the phase *apud iudicem*).

The formulary process was later extended to disputes between Roman citizens. In particular, the *Lex Aebutia* introduced the formulary process in Rome, however, the *legis actiones* were not totally dismissed because the formulary process in Rome at the start was only facultative. Indeed, it is in the years of the Principate of Augustus that after the enactment of the *Lex Iulia iudiciorum privatorum* the formulary process becomes the new mandatory process in place of *legis actiones*. It is during this time that the *iudicia bonae fidei* became part of the *ius civile*.

2.4 *The* ius gentium *and the* bona fides *Dimension in Roman Law*

In the previous section it has been illustrated how the *bona fides* found its legal dimension during the early Republic and developed through the growing importance and influence of international trade and commerce. Undeniably disputes between *peregrini* and Roman citizens as well as between *peregrini* were settled by virtue of the *bonae fidei iudicia*. In other words, the formulary process that has been explained

[19] The *praetor urbanus* was a judge whose jurisdiction was empowered by the *leges Liciniae Sextiae* enacted on the 367 B.C. This judge had the *imperium* (the power) of *dicere ius*, namely the exercise of its jurisdiction was expressed by the pronunciation of at least one of these three verbs during the *legis actiones*: *do*, *dico*, *addico* (the so called *tria verba praetoris*). On the other hand, the *praetor peregrinus* was empowered to solve disputes related to commercial transactions between Romans and *peregrini* (Marrone 1994).

[20] The formula contained different elements some of them were essential in order to create a valid formula such as the *nominatio* (i.e. the appointment of the judge); the *intentio* (namely, the plaintiff's claim); the *demonstratio* (it was a clause stating the facts) while others were facultative and they depend on the nature of the claim for instance the *condemnatio* (it was a statement directed to the judge, namely the *apud iudicem* phase to absolve or condemn the defendant; here if the subject matter of the claim was the quantification of an amount of money it usually contained the clause *ex fide bona*, therefore a sort of equity decision); the *exceptio* (essentially, the defendant's specific grounds of defence and here the claimant should have insert a counter exception referred to as *replicatio*); and the *praescriptio* (namely, to limit the cause of action if the nature of the claim required this clause). For further reference see du Plessis (2010).

before. The Romans defined this new *ius* as a part of the *ius civile*, although it was different due to the fact that it was not based on the *legis actiones* (*i.e.* the Roman process that was reserved only for the Roman citizens). It is during the reign of the emperor Hadrian that this new area of *ius* was defined as *ius gentium*.

To this end, it is interesting to restate here a well-known definition of *ius gentium* provided by Gaius in his first book of the *Istitutiones* in the following terms:

> [Ius] quod vero naturalis ratio inter omnes homines constituit, id apud omnes populous peraeque costoditur vocaturque ius gentium, quasi quo iure omnes gentes utuntur.[21]

For the first time, the understanding of the law here goes beyond the single *civitas* through the recognition that there is a set of rules capable of being applied to different populations. This uniformity of application of the law is connected foremost to a universal conception of legal relationships that is justified by the fact that all the populations recognise the application of the law with the same legal effects. In essence, the universality of this *ius* is capable of directly connecting it to what Gaius defined as a *naturalis ratio*, essentially a natural law as opposed to the positive law.

It can be said that *ius gentium* is informed by a duality: on the one hand, it is a doctrinal idea based on the recognition of a unified law that is equally applicable to all the populations of the Mediterranean Sea, and this feature gives rise to a supreme universality of the law that is based on the understanding of the *ius gentium* as natural law; on the other hand, the *ius gentium* is a positive and pragmatic concept in relation to the Roman legal system that has started to be formed through the relationships between Roman citizens and *peregrini*. The pragmatic conception of *ius gentium* has enlarged the dimension of the *ius* through a dual opposition of *ius gentium* and *ius civile*, but at the same time has set up a supreme law that is above the particular laws of any population and it is still part of the Roman legal system (Schipani 1999).

This understanding of the *ius gentium* as a natural law and its universal character confirms the importance of the *bona fides* in the formation and entrustment of any legal relationship that was formed during the Roman expansion in the Mediterranean Sea. Therefore, in my view it should be highlighted that the same inclusion of the *bona fides* into the living principles of the *ius*[22] gives rise, on the one hand, to its binding nature and objective qualification in terms of an assessment criteria of the parties' conducts, and on the other hand allows a reflection on its supplementing and specific nature as a *lex specialis* that makes the *bona fides* the new judicial parameter to uphold a decision when the *legis actiones* cannot be applied. This latter feature confers upon the *bona fides* the quality of a superior legal principle with a supplementing nature, something that will be used in the modern evolution of good

[21] As it has been translated by Edward Poste (1994, p. 25) in the following terms: 'the rules prescribed by natural reason for all are observed by all nations alike, and are called gentile law', namely the law of the *gentes* that are in this context intended as the different populations.

[22] Here the term *ius* is used in its objective understanding as *ius civile* and *ius gentium* (Bravo González and Bravo Valdés 2004, p. 29).

faith into the *lex mercatoria* when the international arbiter will find through the *bona fides* the concrete rule to apply in order to resolve the dispute, and therefore to *dicere ius*.

2.5 *The* ius gentium *and the New* lex mercatoria

The Roman *ius gentium* was developed during the medieval time through International law, namely the law of nations. It is the so-called *lex mercatoria* that takes into account the needs for a regulation of commercial relationships, which presents an international character to a high degree. The *lex mercatoria* is composed of rules that are derived from customs, and that have a uniform and universal application to merchant dealings. In particular, these rules are internationally uniform or one could say they contribute to uniformity of national laws, and are based on the degree of diffusion of commercial practices that were formally recognised in international arbitration.[23] Indeed, the arbiter as a private judge that is selected by the parties started to apply the customs and commercial practices in accordance to good faith criteria in order to resolve private disputes mainly on international commercial contracts similar to the ancient *praetor peregrinus*, who was deputed to *ius dicere* under the universal conception of *ius gentium*. In the modern age the reference to the "new *lex mercatoria*" is made in relation to a spontaneous law of entrepreneurs or merchants that is formed and followed without the mediation of the legislative power, namely the State. Its creation is based on commercial customs and practices that are observed during commercial transactions at an international level and is formally recognised through the rule that is imposed by the arbiter in the international arbitration procedure.

2.6 *Equity and* bona fides

It is also important to highlight that the *bona fides* in Rome was never associated with the similar, but opposite concept of equity. The original meaning of equity was established by ancient Greeks through the thinking of Plato and Aristotle who made reference to equity as something closely related to justice and as a kind of justice itself.[24] Equity to ancient Greeks was the legal instrument through which law could be corrected and aligned to justice in order to satisfy the private interests of the parties in a concrete and specific case that law had not pre-configured. To this end, the equivalent for equity in Roman terms was *aequitas* which was never identified through *bona fides*. In my opinion, the Roman jurist that better reflects this idea is

[23] Costa (1990).

[24] Jolowicz (1957).

the *praetor* Celsus who is famous for one important verse that was reported by Ulpian in his *Istitutiones* according to which *ius est ars boni et aequi*.[25] This meant that the law should follow a *recta ratio*, namely that law has been created to provide justice (*aequum*) and to be the measure through which men can live together (*bonum*). It is a law made for men that can reflect also the meaning of *ius gentium* as a universal conception of law that calls for a universal application despite the difference among legal systems. Viewed like this, law is never an imposition, but always a categorisation of behaviors in order to distinguish what is legal from what is illegal.

For our purpose, it means that while the *bona fides* was the general principle through which the *praetor* could identify the legal rule to be applied to the concrete case, then the concrete application of the rule to the concrete case represented that idea of *aequitas* as a form of justice to correct the law (namely, a law that was designed for the peaceful coexistence of men).[26]

2.7 *Concluding Remarks on* bona fides

The *bona fides* principle was developed from the early Roman Republic as an objective principle in order to guarantee fairness in commercial transactions between Romans and *peregrini*. Nonetheless, this private dimension of *bona fides* does not mirror the original meaning that initially was merged into *fas*. In the ancient period of Roman legal history *fas* and *ius* were closely related to each other, and the *bona fides* principle was a derivation of such connection. The idea of *potestas* of the *pater familia* that was exercised over items and people who were under his influence is clearly an expression of this idea. Religious aspects informed the ancient *mores* (moral values and virtues), which meant that the *pater familia* could exercise his power in consideration of his role in society that was agreed specifically on a religious basis and founded on the conception of trust.

For this reason, at least at the starting point of Roman legal history the *bona fides* had a public dimension.

[25] The passage of Ulpian is reported in the *Corpus Iuris Civilis* of the Emperor Justinian under D.1.1.1.pr.: '(…) *celsus definit, ius est ars boni et aequi*'. Furthermore, Ulpian continues to describe what does this sentence mean under D.1.1.1.1: '*Cuius merito quis nos sacerdotes appellet: iustitiam namque colimus et boni et eaqui notitiam profitemur, aequum ab iniquo separantes, licitum ab illicito discernentes, bonos non solum metu poenarum, verum etiam praemiorum quoque exhortation efficere cupientes, veram nisi fallor philosophiam, non simulatam affectantes*'.

[26] To this end, the *aequum* under Roman law was close to the equity conception of ancient Greeks. Furthermore, on this understanding of equity as a form of correction of the law is not by chance that in England the equitable jurisdiction was initially implemented by the common law courts, and only later by the special court of the Chancery. This in order to distinguish how equity was applied as a form of justice in order to correct the law, but was never considered as a law itself.

3 The Evolving Principle of Good Faith in International and European Union Law

We have seen that the principle of good faith has evolved from a public conception of trust that in Roman law was especially connected to the sacredness of *fas* until a private and objective conception of *bona fides* that becomes in the modern age a legally binding principle to be observed during the life of private transactions. The latter meaning that is informed by a principle of universality has lead to the modern creation of the *lex mercatoria* that was the product of the decisions of the international arbiter.[27] Here, the *bona fides* dimension of international private transactions dominated the scene again.

Nonetheless, the *lex mercatoria* started to have its own evolution in the modern age and a system of harmonising rules (UPICC, PECL, CFR), legislative acts (CESL) and treaty (CISG) have started to develop and recognise the private dimension of *bona fides* sometimes as a general clause and other times as a general principle. It is important to highlight that all these documents are connected and intimately close to each other because they are all progressive stratification and evolution of international private provisions that aim to harmonise commercial transactions (Alpa 2009, p. 10). Furthermore, the majority of these acts have a soft law nature or otherwise a non-binding nature (*i.e.* UPICC, PECL, CFR) apart from the CISG.

Indeed, the first act that inspired all the others is the United Nations Convention on Contracts for the International Sale of Goods that is an international private law convention, and therefore an international treaty that has a binding effect. Particularly, under article 7 (1) CISG good faith is taken into account in international trade.[28] Historically, when this provision was initially drafted in 1978 by the United Nations Commission on International Trade Law (UNCITRAL), the working group proposed an article 5 according to which: "in the course of the formation of the contract the parties must observe the principles of fair dealing and act in good faith". This means that the principles of good faith and fair dealing were considered desirable standards in international commerce although it was not clear what form of sanction would be derived from a potential breach of good faith. There was no uniformity of views on the point, but the simple fact that for the first time a provision included good faith directly in international trade, this would force the parties' attention to it.[29] At the Vienna Conference small amendments were eventually implemented into the wording of the final article 7 (1) from the UNCITRAL Draft Convention that originally incorporated a different wording where also the concept of fair dealing was taken into account.

[27] Cuniberti (2014).

[28] Article 7 (1) CISG: "In the interpretation of this Convention, regard is to be had to its international character and to the need to promote uniformity in its application and the observance of good faith in international trade".

[29] Bianca and Bonell (1987).

This fact signifies a clear indication that good faith would play a bigger role in international trade. Specifically, the Secretariat commentary on the provision are self-explanatory in this sense: "The principle of good faith is, however, broader than these examples and applies to all aspects of interpretation and application of the provisions of this Convention".[30] I term this approach to good faith as "inclusive approach", namely in this light it can be appreciated how the *bona fides* is working as a general principle rather than a general clause. Indeed, general clauses of good faith can be found in single provisions of the CISG.[31]

Consequently, in 1994 the International Institute for the Unification of Private Law adopted and published the *Unidroit* Principles of International Commercial Contracts[32] seeking to crystallise a shared understanding of the *bona fides* principle. These principles are one of the most important instances that aim for the first time to the codification of the *lex mercatoria* (Bortolotti 2016, p. 1262). Indeed, the UPICC is a system of rules that aims to establish uniformity among international commercial contracts. This according to Bortolotti (2016) can fill in the 'empty box' and create within 'the *lex mercatoria* a legal framework which could be compared as to its certainty and foreseeability with national system law'. Therefore, the UPICC represent a vital instrument, although not binding to allow private parties to place contracts within an autonomous and neutral legal framework capable of superseding the different national or domestic legislations.

One of the main objectives of the UPICC is the regulation of commercial transactions and trade by virtue of a uniform application of the UPICC's provisions to guarantee homogenous recognition of fundamental legal principles. Among these principles, one of the most informing principle that is mentioned is the one of good faith and fair dealing under section 1.7.[33] It is a mandatory and fundamental provision that must be observed in any commercial transactions between private parties through the life of the contract including the negotiation process and it is expressly described as a fundamental idea that informs every provision of the principles as stated in the UPICC comment to section 1.7. This is another international instance of what I term 'inclusive approach' of good faith, namely good faith as a general principle from which all the other provisions are informed.[34] The common feature that both tools share is that they apply only to commercial contracts or international trade agreements.

Furthermore, the importance of the principle of good faith in its objective form, but this time in relation to the contract in general is introduced into the Principles of

---

[30] Mazzetta (2014), p. 127.

[31] On this point, it is interesting to note how the same author (Mazzetta 2014, p. 128) on CISG Article 7 (1) mentions the 2008 UNCITRAL Digest of case law on the CISG comments on good faith that although good faith is expressly referred to only in article 7 (1) there are numerous rules in the Convention that reflect the good faith principle. In particular article 16 (2) (b), 21 (2), 29 (2), 37 and 46, 40, 47 (2), 64 (2), 82, 85 and 88.

[32] Subsequently, two other editions were released respectively in 2004 and 2010.

[33] According to section 1.7 *Unidroit* Principles 2010: '(1) Each party must act in accordance with good faith and fair dealing in international trade. (2) The parties may not exclude or limit this duty.'

[34] The next paragraph will illustrate the difference between general principle and general clause.

European Contract Law that were for the first time elaborated in 1995 by a working group on European contract law chaired by Prof. Ole Lando. In particular, the PECL were firstly aimed to constitute the basis for a European Code of contract law in order to form a harmonised code beyond domestic legislations of Member States in Europe,[35] although the natural development of such initiative was later continued by the CFR in 2007. However, for our purpose the first part of the PECL that was completed in 1995 clearly stated the importance of good faith and fair dealing under section 1.106 (now, 1:201).[36] This is an instance of good faith as a general clause that is directly recognised into a provision and that imposes onto the contractual parties a duty to act in good faith. It is a standard social clause by which the judge is invited to evaluate and assess the conducts of the private parties in their course of affairs. This is what I term 'private approach' to good faith, namely the standardisation of good faith into a clause that serves as a parameter for the juridical application of social justice. Here, good faith starts to lose its universal vocation that was derived from Roman law and that was represented by the construction of this principle as a general universal principle.

Finally, always in relation to European Union's proposals and initiatives, it is helpful to highlight two further systems of rules, namely the CESL and the CFR. The first one is a withdrawn proposal of a Regulation for a Common European Sales Law that was adopted on the 16th of December 2014 in order to benefit small businesses trying to trade online across Europe and to promote a digital single market. Nonetheless, this proposal was not taken into consideration due to the misconception of its title "Common European Sales Law". Indeed, national legislators argued that their legal systems were evolved enough in terms of providing consumers of online purchases with protection. For this reason, the European Commission inserted in its priorities for 2015 to modernise this proposal and to make a new proposal as part of the Digital Single Market Strategy that could operate as an optional regime or instrument, so that national legislations would not be substituted. Specifically, the European Commission proposed a new directive on contracts for online purchases and a directive on the supply of digital content.[37] Nonetheless, none of these proposals contain what the original proposed CESL was aiming at establishing, namely a legal framework on general contract law (formation, validity, interpretation, obligations of the parties, remedies for non-performance, prescription etc.). Indeed, it is inside this original proposal that under the recitals 31 of the Preamble to the Regulation, the principle of good faith and fair dealing is taking into account.[38] In particular, I would like to highlight the sentence of recital 31 which

---

[35] Beale (2008), p. 11.

[36] According to section 1:201 of the Principles of European Contract Law: '(1) Each party must act in accordance with good faith and fair dealing. (2) The parties may not exclude or limit this duty'.

[37] In December 2015, the European Commission proposed a directive on contracts for online and other distances sales of goods (online sale of goods directive) and a directive on the supply of digital content. In particular, the first act was intended to replace the existing Consumer Sales Directive with regard to distance sales (both online and offline).

[38] CESL Preamble, recital 31: "The general principle of good faith and fair dealing should provide guidance on the way parties have to cooperate. As some rules constitute specific manifestations of

says "(…) the general principle of good faith and fair dealing should set a standard of conduct which ensures an honest, transparent and fair relationship." in order to provide the reader with a clear evidence of this phenomenon of "privatisation" of the principle of good faith. Indeed, the CESL then codifies the principle of good faith as a general clause under article 2 and determines under paragraph 2 the effects of its breach.[39]

Finally, we have to examine the CFR. The process of drafting the CFR started after the Tartu conference that was held on the 15th of November 2007 on "Developments in European Law: European Initiatives (CFR) and Reform of Civil Law in New Member States". Indeed, teams of researchers were contracted in 2005 with the European Commission to deliver in 2007 a first proposal for a possible model for a European Code of contract law (we have seen how the PECL constituted a first approach in this sense). Then in 2009 the final edition of CFR was published as a master copy. Here the good faith is taken into account in contractual relationship in terms of general principle, therefore, it is probably the sole instance that is closest to the Roman tradition and definition of good faith as a universal principle. Indeed, under Book I section 1:102 on "Interpretation and Development"[40] the *bona fides* and fair dealing are mentioned as an inspiring criteria that should be followed in the interpretation of the CFR provisions. This statement can directly show how the good faith is informing many CFR provisions and their same interpretation as a general principle. In this light, the CFR codifies the principle of good faith as a general principle under section 1:103 on "Good faith and fair dealing".[41]

---

the general principle of good faith and fair dealing, they should take precedent over the general principle. The general principle should therefore not be used as a tool to amend the specific rights and obligations of parties as set out in the specific rules. The concrete requirements resulting from the general principle of good faith and fair dealing should depend, amongst others, on the relative level of expertise of the parties and should therefore be different in business-to-consumer transactions and in business-to-business transactions. In transactions between traders, good commercial practice in the specific situation concerned should be a relevant factor in this context. The general principle of good faith and fair dealing should set a standard of conduct which ensures an honest, transparent and fair relationship. While it precludes to a party from exercising or relying on a right, remedy or defence which that party would otherwise have, the principle as such should not give to any general right to damages. Rules of the Common European Sales Law constituting specific manifestation of the general principle of good faith and fair dealing, such as avoidance for fraud or the non-performance of an obligation created by an implied term, can give rise to a right to damages, but only in very specific cases".

[39] CESL, Article 2: "1. Each party has a duty to act in accordance with good faith and fair dealing. 2. Breach of this duty may preclude the party in breach from exercising or relying on a right, remedy or defence which that party would otherwise have, but shall not give directly to remedies for non-performance of an obligation".

[40] CFR, Book I, Section 1:102 "Interpretation and development": '(…) (3) In their interpretation and development regard should be had to the need to promote: (a) uniformity of application; (b) good faith and fair dealing; and (c) legal certainty'.

[41] CFR I – 1:103: "1. The expression "good faith and fair dealing" refers to a standard of conduct characterised by honesty, openness and consideration for the interests of the other party to the transaction or relationship in question. 2. It is, in particular, contrary to good faith and fair dealing for a party to act inconsistently with that party's prior statements or conduct when the other party has reasonably relied on them to that other party's detriment".

Indeed, it should be noted that the CFR's aim is to present model rules or general principles because the law of every member state cannot be summarised in one single code. One of this examples is the principle of good faith.[42]

These scholarly principles and binding instruments (*i.e.* CISG) illustrate for the first time how international as well as European principles in contract law are based on the ancient inheritance of Roman law and specifically on the informing principle of good faith or better the *bona fides*[43] in its objective dimension as a binding legal principle that parties must follow during negotiations as well as in the formation of the contract. Particularly, *bona fides* is taken into account both as a general principle and as a general clause in order to assess the conducts of private parties or informing the system of provisions in international and European commercial transactions as well as private contractual relationships in order to generally guarantee the preservation of a fair dealing and correctness in the performance of the contract. However, this comparative analysis of international provisions on good faith has also shown how the principle has been taken into account the majority of times in Europe as a general clause (CESL, PECL), with the only exception of the CFR. This is a significant element in order to qualify what I term "private" approach to good faith and the conclusion of this Chapter will give consolidating remarks on this point.

4 The Private Dimension of the Principle of Good Faith or the 'Private' Approach to Good Faith

In this section I set out how the principle of good faith has changed its original role in order to become a parameter by which to assess the validity of a contract. Specifically, it can be said that from a public dimension, the *bona fides* has been constructed as a private law tool in order to address the possible information asymmetry that new forms of commerce have brought about and affecting relations between a presumed weak party, called the consumer, and a presumed strong party that is the entrepreneur or business operator.

In such instances of information asymmetry, the *lex mercatoria* is not sufficient enough to guarantee fair dealing as the lawmaker had intervened in order to impose social justice and protect private interests by virtue of rendering the contract void, and protecting the interests of the weaker contractual party.

By way of example, in the Italian legal system this new function of the *bona fides* can be seen in respect of at least three different instances: subcontracting,[44]

[42] Beale (2008).

[43] Schipani (1999).

[44] In accordance with section 9 Law, 18 June 1998, n. 192 on the subcontracting, it is expressly provided that the agreement by which it is committed the abuse of economic dependence between enterprises is void because it is against the principles of good faith and fair dealing in commercial relations. The instance of subcontracting is considered as having a general application to any other commercial contract that is characterised by information asymmetry between enterprises (Russo 2009), although this conclusion is not completely accepted by the Italian jurisprudence.

franchising[45] and late payment in commercial transactions.[46] In all these instances the Italian judge in cases of unfair dealing is entitled to intervene either to declare the term void or to rebalance the relationship between the private parties by modifying the unfair contractual term. This is a specific interference by the judge with the private autonomy of the parties in order to protect a superior interest of substantive justice in the economy of the contract, restoring *bona fides*.[47] Furthermore, the Italian law constitutes a perfect instance in order to show how the Lawmaker has directly intervened in order to protect the interest of private parties during the negotiation phase by virtue of implementing a general clause of good faith that must be followed during negotiations in accordance with article 1337 of the Italian Civil Code.[48] Here the good faith is taken in its objective dimension[49] in order to generate a form of contractual responsibility on the party who fails to provide information during the negotiation phase of a contract as well as behaves negligently by

[45] Under the Law, 6 May 2005, n. 129 on the Franchising Agreement, the franchisor has to behave in good faith and in a fair fashion in order to protect the interests of the franchisee. In particular, the good faith must be observed during the negotiation of the franchise agreement (*i.e.* pre-contractual phase) as well as after entering into the agreement. Furthermore, the good faith during the negotiation phase is characterised by a specific information duty that must be followed by the franchisor.

[46] In particular, section 7 of the Legislative Decree, 9 October 2002, n. 231 (the Italian national act of implementation of Directive 2000/35/EU on combating late payment in commercial transactions) provides that if a term on the payment date or on the effects caused by a late payment is unfair and it is expressly against the interests of the creditor, then the contractual clause is void by taking into account the commercial practices, the conditions of the private parties and the commercial relationships between them. Therefore, the Italian judge in the case of an unfair term in relation to payment conditions is entitled either to declare the nullity of the entire agreement as well as to save the contractual effects of the clause by intervening in its discretion to modify the term and rebalanced the interests of the parties to guarantee a fair dealing (D'Adamo 2004).

[47] In addition to this role of the judge to restore good faith between contractual parties, it is also interesting to highlight that under Italian law the factoring discipline is permeated by the good faith that is interpreted as a general clause under articles 1175 and 1375 of the Italian Civil Code. Indeed, in a factoring agreement the debtor has to inform the factor in relation to the inexistence of the credit and the omission to provide such information can generate a contractual responsibility in order to protect the trust of the factor (Breccia 1991, p. 376).

[48] Article 1337 of the Italian Civil Code states that: "*Le parti, nello svolgimento delle trattative e nella formazione del contratto, devono comportarsi secondo buona fede*".

[49] According to Hesselink (2011, p. 619): 'most systems make a distinction between subjective good faith and objective good faith. Subjective good faith is usually defined as a subjective state of mind: not knowing nor having to know of a certain fact or event. It is of relevance particularly in property law (*bona fide* acquisition). Objective good faith, the concept that the general good faith clauses refer to, is usually regarded as a norm for the conduct of contracting parties: 'acting in accordance with or contrary to good faith'. Some systems have even emphasized this distinction by introducing separate terminology for objective good faith (*Treu und Glauben, correttezza, redelijkheid en billijkheid*). In France, however, such a distinction is not usually made. The English common law traditionally does not recognise a concept of objective good faith. However, the concept has recently been introduced into English law by statute [it is the Unfair Terms in Consumer Contracts Regulations 1994 in order to implement the Directive 93/13/EEC]'. It is interesting to highlight, how the English common law as the Italian law have constructed the principle of good faith as a form of social justice to be imposed directly by the lawmaker.

undermining the functioning of the same negotiations and, therefore, compromising the interests of the other party.[50]

4.1 The Good Faith as a General Principle or General Clause

From this comparative study it has emerged that the good faith can be constructed both as a general principle or a general clause. Therefore, a clarification has to be made because while it is common to make reference to the principle of good faith, there is a difference between general clauses and general principles. The general principle is the meaning that is based on the enacted provisions of a legal system and that informs the same existence of the latter (for instance, the fundamental principles of a legal system are based on the provisions of a written or unwritten constitution; the agreed European constitutional traditions are based on a simultaneous interpretation of the fundamental Treaties, etc.). General clauses are provisions that are drafted in the form of open textured terms and refer to a consolidated standard of conduct or models as well as shared evaluations of a social context from which the judge by virtue of interpretation creates the specific rule that determines the dispute.

The peculiarity of good faith is that it can be considered both as a general principle as well as a general clause. It is a general principle because it is the *genus* on which the professional diligence, the information duties *in contrahendo* as well as the abuse of rights are specifications; on the other hand, it is a general clause because it represents a consolidated standard of conduct within a specific social context in which the conduct of the contractual party takes place.

In particular, we have seen as the UPICC, the CISG at international level for commercial contracts as well as the CFR at European level make reference to the conception of *bona fides* or good faith in the form of a general principle upon which the other provisions are informed. This is an instance of 'inclusive' approach, namely to construct the principle of good faith in its original terms as a universal one.

[50] Roppo (2001), p. 175. In particular, this objective dimension of the good faith that is imposed through a paternalistic approach implemented by the State must be differentiated under Italian law from a subjective dimension of good faith that is centred only on subjective intentions of contractual parties and their subjective state of mind (Roppo 2001, p. 176; Piraino 2015, p. 1). In other words, it means that in the former circumstance the lawmaker has imposed the good faith as a general clause to restore justice in a contractual relationship, whereas in the latter case the lawmaker has only recognised the good faith as a subjective state of mind of the party in terms of its ignorance or false configuration of an economic interest by which the law connects the production of legal effects. For instance, in the agency contract under Italian law the principal cannot benefit from the state of ignorance or good faith by which the agent has acted on its behalf in accordance with article 1391, second paragraph, of the Italian Civil Code. This circumstance can directly show how the good faith constructed in subjective terms can prevent possible frauds. Furthermore, it should be highlighted as the good faith constructed in subjective terms is never capable of diminishing or avoid the application of good faith in objective terms that is imposed directly by the lawmaker (Roppo 2001, p. 176).

4.2 *Distance Marketing of Financial Services and the Implementation of Good Faith in the Italian Consumer Code*

The Italian legal system affords consumer protection among others by means of article 36 of the Legislative Decree 6 September 2005, n. 206 (Italian Consumer Code). Here the lawmaker provides the consumer with a specific protection by declaring the nullity of unfair terms. The terms of the contract entered into between the consumer and the business operator are considered unfair if those terms create a significant imbalance of rights and obligations between the parties (article 33), despite those terms have been negotiated in good faith.[51] To this end, the nullity of the unfair term represents a form of protection that is afforded to the consumer, so that the unfair terms are severed from the contract which otherwise maintains its legal effects. This remedy is implemented for the sole benefit of the consumer and the judge is entitled to activate such procedure without being specifically asked for his intervention.

Hence, the good faith as a general principle has been developed and has found a new dimension by becoming a protection tool for the interests of the consumer by virtue of its interpretation as a general clause. In this light, the judge has given 'citizenship' to good faith to evaluate the interests of private parties in specific contracts that are categorised under the paradigm of business to consumer contracts.

In recent decades, this consumer oriented approach has been derived from the implementation of legislative acts of the European Union, specifically in the financial markets sector. Among those secondary legislation acts, the Directive on distance marketing of consumer financial services (Directive 2002/65/EC) provides, *inter alia*, certain provisions to protect the consumer in financial services. In this light, under article 67-*septiesdecies* of the Italian Consumer Code, which in turn implements the Directive 2002/65/EC, imposes an obligation to the supplier of financial services, who must provide the consumer with comprehensive information before the conclusion of a contract of financial services.[52] In case of failure to provide such information and disclosure the Italian Consumer Code entitles the consumer to seek the nullity of such contract.[53] It is interesting to highlight that in the

[51] Under Italian law the law maker has provided two specifications of the general principle of good faith through professional diligence (article 1176 of the Italian Civil Code) and information duties in the negotiations of the contract (article 1337 of the Italian Civil Code). Specifically, good faith and correctness under Italian law are overlapping concepts when the lawmaker and the interpreter make reference to the good faith in objective sense (articles 1175 and 1375 of the Italian Civil Code). Therefore, the judge when is referring to the principle of good faith under Italian law is always considering the objective dimension of good faith (Gallo 2009).

[52] See articles 3, 4 and 5 of the Directive 2002/65/EC.

[53] Indeed, under article 1337 of the Italian Civil Code: 'Le parti nello svolgimento delle trattative e nella formazione del contratto devono comportarsi secondo buona fede'. For this reason, the information duties in the negotiation phase are an essential aspect of the good faith in an objective sense and the provision of the Italian Consumer Code can also be seen as a specification of the general provision that is contained in the Italian Civil Code.

Italian legal system the conception of good faith is constructed in a broad sense as a general principle. We have seen that under the Italian Consumer Code the principle of good faith is specified through the information obligation imposed on the supplier of financial services during the negotiation phase. This is also an implementation of a duty of good faith in pre-contractual negotiations that is imposed by the same Directive concerning the distance marketing of consumer financial services under article 3 (2).[54] Nevertheless, this is only a specification of the general principle of good faith under Italian law because the good faith has been perceived as the real foundation of the entire Italian legal system when scholars and jurisprudence have agreed on associating the principle of good faith to the fundamental solidarity duties under Article 2 of the Italian Constitution.[55,56] Indeed, according to this opinion good faith is a general clause that represents a direct specification of a general principle that is broader and capable of extending to any general clause. For instance, article 1375 of the Italian Civil Code provides that the contractual party must act in good faith during the performance of the contract. This means that the good faith is constructed as a general clause that directly constitutes a specification and application of a general solidarity principle. Indeed, it is only through the solidarity principle that the egoistic interests of the contractual parties can be mitigated and rectified.[57] Therefore, it can be said that constitutional traditions have brought the good faith among the most important values of the Italian State, so that the information duties in the pre-contractual phase can also be interpreted as a specification of a general obligation that is imposed to every Italian citizen in terms of providing information to benefit the other party and not to act in bad faith.

5 Conclusions

This Chapter has provided a thorough overview of the origins of *bona fides* and it has outlined an important development towards a particular meaning of good faith that is no longer applicable in the sense of a universal paradigm.

From the *bona fides* in the *ius gentium* to the fairness of commercial dealings through the *lex mercatoria*, good faith has informed the evaluation criteria of

---

[54] Article 3 (2) Directive 2002/65/EC: 'The information referred to in paragraph 1, the commercial purpose of which must be made clear, shall be provided in a clear and comprehensible manner in any way appropriate to the means of distance communication used, with due regard, in particular, to the principles of good faith in commercial transactions, and the principles governing the protection of those who are unable, pursuant to the legislation of the Member States, to give their consent, such as minors.'

[55] Article 2 of the Italian Constitution: "La Repubblica riconosce e garantisce i diritti inviolabili dell'uomo, sia come singolo, sia nelle formazioni sociali ove si svolge la sua personalità, e richiede l'adempimento dei doveri inderogabili di solidarietà politica, economica e sociale".

[56] Bianca (2004), p. 102.

[57] Piraino (2015), p. 44.

conducts and it has been considered as the legal instrument through which the legal sanction could be applied in case of breach of good faith by a contractual party.

In particular, the Italian lawmaker makes reference to the principle of good faith, and takes into account the principle of good faith both in its objective and subjective forms by constructing *bona fides* both as a general principle and as a consolidated social standard through which to restore social justice into private relationships. In this latter case, it is the judge that is deputed to restore justice. However, we have also pointed out that the *bona fides* dimension in Italy has been perceived also as part of the most important values of the Italian constitution. This is a clear instance of what I term 'inclusive' approach to good faith.

The same reference to good faith as a general principle is contained at international level for commercial contracts both in the UPICC and CISG in order to proclaim good faith as an overarching principle of the entire system of rules. Furthermore, at European level different efforts have been put to draft a European code of contract law (PECL, CFR), but still today the approaches to good faith change from legal system to legal system in Continental Europe up to the total absence of the principle of good faith in objective terms and as a general principle in the English common law. At European level only the CFR takes into account the *bona fides* as a general principle, whereas the PECL and CESL construct the principle in terms of general clauses.

This is not only a words play, but it signifies how *bona fides* has lost its role of informing principle in universalistic terms. This is what I term 'private" approach to good faith. It means that the CESL and the PELC at European level are more concerned into taking into account a standardisation of good faith as a social model to be applied in the concrete case by the judge.

As opposed to this "private" approach to good faith, I have highlighted the presence of an "inclusive" approach to good faith where the principle is still taken into account in universalistic terms. It is not by chance that this recognition is implemented in the CFR, UPICC and CISG. Indeed, these are acts informed by a high principle of internationalization and uniformity. In other words, they preserve the original meaning of *bona fides* in Roman law where it was one of the most important general principles of Roman society, and its universality was centred on its conceptualisation as a value of the society (for instance, it is the same approach that is still taken by the Italian legal system through its constitution).

Furthermore, under the Italian Civil Code as well as the Italian special laws (*i.e.* the Italian Consumer Code) the good faith appears also as a general clause, representing a consolidated standard of conduct, an interpretation tool for contractual law. Indeed, judges prefer to use *bona fides* as a general clause, and this approach seems to be followed also at European level. National courts as well as private arbitrators appointed by the parties use general clauses in order to find the *ratio decidendi*, namely the general rule that must be applied to the concrete case. This technique allows either to supplement the possible lack of protection of a legal system or to create social justice in commercial or contractual relationships fort instance by modifying or terminating the contract that has become onerous for one party. Hence, the judge becomes a present day arbitrator comparable to the *praetor peregrinus* in the third century B.C., who is used to making reference to the general clauses through the *ius commune* of international commerce as expressed by the *lex mercatoria* that in turn postulates honest and fair business practices based on good faith.

However, it can be said that the use of good faith as a general clause rather than a general principle has changed its original meaning. Nowadays *bona fides* has become a particular and specific principle to protect particular interests of the contractual parties, often consumers. It has become a protection tool instead of a legal instrument through which the law could be seen as universal in its application. The latter meaning is still preserved by lawmakers when they need to justify and give emphasis to new legislation, while judges are now used to derive from the law a substantive application of *bona fides*. This application of the principle of good faith that developed from a general principle into a general clause for the determination of a concrete dispute is far from the ancient and original conception of good faith in Roman legal history (indeed, also the *praetor* was applying to the concrete case general principles of the *ius commune* that were not written as opposed to a modern conception of general clauses that are codified by virtue of a standardisation of the good faith in terms of social model). It seems that contemporary interpretation and understanding of *bona fides* is more closely related to the conception of equity as a form of correctness of the law instead of a universal form of understanding of the law. It is a form of privatisation of good faith.

The comparison of different legal meanings rather than different legal systems as pursued in the chapter by way of a comparative study using a timeline rather than separate legal systems has allowed to discover the evolution of good faith and to categorise different meanings in terms of general clauses and general principles. These categories and meanings can actually be compared and can also be used to compare different legal provisions of different legal systems. Indeed, in the case of vague concepts as well as law in general it is the meaning and not the single provisions that are actually the subject matter of the comparison. This novel methodology should be implemented in the study of comparative law in order to discover what I term 'legal constant/s'. This latter concept refers to the constant legal meaning that can be found inside different legal provisions. In this light, the differences that exist among European Member States in terms of approaching the subject of good faith are no more seen as obstacles, but as opportunities of finding a legal constant. In terms of *bona fides*, the legal constant of this comparative study has outlined its categorisation in terms of a universalistic principle and a general principle. It is not by chance that the CFR has stated the good faith as a general principle, because seen in this way it represents the legal constant of the EU Member States. Furthermore, it is the general principle or if one might say according to this new understanding: it is the legal constant that informs all the other provisions under the UPICC and CISG.

As a last remark it can be said that the central question today in relation to good faith is no longer the Kantian quest of *quid est ius*?, but the particular answer to the essential question *quid est iuris*?. One possible concern is that it can bring the law of contract as well as the law in general towards egoistic purposes based on desires and wishful thinking rather than focusing on the protection of universal rights. In other terms, when we take into account rights in general many times we forget that there are also correlative duties to carry out. In the end, no one can benefit from a right without assuming at the same time also duties and responsibilities. This is an essential assumption of the identification of the State, but this dogma has recently been eroded by egoistic desires that call for specific answers. It can be said that the *Res Publica* that in Roman law was an object of public domain because the same society was identified through the State, so that the Roman State was the State of the *gentes* (namely, of all the populations through the *ius gentium*), has developed into an unknown State. Today, the State is an unknown as well as the rights are the rights of unknowns, who pursue their individualistic desire and needs. Under this light, the evolution of good faith as a general clause in terms of protecting the consumer represents the more intimate instance of this wishful thinking discourse. A discourse where the rights of the consumer do not belong to a specific person, but to a legal category that is composed of millions of individuals who are unknowns in the eyes of the law. A law that in Roman law was the expression of justice in universalistic terms through good faith as a general principle. This was the 'inclusive' approach that looked firstly into social justice in order to answer the needs of individuals in universalistic rather than individualistic terms.

References

Alpa G (2009) Il draft common frame of reference del diritto privato europeo. Cedam, Milano

Beale H (2008) European initiatives (CFR) and reform of civil law in new member states, vol XIV. Law Review University of Tartu

Bianca CM (2004) Il Diritto Civile. L'Obbligazione. Giuffrè, Milano

Bianca CM, Bonell MJ (1987) Commentary on the international sales law the 1980 Vienna sales convention. Giuffrè, Milano

Biondi B (1972) Istituzioni di Diritto Romano. Giuffrè, Milano

Bortolotti F (2016) Towards a transnational commercial law: the essential role of the Unidroit principles. In: Eppur si muove: the age of uniform law, vol 2. International Institute for the Unification Private Law, Rome

Bravo González A, Bravo Valdés B (2004) Derecho Romano Primer Curso. Porrúa, México

Breccia U (1991) Le Obbligazioni. Giuffrè, Milano

Brown L (1993) The new shorter Oxford English Dictionary on historical principles, vol 1. A-M Clarendon Press, Oxford

Costa A (1990) Voce Arbitrato, (VI) Arbitrato nel Commercio Internazionale. Enciclopedia Giuridica, Roma

Cuniberti G (2014) Three theories of *lex Mercatoria*. Columbia J Transnl Law 52(2)

D'Adamo G (2004) Le nullità di cui all'art. 7 d. lgs. 9 ottobre 2002, n. 231 in materia di ritardi di pagamento nelle transazioni commerciali. Responsabilità comunicazione impresa

du Plessis P (2010) Borkowski's textbook on Roman law. Oxford University Press, Oxford

Gallo P (2009) Contratto e Buona Fede. Utet, Milano

Grosso G (1965) Lezioni di Storia del Diritto Romano. Giappichelli, Torino

Hesselink MW (2011) The concept of good faith. In: Hartkamp AS, Hesselink MW, Hondius EG, Mark C, du Perron CE (eds) Towards a European Civil Code, 4th edn. Kluwer Law International

Johnston D (1999) Roman law in context. Cambridge University Press, Cambridge

Jolowicz HF (1957) Roman foundations of modern law. Oxford University Press, Oxford
Jolowicz HF (1972) Historical introduction to the study of Roman law. Cambridge University Press, Cambridge
Kent RG (1938) Varro on the Latin language, volume I, Books 5–7 translated by Kent. Harvard University Press, Cambridge
Marrone M (1994) Istituzioni di Diritto Romano. Palumbo, Palermo
Mazzetta FG (2014) The good faith principle: Vexata Quaestio. In: International sales law: a global challenge. Cambridge University Press, Cambridge
Miller W (2016) Cicero *De Officiis* with an English translation. Wentworh Press, Brisbane
Mousourakis G (2003) The historical and institutional context of Roman law. Ashgate, Hampshire
Mousourakis G (2007) A legal history of Rome. Routledge, New York
Orestano R (1961) Introduzione allo Studio Storico del Diritto Romano. Giappichelli, Torino
Piraino F (2015) La buona fede in senso oggettivo. Giappichelli, Torino
Poste E (1994) Istitutionum Iuris Civilis Commentarii Quatuor or elements of Roman law by Gaius with a translation and commentary by Edward Poste. Gaunt & Sons, Holmes Beach
Roppo V (2001) Il Contratto. Giuffre, Milano
Russo E (2009) Imprenditore debole, imprenditore – persona, abuso di dipendenza economica, "terzo contratto". Contratto e Impresa
Schipani S (1999) La Codificazione del Diritto Romano Comune. Giappichelli, Torino
Watson A (1992) The state, law and religion: Pagan Rome. The University of Georgia Press, Athens
Zimmermann R, Whittaker S (2000) Good faith in European contract law. Cambridge University Press, Cambridge

Private and Public in the Design of Commercial Law: Lessons from the History of Bills of Exchange

Janwillem Oosterhuis

Contents

Abstract This chapter provides a historical perspective on the interaction between private and public actors in the area of commercial law, to identify lessons about an appropriate design of commercial law. Historically private actors generally have borne responsibility for creating rules to regulate their transactions whereas public actors often have supported and subsequently codified this private regulation. A central theme in this contribution is whether private actor solutions need public actor intervention to thrive. Although public actor intervention might not be necessary per se for clarity, predictability and the wide use of private actor solutions, that still leaves the possibility open that public actor intervention still might have those effects on private actor solutions. The history of bills of exchange is used to address these questions, because it provides a vivid interaction between private and public actors. It will be concluded that from a historical perspective, private actors appear

I am particularly grateful to Anna Beckers and Nicole Kornet for the stimulating exchange of ideas about the appropriate design of commercial law when working together on our chapter Who does What in Commercial Law? The Case for a Multi-Level & Multi-Actor Approach to Regulating Commercial Transactions, Beckers (2015). For critical remarks on the history of bills of exchange in the Early Modern Period, I would like to thank Bram Van Hofstraeten.

J. Oosterhuis (✉)
Faculty of Law, University of Maastricht, Maastricht, The Netherlands
e-mail: janwillem.oosterhuis@maastrichtuniversity.nl

M. Heidemann, J. Lee (eds.), *The Future of the Commercial Contract in Scholarship and Law Reform*, https://doi.org/10.1007/978-3-319-95969-6_14

to be pre-eminently suited to creating relevant legal rules, regardless of the level—local, regional, global—where these rules are used, provided a relatively efficient enforcement mechanism exists. Although it can be assumed that public actor intervention will generally create more legal certainty for a private actor solution, the actual effects of this legal certainty are very difficult to establish. Moreover, public actor intervention does not appear to be necessary per se for a wide use of clear and predictable private actor solutions.

1 Introduction

Commercial law constitutes a complex amalgamation of private and public actors at different levels of governance developing rules for different types of commercial contracts. Chronologically, certain waves can be detected with respect to who develops the rules for commercial transactions. It can be seen that historically, private actors have borne responsibility for creating rules to regulate their transactions and that this private regulation has been supported and subsequently codified by public actors. However, as European and global trade increases and economic integration progresses, there is not only renewed attention for regulation of commercial transactions at a level other than the national, but also a revival of rules created by private actors that suit with their commercial activities—although these rules must fit within the frameworks primarily provided by public actors. The proper role of the public actor—whether the European Union or international political institutions—in this context, is the subject of much discussion in the literature,[1] an example being the late proposal for a Common European Sales Law (CESL) that would apply to cross-border business-to-business sales contracts.[2] In light of the complexity and fragmentation of the current regulatory environment as well as the regulatory activity of European and international actors, it is highly relevant to consider who is best qualified to develop the rules for commercial contracts and at what level such rules should be implemented.[3]

This contribution will provide a historical perspective on the interaction between private and public actors in the area of commercial law, to identify lessons about an appropriate design of commercial law. Although no separate normative framework will be developed, facilitating the exchange of goods or services in a market will be used to assess whether private and public actors were successful in their regulation of commercial law.[4]

[1] Whether or not the European Union is the right—public—actor is amongst others extensively discussed in literature on proportionality and subsidiarity. See for an overview, instead of many, Jansen and Rademacher (2012), pp. 299–313.

[2] See e.g. Schwenzer (2012); the various contributions to Magnus (2012) and Kornet (2012). See also the contribution of Anagnostopoulou in this volume.

[3] See e.g. Beckers et al. (2015).

[4] For a normative framework taking the exchange of goods and services as starting point, see e.g. Beckers et al. (2015), pp. 131–145.

A central theme in this contribution is whether private actor solutions need public actor intervention to thrive. As mentioned already above, historically private actors generally have borne responsibility for creating rules to regulate their transactions whereas public actors often have supported and subsequently codified this private regulation. This apparent regularity might suggest that private actor solutions are in need of some kind of public actor intervention to let a private actor solution thrive or at least have lasting effect. A first question is whether such hypothesis—private actor solutions need public actor intervention to thrive—is plausible, taking the history of commercial law into account. Put in a different way: are there historical examples where private actor solutions were widely used despite a lack of public actor intervention? However, even if public actor intervention might not be necessary per se for clarity, predictability and the wide use of private actor solutions, that still leaves the possibility open that public actor intervention might nonetheless have those effects on private actor solutions. In other words, is one of the effects of public actor intervention that private actor solutions for commercial transactions will be clearer, more predictable and wider used? The history of bills of exchange is used to address these questions, because it provides a vivid interaction between private and public actors.

It will be concluded that from a historical perspective, private actors appear to be pre-eminently suited to creating relevant legal rules, regardless of the level—local, regional, global—where these rules are used, provided a relatively efficient enforcement mechanism exists. Although it can be assumed that public actor intervention will generally create more legal certainty for a private actor solution, the actual effects of this legal certainty are very difficult to establish. Moreover, public actor intervention does not appear to be necessary per se for a wide use of clear and predictable private actor solutions.

2 Bills of Exchange: A Historical Perspective

2.1 *Private Supremacy in the Middle Ages*

Between the thirteenth and seventeenth centuries, merchants developed their own, varying customs to solve commercial problems[5]; one of them being the fact that trade to a distant place necessarily requires a return trade. Traditionally merchants sold their goods at a fair, such as those of the Champagne in the high Middle Ages, bought a return cargo with the proceeds, and sold this cargo at home with a view to making a profit. Bills of exchange have their origins in a new mechanism for making

[5] It is submitted that no *lex mercatoria* existed in the sense of 'an autonomos system of legal rules applying to merchants throughout the civilized world, akin in status to civil or canon law', or 'a corpus of international rules accepted by merchants everywhere, and was for that reason part of the *jus gentium* or law of nations', Baker (1999), p. 81. See for other rebuttals of such a *lex mercatoria*, i.a. Ewart (1903), Epstein (2004), Donahue (2004), Kadens (2004) and Kadens (2012).

returns that became possible with the transition to a regime of sedentary merchants and the development of an agency merchant system between the thirteenth and seventeenth centuries.[6] For the sake of clarity a basic example: a merchant from Venice could ship spices to his representative in Bruges, who would sell the spices. To obtain payment from the buyer in Bruges, the Venetian merchant would ask his representative (the remitter or deliverer) in Bruges to have the money delivered to a merchant in Bruges, e.g. trading wool to Venice, who, importantly had a representative in Venice. This wool merchant of Bruges (the drawer or taker), who was required to transfer the payment to the Venetian merchant, would draw a bill of exchange on his representative in Venice (the drawee), ordering the Venetian representative to pay a certain sum of money upon presentation of the bill at maturity. The representative of the Venetian spice merchant in Bruges would then send this bill of exchange to the Venetian merchant (the payee), who would present the bill to the wool merchant's Venetian representative upon its maturity to obtain payment.[7] Likewise, when the merchant from Bruges would ship wool to Venice and have it sold there by his representative, a similar set of transactions could be made. The problem of making returns could thus be solved by relying on a system of bills of exchange.[8] Apart from facilitating payment between merchants trading at a distance, the advantage of these bills of exchange was that since around the seventeenth century and particularly in Antwerp, they became negotiable instruments.[9] In the above example, the Venetian merchant could, instead of obtaining payment himself, transfer title to the bill and thereby all rights under it to another merchant who would become the holder of the bill in order to meet his own payment obligation. This subsequent holder would then be entitled to obtain payment under the bill from the drawee upon its maturity. Although a similar—functional—problem thus had to be solved by medieval merchants in different locations, no universal commercial custom arose: the law of bills of exchange varied from country to country, or rather even from city to city.[10]

This historical development shows that with the backing of the local courts and city councils, merchants were perfectly capable of developing their own rules to resolve a particular commercial problem.[11] Bills of exchange are, therefore, indeed an example of law developing from commercial practice, into local and regional customs. It also shows that despite the diversity of local rules on bills of exchange,

[6] See De Roover (1953), pp. 29–42; Spufford (1987), pp. 825–826; Rogers (1995), pp. 32–33.

[7] See Rogers (1995), pp. 33–34; Goode and McKendrick (2010), pp. 516–517. See also Asser (1987), pp. 112–114.

[8] Rogers (1995), p. 34.

[9] Van der Wee (1977), pp. 328–332, 348–350. See also Rogers (1995), p. 94; Asser (1987), p. 122; De Ruysscher (2009b), pp. 265–277.

[10] See e.g. Kadens (2004), pp. 57–58; Baker (1999), p. 85; Ewart (1903), p. 152; Asser (1987), pp. 116–122, 124–130.

[11] See Gelderblom (2013), p. 138; Kadens (2004), pp. 51–54; Epstein (2004), pp. 16–20. For the high Middle Ages impartial legal enforcement is more problematic, see e.g. Greif (2004), pp. 116–119.

the system of bills of exchange could function effectively for merchants trading throughout Europe.

2.2 *From Private Usage to Early Modern Public Intervention*

In the Early Modern Period, many cities of commerce started to codify or at least record their laws, including commercial customs, to avoid the time-consuming judicial investigations by a group of sworn witnesses (*turben*) to confirm the validity of a contested (commercial) practice.[12] Famous examples are customs of Italian city states, such as Genoa and Venice,[13] but since around 1300 customary law also started to be privately recorded in towns in Flanders and Brabant. In certain cities, such as Bruges, and initially also Antwerp, foreign merchants of some privileged nations could have their commercial disputes decided before their own consular courts relying on their own customs. However, in Antwerp, and since 1413 also in Amsterdam, local customs were aligned to business practice by frequently using *turben*, produced by local and foreign merchants. In contrast to ordinary testimonies by witnesses a *turbe* had legal force.[14] Particularly in Antwerp the city's local customs seem to have gained universal acceptance by local and foreign residents. However, only in 1547 a first full set of the Antwerp customs was edited, following the order of Charles V of 1531 to record the customary law for the Low Countries. This first edition was rejected by the government and edited again in 1570, 1582, and 1608.[15] In recording these customs both local and foreign merchants—private actors—thus played a vital role, though the actual rule setting was done via public actors—the city and the central government—at a local level. The Antwerp customs, however, had a more regional impact, as it was one of the sources of the Amsterdam commercial customs, including the law on bills of exchange.[16]

The actual effect of the recording of the Antwerp customs on its market for bills of exchange is very hard—if at all—to establish, because the functioning of a market depends on many variables, which are difficult to isolate.[17] The 1582 edition of the customs, for example, slightly improved the payee's position towards the remitter (or deliverer) when the payee acted in his own name. In that case the remitter could no longer revoke the bill of exchange.[18] However, even if after such change

[12] Gelderblom (2013), pp. 135–136.

[13] Gelderblom (2013), p. 138.

[14] Gelderblom (2013), p. 135.

[15] Gelderblom (2013), p. 135; Asser (1987), p. 106.

[16] See Lichtenauer (1956), pp. 87–88; Asser (1987), pp. 106–107; De Ruysscher (2009a), pp. 478–479. See also Van der Wee (1977), pp. 328–332, 335–336, 344.

[17] On the fundamental problem of statistical identification in modern empirical economics, see Helland and Klick (2011), pp. 108–109. Compare also Olson (1982), pp. 137–140. On the problem of isolating factors that influence economic development, see Helland and Klick (2011), p. 100.

[18] See De Ruysscher (2009b), p. 259.

in the rules also a corresponding change in the practice concerning bills of exchange could be established, for instance by extensive archival research,[19] the problem still remains to what extent such change can be attributed to the new regulation.

Apart from introducing changes in the rules themselves, the recording of the Antwerp customs generally promoted legal certainty and uniformity within the Antwerp market for bills of exchange. Theoretically such legal uniformity leads to lower transaction costs and thus more trade.[20] However, also this general effect of legal uniformity—here the recording of the Antwerp customs for its market—is almost impossible to measure, again because of the number of variables that determine the amount of trade and the difficulty to isolate these variables.[21] Nevertheless, taking the number of judicial decisions in Antwerp as indicator, trade even seemed to diminish upon recording the Antwerp customs, as the number of decisions in commercial matters adjudicated before the Antwerp court declined.[22] Admittedly the number of commercial legal disputes depends importantly on the number of commercial transactions, i.e. the amount of trade, and to a lesser extent on the actual content of the law.[23] The most plausible explanation appears to be simply a downward economic trend.[24] This serves to illustrate that the actual effect of recording customs—i.e. public actor intervention—on a market is extremely difficult, if not impossible, to establish. Rather, although the Antwerp council intervention had indeed the effect that the Antwerp customs were officially recorded, wide use and acceptance appears to hold primarily for the printed edition of the Antwerp customs: the 1582 version of the customs was widely referred to, but not for instance the 1608 edition. Proliferation of customs could thus very well result of the printing of these customs and not of public actor intervention per se.[25]

Public actor intervention to promote the market interest by interfering in commercial practice might even have the opposite effect of disturbing a market. An example from the English history of bills of exchange can serve to illustrate this point. For England it appears that between the thirteenth and seventeenth centuries

[19] Whereby particularly also non-legal sources need to be incorporated in such research, as legal sources only give a distorted, viz. legal, picture of actual commercial practice, see De Ruysscher (2009b), pp. 12–13, 245.

[20] In 1937, the basis for a transaction cost theory was already laid down by Coase (1937). See briefly on the development and impact of neo-institutionalism and particularly the transaction cost theory, Screpanti and Zamagni (1993), pp. 384–388. For an overview of empirical studies addressing the costs of legal uncertainty, see Wagner (2005), pp. 31–32, 35–37. Most of these studies concentrate on explaining cross-country variations in growth due to difference in legal uncertainty within a country. See also Smits (2005), pp. 169–170.

[21] See note 17.

[22] Although there might be a relation between the amount of trade and the number of commercial legal disputes, such relation does not say anything about the actual popularity of a specific legal instrument, such as a bill of exchange, see De Ruysscher (2009b), p. 264.

[23] See e.g. the large empirical study on trends and developments in Dutch private and administrative legal disputes between roughly 2002 and 2012, Diephuis et al. (2013).

[24] See De Ruysscher (2009b), pp. 137–141.

[25] Fundamentally De Ruysscher (2009a), see e.g. 464.

in general commercial transactions, including exchange transactions,[26] were adjudicated by common law courts,[27] but also by the courts of fairs (piepowder), markets, and towns.[28] In 1622, the *Consuetudo, vel Lex Mercatoria* by Gerard Malynes appeared. This survey of local and foreign commercial customs also pointed out the great variety in customs as to bills regarding formation, times of running, falling due, days of grace, etc.[29] From the seventeenth and eighteenth centuries onwards, also in England bills of exchange were no longer considered just a contract between deliverer and taker, but an instrument that created and embodied an obligation for the drawee to pay money to the payee or any other holder[30]—as had been the case in Antwerp earlier during the seventeenth century.[31] Chief Justice Holt importantly harmonized this negotiability of bills of exchange with the existing principles of common law. However, in commercial practice this negotiability was soon extended to promissory notes in general. Thereupon Chief Justice Holt tried to keep the assignment of promissory notes within the general principles of the common law and outside of the law merchant, basically by restricting negotiability to bills of exchange. In response, parliament passed the Statute of Anne in 1704 (or Bills of Exchange Act), making promissory notes negotiable in the same manner as bills of exchange.[32] This, however, undermined the distinction between bills of exchange and promissory notes, which created numerous conceptual difficulties in the law of negotiable instruments, and consequently legal uncertainty in commercial practice.[33] It was not until 1764, that the courts fully developed a new framework for the negotiability of written instruments.[34] Here, statutory intervention did more harm than good, resulting in confusion in legal and commercial practice. This is to illustrate that public actors should be careful when incorporating commercial usages into existing law.

2.3 *Public Dominance in Eighteenth to Twentieth Centuries' Commercial Law*

It was merely the eighteenth and nineteenth centuries that witnessed the emergence of nation states as public actors. Legal rules regulating contractual relations were laid down, inter alia, in general civil codes such as the Prussian *Allgemeines*

[26] See Rogers (1995), pp. 44–68; Baker 1979, pp. 308–313.
[27] Rogers (1995), pp. 12–20.
[28] See Baker (1999), pp. 85–86; Rogers (1995), pp. 20–31.
[29] See Baker (1999), p. 85; Gelderblom (2013), p. 138; Ewart (1903), p. 152.
[30] See Rogers (1995), pp. 94, 194–195.
[31] See Van der Wee (1977), pp. 328–332, 348–350; De Ruysscher (2009b), pp. 265–277.
[32] See Rogers (1995), pp. 177–186; Dylag (2010), pp. 158–165.
[33] See Rogers (1995), pp. 186–188; Dylag (2010), pp. 165–174.
[34] Dylag (2010), pp. 168–174.

Landrecht of 1794, the French *Code civil* of 1804, and the Dutch *Burgerlijk Wetboek* of 1838—essentially a copy of the French *Code civil* valid until then—later replaced by the new *Burgerlijk Wetboek* of 1992, or in separate statutes confined to a particular area, such as the English Sale of Goods Act 1893, succeeded by the Sale of Goods Act 1979. Legal rules on typical commercial usages, customs, contracts, and institutions—such as commercial records, partnerships and companies, maritime commerce and also bills of exchange—were often laid down in separate commercial codes such as the French *Code de commerce* (1807) and the Dutch *Wetboek van Koophandel* (1838)—the latter again more or less a copy of the French *Code de commerce* valid until then.[35] The German *Allgemeines Deutsches Handelsgesetzbuch* of 1861 was a mix of provisions on general contract law and specific commercial rules: no common German codification existed yet.[36] Many of these commercial codes were—at least partly—a codification of existing commercial usages[37] or drawing upon even earlier codifications of such usages, including certain international maritime usages, like the French *Ordonnance sur le commerce* (1673) and *Ordonnance de la marine* (1681) respectively of Jean Baptiste Colbert (1619–1683) and Louis XIV (1638–1715).[38]

As discussed previously, these mainly local usages had been developed by and for private actors, the merchants, even if public actors, such as city councils or lords, recorded and thereby—to a certain extent—transformed them.[39] Importantly, since the French revolution, states generally abolished different classes in society, including a 'merchant class'. This is reflected in several civil and/or commercial codes after the French revolution: importantly in the *Code de Commerce* (1807) itself but also in the *Allgemeines Deutsches Handelsgesetzbuch* (1861), where the definition of commercial law was centred around (persons performing) commercial acts—i.e. taking an objective approach—and no longer around the person of the merchant—i.e. taking a subjective approach.[40]

These civil and/or commercial codes were to create legal certainty in the emerging national markets—like in France—or interregional markets—like in the German Confederation.[41] In variations, the argument of legal certainty has been used to justify and defend the introduction of rather different commercial

[35] E.g. Flume (2014), pp. 53–56; Klomp (1998), pp. 13–24.

[36] Flume (2014), pp. 56–59.

[37] E.g. Flume (2014), pp. 50–51, 56–57; Rückert (1993), pp. 24–25.

[38] E.g. Gelderblom (2013), pp. 133–139; Flume (2014), pp. 49–50; Klomp (1998), pp. 94–97.

[39] See Van Hofstraeten (2015).

[40] Flume (2014), pp. 53–54, 59–60. With the German *Bürgerliches Gesetzbuch* of 1900 a general law of contract was introduced, and the *Handelsgesetzbuch* of 1896 had thus regained more a specific commercial character than its predecessor, the *Allgemeines Deutsches Handelsgesetzbuch*. Indeed, merchants or entrepreneurs again became identified as such by the HGB, see Flume (2014), pp. 65–67. On the problematic side of this distinction between businesses and consumers in contemporary European contract law, see recently Maren Heidemann (2016), pp. 667–668.

[41] E.g. Bergfeld (1987), pp. 101–103; Kanning (2003), p. 61.

instruments,[42] such as the *Code de commerce* (1807),[43] the *Allgemeines Deutsches Handelsgesetzbuch* (1861),[44] and the Sale of Goods Act 1893.[45] Because these codes are embedded in national legal systems, they also imply the enforcement of agreements between private actors.[46] For these civil and commercial codes—and for Europe obviously many more could be listed here—the regulation of commercial relations thus took place by a public actor—the national legislator—on a national level in the form of legislation.

Already in the seventeenth century, Louis XIV had tried to establish legal unity in commercial matters with his *Ordonnance sur le commerce* (1673), which also contained rules on bills of exchange. The origins of these rules were partly based on the customs of Amsterdam and thus Antwerp.[47] Indeed, in the seventeenth and eighteenth centuries Dutch rules concerning negotiable credit instruments—including bills of exchange—transformed financial law throughout the European continent.[48] But as late as the nineteenth century, there were still wide divergences in actual practice on even the most basic principles of law relating to bills of exchange in e.g. Dutch, French, German and English law, for instance in respect of formation, times of running and falling due, and days of grace.[49] Probably more fundamentally, on a dogmatic level roughly three traditions could be distinguished: (i) the French one, whereby the bill of exchange was considered to produce evidence of the agreement between drawer and remitter; (ii) the German one, whereby the bill of exchange was considered to be a payment promise, completely abstract from the underlying legal relationship between drawer and remitter, and; (iii) the English one, that rejects the abstraction from the underlying agreement between drawer and remitter, but also rejects any appeal to the underlying agreement as far as it concerns a holder in due course.[50] These varying rules and traditions on bills of exchange were, inter alia, laid

---

[42] On the introduction and different structures of a.o. the *Code de commerce*, the *Allgemeines Deutsches Handelsgesetzbuch*, and the Sale of Goods Act 1893, see Flume (2014), pp. 43–83.

[43] Chaptal M, ministre de l'intérieur (4 December 1801), in: Locré (1837), p. 2: 'Il vous [les commissaires-rédacteurs] était réservé de donner à la France une législation uniforme; mais, jusqu'aujourd'hui, l'ensemble des lois françaises n'a présenté qu'un chaos qui se compose de coutumes locales, dont la plupart sont contraires entre elles, et de réglemens qui, presque tous, ont été déterminés par l'empire des circonstances.'

[44] Although introduction of the *Allgemeines Deutsches Handelsgesetzbuch* (ADHGB) also had the more general and political goal of unifying German law, see Bergfeld (1987), pp. 101–103, 105. See also Wieacker (1974), p. 90.

[45] Chalmers (1981), p. viii: 'Legislation, too, is cheaper than litigation. Moreover, in mercantile matters, the certainty of the rule is often of more importance than the substance of the rule.'

[46] See e.g. North (1991), p. 97; Greif (2004), pp. 109–110.

[47] For instance, via the French translation book of Johannes Phoonsen (1631–1702) on the customary exchange law and practice of Amsterdam. See Asser (1987), p. 107; Gelderblom (2013), pp. 138–139.

[48] See fundamentally De Ruysscher (2011).

[49] See e.g. Asser (1880), p. 2; Baker (1999), p. 85; Ewart (1903), p. 152; Asser (1987), pp. 116–122, 124–130.

[50] See e.g. Wallert (1996), p. 162; Schmoeckel (2008), p. 100.

down in civil and commercial codes—the Prussian *Allgemeines Landrecht* (1794), the French *Code de Commerce* (1807), the Dutch *Wetboek van Koophandel* (1838)[51]—or separate codes—such as the *Allgemeine Deutsche Wechselordnung* of 1869,[52] the Scandinavian Bills of Exchange Act of 1880[53] and the English Bills of Exchange Act 1882.[54] Although content wise these codes were generally a continuation of the—now nationally—existing rules on bills of exchange, formally and eventually it was now the nation state that acted as the rule maker, and not just in the marginal sense of recording rules made by private actors. This role became particularly poignant when national legislatures decided to follow a foreign example, such as the Dutch following the *Code de Commerce* or the Scandinavians following the *Wechselordnung*.

Here again a distinction can be made between introducing certain commercial rules and more generally providing legal certainty. National legislatures indeed actively shaped the rules applicable to bills of exchange. In particular, in light of the negotiability of bills, legislation was able to further secure the reliability of the system of bills of exchange, for instance by protecting the legitimate interests of subsequent holders of a bill.[55] In this way, the public actor can be seen to promote the market interest. However, the actual effect on commercial practice of these now codified rules is difficult to establish, as has been discussed above for the effect on commercial practice of recording customs during the Early Modern Period.[56] Literature on bills of exchange focuses understandably on legal changes in the laws on bills of exchange and discusses possible consequences for commercial practice only on a general level.[57]

Admittedly, the introduction of civil and/or commercial codes did also lead to a wider use of the previous commercial usages and customs in the relevant areas. The—often already prevailing or dominant—usage in a region or country would now become a statutory rule, generally trumping all other usages or customs on the same subject. However, it appears to be very hard to determine to what extent the legal certainty created by the above-mentioned national civil and/or commercial codifications contributed to an increase in trade. In the second half of the nineteenth century and at the beginning of the twentieth century, many European states indeed faced an enormous increase in trade, internally as well as internationally. However, internally this increase in trade but also its changing character, have been attributed to, inter alia, the expansion of railway networks that started to connect once isolated markets effectively creating unified national markets.[58]

---

[51] See e.g. Wallert (1996), pp. 129–145.

[52] Before the *Allgemeine Deutsche Wechselordnung* of 1869/71, numerous local laws on bills existed, more than fifty in 1847, Brox (2005), pp. 228–229. See extensively on the introduction of the *Wechselordnung*, Kuntze (1862) and Von Pannwitz (1999).

[53] See e.g. Asser (1880).

[54] Although it had already a predecessor in the Bills of Exchange Act 1704, see Goode and McKendrick (2010), p. 521.

[55] See e.g. Meyer (1909) and Wallert (1996), pp. 137–138, 144; Asser (1880), pp. 5–9.

[56] See 2.2 From Private Usage to Early Modern Public Intervention.

[57] See e.g. Wallert (1996), pp. 123–204.

[58] See e.g. for England: Deane (1973), pp. 209–216; Deane and Cole (1969), pp. 238–241; Aldcroft (1992), pp. 66–69; Mathias (1983), pp. 261–262; for Germany: Hoffmann (1963), pp. 104–105;

The economic history surrounding the introduction of the *Allgemeines Deutsches Handelsgesetzbuch* in 1861, can help to exemplify this point. Studies in the economic history of the German Confederation confirm that cross-border trade did increase after 1861.[59] Importantly, in 1834 a German Customs Union had been introduced, removing all custom duties between eighteen states, with a combined population of nearly 23.5 million.[60] Moreover, in the course of the nineteenth century a growing railway and telegraph network began to connect the once isolated territories with each other. As a result of better means of transport, in particular railways, interregional markets for generic goods such as coal and wheat started to emerge and states intertwined both socially and economically.[61] The trade between the industrial, western Prussian provinces Westphalia and Rhineland and the initially more agricultural oriented states in the South—Baden, Württemberg, and Bavaria—had already been significant before the introduction of the *Allgemeines Deutsches Handelsgesetzbuch*[62]: as from 1861, this trade would only intensify.[63] However, in the literature on economic history this increase in cross-border trade is attributed to regional specialisation—not to the introduction of the *Allgemeines Deutsches Handelsgesetzbuch*. After 1860, the Ruhr area became heavily industrialised and an export house for industrial products to the rest of the German territories, including and increasingly to the South—Baden, Württemberg, and Bavaria: specialised in producing and exporting foodstuffs and raw materials to the North.[64] The legal milestone of a uniform commercial code is mentioned only in as far as it facilitated labour mobility between states.[65] The commercial code was in any case not considered as a significant legal change for trade—contrary to for instance the introduction of the Customs Union in 1834, less than three decades ago.[66]

In any case, nation states were now pre-eminently being in the position to promulgate a nationwide code. The wide use of a particular usage seemed thus to have become linked with the fate of a nation state. The challenges faced due to the increase and changes in internal trade had indeed to be met importantly by these codes, many of which were modified in the course of the nineteenth to twenty-first centuries.[67]

Pierenkemper and Tilly (2004), pp. 58–68, 76–80; Henderson (1975), p. 51; for France: Labrousse (1954), p. 9; Price (1981), pp. 20–26, 27–37, 109–119; Bouvier (1997), pp. 652, 668–669.

[59] Detailed Tipton (1976), pp. 17–80; more in general Zorn (1963, 1973, 1978).

[60] See for instance Henderson (1975), pp. 31–43; Pierenkemper and Tilly (2004), pp. 34–36.

[61] In 1831 the first (industrial) railroad was built, near Essen, and stretched just over 7 km. By 1900 the German territories were connected by 51,000 km of railroad. See Pierenkemper and Tilly (2004), pp. 58–68, 76–80; Kanning (2003), pp. 70–76.

[62] Dumke (1977), p. 479.

[63] See Tipton (1976), pp. 39–80; Zorn (1963), pp. 328–330.

[64] See Tipton (1976), pp. 39–80; Zorn (1963), pp. 328–330.

[65] Zorn (1973), pp. 329–330.

[66] See for instance Pierenkemper and Tilly (2004), pp. 34–36; Henderson (1975), pp. 31–43.

[67] See e.g. the overview in Flume (2014), pp. 56, 64–65. On the recent reform of the *Code civil* and its impact on commercial law, see e.g. the contribution of Pédamon in this volume.

2.4 Public Versus Private Actors in the Globalization of Trade

Inclusion of certain private actor usages in a code or treaty, however, does not necessarily mean that these usages would not have been widely used without the intervention of a public actor. To illustrate this point, some international instruments will be discussed, both from public and private actors. The question then is which instruments are—likely or presumably—wider used in international trade: the public or the private actor instruments.

The enormous increase in international trade since the second half of the nineteenth century was not only due to for instance technological progress. In the eighteenth century, the mercantilism of for example Colbert had already been replaced by a *laissez-faire* policy.[68] But towards the end of the nineteenth century, trade would importantly be liberalised through a series of bilateral and sometimes multilateral treaties.[69] These increasing cross-border commercial relations generally fell under the remit of national codifications—such as the *Code de commerce* (1807), the *Wetboek van Koophandel* (1838), the *Allgemeines Deutsches Handelsgesetzbuch* (1861), and the Sale of Goods Act 1893—which in turn underlined the importance of rules on conflicts of laws. The rise of and need for private international law is illustrated by the Hague Conference on Private International Law, first held in 1893, which aimed to unify national rules on conflict of laws, including those in the field of commercial law.[70] Importantly, several still existing international, private organisations were set up to facilitate this globalizing trade, such as the Grain and Feed Trade Association (GAFTA, 1871),[71] the International Law Association (1873),[72] and the International Maritime Committee (1896).[73] Moreover, with the enormous increase in international trade since the 1870s, the documentary credit, including the use of bills of exchange, became a truly global phenomenon, and it was also thought necessary to create unified rules dealing with bills of exchange.[74]

---

[68] See e.g. Screpanti and Zamagni (1993), pp. 25–27, 42–43.

[69] See e.g. Deane and Cole (1969), p. 47; Wintle (2000), pp. 147–150; Van Zanden and Van Riel (2004), pp. 183–187; Bairoch (1989), pp. 36–45.

[70] The Hague Conference has currently 82 Members: 81 States and the EU, see https://www.hcch.net/en/instruments/conventions/status-table/?cid=29. The activities of the Hague Conference are also extended to e.g. family law and the law of succession. See Schmitthoff (1981), pp. 26–27.

[71] Currently the Gafta has over 1650 members in 94 countries, including traders, brokers, superintendents, analysts, fumigators, arbitrators, individuals, professionals and branches of members, see http://www.gafta.com/Membership.

[72] The ILA's membership, presently around 4000, ranges from lawyers in private practice, academia, government and the judiciary, to non-lawyer experts from commercial, industrial and financial spheres, and representatives of bodies such as shipping and arbitration organisations and chambers of commerce, see http://www.ila-hq.org/index.php/about-us/aboutus2.

[73] In 2011 the IMC (or CMI) members were 56 National Maritime Law Associations, with memberships ranging from 10 to 3600. See http://comitemaritime.org/Relationship-with-UN-organisations/0,27114,111432,00.html. Schmitthoff (1981), pp. 26–29.

[74] See e.g. Wallert (1996), pp. 165–166; Goode and McKendrick (2010), p. 1353.

The First World War abruptly put these initiatives for internationally unified rules on hold. Rather, during the war many European governments took a firm grip on economic activities with also far reaching consequences for international trade.[75] Admittedly, it is since the First World War that public actors took a firmer grip on the regulation of international commercial law, though with varying success. In the wake of the war, several international organizations were set up, most notably the League of Nations in 1919, a public actor, but also for instance the International Institute for the Unification of Private Law (UNIDROIT) in 1926 as an auxiliary organ of the League of Nations. At the time, the Institute directed its activities mainly towards international conventions, and can thus be considered a public actor as well. Several international treaties regulating certain commercial transactions were indeed concluded. Unlike the national civil and commercial codes, these regulations are more specific and thus limited in application to specific (aspects of) commercial relations, but on the other hand they are meant to regulate matters at a global level. In respect of the latter, success varied considerably. For example, the Hague Visby Rules (International Convention for the Unification of Certain Rules of Law relating to Bills of Lading) of 1924 can be said to have lived up to this global aspiration, with 86 ratifying countries[76]; the amendments of 1968 and 1979, however, have only been ratified by 24 and 19 countries respectively, making those less effective in a global setting.[77]

Importantly, under the auspices of the League of Nations, also the Geneva Convention providing a Uniform Law for Bills of Exchange and Promissory Notes (1930) was adopted.[78] However, this convention was primarily modelled after the German *Wechselordnung* of 1869 and thus realized the harmonization of laws on negotiable instruments of only a limited number of civil law jurisdictions.[79] The common law rules relating to bills of exchange, cheques, and promissory notes had been codified in the Bills of Exchange Act 1882, and this Act was subsequently adopted throughout the common law world and continued to be applied.[80]

Here it is important to emphasise the relevance of regulatory efforts developed by private actors. The International Chamber of Commerce (ICC), founded in 1919 by entrepreneurs, is by essence a private actor.[81] The ICC published several model

---

[75] Fundamentally on the economics of World War I, Broadberry, Harrison (2005). On the influence of World War I on private law, see Lobban and Van Boom (2014), and specifically on the World War I's influence on unforeseen circumstances, see Oosterhuis (2014).

[76] The Hague Visby Rules (1924), have as their premise that a carrier has greater bargaining power than the shipper, and that to protect the interests of the shipper/cargo-owner, the law should at least impose a set of minimum obligations upon the carrier. See e.g. Goode and McKendrick (2010), p. 1144.

[77] See http://comitemaritime.org/Uploads/Publications/CMI_YBK_Part_III.pdf.

[78] See e.g. Wallert (1996), pp. 166–169; Schmitthoff (1981), pp. 24–26. In 1936 eighteen states had ratified or acceded the convention. See https://treaties.un.org/pages/LONViewDetails.aspx?src=LON&id=551&chapter=30&clang=_en.

[79] See Schmoeckel (2008), p. 100.

[80] See Goode and McKendrick (2010), p. 521.

[81] The ICC currently has over 6.5 million members in more than 130 countries. See https://iccwbo.org/about-us/who-we-are/.

contracts and standard conditions such as the Uniform Customs and Practice for Documentary Credits (UCP) (1933, latest, 6th version 2007, UCP 600)—a set of rules on the issuance and use of letters of credit—and the International Commercial Terms (INCOTERMS) (1936, latest, 8th version 2010)—a series of pre-defined commercial terms widely used in international commercial transactions. Also the GAFTA, already mentioned, is involved in providing model contracts and rules for the transactions that take place within the grain and feed trade. These efforts have often filled regulatory gaps with a view to providing commercial parties with clear rules that offer predictability in a way that aligns with their commercial interests. Therefore, after the First World War, both public and private actors, in particular the League of Nations and the ICC addressed the need for unified rules dealing with bills of exchange. However, at the time, private actor attempts to address the need for unified rules dealing with bills of exchange appeared to be more successful.

The Second World War interrupted the increase of international trade once more, but after the war a second wave of international instruments and institutions was created, again with varying success. Following the demise of the League of Nations, the UNIDROIT was re-established in 1940.[82] Initially the Institute directed its activities again mainly towards international conventions, such as the Hague Uniform Laws on the International Sale of Goods (1964). The United Nations Commission on International Trade Law (UNCITRAL), established in 1966, subsequently used the Hague Uniform Laws (1964) as a source of inspiration for the UN Convention on the International Sale of Goods (CISG) (1980): 87 states are party to the CISG per July 2017.[83] Other international conventions were less successful. In the area of carriage of goods, the United Nations created the Hamburg Rules (1978) to offer an alternative to the Hague Visby Rules, which was perceived to be too carrier-friendly, and the Convention on Multimodal Transport (1980) in response to the changing nature of transportation modalities. However, 34 states are party to the Hamburg Rules, and Convention on Multimodal Transport has not even entered into force yet.[84]

Importantly, UNCITRAL also drafted the United Nations Convention on International Bills of Exchange and International Promissory Notes (New York, 1988) with a view to 'overcom[ing] the major disparities and uncertainties that currently exist in relation to instruments used for international payments'.[85] The Convention was adopted by the General Assembly on 9 December 1988, however,

[82] Currently 63 States are members of UNIDROIT, see http://www.unidroit.org/about-unidroit/membership.

[83] See http://www.uncitral.org/uncitral/en/uncitral_texts/sale_goods/1980CISG_status.html. See also e.g. Schmitthoff (1981), pp. 24–26; Hartkamp (2011), pp. 240–241.

[84] See https://treaties.un.org/pages/ViewDetails.aspx?src=TREATY&mtdsg_no=XI-D-3&chapter=11&lang=en; https://treaties.un.org/pages/ViewDetails.aspx?src=TREATY&mtdsg_no=XI-E-1&chapter=11&clang=_en. The Hague Visby Rules and the Hamburg Rules are eventually to be replaced by the Rotterdam Rules (2009, not yet in force).

[85] See II. Explanatory Note by the UNCITRAL Secretariat on the United Nations Convention on International Bills of Exchange and International Promissory Notes, p. 42 (<http://www.unc itral.org/pdf/english/texts/payments/billsnotes/Bills_of_Exchange_expl_Note.pdf>). See also e.g. Goode and McKendrick (2010), p. 521; Schmitthoff (1981), p. 25; Schoordijk (1989).

by July 2017, only five states have acceded to the Convention (Guinea, Gabon, Honduras, Liberia, and Mexico) and consequently the convention has not yet entered into force.[86] The idea that commercial actors are in need of an international regulation of the law concerning bills of exchange has so far proven to be false.[87]

In this respect it is illustrative to again give an example of a private actor and its regulatory efforts. The International Air Transport Association (IATA, 1945) successfully provides model contracts and rules for air transport on a global scale, as it represents over 275 airlines or 83% of total air traffic per July 2017.[88]

If anything can be deduced from the above overview, than it must be that public actor intervention does not seem to be a condition for the wide use of commercial practice or usage: particularly the GAFTA, ICC, IATA illustrate that private actors are very well able to organise their trade or trade in general. Rather, public actor intervention reveals a mixed picture: some international conventions have been quite successful in terms of use and/or acceptance, such as the Hague-Visby Rules of 1924 and the CISG, where other instruments or amendments have been less successful, such as the amendments to the Hague-Visby Rules of 1969 and 1978, the Hamburg Rules (1978) or the Convention on Multimodal Transport (1980). These international conventions are by nature intergovernmental: joining these conventions is and cannot be imposed on individual states. Widespread participation in these conventions admittedly also depends on whether a particular convention indeed represents more or less internationally shared usages or customs, as can be said for instance of the CISG.[89]

3 Lessons and Conclusions for the Design of Commercial Law

From this concise history of bills of exchange, it is possible to draw three main conclusions in relation to an appropriate design of commercial law. Firstly, the example of bills of exchange shows that private actors are capable of creating clear and predictable rules themselves through practice resulting in the development of customs, however, these rules can only exist and function with the recognition and support of an effective enforcement system, previously courts at fairs, city councils, and later national courts.

Secondly, the historical development shows that while private actors have essentially been responsible for the creation of a solution to a commercial problem—in this case study the creation of an effective payment mechanism between merchants

[86] See http://www.uncitral.org/uncitral/en/uncitral_texts/payments/1988Convention_bills_status.html.

[87] See Schmitthoff (1981), p. 31. See also Goode and McKendrick (2010), p. 1354.

[88] See http://www.iata.org/about/Pages/index.aspx.

[89] See e.g. Cordes (2016), pp. 468–470.

trading with each other at a distance—these rules are often subsequently recorded or codified by public actors, frequently also with a view to promoting clarity and predictability. However, whether these unificatory endeavours by recording or codifying commercial law indeed significantly promoted trade and more specifically the use of bills of exchange, is generally very difficult to establish, because the functioning of markets depends on many, hard to isolate variables. Introduction of certain rules by public actors may have a positive effect of supporting the system created by merchants, and thus promote the interests of the market, although these effects are difficult to establish as well, for the same reasons. Moreover, the introduction of certain rules might even distort the proper functioning of a market. There are many possible reasons for public actors to regulate in certain areas, for example to support corporate social responsibility.[90] However, from a historical perspective, public actor regulation aiming to create legal clarity or change certain usages mainly with a view to foster trade or promote market interest should be considered very carefully and only introduced reluctantly. In this respect, the European Commission's withdrawal in 2014 of the Proposal for a Common European Sales Law (CESL) (2011) seems a wise decision.[91] Here, the EU—a public actor—sought to regulate commercial sales law at a European level. The main justification of this public actor intervention was to increase cross-border trade by creating legal certainty[92]—although the CESL only had an opt-in character.[93] Moreover, the regulation itself deviated from existing commercial sales law of the member states.[94] These two elements made this public actor intervention a questionable enterprise from a historical perspective.

Thirdly, the overview demonstrates that the level at which rules are made or set appears to depend on the market for which these rules are meant. In the Middle Ages and the Early Modern Era, the level was local, with occasional regional—European—implications, parallel to the commercial ties that existed in those days. They reflected the local preferences of a particular market, which is illustrated by the diversity of local customs that existed for different fairs and cities. As the local preferences of commercial communities converged, through increasing trading ties

---

[90] See e.g. the contribution of Andhov in this volume.

[91] See e.g. the contribution of Andhov in this volume.

[92] Proposal for a Regulation of the European Parliament and of the Council on a Common European Sales Law (COM/2011/0635 final) (2011) (CESL), Explanatory Memorandum, 2–4: 'In cross-border transactions between a business and a consumer, contract law related *transaction costs* and legal obstacles stemming from differences between different national mandatory consumer protection rules have *a significant impact*. (…) The value of the trade foregone each year between Member States due to differences in contract law alone amounts to tens of billions of Euros. (…) The overall objective of the proposal is to improve the establishment and the functioning of the internal market by facilitating the expansion of cross-border trade for business and crossborder purchases for consumers. This objective can be achieved by making available *a selfstanding uniform set of contract law rules* including provisions to protect consumers, the *Common European Sales Law*, which is to be considered as a second contract law regime within the national law of each Member State.' [italics JO].

[93] See e.g. Bull (2016), pp. 105–113.

[94] See e.g. Kornet (2012) and the contribution of Anagnostopoulou in this volume.

but also through the unification of nation territories, regulation took place at an increasingly higher level. The Geneva Convention providing a Uniform Law for Bills of Exchange and Promissory Notes (1930) led to a further convergence of laws in a number of civil law systems possibly demonstrating a further convergence of preferences. The failure of the United Nations Convention on International Bills of Exchange and International Promissory Notes (New York, 1988) could be interpreted as evidence of continuing divergence of preferences between, broadly speaking, common law and civil law countries and therefore the appropriate level of regulation. However, here it appears that in certain cases—particularly in well-defined markets, such as the one for bills of exchange or more generally documentary credit—regulation by public actors is not necessary to promote clarity, predictability and the market interest, as the success of the Uniform Customs and Practice for Documentary Credits (UCP 600, 2007) shows.

In conclusion: this case study illustrates that private actors appear to be pre-eminently suited to creating relevant legal rules, regardless of the level—local, regional, global—where these rules are used, provided a relatively efficient enforcement mechanism exists. The effects of public actor intervention with the sole purpose of supporting trade or promoting a market interest through creating legal certainty or changing particular rules, are difficult to establish, if at all, and might even have an adverse effect on a market. Possible success of public actor regulation in the area of commercial law seems to depend largely on a specific market, and should therefore be carefully considered.

References

Aldcroft D (1992) The railway age. In: Digby A, Feinstein CH, Jenkin D (eds) New directions in economic and social history, vol 2. MacMillan, Basingstoke, pp 64–80

Asser TMC (1880) De Scandinavische Wisselwet van 1880, vergeleken met het Duitsche, het Nederlandsche en het Belgische Wisselregt. Gebr. Belinfante, Den Haag

Asser WDH (1987) Bills of exchange and agency in the 18th century law of Holland and Zeeland. Decisions of the Supreme Court of Holland and Zeeland. In: Piergiovanni V (ed) The courts and the development of commercial law. Comparative studies in continental and Anglo-American legal history, vol 2. Duncker & Humblot, Berlin, pp 101–130

Bairoch P (1989) European trade policy, 1815–1914. In: Peter M et al (eds) The industrial economies: the development of economic and social policies. The Cambridge economic history of Europe: from the decline of the Roman Empire, vol 8. Cambridge University Press, Cambridge, pp 1–160

Baker JH (1979) The law merchant and the common law before 1700. Camb Law J 38:295–322

Baker JH (1999) The law merchant as a source of English law. In: Swadling W, Jones G (eds) The search for principle: essays in honour of Lord Goff of Chieveley. Oxford University Press, New York, pp 79–96

Beckers A, Kornet N, Oosterhuis J (2015) Who does what in commercial law? The case for a multi-level & multi-actor approach to regulating commercial transactions. In: Akkermans B, Hage J, Kornet N, Smits J (eds) Who does what? On the allocation of regulatory competences in European private law. Ius Commune Europaeum, vol 137. Intersentia, Cambridge, pp 125–175

Bergfeld C (1987) Preußen und das Allgemeine Deutsche Handelsgesetzbuch. Zeitschrift für Europäische Rechtsgeschichte, Ius Commune XIV. Veröffentlichungen des Max-Planck-Instituts für Europäische Rechtsgeschichte, Frankfurt am Main pp 101–114
Bouvier J (1997) Le mouvement d'une civilisation nouvelle 1852–1914. In: Duby G (ed) Histoire de la France des origines à nos jours. Larousse, Paris, pp 645–690
Broadberry S, Harrison M (eds) (2005) The economics of World War I. Cambridge University Press, Cambridge
Brox H (2005) Handels- und Wertpapierrecht. C.H. Beck, München
Bull W (2016) Optional instruments of the European Union: a definitional, normative and explanatory study. Intersentia, Antwerp
Chalmers MDES (1981) Sale of Goods Act 1893, introduction to the first edition. In: Chalmers MDES, Mark ML, Mance JH (eds) Chalmers' Sale of Goods Act, 1979: including the Factors Acts 1889 & 1890, 18th edn. Butterworths, London
Coase R (1937) The nature of the firm. Economica 4:386–405
Cordes A (2016) Das Recht des Warenkaufs: Eine Rechtsvergleichende Darstellung 1936 & 1958, Ernst Rabel (1874–1955). In: Dauchy S et al (eds) The formation and transmission of Western Legal Culture: 150 books that made the law in the age of printing. Studies in the history of law and justice, vol 7. Springer, Cham, pp 467–470
Deane P (1973) The industrial revolution in Great Britain. In: Cipola CM (ed) Fontana economic history of Europe, vol 4.1. Collins, London, pp 161–227
Deane Ph, Cole WA (1969) British economic growth 1688–1959. Cambridge University Press, Cambridge
De Roover R (1953) L'évolution de la lettre de change XIVe-XVIIIe siècles. Armand Collin, Paris
De Ruysscher D (2009a) Antwerp commercial legislation in Amsterdam in the 17th century: legal transplant or jumping board? Tijdschrift voor Rechtsgeschiedenis 77:459–479
De Ruysscher D (2009b) Naer het Romeinsch recht alsmede den stiel mercantiel: Handel en recht in de Antwerpse rechtbank (16de-17de eeuw). UGA, Kortrijk-Heule
De Ruysscher D (2011) Innovating financial law in early modern Europe: transfers of commercial paper and recourse liability in legislation and *Ius Commune* (sixteenth to eighteenth centuries). Eur Rev Priv Law 5:505–518
Diephuis BJ et al (eds) (2013) Rechtspleging civiel en bestuur 2012: ontwikkelingen en samenhangen. Boom Lemma, Den Haag. https://www.wodc.nl/onderzoeksdatabase/2415-rechtspleging-civiel-en-bestuur-2012.aspx
Donahue C (2004) Medieval and early modern Lex Mercatoria: an attempt at the Probatio Diabolica. Chicago J Int Law 5:21–37
Dumke RH (1977) Intra-German trade in 1837 and regional economic development. Vierteljahrschrift für Sozial- und Wirtschaftsgeschichte 64:468–496
Dylag M (2010) The negotiability of promissory notes and bills of exchange in the time of Chief Justice Holt. J Legal Hist 31(2):149–175
Epstein RA (2004) Reflections on the historical origins and economic structure of the law merchant. Chicago J Int Law 5:1–20
Ewart JS (1903) What is the law merchant? Columbia Law Rev 3:135–154
Flume JW (2014) Law and commerce: the evolution of codified business law in Europe. Comp Legal Hist 2(1):45–83
Gelderblom O (2013) Cities of commerce: the institutional foundation of international trade in the low countries, 1250–1650. Princeton University Press, Princeton
Goode RM, McKendrick E (2010) Goode on commercial law. Penguin, London
Greif A (2004) Impersonal exchange without impartial law: the community responsibility system. Chicago J Int Law 5:109–138
Hartkamp AS (2011) Principles of contract law. In: Hartkamp AS et al (eds) Towards a European Civil Code. Ars Aequi, Arnhem, pp 239–259
Heidemann M (2016) Identities in contract: merchant law in Europe and the future of European contract law. Maastricht J Eur Comp Law 23(4):667–701

Helland E, Klick J (2011) Legal origins and empirical credibility. In: Faure M, Smits J (eds) Does law matter? On law and economic growth. Intersentia, Antwerp, pp 99–113
Henderson WO (1975) The rise of German industrial power 1834–1914. Temple Smith, London
Hoffmann WG (1963) The take-off in Germany. In: Rostow WW (ed) The economics of take-off in to self-sustained growth. MacMillan, London, pp 95–118
Jansen N, Rademacher J (2012) European civil code. In: Smits JM (ed) Elgar encyclopedia of comparative law. Edward Elgar, Cheltenham, pp 299–313
Kadens E (2004) Order within law, variety within custom: the character of the medieval merchant law. Chicago J Int Law 5:39–65
Kadens E (2012) The myth of the customary law merchant. Texas Law Rev 90:1153–1206
Kanning AJ (2003) Unifying commercial laws of nation-states: coordination of legal systems and economic growth. Maastricht University Library
Klomp RJQ (1998) Opkomst en ondergang van het handelsrecht: over de aard en de positie van het handelsrecht, in het bijzonder in verhouding tot het burgerlijk recht, in Nederland in de negentiende en twintigste eeuw. Ars Aequi Libri, Nijmegen
Kornet N (2012) The common European sales law and the CISG - complicating or simplifying the legal environment? Maastricht J Eur Comp Law 19:164–179
Kuntze JE (1862) Deutsches Wechselrecht auf Grundlage der allgemeinen Deutschen Wechselordnung und der Nürnberger Novellen. Hinrich'sche Buchhandlung, Leipzig
Labrousse E (1954) Aspects de l'évolution économique et sociale de la France et du Royaume-Uni de 1815 à 1880: d'après les notes du cours. Centre de Documentation Universitaire, Paris
Lichtenauer WF (1956) Geschiedenis van de wetenschap van het handelsrecht in Nederland tot 1809. Geschiedenis der Nederlandsche rechtswetenschap, vol 5.1. Noord-Hollandsche Uitgevers Maatschappij, Amsterdam
Lobban M, Van Boom WH (eds) (2014) Special issue the Great War and private law. Comp Legal Hist 2(2):163–324
Locré JG (1837) Code de commerce. Législation civile, commerciale et criminelle, ou commentaire et complément des codes français, vol 11. Wahlen, Bruxelles
Magnus U (ed) (2012) CISG vs regional sales law unification. With a focus on the new common European sales law. Sellier, Munich
Mathias P (1983) The first industrial nation: an economic history of Britain 1700–1914. Routledge, London
Meyer F (1909) Das Weltwechselrecht: Im Auftrage der Aeltesten der Kaufmannschaft von Berlin. Die geltenden Wechselrechte in vergleichender Darstellung, vol 1. A. Deichert'sche Verlagsbuchhandlung Nachf, Leipzig
North DC (1991) Institutions. J Econ Perspect 5:97–112
Olson M (1982) The rise and decline of nations: economic growth, stagflation, and social rigidities. Yale University Press, New Haven
Oosterhuis J (2014) Unexpected circumstances arising from World War I and its aftermath: 'Open' versus 'Closed' legal systems. Erasmus Law Rev 7(2):67–79
Pierenkemper T, Tilly R (2004) The German economy during the nineteenth century. Berghahn Books, New York
Price R (1981) An economic history of modern France, 1730–1914. MacMillan, London
Rogers JS (1995) The early history of the law of bills and notes: a study of the origins of Anglo-American commercial law. Cambridge University Press, Cambridge
Rückert J (1993) Handelsrechtsbildung und Modernisierung des Handelsrechts durch Wissenschaft zwischen ca. 1800 und 1900. In: Scherner KO (ed) Modernisierung des Handelsrechts im 19. Jahrhundert. Verlag Recht und Wirtschaft, Heidelberg, pp 19–66
Schmitthoff CM (1981) Commercial law in a changing economic climate. Sweet & Maxwell, London
Schmoeckel M (2008) Rechtsgeschichte der Wirtschaft. Mohr Siebeck, Tübingen
Schoordijk HCF (1989) Verweermiddelen en derdenbescherming onder United Nations Convention on International Bills of Exchange. Kluwer, Deventer

Schwenzer I (2012) The proposed common European sales law and the convention on the international sale of goods. Unif Comm Code Law J 44:457–481
Screpanti E, Zamagni S (1993) An outline of the history of economic thought. Clarendon Press, Oxford
Smits J (2005) Diversity of contract law and the European internal market. In: Smits J (ed) The need for a European contract law: empirical and legal perspectives. Europa Law Publishing, Groningen, pp 151–186
Spufford P (1987) Coinage and currency. In: Postan MM et al (eds) Trade and industry in the middle ages. The Cambridge economic history of Europe: from the decline of the Roman Empire, vol 2. Cambridge University Press, Cambridge, pp 788–863
Tipton FB (1976) Regional variations in the economic development of Germany during the nineteenth century. Wesleyan University Press, Middletown
Van der Wee H (1977) Monetary, credit and banking systems. In: Clapham JH et al (eds) The economic organization of early modern Europe. The Cambridge economic history of Europe: from the decline of the Roman Empire, vol 5. Cambridge University Press, Cambridge, pp 290–392
Van Hofstraeten B (2015) Jurisdictional complexity in Antwerp company law (1480–1620). In: Donlan SP, Heirbaut D (eds) The laws' many bodies: studies in legal hybridity and jurisdictional complexity, c1600–1900. Comparative studies in continental and Anglo-American legal history, vol 32. Duncker & Humblot, Berlin, pp 57–80
Van Zanden JL, Van Riel A (2004) The strictures of inheritance: the Dutch economy in the nineteenth century. Princeton University Press, Princeton
Von Pannwitz K (1999) Die Entstehung der Allgemeinen Deutschen Wechselordnung: Ein Beitrag Zur Geschichte Der Vereinheitlichung Des Deutschen Zivilrechts Im 19. Jahrhundert. Rechtshistorische Reihe, vol 193. Peter Lang, Frankfurt am Main
Wagner H (2005) Economic analysis of cross-border legal uncertainty; The example of the European Union. In: Smits J (ed) The need for a European contract law: empirical and legal perspectives. Europa Law Publishing, Groningen, pp 25–51
Wallert JAF (1996) Ontwikkelingslijnen in praktijk en theorie van de wisselbrief 1300–2000. Nederlands Instituut voor het Bank- en Effectenbedrijf etc., Amsterdam
Wieacker F (1974) Der Kampf des 19. Jhs. um die Nationalgesetzbücher (1970). In: Wieacker F (ed) Industriegesellschaft und Privatrechtsordnung. Athenäum-Fischer-Taschenbuch-Verlag, Frankfurt am Main, pp 79–93
Wintle MJ (2000) An economic and social history of the Netherlands, 1800–1920: demographic, economic, and social transition. Cambridge University Press, Cambridge
Zorn W (1963) Wirtschafts- und sozialgeschichtliche Zusammenhänge der Deutschen Reichsgründungszeit (1850–1879). Historische Zeitschrift 197:318–342
Zorn W (1973) Die Wirtschaftliche Integration Kleindeutschlands in den 1860er Jahren und die Reichsgründung. Historische Zeitschrift 216:304–334
Zorn W (1978) Zwischenstaatliche wirtschaftliche Integration im Deutschen Zollverein 1867–1870. Ein quantitativer Versuch. Vierteljahrschrift für Sozial- und Wirtschaftsgeschichte 65:38–76

ICSID Arbitration Clauses in Contracts: Time for a Revival?

Hendrik Puschmann and Andreas Geroldinger

Contents

This chapter is based on a paper H. Puschmann delivered at the Institute of Advanced Legal Studies in London on 22 September 2016. We are grateful to Hannah Davies, Alicia Mendonca, Ian Meredith, Dr Wojciech Sadowski and Dr Rumiana Yotova for commenting on various iterations of this piece. Special thanks are due to Meg Kinnear, the Secretary-General of ICSID, for her helpful feedback on our underlying hypothesis. Any errors or omissions are, of course, our own.

H. Puschmann (✉)
Farrer & Co, London, UK

Clare Hall, Cambridge, UK

Johannes Kepler Universität Linz, Linz, Austria
e-mail: Hendrik.Puschmann@farrer.co.uk

A. Geroldinger
Faculty of Law, Department of Civil Law, Johannes Kepler University, Linz, Austria
e-mail: andreas.geroldinger@jku.at

M. Heidemann, J. Lee (eds.), *The Future of the Commercial Contract in Scholarship and Law Reform*, https://doi.org/10.1007/978-3-319-95969-6_15

Abstract This brief chapter deals with a particular aspect of ICSID investor-state arbitration. ICSID is widely known, and frequently used, as a mechanism for resolving disputes arising out of investment treaties. Another, far less well-known use of ICSID is in contractual agreements to arbitrate. This second option is rarely employed. This is somewhat surprising as, from an investor perspective, ICSID has significant potential advantages over other types of dispute resolution. The most tangible of these are its narrow, self-contained review mechanism and the straightforward enforceability of awards. The central point of this chapter is, therefore, that contractual ICSID arbitration agreements are an under-utilised instrument. More research is needed into ICSID as a contractual tool.

1 Introduction

This chapter is about the 1965 Convention on the Settlement of Investment Disputes between States and Nationals of Other States, commonly known as ICSID or the Washington Convention—though we simply refer to it as the Convention—after the International Centre for the Settlement of Investment Disputes at the World Bank in Washington D.C., the custodian of the Convention. ICSID is probably the most well-established and best-known mechanism for resolving disputes between states and foreign investors. It offers significant advantages to investors seeking to hedge their exposure to sovereign risk.[1] Thus, ICSID awards are not subject to appeal and can only be reviewed on very narrow procedural grounds. In addition, and perhaps more importantly, Contracting States must enforce the awards as though they were domestic court judgments.[2]

ICSID is often included as a dispute resolution option in bilateral (or multilateral) investment treaties (BITs), and commonly relied on by investors to enforce their rights under such treaties. However, an investor, or investors, from one Contracting State can also agree with another Contracting State or its organs to submit contractual disputes to ICSID arbitration.[3] Given the clear advantages this brings, we would have expected it to be done frequently. However, this does not

[1] The relative advantages of ICSID against other dispute resolution mechanisms are almost invariably discussed primarily from the vantage point of investors. This is because it is essentially always the investor rather than the host state who initiates investor-state arbitration proceedings. In a treaty scenario, it is not actually possible for the host state to initiate arbitration against an investor. Under a private-law contract it is theoretically possible. However, we do not know of any instances where this actually happened. This may well change, though, if investors become more mindful of ICSID arbitration as a contractual tool, as we think they probably should.

[2] See Sect. 3 below.

[3] We are talking here not about the contractual submission to ICSID arbitration of a treaty claim (though that is, of course, also possible) but the submission to ICSID arbitration of a contractual claim by way of an arbitration agreement (as opposed to an umbrella clause in an investment treaty). Although this can be done by way of a separate arbitration agreement, it will ordinarily take the form of an arbitration clause in the contract itself.

appear to be the case. We looked hard for a convincing explanation of why, from an investor perspective, contracts with sovereign counter-parties do not include ICSID arbitration clauses more frequently. We could not find any. On this basis, contractual ICSID arbitration is, in our view, probably an under-used tool (though this is, for now, no more than a working hypothesis that awaits verification by further research).

The remainder of this chapter is divided into a further five sections. Section 2 outlines the circumstances in which a contractual dispute may be submitted to ICSID arbitration. We place particular emphasis on the question whether and in what circumstances a state-controlled company could validly submit to ICSID arbitration, as this is a largely unsettled issue. Section 3 provides an overview of the potential advantages investors would gain from having ICSID clauses in their contracts with sovereign counter-parties. Section 4 charts the use of ICSID in private-law contracts, offering circumstantial evidence to support our assumption that it is not a widely used instrument and that its use is moreover in decline. Section 5 is an inquiry into the reasons why (given its potential advantages) ICSID is not more frequently deployed in contracts. We come to the conclusion that there is no good explanation, at least none that is obvious. Section 6, finally, sets out our overall conclusion and makes the case for further research being undertaken on this issue.

2 Contractual Jurisdiction Under the ICSID Convention

The basis for ICSID's jurisdiction over contractual claims can be found in Art. 25(1) of the Convention:

> The jurisdiction of the Centre shall extend to any legal dispute arising directly out of an investment, between a Contracting State (or any constituent subdivision or agency of a Contracting State designated to the Centre by that State) and a national of another Contracting State, which the parties to the dispute consent in writing to submit to the Centre.

It is clear, and has never been disputed, that this submission can be made by way of an arbitration agreement in (or pertaining to) a contract, as opposed to a treaty. Broadly speaking, a valid contractual ICSID arbitration agreement must meet three requirements—it must:

1. Be between an investor who is a "national" of one Contracting State and another Contracting State or a designated "constituent subdivision or agency". Any such subdivision or agency must consent to submitting to the jurisdiction of ICSID and moreover, pursuant to Art. 25(3) of the Convention, seek approval by the designating Contracting State unless that state has notified ICSID that this is not required.
2. Pertain to an "investment" for the purposes of the Convention.
3. Be in writing.

Each of these requirements has been extensively discussed in both the awards of ICSID tribunals and commentaries.[4] We have little to add to this body of (quasi) case law and literature except, tangentially, on the subject of what entities could constitute an agency or subdivision for ICSID purposes. It may nevertheless be helpful to highlight some other salient points here for ease of reference:

2.1 Agreement Between Nationals of One Contracting State and Another Contracting State or Its Designated Constituent Subdivision or Agency

The definition of "national" in public international law is broad indeed. It includes, for instance, nationals of (or companies based in) a Contracting State that make investments in the host state via entities in third states.[5]

In terms of the host Contracting State, the concept of a constituent subdivision or agency is rather broad and will largely depend on the internal constitutional order of the state concerned.[6] The legal nature of the entity—ministry, non-ministerial public body, province or municipality etc.—is irrelevant, so long as the state has notified the Centre that this entity is a designated subdivision or agency for the purposes of the Convention. As Schreuer puts it in his authoritative commentary of the Convention, "[d]esignation would almost certainly preclude the Contracting State or the designated entity from arguing that the Convention requirements were not fulfilled because the entity was not a 'constituent subdivision or agency.'"[7]

The limits of this hypothesis have not really been tested. In particular, it is an open question to what degree it applies to companies owned or controlled by the Contracting State in question.[8] This is a particularly important question in the context of states as parties to contracts. Much of the commercial activity of governments is channelled through state-owned/controlled enterprises, and this proportion appears to be on the increase.[9] Many (if not most) of the contracts for which ICSID

[4] Schreuer et al. (2009) is the most extensive and comprehensive commentary. McLachlan et al. (2017) provides probably the most up-to-date summary of the interpretation of Art. 25 (and many other Convention provisions), albeit in the context of treaty arbitration rather than contractual arbitration. The best available overview of the scope of ICSID jurisdiction specifically over contractual disputes is provided by Reed et al. (2011), pp. 24–44.

[5] See, e.g., *Siemens AG v. Argentine Republic* (Jurisdiction) ICSID Case No. ARB/02/8, in particular at para. 137, 142 and 150. Cf also Art. 25(2) of the Convention, which defines the meaning of "national".

[6] See e.g. Amerasinghe (1976), pp. 227–267, see esp. p. 233 et seq.

[7] Schreuer et al. (2009), p. 154.

[8] Several state-owned or -controlled companies (particularly energy, shipping and mining companies) appear to have been so registered. See Reed et al. (2011), p. 33.

[9] See e.g. Cuervo-Cazurra et al. (2014), pp. 919–942.

arbitration could conceivably be stipulated will therefore be not with the state itself or its ministries and agencies, but with state-owned/controlled companies.

It seems fairly clear that the rule postulated by Schreuer applies to companies performing public functions on behalf of the Contracting State.[10] Such companies would substantively be organs or agencies of the state in question, even if they are not as a matter of form.

It is far less clear whether a company that does not perform any public function, but merely happens to be owned or controlled by a Contracting State, can validly consent to ICSID arbitration. On one hand, it is arguable that this would be outside the scope of the Convention, given that (i) such companies would not be constituent subdivisions or agencies of the state properly so called, and (ii) the intention of the drafters of the Convention seems to have been to exclude them from its scope.[11]

On the other hand, however, in a contract scenario the Contracting State in question must not only have designated the company as a subdivision or agency for ICSID purposes.[12] It will moreover (through the company itself) have agreed expressly with the investor for claims against the company to be submitted to ICSID arbitration.[13] In addition the Contracting State will have approved the company's consent according to Art. 25(3) of the Convention (or have waived its right to do so). It would almost certainly be inequitable for the state to be allowed to renege on that agreement subsequently. Permitting the state to do so could, after all, have far-reaching negative consequences for the investor who would, in all likelihood, be forced to make their claim in the courts of the host state (assuming the arbitration agreement does not provide for an alternative set of rules to apply in such a scenario).[14]

Therefore, it seems to us to be by far the stronger argument that Schreuer's rule applies in this scenario as well. In designating the company as a subdivision or agency, and contracting with the investor on this basis, both the state and the company waive the right to plead that the company is not, in fact, a subdivision or agency for ICSID purposes. The English-law doctrine of contractual estoppel can

---

[10] See Schreuer et al. (2009), p. 153; Waibel (2015), p. 1242.

[11] See "Summary Record of Proceedings, Bangkok Consultative Meetings of Legal Experts, April 27-May 1, 1964" published in ICSID Secretariat (1968), pp. 458–553; see in particular p. 507. See also Waibel (2015), p. 1242.

[12] This is a *sine qua non* condition for any entity other than the state itself to become a party to an ICSID arbitration. If designation has not occurred, the tribunal will lack jurisdiction. See *Cable Television of Nevis, Ltd and Cable Television of Nevis Holding Ltd v. Federation of St Kitts and Nevis*, ICSID Case No. ARB 95/2 (Award). However, the position might be different if the state had given a binding contractual promise to the investor to designate the entity in question. See note 19 below.

[13] The consent of the company (or other entity) in question is unlikely ever to be an issue in contractual ICSID arbitration. The entity will be party to a contract containing an ICSID arbitration provision, which will almost certainly amount to consent.

[14] Including such an alternative in the contract might, in any event, be sensible to hedge against any residual risk of ICSID (or rather the tribunal constituted under the Convention) declining jurisdiction.

usefully be applied by analogy here.[15] It is unlikely that this "liberal" approach would unduly widen the scope of ICSID's jurisdiction.[16] Contracting States are, according to the *travaux préparatoires* to the Convention, responsible for the compliance with any award rendered against a designated state entity.[17] They will thus not lightly designate companies as subdivisions/agencies or exercise their right according to Art. 25(3) of the Convention to waive the requirement of approving the consent of such companies to submit to ICSID arbitration.

Given that arbitration is fundamentally a party-driven process, it is doubtful that any tribunal would have jurisdiction to decline jurisdiction on its own initiative absent a party challenge.[18] On this basis, it is a reasonable working assumption that ICSID clauses can, in principle, be included in contracts with any entity that is part of, or owned or controlled by, a Contracting State, so long as the designation of that entity as an agency or subdivision has been notified to ICSID.[19] Still, these are uncharted waters. It seems unlikely that a test case will come along any time soon.

2.2 *Pertaining to an "Investment"*

As with "national", the term "investment" is a broad concept that has been the subject of much case law and countless scholarly works,[20] and so it is not necessary to include a detailed discussion here. Briefly, tribunals decide whether an "investment" exists on a case-by-case basis. They usually take into account a list of factors known as the

[15] The doctrine essentially states that: "There is no reason in principle why parties to a contract should not agree that a certain state of affairs should form the basis for the transaction, whether it be the case or not. For example, it may be desirable to settle a disagreement as to an existing state of affairs in order to establish a clear basis for the contract itself and its subsequent performance. Where parties express an agreement of that kind in a contractual document neither can subsequently deny the existence of the facts and matters upon which they have agreed, at least so far as concerns those aspects of their relationship to which the agreement was directed. The contract itself gives rise to an estoppel". *Peekay Intermark Ltd v. Australia and New Zealand Banking Group Ltd* [2006] EWCA Civ 386 per Moore-Bick LJ at 56.

[16] See the concerns raised in the ICSID Convention's drafting process; see note 10.

[17] See Schreuer et al. (2009), p. 1101.

[18] An instance of "negative *Kompetenz-Kompetenz*", as it were.

[19] Or, conceivably, if the state undertakes to do so as part of its contractual obligations towards the investor. However, it is yet another open question whether an ICSID tribunal would take jurisdiction on this basis if the designation was not then, in fact, made. It may be arguable that the state would effectively be contractually estopped from disputing jurisdiction, but there appears to be no available case law or commentary supporting this position. In any event, if only the state-owned company (and not the state) undertakes contractually to procure notification under Art. 25(3), the estoppel argument could be defeated if the host state could show that the company consented to ICSID arbitration without being properly authorised to do so. It would therefore certainly be prudent for investors to insist on designation to occur as a condition precedent to the contract taking effect.

[20] See e.g. Williams and Foote (2011).

"modified *Salini* test".[21] These include the contribution of capital, the assumption of a specific, investment-type risk and the duration of the investment. As a rule of thumb, the larger the scale and the longer the term of the investment, the more likely it is to be an "investment" for Convention purposes. There is also the requirement that the investment must have a "nexus" to the host state, though that nexus can be quite weak and need not entail actual performance of any obligations within the host state.[22]

Moreover, while purely passive, indirect investments do not count, so to speak, the threshold for a passive investment becoming "active" is low. It is likely that any expenditure on an asset acquired passively will turn that asset into an "active" investment.[23]

Schreuer points out that "[i]nvestment in the sense of Art. 25 [...] can cover almost any area of economic activity",[24] and hence more or less any kind of commercial contract: loans, bonds, share purchase agreements, agreements for the sale of goods, etc. Even financial derivatives such as an oil price hedge have been held to be "investments" for ICSID purposes.[25]

In any event, according to Schreuer, a "clause in an agreement by which the parties consent to submit disputes to the Centre is a strong indication that they consider their transaction an investment."[26] Therefore, in theory at least, any commercial contract with a state entity can be made subject to ICSID arbitration, regardless of its subject matter, so long as it does not obviously flaunt the broad criteria of an investment for ICSID purposes.

2.3 *In Writing*

This point is quite self-explanatory. The writing requirement is moreover exceedingly unlikely to be grounds for disputing a tribunal's jurisdiction. We do not know of a single case relating to ICSID where this argument was run (let alone run successfully). As Schreuer notes, "[t]he need to put consent into writing has not led to difficulties in practice".[27]

---

[21] First set out in *Salini Costruttori SpA and Italstrade SpA v. Morocco*, Case No ARB/00/4 (Jurisdiction) and subsequently modified and supplemented by other tribunals.

[22] See e.g. *Deutsche Bank AG v. Democratic Socialist Republic of Sri Lanka*, ICSID Case No. ARB/09/2.

[23] See the recent English High Court decision in *Gold Reserve Inc. v. Bolivarian Republic of Venezuela* [2016] EWHC 153 (Comm), though obviously this can only be persuasive at best outside of England and Wales.

[24] Schreuer et al. (2009), pp. 125–126.

[25] As was the case in *Deutsche Bank v. Sri Lanka* (note 22).

[26] Schreuer et al. (2009), p. 119.

[27] Schreuer et al. (2009), p. 191. The writing requirement is exceedingly unlikely to be an issue in the context of contractual disputes. Those contracts (almost invariably in writing) will likely themselves contain the submission to ICSID jurisdiction (in the form of an arbitration clause).

3 Potential Advantages to Investors of Submitting Contract Claims to ICSID

In their leading guide to ICSID arbitration, Reed et al highlight four potential advantages (to investors) of using ICSID over either litigation or non-ICSID arbitration[28]:

1. The "[n]eutral and self-contained system" of the Convention, which operates without reference or recourse to any national arbitration law or court system.
2. The "[i]ncreasing transparency" of ICSID arbitration, and especially the fact that "the existence, current status and ultimate disposition of ICSID arbitrations are matters of public record".[29]
3. ICSID's "[c]lear and reasonable cost schedules".
4. The "World Bank factor", meaning that states tend to settle ICSID awards against them voluntarily because not to do so means risking "indirect political consequences in terms of credibility with the World Bank".[30]

These are good points, albeit that the exact extent to which each of them matters in the context of contractual arbitration is open to a certain amount of debate. Thus, the heightened confidentiality of non-ICSID arbitration may actually be preferable to investors who do not want their contractual disputes to become a matter of public record. Moreover, while the ICSID cost schedules are both clear and reasonable, that is mainly an advantage vis-à-vis UNCITRAL ad-hoc arbitration,[31] which under many BITs is an alternative option to ICSID. The advantage is less clear-cut in a contractual context, where the parties may choose to apply the rules of an institution other than ICSID, which will invariably also have a (hopefully clear and reasonable) cost schedule. Finally, as to the "World Bank factor", Reed et al themselves note that there have recently been instances of states refusing to pay ICSID awards.[32]

[28] Reed et al. (2011), pp. 14–17.

[29] This is not, of course, the case with arbitrations under essentially all other rules, or ad-hoc arbitrations. These are usually subject to extensive confidentiality obligations—set by the law of the seat of arbitration and/or the rules themselves—which mean that these things are not a matter of public record. See e.g. Blackaby et al. (2015), p. 124 et seq.

[30] Friedland (2007), pp. 157–158, suggests an overlapping but somewhat different list of potential advantages. To him, (i) the "World bank factor" comes first, followed by (ii) the Convention's straightforward enforcement mechanism, (iii) the "neutral, specialized" nature of arbitration—a highly intangible factor—(iv) the lack of a route to appealing awards, and finally (v) the institution's reasonable fee base.

[31] The UNCITRAL Rules do not contain a cost schedule. Instead, the Tribunal has broad discretion to set its fees so long as they are "reasonable"; see Art. 41. UNCITRAL arbitrations being ad-hoc, there are obviously no institutional fees.

[32] Reed et al. (2011), p. 17. This is discussed further in Sect. 4 below.

Be that as it may, there will, in any case, be two very tangible potential advantages to investors in stipulating ICSID arbitration in their contracts.[33] Both fall under the "neutral and self-contained system" heading above. They are (i) the Convention's limited annulment mechanism; and (ii) probably more importantly the more straightforward international enforceability of ICSID awards compared to court judgments and non-ICSID arbitration awards:

3.1 Annulment

It is almost universally the case that judgments and arbitral awards are open to some level of review by the courts. Judgments can, of course, usually be appealed on the merits. This is true of arbitral awards in a minority of jurisdictions only.[34] But even in jurisdictions following the UNCITRAL Model Law, under which awards are not appealable, awards tend to be open to review on procedural grounds, often by several layers of the court hierarchy.[35]

This is not the case under the ICSID Convention, which stipulates at Art. 53(1) that awards:

> shall be binding on the parties and shall not be subject to any appeal or to any other remedy except those provided for in this Convention. Each party shall abide by and comply with the terms of the award except to the extent that enforcement shall have been stayed pursuant to the relevant provisions of this Convention.

The only review mechanism available is the constitution of an ad-hoc ICSID committee with a mandate pursuant to Art. 52(1) of the Convention to consider annulling the award on five grounds:

(a) that the Tribunal was not properly constituted;
(b) that the Tribunal has manifestly exceeded its powers;
(c) that there was corruption on the part of a member of the Tribunal;

---

[33] On a separate but related point, we note in passing that if opting for ICSID arbitration makes sense, it is advantageous for investors to have an ICSID arbitration clause even where the Convention may, in any event, be applicable pursuant to an umbrella clause in an investment treaty. Jurisdiction arising out of umbrella clauses is far from a unanimously accepted doctrine, so there is always a risk of the host state disputing jurisdiction. Arbitration clauses/agreements are not subject to the same degree of risk. Cf Schreuer et al. (2009), p. 263: "The exact meaning and effect of umbrella clauses has been", and continues to be, "the subject of much debate and disagreement in arbitral practice." See also McLachlan et al. (2017) at p. 128 et seq. for a lucid summary of the topic.

[34] The best-known example being England and Wales; see Sect. 45 and 69 of the Arbitration Act 1996, though these provisions are not mandatory.

[35] Cf, e.g., the German regime, which follows the Model Law: set-aside applications on procedural grounds are heard by the Higher Regional Courts (*Oberlandesgerichte*), from where an appeal lies to the Federal Supreme Court (*Bundesgerichtshof*), with possible additional references to the Federal Constitutional Court (*Bundesverfassungsgericht*). See s. 1062 of the German Code of Civil Procedure (*Zivilprozessordnung*).

(d) that there has been a serious departure from a fundamental rule of procedure; or
(e) that the award has failed to state the reasons on which it is based.[36]

There is no appeal against decisions of the ad-hoc committee. Moreover, the grounds for annulment are exceedingly narrow, considerably narrower than even under the Model Law, in particular because the Model Law allows awards to be set aside on grounds of public policy.[37]

The limited ambit of the annulment mechanism is a major potential advantage for investor claimants. It curtails the scope of respondent states for challenging awards made against them. This also limits the scope for delaying enforcement by way of such challenges. This is not to say that the ICSID mechanism eradicates that risk. State respondents do appear to mount challenges as a means of delaying enforcement.[38] However, ICSID ad-hoc committees are usually cautious when staying enforcement pending the outcome of an annulment application and will enquire whether the application is merely tactical.[39] In any event, the scope for successful delaying tactics by way of an annulment application in ICSID proceedings appears to be a far cry from the sometimes absurd delay that parties seeking to frustrate enforcement have been able to achieve in other forae.[40]

3.2 *Enforceability*

There are two aspects to this point. First, it is an obvious advantage to investors that they will be able to enforce an ICSID award against the host state at large (cf. note 17). In contrast, other types of awards or court judgments arising out of contracts

[36] Art. 52(1) of the Convention. Note, furthermore, the limited jurisdiction of the tribunal (or, in certain circumstances, a newly constituted tribunal) to rectify, supplement interpret or revise its award; see Arts. 49 and 51 of the Convention. These are not, however, review mechanisms properly so called.

[37] See Art. 34(b)(ii) of the Model Law. Nigh on every seat of arbitration allows awards to be set aside on grounds of public policy. This is true even of Switzerland, which has narrower grounds for annulment than the Model Law—the narrowest of any commonly used arbitration jurisdiction. See section 190(2) of the Swiss Private International Law Act (*Bundesgesetz über das internationale Privatrecht*, or *IPRG*).

[38] See note 55 below.

[39] Art. 54 of the Convention effectively provides that beyond an initial 30-day period the committee has discretion in deciding whether to stay enforcement. There is no presumption that the stay should continue beyond the initial 30 days; see *Vivendi II Compania de Aguas del Aconquija SA and Vivendi Universal SA v. Argentine Republic* Decision on the Argentine Republic's Request for a Continued Stay of Enforcement of the Award rendered on 20 August 2007 at para 38. It has, moreover, been held that a continued stay should only be granted rarely. See ICSID ad hoc committee, *SGS Societe Generale de Surveillance SA v. Republic of Paraguay,* Decision on Paraguay's Request for the Continued Stay of Enforcement of the Award, ICSID Case ARB/07/29, 22 March 2013.

[40] Cf, for instance, *IPCO (Nigeria) Ltd v. Nigerian National Petroleum Corporation* [2015] EWCA Civ 1144.

may only be enforced against the entity—such as a state owned company—that is party to the contract with the investor. Secondly, court judgments usually depend on bilateral or multilateral treaties to render them enforceable abroad, at least in practice (it is theoretically possible to enforce a judgment in the absence of such treaties, but, as we know from experience, this is often very much an uphill struggle). Non-ICSID foreign arbitral awards—and this includes awards under the ICSID Additional Facility[41]—are enforceable in most countries of the world under the 1958 New York Convention on the Recognition and Enforcement of Foreign Arbitral Awards with its more than 150 signatories,[42] and with some jurisdictions following a similar regime even though they are not signatories.[43] However, recognition and enforcement under the New York Convention is subject to exceptions set out in Art. V, which mirrors Art. 34 of the Model Law cited above. The most significant of these is Art. V(2)(b)—non-enforcement on grounds of public policy. Some jurisdictions treat this as a means of blocking enforcement in a broad range of instances.[44] Examples of jurisdictions that construe, or have construed, public policy particularly broadly (though to varying degrees) include India, Indonesia, Kenya, Pakistan and Nigeria.[45]

In contrast, there is no public-policy exception, or any other exceptions for that matter, when it comes to enforcing "pecuniary obligations" under ICSID awards. Under Art. 54(1), ICSID Contracting States agree to "recognize an award rendered pursuant to this Convention as binding and enforce the pecuniary obligations imposed by that award within its territories as if it were a final judgment of a court in that State."[46]

Non-pecuniary obligations, such as tribunal orders for specific performance, do not benefit from this simplified enforcement mechanism. In practice, tribunal orders for non-pecuniary obligations are rarely sought and even more rarely granted in

---

[41] It moreover includes ICSID awards themselves if they are being enforced in a jurisdiction that is not a Contracting State to the Convention.

[42] See http://www.newyorkconvention.org/countries. Accessed 12 January 2018.

[43] E. g. Taiwan (Arbitration Law of the Republic of China of 2002). We understand that Kosovo has recently enacted a similar law.

[44] This is partially facilitated by the fact that there is no uniform concept of public policy, and New York Convention signatories are left to define the term individually. Most keep it quite vague; tellingly, no signatory jurisdictions have defined public policy statutorily, except for the UAE and Australia. See the excellent 2015 report on public policy of the IBA Sub-Committee on Recognition and Enforcement of Arbitral Awards (2015), pp. 2–3.

[45] IBA Sub-Committee on Recognition and Enforcement of Arbitral Awards (2015), country-specific chapters on those jurisdictions.

To put this into context, though, most jurisdictions interpret public policy narrowly and moreover accord the recognition of foreign awards public policy status in itself. See, for instance, the recent judgment of the English High Court in *Pencil Hill Ltd v. US Città Di Palermo S.p.A.* (unreported) QBD (Merc) (Manchester), 19 January 2016. The Court held that the public policy of recognising foreign awards should be given greater weight than the public policy of blocking the enforcement of penalties that are contrary to English law.

[46] Note, however, that ICSID awards are not exempt from state immunity from execution. See Art. 55 of the Convention.

Bilateral Investment Treaty (BIT) arbitrations.[47] They may, however, be a more prominent feature of contractual ICSID arbitrations (though no data seems to exist on this question). Even so, in most cases investor claimants are inherently likely to bring monetary claims. Therefore, having a simplified mechanism available for the enforcement of such claims is a clear advantage for investors.

4 The Degree of Utilisation of the ICSID Convention for Arbitration Clauses in Contracts

We can offer no hard data on the degree to which investors with sovereign counterparties utilise the option of ICSID arbitration clauses. We doubt that such data exists. There are, however, several reasons that lead us to suspect that investors are not making much use of this tool:

Schreuer's commentary notes that arbitration agreements were "the traditional way of expressing consent" to ICSID arbitration, which only "[m]ore recently [...] has been largely displaced by consent expressed through treaties and legislation".[48] So it appears that arbitration agreements between investors and host states are not used nearly as frequently as they once were.

Proceedings arising out of contractual arbitration agreements between investors and states account for only a small proportion of ICSID's current total case load. In 2010, when the ICSID Secretariat started publishing caseload statistics online, the proportion of contract-based arbitrations registered with the Secretariat was 22%. It has since declined further to 16.8%.[49]

Moreover, ICSID describes all such cases as having arisen under "Investment Contract[s] between the Investor and the Host-State". That term is normally used to denote a fairly narrow range of contracts. Bishop et al., in a comprehensive survey of investment contracts and disputes arising out of them, identify three categories.[50] First, concession, production, licence and service agreements relating to oil and gas. Secondly, joint ventures between investors and state entities. Thirdly, build, operate and transfer agreements relating to infrastructure projects (a relatively new form of contract mainly employed by Asian governments).

We have had a number of informal conversations with clients who have exposure to sovereign risk. Their feedback has been that this is not an instrument that is ordinarily used in "the market". In some cases, sovereign risk professionals were not even aware that it was an option to put ICSID clauses into contracts. Even in terms

[47] See e.g. Kröll (2015), p. 1496; Li (2015), p. 204; Schreuer (2004), p. 325.

[48] Schreuer et al. (2009), p. 192. See also Reed et al. (2011), p. 13; Waibel (2015), p. 1224. Friedland (2007), p. 157, even asserts that ICSID was originally used "almost exclusively" as a contractual rather than treaty-based tool.

[49] The Secretariat's caseload statistics are available at: https://icsid.worldbank.org/en/Pages/resources/ICSID-Caseload-Statistics.aspx. Accessed 12 January 2018.

[50] Bishop et al. (2014), pp. 213–316.

of some of the categories of investment contracts described above, our sources indicated that ICSID clauses are far from being a common feature.

In summary, while there is not much data on the degree of utilisation of ICSID in contracts, it appears that (i) this is not a commonly used tool, (ii) its usage has declined over time, and (iii) it is only used (or at any rate, only used regularly) for a narrow range of investment contracts, as opposed to "ordinary" commercial contracts involving states and state entities.

In other words, ICSID is not put into contracts nearly as much as it could be. In particular, given the wide scope of the term "investment", touched on above,[51] ICSID tribunals would—if the parties so agreed—surely take jurisdiction over a much wider universe of disputes than those arising out of what are commonly referred to as investment contracts. For example, the acquisition of state-owned assets or shares in companies being privatised could feasibly be brought under the jurisdiction of ICSID tribunals. As could sovereign bonds or loan agreements with states and any number of other long-term commercial arrangements involving a sovereign (or state owned/controlled) counter-party.

5 Why Do Investors Appear Not to Use the ICSID Convention for Contractual Disputes?

There does not seem to be any literature on this question, so we can only speculate about the reasons why ICSID clauses are not used as much as perhaps they should be from an investor perspective. It may be due to a lack of bargaining power,[52] though instinctively we find this hard to believe. It would mean that host states inherently have the upper hand in negotiating contracts with investors. Given how keen many governments are to attract foreign investment,[53] this seems unlikely.

Maybe, as one colleague with whom we discussed the question speculated, the advantages of the ICSID Convention over other dispute resolution routes, particularly non-ICSID arbitration, exist more in theory than in practice. So perhaps it is just not worth the investors' while to push the sovereign counter-party for an ICSID arbitration clause. This colleague cited two principal reasons in support of his hypothesis. First, he suspects that enforcement under the ICSID Convention may not be as straightforward as the legal framework suggests. Secondly, in his experience (which is significant; he is an acclaimed expert in the field) ICSID tribunals tend to show a degree of pro-host state bias. Both are valid concerns, but there is no conclusive evidence for either:

---

[51] Which moreover has significantly expanded over the past few decades. See e.g. McLachlan et al. (2017), p. 217 et seq.

[52] Cf. e.g. Waibel (2015), p. 1225.

[53] Cf, e.g., Shyam (2016), Vukšić (2013), p. 351 et seq.; Wells and Wint (2001).

5.1 Host States Resisting Enforcement?

In terms of host states seeking to circumvent or delay enforcement, there are a number of examples. Thus, it is well known that Argentina regularly and (fairly) successfully uses the ICSID annulment mechanism to delay the enforcement of awards against it.[54] And some states—notably Argentina again—have recently simply declined to comply with their enforcement obligations,[55] albeit that we understand Argentina now to have paid nearly all outstanding awards[56] following a change of government.

However, there is insufficient data to assess the magnitude of this risk to investors, let alone its effect on their choice of dispute resolution provisions for contracts with state entities. As one expert notes, "it is difficult to have a clear picture of the effectiveness of the ICSID mechanism" for enforcing awards.[57]

In any event, the question is not whether enforcing ICSID awards is risk-free. It is whether there is less inherent risk to the investor than in enforcing other types of awards or judgments. As noted above, that appears to be the case (though there is no conclusive evidence of this position, either).[58]

5.2 Pro-Host State Bias?

As to the real or perceived pro-host state bias of ICSID tribunals, there is by no means a consensus among scholars or practitioners that ICSID is biased in favour of host state respondents. If anything, recent scholarly works appear to point towards the absence of such a bias.[59] Some scholars even claim to have identified systemic pro-investor bias.[60] As the author of one particularly thorough empirical inquiry into arbitrator behaviour in investor-state arbitration concludes:

> the results of empirical research on possible bias will vary according to the questions asked, methods used, project design, and inferences drawn. Given the diversity of approaches, it is not surprising that there is mixed (often inconclusive) evidence regarding possible bias in investment arbitration.[61]

---

[54] See e.g. Minorini Lima (2015), pp. 121–136. Argentina's latest annulment application, against an award in favour of several (insolvent) Spanish companies, was lodged in November 2017; see Jones (2017).

[55] Other examples are Congo, Georgia, Liberia, Senegal, Zimbabwe and the autonomous province of Kurdistan in Iraq. See (i) Joubin-Bret (2015), pp. 99–112, see especially pp. 102–105, and (ii) Petrochilos et al. (2010), p. 142.

[56] That is, those not being challenged. See note 55 above.

[57] Joubin-Bret (2015), p. 112.

[58] See Sect. 3 above.

[59] E.g. Frank (2014).

[60] Broad (2015).

[61] Van Harten (2012), p. 251.

Moreover, even assuming ICSID tribunals are more likely than not to be biased in favour of state actors, and this bias is consistent enough to drive investors' choice of forum for their contractual disputes with sovereign counter-parties, would it not be likely that non-ICSID tribunals would tend to display the same bias when adjudicating disputes between investors and states or state entities?

6 Conclusions

We have not found a convincing, empirically tested explanation of why investors do not to use ICSID clauses in contracts with sovereign counter-parties more frequently, despite the obvious and tangible advantages it has over other forms of dispute resolution. It is at least possible, then, that investors are either not aware of this option or have insufficient information regarding it. By this we mean that some investors may simply not know that they can put ICSID arbitration clauses into many types of "ordinary" commercial contracts with states or state entities (as opposed to investment contracts in the narrow sense of the term).[62] It might be that ICSID as a contractual dispute resolution mechanism has simply gone out of fashion in the post-Cold War world, where the Convention is almost exclusively associated with treaty-based disputes, at least in the public eye.

If so, perhaps what is needed is a more active debate about the pros and cons, the limits and practicalities of ICSID specifically as a contractual tool.[63] The obvious first step towards such a debate is empirical research into the degree to which ICSID clauses are used in commercial contracts with sovereigns and the reasons they are or are not used. This kind of survey would be invaluable for "users" of ICSID arbitration, practitioners and scholars alike. It would provide a sound basis for setting out recommendations to investors as to the types of contracts in which ICSID clauses may (and, from an investor perspective, should) be used.

---

[62] This is certainly corroborated by the informal conversations we have had on the subject, as noted above.

[63] This is not to say that there is not plenty of information out there. For instance, in addition to the sources quoted above, the ICSID Secretariat maintains (and regularly updates) a set of model clauses for contracts on its website (http://icsidfiles.worldbank.org/icsid/icsid/staticfiles/model-clauses-en/main-eng.htm. Accessed 12 January 2018). Reed et al. (2011), pp. 43–51, contains a fairly current (and very user-friendly) guide to drafting such clauses, as does Friedland (2007), pp. 157–170. Another thorough and detailed guide—even if by now somewhat dated—is Delaume (1992). The issue is that all of this literature is focussed on the mechanics of using ICSID contractually, rather than how it is actually being used, or why and in what circumstances it makes sense to do so.

References

Amerasinghe CF (1976) Jurisdiction Rationae Personae under the convention on the settlement of investment disputes. In: Royal Institute of International Affairs (ed) British year book of international law 1975, vol. 47(1). Oxford University Press, Oxford, pp 227–267

Bishop RD, Crawford J et al (2014) Foreign investment disputes: cases materials and commentary. Kluwer Law International, Alphen aan den Rijn

Blackaby N, Partasides C et al (2015) Redfern and Hunter on international arbitration, 6th edn. Oxford University Press, Oxford

Broad R (2015) Corporate bias in the World Bank Group's International Centre for settlement of investment disputes: a case study of a global mining corporation Suing El Salvador. Univ Pa J Int Law 36(4):851–874

Cuervo-Cazurra A, Inkpen A et al (2014) Governments as owners: state-owned multinational companies. J Int Bus Stud 45(8):919–942

Delaume G (1992) How to draft an ICSID arbitration clause. ICSID Rev Foreign Invest Law J 7(1):168–195

Frank S (2014) Conflating politics and development? Examining investment treaty arbitration outcomes. Va J Int Law 55(1):13–69

Friedland P (2007) Arbitration clauses for international contracts, 2nd edn. JurisNet, Huntington

IBA Sub-Committee on Recognition and Enforcement of Arbitral Awards (2015) Recognition and Enforcement of Arbitral Awards - Study on Public Policy. http://www.ibanet.org/LPD/Dispute_Resolution_Section/Arbitration/Recogntn_Enfrcemnt_Arbitl_Awrd/publicpolicy15.aspx. Accessed 12 Jan 2018

ICSID Secretariat (ed) (1968) History of the ICSID convention, vol II. World Bank, Washington

Jones T (2017) Argentina seeks to Annul Airlines Award. Glob Arbitr Rev. 24 November 2017. https://globalarbitrationreview.com/article/1151034/argentina-seeks-to-annul-airlines-award (requires subscription). Accessed 20 Jan 2018

Joubin-Bret A (2015) The effectiveness of the ICSID mechanism regarding the enforcement of arbitral awards. In: Fouret J (ed) Enforcement of investment treaty arbitration awards. Globe Law and Business, London, pp 99–112

Kröll S (2015) Enforcement of awards. In: Bungenberg M, Griebel J et al (eds) International investment law. Nomos, Baden-Baden, pp 1482–1504

Li F (2015) The divergence and convergence of ICSID and non-ICSID arbitration. PhD thesis, University of Glasgow

McLachlan C, Shore M et al (2017) International investment arbitration: substantive principles, 2nd edn. Oxford University Press, Oxford

Minorini Lima I (2015) Argentina. In: Fouret J (ed) Enforcement of investment treaty arbitration awards. Globe Law and Business, London, pp 121–136

Petrochilos G, Noury S et al (2010) Convention of the settlement of disputes between states and nationals of other states (Washington/ICSID Convention) 1965. In: Mistelis L (ed) Concise international arbitration. Kluwer Law International, Alphen aan den Rijn, pp 33–170

Reed L, Paulsson J et al (2011) Guide to ICSID arbitration, 2nd edn. Kluwer Law International, Alphen aan den Rijn

Schreuer C (2004) Non-Pecuniary remedies in ICSID arbitration. Arbitr Int 20(4):325–332

Schreuer C, Malintoppi L et al (2009) The ICSID convention: a commentary, 2nd edn. Cambridge University Press, Cambridge

Shyam A (2016) ET 500: State govts' race to attract foreign investment intensifies. https://economictimes.indiatimes.com/markets/stocks/news/et-500-making-a-state-ment/articleshow/55634574.cms. Accessed 12 Jan 2018

Van Harten G (2012) Arbitrator behaviour in asymmetrical adjudication: an empirical study of investment treaty arbitration. Osgoode Hall Law J 50(1):211–268

Vukšić G (2013) Developing countries in competition for foreign investment. J Int Trade Econ Dev 22(3):351–376

Waibel M (2015) Investment arbitration: jurisdiction and admissibility. In: Bungenberg M, Griebel J et al (eds) International investment law. Nomos, Baden-Baden, pp 1212–1287

Wells LT, Wint AG (2001) Marketing a country: promotion as a tool for attracting foreign investment. https://hbswk.hbs.edu/item/marketing-a-country-promotion-as-a-tool-for-attracting-foreign-investment. Accessed 12 Jan 2018

Williams DAR, Foote S (2011) Recent developments in the approach to identifying an 'investment' pursuant to Article 25(1) of the ICSID Convention. In: Brown C, Miles K (eds) Evolution in investment treaty law and arbitration. Cambridge University Press, Cambridge, pp 42–64

Object and Purpose as Interpretation Tool in International Commercial Law Conventions: How to Make the 'Top Down Approach' Work

Maren Heidemann

Contents

Abstract By creating unworkable rules based on misaligned object, content and purpose states fail to achieve their public policy goals by exceeding the limits of their remit and are responsible for the continued necessity for a spontaneous, non-state informal private legal order in cross border trade, the so-called bottom up approach to self-regulation. This in turn appears to prompt a need for state regulation in order

---

M. Heidemann (✉)
Institute of Advanced Legal Studies, School of Advanced Studies, University of London, London, UK

M. Heidemann, J. Lee (eds.), *The Future of the Commercial Contract in Scholarship and Law Reform*, https://doi.org/10.1007/978-3-319-95969-6_16

to safeguard the very public policy goals. Only a reflection on the relationship between object and purpose can be a basis for successful modern treaty law in the area of international private commercial law. This chapter examines the role of object and purpose as recognized by Art. 31 of the 1969 Vienna Convention on the Law of Treaties, VCLT. The author looks at object and purpose separately and explains the meaning of each of these two terms with regard to selected international conventions regulating private commercial law including tax treaties. In combination with interpretation rules contained in the commercial law conventions themselves, an expanded meaning and use of object and purpose of a treaty can be discerned and used to form a reinforced comprehensive autonomous interpretation method. While the purpose of any convention is discernible by recourse to the texts and materials of a treaty, the object plays a decisive role in successful drafting, application and interpretation of a commercial law treaty. The author argues that it is exclusively the international character of the object that requires the creation of transnational substantive uniform law and other types of international commercial law.

1 Introduction

The decades following World War II have seen worldwide efforts to establish a legal framework facilitating international trade. This framework is generally intended to create a comprehensive infrastructure for merchants.[1] The four general areas can be said to consist of public law import and export rules, private law substantive commercial contract law, transnational commercial adjudication and enforcement and a supportive system of international taxation. Progress has been made in all these areas. The degree to which the resulting legal landscape is truly transnational varies, though, and elements of this global structure appear in different costumes, national, international and transnational, public and private. While the General Agreement on Tariffs and Trade (GATT) and the World Trade Organisation (WTO) have provided a world wide network of trade agreements dealing with trade barriers, international organisations have promoted the adoption of conventions providing substantive commercial contract law for cross border contracts. International adjudication has not manifested in the shape of an international commercial court yet, but rather employing a system of informal incentives to promote convergence across national court systems by offering databases of international commercial case law using the substantive contract law conventions. A great amount of international commercial dispute settlement remains entrusted to the arbitration centers around the world. The desire to regulate and control international trade and commerce is growing, however, revealing a tension between the public and the private sector when it comes to finding the most promising avenues to achieving fairness, justice and ethical observance in the newly globalized world of trade. One strand of debate is therefore

[1] See Van Alstine (1998), p. 689.

whether the so called top down approach (formal state legislation) is better than the so called bottom up approach (evolutionary often uncodified and customary law originating from private sources of traditional self governance) to legislating and rule making in the sphere of commercial dealing. This includes taxation which of course seems doubtlessly reserved to the public law and top down method. At present, it is not obvious which of the two seems to be the most successful in promoting trade for the benefit of both national and international interests. While the 'top down approach' is generating substantial zealousness and output at present, some undeniable short comings of this philosophy seem to perpetuate the need to sustain the opposite number, the 'bottom up approach' to transnational commercial law. This chapter identifies as one of these short comings the lack of clarity in the object and purpose of public international law instruments regulating international commercial relationships.[2] Object and purpose of international treaties are an element of the (autonomous) interpretation method as incorporated in Art 31 (1) of the 1969 Vienna Convention on the Law of Treaties (VCLT).[3] The autonomous interpretation method is instrumental for the successful application of international law and is yet reserved to formal conventions adopted among state signatories. This tool, the interpretation rule applicable to an international treaty, constitutes the interface between public and private commercial contract law and other relevant commercial regulatory law. This chapter explores the role of the component of 'object and purpose' of a convention for the successful application and enforcement of treaty law regulating transnational commercial contract law and in three of the four areas of activity mentioned above—substantive contract law, its enforcement and its taxation.

International commercial contracts have been subject to international legislation all through the past century. The result has often been cast in the form of an international convention containing substantive rules of contract law. Examples are the 1964 Hague Convention relating to a Uniform Law on the International Sale of Goods (ULIS) and the Convention relating to a Uniform Law on the Formation of Contracts for the International Sale of Goods (ULF) as well as the 1980 United Nations Convention of Contracts for the International Sale of Goods (CISG). These conventions incorporate rules which commit the contracting state parties to adopt the conventions according to their respective national implementation procedures, including reservation clauses and all rules normally to be expected in international treaties. The operative part of the conventions, however, can be said to stand out from the majority of treaties in that it consists of substantive rules of private contract law. This is remarkable in two ways. For one thing, these rules of substantive contract law are intended to operate only between private parties. There may be occasions where states may choose to interact in this way, but this will be rare. The

[2] Along with Jonas and Saunders (2010), p. 569: "Scholars debate why states comply with their international law obligations despite the lack of strong enforcement mechanisms, and one of the critical factors recognized by multiple theories is whether the law is *clear*.'[...] Vague terms such as object and purpose erode the law's capacity to guide state behavior."

[3] See for the drafting history of this provision Buffard and Zemanek (1998), Crnic-Grotic (1997) and Klabbers (2001).

rules are meant to govern contracts for the sale of goods across borders between private parties. For another thing, these contractual rules complement or replace state rules on contractual relations between private individuals. This effect is not as apparent in comparable conventions such as the Warsaw convention[4] on the liability of air carriers and of the Hague-Visby rules[5] on the liability of sea carriers. The rules contained therein do not constitute the actual underlying liability rules, they only specify that liability should arise from a certain situation and attributed to the carrier. They do not seek to establish a separate regime of tort law. The above mentioned sales law conventions do exactly that. They create a directly applicable separate regime of contract law for international sale of goods. This was one of the reasons why contract formation in particular was hard to agree and took two conventions (ULF and CISG) to be introduced at transnational level by the signatory states. Contract laws differ a lot around the globe and they depend not only on isolated rules within each jurisdiction but are an integral part of a whole network of rules that do not easily function in isolation but depend on a background of contextual and enforcement rules. Acknowledging this difficulty in creating a transnational commercial contract law, databases were established hosted by a number of international organisations (the Institute for the Unification of Private Law, UNIDROIT and the United Nations Commission on Trade Law, UNCITRAL) and academic institutions (most prominently the Pace University) which compile court decisions referring to international conventions and other instruments such as model laws providing uniform law.[6] This is an attempt to create a comprehensive legal infrastructure at transnational level which is naturally present at the national level of domestic law. The obstacle faced by this attempt, however, is the fact that using these databases is not only non-mandatory but even hard to justify for each national court using the uniform sales laws. It is this fact that highlights the inherent conflict contained in uniform sales conventions. The states who are the signatory parties to the conventions effectively have no direct interest in the correct use and application of its operative part. The same is true for the below mentioned tax law conventions.[7] The signatory states may be able to monitor and demand the adherence to the implementation rules contained in the sales law treaties but they will not have an interest in the correct application of the substantive rules of contract law contained therein, even less so than in the case of the tax law conventions. It is the aim of this chapter to analyse this conflict of interest, its reasons and effects on uniform law and the practice of international commercial contracts.

[4] Convention for the Unification of Certain Rules Relating to International Carriage by Air, Signed at Warsaw on 12 October 1929—Warsaw Convention 1929 as amended by the Montreal Convention 1999. Text available from IATA at https://www.iata.org/policy/Documents/MC99_en.pdf.

[5] The Hague-Visby Rules—The Hague Rules as Amended by the Brussels Protocol 1968.

[6] UNIDROIT maintains a database on all its texts including the UNIDROIT Principles of Commercial contracts on its website, see Sect. 2.2 below.

[7] See Sect. 5 below.

2 Interpretation of Uniform Laws

Uniform laws are a number of conventions, model laws and 'principles' that have been drafted, adopted and enacted to provide uniform law for international commercial contracts. Typically, they contain their own interpretation rules. These rules relate to the interpretation of the convention or model law itself and also in parts to the construction of the contractual relationship. It can be observed that the interpretation rules relating to the legal instrument itself differ according to the legal nature of the instrument. They also fall into two categories which can be called a method rule and an actual interpretation rule. The method rule stipulates the method to be chosen in order to 'fill gaps' left by the instrument, matters that are not covered by the instrument itself. Which laws or legal rules should apply in such instances and how to arrive at them is the subject of the method rules. The way to interpret the rules contained within the uniform instrument is the subject of the interpretation rules.

2.1 Method Rules

The method of how to progress from the text of the substantive contract law convention to legal rules outside the convention has been a prime concern for drafters of contract law conventions. The first law of this kind was created with the 1964 Hague Convention relating to a Uniform Law on the International Sale of Goods (ULIS). It contained the method rule as a 'point of departure' within the development and successive enactments of later conventions dealing with private contract law. Art 17 ULIS reads:

> Questions concerning matters governed by the present Law which are not expressly settled therein shall be settled in conformity with the general principles on which the present Law is based.

This rule can be viewed as a semi perfect design for the use of uniform law. The rule stipulates to resort to underlying general principles on the encounter of a gap in ULIS.[8] It would be perfect if it then went on to stipulate horizontal progression to the use of other relevant uniform or international law in order to reflect the international character of the contract it regulates. However, ULIS stopped short of this. This is because later developments of uniform contract law show that this next step went too far in the eyes of the state drafters of this law.

The next uniform law on international commercial contracts to be adopted as an international treaty was the 1980 United Nations Convention on the International Sale of Goods (CISG). Article 7 CISG reads:

> (1) In the interpretation of this Convention, regard is to be had to its international character and to the need to promote uniformity in its application and the observance of good faith in international trade.

[8] This technique is advocated by Van Alstine (1998).

> (2) Questions concerning matters governed by this Convention which are not expressly settled in it are to be settled in conformity with the general principles on which it is based or, in the absence of such principles, in conformity with the law applicable by virtue of the rules of private international law.

Art. 7 (2) CISG introduces the next step in finding the applicable law to an international commercial contract by pointing to the traditional method of applying national rules of private international law. These always point to a domestic law rather than to other tailor made transnational uniform rules for commercial contracts, for instance the UNIDROIT Principles for Commercial Contracts (UPICC). Franco Ferrari has set out that at present the UPICC cannot be used to complement CISG[9] on the encounter of gaps. Gaps (*lacunae*) occur as *lacunae intra legem* and *lacunae praeter legem*. The former are an effect of the limited scope of a legal instrument and the latter are matters where no rule of it can be considered to address a specific question of law that arises out of a dispute governed by the legal instrument. These are the type of gaps covered by Art. 7 (2) CISG and Art. 17 ULIS. It can be observed, that uniform rules for international commercial contracts that have not amounted to international treaties such as the UPICC and others contain the same method rule as ULIS does. Art 1.6. UPICC reads:

> (Interpretation and supplementation of the Principles)
> (1) In the interpretation of these Principles, regard is to be had to their international character and to their purposes including the need to promote uniformity in their application.
> (2) Issues within the scope of these Principles but not expressly settled by them are as far as possible to be settled in accordance with their underlying general principles.

This may still not allow resorting to other relevant uniform law instruments outside the one containing the method rule. Therefore, there is currently no available network or range of international uniform laws that can be resorted to horizontally and thereby remaining within an international law setting in the way of a hierarchy formed by the degree of specialisation of each set of rules in relation to the case in hand. Instead, at the end of each application of a method rule by state courts stands domestic national law. This may not be the best solution for an international commercial dispute involving substantive private law. The question is of course what is meant by 'the best solution'. This is discussed below.

2.2 *Integrated Interpretation Rules*

While ULIS only contained the method rule, subsequent uniform law conventions, model laws and principles of substantive commercial contract law also provide for an interpretation rule. It usually precedes the method rule within the same Article as can be seen from the above quoted instruments. These interpretation rules do not relate to

[9] Ferrari (1998, 2007).

the interpretation of the contracts governed by the legal rules of the convention or model law as the case may be but to the interpretation of the rules that the instruments consist of. This must be seen as a deviation from domestic law where interpretation rules relating to the law itself are usually part of general legal doctrine and judicial practice and not contained in any codification itself. For uniform law it was deemed necessary to expressly state interpretation rules in order to reinforce and preserve the aims and objectives that were to be pursued with their adoption. What are these aims and objectives? The answer to that may seem straightforward. Both Art. 1.6. UPICC and Art. 7 (1) CISG, for instance, specify 'the need to promote uniformity in [the] application' of these two instruments. But can 'the international character' of these rules as well as 'the observance of good faith in international trade' (Art. 7 (1) CISG) be regarded to be an aim of the convention? Based on a purely textual understanding this may not be entirely unequivocal. The UPICC also mention 'their purposes' in the plural, suggesting that there must be more purposes that are not mentioned in the interpretation rule itself. Where and how can these purposes be found relying on an internationally accepted method? In the case of formal public international law such as CISG and other substantive law conventions adopted by UNCITRAL, for instance, the answer will be found by looking at the preamble of the conventions as well as by applying Art. 31-33 of the 1969 Vienna Convention on the Law of Treaties (VCLT).[10] These latter provisions contain interpretation rules applicable to international treaties which CISG and other uniform law conventions doubtlessly are.[11] However, are these rules meant to govern substantive law disputes between private parties and are they suitable for this purpose? This question reveals an unique tension present in substantive law conventions which arises from their legal nature as treaties concluded between state parties and their substantive law content which almost exclusively binds individual private commercial parties except in rare cases where states may act commercially and remain in an 'eye level' position with a commercial party. This raises questions as to the object and purpose to be pursued with these conventions in the sense of Art. 31 (1) of the VCLT which reads:

> General rule of interpretation
> 1. A treaty shall be interpreted in good faith in accordance with the ordinary meaning to be given to the terms of the treaty in their context and in the light of its object and purpose.
> 2. The context for the purpose of the interpretation of a treaty shall comprise, in addition to the text, including its preamble and annexes:
> (a) any agreement relating to the treaty which was made between all the parties in connection with the conclusion of the treaty;
> (b) any instrument which was made by one or more parties in connection with the conclusion of the treaty and accepted by the other parties as an instrument related to the treaty.
> 3. There shall be taken into account, together with the context:
> (a) any subsequent agreement between the parties regarding the interpretation of the treaty or the application of its provisions;

[10] Done at Vienna on 23 May 1969. Entered into force on 27 January 1980. United Nations, Treaty Series, vol. 1155, p. 331.

[11] See for further detail Sect. 4.2 below.

(b) any subsequent practice in the application of the treaty which establishes the agreement of the parties regarding its interpretation;
(c) any relevant rules of international law applicable in the relations between the parties.
4. A special meaning shall be given to a term if it is established that the parties so intended.

The interpretation rules in uniform law instruments which are integrated into their text contain additional criteria compared to the VCLT when they mention the need to promote uniformity in the application of the substantive law conventions or the observance of good faith in international trade. When viewed together with the VCLT, this can be considered to constitute a novel interpretation standard for use with substantive law conventions and uniform law. This comprehensive standard requires a rule of uniform law to be viewed as a stand alone rule within the context of the actual legal instrument in the sense of an autonomous interpretation and also as part of a transnational system of adjudication. In the absence of a transnational commercial court this is created by the multitude of national court decisions which are collected and publicised by the various public and private databases provided by international legal drafters such as the UN Commission on International Trade Law (UNCITRAL)[12] and the Institute for the Unification of Private Law (UNDROIT)[13] as well as by academic institutions[14] or even collections provided by international arbitration centers.[15] The difficulty with this understanding of uniformity is that while it may be maintained that recourse to any of the national case law is mandatory pursuant to Art. 7 (1) CISG and similar interpretation rules in other formal conventions, each of the domestic decisions have no binding force in the way of judicial precedent outside the jurisdiction of each body of adjudication. This creates a tension between the expectation created within uniform law conventions by way of their integrated interpretation rules and traditional legal doctrine and practice resisting of any influence of foreign courts as a matter of asserting sovereignty.[16]

The tension is well illustrated by a closer analysis of the criterion of object and purpose of a uniform instrument in the context of international treaty law.

3 Object and Purpose in Public International Law

The VCLT determines as one of the first criteria for the interpretation of a rule of an international treaty the 'object and purpose' of a convention as a standard for the contextual analysis of the meaning of a treaty provision.[17] This criterion is only

[12] Maintaining their database CLOUT.

[13] Maintaining their database Unilex.

[14] Such as the Pace University database or 'lex mercatoria' at the University of Oslo.

[15] Such as the International Chamber of Commerce (ICC) in Paris.

[16] The current 'Brexit' debate as it is conducted in the UK is a discouraging confirmation of this reluctance. See also Fredman (2015) and Roberts (2011).

[17] See Art. 31 (1) VCLT as quoted above. The expression "object and purpose" appears in seven further provisions of the VCLT. It has most often been discussed in case law of the ICJ in order to determine questions of the validity of reservations to treaties (as a compatibility test providing an

seemingly starightforward and it not necessarily easy to determine even if primarily established by recourse to the preamble of the treaty as suggested by the VCLT.[18] It is useful to leave conventional practice to one side[19] and analyse the object and the purpose of a treaty separately.

3.1 *The Purpose of a Convention*

The purpose or objective of a convention can be established by recourse to the express terms of the preamble[20] or any material setting out the intentions of the drafters and contracting parties. If no express recorded declarations are made, it is less obvious how to establish the purpose of a treaty in order to shed light on any of its rules according to Art. 31-33 VCLT. In the case of CISG, the brief preamble reads:

> THE STATES PARTIES TO THIS CONVENTION,
> BEARING IN MIND the broad objectives in the resolutions adopted by the sixth special session of the General Assembly of the United Nations on the establishment of a New International Economic Order,
> CONSIDERING that the development of international trade on the basis of equality and mutual benefit is an important element in promoting friendly relations among States,
> BEING OF THE OPINION that the adoption of uniform rules which govern contracts for the international sale of goods and take into account the different social, economic and legal systems would contribute to the removal of legal barriers in international trade and promote the development of international trade,
> HAVE AGREED as follows:

This preamble or mission statement refers sweepingly to visionary and long term goals and objectives decidedly of a public policy nature. They are easy to establish and determine.

The preamble to predecessor ULIS, however, is extremely brief and says nothing about the objectives pursued with the convention. It reads:

> The States signatory to the present Convention, Desiring to establish a uniform law on the international sale of goods, Have resolved to conclude a convention to this effect and have agreed upon the following provisions:...

The preamble is identical to that of the ULF. The absence of express statements of the pursued objectives might reflect the difficulty of arriving at these uniform provisions in the first place. It makes the questions of the aims pursued more poignant. Given that the uniform laws mentioned in this section provide substantive

alternative to the unanimity rule, Art. 19 (c) VCLT) and of states' obligations under a treaty prior to its entry into force, Art. 18 VCLT. See Buffard and Zemanek (1998), Jonas and Saunders (2010) and Linderfalk (2003).

[18] Art. 31 (2) VCLT.

[19] Linderfalk (2003), p. 433.

[20] Buffard and Zemanek (1998), p. 318.

rules of contract law only and no agreements on the declared policies in the preamble to CISG begs the question how the uniform laws are suitable to achieve the stated aims or if no aim is stated, what the actual motivation for the signatory states was to adopt them in the first place. The tension arises from the discrepancy between the identity of the obligated parties under the convention and the addressees of the actual rules. Only states can be bound by treaties. The addressees of these contract law conventions, however, are private parties who will become bound by the contracts they conclude, not by the convention itself. On the other hand, these private parties cannot hold a state to account for breach of a rule of the convention by a contractual partner and cannot expect a state to enforce the convention against a contractual party under the uniform laws. While none of these scenarios is unthinkable, they are highly unlikely. The signatory states have stopped short of allowing an international adjudication body to settle contractual disputes arising under the sales law conventions and therefore completing the transnational merchant law regime. Traders have no standing before the International Court of Justice (ICJ) to bring a contractual claim under CISG, ULF or ULIS. It is hard to imagine a scenario where a state could be made responsible for not applying or misapplying a rule of CISG or ULF as they hardly ever do apply these rules. It would be the independent national courts who apply the rules apart from the merchants themselves and private dispute settlement bodies. It is also hard to imagine a state pursuing a private party's contractual claim before the ICJ. What interest and legitimation would states have to do that when they profess to respect private dealing and the freedom of contract? It is clear that states have provided a substantive private law regime for exclusive use by international merchants without any involvement of the signatory states other than the general commitment to implement the conventions nationally. The proceeds of the private commercial contracts concluded under CISG or ULIS do not directly benefit the states but the merchants. Even if the resulting increase in turnover and possibly tax revenue are considered to be the economic benefit, these are hard to quantify and predict at any point in the life of these conventions. This raises the question of the suitability of the instruments to achieve the purposes set out in the preamble of CISG as well as—in the absence of a preamble—the question of the actual motivation behind the adoption of ULF and ULIS. Both questions impact on the usefulness of the purpose of the treaty as a tool for the interpretation of its rules and terms.

By contrast, the 1999 Montreal Convention amending the Warsaw Convention has the following preamble:

> THE STATES PARTIES TO THIS CONVENTION
> RECOGNIZING the significant contribution of the Convention for the Unification of Certain Rules Relating to International Carriage by Air signed in Warsaw on 12 October 1929, hereinafter referred to as the "Warsaw Convention", and other related instruments to the harmonization of private international air law;
> RECOGNIZING the need to modernize and consolidate the Warsaw Convention and related instruments;

> RECOGNIZING the importance of ensuring protection of the interests of consumers in international carriage by air and the need for equitable compensation based on the principle of restitution;
> REAFFIRMING the desirability of an orderly development of international air transport operations and the smooth flow of passengers, baggage and cargo in accordance with the principles and objectives of the Convention on International Civil Aviation, done at Chicago on 7 December 1944;
> CONVINCED that collective State action for further harmonization and codification of certain rules
> governing international carriage by air through achieving an equitable balance of interests;

This preamble is a lot more focussed and closely related to the actual content of the convention. It recognizes openly that it is made in the interests of consumers, not states. The "equitable balance of interests" mentioned therein is that of the contracting private parties, not that of the signatory states.

3.2 *The Object of a Convention*

It might be less common to expend much thought on the object of a convention than on its objective or purpose since the answer may appear to be obvious at first glance. In many cases, however, taking a closer look at the object of a treaty may reveal inconsistencies or difficulty to specify the object. While the reference to 'object and purpose' in Art. 31 (1) VCLT may be understood to be a mere turn of a phrase,[21] determining the object of a convention using an extrinsic fact based, non-normative meaning of the term object[22] can be revealing as to the convention's purpose as well as to its content. For instance, the object of CISG is international commercial contracts for the sale of goods. This is not identical with the purposes and declared objectives in the preamble. The object of CISG is neither the 'development of international trade' as a whole, nor the 'friendly relations among States'. In fact, the object that CISG regulates is not state related at all. The object of CISG is contractual relations between private individuals, the international commercial contract for the sale of goods. These contracts may be infused with 'equality and mutual benefit'

[21] Linderfalk (2003), p. 433; Buffard and Zemanek (1998), pp. 315–316; Jonas and Saunders (2010), p. 580, who call it the 'unitary view'.

[22] I.e. synonymous with objective, aim or goal as gleaned from the actual rules of a treaty. Linderfalk (2003), and Buffard and Zemanek (1998) explain in detail how the term object or the French *objet* has been understood in scholarship deriving meaning either from the normative content of the convention or likening the term encyclopedically to that of objective or aim (French *but*). Authors have not stepped out of the actual normative context, created by the convention, however, thereby creating a self referring technique, or circular argument, for the establishment of meaning under Art 31 VCLT and presupposing a similar meaning of both terms, also sometimes suggesting that they are interchangeable. This is criticized by Jonas and Saunders (2010), pp. 573–574, commenting on Art. 31 VCLT: "The text of a treaty must be interpreted in light of the treaty's object and purpose, but the treaty's object and purpose must be discovered through interpretation of the text itself. This circularity problem is discussed in detail [further down in their text]."

in the spirit and through the application of CISG. But this does not automatically lead to the same effect on a state level or within global trade as a whole. It is not impossible that CISG has had and will have this effect or contribute to the declared objectives in the preamble. But this is a question of the causal link between the object and the purpose of a treaty. Looking at other conventions can offer a comparison. A typical public international law convention may be the 1951 United Nations Geneva Convention Relating to the Status of Refugees (the Geneva Convention). The object of this treaty is the status of refugees. This is something that only states can grant. Here, states agree among each other on how to adapt and apply their laws to refugees who are defined in Art. 1 of the Geneva Convention. Subsequent Articles read: "The Contracting States shall accord…", "The Contracting States shall apply…", "granted by a Contracting State to refugees…". Here, the states are clearly bound[23] by and acting under the treaty in question. The convention regulates a horizontal commitment between states which can only be fulfilled by the contracting parties, the signatories.[24] The CISG, by contrast, does not contain a single word that would oblige a state in relation to another signatory party to do something that only a state can do. The same is true (surprisingly) of another example which could be contextualised between CISG at one end and the Geneva Convention at the other—bilateral Double Tax Conventions (DTCs). They deal with a subject that is commercially significant and yet essentially reserved to state acting. Interestingly, the tax law conventions remain entirely vague on this point. Their object is double taxation and double non-taxation. Their purpose is the avoidance of those two objects.[25] This can only be gleaned from the full title of the DTCs in the absence of a preamble. Notably, their object is not the distribution of revenue between the participating states. Instead, the first mentioned object impacts on the tax payer, the second impacts on the state. The interests of those two parties are definitely contrary to each other in this case. It could be assumed therefore that the purpose of DTCs is to balance these interests against each other. Or, it could be assumed that the two objects remain irreconcilable. The first assumption could be verified by comparing the content of the treaties with this purpose. The second could be understood to

[23] So is the refugee according to Art. 2 Geneva Convention.

[24] The criterion of object and purpose was in fact initially developed from case law—see in more detail Buffard and Zemanek (1998), p. 316—in the ICJ's Advisory Opinion *Reservations to the Convention on the Prevention and Punishment of the Crime of Genocide*, ICJ, Reports 1951, 15–30. See for a more recent case discussion concerning the 1948 Genocide Convention, *Bosnia and Herzegovina v. Serbia and Montenegro (Bosnia v. Serbia),* ICJ Reports 2007, Gibney (2007–2008): Gibney suggests applying the object and purpose (compatibility) test to the question of attribution and state responsibility where the actual acts of genocide are not carried out by the state itself: "If the Court had applied the same kind of "object and purpose" analysis to this issue (which it did not), it is next to impossible to imagine that it would have reached the result that it did. Thus, the question that the ICJ should have asked (but did not) is this: in what way is providing massive amounts of military, economic and political assistance to paramilitary forces with genocidal designs at all consistent with the object and purpose of the Genocide Convention?…", Gibney (2007–2008), p. 146.

[25] See Sect. 5.3 below.

stifle the achievement of the pursued aim. In the following, it is attempted to develop conclusions drawn from these tensions which are inherent in treaties due to their object and purpose in respect of the interpretation of the rules of international conventions in the area of commercial law and in respect of recommendations for the further development of public policies.

4 The Effect of Object and Purpose on the Interpretation of Contract Law Conventions

Art. 31 VCLT is the more general and complementary rule to the integrated interpretation rules in the above mentioned contract law conventions. As the VCLT was only adopted in 1969 and entered into force in 1988, older conventions such as ULIS and ULF and also some DTCs may not be governed by this rule therefore. It may nevertheless be regarded as a rule of customary international law which has only been codified or 'restated' in the VCLT. It could also be argued that the convention applies to all treaties from the point of its entering into force regardless of the adoption date of the treaty rule to be interpreted.

4.1 CISG

The object and purpose rule of Art. 31 (1) VCLT is to be applied together with Art. 7 CISG when applying and interpreting a rule of CISG. Art. 7 will have to be treated as the *lex specialis* rule in relation to the VCLT rule and therefore prevail.

4.1.1 Art. 7 (1) CISG

Art. 7 (1) CISG can be understood to reinforce the purposes mentioned in the preamble. It clarifies the aspiration expressed in the preamble to conduct "international trade on the basis of equality and mutual benefit" by emphasizing the requirement to observe good faith. This is an important link to be established between the profession expressed in the preamble by the signatory states and its (desired) execution by the individual merchants who, as mentioned above, are not bound by the convention itself, but rather by their contracts. Art. 31 (1) VCLT can underpin this legal link and counteract the impression that the states have chosen an unlikely tool to achieve their objectives expressed in the preamble which would typically be pursued by means of bilateral or multilateral trade agreements such as GATT. It shows a way of how to achieve public policy ends with private law means. The other component of Art. 31 (1) VCLT, the object of the convention adds another reinforcing tool for users of the convention. The object of CISG is the international commercial contract for the sale of goods. The seemingly inconspicuous component, the object of an international treaty, adds powerful potential to the wording of Art. 7 (1) CISG. In addition to the international character of the convention itself which is to be considered there, the international character of the object is to be borne in mind. This forms the context mentioned in Art. 31 (1) VCLT. Specifying and considering the object of the convention reinforces the effect of Art. 7 CISG. CISG is a *lex specialis* to domestic contract law in so far as domestic law usually only extends to contracts in general. While national legal systems provide for rules to apply to contracts with an international element they rarely distinguish commercial contracts from private transactions and provide substantive rules of contract law but conflict rules which point to a national (domestic or foreign) legal system to apply to the contract. CISG provides substantive transnational uniform rules which apply directly to the cross border commercial contracts. The signatory states of CISG have thereby acknowledged that the international commercial contract for the sale of goods is a separate contract type. In order to observe this international character and the context of the rules of CISG pursuant to Art. 31 VCLT, it may therefore easily be assumed that Art. 7 (1) CISG provides a mandatory obligation to refer to national court judgments as communicated by the above mentioned official databases in order to promote uniformity in international merchant law. As before, however, neither the individuals adjudicating on the basis of CISG nor the litigating parties are state parties who have committed themselves to CISG and the VCLT but they are independent national judges or arbitrators or private merchants. It is therefore far from obvious that these users can rely on Art. 7 CISG in order to adhere to an international rule of judicial precedent other than spontaneously or relying on persuasive authority and even in spite of or contrary to traditional legal doctrine in order to create uniformity (of application) in the international sale of goods.[26] The fact that in many jurisdictions CISG will only be in force as part of national law[27] unsettles the public international law based interpretation standard even further by removing it from its international origin. Only the object itself, viewed in the context of Art. 7 CISG can be relied on as justification for the mandatory reference to foreign court decisions in the way of international precedent or, less aspirational, international judicial accord (*Entscheidungsharmonie*) and thereby giving effect to the international character of both CISG and the object it regulates according to Art. 7 (1) CISG. There will be other examples of how the international character of both CISG and its object can influence an interpretation of a rule of CISG, for instance when taking into account a shared understanding of a term of a contract concluded under CISG or a specific objectively determined meaning of a contractual term in the light of its international character.

[26] See Roberts (2011) and Baasch-Andersen (2005).

[27] Many jurisdictions require international law to be implemented into national law and do not apply it directly. This is so in both so called monist and dualist systems, see Klabbers (2013), pp. 288–303; Aust (2013), pp. 163–177; Crawford (2012), pp. 48–111.

4.1.2 Art. 7 (2) CISG

The international character of both CISG and its object can be understood to demand a particular use of the method rule. Again, the main difficulty lies in the tension arising from the absence of an international commercial court for the adjudication of cases under CISG and the resulting need for national judges to transcend their national judicial boundaries in order to apply Art. 7 CISG correctly. The problem will almost certainly not arise in arbitration proceedings because the method rule can easily be complemented by further reference to suitable uniform or customary law when the underlying general principles to CISG have not yielded an acceptable answer to the problem in hand. The provisions of the VCLT and CISG can even be understood to require an extension of the method rule to allow horizontal reference to suitable uniform law or general principles outside CISG in order to appropriately consider the international character of the object. They can therefore serve as a legal basis allowing to expand the codified method rule beyond the limits set by current legal doctrine which is to disallow an exclusive horizontal recourse to transnational substantive law applying to cross border commercial contracts.[28]

4.2 The UNIDROIT Ottawa Conventions

In 1988, UNIDROIT called a diplomatic conference in Ottawa, Canada, where two conventions on international leasing and factoring contracts were adopted. These contain for the first time the express reference to 'object and purpose' of the conventions in their interpretation rules. The two conventions contain identical integrated interpretation and method rules which read as follows:

> UNIDROIT Convention on International Factoring (Ottawa, 28 May 1988)
> Article 4
> 1. - In the interpretation of this Convention, regard is to be had to its object and purpose as set forth in the preamble, to its international character and to the need to promote uniformity in its application and the observance of good faith in international trade.
> 2. - Questions concerning matters governed by this Convention which are not expressly settled in it are to be settled in conformity with the general principles on which it is based or, in the absence of such principles, in conformity with the law applicable by virtue of the rules of private international law.
>
> UNIDROIT Convention on International Financial Leasing (Ottawa, 28 May 1988)
> Article 6
> 1. - In the interpretation of this Convention, regard is to be had to its object and purpose as set forth in the preamble, to its international character and to the need to promote uniformity in its application and the observance of good faith in international trade.
> 2. - Questions concerning matters governed by this Convention which are not expressly settled in it are to be settled in conformity with the general principles on which it is based or, in the absence of such principles, in conformity with the law applicable by virtue of the rules of private international law.

[28] As this is not possible under current state private international law.

The rules make it clear where the object and purpose of the conventions are to be found. The method rules, just as in the other UN conventions mentioned above, may be seen to add an important innovation consisting of only two words—'rules of' private international law. This is understood to allow the applying lawyers or arbitrators a wider choice of conflict rules to arrive at the applicable law. For instance, they may choose to disregard the Rome I Regulation[29] in determining the applicable law even though they would otherwise be bound by it. The expression 'rules of law' is used to denote both formal and informal so called non-state law, while the term 'law' refers to a state's law only. The national conflict of laws do, however, not currently allow the application of non-state transnational law within a national jurisdiction as governing law.[30] National law might be less specialized or simply not sufficiently neutral to be mutually acceptable and therefore not the prime choice to govern an international commercial contract. By choosing the wording in the method rules, the drafters have attempted to optimise the flexibility available within the current scope for a convention to be formally adopted at international level.

The preamble of the factoring convention reads:

> THE STATES PARTIES TO THIS CONVENTION,
> CONSCIOUS of the fact that international factoring has a significant role to play in the development of international trade,
> RECOGNISING therefore the importance of adopting uniform rules to provide a legal framework that will facilitate international factoring, while maintaining a fair balance of interests between the different parties involved in factoring transactions,
> HAVE AGREED as follows:

The preamble of the leasing convention reads:

> THE STATES PARTIES TO THIS CONVENTION,
> RECOGNISING the importance of removing certain legal impediments to the international financial leasing of equipment, while maintaining a fair balance of interests between the different parties to the transaction,
> AWARE of the need to make international financial leasing more available,
> CONSCIOUS of the fact that the rules of law governing the traditional contract of hire need to be adapted to the distinctive triangular relationship created by the financial leasing transaction,
> RECOGNISING therefore the desirability of formulating certain uniform rules relating primarily to the civil and commercial law aspects of international financial leasing,
> HAVE AGREED as follows:

Other than in the CISG both conventions expressly recognise the interests of the contracting parties rather than those of the signatory states or any visionary public policies as the purposes of the conventions.

---

[29] Regulation (EC) No 593/2008 of the European Parliament and the Council of 17 June 2008 on the law applicable to contractual obligations (Rome I).

[30] Within the EU this is currently determined by Articles 3 and 4 Rome I Regulation.

4.3 UNCITRAL and UNIDROIT Principles and Model Laws

Where the texts are not intended to be formally adopted, the phrasing allowing non-state law into the dispute settlement process is more pronounced. This is the case in the UNCITRAL Model Law on international arbitration and the UPICC. The interpretation rules there read as follows:

> UPICC
> ARTICLE 1.6 (Interpretation and supplementation of the Principles)
> (1) In the interpretation of these Principles, regard is to be had to their international character and to their purposes including the need to promote uniformity in their application.
> (2) Issues within the scope of these Principles but not expressly settled by them are as far as possible to be settled in accordance with their underlying general principles.

> The UNCITRAL Model Law on international arbitration (as revised 2006)
> Article 2 A.
> International origin and general principles (As adopted by the Commission at its thirty-ninth session, in 2006)
> (1) In the interpretation of this Law, regard is to be had to its international origin and to the need to promote uniformity in its application and the observance of good faith.
> (2) Questions concerning matters governed by this Law which are not expressly settled in it are to be settled in conformity with the general principles on which this Law is based.

These two instruments will not be subject to the VCLT. Therefore, it can be assumed that elements of Art. 31 (1) VCLT have been added to the texts in order to clarify the application process. In the absence of the confines of state law, however, it is surprising that the method rules do not go further in pointing to other suitable transnational commercial law but exclusively to those general principles on which the rules are based rather than all those which might best aid the dispute settlement process. Instead, the instruments remain self-contained and self-referring.

4.4 Conclusion

When viewed together, the interpretation standards employed in the contract law conventions adopted by the United Nations and those prepared by UNIDROIT can become a rather elaborate comprehensive standard suitable to deal with transnational commercial contracts by applying uniform law. The method rules, however, appear to fall short of their potential because they do not tie in with each other beyond the actual convention they are part of nor indeed with other sources of private commercial law at transnational level. The method rules do not have any effect beyond the individual conventions to form a comprehensive set of tools in transnational commercial law and thereby creating the "New International Economic Order" mentioned in the preamble to CISG. Such an effect does not seem to be intended either as could be taken from the method rules in the UPICC and UNCITRAL Model Law where the drafters could have exercised more discretion than in the formally adopted contract law conventions. Once again, the tension between the intentions and inherent ways of state acting and the needs of private merchants could be at the heart of this phenomenon. The new economic order is no new legal order after all. This might indicate the limits of legislating for private dealing and substantive transnational contract law by means of international conventions.

5 The Effect of Object and Purpose on the Interpretation of Tax Law Conventions

Taxation is an important factor for international trade. Outside the EU, which has developed certain shared rules on Value Added Tax (VAT)[31] and transfer pricing,[32] double taxation conventions (DTCs) are the only transnational source of law that applies to cross border transactions. DTCs are almost exclusively bilateral conventions[33] and therefore a large number of them exist. Some of them are based on the Model Tax Convention published by the Organisation for Economic Development and Co-operation (OECD), the OECD Model Convention.[34] The United Nations also offer a Model Tax Convention, the UN Model.[35] The model conventions leave room for a preamble and both recommend that

> States wishing to [insert a preamble] may follow the widespread practice of including in the title a reference to either the avoidance of double taxation or to both the avoidance of double taxation and the prevention of fiscal evasion.[36]

5.1 *Interpretation Rules in DTCs*

The OECD Model DTC contains an integrated interpretation rule in its Art. 3 (2) which reads:

> As regards the application of the Convention at any time by a Contracting State, any term not defined therein shall, unless the context otherwise requires, have the meaning that it has at that time under the law of that State for the purposes of the taxes to which the Convention applies, any meaning under the applicable tax laws of that State prevailing over a meaning given to the term under other laws of that State.

---

[31] Council Directive 2006/112/EC of 28 November 2006 on the common system of value added tax, OJ L 347, 11.12.2006, pp. 1–118.

[32] Parent Subsidiary Directive.

[33] Multilateral DTCs exist among Scandinavian countries and have been proposed by some European states to no avail so far, see Townsend (2001), p. 223.

[34] The Model gets updated on a regular basis. This chapter refers to the (penultimate) ninth version of it which is available from the OECD, "Model Tax Convention on Income and on Capital 2014 (Full Version)", at http://www.oecd.org/ctp/treaties/model-tax-convention-on-income-and-on-capital-2015-full-version-9789264239081-en.htm. This publication also contains a list of all DTCs in force worldwide.

[35] United Nations Model Double Taxation Convention between Developed and Developing Countries, available at http://www.un.org/esa/ffd/wp-content/uploads/2014/09/DoubleTaxation.pdf.

[36] Identical text of footnote 1 to the preamble left blank of the UN and OECD Model.

The text shows no resemblance to the wording in the above mentioned contract law conventions. No sign of an intended uniformity in application or the observance of an international character of the convention. Instead, the Model gives priority to the contracting states to take recourse to their national laws instead of seeking to establish a shared or international understanding of a term contained in the convention but "not defined therein" and "unless the context otherwise requires". Not surprisingly the practical application of the Model or the DTCs based thereon shows very little attempt to achieve any kind of uniformity or shared understanding of a term across the bilateral scope of the conventions.[37] In the same way as with the contract law conventions, the absence of a joint adjudication and lack of a 'judicial precedent' across national boundaries are the reasons for the absence of a joint standard of interpretation. Whether or not DTCs are subject to the VCLT is not straightforward. Even though many of them have been concluded before the VCLT entered into force and not all states are parties to it, it can be argued that the standard contained in Art. 31-33 VCLT applies to them by way of custom and subsequent acceptance.[38] Rather, it would take some justification to maintain an interpretation of a DTC that directly contradicts the VCLT provisions. A rather comprehensive discussion of the interpretation standard provided by the interpretation rule contained in the DTC between Germany and the UK can be seen in the *Memec* case series.[39] More modern DTC texts steer in a more promising direction. The interpretation rule in the 1991 German-Swedish DTC for instance, reads:

> Artikel 3 - Article 3 *Allgemeine Begriffsbestimmungen* (General definitions) (2) *Dieses Abkommen ist bei seiner Anwendung durch beide Vertragsstaaten übereinstimmend aus sich selbst heraus auszulegen. Ein in diesem Abkommen nicht definierter Ausdruck hat jedoch dann die Bedeutung, die ihm nach dem Recht des anwendenden Staates zukommt, wenn der Zusammenhang dies erfordert und die zuständigen Behörden sich nicht auf eine gemeinsame Auslegung geeinigt haben (Artikel 39 Absatz 3, Artikel 40 Absatz 3)*.(An interpretation of this convention is to be derived from the convention itself when applied by both

---

[37] See Townsend (2001) for US judicial practice. A "shared understanding" seems to be generally acknowledged in US doctrine and judicial practice on the basis on a contractual conception of treaties. However, cases like *United States v. Alvarez-Machain* 504 U.S. 655 (1992) (see on this also Bederman 1994) and *National Westminster Bank, PLC v. United States* 144 Fed.Cl. 120 (1999) (*NatWest*) demonstrate how the contractual model has been taken to an extreme so that "a foreign nation's wishes in the treaty interpretation process are to be utterly ignored when they conflict with the interpretation supported by the United States government" Bederman (1994), p. 1010. In both cases the partner state was deemed to have agreed to the respective US practice by having had knowledge of it at the time of contracting, i.e. the *Ker* doctrine concerning forcible abductions and extradition agreements in *Alvarez* and the Treas. Reg. sections 1.861-8 and 1.882-5 expressly mentioned in the Technical Explanations accompanying the DTC negotiating documents in *NatWest*, see Townsend (2001), p. 242. See Lang et al. (1998) for European judicial practice in the German speaking jurisdictions.

[38] It is accepted in case law of the ICJ and scholarship that the VCLT restated existing custom in international law. See for instance *Arbitral Award of 31 July 1998 (Guinea-Bissau v Senegal),* ICJ Reports 1001, 53; *Genocide (Bosnia v Serbia),* ICJ Reports 2007, 43, 109-10; Buffard and Zemanek (1998), p. 318; Crawford (2012), p. 380.

[39] *Memec plc v Inland Revenue Commissioners (IRC)* Simons Tax Cases Ch D [1996] STC, 1336 (Chancery Division); *Memec plc v Inland Revenue Commissioners (IRC)* CA [1998] STC, 754.

contracting states. A term which is not defined in this convention however, has the meaning which it has according to the law of the applying state if the context so requires and if the competent authorities have not reached an agreement on a joint interpretation, Art. 39 (3) and Art. 40 (3).)

The autonomous interpretation standard is incorporated in this interpretation rule, qualified by the condition that the convention be 'applied by both contracting states.' Under this newer DTC, the tax payer can also seek the correct application of the DTC (i.e. the correct taxation) regardless of a double taxation effect of a misinterpretation.[40]

The role of the object and purpose of a DTC within this interpretation rule is discussed below.

5.2 *The Purpose of DTCs*

Using the aforementioned method, the purpose of a convention should be found in the preamble as a starting point. The 'model preamble' is notably very brief. It is used for instance in the DTC concluded between the UK and Germany which reads:

> The United Kingdom of Great Britain and Northern Ireland and the Federal Republic of Germany,
> Desiring to conclude a new Convention for the avoidance of double taxation and the prevention of fiscal evasion,
> Have agreed as follows:...

This DTC displays almost the identical text already in its title. The brevity of these points of reference are contrasted by the much more wordy Introduction to the text of the UN Model:

---

[40]Artikel 40 *Verständigung*—[direct conciliation between fiscal authorities initiated by taxpayer]

(1) *Ist eine Person der Auffassung, daß Maßnahmen eines Vertragsstaats oder beider Vertragsstaaten für sie zu einer Besteuerung führen oder führen werden, die diesem Abkommen nicht entspricht, so kann sie unbeschadet der nach dem innerstaatlichen Recht dieser Staaten vorgesehenen Rechtsbehelfe ihren Fall der zuständigen Behörde des Vertragsstaats, in dem sie ansässig ist, oder, sofern ihr Fall von Artikel 38 Absatz 1 erfaßt wird, der zuständigen Behörde des Vertragsstaats unterbreiten, dessen Staatsangehöriger sie ist.* [A person is entitled to refer his or her case to the authorities of his or her state of residence or nationality irrespective of national procedure if they think that measures taken by one or both contracting states will lead to a taxation that does not comply with this convention.]

(2) *Hält die zuständige Behörde die Einwendung für begründet und ist sie selbst nicht in der Lage, eine befriedigende Lösung herbeizuführen, so wird sie sich bemühen, den Fall durch Verständigung mit der zuständigen Behörde des anderen Vertragsstaats so zu regeln, daß eine dem Abkommen nicht entsprechende Besteuerung vermieden wird. Die Verständigungsregelung ist ungeachtet der Fristen des innerstaatlichen Rechts der Vertragsstaaten durchzuführen.* [If the competent authority considers the complaint justified... they can seek an understanding with... the other contracting state, in order to resolve the case in such a way that a taxation that does not comply with this convention is avoided]. [Note the 'negative' formulation.]

> The prevention or elimination of international double taxation—i.e., the imposition of similar taxes in two or more States on the same taxpayer in respect of the same base—whose effects are harmful to the exchange of goods and services and to the movement of capital and persons, constitutes a significant component of such a climate. Broadly, the general objectives of bilateral tax conventions may today be seen to include the full protection of taxpayers against double taxation (whether direct or indirect) and the prevention of the discouragement which taxation may provide for the free flow of international trade and investment and the transfer of technology. They also aim to prevent discrimination between taxpayers in the international field, and to provide a reasonable element of legal and fiscal certainty as a framework within which international operations can be carried on. With this background, tax treaties should contribute to the furtherance of the development aims of the developing countries. In addition, the treaties have as an objective the improvement of cooperation between taxing authorities in carrying out their duties.[41]

The UN Model thereby reveals that its aim is predominantly to regulate the taxation between developed and developing countries. This is in direct response to OECD findings published in 1965 which stated:

> the traditional tax conventions have not commended themselves to developing countries. [...] the essential fact remains that tax conventions which capital-exporting countries have found to be of value to improve trade and investment among themselves and which might contribute in like ways to closer economic relations between developing and capital-exporting countries are not making sufficient contributions to that end ... Existing treaties between industrialized countries sometimes require the country of residence to give up revenue. More often, however, it is the country of source which gives up revenue. Such a pattern may not be equally appropriate in treaties between developing and industrialized countries because income flows are largely from developing to industrialized countries and the revenue sacrifice would be one-sided. But there are many provisions in existing tax conventions that have a valid place in conventions between capital-exporting and developing countries too.[42]

The OECD Model itself is advertised with the following text:

> International juridical double taxation – generally defined as the imposition of comparable taxes in two (or more) States on the same taxpayer in respect of the same subject matter and for identical periods – has harmful effects on the international exchange of goods and services and cross-border movements of capital, technology and persons. In recognition of the need to remove this obstacle to the development of economic relations between countries, as well as of the importance of clarifying and standardising the fiscal situation of taxpayers who are engaged in activities in other countries, the OECD Model Tax Convention on Income and on Capital provides a means to settle on a uniform basis the most common problems that arise in the field of international juridical double taxation.[43]

Even this brief overview shows that the purpose of DTCs extends beyond those contained in their titles and preambles. The OECD Intro text explains the rationale behind avoiding double taxation which is explained as serving the tax payer and thereby contributing to a smoother functioning of "economic relations between

[41] UN Model, Introduction A. 2.

[42] 1964 report of the OECD Fiscal Committee paras 164–165 quoted after UN Model, Introduction A. 3.

[43] http://www.oecd.org/ctp/treaties/model-tax-convention-on-income-and-on-capital-2015-full-version-9789264239081-en.htm.

countries." In the UN Intro text, however, which interestingly relies on previous OECD work, certain details of the resulting allocation of tax revenue are criticized as disadvantageous to developing countries who typically are source countries and not countries of residence. This observation draws on the actual model which has become a world wide standard and which uses the residency status of the tax payer as the preferred and default defining factor for the determination of the tax base. The alternative, using the source of the arising income as a determinant for the tax base has been discussed vividly at the outset of the international co-operation work in this area of law.[44] The general antagonism between 'capital exporting' industrialised countries and the more dependent developing or emerging markets continues. Initiatives promoted by the OECD and G20[45] clearly prevail at present and define the parameters and standards in international taxation.

DTCs are therefore not intended to provide uniform law for international taxation. They do not provide a common standard of taxation, neither in respect of the tax base nor the rates. States cannot agree on these common standards. DTCs are also no agreements as to the distribution of the arising revenue. For the purposes of this enquiry the point of note is the discrepancy between the aims that are stated expressly in the DTCs and the aims that are actually pursued as well as of course the resulting question whether the actual content and the practice of application serves or achieves any of these aims. The question is whether the purpose and content of the conventions are in alignment and how this impacts on the application of the conventions in terms of the interpretation.

Of the many examples of inconsistencies in the interpretation of DTCs only one or two can be mentioned here. Two issues may serve to illustrate the complex picture that arises from the shortcomings of international alignment of the actual purposes of DTCs—the residency status of taxpayers and the qualification of the proceeds of partnerships.

5.2.1 Residency Status

The residency status remains the most important anchor for the determination of tax base and liability. Nevertheless, no uniform definition of this status is currently in use. States use definitions that range from nationality to 'having a permanent home available to them.' The DTCs are aspiring to provide a platform for "clarifying and standardising the fiscal situation of taxpayers" and to this end incorporate what I would term a 'DTC residency'. In the case of the above mentioned UK/Germany DTC this is Art. II (1) (h) (i)–(iii) which defines a person's residency status in four subsections of subsection (ii). This means that the ordinary residency status in the contracting states exists alongside the DTC status which in the case of the UK/ Germany DTC means that the German tax payers go by the 'permanent home'

[44] Vogel (1990).

[45] Such as the OECD's "BEPS" Action Plan and the resulting multilateral conventions, see OECD (2013), see on this Heidemann (2017).

status whereas British tax payers are subject to a much more complex status based on time spent, domicile and intention to stay.[46] The OECD Convention on Mutual Administrative Assistance in Tax Matters as amended in 2010, however, has prompted the adoption of a number of national tax laws for the purpose of the exchange of tax relevant information requiring the co-operation of the tax payer which do not make this pre-existing distinction of double layered residency status or expressly refer to the DTC defined tax status. The above declared purpose of providing foreseeability for the tax payer is thereby diluted and reversed. This begs the question of course, if the interests of the tax payer are to be served at all in these conventions or those of the contracting states only. As with the above mentioned contract law conventions the fact that states agree to an international treaty in an area that is directly affecting and involving private parties but without giving them a role in the negotiation or application practice within the text of the operative part makes it unlikely for a purpose to have legal effect outside the state operated sphere. As with the contract conventions, objectives are being described which are decidedly part of public policies and state reserved areas of operation such as the 'development of economic relations' and 'settle on a uniform basis the most common problems that arise in the field of international juridical double taxation' (OECD Model) or 'tax treaties should contribute to the furtherance of the development aims of the developing countries'. In addition, the treaties have as an objective 'the improvement of cooperation between taxing authorities in carrying out their duties' (UN Model). The interests of the tax payer are described as a means to serve these aims, not as an end in itself or a guarantee given to trading and migrating individuals.[47] This is very similar to the expectations expressed in the contract law conventions. It almost insinuates that the merchants and international tax payers are at the service of the sates in order to further their interests. The question arises to what extent the nexus between the states and their citizens can get lost in this way before the damage to private trading creates exactly those harmful effects described in the above-quoted OECD Model introduction which it set out to remove in the first place.

5.2.2 Partnerships

The OECD acknowledged the difficulty of taxing partnerships across borders by way of their partnership report.[48] A specific detail of the taxation of partnerships was the subject of the *Memec* case series where an English company sought to claim tax relief in respect of trade tax paid by their German subsidiary before the British courts. They lost their case due to the silent partnership structure they had chosen

[46] The UK Guidance Notes are available at https://www.gov.uk/government/publications/rdr3-statutory-residence-test-srt.

[47] Such a guarantee would be what Tammelo described as justice in his 1969 article commenting on the drafting process of the VCLT, Tammelo (1969), see section 6 below, note 58.

[48] OECD (1999).

for their German investment which was treated as giving rise to dividends rather than business profits according to the UK/German DTC. The British judges in both instances demonstrated a meticulous method of interpretation based on *Fothergill*[49] by which they arrived at this conclusion and which included reference to respective German court decisions.[50] They also inadvertently confirmed the unfortunate fact that there is no meaningful practice of cross border judicial exchange or precedent as explained above in order to form a uniform or shared understanding of a term of the DTCs.[51] The crucial point that was missed by the judges (and in fact academia) is that Germany along with most civil law countries distinguishes 'typical' from 'atypical' silent partnerships and classes the latter category as generating business profits. The DTC would have required the respective term of silent partnership to be interpreted in the light of this discrepancy. The British judges acknowledged in the light of *Fothergill* the general necessity of giving a specifically international meaning to a term whereas there is no such acknowledgement in any German decision about the 'atypical' silent partnership. Instead, the interpretation rule of Art II of the UK/German DTC is effectively applied like a conflict rule pointing to German law. The result when seen under the aspect of the purpose of the DTC reinforces the conclusion that interpreting DTCs according to an international standard has no place outside the immediate interest of avoiding double taxation and double non-taxation. No decisions have been made in respect of a meaningful distribution of arising revenue between the contracting states by way of the DTCs and therefore no uniform standards are being supported in their application. It is clear that the maintenance of conflicting, contradictory and arbitrary taxation results and legal reasoning rather adds to than diminishes obstacles in trade on the part of the merchants. On the part of the states this practice seems to avoid conflict only thanks to the isolation they maintain in respect of the full understanding of each other's tax regimes thereby abstaining from any serious attempt to create a uniform standard of international taxation. This would have to include decisions as to the distribution of the available revenue and therefore involve mutual concessions in the way suggested by the Introduction to the UN Model Convention quoted above.

5.3 *The Object of DTCs*

The object of DTCs may not be as straight forward to determine as their preambles suggest. Is the object double taxation and double non-taxation or is the object the international tax payer? Or is the object multiple residency? Just as the purpose of DTCs, the object is indeterminate or debatable. The impression is that in this area of

---

[49] *Fothergill v Monarch Airlines* [1981] AC 251; [1980] 2 All ER 696; [1980] 3 WLR 209; [1980] 2 Lloyd's Rep 295.

[50] For details see Heidemann and Knebel (2010).

[51] Lang et al. (1998) found a very small number of reference to foreign court decisions by German courts in their analysis of cases arising under DTCs.

law or regulation, there is a fundamental lack of alignment of the object, purpose and content of the treaty, partly caused by a lack of explicitness. A lack of agreement or a reluctance to uncover disagreement is obfuscated and smoothed over by a lack of enforcement of the convention itself.[52] Considering carefully what the object of the intended regulation is and whether it is compatible with one or more other objects to be pursued in one and the same convention must be a starting point for the definition of purpose and content of a treaty if it is to be successfully applied and complied with. Attainability and viability of each component may have to be re-evaluated and placed in a realistic relationship with each other.

6 Conclusions

The above analysis shows that the starting point for a successful interpretation of public international law conventions is the determination of the object. The object delimits the purposes and objectives that appear to be attainable with the convention. Both form an important and often underestimated component of treaty interpretation as embodied in the VCLT. In the area of conventions which seek to provide substantive commercial contract law and other commercial law related infrastructure for private cross border trade the relationship between the signatory states and the object and purpose of the conventions they conclude is very complex. Not only should states ask themselves whether they are the right actors[53] to employ the respective tool for the purposes they seek to achieve but also whether the desired policies are achievable at all with the chosen instrument. The impact of a well defined or misaligned object and purpose on the interpretation and enforcement of the treaty forms an important factor for success or failure of a treaty. A lack of underlying consent or unrealistic expectations can be reasons for poorly chosen objects and purposes.[54]

In the case of contract law conventions the fact that the object, international commercial contracts—a form of acting usually not practiced by states—is employed to achieve a public policy aim (friendly economic relations between countries) which

[52] States seek to apply their national law instead, using the interpretation rule in the Model and the respective DTCs based on that as explained above, and see Townsend (2001).

[53] Tammelo, writing at the time the VCLT was being drafted by the International Law Commission, ILC, observed: "…it has become obvious that the organization of the world into States as they exist today has become increasingly obsolescent. Contemporary States are not internally organized in such a way that their governments would be sufficiently capable of responsible and efficient action in the interest of their own citizens and for the sake of mankind.", Tammelo (1969), p. 85.

[54] Another argument why the criterion 'object and purpose' may indeed be ill chosen, an opinion held by contemporary scholars and indeed drafters at the time, see Tammelo (1969), p. 81 who would have preferred 'justice' as a criterion to temper the 'plain terms rule' (see also note below), Buffard and Zemanek (1998), pp. 319–321 and Klabbers (2001), p. 306, who reports on the making of the 'object and purpose' criterion in Art. 18 VCLT in the context with the obligations of states during the time between signing, ratification and entry into force of a convention.

in turn is not normally pursued by private merchants and by way of commercial contracts creates a misalignment of object and purpose. This leads to a lackluster enforcement infrastructure where states eventually sabotage their own 'product' including the interpretation rule by disallowing a transnational commercial court and non-state governing law. The intended policy aims may not be achievable with the tool of a substantive international commercial contract law regime. This begs the question of why these aims had to be published in preambles and other material in order to justify the adoption of CISG and other conventions. The chosen tool in turn does not get the support by its creators that it would need to strive fully[55] because it may be the product of the spur of the moment where private acting was appreciated perhaps not at all as a vehicle for achieving public policies but rather as a consequence of such policies and of prior efforts to create a globalised world of trade and friendly relations, an expression of success rather than a precondition, therefore the actual aim itself. The preambles of the Ottawa conventions are an expression of this attitude. They focus on the actual object of the conventions which are two special types of cross border commercial contract. They can still not explain the role and interest of the states in agreeing to those substantive rules of contract law because the distinctive feature has to be the international character of the object which is the only reason why uniform rules are needed. This is not clear in the preambles of these conventions. Instead, they suggest that leasing and factoring contracts need optimising without giving a point of reference.[56] This gives justified reason to question the mandate of the drafting institutions. The mandate cannot be to create a transnational system of law to be imposed on international merchants and to replace national laws as an expression of trade policies or even to provide a 'better law' for the sake of it. The mandate must be to respond to the needs of international trade to rely on a specialised legal infrastructure which inevitably has to transcend national judicial boundaries in order to support the cross border activities that have already transcended these boundaries with the consent of the jurisdictions involved. While the desired legal regime would certainly be self-contained as proclaimed by UNCITRAL[57] its only justification is the international character of its object and its role as a *lex specialis* for transnational as opposed to purely domestic transactions.[58] An exception to this would be where national law lacks a suitable legal framework in the area of trade law. This does not explain the adoption of a general standard through the UN, though.

---

[55] CISG is still most often opted out of in international commercial contracts.

[56] The Annex—Explanatory Note by the UNCITRAL Secretariat on the United Nations Convention on International Bills of Exchange and International Promissory Notes says in its section A4.: "The United Nations Convention on International Bills of Exchange and International Promissory Notes is the result of a movement to establish a modern, self-contained international legal regime that would apply world-wide."

[57] See previous note.

[58] Such a regime ought to be employed to deliver "justice" in international relations as Tammelo put it: "The phrase 'international.., justice' in Art. 1 (1) [of the UN Charter] can be understood to mean justice between men in their international concerns, that is, men in their international roles and affected by international events." Tammelo (1969), p. 85.

In the case of tax law conventions the public policies to be achieved by way of seemingly enabling and protective tools such as the avoidance of double taxation are employed without any role to play for the international tax payer. This is because there is no genuine consent among states to share revenue. DTCs should really be agreements between two or more states to split the proceeds of international trade. It should not be up to the tax payer to guarantee the correct allocation of funds because this is a genuinely governmental role and prerogative. The DTCs are an expression of compromise rather than active co-operation. This is why enforcement is directed against the tax payer rather than against the partner state as it helps to avoid the question of fair distribution of tax revenue as suggested by the drafters of the UN Model. The limited scope and incomplete interpretation rules effectively help to self defeat the tools which were not very ardently desired in the first place but necessary concessions for fear of overburdening and stifling international trade intolerably. This explains why the objective of avoiding tax evasion (double non-taxation) serving the state is pursued in the same convention as the enabling function serving the tax payer but directly disempowering the conceding state by giving up revenue. The interplay of object and purpose reveals both the true intentions behind a convention as well as a clear path ahead. Clearly stated objects and reasonably related and achievable purposes tailored to fit the object are essential for the success of a legal tool such as a trade enhancing treaty. Some objects such as sharing revenue never get openly discussed and successfully agreed. Some purposes, despite being formally agreed, may not be fully endorsed by all contracting states but a product of compromise and strategy. If the resulting treaty can only be realised by a private party who is not directly bound by it no surprise should arise from the resulting sense of futility.

7 Outlook

The so-called top down approach in international and transnational legislation for cross border trade is clearly the preferred method among the governments of the world. This is true of the UN whose New Economic Order declared in 1974 presupposes state acting in order to achieve the public policy ends described therein and assigns the required activity to states only. It is also true for the EU where despite increased stake holder participation legislative initiatives in the area of private and commercial law take the form of administrative acts culminating in the recently withdrawn Common European Sales Law (CESL) proposal.[59] Due to the fragmented nature of the "top down approach" to international commercial law regulation on the part of state legislation, as well as the lack of attention and good will shown to the objects in relation to the purposes of this legislation, the prevailing method of providing a transnational commercial legal infrastructure will have to remain the "bottom up

[59] Proposal for a Regulation on a Common European Sales Law for the European Union COM(11)635.

method". This means that merchants will continue to rely on informal self regulation and private dispute settlement. Some parameters of state acting may have to be reviewed so that public policies can be realised with the means of private law such as equality, fairness, welfare and the principle of consent on which treaty law and its interpretation are based. One starting point for this review can be the recognition of the international character of the objects of legislation in this area. These objects require specialised autonomous transnational uniform law whether these consist of cross border transactions or migrating merchants or private parties. If this is observed, top down regulation may be successful and actually achieve the desired public policy ends as the ones proclaimed by the UN on 1 May 1974.[60] An object-based technique as proposed in this chapter would then possibly achieve justice as expressed by Tammelo in 1969:

> The phrase 'international.., justice' in Art. 1 (1) [of the UN Charter] can be understood to mean justice between men in their international concerns, that is, men in their international roles and affected by international events. This interpretation would harmonise with the requirement of international peace and security expressed in the same provision, for it appears that international conflicts can best be managed when the greatest possible regard is paid to what is due to individual human beings under the relevant criteria of justice.[61]

References

Aust A (2013) Modern treaty law and practice, 3rd edn. Cambridge University Press, Cambridge, New York

Baasch-Andersen C (2005) The uniform international sales law and the global jurisconsultorium. J Law Commerce 24:159–179

Bederman DJ (1994) Revivalist canons and treaty interpretation. UCLA Law Rev 41(4):953–1034

Buffard I, Zemanek K (1998) Object and purpose of a treaty: an enigma. Austrian Rev Int Eur Law 3

Crawford J (2012) Brownlie's principles of public international law, 8th edn. Oxford University Press, Oxford

Crnic-Grotic V (1997) Object and purpose of treaties in the Vienna Convention on the Law of Treaties. Asian Yearb Int Law 7:141–174

Ferrari F (1998) Das Verhältnis zwischen den Unidroit-Grundsätzen und den allgemeinen Grundsätzen internationaler Einheitsprivatrechtskonventionen. Juristenzeitung 1:9–17

Ferrari F (2007) The interaction between the United Nations Conventions on contracts for the international sale of goods and domestic remedies. Rabels Zeitschrift für ausländisches and internationales Privatrecht 71:53–71

Fredman S (2015) Foreign fads or fashions? The role of comparativism in human rights law. ICLQ 64(3):631–660

Gibney M (2007–2008) State responsibility and the object and purpose of the genocide convention. Int Stud J 4(2–3):141–150

Heidemann M (2017) Is internationalisation going too far? – Constitutional challenges of international data exchange programmes. EBLR 28(6):847–878

[60] Doc. 3201 (S-VI). Declaration on the Establishment of a New International Economic Order, available at http://www.un-documents.net/s6r3201.htm.

[61] Tammelo (1969), p. 85.

Heidemann M, Knebel A (2010) Double taxation treaties: the autonomous interpretation method in German and English Law; as demonstrated by the case of the silent partnership. Intertax 38(3):136–152
Jonas DS, Saunders TN (2010) The object and purpose of a treaty: three interpretive methods. Vanderbilt J Transnatl Law 43(3):565–610
Klabbers J (2001) How to defeat a treaty's object and purpose pending entry into force: toward manifest intent. Vanderbilt J Transnatl Law 34(2):283–332
Klabbers J (2013) International law. Cambridge University Press, Cambridge
Lang M, Mössner JM et al (1998) Die Auslegung von Doppelbesteuerungsabkommen in der Rechtsprechung der Höchstgerichte Deutschlands, der Schweiz und Österreichs. Linde Verlag, Wien
Linderfalk U (2003) On the meaning of the object and purpose criterion, in the context of the Vienna Convention on the Law of Treaties, Article 19. Nordic J Int Law 72(4):429–448
OECD (1999) The application of the OECD model tax convention to partnerships. OECD Publications, Paris
OECD (2013) Action plan on base erosion and profit shifting. OECD Publishing, Paris
Roberts A (2011) Comparative international law? The role of national courts in creating and enforcing international law. ICLQ 60(1):57–92
Tammelo I (1969) Treaty interpretation and considerations of justice. Revue Belge de Droit International/Belg Rev Int Law 5(1):80–86
Townsend JA (2001) Tax treaty interpretation. Tax Lawyer 55(1):219–308
Van Alstine MP (1998) Dynamic treaty interpretation. Univ Pa Law Rev 146(3):687–794
Vogel K (1990) World wide vs source taxation of income - a review and reevaluation of arguments. In: McLure et al (eds) Influence of tax differential on international competitiveness. Proceedings of the VIIIth Munich Symposium on International Taxation. Kluwer, Deventer, Boston, pp 117 et seq

Commercial Law, Investor Protection, EU and Domestic Law

Mads Andenas

Contents

M. Andenas (✉)
Institute of Private Law, Faculty of Law, University of Oslo, Oslo, Norway

Institute of Advanced Legal Studies, School of Advanced Study, University of London, London, UK
e-mail: mads.andenas@jus.uio.no

M. Heidemann, J. Lee (eds.), *The Future of the Commercial Contract in Scholarship and Law Reform*, https://doi.org/10.1007/978-3-319-95969-6_17

Abstract This chapter explores the interface between private, commercial and public law in the field of European regulation of financial markets and institutions. Financial regulation has an impact on commercial contract law, tort law, company law and other aspects of domestic law. Some regulatory rules, typically those about the conduct of business or investor protection rules, have been limited to investor or consumer protection. The relevance of EU regulatory conduct of business rules for contract law in general is one of the main topics of the chapter. The main part of this chapter discusses the extent to which national courts have used the remedies based on general contract law as tools to enforce the EU conduct of business rules. The author argues that European financial market regulation will continue to contribute to the breaking down of the traditional autonomy of general contract law and transform contract law into a regulatory tool to govern financial transactions. The traditional autonomy of commercial law had a particular role to play in the domestic context, also in protecting party autonomy against regulatory intervention. This is less and less relevant today, especially on the European and international levels.

1 The Future of Commercial Law and the Role of EU Private and Regulatory Law

Private, commercial and public law are the three mirrors that create the repeating triangles of European regulation of financial markets and institutions. The mirrors of European and international law make the patterns ever more varied and in need of clarification and simplification to provide effective legal regimes. Financial regulation has an impact on commercial contract law, tort law, company law and other aspects of domestic law. Some regulatory rules, typically those about the conduct of business or investor protection rules, have been limited to investor or consumer protection. Member States may extend investor protection to smaller businesses otherwise falling into a commercial law category. When EU law contains the investor protection rules and the general contract law, including the commercial contract, remains at the national level, the reach of investor protection adds a new jurisdictional divide bringing with it its own set of legal issues.

The codification of commercial law in the nineteenth and early twentieth centuries provided the foundation of general contract law in many countries, and also in international legislative collaboration and the development of a transnational *lex mercatoria* or *law merchant*.[1]

The international and UN based harmonisation has created a body of international commercial law. The work on the UNIDROIT Principles of International

[1] It also played a central role in national legal unification, as Schulze and Zoll (2018), p. 25 mention, 'Spain and Germany in the nineteenth century and, to some extent, through the General Commercial Code in the USA' in the twentieth century.

Commercial Contracts (PICC) 1994 began in 1980, following the UNIDROIT Convention relating to a Uniform Law on the International Sale of Goods (1964) and UNIDROIT International Convention on Travel Contracts (1970), and followed by the UNIDROIT Convention on Agency in the International Sale of Goods (1983), the UNIDROIT Convention on Factoring (1988), the UNIDROIT Model Franchise Law (2002) and the UNIDROIT Convention on Substantive Rules for Intermediated Securities (2013).

The United Nations Convention on the Recognition and Enforcement of Foreign Arbitral Awards (1958) and the United Nations Convention on Contracts for the International Sale of Goods (1980) (CISG) are both promulgated by the United Nations Commission on International Trade Law. Together with the UNIDROIT sources are they the core international commercial law sources. They are supported by a series of other conventions and texts including the Convention on the Limitation Period in the International Sale of Goods (1974), the UNCITRAL Model Law on International Commercial Arbitration (1985) and Uniform Rules on Contract Clauses for an Agreed Sum Due upon Failure of Performance (1983).

UNCITRAL has endorsed many of the UNIDROIT conventions and other texts, and the texts mentioned here constitute the main part of the core of a written international commercial law.[2] The texts are ratified and transposed or used as models for domestic legislation. They contribute to the formation of an international contract law, which remains based on commercial law.

EU harmonisation has from an early stage included commercial law which was considered to have particular importance for free movement.[3] One example is the law on commercial agents. Commercial agents' right of establishment and to provide services was provided for in 1964.[4] The 1986 Directive on the coordination of the laws of the Member States relating to self-employed commercial agents provided for 'the coordination of the laws of the Member States relating to self-employed commercial agents'[5] as explained in the preamble by the differences in national laws concerning commercial representation. These differences substantially affected the conditions of competition and the carrying-on of that activity within the Community and were detrimental both to the protection available to commercial agents vis-à-vis their principals and to the security of commercial transactions. The differences also inhibited the conclusion and operation of commercial representation contracts where principal and commercial agent were established in different Member States. A functioning single market necessitated approximation of the legal systems of the Member States. Conflict of laws rules did not remove the inconsistencies for commercial representation, and could not possibly do so even if they were made uniform. In the preamble it is also stated that the legal relationship between commercial agent and principal must be given priority.

[2] See the analysis in Heidemann (2007, 2012).

[3] More generally on the reach of free movement, see Andenas and Snell (2002).

[4] Directive 64/224/EEC OJ No 56, 4. 4. 1964, p. 869/64.

[5] 86/653/EEC OJ L 386/17 21.12.1986.

At the EU level, there are still no comprehensive rules on business-to-business unfair commercial practices. There is an extensive regulation of business-to-consumer commercial practices in the Directive on Unfair Commercial Practices from 2005.[6] Under the original procedures and competences of the Treaty of Rome, harmonisation measures required unanimity in the Council. But the questions of EU competences were not as controversial, and the European Commission envisaged harmonisation of business-to-business unfair commercial practices. Of the six original Member States, four (Belgium, Germany, Italy and Luxemburg) had codifications, and in the two remaining (France and the Netherlands), unfair competition is an unlawful act under general tort law. The only outcome was the Council Directive 84/450/EEC concerning misleading and comparative advertising.[7] The only EU regulation on business-to-business (B2B) commercial practices are the surviving rules on misleading and comparative advertising.[8]

In 1992 the work on the Principles of European Contract Law (PECL) began, 2 years after the work on the UNIDROIT PICC. Article 1:101 PECL provides about the application of the principles that they are

(1) intended to be applied as general rules of contract law in the European Communities.
and
(2) that they will apply when the parties have agreed to incorporate them into their contract or that their contract is to be governed by them.

PECL keeps the focus on general contract law, based on sources of commercial law. It makes no mention of the term 'consumer'. That had to change in subsequent work on law, and for pressing reasons. Much of the fragments of an EU contract law concerned consumer rights. Originally, the EU policy aim was to guarantee minimum standards of consumer protection to facilitate free movement in the Internal Market.

The general EU codifications have not materialised. The Draft Common Frame of Reference (Principles, Definitions and Model Rules of European Private Law, DCFR, 2008) was an academic project supported by the European Commission and European Parliament. It contained model rules on several areas of private law and was seen an embryo of a European Civil Code. Any wider codification plans met with fierce opposition and the Commission focused on a more narrow project, cross-border sales and proposed a Common European Sales Law (CESL). In parallel the adoption of the Consumer Rights Directive (2011), and development and consolida-

[6] Directive 2005/29/EC. The directive provides for full or positive harmonisation.

[7] Directive 84/450/EEC concerning misleading and comparative advertising, amended by Directive 97/55/EC to include provisions on comparative advertising. Directive 2005/29/EC concerning business-to-consumers unfair commercial practices in the internal market repealed the application on B2C relations in Directive 84/450/EEC. The remaining provisions of Directive 84/450/EEC, the provisions on B2B misleading advertising and the provisions on comparative advertising are consolidated in Directive 2006/114/EC concerning misleading and comparative advertising.

[8] The regulation of misleading advertising only provides for minimum harmonisation.

tion of other private law directives and regulatory directives has contributed to a body of private law of a more regulatory nature, with different concepts and rules specific to the different areas. CESL was withdrawn in 2015 but the legal landscape has been shaped by the new Package Travel Directive and Commissions proposals for Directives on the Online Sale of Goods and on the Supply of Digital Content. The jurisprudence of the CJEU has continued to develop the legislation on consumer guarantees and the control of contract terms.

Restitution and tort law are subject to similar developments of a new regulatory private law. The Directive on liability for defective products was adopted in 1985, at the same time as state liability and private party liability for breaches of EU law developed in the CJEU jurisprudence. Contract and tort liability for breach of competition law, the remedies directives on public procurement, liability for state aid, legal protection and enforcement of patents and other intellectual property rights.

Schulze and Zoll mention that 'at European level, the extension of contract law acquis beyond the PECL has however allowed one to find the starting points in consumer law and individual aspects of commercial law in order to develop the concepts and principles of European contract law from "the specific to the general".[9] They refer to the nineteenth and twentieth century experiences with the codifications of commercial law, and find it 'somewhat astonishing' that 'only recently, has a discussion started on whether a codification of commercial contract law or a codification of business law relevant to the internal market can be of primary importance for European integration'.[10] This is representative of the view of many academic contract lawyers who have worked primarily with commercial law and subscribes to this as the general and residual. In spite of many commercial lawyers' theoretical commitment to the international, there has been less interest in making use of EU law in the development of general contract law or commercial contract law.

This fragmentation threatens the effectiveness of EU law. The codification route has not been viable. In the EU's history, the CJEU has stepped into the breach when the EU legislator has not been able to resolve the challenges. Courts have traditionally several mechanisms for ameliorating fragmentation in the legal system. To some extent that could be seen as a typical task for courts. Developing general principles based on legislation and its own jurisprudence and other sources of law is one response.

The relationship between the emergence of a new general European private law and national private law remains unresolved at many levels. Modernization of private law primarily takes place at the EU level. National private law relies for its own modernisation on this process to an increasing degree. The nature of general private law changes with consequences for foundational concepts as party autonomy. EU private law is typically mandatory, and national private law, which often has a default or declaratory character, takes an increasingly residual role in relationship to EU law. The scope for domestic law is narrowing and increasingly more limited to giving effect to EU law and gap-filling.

---

[9] Schulze and Zoll (2018), p. 25.

[10] Schulze and Zoll (2018), p. 25.

The relevance of EU regulatory conduct of business rules for contract law in general is one of the topics of this chapter. Much of the modernisation of contract law takes place at a European level. With the emphasis on investor or consumer protection of much EU legislation, this entails particular problems for general contract law and commercial law. The sophisticated balancing of the interests of the parties and markets in banking, insurance and investments services contracts may be a good starting point for modern general contract law. Core concepts and main rules of contract and property law have been adapted to modern business transactions, but may still owe much to their origins. They may have come about to deal with the needs of a very different kind. When *Benjamin's Sale of Goods*, now in its tenth edition,[11] was first published in 1868, it contained a comprehensive survey of the English case law, in which horses had a prominent place. The law of moveables still rely on basic concepts from Roman property law much of which sprang out of cases on slaves.[12]

Another main topic is the relevance of the principles about the application of the EU regulatory conduct of business rules outside investor protection. Does the application of EU regulatory rules outside conduct of business rules and investor protection, follow the same model?

Core questions for future research include which is the role of general principles in the emergence of a new general European private law, their reception in national legal orders and their role in the modernization of national private law.

One reasonable prediction is that the outcome will be a gradual and parallel emergence of a new general European private law and modernization of general national private law, both increasingly organised around general principles. The role of principles in securing coherence at either level and between them is increasingly important. Principles have gap-filling residual functions but could also be granted constitutional rank within the legal orders. In the relationship between legal orders, such lex superior status may resolve conflicts.

The role of general principles may increase due to the failure of legislators at EU and Member State levels in the private law field. There is a spectacular gap created by the technical, fragmented and specialised EU regulatory private law, and the slow responses to market, technological and general social change in private law legislation promulgated by member states.

The problem of fragmentation of EU law has not been adequately addressed by the EU legislator. Unification requires resources. There are also strong interests at the EU and national level which make this more difficult to resolve. Different EU institutions and departments within them such as DGs in the Commission, in individual cases or in general, want to retain autonomy from a unified regime. National governments may not wish the strengthened impact that a uniform EU regime could have. The result is different approaches to private law, including contract law, tort law and property law. One example of fragmentation is in the different approaches

[11] Bridge (2017).

[12] Watson (1992) and Watson (1982).

of the CESL and the consolidated Consumer Law Directive which were proposed by the Commission in the same term. Systematic approach, terminology and certain general or common substantive rules differed. Whilst the CESL reflected a traditional and outdated view of national contract law, the Consumer Law Directive revitalised the *aquis communautaire* of consumer law by providing for a horizontal tool to regulate consumer contracts. Restricted to consumer contracts, the Consumer Rights Directive increases the potential of influencing the judicial interpretation of national law. It will be explored how the judicial dialogue between national judges and the Court of Justice may foster a process of convergence from the EU sectorial regulatory contract law to the national general contract law. There are several attempts to respond to fragmentation in EU law. A critical perspective on some of the academic initiatives, including the Draft Common Frame of Reference (DCFR), will explore the extent to which they were able to address the pressing problems and new developments or reverted to find common solutions based on the general private law disciplines in national laws. Problems with the DCFR and outcomes of similar groups is their basis in outdated national law.

EU law becomes the active force where most pressing problems and modern challenges are dealt with. Domestic law increasingly takes a residual role. That the law to deal with new technological and market developments to a large extent is promulgated at an EU level poses problems for general private law at the domestic level. The old and not the updated private law disciplines remain at the national level and the most dynamic fields have moved up to the EU level. If limited to national law in a narrow sense, the general private law disciplines are generated on the basis of an ever narrower and more outdated basis.

The responses to EU law in general private law at national level is another area of exploration. One cannot assume that these are uniform, either between national systems or between disciplines between or across the national systems.

This includes the role of the private law case law of the CJEU, its application by national courts and the further interactions between the CJEU and national courts.

Of particular interest is how EU sectorial contract and tort law is applied when general private law is applied in national courts. National courts will apply or take account of EU legislation and also CJEU jurisprudence. At a national level, this could lead to a sectorialisation of national law. One needs to investigate how such EU influences impact on the general private law in the Member State legal system.

General principles of law are important in the development of EU law and in the relationship with the national legal orders. At the EU level, general principles of civil law are developed by the CJEU. Article 340 (2) TFEU (ex Article 288 TEC) has the same words as the Treaty of Rome: "In the case of non-contractual liability, the Union shall, in accordance with the general principles common to the laws of the Member States, make good any damage caused by its institutions or by its servants in the performance of their duties". The CJEU has developed the law of damages for breach of EU law on the basis of this provision.

The CJEU needs to take into account general principles of civil law in a much wider field, as exemplified for contract law by C-412/06 *Annelore Hamilton v. Volksbank Filder* [2008] ECR I-2383, and for general tort law by *Kolassa* C-375/13:EU:C:2015:37.

The main hypothesis is that the responses to the fragmentation of private law across the EU and national jurisdictions need to be found in the law developed through the interpretation and enforcement of the law by courts, public agencies and legal doctrine.

There is a traffic both ways, between the national and the EU levels. There is also traffic between the sectorial and specific and the general, across these levels.

Principles of EU law and principles of domestic law may be vectors for the application of rules of financial market regulation beyond investor protection. The Danish Supreme Court judgment in the *Ajos* case[13] indicate resistance to rely on the general principles route to the extent done by the CJEU.[14] The Supreme Court had referred several questions to the Court of Justice of the European Union. The Supreme Court then rejected an interpretation of national law which would be consistent with EU law. It refused to disapply an incompatible statutory provision on the basis of the general principle of EU law prohibiting discrimination on grounds of age. The CJEU's preliminary ruling was not followed.

There may be a wider resistance in national courts against relying too much on general principles, and this applies also to following that route in providing remedies in tort or contract for breach of regulatory rules.[15] EU legal principles are highly controversial in national courts, and their application by the CJEU is resisted in important cases, see most recently the *Ajos* judgment (2016) of the Danish Højesteret that declined to follow the CJEU Grand Chamber ruling in C-441/14: EU:C:2016:278. But the CJEU reply in judgments subsequent to the *Ajos* case shows that general principles rarely stand on their own. They are based in the EU Treaties, on directives and on other sources of law that national courts can hardly choose to disregard. The CJEU delivered its preliminary ruling in the Grand Chamber in the case of *Egenberger* in 2018, tying the general principles to the words of the treaty, directives and other less disputed sources of law.[16] Much of the same arguments had been available in *Ajos,* and had the CJEU used this in the way it did in *Egenberger*, the Danish Supreme Court would have found itself bound to follow the CJEU.

The conclusion is that European financial market regulation will continue to contribute to the breaking down of the traditional autonomy of general contract law and transform contract law into a regulatory tool to govern financial transactions. The traditional autonomy of commercial law will not change this. That autonomy has had a particular role to play in the domestic context, protecting party autonomy

[13] Sag 15/2014, judgment of 06.12.2016. See Holdgaard et al. (2018).

[14] Case C-441/14 *Dansk Industri (DI), acting on behalf of Ajos A/S v Estate of Karsten Eigil Rasmussen*, EU:C:2016:278.

[15] As developed in C-144/04 *Mangold* and C-555/07 *Kücükdeveci.*

[16] C-414/16 *Egenberger.*

against regulatory intervention. It has less relevance on the European and international levels.

2 The Interface Between Private, Commercial and Public Law in the Field of European Regulation of Financial Markets and Institutions

Some regulatory rules, typically those about the conduct of business or investor protection rules, have been limited to investor or consumer protection. So who is the 'consumer' who is covered by the protection?[17]

Member States may extend investor protection to smaller businesses otherwise falling into a commercial law category. There is no consistent and uniform definition of consumer in the laws of the EU Member States. The EU directives and regulations define 'consumer' separately for its own purposes. Those definitions converge, but some differences continue to exist. The notion of consumer has been defined in several directives in the area of contract law, as well as in the Regulation Brussels I and Rome I (in the area of procedural law), which include specific rules for consumer protection.[18] A majority of current EU directives define the consumer as a 'natural person who is acting for the purposes which are outside his trade, business and profession'. The definition is therefore a negative one. The directives also diverge in the definition of economic activity, some also including a 'craft'. The notion of consumer in EU law does not apply to legal persons, even if they have a non-business character, as would be the case for non-profit associations. This has also been emphasised in the case law of the Court of Justice on several occasions. There is an exception, namely the Package Travel Directive 90/314/EEC, which uses a broader notion of the consumer by including companies and business travellers as purchasers and users of travel services.

Because of the minimum harmonisation character of the larger part of the consumer acquis, many Member States extended the scope of their consumer protection law beyond the definition of 'consumer' in EU law.

The relevance of EU regulatory conduct of business rules for contract law in general is one of the topics of this chapter. Another is the relevance of the principles about *the application* of the EU regulatory conduct of business rules outside investor protection, including the effect of conduct of business rules on contract law, as a model for giving effect to other EU and regulatory rules on commercial law.

---

[17] One of the earlier authorities in the line of rulings on that concept is C-361/89 *Criminal proceedings against Patrice Di Pinto.—Reference for a preliminary ruling: Cour d'appel de Paris.* 1991 ECR I-01189.

[18] See about some of the conflicts between these two systems in Rühl (2018).

3 National Courts, Remedies Based on General Contract Law and the Enforcement of EU Conduct of Business Rules

Starting from the analysis of the legal nature of the duties derived from EU conduct of business rules and the role played by contract law in the governance of financial markets, this main part of the chapter shows that, after the global financial crisis, national courts have used the remedies based on general contract law as tools to enforce the EU conduct of business rules.[19] The case law provides evidence of a gradual process of Europeanisation and modernisation of the general law of contract.

Following the global financial crisis, the European Commission proposed more than 40 new legislative measures to increase the stability of the financial system, the integrity of financial markets and investor protection.[20] The cascade of rules adopted by the EU between 2009 and 2015 not only reshuffled the prudential requirements for credit and investment firms and the conduct of business rules, which apply to financial services providers, but also the architecture of financial supervision and enforcement.

However, the lack of harmonisation of contract law-related rules—including the rules on the formation, performance, breach of contract and other contractual remedies—remains a distinctive feature of EU financial regulation.[21] Whereas the EU regulates financial products, services and capital requirements heavily, it does not regulate the content of contracts between financial market participants nor does it require Member States to establish contractual remedies or private rights of action for the loss suffered by clients as a result of the firm's violation of conduct of business rules.

The EU post-crisis legislation has gradually restricted the scope for self-regulation by key market players.[22] How this restriction is transposed directly into a limitation of their freedom of contract is still to be clarified. National private law remains, formally speaking, untouched by the provisions of the EU legislation of the new post-crisis reforms.[23] The lack of EU harmonisation of national private law

---

[19] See Andenas (1994) on the background for and adoption of the first conduct of business rules in the Investment Services Directive. The chapter builds in the following on Andenas and Della Negra (2017).

[20] European Commission, Regulating Financial Services for Sustainable Growth. Brussels, 2.6.2010 COM(2010) 301 final.

[21] New tortious liability regimes have been introduced by Article 21 of Directive 2011/61/EU of the European Parliament and of the Council on Alternative Investment Fund Managers (AIFMD) O.J. L 174/1 (2011) and Article 35 of Regulation (EU) No 462/2013 of the European Parliament and of the Council on Credit Rating Agencies O.J. L 146/1 (2013). See the discussion on regulator liability in Andenas and Fairgrieve (2002) and Andenas (2015).

[22] Pagliari (2012).

[23] See, for an exception, Article 12(3) of the Regulation (EU) No 648/2012 of the European Parliament and of the Council of 4 July 2012 on OTC derivatives, central counterparties and trade repositories (EMIR), O.J. L 201/1 (2012).

remedies could suggest that the EU prefers a public law-based system of regulation and enforcement of financial regulation.[24] It does not rule out the possibility that EU conduct of business rules can influence, by way of judicial interpretation, or even more directly determine the nature, role and function of national contract law.

The understanding of how EU regulatory standards can interfere with general private law,[25] is important from a practical and theoretical perspective. From a practical perspective, the lack of an express private remedy for the breach of regulatory duties derived from EU law begs the question, recurrent among courts and adjudicators after the global financial crisis: whether any remedy, based on general private law, can be granted to clients, and, if so, on what legal basis (e.g. principle of effectiveness of EU law). From a theoretical perspective, the interaction between regulatory and private law duties, requires a clarification of whether, and to what extent, the general categories of private law (e.g. freedom of contract, good faith, privity of contract) can be adapted, adjusted and modelled in order to provide redress to clients who suffered a loss as a result of the firms' breach of conduct of business rules.[26]

Against this background, the hypothesis is that EU financial regulation, in particular conduct of business rules, has an impact on general private law, both on the principle of freedom of contract and on the remedies for breach of contractual obligations.

First, while it does not directly limit the parties' freedom to enter into contracts or to draft contracts in a specific way, EU financial regulation indirectly leads financial services providers to draft standard contract terms in ways that do not conflict with national law transposing EU law, and in particular the Investment Service Directive[27] and MiFID I[28]—the "new constitution" in the area of investment services and secondary capital markets.[29]

Second, the EU conduct of business rules, as transposed by the relevant national laws, can be used by national courts and adjudicating bodies as a tool to interpret, in a purposive way (i.e. in order to achieve the client protection objective), the general contract law. The influence of EU law on freedom of contract and remedies is not, however, homogeneous. Whereas in some jurisdictions (e.g. Italy, Spain, France) there is a trend towards gradual integration of EU financial regulation and national contract law, in others (e.g. United Kingdom) national statute law and case law preserve the distinction between regulatory and contract duties.

[24] Tridimas (2011), see also Andenas (2011) and for a different rights regime and the role of courts, Andenas and Bjorge (2013).

[25] See Lipari (2008a, b).

[26] For the importance of 'the law' and 'the legal system' in the governance of financial markets, see Pistor (2013).

[27] Council Directive 93/22/EEC of 10 May 1993 on investment services in the securities field (ISD), O.J. L 141/27 (1993).

[28] Directive 2004/39/EC on markets in financial instruments (MiFID I) O.J. L 145/1 (2004).

[29] Grundmann and Hollering (2008), p. 58.

The rest of this chapter is organised as follows. Section 4 provides a theoretical framework for understanding the problems related to the legal nature and purpose of EU conduct regulation.[30] Section 5 illustrates and explains the subsidiary role played by contract law rules in EU financial regulation by analysing EU law on retail financial contracts (e.g. consumer credit, payment services) and non-retail financial contracts (e.g. MiFID II[31], EMIR). Section 6 explains the concept of retail financial regulation and Sect. 7 non-retail or wholesale which does in no way correspond to different concepts of commercial law but has certain similarities. Section 8 describes the function of contract law in the case law of the Court of Justice of the European Union (CJEU) by looking at two important cases, *Peter Paul* and *Bankinter v Genil*, where the CJEU had the opportunity to consider the impact of EU prudential and conduct regulation on private law. Section 9 gives an account of the impact of EU statute and case law on national contract law in several EU jurisdictions. This comparative analysis brings to light national divergences and convergences and shows different models of interaction between EU financial regulation and national contract law. Section 10 illustrates the increasing role played by alternative dispute resolution mechanisms in the resolution of disputes involving retail clients. Section 11 draws conclusions from the preceding research and advocates a high degree of harmonisation of contract law rules for investment contracts to enhance legal certainty and legal integration between Member States.

4 The Legal Nature and Purpose of Financial Regulatory Duties

4.1 The Legal Nature of Financial Regulatory Duties

The legal nature of duties of conduct has provoked much debate in the literature. Some Authors consider conduct of business rules to be regulatory rules; others see them as "contract related supervision rules"[32] or as hybrid duties between contract and administrative law.[33]

There is also intense debate over the relationship between financial regulatory duties and contract law duties (or obligations). Some authors claim that these duties should be kept separate;[34] others claim that the regulatory duties should produce

[30] For a recent analysis, on the impact of EU prudential regulation on national contract law, see Hadjiemmanuil (2015).

[31] Directive 2014/65/EU on markets in financial instruments (MiFID II) O.J. L 173/349 (2014). MiFID II will enter into force and repeal MiFID I with effect from 3 January 2018.

[32] See Cherednychenko (2015) and Ferrarini (2005).

[33] Köndgen (2011), p. 40.

[34] Hudson (2013), p. 13.

radiating effects on contractual duties;[35] others argue that there is a necessary complementarity between them since they functionally integrate with each other.[36]

4.2 *The Purpose of Financial Regulatory Duties*

Seeking to further clarify the relationship between financial regulatory duties and contract law duties, some scholars have recently focussed on the purpose of the duty (i.e. safety and soundness of individual firms, financial stability or client protection), rather than its legal nature (private or public law). From this purposive perspective, there may be convergences (especially in the field of client protection regulation) or divergences (especially in the field of micro and macro prudential regulation) between different kinds of duties.[37] For example, the investment firm's duty to "act honestly, fairly and professionally in accordance with the best interests of its clients" (Article 19 of the MiFID I and Article 24 of the MiFID II) does not differ, in its substance, from the duty to negotiate in good faith and to perform contractual obligations in good faith, both of which exist in a number of national jurisdictions and in the projects for the harmonisation of European contract law.[38]

However, it is much more difficult to find convergent purposes or goals between financial regulation and contractual duties in relation to micro and macro prudential regulatory rules. After the global financial crisis, financial stability became the key concern for international and EU regulators. Financial stability is not just conceived of as instrumental in reducing the vulnerability of individual institutions, especially in times of capital shortfalls, but also as a public good in itself, which ensures medium- and long-term growth.[39] The rules imposed on credit and investment firms to protect clients may be in conflict with rules, now enshrined in the Capital Requirements Regulation (CRR)[40] and Capital Requirements Directives (CRD IV),[41] which mandatorily require them to hold certain levels of capital and liquidity and set up efficient governance and organisational mechanisms to control financial risks. In fact, these financial regulatory rules pursue conflicting interests, which are intrinsically connected to the basic objectives of prudential regulation: on the one hand, maintaining the safety and soundness of financial institutions and the financial system as a whole; on the other hand, protecting the depositors and other creditors of financial institutions.

---

35 See Haar (2011).

36 See Cherednychenko (2015); Zoppini (2013), p. 523.

37 See Grundmann (2015).

38 See how the last remaining jurisdictions are subjected to the regulatory regime, Andenas and Cortesi (2017).

39 See Andenas and Chiu (2013), p. 335.

40 Regulation 575/2013.

41 Directive 2013/36/EU.

The difference between financial conduct of business and prudential rules suggests that a cautious approach should be adopted when interpreting the EU financial regulatory standards. Whilst there may be a convergence of purposes between financial regulation and contract law with regard to conduct of business regulation, divergence may still exist when it comes to prudential regulation because the protective contract law rules (e.g. good faith) may conflict with the prudential objectives pursued by financial regulation.

5 The Role of Contract Law in the Regulation of Financial Transactions

Having examined the most prominent views in European academia on the legal nature and purpose of EU financial regulatory duties, it is necessary to analyse in more detail the role played by the law of contract in EU financial regulation. The law of contract—including the default and mandatory rules governing the formation, performance, and breach of contract—has traditionally played a subsidiary role in EU financial regulation. Ever since the adoption of the Investment Services Directive (ISD)[42] in 1993, the EU legislator has focussed on the regulation of conduct of business rules, i.e. by regulated financial instruments and services,[43] without interfering in the regulation of the contract between investment firms and clients. In fact, similar to other sectors of the internal market, the liberalisation of financial services has gradually required more regulation, supported by administrative agencies, in order to increase competition and to protect weaker parties. As a result, liberalisation has paradoxically produced its opposite, namely regulation.

This regulatory technique, however, has not directly changed nor has it harmonised the national law of contract. This is for the following reasons.

First of all, given that the EU does not enjoy express competence in the field of private law, it is easier to harmonise administrative sanctions than contract law duties and civil law remedies.[44] Second, there is a wide belief in the financial industry and among scholars that the harmonisation of civil law remedies could give rise to opportunistic litigation by professional clients and endanger the efficiency of financial markets.[45] The resistance of the industry, coupled with the disagreement among Member States, is one of the reasons why the 2010 Commission proposal, put forward in the context of the MiFID I review, to introduce a principle of civil liability for financial firms who caused losses to clients was eventually dropped.[46] Third, from a more theoretical perspective, the EU has traditionally been much more concerned to regulate the economic activity of market participants than the

[42] (93/22/EEC).

[43] See Andenas (1994).

[44] Tridimas (2011), p. 794.

[45] MacNeil (2015).

[46] See Moloney (2012a), p. 421.

legal acts that enable such activity, not only in the field of financial services but also in telecommunications, transport and energy.[47]

This regulatory approach has resulted in the establishment of vertical, sectoral or silo-type regimes which govern the technicalities and specificities of different economic activities for the overriding purpose of increasing the functioning of the internal market.[48] In fact, the Directives and the Regulations adopted on the basis of the 1999 Commission's Financial Services Action Plan (FSAP), and those adopted after the global financial crisis, between 2009 and 2015, have all relied on Article 95 TEC (now Article 114 TFEU), which is the classical legal basis for measures aimed at strengthening the functioning of the internal market. The rationale for this legislative choice rests on the assumption that the greater the harmonisation of national laws, the higher the level of market integration.[49]

A remarkable novelty is that after the global financial crisis, this provision was also used as an 'institution-building tool' to set up new EU bodies entrusted with micro- and macro-prudential financial supervision, such the European Supervisory Authorities (ESAs)—the European Banking Authority (EBA), the European Securities and Markets Authority (ESMA) and the European Insurance and Occupational Pensions Authority (EIOPA)—and the European Systemic Risk Board (ESRB) which together compose the new European System of Financial Supervision (ESFS).[50] In the landmark case C-270/12, *UK* v. *Parliament and Council*, the Court of Justice of the European Union (CJEU) held that Article 114 TFEU was an appropriate legal basis for the adoption of Article 28 of Regulation No 236/2012 on short-selling[51] as this provision improves the conditions for the establishment and functioning of the internal market in the financial field.[52]

More critically, in 2014, the Single Resolution Board (SRB) and the Single Resolution Fund (SRF), as part of the new Single Resolution Mechanism (SRM), were set up on the basis of Article 114 TFEU. In fact, in order to accommodate the concerns of some Member States about the appropriateness of this legal basis, it was agreed that the complex arrangements concerning the transfer to and the mutualisation of contributions to the SRF would be included in an intergovernmental agreement signed by the participating Member States.

However, whereas this "internal market-driven" substantive and institutional legislation has led to an increase in the level of harmonisation of both retail and wholesale segments of the market, it has not introduced harmonised rules on contracts between market participants. As a result of the lack of EU harmonisation of national

[47] Jannarelli (2003).

[48] See, in particular, Comparato et.al. (2016).

[49] In more detail, on the relationship between harmonisation of laws and financial integration, see Moloney (2014), p. 27; Avgouleas and Arner (2017); Buckley et al. (2017).

[50] For the analysis of the impact of the acts adopted by the ESAs and national competent authorities on general contract law see Della Negra (2016a), pp. 139 et seq.; Svetiev and Ottow (2014); Cherednychenko (2014).

[51] Regulation (EU) No 236/2012 on short selling and certain aspects of credit default swaps O.J. L 86/1 (2012).

[52] CJEU, case C-270/12, *UK* v. *Parliament and Council*, EU:C:2014:18.

contract law, three different levels of rules govern financial transactions:[53] the rules that the parties design themselves (self-regulation); EU legislative (directives, regulations, decisions) and non legislative rules (ESMA's decisions, guidelines, recommendations); and national rules (e.g. in contract, tort and property law), whether they transpose EU rules or not.

This classification is not only illustrative of the complexity which characterises the regulation of financial transactions but also of the need for lawyers to adopt a flexible approach when interpreting financial contract clauses and regulation. In fact, in this field the boundaries between contract and administrative law have become particularly blurred. For a contract lawyer, an interest rate swap is a contract, but for an administrative lawyer, it is a financial instrument. Can the regulatory duties imposed on a swap dealer be more intense than those laid down by general contract law? Should national courts and adjudicating bodies interpret the general law of contract in light of EU financial regulation even if there is no express EU rule regulating such contracts? As we will see below, national courts have given very different answers to these questions.

Another important distinction should be drawn between retail and non-retail financial transactions. The nature of the client (retail, professional, eligible counterparty), together with the type of service (execution-only, portfolio management, investment advice) and the financial instrument (complex, non-complex), is one of the criteria used by the MiFID I and MiFID II to customize the duties of conduct.[54]

6 Retail Financial Regulation

The notion of retail includes all clients, both natural and legal persons, that are not professional clients; that is, who do not possess the experience, knowledge and expertise to make their own investment decisions and properly assess the risks that are incurred.[55] It follows that the notion of retail client includes also that of consumer which, according to the relevant EU law, refers to any natural person who, acts for purposes which are outside his trade, business, craft or profession.[56] This means that the EU financial directives applying to retail clients also apply to

[53] For the notion of transaction see, in particular, Williamson (1979); Moeslein and Riesenhuber (2009).

[54] See Kruithof and van Gerven (2010).

[55] See Article 4(1)(11) of MiFID II, referring to Annex II.

[56] See in particular Article 2(1) of Directive 2011/83/EU of the European Parliament and of the Council of 25 October 2011 on consumer rights, amending Council Directive 93/13/EEC and Directive 1999/44/EC of the European Parliament and of the Council and repealing Council Directive 85/577/EEC and Directive 97/7/EC of the European Parliament and of the Council (consumer rights directive). See also generally on the notion of consumer in EU legislation Heidemann (2016).

consumers and that, conversely, EU consumer directives apply to retail clients in so far as they are natural persons.

Among consumer directives, the Distance Marketing of Consumer Financial Services Directive,[57] the Payment Services Directive,[58] the Consumer Credit Directive[59] and the Mortgage Credit Directive[60] are the most important for our purposes. Although these directives do not provide a comprehensive harmonised framework of contractual rights and duties, they do regulate consumer contractual rights and remedies. In particular, Article 6 of the Distance Marketing of Consumer Financial Services Directive and Article 14 of the Consumer Credit Directive confer on the consumer the right of withdrawal; Articles 60 and 75 of the Payment Services Directive harmonise the payment service provider's liability to the payer for unauthorised payment transactions and for non-execution or defective execution of the payment transaction; and Article 14 of the Mortgage Credit Directive imposes detailed pre-contractual information duties on the creditor.[61]

These provisions reveal that the consumer financial directives have been drafted from the perspective of the private law relationship between a consumer and a service provider[62] for the main purpose of increasing the protection of the investor vis-à-vis financial service providers.

7 Non-retail Financial Transactions

Unlike the EU consumer and retail financial regulation, EU non-retail financial regulation is drafted from the perspective of public enforcement via supervisory authorities of the investor protection provisions contained therein. The Prospectus

[57] Directive 2002/65/EC concerning the distance marketing of consumer financial services O.J. L 271/16 (2002).

[58] Directive 2007/64/EC of the European Parliament and of the Council of 13 November 2007 on payment services in the internal market amending Directives 97/7/EC, 2002/65/EC, 2005/60/EC and 2006/48/EC and repealing Directive 97/5/EC O.J. L 319/36 (2007).

[59] Directive 2008/48/EC of the European Parliament and of the Council of 23 April 2008 on credit agreements for consumers and repealing Council Directive 87/102/EEC O.J. L 133/66 (2008).

[60] Directive 2014/17/EU of the European Parliament and of the Council of 4 February 2014 on credit agreements for consumers relating to residential immovable property and amending Directives 2008/48/EC and 2013/36/EU and Regulation (EU) No 1093/2010 O.J.L 60/34 (2014).

[61] The Recital 58 of the Mortgage Credit Directive specifies that "Without prejudice to private contract law, Member States should ensure that creditors cannot terminate a credit agreement because they realised, after the signature of the credit agreement, that the assessment of creditworthiness was incorrectly conducted due to incomplete information at the time of the creditworthiness assessment".

[62] See Cherednychenko (2010).

Directive,[63] the Transparency Directive,[64] MiFID I[65] and MiFID II[66] require Member States to establish effective sanctions for a firm's failure to comply with specific conduct of business rules but they do not provide private law remedies to (retail and non-retail) investors who may have been affected by the firm's violation of these rules. However, these Directives do not expressly prevent Member states from introducing or preserving private law remedies or mandatory rules which ensure a high level of investor protection. The EMIR, on the other hand, specifies that an infringement of its rules shall not affect the validity of an Over-The-Counter (OTC) derivative contract and shall not give rise to any right to compensation from a party to an OTC derivative contract (Article 12(3)). In such cases, a national provision establishing the nullity of an OTC derivative contract in cases where a firm infringes conduct of business rules would be in breach of EU law.

There are two reasons for this public enforcement approach to the regulation of the B2B segment of the market. First of all, it must be kept in mind that the primary aim of these directives is to maintain the stability of financial markets. Maintaining a stable financial market increases the efficiency of financial markets and therefore indirectly enhances investor protection against banking crises, misselling practices and fraud. Even if investor protection has attracted more attention since the global financial crisis,[67] it is doubtful whether the EU legislation can be interpreted in light of this exclusive objective. Rather, it seems that this objective needs to be counter-balanced with that of ensuring financial stability. This problem, as we will be shown below, is particularly relevant for national courts and adjudicating bodies when deciding whether the EU conduct of business rules pursue similar or divergent goals with respect to general contract law.

Second, the public enforcement approach to financial regulation seeks to overcome divergences existing at the national level as regards the legal qualification of financial contracts (e.g. mandate, sale, *sui generis* contract) and the remedies for breach of these contracts (e.g. pre-contractual liability, contractual liability, nullity). In fact, by regulating the economic activity (e.g. financial instruments, financial services) instead of the legal mechanisms used to carry out such activities (e.g. the contract), EU law ensures that regulation will apply in Member States despite the

[63] Article 25 of Directive 2003/71/EC on the prospectus to be published when securities are offered to the public or admitted to trading O.J. L 345/64 (2003). Art. 6 requires Member States to ensure that their laws, regulations and administrative provisions on civil liability apply to those persons responsible for the information given in a prospectus.

[64] Article 24 of Directive 2004/109/EC on the harmonisation of transparency requirements in relation to information about issuers whose securities are admitted to trading on a regulated market and amending Directive 2001/34/EC O.J. L 390/38. Art. 7 requires Member States to ensure that their laws, regulations and administrative provisions on liability apply to issuers.

[65] Article 51 of MiFID I.

[66] Article 69 of MiFID II.

[67] See the recitals Nos. 77, 156, 177; Art. 24(6), 74(2) and 75(1) of MiFID II. See in particular Moloney (2012b).

relevant divergences across national jurisdictions. This means that EU financial regulation is insensitive to national contract law, i.e. national contract law cannot set lower standards of protection than EU law. It does not mean, however, that national contract law is insensitive to EU financial regulation as the rules of conduct imposed by EU law on credit and investment firms may drive the interpretation of traditional categories of contract law.[68]

How can the influence of EU law on national contract law be legally conceptualised?

From the perspective of EU law, the problem arises when EU legislation (e.g. MiFID I, MiFID II) does not expressly require Member States to establish private law rights and remedies between the parties to a transaction but similarly does not prevent Member States from doing so. In these circumstances, if the Member State does not lay down a specific remedial consequence for the firm's failure to respect the national law transposing EU law, can the firm's breach give rise to a remedy based on general contract law?

Some have argued that since directives lack horizontal direct effect they cannot be used by courts in order to provide a private law remedy to an investor (e.g. compensation). In contrast, other scholars have claimed that, notwithstanding the lack of horizontal effect of directives, the national judge has a duty to interpret national law, including contract law, in light of EU law in accordance with the principle of "harmonious interpretation".[69] Notably, the duty to interpret national law in light of EU law applies even if the provision was not enacted for the specific purpose of transposing the directive, provided that it does not lead to an interpretation *contra legem* of national law and does not have the effect of determining or aggravating the liability in criminal law of persons who act in violation of the directive.[70] Thus, while the provisions laid down in EU directives cannot be directly applied in horizontal relationships, they may be relied upon by the investor in order to have the conformity of national law with the directive reviewed.[71] To support this argument it must be remembered that since the global financial crisis the level of detail and prescription of the duties imposed on financial services providers under EU law has significantly increased[72] despite the lack of private law remedies for the breach of these duties. The intensification of conduct of business rules is a clear sign that, even in the con-

[68] See Della Negra (2016b).

[69] See Moeslein (2015), p. 551.

[70] CJEU, case C-168/95, Luciano Arcaro ECLI:EU:C:1996:363, para 42; case C-105/03, Pupino, ECLI:EU:C:2005:386, para 45.

[71] See also Della Negra (2016b), p. 120. In the case law, see the judgment of the Court of Appeal of Turin of 27 November 2009 available at www.ilcaso.it which held that the provisions of the Italian consolidated text of finance (Legislative Decree No 58/1998) must be interpreted in light of Art. 47 of the Italian Constitution and MiFID I. For a different view, see the judgment of the Scottish Court of Session in *Grant Estates Limited v The Royal Bank of Scotland plc.* [2012] CSOH 133, of 21 August 2012 which refused to interpret the national contract law in light of the purposes of MiFID I.

[72] See Moloney (2015).

tractual relationship with the firm, investor protection is assuming crucial importance.

8 The Case Law of the Court of Justice

8.1 The Peter Paul *Judgment*

The CJEU addressed the complex problem of the horizontal effect of EU financial regulation in the *Peter Paul* judgment in 2004[73] and the *Genil v Bankinter* judgment in 2013.[74] The former concerned the interpretation of Directive 1994/19/EC on deposit guarantee schemes[75] and the latter, the interpretation of MiFID I.

In *Peter Paul*, the plaintiffs claimed damages from the German state for deficient prudential supervision by the supervisory authority. However, they were precluded from claiming compensation for loss resulting from defective supervision because a specific banking law rule provided that the functions of the competent supervisory authority were to be carried out only in the public interest. The CJEU noted, interpretating the recitals of several banking directives (Directives 77/780, 89/299 and 89/646), that

> it does not necessarily follow either from the existence of such obligations or from the fact that the objectives pursued by those directives also include the protection of depositors that those directives seek to confer rights on depositors in the event that their deposits are unavailable as a result of defective supervision on the part of the competent national authorities.[76]

Moreover, the CJEU held that the very objective of harmonisation pursued by these directives was the mutual recognition of authorisations and of prudential supervision systems. Therefore, the CJEU concluded that a national rule which precludes individuals from claiming compensation for damage resulting from defective supervision on the part of a supervisory authority was compatible with EU law.[77]

This conclusion was based on a rather restrictive interpretation of the "conferring right" quality of the banking directives' provisions. Whilst it is undisputed that these directives did not confer enforceable rights on depositors, it could be argued that they took into account their legal interests at least in the sense that prudential

[73] CJEU, case C-222/02, *Peter Paul,* ECLI:EU:C:2004:606.

[74] CJEU, case C-604/11, *Bankinter*, ECLI:EU:C:2013:344.

[75] Directive 1994/19/EC on deposit guarantee schemes of the European Parliament and of the Council of 30 May 1994 on deposit guarantee schemes, O.J. 1994 L 135/5, recently replaced by Directive 2014/49/EU of the European Parliament and of the Council of 16 April 2014 on deposit guarantee schemes, 2014 O.J. L 173/149.

[76] CJEU, case C-604/11, case C-604/11, *Bankinter*, para 40.

[77] See, for instance, about the law before the *Bankinter* judgment, Andenas and Fairgrieve (2002) and about other aspects, D'Ambrosio (2015).

authorities, when exercising supervision, should balance the interest in the stability of the individual bank with the interest in the protection of its depositors.[78]

8.2 *The* Bankinter *Judgment*

In the *Genil v Bankinter* case, the referring court asked the CJEU, among other things, whether the omission of the appropriateness and suitability test provided for by Article 19(4) and (5) of MiFID I in relation to the supply of an interest rate swap to a retail investor could determine the absolute nullity of the contract between the firm and the client. The CJEU noted that, even if MiFID I lays down administrative sanctions for a firm's breach of national provisions transposing the directive, it does not require the Member States to stipulate contractual consequences for this breach. Therefore, the CJEU held that it is for the internal legal order of each Member State to determine the contractual consequences of non-compliance with the obligations, subject to the principles of equivalence and effectiveness.[79] Interestingly, the CJEU did not refer to or quote the *Peter Paul* judgment in support of its argument. This shows that the *Peter Paul* judgment could be a precedent for the interpretation of the contractual effects of prudential regulation but not conduct regulation.[80] In its concise reasoning, the CJEU made two important points. First, MiFID I does not prohibit Member States from preserving or introducing contract law remedies for a firm's failure to respect national laws transposing MiFID I; second, the national contractual remedies must respect the EU principles of effectiveness and equivalence. Yet, the CJEU did not clarify one of the most problematic aspects which emerged across national jurisdictions in the wake of the financial crisis: does EU law require Member States to provide contract law remedies, alongside administrative sanctions, for a firm's breach of national laws transposing MiFID I?

The reasoning of the CJEU suggests that the question should be answered in the affirmative, for the following reasons. First of all, the CJEU twice underlined the importance of the "investor protection" objective in MiFID, by referring to its recitals Nos 2 and 31 and by stressing that MiFID's provisions on conduct of business rules (Art. 19 seq.) should be interpreted in light of this objective.[81] This is even more true with regard to the new MiFID II which has included further references in its recitals to the need to improve the protection of investors and consumers of financial services.[82]

[78] See Tison (2005).

[79] CJEU, case C-604/11, *Bankinter*, para 57.

[80] See in this sense Moeslein (2015), p. 552.

[81] CJEU, case C-604/11, *Bankinter*, para 39.

[82] See the recitals Nos. 77, 156, 177; Art. 24(6), 74(2) and 75(1) of MiFID II.

Second, from a more literal perspective, the judgment itself provides further support for the argument made here. In paragraph 57 of the judgment, the CJEU held that MiFID "does not state either that the Member States must provide for contractual consequences in the event of contracts being concluded which do not comply with the obligations under national legal provisions transposing Article 19(4) and (5) of Directive 2004/39, or what those consequences might be. In paragraph 58, however, the CJEU concluded that it was up to the internal legal order of each Member State to determine the contractual consequences of non-compliance with those obligations, subject to observance of the principles of equivalence and effectiveness. The different wording used in these two instances suggests that Member States may choose an appropriate contractual remedy for the firm's failure to comply with MiFID, but that they may not choose to provide *no* remedy if this would undermine the effectiveness of MiFID.[83]

Third, if the ruling were interpreted as leaving Member States free to decide whether or not to establish contractual remedies for a firm's breach of MiFID, this would mean that Member States could circumvent the principle of effectiveness of EU law by simply refusing to provide a contractual remedy. This result would, however, conflict with the principle of effectiveness of EU law, which requires that national law (whether public or private) should not make impossible or excessively difficult the exercise of rights conferred on the individual by EU law.[84] Thus, the Member State should be able to prove that despite the lack of private law remedies the protection of individual investor rights against the financial service provider are sufficiently protected by other legal remedies (e.g. administrative sanctions).

It is likely that the CJEU's restrictive answer can be explained by the narrow formulation of the question referred for a preliminary ruling by the national court.[85] But the restrictive approach upheld by the CJEU could also be interpreted as a paradigmatic sign of the CJEU's reluctance to encroach on the very sensitive issue of the interplay between EU law and national contract law, regulation and private autonomy.[86]

In conclusion, it is argued here that on the basis of the *Bankinter v Genil* ruling Member States have a duty to provide investors with private law remedies for a firm's failure to respect the EU conduct of business rules unless the Member State proves that other legal remedies already ensure full compliance with the principle of effectiveness under EU law.

[83] See Grundmann (2013), p. 278.

[84] See, in particular, Dougan (2011).

[85] Grundmann (2013), p. 267.

[86] Cherednychenko (2015), p. 505.

9 The Impact of EU Financial Regulation on National Private Law

9.1 *The Impact of EU Financial Regulation on National Legislation*

The interpretation of the *Bankinter v Genil* judgment proposed here would increase convergence in the judicial interpretation of the complex relationship between EU financial regulation and national contract law across Member States.

In the absence of any express EU law provision, Member States have adopted various perspectives on the relationship between EU financial regulation and national contract law. The divergences in national legislation can be summarised in three models. Some Member States, like Spain and France, have decided not to introduce any specific contractual remedies for a firm's failure to respect its conduct of business rules; other Member States, such as Italy, have not introduced any specific contractual remedies but, nevertheless, set out certain rules regarding the form of investment contract and the burden of proof in compensation claims;[87] other Member States, such as the United Kingdom, have introduced an express private cause of action for a firm's failure to comply with the conduct of business rules.[88]

9.2 *The Impact of EU Financial Regulation on National Case Law*

9.2.1 The Challenges of Complex Financial Disputes for the National Judge

However, beyond the "law on the books" (i.e. *statute* law), the "law in action" (i.e. *case* law) shows a much more variegated reality. In the wake of the financial crisis, national courts have had to deal with financial disputes involving complex financial instruments (e.g. interest rate swaps, collateralised debt obligations), jurisdictional clauses and bankruptcies. The recurrent issue in the litigation concerns the role and function of the traditional categories of private law (e.g. liability, debt, guarantee, promise) in view of the rapid evolution in financial instruments, market practices and societal customs.[89]

---

[87] See Articles 23(1) and (6) of the Italian consolidated text of finance (Legislative Decree No 58/1998).

[88] Section 138D of FSMA (replacing the former Section 150 of FSMA). On the interpretation of this provision see, in particular, *Titan Steel Wheels Ltd v The Royal Bank of Scotland Plc* [2010] EWHC 211 (Comm).

[89] See Renner (2011).

For example, derivative contracts have *de facto* transformed the contractual promise into a matter of risk management. The functioning of a derivate contract, such as for example a credit default swap (CDS), does not substantially differ from a traditional insurance contract regulated by national civil codes: the seller of the CDS compensates the buyer in the event of a loan default (by the debtor) or other credit event. What is remarkably different, however, when compared to traditional insurance contracts, is the systemic relevance of these contractual arrangements, as well as the fact that they are highly standardised throughout global financial markets.[90]

Ninety percent of all OTC derivatives are governed by the standardised documentation published by the trade association, the International Swaps and Derivatives Association (ISDA).[91] The complexity of financial instruments and practices raises important new challenges for the national judge. First, whilst the contract terms are global, the assets of the parties and the adjudicating courts remain local. Second, such contracts are not individually negotiated and the parties to the contract are not the original drafters of the contract terms. This means that, in order to understand the context of the transaction, the judge should refer to the intention of the original drafters of the terms rather than that of the actual contracting parties.[92] Third, as we mentioned above, the regulatory architecture of such contracts is multi-layered: it comprises self-regulation (standard contract terms), general contract law and financial regulation. But whilst self-regulation and financial regulation are rapidly evolving, the latter following the former, the general law of contract remains formally enshrined in civil codes adopted in the nineteenth and twentieth centuries or in the case law. What role should the traditional categories of private law play in the adjudication of complex financial disputes in the post-crisis era? What is the relationship between these categories and financial regulatory standards?

The recurrent issue tackled by national courts since the financial crisis is whether, in the absence of EU law provisions, a firm's failure to comply with conduct of business rules may give rise to a remedy based on general contract law. The solutions adopted by national courts are very diverse even within the same jurisdiction.[93]

9.2.2 The National Adjudication Techniques

Two general approaches can be identified in the case law.

Some national courts maintain a strict separation between financial regulatory standards and private law standards and therefore refuse to enforce regulatory standards through private law remedies. In the UK, for example, national courts have

[90] See about the regulatory response in Solvency II, Andenas et al. (2017).

[91] See in particular Braithwaite (2012), p. 784.

[92] See Choi and Gulati (2006).

[93] See for an overview, Busch (2012).

refused, bar a few rare cases,[94] to grant remedies based on general common law to clients who suffered a loss as a result of a firm's failure to comply with the pre-MiFID[95] and MiFID-derived conduct of business rules.[96] The U.K. court approach is based on the idea that the autonomy of general common law, and consequently, the principle of private autonomy should be protected against the 'intrusions' of EU-derived regulatory standards. Separating financial regulation and contract law is instrumental in achieving greater private autonomy, which helps to foster financial innovation and strengthen commercial and legal certainty.[97] To achieve these objectives, UK Courts attach a crucial importance to the contractual documentation freely agreed between the parties,[98] i.e. by deciding that in the absence of advisory agreement no duty to advise can arise at common law[99] and that, in the absence of an express contractual provision, regulatory duties cannot be incorporated into the contract and cannot be actionated by way of contractual remedies.[100]

Other national courts have held that a firm's failure to comply with its conduct of business rules may give rise to an implied remedy based on general contract law. The underpinning rationale is that general contract law should support EU-derived regulatory standards in order to increase the protection of retail clients. To achieve this objective, national courts, rather than focussing on contractual documentation, focus on the purposive interpretation of national private law in light of EU-derived regulatory standards (suitability and appropriateness rules).

However, the courts' approach differ with regard to the type of remedy awarded to retail investors (e.g. absolute nullity, avoidance for mistake, liability).

In Italy, between 2005 and 2007, several courts held that a firm's failure to comply with the national rules implementing the ISD (when providing financial services to retail clients in relation to Cirio, Parmalat and Republic of Argentina bonds[101]) provoked the absolute nullity of the contract for the breach of mandatory rules pursuant to Article 1418(1) of the Civil Code.[102] This judicial reasoning was based on the premise that financial regulatory duties are tantamount of mandatory contract

---

[94] *Loosemore v Financial Concepts* [2001] Lloyd's Rep. P.N. 235; *Seymour v Caroline Ockwell & Co.* [2005] EWHC1137 (QB); *Shore v Sedgwick Financial Services Ltd* [2007] EWHC 2509 (QB); *Rubenstein v HSBC Bank plc* [2012] EWCA Civ 1184.

[95] See, inter alia, *JP Morgan Chase Bank v Springwell Navigation Corporation* [2008] EWHC 1186 (Comm) 2008 WL 2148250; *Green v Royal Bank of Scotland Plc* [2012] EWHC 3661 (QB).

[96] See, inter alia, *Crestsign Ltd v National Westminster Bank plc and Royal Bank of Scotland plc* [2014] EWHC 3043 and *Thornbridge Ltd v Barclays Bank Plc* [2015] EWHC 3430 (QB).

[97] See Bridge and Braithwaite (2013).

[98] See Alexander (2017).

[99] *JP Morgan Chase Bank and Others v Springwell Navigation* [2008] EWHC 1186 (Comm), para 440.

[100] *Clarion Ltd v National Provident Institution [2000] 1 WLR 1888.*

[101] See Capriglione (2006).

[102] See, in particular, Trib. Mantova, 18 March 2004 and Trib. Mantova, 12 November 2004. Available on www.ilcaso.it.

terms, because of their public order (*ordre public*) nature and therefore determines the nullity of the contract.[103]

By contrast, other courts have held that a breach of the conduct of business rules gives rise to avoidance of the contract for mistake or fraud[104] or determines pre-contractual[105] or contractual liability[106] of the financial service provider.[107]

In 2007, the Plenary Session of the Italian Supreme Court held, in two landmark judgments,[108] that a breach of the conduct of business rules would not engender the absolute nullity of the contract because conduct of business rules, whilst mandatory, do not qualify as imperative rules under Article 1418(1) of the Civil Code. According to the Supreme Court, violation of these rules by the financial service provider could only give rise to pre-contractual or contractual liability; thus it falls to the plaintiff to prove the loss suffered as a result of an alleged breach of these rules. These judgments are based on a theoretical and formalistic distinction between rules of conduct, which govern the parties' behaviour before, during and after the conclusion of the contract, and rules of validity, which govern the formal and structural requirements of the contract. However, this distinction is not expressly laid down in the law and, more importantly, it risks undermining the effective protection of retail investors who may find it difficult to prove the firm's breach of conduct of business rules.[109] It must be noted, however, that in some recent judgments Italian courts have declared null and void OTC interest rate swaps (not based on International Swaps and Derivatives Association, ISDA, model agreements) for a lack of consideration (*causa*) pursuant to Article 1418(2) of the Civil code.[110] Interestingly, in such cases the contract was not annulled for mere lack of information but because this lack of information meant that the investors could not have been aware of the imbalance of power vis-à-vis the financial firm. As a result, the likelihood of monetary risk protection was frustrated, inexistent or reduced by the contract.

In the wake of the global financial crisis, Spanish courts have faced a wave of financial litigation concerning the mis-selling of *participationes preferentes*, interest rate swaps and Lehman Brothers' products. Similarly to Italian courts, the Spanish courts have had to seek the most appropriate contractual remedy for a firm's failure to respect MiFID's suitability and appropriateness tests.[111] Unlike in Italy

[103] See for this thesis Tison (2010).

[104] See, in particular Trib. Roma, 16 May 2005, Trib. Bologna, 18 December 2006. Available on www.ilcaso.it.

[105] See Cass. 29 settembre 2005, n. 19024. Available on www.ilcaso.it.

[106] See in particular Trib. Firenze, 18.10.2005; Trib. Genova, 19.10.2006. Available on www.ilcaso.it.

[107] For an overview of the case law see Roppo (2005), p. 896; Greco (2010).

[108] Cass. Sez. Un., 19 dicembre 2007, nn. 26724 e 26725 commented, inter alia, by Scoditti (2008), Lucchini-Guastalla (2008) and Roppo (2008).

[109] See Alpa (2008).

[110] See Corte App. Milano, 18 September 2013; Corte App. Torino, 22 April 2016. Available on www.ilcaso.it.

[111] See Zunzunegui (2014).

and in the United Kingdom, the most important remedy applied by national law is the avoidance of the contract for mistake pursuant to Article 1265 of the Civil code. In a recent string of cases, the Spanish Supreme Court, referring to the judgment of the CJEU in *Bankinter v Genil*, held that a firm's failure to carry out the appropriateness test required by MiFID I could give rise to an error invalidating the consent of the client.[112] In particular, the Supreme Court has clarified that while the lack of performance of such assessment does not itself imply the existence of an error invalidating consent, it does not preclude its presumption. Thus, the error must take place in relation to the subject-matter of the contract. In swaps contracts, the error must concern the risks associated with that instrument. This means, then, that the provision of understandable and appropriate information, comprising "guidelines and warnings about the risks associated with those instruments", becomes essential for a retail client to legitimately give his consent.

In France, civil courts have consistently held that an investment firm's failure to respect MiFID's conduct of business rules, as transposed by Article L. 533 of the *Code monétaire et financier*, leads to a breach of the investment contract pursuant to Article 1147 of the Civil Code. The Supreme Court has specified that the duty of a bank to warn its client(s) of the risks associated with a transaction only lies where the financial instrument is of a so-called "speculative nature" (*caractère speculatif*)—i.e. instruments subject to a high level of exposure, traded on future markets—or where the client is not a sophisticated investor (*investisseur averti*) and is therefore unable to assess his/her financial exposure.[113] Thus, in the absence of a specific remedy provided under the "*droit spécial*" the judge must apply the remedies of the "*droit général*".[114]

Similarly, the Dutch Supreme Court in *Levob v. B*, *De Treek v. Dexia* and *Stichting Gedupeerden Spaarconstructie v. Aegon*[115] held the banks responsible for breaching the duty of care. Even if the duty to know one's client had not been included in the financial supervision legislation then in force, the Supreme Court held that private law duties of care could extend further than the public law duties of care contained in the conduct of business rules.[116]

A similar solution has been adopted by the German civil courts.[117] According to the German Supreme Court, a firm's failure to comply with its conduct of business rules does not determine per se the avoidance of the contract but it may give rise to pre-contractual liability and breach of contract.[118]

---

[112] See judgments of the Supreme court 4 February 2016, 323/2016; 20 January 2014, No 840/2013, 15 September 2015, No 491/2015, / July 2014, No 384-384/2014.

[113] Cass. com., 5 Novembre 1991, n° 89-10005 (*Buon* case); Cass. com, 19 September 2006, n° 05-15.305 (*Benefic* cases); Com., 26 February 2008, *Bull.* 2008, IV, n° 42, pourvoi n° 07-10.761; Com., 1 July 2008, pourvoi n° 07-16.461.

[114] See Mazeaud (2004), p. 703.

[115] HR 5 June 2009, NJ 2012, 182, 183 and 184.

[116] Cherednychenko (2010), p. 421.

[117] See on this debate Grundmann (2001), p. 266.

[118] See, in particular, BGH, 22.3.2011, XI ZR 33/10 commented by Haas (2011), 318031.

9.2.3 The (Regulatory) Implications of Adjudication Techniques

The foregoing overview on the national case law has brought to light differences between the continental and common law approaches to dispute resolution. The continental courts promote a gradual integration between regulatory and contract law duties. The common law courts, instead, seem to separate these two sets of duties. Both approaches have regulatory implications. The continental approach attaches to courts the role of supplementing financial regulation, supervision and public enforcement, by compensating clients who suffered a loss as a result of mis-selling of financial instruments. By contrast, the common law approach is instrumental to foster financial innovation and market efficiency because it assigns primary importance to the parties' agreement and self-responsibility.[119]

The difference between these two approaches, whilst reflecting historical divergences between civil and common law that cannot be investigated in this chapter, should, nevertheless, not be over-emphasised because the factual context of the disputes is very different.

The UK courts adjudicate high level claims disputes which involve, almost always, sophisticated retail clients (i.e. firms) or non-retail clients, who are supposed to have a sufficient knowledge, experience and financial resources to understand the terms and conditions of financial agreements; by contrast, the disputes before civil law courts, especially in Italy and Spain, often involve small claim disputes concerning unsophisticated retail clients who do not have any knowledge and experience of securities markets (i.e. retired persons).[120]

This context-driven consideration suggests that the role of private law-making and enforcement in financial markets should be analysed taking into account, besides national courts, also other institutional mechanisms, such as out-of-court dispute resolution, which can support courts in the 'management of conflict between firms and clients.[121]

10 The Role of Alternative Dispute Resolution (ADR) Mechanisms

10.1 The Influence of EU Law on ADR: From Convergence to Harmonisation

Since the outbreak of the global financial crisis, Alternative Dispute Resolution (ADR) mechanisms have also assumed increasing importance in the adjudication of retail client disputes. At the EU level, the out-of-court resolution of financial

[119] See, on the impact of courts on contractual innovation, Gilson et al. (2013).

[120] See Della Negra (2016b).

[121] See Micklitz (2015).

disputes has has become an essential element of retail financial market regulation, first, through the establishment of the FIN-NET network, and, second, through 'light-touch' harmonisation of national laws.[122] In 2001 the European Commission launched the FIN-NET network to facilitate cross-border retail client dispute resolution. The FIN-NET, however, is a mechanisms of coordination which does not introduce any harmonisation of the institutional rules governing ADR at the national level. An important step towards legislative harmonisation was made by the MiFID I which required Member States to establish "efficient and effective complaints and redress procedures for the out-of-court settlement of consumer disputes" (Art. 53). The MiFID II reiterated the same principle but did not introduce any specific requirement on how Member States should design ADRs and what remedies they can grant. Therefore, these ADR shall remain subject to the principles laid down by the new Directive on consumer ADR adopted in 2013 which encourages Member States to develop ADR networks, such as the financial dispute resolution network 'FIN-NET' in the area of financial services, and to foster the inclusion of national ADR mechanisms in this network.[123]

A remarkable novelty of the MiFID II is that it requires Member States to set up mechanisms

> to ensure that compensation may be paid or other remedial action be taken in accordance with national law for any financial loss or damage suffered as a result of an infringement of this Directive or of Regulation (EU) No 600/2014[Article 69].[124]

Although this innovative provision does not confer an express private law remedy to clients it certainly strengthens the private enforcement of MiFID II conduct of business rules, namely by 'importing' in EU law the UK enforcement model of the 'consumer redress scheme' of Section 404 of the UK Financial Services and Markets Act (FSMA) which provision empowers the UK supervisory body, the Financial Conduct Authority to require financial firms to establish and operate a consumer redress scheme when there may have been a widespread or regular failure by relevant firms to comply with its conduct of business rules, consumers have suffered (or may suffer) loss or damage and it considers that it is desirable to make rules for the purpose of securing that redress is made to the consumers.

10.2 The National Models of ADR

However, the institutional nature and remedies awarded by national ADR schemes differ significantly from one country to another. Some ADR schemes are public or publicly funded (*Arbitro Bancario e Finanziario*, ABF in Italy); others are private or

---

[122] See Della Negra (2014).

[123] See Recital No 53 of Directive 2013/11/EU of the European Parliament and of the Council of 21 May 2013 on alternative dispute resolution for consumer disputes and amending Regulation (EC) No 2006/2004 and Directive 2009/22/EC (Directive on consumer ADR).

[124] See, with more detail on the interpretation of this provision, Della Negra (2016a), p. 155.

privately funded (*Ombudsman-giurì bancario* in Italy). Some provide mere recommendations to investment firms (*Comisionado para la Defensa del Cliente* in Spain); others adjudicate the dispute through a binding determination (ABF and Financial Ombudsman Service, FOS in the UK). It is also important to note that some "adjudicative" ADRs, like the ABF, seriously take into account statute law and case law,[125] whilst others, in particular the FOS, determine the complaint by reference to what is

> fair and reasonable in all the circumstances of the case.[126]

The British courts have emphasised the importance of this 'informal' approach to dispute resolution by holding that the FOS is not bound by common law[127] and that its determinations can be set aside by means of judicial review only if

> his opinion as to what is fair and reasonable in all the circumstances of the case is perverse or irrational.[128]

The nature of the FOS' adjudication, together with its broad competence (up to £ 150,000), gives to retail unsophisticated investors, who could not afford access to courts, an effective way to protect their rights vis-à-vis financial firms.[129]

11 Conclusions

This research, based on an analysis of the statute law and case law in several Member States, has underlined two important findings.

First, in most European countries judicial enforcement of EU financial regulation has provided certain options to investors in terms of compensation and deterrence. In Italy and Spain, in particular, national courts have played a fundamental role in protecting investors against mis-selling practices, often compensating for the weaknesses of public enforcement and supervision. Although it could be argued that an excessive level of litigation may endanger market efficiency, in several countries national courts have been successful in compensating retail investors for the losses suffered as a result of widespread misselling practices.[130]

Second, the general law of contract, which is often neglected in academic studies on financial regulation, has proved to be an adaptable and flexible tool to achieve a

---

125 See Dolmetta (2013).

126 See Section 228 FSMA 2000. The FOS shall take into account, among other things, the relevant law and regulations (DISP 3.6.4 of FCA Handbook Dispute Resolution Complaints). See Alpa (2008), p. 910.

127 See *R. (on the application of London Capital Group) v Financial Ombudsman Service Ltd* [2013] EWHC 2425 (Admin).

128 See *R. (on the application of IFG Financial Services Ltd v Financial Ombudsman Services Ltd v Mr and Mrs Jenkins* [2005] EWHC 1153 (Admin).

129 See, for the impact of the FOS adjudication of payment protection insurance (PPI)-related disputes, Ferran (2012).

130 See Perrone and Valente (2012).

high level of investor protection. The case law in several EU countries (e.g. Italy, Spain, France, Germany, Netherlands) shows an ongoing process of 'Europeanisation' and 'modernisation' of general contract law and its traditional categories (e.g. liability, validity) which suggests gradual convergence between financial regulatory standards and contractual standards.[131]

This judicial development should be normatively welcomed. The traditional categories of contract law should not represent an outdated toolbox. On the contrary, they can be effectively used as flexible theoretical tools to enhance legal and commercial certainty by conceptualising a rapidly evolving reality.[132]

One important implication of these ongoing processes (Europeanisation and modernisation) is the growing interdependence and integration between financial regulatory standards and contractual standards. EU law has designed financial regulation as a self-sufficient body of law, which should theoretically at least steer the parties' behaviour without needing to rely on traditional contract law.[133] As mentioned above, this regulatory technique aims to set limits to the economic activity of market participants by overcoming the different private law regulations existing at the national level.[134] However, after the global financial crisis and the widespread mis-selling scandals, fraud and bankruptcies which followed, there was a pressing need to ensure a high level of investor protection and the effectiveness of EU law. For these reasons, the remedies based on the general law of contract have become necessary tools to support and complement the financial regulatory tools (i.e. information duties) and provide a high level of investor protection.

The national judge-made modernisation of general contract law cannot overcome the high degree of divergence in private law-making and enforcement that has arisen across national jurisdictions. The regulatory approach of Member States and the judgments of national courts still differ significantly as regards the kinds of private law remedy that investors can rely on to recoup losses suffered as a result of a firm's failure to comply with EU conduct of business rules, as transposed in national law. In fact, whereas the modernisation of contract law is visible in continental Europe, in the UK national courts have maintained a more conservative approach when interpreting contract clauses and have refused to interpret the general common law in light of the objectives of EU financial regulation.

Although the EU is still struggling to introduce harmonised rules on the civil liability of financial service providers, there is some evidence of a new trend towards the strengthening of private enforcement of conduct regulation. The innovative provision of Article 69 of the MiFID II, read in light of the *Bankinter* judgment, suggests that Member States should introduce mechanisms (judicial and extra-judicial) to confer on individual clients the right to enforce EU-derived regulatory standards, thus strengthening the effectiveness of EU financial regulation. It is the author's

[131] See Della Negra (2014), p. 592.

[132] See Lipari (2008a, b).

[133] See Micklitz and Svetiev (2012).

[134] See also Azoulai (2015).

conviction that, the effective enforcement of EU conduct regulation is a necessary precondition to ensure the credibility of EU client protection regulation, strengthen the investors' confidence in the EU financial markets and mitigate the systemic risk arising from misconduct by firms.

In this process European financial market regulation will break down the traditional autonomy of general contract law. To an increasing degree it will transform contract law into a regulatory tool to govern financial transactions. The traditional autonomy of commercial law will not change this. It is not a relevant dichotomy for the context of modern financial markets.

References

Alexander K (2017) Bank civil liability for misselling and advice. In: Busch D et al (eds) A bank's duty of care. Hart Publishing, Oxford, p 253 et seq

Alpa G (2008) Gli obblighi informativi precontrattuali nei contratti di investimento finanziario. Per l'armonizzazione dei modelli regolatori e per l'uniformazione delle regole di diritto comune. Contratto e Impresa (3):131 et seq

Andenas M (1994) Rules of conduct and the principle of subsidiarity. Company Lawyer 15:60 et seq

Andenas M (2011) Harmonising and regulating financial markets. In: Andenas M et al (eds) Theory and practice of harmonisation. Edward Elgar Publishing, Cheltenham (UK), Northampton (MA), pp 180–198

Andenas M (2015) The ECB and NCA liability within the single supervisory mechanism. Bank of Italy Legal Research Papers (Quaderni di ricerca giuridica) 3–6

Andenas M, Bjorge E (2013) National implementation of ECHR rights. In: Føllesdal A, Peters B, Ulfstein G (eds) Constituting Europe: the European Court of Human Rights in a national, European and global context. Cambridge University Press, Cambridge, pp 181–262

Andenas M, Chiu I (2013) Financial stability and legal integration in financial regulation. Eur Law Rev 38(3):335–359

Andenas M, Cortesi I (2017) The creation of a Vatican financial regulatory framework. Law Econ Yearly Rev 6:242–264

Andenas M, Della Negra F (2017) Between contract law and financial regulation: towards the Europeanisation of general contract law. Eur Bus Law Rev 28(4):499–521

Andenas M, Fairgrieve D (2002) Misfeasance in public office, governmental liability, and European influences. Int Comp Law Q 51(4):757–780

Andenas M, Snell J (2002) Exploring the outer limits: restriction on the free movement of goods and services. In: Andenas M, Roth WH (eds) Services and free movement in the EU law. Oxford University Press, Oxford, pp 69–141

Andenas M, Avesani R, Manes P, Wood P (2017) Solvency II: a dynamic challenge for the insurance market. Societa Editrice Il Mulino

Avgouleas A, Arner D (2017) The Eurozone debt crisis and the European banking union: "hard choices," "intolerable dilemmas," and the question of sovereignty. Int Lawyer 50(1):29 et seq

Azoulai L (2015) The complex weave of harmonization. In: Chalmers D et al (eds) The Oxford handbook of European union law. Oxford University Press, Oxford

Braithwaite JP (2012) Standard form contracts as transnational law: evidence from the derivatives markets. Mod Law Rev 75(5):779–805

Bridge M (ed) (2017) Benjamin's sale of goods. Sweet & Maxwell, London

Bridge M, Braithwaite J (2013) Private law and financial crises. J Corp Law Stud 13(2):361–399

Buckley RP, Avgouleas E, Arner DW (eds) (2017) Reconceptualising global finance and its regulation. Cambridge University Press, Cambridge
Busch D (2012) Why MiFID matters to private law—the example of MiFID's impact on an asset manager's civil liability. Cap Mark Law J 7(4):386–413
Capriglione F (2006) Crisi di sistema ed innovazione normativa: Prime riflessioni sulla nuova legge sul risparmio (l. N. 262 del 2005). Banca, borsa e titoli di credito 69(2):125–179
Cherednychenko O (2010) The regulation of retail investment services in the EU: towards the improvement of investor rights? J Consum Policy 33:408 et seq
Cherednychenko O (2014) Public supervision over private relationships: towards European supervision private law? Eur Rev Priv Law 22(1):37–60
Cherednychenko O (2015) Contract governance in the EU: conceptualising the relationship between investor protection regulation and private law. Eur Law J 21(4):500–520
Choi SJ, Gulati GM (2006) Contract as statute. Mich Law Rev 104:1129–1173
Comparato G, Micklitz H-W, Svetiev Y (2016) The regulatory character of European private law. In: Twigg-Flesner C (ed) Research handbook on EU consumer and contract law. Edward Elgar, London, p 35
D'Ambrosio R (2015) The liability of the ECB and the NCAs within the single supervisory mechanism. Quaderni di Ricerca Giuridica della Consulenza Legale della Banca d'Italia 78
Della Negra F (2014) The private enforcement of the MiFID conduct of business rules. An overview of the Italian and Spanish experiences. Eur Rev Contract Law 10(4):571–595
Della Negra F (2016a) The effects of ESMA's powers on domestic contract law. In: Andenas M et al (eds) Regulating and supervising European financial markets. More risks than achievements? Springer, Heidelberg, New York
Della Negra F (2016b) The transformation of the retail financial transactions in the EU and the role of contract law. In: Comparato G et al (eds) European regulatory private law – autonomy, competition and regulation in European private law. EUI, Florence, p 117 et seq
Dolmetta A (2013) Trasparenza dei prodotti bancari. Regole. Zanichelli, Bologna
Dougan M (2011) The vicissitudes of life at the coalface: remedies and procedures for enforcing union law. In: Craig P et al (eds) The evolution of EU law. Oxford University Press, Oxford, p 424 et seq
Ferran E (2012) Regulatory lessons from the payment protection insurance mis-selling scandal in the UK. Eur Bus Organ Law Rev 13(4):247–270
Ferrarini G (2005) Contract standards and the markets in financial instruments directive (MiFID): an assessment of the Lamfalussy regulatory architecture. Eur Rev Contract Law 1(1):19–43
Gilson RJ, Sabel CF et al (2013) Contract and innovation: the limited role of generalist courts in the evolution of novel contractual forms. N Y Univ Law Rev 88(1):170–215
Greco F (2010) Informazione pre-contrattuale e rimedi nella disciplina dell'intermediazione finanziaria. Giuffrè, Milano
Grundmann S (2001) Commentary to §§ 31 et seq, Bankrecht VI – Wertpapierhandelsgesetz. In: Ebenroth C et al (eds) HGB-Kommentar, vol 2. C H Beck, Munich, p 229 et seq
Grundmann S (2013) The *Bankinter* case on MiFID regulation and contract law. Eur Rev Contract Law 9(3):267–280
Grundmann S (2015) The banking union translated into (private law) duties: infrastructure and rulebook. Eur Bus Organ Law Rev 16(3):357–382
Grundmann S, Hollering J (2008) EC financial services and contract law - developments 2005–2007. Eur Rev Contract Law 4(1):45–64
Haar B (2011) From public law to private law: market supervision and contract law standards. In: Grundmann S et al (eds) Financial services, financial crisis and general European contract law: failure and challenges of contracting. Kluwer Law International, Alphen aan den Rijn, pp 259–279
Haas M (2011) In: Lindenmaier-Möhring (ed) Kommentierte BGH-rechtsprechung (lmk). CH Beck, Munich

Hadjiemmanuil C (2015) The banking union and its implications for private law: a comment. Eur Bus Organ Law Rev 16(3):383–400
Heidemann M (2007) Methodology of uniform contract law - the UNIDROIT principles in international legal doctrine and practice. Springer, Berlin, Heidelberg, New York
Heidemann M (2012) Does international trade need a doctrine of transnational law? Some thoughts at the launch of a European contract law. Springer, Berlin, Heidelberg, New York
Heidemann M (2016) Identities in contract – merchant law in Europe and the future of European contract law. Maastricht J Eur Comp Law 23(4):667–701
Holdgaard R, Elkan D, Krohn Schaldemose G (2018) From cooperation to collision: the ECJ's Ajos ruling and the Danish Supreme Court's refusal to comply. Common Mark Law Rev 55(1):17–53
Hudson A (2013) Law of finance. Sweet and Maxwell, London
Jannarelli A (2003) La disciplina dell'atto e dell'attività: I contratti tra imprese e tra imprese e consumatori. In: Lipari N (ed) Trattato di diritto privato europeo. Cedam, Padova
Köndgen J (2011) Policy responses to credit crises: does the law of contract provide an answer? In: Grundmann S et al (eds) Financial services, financial crisis and general European contract law: failure and challenges of contracting. Kluwer Law International, Alphen aan den Rijn, pp 35–60
Kruithof M, van Gerven W (2010) A differentiated approach to client protection: the example of MiFID. Ghent University Financial Law Institute Working Papers 2010/07, https://papers.ssrn.com/sol3/papers.cfm?abstract_id=1622682
Lipari N (2008a) Parte generale del contratto e norme di settore nel quadro del procedimento interpretativo. Rivista trimestrale di diritto e procedura civile 1(1)
Lipari N (2008b) Categorie civilistiche e diritto di fonte comunitaria. Rivista trimestrale di diritto e procedura civile (1):20 et seq
Lucchini-Guastalla E (2008) Violazione degli obblighi di condotta e responsabilità degli intermediari finanziari. Responsabilità civile e previdenza (2)
MacNeil I (2015) Enforcement and sanctioning. In: Ferran E et al (eds) Oxford handbook on financial regulation. Oxford University Press, Oxford, p 293
Mazeaud D (2004) Droit commun du contrat et droit de la comsommation nouvelles frontières? – etudes de droit de la consommation – liber amicorum jean calais-auloy. Dalloz, Paris
Micklitz H-W (2015) The transformation of enforcement in European private law: preliminary considerations. Eur Rev Priv Law 23(4):491–524
Micklitz H-W, Svetiev Y (2012) A self-sufficient European private law – a viable concept? EUI Working Papers Law 31:23 et seq
Moeslein F (2015) Third parties in the European banking union: regulatory and supervisory effects on private law relationships between banks and their clients or creditors. Eur Bus Organ Law Rev 16(3):547–574
Moeslein F, Riesenhuber K (2009) Contract governance – a draft research agenda. Eur Rev Contract Law 5:248 et seq
Moloney N (2012a) Liability of asset managers: a comment. Cap Mark Law J 7(4):414–422
Moloney N (2012b) The investor model underlying the EU's investor protection regime: consumers or investors? Eur Bus Organ Law Rev 13(2):169–193
Moloney N (2014) EU securities and financial markets regulation, 3rd edn. Oxford University Press, Oxford
Moloney N (2015) Regulating the retail markets. In: Ferran E et al (eds) Oxford handbook on financial regulation. Oxford University Press, Oxford, p 739 et seq
Pagliari S (2012) Who governs finance? The shifting public-private divide in the regulation of derivatives, rating agencies and hedge funds. Eur Law J 18(4):44–61
Perrone A, Valente S (2012) Against all odds: investor protection in Italy and the role of courts. Eur Bus Organ Law Rev (13):21 et seq
Pistor K (2013) A legal theory of finance. J Comp Econ 41(2):315–330

Renner M (2011) Death by complexity: the financial crisis and the crisis of law. In: Kjaer PF et al (eds) The financial crisis in constitutional perspective. The dark side of functional differentiation. Hart Publishing, Oxford, p 105 et seq
Roppo V (2005) La tutela del risparmiatore fra nullità, risoluzione e risarcimento, (ovvero, l'ambaradan dei rimedi contrattuali). Contratto e impresa (3):896–910
Roppo V (2008) Nullità virtuale del contratto dopo la sentenza Rordorf. Danno e responsabilità (5):536 et seq
Rühl G (2018) The unfairness of choice-of-law clauses, or: the (unclear) relationship between Article 6 Rome I Regulation and the Unfair Terms in Consumer Contracts Directive: VKI v. Amazon. Common Mark Law Rev 55(1):201–224
Schulze R, Zoll F (2018) European contract law, 2nd edn. Hart Publishing, Oxford
Scoditti E (2008) La violazione delle regole di comportamento dell'intermediario finanziario e le sezioni unite. Foro italiano (1):748 et seq
Svetiev Y, Ottow A (2014) Financial supervision in the interstices between private and public law. Eur Rev Contract Law 10(4):496–544
Tison M (2005) Do not attack the watchdog! Banking supervisor's liability after Peter Paul. Common Mark Law Rev 42(3):639–675
Tison M (2010) The civil law effects of MiFID in a comparative law perspective. Financial Law Institute Working Paper 2010, 5
Tridimas T (2011) EU financial regulation: federalization, crisis management and law reform. In: Craig P et al (eds) The evolution of EU law. Oxford University Press, Oxford, p 793
Watson A (1982) Slave law: history & ideology. Yale Law J 91:1034 et seq
Watson A (1992) Thinking property at Rome - symposium on the law of slavery: comparative law and slavery. Chicogo-Kent Law Rev 68(3):1355 et seq
Williamson OE (1979) Transaction-cost economics: the governance of contractual relations. J Law Econ 22:235 et seq
Zoppini A (2013) Diritto privato vs diritto amministrativo (ovvero alla ricerca dei confini tra stato e mercato). Rivista diritto civile (3):515–530
Zunzunegui F (2014) Misselling of preferred shares to Spanish retail clients. J Int Bank Law Regul 29(3):174–186

Kolibri 360 GmbH
Ferdinand-Jühlke-Straße 7
99095 Erfurt, Deutschland
produktsicherheit@kolibri360.de